KEEPING TIME

KEEPING TIME

Readings in Jazz History

Second Edition

Edited by
Robert Walser

New York Oxford
Oxford University Press

Oxford University Press is a department of the University of Oxford.
It furthers the University's objective of excellence in research,
scholarship, and education by publishing worldwide.

Oxford New York
Auckland Cape Town Dar es Salaam Hong Kong Karachi
Kuala Lumpur Madrid Melbourne Mexico City Nairobi
New Delhi Shanghai Taipei Toronto

With offices in
Argentina Austria Brazil Chile Czech Republic France Greece
Guatemala Hungary Italy Japan Poland Portugal Singapore
South Korea Switzerland Thailand Turkey Ukraine Vietnam

For titles covered by Section 112 of the US Higher Education Opportunity Act, please visit www.oup.com/us/he for the latest information about pricing and alternate formats.

Published by Oxford University Press
198 Madison Avenue, New York, New York 10016
http://www.oup.com

Library of Congress Cataloging-in-Publication Data
Keeping time : readings in jazz history / edited by Robert
Walser. -- Second edition.
pages cm
ISBN 978-0-19-976577-5
1. Jazz--History and criticism. I. Walser, Robert, editor of compilation.
ML3507.K4 2014
781.6509--dc23

2013048713

Printing number: 9 8 7 6 5 4 3 2 1

Printed in the United States of America
on acid-free paper

Contents

PART 3 The Thirties

PART 4 The Forties

PART 5 The Fifties

Preface

To the First Edition

> Perhaps more than any other people, Americans have been locked in a deadly struggle with time, with history. We've fled the past and trained ourselves to suppress, if not forget, troublesome details of the national memory, and a great part of our optimism, like our progress, has been bought at the cost of ignoring the processes through which we've arrived at any given moment in our national experience.
>
> —Ralph Ellison[1]

When jazz musicians "keep time," they organize the flow of experience. Their sense of what is happening, what has happened, and what will happen is framed by their unspoken collective agreements on the tempo and rhythmic feel of their performance. Jazz historians, critics, and fans also keep time: their activities are framed by their collective understandings of jazz history. What we know about the past provides the basis for our evaluations of the present, and what is evoked for us by a word like "jazz" depends on the effects of many perceptions, arguments, constructions and reconstructions, some ongoing, some apparently vanished. *Keeping Time* assembles a great variety of ways in which people have understood and cared about jazz. It records a history not of style changes, but of values, meanings, and sensibilities.

It is often said that recordings are the primary documents of jazz history, but written documents can help us understand the disparate reactions of those who heard those recordings as contemporaries, so that we do not take our own reactions to be the only possible or rational ones. These selections include the words of many who have been hailed as jazz's greatest musicians—Louis Armstrong, Miles Davis, Duke Ellington, Sidney Bechet, Jelly Roll Morton, Dizzy Gillespie—but they also engage with music usually ignored by jazz historians—for example, that of Paul Whiteman, whose music defined the jazz of the Jazz Age for most Americans in the 1920s. The present jazz canon has been constructed over time, and for historians, knowing what was left out is often as important as learning about what has been included.

In retrospect, it seems that four themes have guided my selections and annotations for *Keeping Time*. First, I wanted to present jazz not only as a virtuosic art form, but as a social practice of great historical significance. Jazz musicians have produced not only great music, but great understandings—of culture, race, gender, nation, the body, creativity, tradition, individuality, cooperation, and community.

1. Ralph Ellison, *Shadow and Act* (New York: Vintage Books, 1972 [1964]), p. 250.

All of the excerpts touch on one or more of these aspects of how jazz has affected the categories and concepts that structure our social experience. Some (those by Ralph Ellison and Scott DeVeaux, for example) show explicitly how the process of constructing jazz histories is itself a social practice that reflects interests and participates in cultural politics.

Second, this anthology includes a wide range of voices beyond the jazz critics who (however vigorous their disagreements at times) have dominated published discussion of the music. There is an emphasis here on reception, on diverse reactions to and uses of jazz, on the actual meanings that have circulated around the music, however distant these were, sometimes, from the intentions of those who made it. In particular, I have foregrounded the voices of African Americans; nearly half of the excerpts included here are statements by black musicians or writers. Together, they underscore the fact that debates over jazz have taken place within communities as well as across them; black understandings of jazz have been no more consistent or monolithic than white interpretations.

Third, I have focused, as much as possible, on the music—on the specific choices, techniques, and rhetoric upon which everything else depends. The musicians' statements included here center on how the music works and what it means, as opposed to, say, biographical statements or colorful stories. Other commentaries, from the musicological formalism of Andre Hodeir to the diverse analytical strategies of Sidney Finkelstein, Albert Murray, Hazel Carby, Samuel Floyd, and Christopher Small, attempt to illuminate the significance of the musical potentials that musicians inherit and the creative options they exercise.

Fourth, I wanted to find writings that would be enjoyable and productive to discuss. This drew me to excerpts that take a stand on what jazz is and why it matters. Thus, although it is aimed at a broad readership, this book should prove useful in classrooms. The primary sources collected here could be used to complement and expand historically-oriented jazz textbooks, such as Frank Tirro's *Jazz: A History* or *Jazz: From Its Origins to the Present* by Lewis Porter and Michael Ullman. Or, used with a text that emphasizes "appreciation," such as *Jazz Styles* by Mark Gridley, *Keeping Time* can enable discussions of many aspects of jazz history that would otherwise be missing. I have not thought it important to offer a prescriptive definition of "jazz," in the belief that the historian's job is to understand how such terms have been used, not to tell people how they should use them.

The selections are roughly organized by decade as a way of partially evading the usual progression of style periods, which tend to make what happened seem as though it had to happen. Tensions, not tendencies, define historical moments, and avoiding style categories underscores each statement's place in history—not just jazz history. Even so, some of the selections range across two or more decades as, for example, a musician looks back over a career.

Each excerpt is preceded by a brief introduction, the purpose of which is to explain the context of the selection and to point out some issues that would seem to deserve discussion. I have marked [RW] footnotes to explain obscure references in the text, to make recommendations for further reading, and to comment on or question some statements; other footnotes are by the original authors. I have corrected myriad misspellings of musicians' names, and many of the selections have been abridged, with cuts not always indicated when ellipses might interfere with readability. Thus, while scholars should still consult the original documents, other readers will be able to engage a great variety of materials conveniently. More information on how the selections have been edited can be found in the Editing Notes at the end of the book.

There are probably already more anthologies devoted to jazz than to any other twentieth-century musical genre. Most focus on one type of material, ranging from the essays of individual critics (Leonard Feather, Martin Williams, Amiri Baraka, Gary Giddins, Ralph Gleason, Gunther Schuller, Andre Hodeir, Eddie Condon, Gene Lees) to collections of interviews (by Art Taylor, Ben Sidran, Nat Hentoff, Jim Merod) to items devoted to a particular musician (Mark Tucker on Duke Ellington, Lewis Porter on Lester Young) or drawn from a single periodical (Frank Alkyer with *Down Beat,* Pauline Rivelli and Robert Levin with *Jazz and Pop,* Art Hodes and Chadwick Hansen with the *Jazz Record*). There are scholarly state-of-the-art compilations (by Krin Gabbard, David Baker, Nat Hentoff, Reginald Buckner and Steven Weiland) and even a set of record liner notes (by Tom Piazza).

And then there is a more eclectic category, to which *Keeping Time* belongs. The most recent examples are two volumes by David Meltzer and Robert Gottlieb, separately edited, independent projects but both entitled *Reading Jazz.* Like the earlier *The Jazz Word* (Cerulli et al., which covered only the 1950s), they include fiction and poetry along with criticism, autobiography, and cultural analysis. Gottlieb is primarily interested in the "quality" of writing about jazz, from the perspective of a professional editor newly become a fan of the music. Meltzer, who is a poet, devotes his book to the thesis that the history of jazz is a history of racialized misunderstandings. Both authors furnish us with a great deal of handy material, though neither does much to contextualize his individual excerpts. My own approach is closer to that of several collections from another era: *Jazzmen* (1939) by Frederic Ramsey, Jr., and Charles Edward Smith; Ralph de Toledano's *Frontiers of Jazz* (1947); Eddie Condon and Richard Gehman's *Eddie Condon's Treasury of Jazz* (1956); Ralph Gleason's *Jam Session* (1958); and Martin Williams's *The Art of Jazz* (1959). Although a great deal of jazz history has passed since these were published, they are all still valuable because they focused more on the history and meanings of the music than on elegant or poetic writing; de Toledano included especially thoughtful, helpful introductions for each item. Given the years that have passed since these earlier collections, the different priorities of the more recent ones, and the countless pages that have been written about jazz, it isn't surprising to find that *Keeping Time* overlaps very little with its predecessors. Even in the few cases when the editors drew from the same sources, we chose different sections, for different reasons.

Perhaps the most important model for this book was Piero Weiss and Richard Taruskin's *Music in the Western World: A History in Documents* (Schirmer, 1984). It was by teaching the Western musical canon with their collection that I realized the extraordinary educational value, at all levels, of source readings. Instead of presenting my students with a stolid and static canon for them to learn about and revere, Weiss/Taruskin helped me to lead them through a historical landscape that was more interesting for being more conflicted. They came to care about early opera or Beethoven's *Eroica* because they could see that other people had once cared enough to argue, sometimes passionately, about them. The letters, reviews, journalism, academic writing, and official documents collected in Weiss/Taruskin helped my students to see multiple sides to each issue—helped them, indeed, to see that there had been issues at all.[2] Over years of playing jazz and teaching its history, I have similarly sought to provide my students with materials that would enable them to relive the

2. Eileen Southern's *Readings in Black American Music* (New York: W. W. Norton, 1971) has been similarly useful.

controversies that have accompanied every moment of jazz history, despite the smooth, seemingly inevitable linear trajectory laid out by most textbooks.

No book keeps time alone: each is in dialogue not only with other books but also with other sites of conversation and contestation. No book can contain all perspectives; an author or editor can hope only to have made some useful points and enabled further discussion. Fewer than a hundred items can't record all that much of a hundred years' worth of history (although this seems luxurious in comparison with *Music in the Western World,* which covered twenty-six centuries with 156).

Thus, *Keeping Time's* coverage is, inevitably, incomplete, frustrating no one more than its editor. Much of what I might have wished to include was never written down. Other materials have vanished, and still more, no doubt, escaped notice, despite my best efforts. Some major musicians (John Coltrane, Charlie Parker) never indulged the autobiographical impulse that left us with so much valuable material by some of their contemporaries. For later decades, some sources, especially autobiographies, don't yet exist. Some of the most famous and influential jazz critics have been excluded, partly because their views are already well represented in print, and partly because, in many cases, the immediate goals of their writing had little to do with accounting for the social significance of the music. Copyright difficulties ruled out a number of attractive prospects. Yet a project I thought would be both useful and quick has taken longer than anything else I have done; ultimately, I can do no better than to echo one of my predecessors of fifty years ago:

> The job of choosing what merited inclusion and what did not was never an easy one. Every reader, except the newcomers in the field, will quarrel with me over one or more choices, and I imagine there will be some who reject most of the book. That is the fate of any anthologist, especially one whose general approach is eclectic—which means that the dead cats and ancient tomatoes come from every direction. If further editions of this book are ever issued, and that is my earnest hope, the complaints of the readers will be weighed in making new selections.[3]

Many statements in this book are controversial, for the excerpts included here trace debates over the meaning and importance of jazz that were sometimes bitterly fought. Some arguments are still alive; others have faded away with time. Many positions now look ridiculous, but the point of historical studies should never be simply to decide which previous writers were right. If we are to study jazz as history, we must try to recover some of the ways in which people related to it and understood their involvement with it—the history jazz has actually had, not the one we think it should have had. The debates of our own time matter no less, since they show us the process of future history being constructed. In opposition to the growing tendency to replace jazz history with jazz appreciation, such an approach demands critical thinking, increases historical engagement, and encourages lively discussion. It does so in part by paying attention not only to those who have played jazz, but also the people who have loved, hated, supported, banned, misunderstood, and argued about the music.

To avoid such controversies, to treat jazz as a timeless art of universal appeal, may seem flattering to those who have been associated with it; ultimately, though, such a view trivializes the music and its makers. "Keeping time" means hanging on to the stormy diversity of opinions that show us how jazz has meant so much to so many. It means respecting the richness of a music that can create so many meanings

3. Ralph de Toledano, *Frontiers of Jazz* (Oliver Durrell, Inc., 1947), p. xiv.

and intersect with so many spheres of life, claiming on its behalf its full social importance. It means recovering different perspectives, becoming familiar with more ways of hearing and relating to jazz, gaining more awareness of those whose lives have been touched by it. Finally, it means learning from the past in ways that affect our understandings and actions in the present, and there is no better vehicle for such learning than jazz.

To the Second Edition

What's new in this edition:

- New selections updating the book to cover developments in jazz history since the 1990s, including:
  - Fred Ho on the potential of jazz to be a revolutionary music
  - A survey of smooth jazz by journalist Sarah Rodman
  - Important theoretical statements by musicians Brad Mehldau, George Lewis, and Vijay Iyer, discussing aesthetics, race, and embodiment
  - George Lipsitz's critique of Ken Burns's landmark documentary film, *Jazz*
  - Three polemical statements by prominent critic Stanley Crouch
  - Analysis of the politics of contemporary jazz by sociologist Herman Gray
  - Exploration of the important Nordic jazz scene by Stuart Nicholson
  - An updated survey of the characteristics of the contemporary audience for jazz
- New coverage of earlier jazz, including:
  - Sherrie Tucker on the female musicians of the swing era
  - Robert Palmer on "Jazz Pop," the predecessor to smooth jazz
  - The burgeoning of jazz theory and pedagogy as reflected in Jamey Aebersold's "Scale Syllabus"
  - Robert Walser on Miles Davis's trumpet playing
- Updates to the headnotes throughout, and a revised index that reflects the new additions, deletions, and editing.

Acknowledgments

To the First Edition

I have called upon many people for help during the book's long gestation and I am pleased to acknowledge their generosity. I am grateful for the financial support for travel and other research expenses provided by a Marion and Jasper Whiting Foundation Fellowship, the Walter Burke Research Initiation Award at Dartmouth College, and UCLA Faculty Senate Grants. The staff at the Institute of Jazz Studies at Rutgers, the State University of New Jersey at Newark, the Center for Black Music Research at Columbia College Chicago, and the William Ransom Hogan Jazz Archive at Tulane University did much to make my research trips pleasant and productive.

I owe a great deal to the labors of a series of smart, diligent, and creative research assistants: Adam Klipple and Luis Scheker at Dartmouth College, Chris Aschan at the Humanities Research Institute at UC-Irvine, and Steve Baur, Dave Kopplin, Francesca Draughon, and David Ake at UCLA. In particular, Adam Klipple helped me work out the book's title, and David Ake's intimate knowledge of jazz, scrupulous scholarship, and enthusiasm for my project have greatly improved it.

For valuable advice, tips, support, and feedback, I am grateful to Kimasi Browne, James Lincoln Collier, Scott DeVeaux, Samuel A. Floyd Jr., Krin Gabbard, Lawrence Kramer, Steven Ledbetter, Dominique-Rene de Lerma, George Lewis, George Lipsitz, Dan Morgenstern, Joel Pfister, Guthrie Ramsey, Nancy Schnog, Barry Shank, George Simon, Mark Tucker, Chris Waterman, and the anonymous reviewers for Oxford University Press. If I have not always taken their advice, I have always learned from it. I thank my editor, Maribeth Payne, for her patience and for choosing tough, helpful referees. Crucial challenges and encouragement came, as always, from my favorite person, Susan McClary.

This book grew from one stray seed, a 1924 copy of *The Etude* magazine that I inherited from my grandfather. The son of a shopkeeper in St. Paul, Minnesota, Gottfried Anton Walser (1900–1979) dreamed of studying music at the University of Minnesota but found himself transplanted to a farm in 1913 when his parents got caught up in a "back-to-nature" craze. The farmland turned out to be sand and my grandfather spent most of his life paying off his parents' debts, his musical opportunities limited to playing the piano at home and the organ at church. He hated the farm; his lifeline to another world was that piano, where he played Beethoven, Grieg, Debussy, and the musical "characteristic sketches" found in each issue of *The Etude.* He was a kind and learned man; he taught me "chopsticks" and encouraged my interests in music and science. I have been fortunate to have had the kind of career he should have had. I wish we had made music together more than we did.

Keeping Time is dedicated to his memory; to that of the musician who has most inspired me to study and perform jazz, Miles Davis; to my friend Christopher Small, who has done as much as anyone to explain why this music matters; and to my teacher Harold Land, who keeps me practicing.

To the Second Edition

This edition of *Keeping Time* was completed fifteen years and 2,000 miles away from where the first one was finished. There have been significant abridgements but the wholly deleted materials are few, and the new materials both speak for themselves and have been spoken for in my individual introductions. But some thanks are in order.

Oxford University Press surveyed at least two handfuls of jazz scholars and teachers to gather suggestions for how first edition of the book was working and for how it might be improved. I am grateful to all who provided their feedback about how *Keeping Time* has actually fared as a resource in their scholarship and teaching. Some of these referees and other specialists who have shared feedback are known to me, for one reason or another, and I am pleased to acknowledge their expert and essential advice.

Several of the new authors included in this edition went beyond the call of duty to make this a better book, especially Sherry Tucker, George Lipsitz, Vijay Iyer, Fred Ho, Stuart Nicholson, and George Lewis. The editorial team at Oxford University Press, especially Janet Beatty and Richard Carlin, has been excellent. And I haven't forgotten that Maribeth Payne talked me into doing this in the first place, for which I'm very glad.

At UCLA, Mitchell Morris was a still of intellectual ferment, always ready to condense interesting ideas and observations from any topic I brought up. Students at Case Western Reserve University served as test subjects for the new materials, and I am pleased to acknowledge their feisty engagement with the selections that appear for the first time in this new edition: Thank you Adam Spektor, Michelle Cheng, and Karl Beheim, as well as Leah Branstetter, who provided useful editing suggestions at the last. Colleagues at Case brought me into a welcoming environment and I am glad to acknowledge their less specific but no less important support, especially that of David Rothenburg, Francesca Brittan, Georgia Cowart, Kathleen Horvath, and Stephen Hefling. And, of course, Susan McClary, who understands better than anyone else what this project has meant to me.

Finally, love and gratitude go to my favorite Spanish expats: Christopher Small, Neville Braithwaite, and Dennis Sanders, all of whom taught me much about music and life. Sadly, all three have now passed on, which reminds us that only in the insights and memories we've been left can time really be kept.

PART 1

First Accounts

1. Sidney Bechet's Musical Philosophy

ONE OF THE GREATEST OF THE EARLY NEW Orleans jazz musicians, Sidney Bechet (1897–1959) was among those who left the city around the time of World War I, bringing the music to an international audience. Although he performed on clarinet throughout his career, he was also the first important player of the soprano saxophone, which became his main instrument. Bechet worked for Duke Ellington for a few months in 1924 and his New Orleans style had a great influence on Ellington's band. His fortunes declined during the 1930s, along with the "hot" style he exemplified, but he became one of the beneficiaries of the New Orleans revival at the turn of the decade.

During the latter part of his life, Bechet narrated his autobiography in a series of taped interviews, which were later transcribed and edited.[1] These selections from the book that resulted, *Treat It Gentle: An Autobiography* (1960), pertain to Bechet's musical philosophy and the heritage that shaped it. Although it is in some sense a document of the 1950s, the book is excerpted here as a firsthand account of the earliest jazz "musicianers." Bechet makes his story vivid and evocative by personifying the musical tradition to which he belonged, allowing him to present jazz as something that is experienced as deeply personal, yet shared socially and rooted historically.

Source: Sidney Bechet, *Treat It Gentle: An Autobiography* (London: Cassell, 1960), pp. 4, 47–48, 104, 203, 63, 176–77, 209, 201. Reprinted by permission of Daniel Bechet.

1. The extent to which Bechet's collaborators rewrote his memoirs is now hard to determine. For an account of the complex process that produced *Treat It Gentle,* see John Chilton, *Sidney Becket: The Wizard of Jazz* (New York: Oxford University Press, 1987), pp. 290–92. See also the thoughtful reviews by Nat Hentoff, "A Need to be Moving," *Metronome,* March 1961, pp. 30–31, and Max Jones, "This Book *Is* Bechet," *Melody Maker,* April 23, 1960, p. 5. [RW]

My story goes a long way back. It goes further back than I had anything to do with. My music is like that. I got it from something inherited, just like the stories my father gave down to me. And those stories are all I know about some of the things bringing me to where I am. And all my life I've been trying to explain about something, something I understand—the part of me that was there before I was. It was there waiting to be me. It was there waiting to be the music. It's that part I've been trying to explain to myself all my life.

There was a hell of a lot of fuss and confusion about the time my father was growing up. It was right around Emancipation time. All the papers were taking sides, running cartoons of apes and things, screaming blood and gunpowder. A lot of people didn't want to lose the Negroes. The Negro, he was three billion dollars worth of property, and here was a law coming that was to take it all away. Who was to do the work then?

Well, they had the war, and it made a bitterness. A lot of people, they never could climb so high again after the war and they had a whole lot to say about that. It was a crime; it was all political; it was the end of America. What would anyone want with a lot of black people being free, people who couldn't even spell their names or read a book? And everything changed upside down . . . the soldiers being brought in to guard, sort of keep order, and making more bitterness just by being there.

But the Negroes, it had made them free. They wouldn't be bought and sold now, not ever again. If they could find a piece of land somewheres it would be theirs, they could work it for themselves—the ones anyway who had heard that slavery was against the law. A lot of Negroes, especially in back places, never did hear about it. But mostly there was this big change: a different feeling had got started.

Go down Moses,
Way down in Egypt land;
Tell old Pharaoh,
Let my people go. . . .

It was years they'd been singing that. And suddenly there was a different way of singing it. You could feel a new way of happiness in the lines. All that waiting, all that time when that song was far-off music, waiting music, suffering music; and all at once it was there, it had arrived. It was joy music now. It was Free Day . . . Emancipation.

And New Orleans just bust wide open. A real time was had. They heard the music, and the music told them about it. They heard that music from bands marching up and down the streets and they knew what music it was. It was laughing out loud up and down all the streets, laughing like two people just finding out about each other . . . like something that had found a short-cut after traveling through all the distance there was. That music, it wasn't spirituals or blues or ragtime, but everything all at once, each one putting something over on the other.

Maybe that's not easy to understand. White people, they don't have the memory that needs to understand it. But that's what the music is . . . a lost thing finding itself. It's like a man with no place of his own. He wanders the world and he's a stranger wherever he is; he's a stranger right in the place where he was born. But then something happens to him and he finds a place, *his* place. He stands in front of it and he crosses the door, going inside. That's where the music was that day—it was taking him through the door; he was coming home.

All those people who had been slaves, they needed the music more than ever now; it was like they were trying to find out in this music what they were supposed to do with this freedom: playing the music and listening to it—waiting for it to express what they needed to learn.

Sometimes when I was playing the music I knew what it was that I was remembering. Other times, I was just being a kid, forgetting a thing almost before it was over. Somehow it seems like I always *understood* more when the music was playing and I was inside it, bringing it on out to itself.

There's a pride in it, too. The man singing it, the man playing it, he makes a place. For as long as the song is being played, *that's* the place he's been looking for. And when the piece is all played and he's back, it may be he's feeling good; maybe he's making good money and getting good treatment and he's feeling good—or maybe he starts missing the song. Maybe he starts wanting the place he found while he was playing the song. Or maybe it just troubles back at him.

Sometimes we'd have what they called in those days "bucking contests"; that was long before they talked about "cutting contests." One band, it would come right up in front of the other and play at it, and the first band it would play right back, until finally one band just had to give in. And the one that didn't give in, all the people, they'd rush up to it and give it drinks and food and holler for more, wanting more, not having enough. There just couldn't be enough for those people back there. And that band was best that played the best *together.* No matter what kind of music it was, if the band could keep it together, that made it the best. That band, it would know its numbers and know its foundation and it would know *itself.*

In the old days there wasn't no one so anxious to take someone else's run. We were working together. Each person, he was the other person's music: you could feel that really running through the band, making itself up and coming out so new and strong. We played as a group then. . . . I guess just about the loneliest a musicianer can be is in not being able to find someone he can really play with that way.

Like I said before, you could ask me, "What's classical music?" I couldn't answer that. It's not a thing that could be answered straight out. You have to tell it the long way. You have to tell about the people who make it, what they have inside them, what they're doing, what they're waiting for. Then you can begin to have an understanding.

You come into life alone and you go out of it alone, and you're going to be alone a lot of the time when you're on this earth—and what tells it all, it's the music. You tell it to the music and the music tells it to you. And then you know about it. You know what it was happened to you.

2. "Whence Comes Jass?"

ONE OF THE EARLIEST PUBLISHED DISCUSSIONS of jazz appeared in the *New York Sun* on August 5, 1917. The author, Walter Kingsley ("the Great Authority on the Subject" according to the *Sun*), was a press agent

---

Source: Walter Kingsley, "Whence Comes Jass? Facts From the Great Authority on the Subject," *New York Sun*, August 5, 1917, p. 3. Later summarized and quoted extensively in "The Appeal of the Primitive Jazz," *The Literary Digest*, August 25, 1917, pp. 28–29.

for New York's Palace Theatre. The first section of his article illustrates how writers frequently projected their fantasies onto the new music: here jazz is positioned midway between the exoticism of the African jungle and the eclecticism of New York's vaudeville and variety shows. Kingsley continues by quoting and summarizing (sometimes inaccurately) the work of a certain Professor William Morrison Patterson, who offers some perceptive comments on rhythm, particularly syncopation.

But when Patterson tries to explain the power of jazz, his theory relies on a contradiction that would plague jazz throughout its history: he refers to "savage," "instinctive" jazz musicians, yet he praises their skills and links their art to modernity. Overall, Kingsley's account of the origins of jazz is closer to the truth than many other versions that have circulated, but this article is of interest mainly as evidence of how jazz was being presented to the attention of white Americans at this time.

Variously spelled Jas, Jass, Jaz, Jazz, Jasz, and Jascz.

The word is African in origin. It is common on the Gold Coast of Africa and in the hinterland of Cape Coast Castle. In his studies of the creole patois and idiom in New Orleans, Lafcadio Hearn reported that the word "jaz," meaning to speed things up, to make excitement, was common among the blacks of the South and had been adopted by the creoles as a term to be applied to music of a rudimentary syncopated type.[1] In the old plantation days, when the slaves were having one of their rare holidays and the fun languished, some West Coast African would cry out, "Jaz her up," and this would be the cue for fast and furious fun. No doubt the witch-doctors and medicine-men on the Congo used the same term at those jungle "parties" when the tomtoms throbbed and the sturdy warriors gave their pep an added kick with rich brews of Yohimbin bark—that precious product of the Cameroons.[2] Curiously enough the phrase "Jaz her up" is a common one today in vaudeville and on the circus lot. When a vaudeville act needs ginger the cry from the advisors in the wings is "put in jaz," meaning add low comedy, go to high speed and accelerate the comedy spark. "Jasbo" is a form of the word common in the varieties, meaning the same as "hokum," or low comedy verging on vulgarity.

Jazz music is the delirium tremens of syncopation. It is strict rhythm without melody. To-day the jazz bands take popular tunes and rag them to death to make jazz. Beats are added as often as the delicacy of the player's ear will permit. In one-two time a third beat is interpolated. There are many half notes or less and many long-drawn wavering tones. It is an attempt to reproduce the marvelous syncopation of the African jungle. Prof. William Morrison Patterson, Ph.D., of Columbia University in his monumental pioneering experimental investigation of the individual difference in the sense of rhythm says:

"The music of contemporary savages taunts us with a lost art of rhythm. Modern sophistication has inhibited many native instincts, and the mere fact that our conventional dignity usually forbids us to sway our bodies or to tap our feet when we hear

---

1. Lafcadio Hearn (1850–1904) was a writer who was best known for introducing the culture and literature of Japan to the West. [RW]

2. Kingsley's "no doubt" signals that he is simply guessing. Similarly, the musical descriptions he offers in the following paragraph are, to put it charitably, vague. [RW]

effective music has deprived us of unsuspected pleasures." Professor Patterson goes on to say that the ear keenly sensible of these wild rhythms has "rhythmic aggressiveness." Therefore of all moderns the jazz musicians and their auditors have the most rhythmic aggressiveness, for jazz is based on the savage musician's wonderful gift for progressive retarding and acceleration guided by his sense of "swing." He finds syncopation easy and pleasant. He plays to an inner series of time beats joyfully "elastic" because not necessarily grouped in succession of twos and threes. The highly gifted jazz artist can get away with five beats where there were but two before. Of course, beside the thirty-seconds scored for the tympani in some of the modern Russian music, this doesn't seem so intricate, but just try to beat in between beats on your kettledrum and make rhythm and you will think better of it. To be highbrow and quote Professor Patterson once more:

"With these elastic unitary pulses any haphazard series by means of syncopation can be readily, because instinctively, coordinated. The result is that a rhythmic tune compounded of time and stress and pitch relations is created, the chief characteristic of which is likely to be complicated syncopation. An arabesque of accentual differences, group-forming in their nature, is superimposed upon the fundamental time divisions."

There is jazz precisely defined as a result of months of laboratory experiment in drum beating and syncopation. The laws that govern jazz rule in the rhythms of great original prose, verse that sings itself, and opera of ultra modernity. Imagine Walter Pater, Swinburne, and Borodin swaying to the same pulses that rule the moonlit music on the banks of African rivers.

3. The Location of "Jass"

ALTHOUGH NEW ORLEANS HAS LONG BEEN proud of its status as "the birthplace of jazz," that was not always the case. In 1918, the editors of the city's leading newspaper hastened to decline this honor.[1] First, however, they condemned jazz in musical terms. They built a "house of the muses" according to the plan of European symphonic music, grouping together and dismissing as inferior all types of music that work according to other principles—especially those that encourage

---

Source: "Jass and Jassism," *The Times-Picayune* [New Orleans], June 20, 1918, p. 4.

1. The *Times-Picayune* had only a slightly larger circulation than the other leading daily, the *Item.*

bodily movement. Their stern reference to people who tap their feet at symphony concerts reflects the process of sacralizing art and taming audiences that took place in the late nineteenth and early twentieth centuries.[2]

We usually think of people as either musical or nonmusical, as if there were a simple line separating two great classes. The fact is, however, that there are many mansions in the house of the muses. There is first the great assembly hall of melody—where most of us take our seats at some time in our lives—but a lesser number pass on to inner sanctuaries of harmony, where the melodic sequence, the "tune," as it most frequently is called, has infinitely less interest than the blending of notes into chords so that the combining wave-lengths will give new aesthetic sensations. This inner court of harmony is where nearly all the truly great music is enjoyed.

In the house there is, however, another apartment, properly speaking, down in the basement, a kind of servants' hall of rhythm. It is there we hear the hum of the Indian dance, the throb of the Oriental tambourines and kettledrums, the clatter of the clogs, the click of Slavic heels, the thumpty-tumpty of the negro banjo, and, in fact, the native dances of a world. Although commonly associated with melody, and less often with harmony also, rhythm is not necessarily music, and he who loves to keep time to the pulse of the orchestral performance by patting his foot upon the theatre floor is not necessarily a music lover.

Prominently, in the basement hall of rhythm, is found rag-time, and of those most devoted to the cult of the displaced accent there has developed a brotherhood of those who, devoid of harmonic and even of melodic instinct, love to fairly wallow in noise. On certain natures, sound loud and meaningless has an exciting, almost an intoxicating effect, like crude colors and strong perfumes, the sight of flesh or the sadic pleasure in blood. To such as these the jass music is a delight, and a dance to the unstable bray of the sackbut gives a sensual delight more intense and quite different from the languor of a Viennese waltz or the refined sentiment and respectful emotion of an eighteenth-century minuet.[3]

In the matter of the jass, New Orleans is particularly interested, since it has been widely suggested that this particular form of musical vice had its birth in this city—that it came, in fact, from doubtful surroundings in our slums. We do not recognize the honor of parenthood, but with such a story in circulation, it behooves us to be last to accept the atrocity in polite society, and where it has crept in we should make it a point of civic honor to suppress it. Its musical value is nil, and its possibilities of harm are great.

2. See Lawrence W. Levine, *Highbrow/Lowbrow: The Emergence of Cultural Hierarchy in America* (Cambridge: Harvard University Press, 1988).

3. "Sadic" is equivalent to "sadistic." Until the eighteenth century, the trombone was often called a "sackbut": here, the archaic word is used for effect. [RW]

4. A "Serious" Musician Takes Jazz Seriously

ONE OF THE FIRST PRESTIGIOUS CONCERT hall musicians to endorse jazz was a Swiss conductor, Ernest Ansermet (1883–1969). In this essay his main topic is Will Marion Cook (1869–1944), an important composer for the black musical theater who led a series of bands in New York from the turn of the century into the 1920s; Cook assembled the New York Syncopated Orchestra (later called the Southern Syncopated Orchestra) and toured the United States and England with it between 1918 and 1920. Ansermet's comments have long been famous, however, because of his early recognition of Sidney Bechet's talent. Although even this enthusiastic report is not entirely free of condescension, Ansermet presents this music as different from European concert music yet not inferior to it. He recognized the cooperative flexibility that kept the performances fresh, and his deep respect for these musicians was extraordinary for the time. Perceptively, he emphasized performance over composition, and tradition as much as instinct. Still, the conductor was troubled by his inability to gauge the musicians' interiority (what they thought and felt, who they really were): he liked what he was hearing, but wasn't sure he understood its source.[1]

The first thing that strikes one about the Southern Syncopated Orchestra is the astonishing perfection, the superb taste, and the fervor of its playing. I couldn't tell whether these artists feel it is their duty to be sincere, or whether they are driven by the idea that they have a "mission" to fulfill, or whether they are convinced of the "nobility" of their task, or have that holy "audacity" and that sacred "valor" which the musical code requires of our European musicians, nor indeed whether they are animated by any "idea" whatsoever. But I can see they have a very keen sense of the music they love, and a pleasure in making it which they communicate to the hearer with irresistible force—a pleasure which pushes them to outdo themselves all the time,

---

Source: Originally published in Switzerland: E. Ansermet, "Sur un Orchestre Nègre," *Revue Romande*, October 1919. Reprinted in Paris, with a translation by Walter E. Schaap, in *Jazz Hot*, November–December 1938, pp. 4–9.

1. For a fuller discussion of this topic, see Robert Walser, "Deep Jazz: Notes on Interiority, Race, and Criticism," in *Inventing the Psychological: Toward a Cultural History of Emotional Life in America*, ed. Joel Pfister and Nancy Schnog (New Haven: Yale University Press, 1997), pp. 271–96.

to constantly enrich and refine their medium. They play generally without written music, and even when they have it, the score only serves to indicate the general line, for there are very few numbers I have heard them execute twice with exactly the same effects. I imagine that, knowing the voice attributed to them in the harmonic ensemble and conscious of the role their instrument is to play, they can let themselves go, in a certain direction and within certain limits, as their hearts desire. They are so entirely possessed by the music they play that they can't stop themselves from dancing inwardly to it in such a way that their playing is a real show. When they indulge in one of their favorite effects, which is to take up the refrain of a dance in a tempo suddenly twice as slow and with redoubled intensity and figuration, a truly gripping thing takes place: it seems as if a great wind is passing over a forest or as if a door is suddenly opened on a wild orgy.

The musician who directs them and who is responsible for creating the ensemble, Mr. Will Marion Cook, is, moreover, a master in every respect, and there is no orchestra leader I so delight in seeing conduct. As for the music which makes up their repertory . . . , it bears the names of the composers (all unknown to our world) or is simply marked *Traditional.* This traditional music is religious in inspiration. It is the index of a whole mode of religion and of a veritable religious art which merits a study of its own. The aforementioned traditional music itself has its source, as could doubtless be easily rediscovered, in the songs the negroes learned from the English missionaries. Thus, all, or nearly all, the music of the Southern Syncopated Orchestra is in origin foreign to these negroes. How is this possible? Because it is not the material that makes Negro music, it is the spirit.

The desire to give certain syllables a particular emphasis or a prolonged resonance, that is to say preoccupations of an expressive order, seem to have determined in negro singing their anticipation or delay of a fraction of rhythmic unity. This is the birth of syncopation. All the traditional negro songs are strewn with syncopes which issue from the voice while the movement of the body marks regular rhythm. Then, when the Anglo-Saxon ballad or the banal dance forms reach Dixieland, land of the plantations, the negroes appropriate them in the same fashion, and the rag is born. But it is not enough to say that negro music consists in the habit of syncopating any musical material whatsoever. We have shown that syncopation itself is but the effect of an expressive need, the manifestation in the field of rhythm of a particular taste, in a word, the genius of the race. This genius demonstrates itself in all the musical elements.

Composed of two violins, a cello, a saxophone, two basses, two clarinets, a horn, three trumpets, three trombones, drums, two pianos, and a banjo section, it (Cook's orchestra) achieves by the manner in which the instruments are played, a strangely fused total sonority distinctly its own, in which the neutral timbres like that of the piano disappear completely, and which the banjos surround with a halo of perpetual vibration. Now the fusion is such (all brasses muted) that it is difficult to recognize the individual timbres, now a very high clarinet emerges like a bird in flight, or a trombone bursts out brusquely like a foreign body appearing. And the ensemble displays a terrific dynamic range, going from a subtle sonority reminiscent of Ravel's orchestra to a terrifying tumult in which shouts and hand-clapping are mixed.

In the field of melody, although his habituation to our scales has effaced the memory of the African modes, an old instinct pushes the negro to pursue his pleasure outside the orthodox intervals: he performs thirds which are neither major nor minor and false seconds, and falls often by instinct on the natural harmonic sounds of a given note—it is here especially that no written music can give the idea of his playing.

It is only in the field of harmony that the negro hasn't yet created his own distinct expression. But even here, he uses a succession of seventh chords, and ambiguous major-minors with a deftness which many Europeans should envy. But, in general, harmony is perhaps a musical element which appears in the scheme of musical evolution only at a stage which the negro art has not yet attained.

All the characteristics of this art, in fact, show it to be a perfect example of what is called popular art—an art which is still in its period of oral tradition. It doesn't matter a whit, after all, whether negro music be written by Russian Jews, German Jews, or some corrupted Anglo-Saxon. It is a fact that the best numbers are those written by the negroes themselves. But with these as with the others, the importance of the writer in the creation of the work is counterbalanced by the action of tradition, represented by the performer. The work may be written, but it is not fixed and it finds complete expression only in actual performance.

I am inclined to think that the strongest manifestation of the racial genius lies in the Blues. The Blues occurs when the negro is sad, when he is far from his home, his mammy, or his sweetheart. Then he thinks of a motif or a preferred rhythm, and takes his trombone, or his violin, or his banjo, or his clarinet, or his drum, or else he sings, or simply dances. And on the chosen motif, he plumbs the depths of his imagination. This makes his sadness pass away—it is the Blues.

There is in the Southern Syncopated Orchestra an extraordinary clarinet virtuoso who is, so it seems, the first of his race to have composed perfectly formed blues on the clarinet. I've heard two of them which he elaborated at great length. They are admirable equally for their richness of invention, their force of accent, and their daring novelty and unexpected turns. These solos already show the germ of a new style. Their form is gripping, abrupt, harsh, with a brusque and pitiless ending like that of Bach's Second Brandenburg Concerto. I wish to set down the name of this artist of genius; as for myself, I shall never forget it—it is Sidney Bechet. When one has tried so often to find in the past one of those figures to whom we owe the creation of our art as we know it today—those men of the 17th and 18th centuries, for example, who wrote the expressive works of dance airs which cleared the way for Haydn and Mozart—what a moving thing it is to meet this black, fat boy with white teeth and narrow forehead, who is very glad one likes what he does, but can say nothing of his art, except that he follows his "own way"—and then one considers that perhaps his "own way" is the highway along which the whole world will swing tomorrow.

5. "A Negro Explains 'Jazz' "

AFRICAN-AMERICAN MUSICIANS WERE NOT often invited to participate in public debates over the nature and meaning of early jazz, so this statement by James Reese Europe (1881–1919) is especially significant. A successful band leader and composer, Europe organized in 1910 an association of black musicians known as the Clef Club, and in 1913 his band became the first black group ever to make recordings. He gained great fame through his association with Irene and Vernon Castle, leaders of the social dance craze of the 1910s, who popularized African-American-derived dances among the white middle class. During World War I, Europe became famous for the quality of his military band and for the concerts he conducted in France. In retrospect, his music is usually taken to represent a transitional moment between ragtime and jazz.

Like so many other people, Europe offered a fanciful explanation of the word "jazz" (evidence for the existence of "Razz's Band" is lacking). But his story includes valuable accounts of how his music was received, and he mentions technical details to explain how certain "peculiar" sounds were produced. With great conviction, Europe advocated the cultivation of "negro music" (though where he refers to "racial" qualities we might today be inclined to write of "cultural" ones), invoking the names of prominent African-American musicians of the time in support of his argument against musical assimilation. This article begins with a brief introduction by Grenville Vernon, under whose byline Europe's statement appeared in the *New York Tribune* in 1919.

Just what is "jazz"? Most of us know it when we hear it, but few of us know its derivation, its reason, or the manner in which the veritable "jazz" is produced, for there are "jazzes" which are not veritable. "Jazz" is, of course, negro; somehow or other all musical originality in America seems to be negro. The negro musically is always a worshipper of rhythm; often he is a rhythomaniac, and "jazz" arises from his rhythmic fervor, combined with a peculiar liking for strange sounds. This at least is the opinion of Lieutenant James Reese Europe, late of the Machine Gun Battalion of the

---

Source: Grenville Vernon, "That Mysterious 'Jazz,' " *New York Tribune,* March 30, 1919, Section 4, p. 5. Subsequently reprinted with slight changes as "A Negro Explains 'Jazz,' " *The Literary Digest,* April 26, 1919, pp. 28–29.

old 15th Regiment. Lieutenant Europe has just returned from more than a year's service in France, which he passed partly in the direction of the band he had organized for his regiment, a band which had a stupendous success in France and which is having equally as great success at home.

"When war broke out I enlisted as a private in Colonel Hayward's regiment, and I had just passed my officer's examination when the Colonel asked me to form a band. I told him that it would be impossible, as the negro musicians of New York were paid too well to have them give up their jobs to go to war. However, Colonel Hayward raised $10,000 and told me to get the musicians wherever I could get them. The reed players I got in Porto Rico, the rest from all over the country. I had only one New York negro in the band—my solo cornetist. These are the men who now compose the band, and they are all fighters as well as musicians, for all have seen service in the trenches.

"I believe that the term 'jazz' originated with a band of four pieces which was found about fifteen years ago in New Orleans, and which was known as 'Razz's Band.' This band was of truly extraordinary composition. It consisted of a barytone horn, a trombone, a cornet, and an instrument made out of the china-berry-tree. This instrument is something like a clarinet, and is made by the Southern negroes themselves. Strange to say, it can be used only while the sap is in the wood, and after a few weeks' use has to be thrown away. It produces a beautiful sound and is worthy of inclusion in any band or orchestra. I myself intend to employ it soon in my band. The four musicians of Razz's Band had no idea at all of what they were playing; they improvised as they went along, but such was their innate sense of rhythm that they produced something which was very taking. From the small cafés of New Orleans they graduated to the St. Charles Hotel, and after a time to the Winter Garden in New York, where they appeared, however, only a few days, the individual musicians being grabbed up by various orchestras in the city. Somehow in the passage of time Razz's Band got changed into 'Jazz's Band,' and from this corruption arose the term 'jazz.'

"The negro loves anything that is peculiar in music, and this 'jazzing' appeals to him strongly. It is accomplished in several ways. With the brass instruments we put in mutes and made a whirling motion with the tongue, at the same time blowing full pressure. With wind instruments we pinch the mouthpiece and blow hard. This produces the peculiar sound which you all know. To us it is not discordant, as we play the music as it is written, only that we accent strongly in this manner the notes which originally would be without accent. It is natural for us to do this; it is, indeed, a racial musical characteristic. I have to call a daily rehearsal of my band to prevent the musicians from adding to their music more than I wish them to. Whenever possible they all embroider their parts in order to produce new, peculiar sounds. Some of these effects are excellent and some are not, and I have to be continually on the lookout to cut out the results of my musicians' originality.

"This jazz music made a tremendous sensation in France. I recall one incident in particular. From last February to last August I had been in the trenches, in command of my machine gun squad. I had been through the terrific general attack in Champagne when General Gouraud annihilated the enemy by his strategy and finally put an end to their hopes of victory, and I had been through many a smaller engagement. I can tell you that music was one of the things furthest from my mind when one day, just before the Allied conference in Paris on August 18, Colonel Hayward came to me and said:

"'Lieutenant Europe, I want you to go back to your band and give a single concert in Paris.'

"I protested, telling him that I hadn't led the band since February, but he insisted. Well, I went back to my band, and with it I went to Paris. What was to be our only concert was in the Théâtre des Champs-Elysées. Before we had played two numbers the audience went wild. We had conquered Paris. General Bliss and French high officers who had heard us insisted that we should stay in Paris, and there we stayed for eight weeks. Everywhere we gave a concert it was a riot, but the supreme moment came in the Tuileries Gardens when we gave a concert in conjunction with the greatest bands in the world—the British Grenadiers' Band, the Band of the Garde Républicain, and the Royal Italian Band. My band, of course, could not compare with any of these, yet the crowd, and it was such a crowd as I never saw anywhere else in the world, deserted them for us. We played to 50,000 people at least, and, had we wished it, we might be playing yet.

"After the concert was over the leader of the band of the Garde Républicain came over and asked me for the score of one of the jazz compositions we had played. He said he wanted his band to play it. I gave it to him and the next day he again came to see me. He explained that he couldn't seem to get the effects I got, and asked me to go to a rehearsal. I went with him. The great band had played the composition superbly—but he was right: the jass effects were missing. I took an instrument and showed him how it could be done, and he told me that his own musicians felt sure that my band had used special instruments. Indeed, some of them, afterward attending one of my rehearsals, did not believe what I had said until after they had examined the instruments used by my men.

"I have come back from France more firmly convinced than ever that negroes should write negro music. We have our own racial feeling and if we try to copy whites we will make bad copies. I noticed that the Morocco negro bands played music which had an affinity to ours. One piece, 'In Zanzibar,' I took for my band, and though white audiences seem to find it too discordant, I found it most sympathetic. We won France by playing music which was ours and not a pale imitation of others, and if we are to develop in America we must develop along our own lines. Our musicians do their best work when using negro material. Will Marion Cook, William Tires, even Harry Burleigh and Coleridge-Taylor are not truly themselves [except] in the music which expresses their race. Mr. Tires, for instance, writes charming waltzes, but the best of these have in them negro influences. The music of our race springs from the soil, and this is true today of no other race, except possibly the Russians, and it is because of this that I and all my musicians have come to love Russian music. Indeed, as far as I am concerned, it is the only music I care for outside of negro."

6. Jazzing Away Prejudice

ALTHOUGH MUSIC IS OFTEN DISMISSED AS mere entertainment, this 1919 editorial argues that musical performances can have profound political effects. It appeared in the *Chicago Defender*, one of the country's leading black newspapers, in response to a concert by James Reese Europe and his band.

With the ringing down of the curtain at the Auditorium last Saturday night there closed a remarkable period of band concerts. If you were not fortunate enough to attend you missed a rare treat. This band had made a wonderful record with the American expeditionary forces in France and with its jazz music had proved a source of great entertainment wherever it went. When it returned to the United States it was given a great ovation by the people of New York City, and Chicago found it equal to advance notice. It has all the artistic finish of any band that has invaded these parts in many years. We doubt seriously that Creatore at his best could have furnished a better entertainment.[1] The audiences were highly responsive and rewarded each number with the most spirited applause. The closing number of the program, "In No Man's Land," in which the house was thrown into darkness and all the noises of the battlefield reproduced, furnished a thriller that was a fitting finale to a splendid evening's entertainment.

We hope the swing of Europe and his band around the country will be nation wide. The most prejudiced enemy of our Race could not sit through an evening with Europe without coming away with a changed viewpoint. For he is compelled in spite of himself to see us in a new light. It is a well-known fact that the white people view us largely from the standpoint of the cook, porter, and waiter, and his limited opportunities are responsible for much of the distorted opinion held concerning us. Europe and his band are worth more to our Race than a thousand speeches from so-called Race orators and uplifters. Mere wind-jamming has never given any race material help. It may be entertaining in a way to recite to audiences of our own people in a flamboyant style the doings of the Race, but the spellbinder's efforts, being confined almost exclusively to audiences of our own people, is of as much help in properly presenting our cause to those whom we desire most to reach as a man trying to lift

---

Source: "Jazzing Away Prejudice," *Chicago Defender*, May 10, 1919, p. 20.

1. Giuseppe Creatore (1871–1952) was a successful conductor, impresario, composer, and band leader. [RW]

himself by pulling at his own bootstraps. Experience has shown that most of our spellbinders are in it for what there is in it. The good they do is nil.

Europe and his band are demonstrating what our people can do in a field where the results are bound to be of the greatest benefit. He has the white man's ear because he is giving the white man something new. He is meeting a popular demand and in catering to this love of syncopated music he is jazzing away the barriers of prejudice.

7. The "Inventor of Jazz"

BORN AND RAISED IN NEW ORLEANS, JELLY Roll Morton (1890–1941; born Ferdinand Lamothe) was working as a pianist in the sporting houses of the city's Storyville district by the time he had reached his twelfth birthday. Morton began traveling around 1904—gambling, shooting pool, hustling, and playing the piano—and by 1917 had ranged as far as New York and Los Angeles. Throughout this period he absorbed many kinds of music—ragtime, blues, hymns, minstrel songs, Tin Pan Alley songs, and Caribbean music with its "Spanish tinge"—blending them together and helping to spread the emerging style that was becoming known as jazz. The recordings Morton made in Chicago in the mid-1920s announced a new fusion of improvisation and composition, leading some historians to hail Morton as the first jazz composer.

These selections are taken from Alan Lomax's *Mister Jelly Roll,* a book based on a series of recorded interviews Lomax conducted with Morton in 1938. Although Lomax admitted to having "polished" the prose, he preserved a remarkable autobiographical statement by one of the most important musicians in jazz. Morton's account evokes the rich diversity of musical life in New Orleans and provides an insider's explanation of how jazz developed and how it works. Morton touches on personal problems of identity—as a light-skinned Creole, and as a man playing an instrument that was largely identified with women—at the same time that his story shows how he belonged to the tradition of piano "professors": boastful, vain, and competitive virtuosi who cultivated

---

Source: Alan Lomax, *Mister Jelly Roll: The Fortunes of Jelly Roll Morton, New Orleans Creole and "Inventor of Jazz"* (New York: Pantheon, 1993) [original publication: New York: Duell, Sloan and Pearce, 1949], pp. 7, 52–53, 76–82, 179–83. Reprinted by permission of Odyssey Productions, Inc. The Alan Lomax Archive.

a dandified image (Morton had a diamond set in one of his front teeth, and bragged that he was "the suit man from suit land"). His claim that he was the "inventor of jazz" and the false birth date he gave in order to support this assertion should be understood in this light, although it's probably true that no one could make a better case than he.

Of course, my folks never had the idea they wanted a musician in the family. They always had it in their minds that a musician was a tramp, trying to duck work, with the exception of the French Opera House players which they patronized. As a matter of fact, I, myself, was inspired to play piano by going to a recital at the French Opera House. There was a gentleman who rendered a selection on the piano, very marvelous music that made me want to play the piano very, very much. The only trouble was that this gentleman had long bushy hair, and, because the piano was known in our circle as an instrument for a lady, this confirmed me in my idea that if I played the piano I would be misunderstood.

I didn't want to be called a sissy. I wanted to marry and raise a family and be known as a man among men when I became of age. So I studied various other instruments, such as violin, drums and guitar, until one day at a party I saw a gentleman sit down at the piano and play a very good piece of ragtime. This particular gentleman had short hair and I decided then that the instrument was good for a gentleman same as it was for a lady. I must have been about ten years old at the time.

So in the year of 1902 when I was about seventeen years old I happened to invade one of the sections where the birth of jazz originated from. Some friends took me to The Frenchman's on the corner of Villery and Bienville, which was at that time the most famous nightspot after everything was closed. It was only a back room, but it was where all the greatest pianists frequented after they got off from work in the sporting-houses. About four A.M., unless plenty of money was involved on their jobs, they would go to The Frenchman's and there would be everything in the line of hilarity there.

All the girls that could get out of their houses was there. The millionaires would come to listen to their favorite pianists. There weren't any discrimination of any kind. They all sat at different tables or anywhere they felt like sitting. They all mingled together just as they wished to and everyone was just like one big happy family. People came from all over the country and most times you couldn't get in. So this place would go on at a tremendous rate of speed—plenty money, drinks of all kinds—from four o'clock in the morning until maybe twelve, one, two, or three o'clock in the daytime. Then, when the great pianists used to leave, the crowds would leave.

New Orleans was the stomping grounds for all the greatest pianists in the country. We had Spanish, we had colored, we had white, we had Frenchmens, we had Americans, we had them from all parts of the world because there were more jobs for pianists than any other ten places in the world. The sporting-houses needed professors, and we had so many different styles that whenever you came to New Orleans, it wouldn't make any difference that you just came from Paris or any part of England, Europe, or any place—whatever your tunes were over there, we played them in New Orleans.

I might name some of the other great hot men operating around New Orleans at this period and a little later. There was Emanuel Perez, played strictly ragtime, who was maybe the best trumpet in New Orleans till Freddie Keppard came along. John Robichaux probably had the best band in New Orleans at the time, a strictly all-reading, legitimate bunch.[1] Before him, there was Happy Galloway. Both men had the same type seven-piece orchestra—cornet, clarinet, trombone, drums, mandolin, guitar, and bass. A guy named Payton had a band that played a very lowdown type of quadrille for the low-class dance halls. Also a lot of bad bands that we used to call "spasm" bands, played any jobs they could get in the streets.[2] They did a lot of ad-libbing in ragtime style with different solos in succession, not in a regular routine, but just as one guy would get tired and let another musician have the lead.

None of these men made much money—maybe a dollar a night or a couple of bucks for a funeral, but still they didn't like to leave New Orleans. They used to say, "This is the best town in the world. What's the use for me to go any other place?" So the town was full of the best musicians you ever heard. Even the rags-bottles-and-bones men would advertise their trade by playing the blues on the wooden mouthpieces of Christmas horns—yes sir, play more lowdown, dirty blues on those Kress horns than the rest of the country ever thought of.[3]

All of these people played ragtime in a hot style, but man, you can play hot all you want to, and you still won't be playing jazz. Hot means something spicy. Ragtime is a certain type of syncopation and only certain tunes can be played in that idea. But jazz is a style that can be applied to any type of tune. I started using the word in 1902 to show people the difference between jazz and ragtime.

Jazz music came from New Orleans and New Orleans was inhabited with maybe every race on the face of the globe and, of course, plenty of French people. Many of the earliest tunes in New Orleans was from French origin. Then we had Spanish people there. I heard a lot of Spanish tunes and I tried to play them in correct tempo, but I personally didn't believe they were really perfected in the tempos. Now take *La Paloma,* which I transformed in New Orleans style. You leave the left hand just the same. The difference comes in the right hand—in the syncopation, which gives it an entirely different color that really changes the color from red to blue.

Now in one of my earliest tunes, *New Orleans Blues,* you can notice the Spanish tinge. In fact, if you can't manage to put tinges of Spanish in your tunes, you will never be able to get the right seasoning, I call it, for jazz. This *New Orleans Blues* comes from around 1902. I wrote it with the help of Frank Richards, a great piano player in the ragtime style. All the bands in the city played it at that time.

Most of these ragtime guys, especially those that couldn't play very well, would have the inspiration they were doing okay if they kept increasing the tempo during a piece. I decided that was a mistake and I must have been right, because everybody grabbed my style. I thought that accurate tempo would be the right tempo for any tune. Regardless to any tempo you might set, especially if it was meant for a dance tune, you ought to end up in that same tempo. So I found that the slow tunes, especially the medium slow tunes, did more for the development of jazz than any other

---

1. Morton means that none of the players improvised. [RW]

2. Spasm bands used mostly homemade instruments. [RW]

3. Kress horns were toy instruments sold by the Kress company in the early years of the twentieth century. They consisted of a cardboard cone and a wooden mouthpiece, although street vendors and spasm band musicians would often substitute a trumpet or clarinet mouthpiece. [RW]

type, due to the fact that you could always hit a note twice in such a tune, when ordinarily you could only hit it once, which gave the music a very good flavor.

About harmony, my theory is never to discard the melody. Always have a melody going some kind of way against a background of perfect harmony with plenty of riffs—meaning figures. A riff is something that gives an orchestra a great background and is the main idea in playing jazz. No jazz piano player can really play good jazz unless they try to give an imitation of a band, that is, by providing a basis of riffs. I've seen riffs blundered up so many times it has give me heart failure, because most of these modern guys don't regard the harmony or the rules of the system of music at all. They just play anything, their main idea being to keep the bass going. They think by keeping the bass going and getting a set rhythm, they are doing the right thing, which is wrong.

Now the riff is what we call a foundation, like something that you walk on. It's standard. But without breaks and without clean breaks and without beautiful ideas in breaks, you don't even need to think about doing anything else, you haven't got a jazz band and you can't play jazz. Even if a tune haven't got a break in it, it's always necessary to arrange some kind of a spot to make a break.

A break, itself, is like a musical surprise which didn't come in until I originated the idea of jazz, as I told you. We New Orleans musicians were always looking for novelty effects to attract the public, and many of the most important things in jazz originated in some guy's crazy idea that we tried out for a laugh or just to surprise the folks.

Most people don't understand the novelty side of jazz. Vibrato—which is all right for one instrument but the worst thing that ever happened when a whole bunch of instruments use it—was nothing at the beginning but an imitation of a jackass hollering. There were many other imitations of animal sounds we used—such as the wah-wahs on trumpets and trombones. Mutes came in with King Oliver, who first just stuck bottles into his trumpet so he could play softer, but then began to use all sorts of mutes to give his instrument a different flavor. And I, myself, by accident, discovered the swats on drums.[4] Out in Los Angeles I had a drummer that hit his snares so loud that one night I gave him a couple of fly swatters for a gag. This drummer fell in with the joke and used them, but they worked so smooth he kept right on using them. So we have "the swats" today—a nice soft way to keep your rhythm going.

A lot of people have a wrong conception of jazz. Somehow it got into the dictionary that jazz was considered a lot of blatant noises and discordant tones, something that would be even harmful to the ears. The fact of it is that every musician in America had the wrong understanding of jazz music. I know many times that I'd be playing against different orchestras and I would notice some of the patrons get near an orchestra and put their hands over their ears. (Of course, I wouldn't permit mine to play that way.) Anyhow, I heard a funny fellow say once: "If that fellow blows any louder, he'll knock my ear drums down." Even Germany and Italy don't want this discordant type of jazz, because of the noise.

Jazz music is to be played sweet, soft, plenty rhythm. When you have your plenty rhythm with your plenty swing, it becomes beautiful. To start with, you can't make crescendos and diminuendos when one is playing triple forte. You got to be able to come down in order to go up. If a glass of water is full, you can't fill it any more; but if you have half a glass, you have the opportunity to put more water in it. Jazz music is based on the same principles, because jazz is based on strictly music. You have the finest ideas from the greatest operas, symphonies, and overtures in jazz

---

4. Later known as "brushes." [RW]

music. There is nothing finer than jazz because it comes from everything of the finest-class music. Take the *Sextet* from *Lucia* and the *Miserere* from *Il Trovatore*, that they used to play in the French Opera House, tunes that have always lived in my mind as the great favorites of the opera singers; I transformed a lot of those numbers into jazz time, using different little variations and ideas to masquerade the tunes.

The *Tiger Rag*, for an instance, I happened to transform from an old quadrille, which was originally in many different tempos. First there was an introduction, "Everybody get your partners!" and the people would be rushing around the hall getting their partners. After a five-minute lapse of time, the next strain would be the waltz strain . . . then another strain that comes right beside the waltz strain in mazurka time.

We had two other strains in two-four time. Then I transformed these strains into the *Tiger Rag* which I also named, from the way I made the "tiger" roar with my elbow. A person said once, "That sounds like a tiger hollering." I said to myself, "That's the name." All this happened back in the early days before the Dixieland Band was ever heard of.[5]

About 1912

It was along about that time that the first hot arrangements came into existence. Up until then, everything had been in the heads of the men who played jazz out of New Orleans. Nowadays they talk about these jam sessions. Well, that is something I never permitted. Most guys, they improvise and they'll go wrong. Most of the so-called jazz musicians still don't know how to play jazz until this day; they don't understand the principles of jazz music. In all my recording sessions and in all my band work, I always wrote out the arrangements in advance. When it was a New Orleans man, that wasn't so much trouble, because those boys know a lot of my breaks; but in traveling from place to place I found other musicians had to be taught. So around 1912, I began to write down this peculiar form of mathematics and harmonics that was strange to all the world.

For a time I had been working with McCabe's Minstrel Show and, when that folded in St. Louis, I began looking around for a job. My goodness, the snow was piled up till you couldn't see the streetcars. I was afraid that I'd meet some piano player that could top me a whole lot, so I wouldn't admit that I could play. I claimed that I was a singer. At that time I kinda figured I was a pretty good singer, which was way out of the way, but I figured it anyhow. Well, I was hired at the Democratic Club where they had a piano player named George Reynolds. He was a bricklayer trying to play piano. He couldn't even read music. In fact, none of the boys couldn't read much and so it was very tough for them to get those tough tunes. They bought sheet music just to learn the words of the songs.

This George Reynolds, that couldn't read, played for me while I sang. Of course, George was a little bit chesty, because all the girls around were making eyes at him (he was a fairly nice-looking fellow); but I thought, if this guy's the best, the other piano players must be very, very terrible. So I asked George to play me one of the numbers I was going to sing. He played it, although he didn't seem very particular about doing it. I told him, "One of these parts here you don't play right. I'd like a little more pep in it." I forget what tune it was, some popular number of that time.

---

5. Morton is establishing that his success predates the fame of the Original Dixieland Jazz Band, which began with their recordings of 1917. [RW]

"Well," he said, not knowing I could play, "if you don't like the way I'm playing, you do better."

"Okay," I said, "if you don't play my tunes right, I can play them myself." So I sat down and showed him his mistakes.

Immediately he had a great big broad smile on his face. Seeing that I was superior to him, he wanted to make friends with me. I didn't object and we gotten to be friends right away. He asked me did I read music. I told him a little bit. So he put different difficult numbers on the piano—he thought they were difficult, but they were all simple to me. I knew them all. By that time he started getting in touch with the different musicians around town that was supposed to be good and they started bringing me different tunes. They brought me all Scott Joplin's tunes—he was the great St. Louis ragtime composer—and I knew them all by heart and played them right off. They brought me James Scott's tunes and Louis Chauvin's and I knew them all. Then Artie Matthews (the best reader in the whole bunch) brought me his *Pastimes* and I played it. So he decided to find out whether I could really read and play piano and he brought me different light operas like *Humoresque,* the *overture* from *Martha,* the *Miserere* from *Il Trovatore* and, of course, I knowed them all.

Finally they brought me *The Poet and the Peasant.* It seems like in St. Louis, if you was able to play this piece correctly, you was really considered the tops. The man that brought it was the best musician in town and he hadn't been able to master this piece. Well, I had played this thing in recitals for years, but I started looking at it like I hadn't ever seen it before. Then I started in. I got to a very fast passage where I also had to turn the page over. I couldn't turn the page, due to the fact that I had to manipulate this passage so fast. I went right on. Artie Matthews grabbed the tune from in front of me and said, "Hell, don't be messing with this guy. This guy is a shark!" I told them, "Boys, I been kidding you all along. I knew all these tunes anyhow. Just listen." Then I swung the *Miserere* and combined it with the *Anvil Chorus.*

You find, though, that people act very savage in this world. From then on it was George Reynolds's object to try to crush me. He couldn't do this, but he made things so unpleasant that I finally took a job out in the German section of town. The manager wanted a band, so I got some men together, although there wasn't many to pick from—clarinet, trumpet, mandolin, drums, and myself. These were not hot men, but they were Negroes and they could read. They didn't play to suit me, but I told them if they played exactly what I put down on paper, they would be playing exactly as I wanted. Then I arranged all the popular tunes of that time—I even made a jazz arrangement of *Schnitzelbank*—and we made some pretty fair jazz for St. Louis in 1912.

St. Louis had been a great town for ragtime for years because Stark and Company specialized in publishing Negro music. Among the composers the Starks published were: Scott Joplin (the greatest ragtime writer who ever lived and composer of *Maple Leaf Rag),* Tom Turpin, Louis Chauvin, Artie Matthews, and James Scott. But St. Louis wasn't like New Orleans; it was prejudiced. I moved on to Kansas City and found it was like St. Louis, except it did not have one decent pianist and didn't want any. That was why I went on to Chicago. In Chicago at that time you could go anywhere you wanted regardless of creed or color. So Chicago came to be one of the earliest places that jazz arrived, because of nice treatment—and we folks from New Orleans were used to nice treatment.[6]

6. Not all musicians agreed; Louis Armstrong and others spoke bitterly about racism in New Orleans at this time and later. [RW]

PART 2

The Twenties

8. Jazzing Around the Globe

"AMERICAN COMPOSERS OF 'JAZZ' TUNES and similar lowly but popular outcroppings of the musical art have accomplished in their field something which American 'highbrow' musicians, in theirs, have never even come within hailing distance of accomplishing. They have utterly vanquished their European rivals."[1] So began a jingoistic celebration of popular song printed by the *New York Times* in 1921, a year before the following round-the-world survey of jazz appeared. In this context, "jazz" referred to Tin Pan Alley popular songs that had absorbed some of the rhythmic influences of ragtime.[2] Relatively few people had heard the collective improvisation for which critics would later reclaim the word.

As he travels ever westward, journalist Burnet Hershey comments with the tone of a condescending sophisticate who accepts national stereotypes and reproduces them (using the word "barbaric" more than once). Yet he also recorded the existence of new musical fusions that were sparked by American music as it spread through mass mediation—sheet music and phonograph records—and through the increasing mobility of people, such as the "Negro bands" he noticed in Paris, the European businessmen in Shanghai, the armies and administrators of the West's colonial possessions around the globe. As other kinds of "jazz" came along later, their dissemination would follow similar trade routes and compound this impact.

Source: Burnet Hershey, "Jazz Latitude," *New York Times Book Review and Magazine,* June 25, 1922, pp. 8–9.

1. T. R. Ybarra, "'Jazz 'er Up!' Broadway's Conquest of Europe," *New* York *Times Book Review and Magazine,* December 18, 1921, p. 3.

2. Named for the clamor of song demonstrators' pianos, Tin Pan Alley was a section of New York's 28th Street where most of the major music publishers had offices; in the early years of the twentieth century, nearly all popular song hits emerged from there.

A new line of latitude one-steps around the globe. Its location is reckoned by the degree of its jazz and computed exactly by the number of minutes and seconds it is distant from its meridian—Tin Pan Alley. To trace it, you don't have to be a student of geography. Even the amateur globe-trotter on an automatic tour won't need his Baedeker to find it, for every ship the traveler takes today throbs with the staccato cacophony of jazz and every stop at a port is punctuated by the syncopation of jazz.[3]

Jazz latitude is marked as indelibly on the globe as the heavy line of the equator. It runs from Broadway along Main Street to San Francisco to the Hawaiian Islands, which it has lyricized to fame; to Japan, where it is hurriedly adopted as some new Western culture; to the Philippines, where it is royally welcomed back as its own; to China, where the mandarins and even the coolies look upon it as a hopeful sign that the Occident at last knows what is music; to Siam, where the barbaric tunes strike a kindred note and come home to roost; to India, where the natives receive it dubiously, while the colonists seize upon it avidly; to the East Indies, where it holds sway in its elementary form—ragtime; to Egypt, where it sounds so curiously familiar and where it has set Cairo dance mad; to Palestine, where it is looked upon as an inevitable and necessary evil along with liberation; across the Mediterranean, where all ships and all shores have been inoculated with the germ; to Monte Carlo and the Riviera, where the jazz idea has been adopted as its own enfant-chéri; to Paris, which has its special versions of jazz; to London, which long has sworn to shake off the fever, but still is jazzing, and back again to Tin Pan Alley, where each day, nay, each hour, adds some new inspiration that will slowly but surely meander along jazz latitude.

I set out on a tour of the world with the wanderer's lure of adventure, strange lands and quaint customs. My trail led along curious rough byways, but all along the route, yawping after me, ululating along with me, blatantly greeting me, was the inevitable jazz. No sooner had I shaken off the dust of some city and slipped almost out of earshot of its jazz bands than zump-zump-zump, toodle-oodle-doo, right into another I went. Never was there a cessation of this universal potpourri of jazz. Each time I would discover it at a different stage of metamorphosis and sometimes hard to recognize, but unmistakably it was an attempt at jazz. If you follow jazz latitude you can pick up the original traces of jazz. You will wonder how from the crude and sensuous dances and savage music there has evolved our new national anthem, jazz, and our National Conservatory of Music, Tin Pan Alley. Natives of far-off tropical lands eagerly nod their approval of Tin Pan Alley's latest masterpieces. They prick up their ears in recognition of something strangely similar to the plaintive melodies of their homelands. Occidental versions of Oriental rhythm and harmony they do not regard as plagiarism nor as an improvement upon their own music, but as their own songs and dances which the West has adopted.

The stepping-off point of jazz to the Orient is San Francisco. Saxophones and trombones have come to drive away the ghosts haunting Barbary Coast from their last resting place behind the boarded bars and fenced-in saloons where ragtime had its American tryout.[4] Here the turkey trot, the bunny hug, and the rest of the "gutter dances" originated and presaged the tango, the Maxixe, the Boston dip, the shimmy, the fox trot, the collegiate glide and the rest of the one-step dance innovations.

---

3. A reference to the popular Baedeker tourist guidebooks. [RW]

4. Named after a part of the North African coastline, and perhaps the pirates who preyed there for centuries, the Barbary Coast was San Francisco's district of ragtime, saloons, and brothels—its equivalent of New Orleans's Storyville. [RW]

Barbary Coast is now a memory, but the rest of the Pacific East is jazzing away to the latest of broadway melodies.

Jazz follows the flag. Ships freighted with jazz—"Made in America"—form the newest product of export to the Orient. Cargoes of jazz are laden on all vessels passing through the Golden Gate. To the Orient they sail, carrying the jazziest song hits, the latest dance steps and the phonograph records, stopping sometimes to unload some of the cargo of choice tunes at Honolulu.

Since Waikiki Beach has been rhapsodized by Tin Pan Alley, jazz has made a hit with the Honoluluans. The Hawaiians appreciate the music written about themselves, and to repay the compliment are now busy fox-trotting along their famous moonlit shores. Incidentally, the sheiks, the kings, the suzerains, the rajahs, the moguls, the nabobs and the local Boards of Alderman of the communities that have been so widely advertised—Honolulu, Kalua, Siam, India, Araby, Hindustan—are exceedingly grateful for the publicity.[5] It helps the tourist trade and the sale of souvenirs, they say, and feel honored that some song writer, who never visited their shores, should have found in them an adequate theme for his inspiration.

Filipino orchestras are the interpreters of jazz on the Pacific Ocean liners. Where music is concerned, the Filipinos are known as the Italians of the East. Add their own barbaric musical strain—a blend of Oriental and Spanish "ear culture"—and you get an idea of their adeptness with the torturous instruments of jazz. The banjo and cornet are still the mainstays of the Filipino jazz bands. The saxophone is only a recent addition.

Nowhere else in the world, outside of New York, have the cymbals, bells, sirens, motor horns, cow bells and all the clap-trap of the original ragtime bands been abandoned. Every jazz band in Asia, Africa or Europe starts with the drum-and-trap accessories as a nucleus. This constitutes the jazz, the rest merely band.

I was in Yokohama only a few hours when I heard the call of the West—a jazz band tuning up, or getting out of tune, in the Grand Hotel. In this most European of Japanese cities there are half a dozen jazz bands. One European troupe, led by an ex-U.S. Navy bandmaster, dispenses ragtime at the leading hotel. The others are Japanese groups who, with that marvelous faculty for imitating the Occident, manage to organize some semblance of jazz.

In Peking I found a diplomatic corps turning to jazz somewhat in the fashion in which the Washington foreign colony has turned to golf. The two leading hotels were filled every day at tea time and dinner. Everybody danced.

The mandarin loves to dance. Jazz to him means harmony of the soul. It is his reed pipe and lyre chosen from a celestial symphony. His son, returned from a Western university, is saturated with the jazz idea. Any observer in China will tell you that whatever the students say ought to be done because it is done in the West is done with a gusto—a gusto peculiarly Chinese.

On a Shipping Board steamer we journey to Hongkong and enter the "most beautiful port in the world" to the tune of "Chong, He Comes from Hongkong," which the Silver State Jazz Fiends have picked out as an appropriate air to make our entry. The jazz fiends are a band of devil-may-care college men from Seattle who have chosen the happy life of the sailor-jazz-bandsmen.

---

5. Tin Pan Alley exoticism and Orientalism were indeed popular at this time; examples might include "The Sheik of Araby" (1921), "Hindustan" (1918), "The Japanese Sandman" (1920), "In a Persian Market" (1920), and "China Boy" (1922). [RW]

Everything in Hongkong is very English. Nowhere throughout the length and breadth of the British Empire is English influence more impressed than in Victoria, otherwise known as Hongkong. Everything except the music and dancing. That is American. Twenty-four days from Tin Pan Alley and when the song hit gets to Hongkong it spreads like a tune in Harlem. Everybody whistles it, hums it, plays it on the graphophone. The sale of American jazz records in the Far East is enormous.

You jazz across the China Sea on a floating jazz palace to Manila, to our own Philippine Islands. No sooner arrived at the Manila Hotel than the strains of a jazz band greet you. The jazz band of jazz bands is to be found here. Our champion one-steppers, officers of the naval and army base, and their partners, American ladies all, dance the very latest from New York and often set the pace with some new step of their own.

Continue Westward Ho, on jazz latitude. Steam on an English vessel to the Malay States and Borneo. No jazz band is aboard, but there is a graphophone and the latest New York records. Stop for a brief spell at Saigon, miniature French metropolis on the edge of mysterious Indo-China. Yes, they're jazzing at the Café Pancrazi and Continental. Painted ladies from Paris who follow the khaki of the French colonials everywhere are busy here spreading the culture of jazz, even into the virgin teakwood forests of Tonkin.

Singapore and at Raffles, that oasis of the globe-trotter (shades of the Johore Sultans!), they're even doing it in Singapore.[6] There was no mistaking the jumble of sound. From the veranda of the big hotel came the diapason. What do you think I heard? "Alexander's Ragtime Band," as unpleasantly reminiscent as the hurdy-gurdy old tunes. It was, in fact, the venerable grandfather of jazz, Irving Berlin's first attempt at syncopation away back in history.

I stopped to reason out the cause for this antique state. It was evident that the further we go away from Manila, the staler the jazz. It takes years for some songs to travel around the world. Some tunes linger a long time en route; others flash around in less than Jules Verne's eighty days. In Cairo we heard some of the new Sheik songs ground out this year in Tin Pan Alley, whereas in Japan—ten days from Seattle—they were still playing old songs. Japan really is the crossroads where jazz ends and ragtime begins.

In Calcutta, as in Bombay and throughout India, where the English civil service man makes his home, and where a handful of white business, army and professional men make up the European colony, jazz is welcomed as a "life-saver." In this country of few diversions, it relieves the tedium of routine existence. India sounds like a paradise of romance, but the colonist, the army officer who has spent many months and years amid the "dirt of Asia," is blasé and weary of the life. He has turned to bridge and poker. Now he gladly seizes upon jazz. And there is always the "stengha"—the whisky-soda, faithful auxiliary of jazz.

Journey along the Indian coast in the Arabian Sea to India's little brother, Ceylon, where you find jazz in its most antiquated state. It isn't jazz, but they think it is. They have only arrived at "Down in Jungle Town." The record, played on a venerable gramophone, was one of the old ones which announced the song and the band.

---

6. Raffles was (and is) a famous nightclub, named for Sir Thomas Stanford Raffles, the British East Indian administrator who founded Singapore in 1819. The Johore Strait separates the main island of Singapore from Malaysia. [RW]

But the one-step is there. On the terrace of the Galle Face Hotel, on the edge of the Arabian Sea, an Arabian moon, swaying cocoanut trees, chirping monkeys and cawing of big birds mingled with the strains of the local band.

Cairo, gay, exotic Cairo, with its population of Orientalized Europeans and its legion of pleasure-seeking Americans. Here jazz comes back into its own again. It comes directly from New York, without stopping in Europe. The idle rich of Europe, the newly rich from South America, wanderers from all corners of the globe, are here. To Egypt jazz is something native. It echoes pleasantly familiar to the Arabs and as far as the cabaret is concerned, you might just as well be in New York. It is jazz, and real jazz, and even in the shade of the Pyramids there is a New Yorker leading a band of jazzers.

From Cairo the road leads to Jerusalem, and in the Holy City there is a jazz band. The bearded patriarchs and the credulous Arabs listen in amazement to the new importation of jazz, come to ruffle the ancient complacency of the Biblical city. They accept it doubtfully.

Paris is exhibiting its own versions of jazz, too—boulevard concoctions of Tin Pan Alley's inventions. The negro band still is the vogue. So essential do some Montmartre dance halls find the black musicians that they have hit upon the ingenious scheme to use their disguise for their own French jazz bands. They may be French colonials, or some longshoremen from Harlem left over from the war—it doesn't matter. These colored folk are placed at the ends of the band, looking like endmen, and rattle tambourines or crash cymbals just to make a racket.[7]

Of London little need be said, for like New York, it has been caught in the whirlpool of jazz, and, try as the English will, they cannot disentangle themselves. They sermonize against it, they editorialize against it, but it only serves to intensify jazz.

Once upon the Atlantic steamer, a French floating chateau, I settle down to thoughts of home. Since I had jazz all the way around the world, I knew I wouldn't miss it here, on the last lap. But what was that? Say, that's a snappy tune. Where did I hear that before? No. I haven't heard it before. It's something new.

So here, heading for Tin Pan Alley, I heard the first strains of new jazz. The masters of noise acrobatics were blaring out Broadway's up-to-the-minute stuff. Nowhere along the route had I heard a song I didn't know. Now I might as well be listening to the pounding of pianos along Tin Pan Alley and the yodeling of its serenaders by radio. It was jazz at its latest.

It made me reconsider jazz latitude. What the world is getting along jazz latitude is old. It travels and gets there, but by that time it is jazz platitude.

---

7. A reference to the conventions of blackface minstrelsy. [RW]

9. "Does Jazz Put the Sin in Syncopation?"

"WHAT INSTINCTS THEN ARE AROUSED BY JAZZ?" Whether she knew it or not, Anne Shaw Faulkner's 1921 diatribe in *The Ladies' Home Journal* could have been cribbed from Plato's *Republic:* "Certainly not deeds of valor or martial courage," she answers, echoing Plato's disparagement of Lydian ethnicity in favor of Dorian martial virtue. In both cases, the power and importance of music are recognized, but only in order that it can be blamed for social problems: Faulkner linked uncorseted bodies and sloppy workmen to what she heard as the undisciplined sounds of jazz.

The heading of this article also identified Faulkner as Mrs. Marx E. Oberndorfer, National Music Chairman, General Federation of Women's Clubs, marking her as a member of that privileged class of philanthropic women who had founded symphony orchestras and campaigned for moral uplift during the late nineteenth and early twentieth centuries. Faulkner's musical analysis is a bit confusing (by "partial tones," she appears to mean complex or unfamiliar timbres) and her "scientific" evidence is vaguely claimed, without citation. But she raises important concerns about how music challenges social values, and how it is variously used on behalf of individual freedom or social harmony; some of her arguments seem all too familiar in the wake of more recent controversies over rap and heavy metal. Surprisingly, she has nothing bad to say about ragtime, which had been bitterly denounced in much the same terms only a few years earlier.

We have all been taught to believe that "music soothes the savage breast," but we have never stopped to consider that an entirely different type of music might invoke savage instincts. We have been content to accept all kinds of music, and to admit music in all its phases into our homes, simply because it was music. It is true that frequently father and mother have preferred some old favorite song or dance, or some aria from opera, to the last "best seller" which has found its way into the home circle; but, after all, young people must be entertained and amused, and even if the old-fashioned parents did not enjoy the dance music of the day, they felt it could really do no harm, because it was music.

Source: Anne Shaw Faulkner, "Does Jazz Put the Sin in Syncopation," *The Ladies' Home Journal,* August 1921, pp. 16, 34.

Therefore, it is somewhat of a rude awakening for many of these parents to find that America is facing a most serious situation regarding its popular music. Welfare workers tell us that never in the history of our land have there been such immoral conditions among our young people, and in the surveys made by many organizations regarding these conditions, the blame is laid on jazz music and its evil influence on the young people of today. Never before have such outrageous dances been permitted in private as well as public ballrooms, and never has there been used for the accompaniment of the dance such a strange combination of tone and rhythm as that produced by the dance orchestras of today.

Certainly, if this music is in any way responsible for the condition and for the immoral acts which can be traced to the influence of these dances, then it is high time that the question should be raised: "Can music ever be an influence for evil?"

In history there have been several great periods when music was declared to be an evil influence, and certain restrictions were placed upon the dance and the music which accompanied it. But all of these restrictions were made by the clergy, who have never been particularly enthusiastic about dancing anyway. Today, however, the first great rebellion against jazz music and such dances as the "toddle" and the "shimmy" comes from the dancing masters themselves. Realizing the evil influence of this type of music and dancing, the National Dancing Masters' Association, at their last session, adopted this rule: "Don't permit vulgar cheap jazz music to be played. Such music almost forces dancers to use jerky half-steps, and invites immoral variations. It is useless to expect to find refined dancing when the music lacks all refinement, for, after all, what is dancing but an interpretation of the music?"

Several of the large dance halls in the big cities are following the lead of the proprietor of one of them in Chicago, who, when he opened his establishment a few years ago, bravely advertised in all the papers that no jazz music and no immoral dances would be allowed on his floor. His announcement was met with ridicule, but his dance hall has become the most popular one in Chicago. The place is crowded every evening, and yet nothing except waltzes and two-steps are allowed on the floor and absolutely no jazz music is tolerated.

That jazz is an influence for evil is also felt by a number of the biggest country clubs, which have forbidden the corset check room, the leaving of the hall between dances, and the jazz orchestras—three evils which have also been eliminated from many municipal dance halls, particularly when these have been taken under the chaperonage of the Women's Clubs.

Still another proof that jazz is recognized as producing an evil effect is the fact that in almost every big industry where music has been instituted it has been found necessary to discontinue jazz because of its demoralizing effect upon the workers. This was noticed in an unsteadiness and lack of evenness in the workmanship of the product after a period when the workmen had indulged in jazz music.

Many people classify under the title of "jazz" all music in syncopated rhythm, whether it be the ragtime of the American Negro or the csardas of the Slavic people. Yet there is a vast difference between syncopation and jazz. To understand the seriousness of the jazz craze, which, emanating from America, has swept over the world, it is time that the American public should realize what the terms ragtime and jazz mean; for the works are not synonymous, as so many people suppose.

Jazz is not defined in the dictionary or encyclopedia. But *Grove's Dictionary of Music* says that "ragtime is a modern term of American origin, signifying in the first instance broken rhythm and melody, especially a sort of continuous syncopation." The *Encyclopedia Britannica* sums up syncopation as "the rhythmic method of tying two beats of the same note into one tone in such a way as to displace the accent."

Syncopation, this curious rhythmic accent on the short beat, is found in its most highly developed forms in the music of the folk who have been held for years in political subjection. It is, therefore, an expression in music of the desire for that freedom which has been denied to its interpreter. It is found in its most intense forms among the folk of all the Slavic countries, especially in certain districts of Poland and Russia, and also among the Hungarian gypsies.

For the same reason it was the natural expression of the American Negroes and was used by them as the accompaniment for their bizarre dances and cakewalks. Negro ragtime, it must be frankly acknowledged, is one of the most important and distinctively characteristic American expressions to be found in our native music. Whether ragtime will be the cornerstone of the American School of Music may be a subject for discussion; but the fact remains that many of the greatest compositions by past and present American composers have been influenced by ragtime. Like all other phases of syncopation, ragtime quickens the pulse, it excites, it stimulates; but it does not destroy.[1]

What of jazz? It is hard to define jazz, because it is neither a definite form nor a type of rhythm; it is rather a method employed by the interpreter in playing the dance or song. Familiar hymn tunes can be jazzed until their original melodies are hardly recognizable. Jazz does for harmony what the accented syncopation of ragtime does for rhythm. In ragtime the rhythm is thrown out of joint, as it were, thus distorting the melody; in jazz exactly the same thing is done to the harmony. The melodic line is disjointed and disconnected by the accenting of the partial instead of the simple tone, and the same effect is produced on the melody and harmony which is noticed in syncopated rhythm. The combination of syncopation and the use of these in-harmonic partial tones produces a strange, weird effect, which has been designated "jazz."

The jazz orchestra uses only those instruments which can produce partial, inharmonic tones more readily than simple tones—such as the saxophone, the clarinet, and the trombone, which share honors with the percussion instruments that accent syncopated rhythm. The combination of the syncopated rhythm, accentuated by the constant use of the partial tones sounding off-pitch, has put syncopation too off-key. Thus the three simple elements of music—rhythm, melody, and harmony—have been put out of tune with each other.

Jazz originally was the accompaniment of the voodoo dancer, stimulating the half-crazed barbarian to the vilest deeds. The weird chant, accompanied by the syncopated rhythm of the voodoo invokers, has also been employed by other barbaric people to stimulate brutality and sensuality. That it has a demoralizing effect upon the human brain has been demonstrated by many scientists.

There is always a revolutionary period of the breaking down of old conventions and customs which follows after every great war; and this rebellion against existing conditions is to be noticed in all life today. Unrest, the desire to break the shackles of old ideas and forms are abroad. So it is no wonder that young people should have become so imbued with this spirit that they should express it in every phase of their daily lives. The question is whether this tendency should be demonstrated in jazz—that expression of protest against law and order, the bolshevik element of license striving for expression in music.

1. By "American School of Music," Faulkner means not an institution but a tradition of distinctively American musical composition. [RW]

The human organism responds to musical vibrations. This fact is universally recognized. What instincts then are aroused by jazz? Certainly not deeds of valor or martial courage, for all marches and patriotic hymns are of regular rhythm and simple harmony; decidedly not contentment or serenity, for the songs of home and the love of native land are all of the simplest melody and harmony with noticeably regular rhythm. Jazz disorganizes all regular laws and order; it stimulates to extreme deeds, to a breaking away from all rules and conventions; it is harmful and dangerous, and its influence is wholly bad.

A number of scientific men who have been working on experiments in musicotherapy with the insane declare that while regular rhythms and simple tones produce a quieting effect on the brain of even a violent patient, the effect of jazz on the normal brain produces an atrophied condition on the brain cells of conception, until very frequently those under the demoralizing influence of the persistent use of syncopation, combined with inharmonic partial tones, are actually incapable of distinguishing between good and evil, between right and wrong.

Dancing to Mozart minuets, Strauss waltzes, and Sousa two-steps certainly never led to the corset check room, which now holds sway in hotels, clubs, and dance halls. Never would one of the biggest fraternities of a great college then have thought it necessary to print on the cards of invitation to the "Junior Prom" that "a corset check room will be provided." Nor would the girl who wore corsets in those days have been dubbed "old ironsides" and left a disconsolate wallflower in a corner of the ballroom. Now boys and girls of good families brazenly frequent the lowest dives in order to learn new dance steps. Now many jazz dances have words accompanying them which would then never have been allowed to go through the mail. Such music has become an influence for evil.

Last winter, at one of the biggest high schools in one of our largest cities, a survey was made of the popular songs of the day by the music supervisor, who suggested that a community sing be held for one assembly each week. He requested the students to bring all the popular songs to school that a choice might be made of what to sing. At the end of two weeks he had in his office over two thousand "best sellers." He asked the student body to appoint from among themselves a committee of six to choose the songs to be sung at the assembly. This committee, after going through the two thousand songs, chose forty as being "fit for boys and girls to sing together." With this evil influence surrounding our coming generation, it is not to be wondered at that degeneracy should be developing so rapidly in America.

In a recent letter to the author, Dr. Henry van Dyke says of jazz: "As I understand it, it is not music at all. It is merely an irritation of the nerves of hearing, a sensual teasing of the strings of physical passion. Its fault lies not in syncopation, for that is a legitimate device when sparingly used. But 'jazz' is an unmitigated cacophony, a combination of disagreeable sounds in complicated discords, a willful ugliness and a deliberate vulgarity."

Never in the history of America have we more needed the help and inspiration which good music can and does give. The music department of the General Federation of Women's Clubs has taken for its motto: "To Make Good Music Popular, and Popular Music Good." Let us carry out this motto in every home in America firmly, steadfastly, determinedly, until all the music in our land becomes an influence for good.

10. Jazz and African Music

"JAZZ IS A CERTAIN WAY OF SOUNDING TWO rhythms at once . . . a counterpoint of regular against irregular beats," wrote composer Virgil Thomson. If some early commentators associated jazz with unusual instruments (the saxophone, the drum set) or timbres (growling, wailing), others, especially composers, identified rhythm as that which made jazz distinctive. But was jazz polymetric, the product of irregular rhythmic units added together? Or was it filled with syncopations that push against a regular framework? Debate continued for decades, with many musical worthies weighing in, as when Aaron Copland argued in 1927 that jazz derived its power from the clash of independent rhythms.[1] But the earliest, arguably most insightful contribution went unnoticed by later writers.

The topic of jazz was both sensational and mysterious when the *Musical Courier* ran this 1922 essay by "Nicholas G. Taylor of Sierra Leone, South Africa." The article is insightful without being accurate: Sierra Leone is in West Africa, not South Africa, and Taylor's musical examples bear no resemblance to the Chindau' (not Chindon) songs he cited.[2] But the relationship of African rhythms to jazz is still frequently misunderstood, and Nicholas G. J. Ballanta-Taylor, author of several scholarly articles on African music, arguably got it right before anyone else. Taylor's direct familiarity with African music helped him to illuminate jazz, but his closing comments invoke broader and long-lived debates over the persistence of African traits in African-American culture: to deny the existence of African retentions is absurd, but to

---

Source: Nicholas G. Taylor, "Jazz Music and Its Relation to African Music," *Musical Courier,* June 1, 1922, p. 7.

1. See Aaron Copland, "Jazz Structure and Influence," *Modern Music* 4:2 (January—February 1927), pp. 9–14; Virgil Thomson is quoted on page 9. Copland credits Don Knowlton ("The Anatomy of Jazz," *Harper's,* April 1926) with having anticipated his points about rhythm, but he actually misinterpreted Knowlton's position, which was closer to that presented by Nicholas Taylor. For critiques of Copland's view, see Roger Pryor Dodge, "Consider the Critics," in Frederic Ramsey and Charles Edward Smith, eds., *Jazzmen* (New York: Harcourt Brace, 1959), pp. 301–42, and Louis Harap, "The Case for Hot Jazz," *Musical Quarterly* 27:1 (January 1941), pp. 47–61.

2. See Natalie Curtis, *Songs and Tales From the Dark Continent* (New York: Schirmer, 1920). For other writings by Taylor, see "Music of the African Races," *West Africa* 14 (1930), pp. 752–53, and "Gathering Folk Tunes in the African Country," *Musical America* 44:23 (1926), pp. 3, 11.

overemphasize them is to slight the agency of African Americans and mistake their creative fusions for passive survivals.

Some think that this "jazz" music is leading the generation to the African jungle, but I believe that the more "jazzy" the music, the more distant it is from that of the African jungle; which of these is nearer the truth could be proved by a reference to the musical examples of Chindon songs contained in the late Natalie Curtis's book, published by G. Schirmer and entitled "Songs and Tales from the Dark Continent."[3]

"Jazz" music makes use of syncopation to a marked degree more than African music pretends to do. It is regular in its accents and the rhythmical contents of its bars; it is mostly of the four-and-eight bar period. All these things, together with the question of idiom, are so foreign to the native African that he scarcely recognizes any connection between "jazz" music and his own. On the other hand, African music is cross-rhythmic, its use of syncopation is decidedly moderate and the rhythmical contents of many a bar of African music is as irregular as it could be. Again, owing to the use of cross rhythms, the periods and phrases are explained in a different method from that employed in "jazz" music.

The American Negroes brought over from Africa this music with its cross rhythms. Here they were surrounded with a different idiom; they had to face different conditions and the atmosphere in which they lived was a decided contrast to the environments that they had about them in their native land. The result is that they began to reduce African music to suit their new conditions and this is how they did it:

When the African says:

Ex. 1

Jazz reduces it to:

Ex. 2

3. Compare Walter Kingsley's "Whence Comes Jass?" (the second selection in this volume), which later appeared under the title "Why 'Jazz' Sends Us Back to the Jungle," in *Current Opinion* 65 (September 1918), p. 165. [RW]

When he says:

Ex. 3

Jazz has it:

Ex. 4

This method of reduction—this system by which everything is to be brought within the confines of man's limited knowledge so as to be suitable to the conditions of his environment—gives the clue as to the only link (and a most important one, too) between African music and "jazz" music. That neither Example 1 nor Example 3 is respectively the same as Example 2 or Example 4 is evident to any thoughtful musician. Thus far has European music been so influenced by African music as to produce "jazz" which is popular American music. And "jazz" music having once been so deduced takes its own course and at the present time has nothing more or less in common with African music. Is it also true of peoples as well as music?

11. The Sexual Politics of Women's Blues

THE MOST-HONORED WOMEN IN JAZZ have been singers, but singers are the least-honored musicians in jazz history. Billie Holiday and Bessie Smith are canonic figures, to be sure, but the cultural significance of Smith and the many other "Blues Queens" of the 1920s and '30s—the meanings they expressed and embodied for their audiences—have seldom been recognized. Yet the advent of commercial recording enabled African-American women's voices to be widely heard and preserved—to enter history—as never before and rarely since. Not until the rap music of the 1980s would a cohort of frankly assertive, sexy, articulate, artistic black women stake out a large share of American popular culture again.

The blues singers' commercial success enabled them to hire the best jazz musicians of the time—Louis Armstrong, Fletcher Henderson, Coleman Hawkins, and others—to accompany and collaborate with them. That fact, along with their mastery of the forms and expressive techniques that were at the heart of jazz, should gain them a more central place in jazz history. Their significance as artists, though, has just as much to do with how they creatively engaged issues of sexuality and migration for their black urban audiences, as this article explains.[1] Although it deals with performers of the 1920s and '30s, this is a document of the 1980s in that its insights reflect the influence of (and contribute to) African-American Studies and feminist theory. Hazel V. Carby (b. 1948) is chair of African and African American Studies at Yale University. She is the author of *Reconstructing Womanhood: The Emergence of the Afro-American Woman Novelist* (New York: Oxford University Press, 1987) and *Racemen: The Body and Soul of Race, Nation, and Masculinity (Cambridge:* Harvard University Press, 1998).

Source: Hazel V. Carby, "'It Jus' Be's Dat Way Sometime': The Sexual Politics of Women's Blues," in Ellen Carol DuBois and Vicki L. Ruiz, eds., *Unequal Sisters: A Multicultural Reader in U.S. Women's History* (New York: Routledge, 1990), pp. 238–49. Originally published in *Radical America* 20:4 (1986), pp. 9–24. Reprinted by permission of Hazel B. Carby. This version incorporates more recent corrections by the author.

1. 'See also Daphne Duval Harrison, *Black Pearls: Blues Queens of the 1920s* (New Brunswick, New Jersey: Rutgers University Press, 1988).

This essay considers the sexual politics of women's blues in the 1920s.[2] Their story is part of a larger history of the production of Afro-American culture within the North American culture industry. My research has concentrated almost exclusively on those black women intellectuals who were part of the development of an Afro-American literature culture and reflects the privileged place that we accord to writers in Afro-American Studies (Carby, 1987). Within feminist theory, the cultural production of black women writers has been analyzed in isolation from other forms of women's culture and cultural presence and has neglected to relate particular texts and issues to a larger discourse of culture and cultural politics. I want to show how the representation of black female sexuality in black women's fiction and in women's blues is clearly different. I argue that different cultural forms negotiate and resolve very different sets of social contradictions. However, before considering the particularities of black women's sexual representation, we should consider its marginality within a white-dominated feminist discourse.

In 1982, at the Barnard conference of the politics of sexuality, Hortense Spillers condemned the serious absence of consideration of black female sexuality from various public discourses including white feminist theory. She described black women as "the beached whales of the sexual universe, unvoiced, misseen, not doing, awaiting *their* verb." The sexual experiences of black women, she argued, were rarely depicted by themselves in what she referred to as "empowered texts": discursive feminist texts. Spillers complained of the relative absence of American-American women from the academy and thus from the visionary company of Anglo-American women feminists and their privileged mode of feminist expression.

The collection of the papers from the Barnard conference, the *Pleasure and Danger* (1984) anthology, has become one of these empowered feminist theoretical texts and Spillers's essay continues to stand within it as an important black feminist survey of the ways in which the sexuality of black American women has been unacknowledged in the public/critical discourse of feminist thought (Spillers, 1984). Following Spillers's lead black feminists continued to critique the neglect of issues of black female sexuality within feminist theory and, indeed, I as well as others directed many of our criticisms toward the *Pleasure and Danger* anthology itself (Carby, 1986).

As black women we have provided articulate and politically incisive criticism which is there for the feminist community at large to heed or to ignore—upon that decision lies the future possibility of forging a feminist movement that is not parochial. As the black feminist and educator Anna Julia Cooper stated in 1892, a woman's movement should not be based on the narrow concerns of white middle class women under the name of "women"; neither, she argued, should a woman's movement be formed around the exclusive concerns of either the white woman or the black woman or the red woman but should be able to address the concerns of all the poor and oppressed (Cooper, 1892).

But instead of concentrating upon the domination of a white feminist theoretical discourse which marginalizes non-white women, I focus on the production of a discourse of sexuality by black women. By analyzing the sexual and cultural politics of black women who constructed themselves as sexual subjects through song, in particular the blues, I want to assert an empowered presence. First, I must situate the historical moment of the emergence of women-dominated blues and establish

2. This paper was originally a presentation to the conference on "Sexuality, Politics and Power" held at Mount Holyoke College, September 1986. The power of the music can only be fully understood by listening to the songs, which should be played as the essay is read.

a theoretical framework of interpretation and then I will consider some aspects of the representation of feminism, sexuality, and power in women's blues.

Movin' On

Before World War I the overwhelming majority of black people lived in the South, although the majority of black intellectuals who purported to represent the interests of "the race" lived in the North. At the turn of the century black intellectuals felt they understood and could give voice to the concerns of the black community as a whole. They were able to position themselves as spokespeople for the "race" because they were at a vast physical and metaphorical distance from the majority of those they represented. The mass migration of blacks to urban areas, especially to the cities of the North, forced these traditional intellectuals to question and revise their imaginary vision of "the people" and directly confront the actual displaced rural workers who were, in large numbers, becoming a black working class in front of their eyes. In turn the mass of black workers became aware of the range of possibilities for their representation. No longer were the "Talented Tenth," the practitioners of policies of racial uplift, the undisputed "leaders of the race." Intellectuals and their constituencies fragmented, black union organizers, Marcus Garvey and the Universal Negro Improvement Association, radical black activists, the Sanctified Churches, the National Association of Colored Women, the Harlem creative artists, all offered alternative forms of representation and each strove to establish that the experience of their constituency was representative of the experience of the race.

Within the movement of the Harlem cultural renaissance, black women writers established a variety of alternative possibilities for the fictional representation of black female experience. Zora Neale Hurston chose to represent black people as the rural folk; the folk were represented as being both the source of Afro-American cultural and linguistic forms and the means for its continued existence. Hurston's exploration of sexual and power relations was embedded in this "folk" experience and avoided the cultural transitions and confrontations of the urban displacement. As Hurston is frequently situated as the foremother of contemporary black women writers, the tendency of feminist literary criticism has been to valorize black women as "folk" heroines at the expense of those texts which explored black female sexuality within the context of urban social relations. Put simply, a line of descent is drawn from *Their Eyes Were Watching God* to *The Color Purple.* But to establish the black "folk" as representative of the black community at large was and still is a convenient method for ignoring the specific contradictions of an urban existence in which most of us live. The culture industry, through its valorization in print and in film of *The Color Purple,* for example, can *appear* to comfortably address issues of black female sexuality within a past history and rural context while completely avoiding the crucial issues of black sexual and cultural politics that stem from an urban crisis.

"There's No Earthly Use in Bein Too-Ga-Tha if It Don't Put Some Joy in Yo Life" (Williams, 1981)

However, two other women writers of the Harlem Renaissance, Jessie Fauset and Nella Larsen, did figure an urban class confrontation in their fiction, though in distinctly different ways. Jessie Fauset became an ideologue for a new black bourgeoisie; her novels represented the manners and morals that distinguished the emergent middle class from the working class. She wanted public recognition for the existence of a black elite that was urbane, sophisticated, and civilized but her representation of this elite implicitly defined its manners against the behavior of the new black proletariat. While it must be acknowledged that Fauset did explore the limitations of a middle-class existence for women, ultimately each of her novels depicts independent women who surrender their independence to become suitable wives for the new black professional men.

Nella Larsen, on the other hand, offers us a more sophisticated dissection of the rural/urban confrontation. Larsen was extremely critical of the Harlem intellectuals who glorified the values of a black folk culture while being ashamed of and ridiculing the behavior of the new black migrant to the city. Her novel, *Quicksand* (1928), contains the first explicitly sexual black heroine in black women's fiction. Larsen explores questions of sexuality and power within both a rural and an urban landscape; in both contexts she condemns the ways in which female sexuality is confined and compromised as the object of male desire. In the city Larsen's heroine, Helga, has to recognize the ways in which her sexuality has an exchange value within capitalist social relations while in the country Helga is trapped by the consequences of woman's reproductive capacity. In the final pages of *Quicksand* Helga echoes the plight of the slave woman who could not escape to freedom and the cities of the North because she could not abandon her children and, at the same time, represents how a woman's life is drained through constant childbirth.

But Larsen also reproduces in her novel the dilemma of a black woman who tries to counter the dominant white cultural definitions of her sexuality: ideologies that define black female sexuality as primitive and exotic. However, the response of Larsen's heroine to such objectification is also the response of many black women writers: the denial of desire and the repression of sexuality. Indeed, *Quicksand* is symbolic of the tension in nineteenth-and early twentieth-century black women's fiction in which black female sexuality was frequently displaced onto the terrain of the political responsibility of the black woman. The duty of the black heroine toward the black community was made coterminous with her desire as a woman, a desire which was expressed as a dedication to uplift the race. This displacement from female desire to female duty enabled the negotiation of racist constructions of black female sexuality but denied sensuality and in this denial lies the class character of its cultural politics.

It has been a mistake of much black feminist theory to concentrate almost exclusively on the visions of black women as represented by black women writers without indicating the limitations of their middle-class response to black women's sexuality. These writers faced a very real contradiction for they felt that they would publicly compromise themselves if they acknowledged their sexuality and sensuality within a racist sexual discourse thus providing evidence that indeed they were primitive and exotic creatures. But because black feminist theory has concentrated upon the literate forms of black women's intellectual activity the dilemma of the place of sexuality within a literary discourse has appeared as if it were the dilemma of most black women. On the other hand, what a consideration of women's blues allows us to see is an alternative form of representation, an oral and musical women's culture that explicitly addresses the contradictions of feminism, sexuality, and power. What has been called the "Classic Blues," the women's blues of the twenties and thirties, is a discourse that articulates a cultural and political struggle over sexual relations: a struggle that is directed against the objectification of female sexuality within a patriarchal order but which also tries to reclaim women's bodies as the sexual and sensuous subjects of women's song.

Testifyin'

Within black culture the figure of the female blues singer has been reconstructed in poetry, drama, fiction, and art and used to meditate upon conventional and unconventional sexuality. A variety of narratives, both fictional and biographical, have mythologized the woman blues singer and these mythologies become texts about sexuality. Women blues singers frequently appear as liminal figures that play out and explore the various possibilities of a sexual existence; they are representations of women who attempt to manipulate and control their construction as sexual subjects. In Afro-American fiction and poetry, the blues singer has a strong physical and sensuous presence. Shirley Anne Williams wrote about Bessie Smith:

the thick triangular
nose wedged
in the deep brown
face nostrils
flared on a last hummmmmmmmm

Bessie singing
just behind the beat
that sweet sweet
voice throwing
its light on me

I looked in her face
and seed the woman
I'd become. A big
boned face already
lined and the first line
in her fo'head was
black and the next line
was sex cept I didn't
know to call it that
then and the brackets
round her mouth stood fo
the chi'ren she teared
from out her womb. . . . (Williams, 1982)

Williams has argued that the early blues singers and their songs "helped to solidify community values and heighten community morale in the late nineteenth and early twentieth centuries." The blues singer, she says, uses song to encourage reflection and create an atmosphere for analysis to take place. The blues were certainly a communal expression of black experience which had developed out of the call and response patterns of work songs from the nineteenth century and have been described as "a complex interweaving of the general and the specific" and of individual and group experience. John Coltrane has described how the audience heard "we" even if the singer said "I." Of course the singers were entertainers but the blues was not an entertainment of escape or fantasy and sometimes directly represented historical events (Williams, 1979).

Sterling Brown has testified to the physical presence and power of Ma Rainey who would draw crowds from remote rural areas to see her "smilin' gold-toofed smiles" and to feel like participants in her performance, which articulated the conditions of their social existence. Brown in his poem "Ma Rainey" remembers the emotion of her performance of "Black Water Blues," which described the devastation of the Mississippi flood of 1927. Rainey's original performance becomes in Brown's text a vocalization of the popular memory of the flood and Brown's text constructs itself as a part of the popular memory of the "Mother of the Blues" (Brown, 1980).

Ma Rainey never recorded "Backwater Blues" although Bessie Smith did but local songsters would hear the blues performed in the tent shows or on record and transmit them throughout the community. Ma Rainey and Bessie Smith were among the first women blues singers to be recorded and with Clara Smith, Ethel Waters, Alberta Hunter, Ida Cox, Rosa Henderson, Victoria Spivey, and Lucille Hegamin they dominated the blues-recording industry throughout the twenties. It has often been asserted that this recording of the blues compromised and adulterated a pure folk form of the blues but the combination of the vaudeville, carnival, and minstrel shows and the phonograph meant that the "folk-blues" and the culture industry were inextricably mixed in the twenties. By 1928 the blues sung by blacks were only secondarily of folk origin and the primary source for the group transmission of the blues was by phonograph, which was then joined by the radio.

Bessie Smith, Ma Rainey, Ethel Waters, and the other women blues singers traveled in carnivals and vaudevilles which included acts with animals, acrobats and other circus performers. Often the main carnival played principally for white audiences but would have black sideshows with black entertainers for black audiences. In this way black entertainers reached black audiences in even the remotest rural areas. The records of the women blues singers were likewise directed at a black audience through the establishment of "race records," a section of the recording industry which recorded both religious and secular black singers and black musicians and distributed these recordings through stores in black areas: they were rarely available in white neighborhoods.

When a Woman Gets the Blues . . .

This then is the framework within which I interpret the women blues singers of the twenties. To fully understand the ways in which their performance and their songs were part of a discourse of sexual relations within the black community, it is necessary to consider how the social conditions of black women were dramatically affected by migration, for migration had distinctively different meanings for black men and women. The music and song of the women blues singers embodied the social relations and contradictions of black displacement: of rural migration and the urban flux. In this sense, as singers these women were organic intellectuals; not only were they a part of the community that was the subject of their song but they were also a product of the rural-to-urban movement.

Migration for women often meant being left behind: "Bye Bye Baby" and "Sorry I can't take you" were the common refrains of male blues. In women's blues the response is complex: regret and pain expressed as "My sweet man done gone and left me dead," or "My daddy left me standing in the door," or "The sound of the train fills my heart with misery." There was also an explicit recognition that if the journey were to be made by women it held particular dangers for them. It was not as easy for women as it was for men to hop freight trains and if money was saved for tickets it was men who were usually sent. And yet the women who were singing the songs had made it North and recorded from the "promised land" of Chicago and New York. So, what the women blues singers were able to articulate were the possibilities of movement for the women who "have ramblin on their minds" and who intended to "ease on down the line" for they had made it—the power of movement was theirs. The train, which had symbolized freedom and mobility for men in male blues songs, became a contested symbol. The sound of the train whistle, a mournful signal of imminent desertion and future loneliness was reclaimed as a sign that women too were on the move. In 1924, both Trixie Smith and Clara Smith recorded "Freight Train Blues." These are the words Clara Smith sang:

I hate to hear that engine blow, boo, hoo.
I hate to hear that engine blow, boo, hoo.
Everytime I hear it blowin, I feel like ridin too.

That's the freight train blues, I got box cars on my mind.
I got the freight train blues, I got box cars on my mind.
Gonna leave this town, cause my man is so unkind.

I'm goin away just to wear you off my mind.
I'm goin away just to wear you off my mind.
And I may be gone for a doggone long long time.

I'll ask the brakeman to let me ride the blind.
I'll ask the brakeman to please let me ride the blind.
The brakeman say, "Clara, you know this train ain't mine."

When a woman gets the blues she goes to her room and hides.
When a woman gets the blues she goes to her room and hides.
When a man gets the blues he catch the freight train and rides.

The music moves from echoing the moaning, mournful sound of the train whistle to the syncopated activity of the sound of the wheels in movement as Clara Smith determines to ride. The final opposition between women hiding and men riding is counterpointed by this musical activity hiding and the determination in Clara Smith's voice. "Freight Train Blues" and then "Chicago Bound Blues," which was recorded by Bessie Smith and Ida Cox, were very popular so Paramount and Victor encouraged more "railroad blues." In 1925 Trixie Smith recorded "Railroad Blues," which directly responded to the line "had the blues for Chicago and I just can't be satisfied" from "Chicago Bound Blues" with "If you ride that train it'll satisfy your mind." "Railroad Blues" encapsulated the ambivalent position of the blues singer caught between the contradictory impulses of needing to migrate North and the need to be able to return for the "Railroad Blues" were headed not for the North but for Alabama. Being able to move both North and South the woman blues singer occupied a privileged space: she could speak the desires of rural women to migrate and voice the nostalgic desires of urban women for home, which was both a recognition and a warning that the city was not, in fact, the "promised land."

Men's and women's blues shared the language and experience of the railroad and migration but what that meant was different for each sex. The language of the blues carries this conflict of interests and is the cultural terrain in which these differences were fought over and redefined. Women's blues were the popular cultural embodiment of the way in which the differing interests of black men and women were a struggle of power relations. The sign of the train is one example of the way in which the blues were a struggle within language itself to define the differing material conditions of black women and black men.

Baaad Sista

The differing interests of women and men in the domestic sphere were clearly articulated by Bessie Smith in "In House Blues," a popular song from the mid-twenties which she wrote herself but didn't record until 1931. Although the man gets up and leaves, the woman remains, trapped in the house like a caged animal pacing up and down. But at the same time Bessie's voice vibrates with tremendous power which implies the eruption that is to come. The woman in the house is only barely restrained from creating havoc; her capacity for violence has been exercised before and resulted in her arrest. The music, which provides an oppositional counterpoint to Bessie's voice, is a parody of the supposed weakness of women. A vibrating cornet contrasts with the words that ultimately cannot be contained and roll out the front door.

Sitting in the house with everything on my mind.
Sitting in the house with everything on my mind.
Looking at the clock and can't even tell the time.

Walking to my window and looking outa my door.
Walking to my window and looking outa my door.
Wishin that my man would come home once more.

Can't eat, can't sleep, so weak I can't walk my floor.
Can't eat, can't sleep, so weak I can't walk my floor.
Feel like calling "murder" let the police squad get me once more.

They woke me up before day with trouble on my mind.
They woke me up before day with trouble on my mind.
Wringing my hands and screamin, walking the floor hollerin an crying.

Hey, don't let them blues in here.
Hey, don't let them blues in here.
They shakes me in my bed and sits down in my chair.

Oh, the blues has got me on the go.
They've got me on the go.
They roll around my house, in and out of my front door.

The way in which Bessie growls "so weak" contradicts the supposed weakness and helplessness of the woman in the song and grants authority to her thoughts of "murder."

The rage of women against male infidelity and desertion is evident in many of the blues. Ma Rainey threatened violence when she sang that she was "gonna catch" her man "with his britches down," in the act of infidelity, in "Black Eye Blues." Exacting revenge against mistreatment also appears as taking another lover as in "Oh Papa Blues" or taunting a lover who has been thrown out with "I won't worry when you're gone, another brown has got your water on" in "Titanic Man Blues." But Ma Rainey is perhaps best known for the rejection of a lover in "Don't Fish in My Sea," which is also a resolution to give up men altogether. She sang:

If you don't like my ocean, don't fish in my sea,
If you don't like my ocean, don't fish in my sea,
Stay out of my valley, and let my mountain be.

Ain't had no lovin' since God knows when,
Ain't had no lovin' since God knows when,
That's the reason I'm through with these no good triflin' men.

The total rejection of men as in this blues and in other songs such as "Trust No Man" stand in direct contrast to the blues that concentrate upon the bewildered, often half-crazed and even paralyzed response of women to male violence.

Sandra Leib (1981) has described the masochism of "Sweet Rough Man," in which a man abuses a helpless and passive woman, and she argues that a distinction must be made between reactions to male violence against women in male and female authored blues. "Sweet Rough Man," though recorded by Ma Rainey, was composed by a man and is the most explicit description of sexual brutality in her repertoire. The articulation of the possibility that women could leave a condition of sexual and financial dependency, reject male violence, and end sexual exploitation was embodied in Ma Rainey's recording of "Hustlin Blues," composed jointly by a man and a woman, which narrates the story of a prostitute who ends her brutal treatment by turning in her pimp to a judge. Ma Rainey sang:

I ain't made no money, and he dared me to go home.
Judge, I told him he better leave me alone.

He followed me up and he grabbed me for a fight.
He followed me up and he grabbed me for a fight.
He said, "Girl, do you know you ain't made no money tonight."

Oh Judge, tell him I'm through.
Oh Judge, tell him I'm through.
I'm tired of this life, that's why I brought him to you.

However, Ma Rainey's strongest assertion of female sexual autonomy is a song she composed herself, "Prove It on Me Blues," which isn't technically a blues song, and which she sang accompanied by a Tub Jug Washboard Band. "Prove It on Me Blues" was an assertion and an affirmation of lesbianism. Though condemned by society for her sexual preference the singer wants the whole world to know that she chooses women rather than men. The language of "Prove It on Me Blues" engages directly in defining issues of sexual preference as a contradictory struggle of social relations. Both Ma Rainey and Bessie Smith had lesbian relationships and "Prove it on Me Blues" vacillates between the subversive hidden activity of women loving women with a public declaration of lesbianism. The words express a contempt for a society that rejected lesbians. "They say I do it, ain't nobody caught me, They sure got to prove it on me." But at the same time the song is a reclamation of lesbianism as long as the woman publicly names her sexual preference for herself in the repetition of lines about the friends who "must've been women, cause I don't like no men" (Leib, 1981).

But most of the songs that asserted a woman's sexual independence did so in relation to men, not women. One of the most joyous is a recording by Ethel Waters in 1925 called "No Man's Mamma Now." It is the celebration of a divorce that ended a marriage defined as a five year "war." Unlike Bessie Smith, Ethel Waters didn't usually growl, although she could; rather her voice, which is called "sweet-toned," gained authority from its stylistic enunciation and the way in which she almost recited the words. As Waters (1951) said, she tried to be "refined" even when she was being her most outrageous.

You may wonder what's the reason for this crazy smile,
Say I haven't been so happy in a long while
Got a big load off my mind, here's the paper sealed and signed,
And the judge was nice and kind all through the trial.
This ends a five year war, I'm sweet Miss Waters once more.

I can come when I please, I can go when I please.
I can flit, fly and flutter like the birds in the trees.
Because, I'm no man's mamma now. Hey, hey.

I can say what I like, I can do what I like.
I'm a girl who is on a matrimonial strike;
Which means, I'm no man's mamma now.

I'm screaming bail
I know how a fella feels getting out of jail
I got twin beds, I take pleasure in announcing one for sale.

Am I making it plain, I will never again,
Drag around another ball and chain.
I'm through, because I'm no man's mamma now.

I can smile, I can wink, I can go take a drink,
And I don't have to worry what my hubby will think.
Because, I'm no man's mamma now.

I can spend if I choose, I can play and sing the blues.
There's nobody messin with my ones and my twos.
Because, I'm no man's mamma now.

You know there was a time,
I used to think that men were grand.
But no more for mine,
I'm gonna label my apartment "No Man's Land."

I got rid of my cat cause the cat's name was Pat,
Won't even have a mailbox in my flat,
Because, I'm no man's mamma now.

Waters's sheer exuberance is infectious. The vitality and energy of the performance celebrates the unfettered sexuality of the singer. The self-conscious and self-referential lines "I can play and sing the blues" situates the singer at the center of a subversive and liberatory activity. Many of the men who were married to blues singers disapproved of their careers, some felt threatened, others, like Edith Johnson's husband, eventually applied enough pressure to force her to stop singing. Most, like Bessie Smith, Ethel Waters, Ma Rainey, and Ida Cox did not stop singing the blues but their public presence, their stardom, their overwhelming popularity, and their insistence on doing what they wanted caused frequent conflict with the men in their personal lives.

Funky and Sinful Stuff

The figure of the woman blues singer has become a cultural embodiment of social and sexual conflict from Gayl Jones's novel *Corregidora* to Alice Walker's *The Color Purple.* The women blues singers occupied a privileged space; they had broken out of the boundaries of the home and taken their sensuality and sexuality out of the private into the public sphere. For these singers were gorgeous and their physical presence elevated them to being referred to as Goddesses, as the high priestesses of the blues, or like Bessie Smith, as the "Empress of the Blues." Their physical presence was a crucial aspect of their power; the visual display of spangled dresses, of furs, of gold teeth, of diamonds, of all the sumptuous and desirable aspects of their bodies reclaimed female sexuality from being an objectification of male desire to a representation of female desire.

Bessie Smith wrote about the social criticism that women faced if they broke social convention. "Young Woman's Blues" threads together many of the issues of power and sexuality that have been addressed so far. "Young Women's Blues" sought possibilities, possibilities that arose from women being on the move and confidently asserting their own sexual desirability.

Woke up this morning when chickens were crowing for day.
Felt on the right side of my pillow, my man had gone away.
On his pillow he left a note, reading I'm sorry you've got my goat.
No time to marry, no time to settle down.

I'm a young woman and ain't done running around.
I'm a young woman and ain't done running around.
Some people call me a hobo, some call me a bum,
Nobody know my name, nobody knows what I've done.
I'm as good as any woman in your town,
I ain't no high yella, I'm a deep killa brown.

I ain't gonna marry, ain't gonna settle down.
I'm gonna drink good moonshine and run these browns down.
See that long lonesome road, cause you know it's got a end.
And I'm a good woman and I can get plenty men.

The women blues singers have become our cultural icons of sexual power but what is often forgotten is that they could be great comic entertainers. In "One Hour Mama" Ida Cox used comedy to intensify an irreverent attack on male sexual prowess. The comic does not mellow the assertive voice but on the contrary undermines mythologies of phallic power and establishes a series of woman-centered heterosexual demands.

I've always heard that haste makes waste,
So, I believe in taking my time
The highest mountain can't be raced
It's something you must slowly climb.

I want a slow and easy man,
He needn't ever take the lead,
Cause I work on that long time plan
And I ain't a looking for no speed.

I'm a one hour mama, so no one minute papa
Ain't the kind of man for me.
Set your alarm clock papa, one hour that's proper
Then love me like I like to be.

I don't want no lame excuses bout my lovin being so good,
That you couldn't wait no longer, now I hope I'm understood.
I'm a one hour mama, so no one minute papa
Ain't the kind of man for me.

I can't stand no green horn lover, like a rookie goin to war,
With a load of big artillery, but don't know what it's for.
He's got to bring me reference with a great long pedigree
And must prove he's got endurance, or he don't mean snap to me.

I can't stand no crowin rooster, what just likes a hit or two,
Action is the only booster of just what my man can do.
I don't want no imitation, my requirements ain't no joke,
Cause I got pure indignation for a guy what's lost his stroke.

I'm a one hour mama, so no one minute papa
Ain't the kind of man for me.
Set your alarm clock papa, one hour that's proper,
Then love me like I like to be.

I may want love for one hour, then decide to make it two.
Takes a hour 'fore I get started, maybe three before I'm through.
I'm a one hour mama, so no one minute papa
Ain't the kind of man for me.

But this moment of optimism, of the blues as the exercise of power and control over sexuality, was short lived. The space occupied by these blues singers was opened up by race records but race records did not survive the depression. Some of these blues women, like Ethel Waters and Hattie McDaniels, broke through the racial boundaries of Hollywood film and were inserted into a different aspect of the culture industry where they occupied not a privileged but a subordinate space and articulated not the possibilities of black female sexual power but the "Yes, Ma'ams" of the black maid. The power of the blues singer was resurrected in a different moment of black power, re-emerging in Gayl Jones's *Corregidora;* and the woman blues singer remains an important part of our 20th century black cultural reconstruction. The blues singers had assertive and demanding voices; they had no respect for sexual taboos or for breaking through the boundaries of respectability and convention, and we hear the "we" when they say "I."

References

Brown, S. (1980). "Ma Rainey." *The Collected Poems of Sterling A. Brown.* New York: Harper and Row.

Carby, H. V. (1986). "On the Threshold of Woman's Era: Lynching, Empire, and Sexuality in Black Feminist Theory." In H. L. Gates, Jr., ed., *"Race," Writing, and Difference* (301–16). Chicago: University of Chicago Press.

Carby, H. V. (1987). *Reconstructing Womanhood: The Emergence of the Afro-American Woman Novelist.* New York: Oxford University Press.

Cooper, A. J. (1892). *A Voice from the South.* Xenia, OH: Aldine Publishing House.

Cox, I. (1980). "One Hour Mama." *Mean Mothers.* Rosetta Records, RR 1300.

Leib, S. (1981). *Mother of the Blues: A Study of Ma Rainey.* Amherst: University of Massachusetts Press.

Rainey, G. (1974). *Ma Rainey.* Milestone Records, M47021.

Smith, B. (n.d.). "In House Blues." *The World's Greatest Blues Singer.* Columbia Records, CG33.

Smith, B. (1972). "Young Woman's Blues." *Nobody's Blues But Mine.* Columbia Records, CG 31093.

Smith, C. (1980). "Freight Train Blues." *Women's Railroad Blues.* Rosetta Records, RR 1301.

Spillers, H. (1984). "Interstices: A Small Drama of Words." In C. Vance, ed., *Pleasure and Danger: Exploring Female Sexuality* (73–100). London: Routledge and Kegan Paul.

Waters, E. (1951). *His Eye Is on the Sparrow.* New York: Doubleday & Co., Inc.

Waters, E. (1982). "No Man's Mama." *Big Mamas.* Rosetta Records, RR 1306.

Williams, S. A. (1979). "The Blues Roots of Contemporary Afro-American Poetry." In M. S. Harper and R. B. Stepto, eds., *Chant of Saints* (123–35). Chicago: University of Illinois Press.

Williams, S. A. (1981). "The House of Desire." In E. Stetson, ed., *Black Sister: Poetry by Black American Women, 1746–1980.* Bloomington: Indiana University Press.

Williams, S. A. (1982). "Fifteen." *One Sweet Angel Chile.* New York: William Morrow and Co., Inc.

12. The Man Who Made a Lady Out of Jazz

PAUL WHITEMAN'S CONCERT OF FEBRUARY 12, 1924, became famous as the night that "made a lady out of jazz." Whiteman's all-white orchestra delivered sedate, polished performances that had little in common with the music of black contemporaries such as Louis Armstrong. But by the early 1920s, Whiteman had become the most famous band leader in the country and had claimed the title "King of Jazz." Later, many historians and audiences would recognize the importance of Jelly Roll Morton, King Oliver, and other black innovators, but Whiteman's orchestral arrangements, with relatively little improvisation, exemplified jazz to millions of people at this time.

Entitled "An Experiment in Modern Music," the concert at New York's Aeolian Hall included the premiere of George Gershwin's *Rhapsody in Blue,* along with music by Victor Herbert, Zez Confrey, and Irving Berlin. Whiteman's Palais Royale Orchestra began with the "Livery Stable Blues," adapted from the first jazz record—the million-selling 1917 recording by the Original Dixieland Jazz Band, a white band from New Orleans. Like the ODJB, Whiteman's performance featured a variety of raucous imitations of barnyard sounds, but he began the concert with this number in order to display the subsequent "improvements" in jazz scoring that had been developed as certain aspects of jazz were repackaged to fit with the white popular music of the time. Later, Whiteman performed the popular song "Whispering" in two versions—"legitimate scoring vs. jazzing"—so as to display a "melodic, harmonious, modern theme jazzed into a hideous nightmare."

In the long run, the experiment might be said to have failed, since jazz concerts developed out of dance styles, not "elevation."[1] But at the time, the program was well received, even though one reviewer called the opening number "exciting and very stupid."[2] The program notes for the concert, including the prefatory statement given below, were written by Hugh C. Ernst, manager of the Whiteman office. Ernst performs

---

Source: Excerpts from the 1924 Aeolian Hall concert program notes by Hugh C. Ernst.

1. See Scott DeVeaux, "The Emergence of the Jazz Concert, 1935–1945," *American Music 7:1* (Spring 1989), pp. 6–29.

2. "Capacity House Fervently Applauds as Jazz Invades Realm of Serious Music," *Musical America,* February 23, 1924, p. 32. See also the enthusiastic review by Henry O. Osgood, "An Experiment in Music," *Musical Courier,* February 21, 1924, p. 39.

"spin control": his characterization of the event as an "experiment" and his delicate negotiation of Whiteman's relationship to jazz betray the controversial status of even this version of the music.

The Why of This Experiment

Introductory

Three or four years ago Mr. Whiteman was requested by a number of his friends to give a concert of popular music but until now he considered it unwise to make the attempt because he did not feel confident that his organization had become sufficiently well known to be taken seriously by those people who are giving their time and effort to arouse in the present generation and in those to come a deeper appreciation of really good music.

Object of the Experiment

The experiment is to be purely educational. Mr. Whiteman intends to point out, with the assistance of his orchestra and associates, the tremendous strides which have been made in popular music from the day of the discordant Jazz, which sprang into existence about ten years ago from nowhere in particular, to the really melodious music of today, which—for no good reason—is still called Jazz. Most people who ridicule the present so-called Jazz and who refuse to condone it or listen to it seriously, are quarreling with the name Jazz and not with what it represents.

What Has Happened

Modern Jazz has invaded countless millions of homes in all parts of the world. It is being played and enjoyed where formerly no music at all was heard.

The greatest single factor in the improvement of American music has been the art of scoring. Paul Whiteman's orchestra was the first organization to especially score each selection and to play it according to the score. Since then practically every modern orchestra has its own arranger or staff of arrangers. As a result there are thousands of young people scoring and composing, who otherwise would perhaps have never dreamed of writing music. These same people are creating much of the popular music of today. They are not influenced by any foreign school. They are writing in the spirit of the times. They are striving only for melodies, harmony and rhythms which agitate the throbbing emotional resources of this young, restless age.

What May Happen

American composers should be encouraged to not only maintain the present standard, but to strive for bigger and better things. Eventually there may evolve an American school which will equal those of foreign origin or which will at least provide a stepping stone which will make it very simple for the masses to understand and therefore enjoy symphony and opera. That is the true purpose of this experiment.

If after the concert you decide that the music of today is worthless and harmful, it is your duty to stamp it down. If it is not, then we welcome anyone eager to assist in its development.

13. "The Jazz Problem"

THE ETUDE (PUBLISHED FROM 1883 TO 1957) was the most popular music teachers' magazine in the United States during the first half of the twentieth century. The garish cover of the August 1924 issue announced the magazine's intention to grapple with what it called "The Jazz Problem"—a phrase that evoked contemporary social crises such as "The Negro Problem" or "The Woman Question."[1] For devotees of classical music, jazz was a controversial topic; some felt that jazz was corrupting young musicians by luring them away from "good music" and encouraging sloppy technique, while others were more inclined to be tolerant of anything that attracted young people to music at all.

To air the debate, the magazine's editors solicited and printed the "Opinions of Prominent Public Men and Musicians," asking them: "Where Is jazz Leading America?" The excerpts given below, beginning with an introductory editorial, are taken from the two-part symposium of August and September, 1924. They show that quite different understandings of the term "jazz" were in circulation (one respondent, bandleader Vincent Lopez, proposed yet another fanciful origin for the word). Although all of the responents were male and white, they belonged to different musical traditions and institutions. These composers, educators, popular songwriters, bandleaders, and orchestral conductors responded to jazz from within their various understandings of music and history. For some of the writers, jazz could not be considered apart from ideas of race; for others, the World War, or modernity more generally, was the key to understanding jazz, whether one approved of it or not.

Where *The Etude Stands* on Jazz

The Etude has no illusions on Jazz. We hold a very definite and distinct opinion of the origin, the position and the future of Jazz. *The Etude* reflects action in the music world. It is a mirror of contemporary musical educational effort. We, therefore, do most emphatically *not endorse* Jazz, merely by *discussing* it.

Source: "Where The Etude Stands on Jazz," *The Etude,* August 1924, p. 515; "Where Is Jazz Leading America?," *The Etude,* August 1924, pp. 517–18, 520; "Where Is Jazz Leading America? Part II", *The Etude,* September 1924, p. 595.

1. See also Edmund Wilson, "The Jazz Problem," *The New Republic,* January 13, 1926, pp. 217–19, which mostly discusses Paul Whiteman.

Jazz, like much of the thematic material glorified by the great masters of the past, has come largely from the humblest origin. In its original form it has no place in musical education and deserves none. It will have to be transmogrified many times before it can present its credentials to the Walhalla of music.[2]

In musical education Jazz has been an accursed annoyance to teachers for years. Possibly the teachers are, themselves, somewhat to blame for this. Young people demand interesting, inspiring music. Many of the Jazz pieces they have played are infinitely more difficult to execute than the somber music their teachers have given them. If the teacher had recognized the wholesome appetite of youth for fun and had given interesting, sprightly music instead of preaching against the evils of Jazz, the nuisance might have been averted.

As it is, the young pupil who attempts to play much of the "raw" jazz of the day wastes time with common, cheap, trite tunes badly arranged. The pupil plays carelessly and "sloppily." These traits, once rooted, are very difficult to pull out. This is the chief evil of Jazz in musical education.

On the other hand, the melodic and rhythmic inventive skill of many of the composers of Jazz, such men as Berlin, Confrey, Gershwin, and Cohan is extraordinary. Passing through the skilled hands of such orchestral leaders of high-class Jazz orchestras conducted by Paul Whiteman, Isham Jones, Waring, and others, the effects have been such that serious musicians such as John Alden Carpenter, Percy Grainger, and Leopold Stokowski have predicted that Jazz will have an immense influence upon musical composition, not only of America, but also of the world.[3]

Because *The Etude* knows that its very large audience of wideawake readers desires to keep informed upon all sides of leading musical questions, it presents in this midsummer issue the most important opinions upon the subject yet published. We have thus taken up the "Jazzmania" and dismiss it with this issue. But who knows, the weeds of Jazz may be Burbanked into orchestral symphonies by leading American composers in another decade?[4]

We do desire, however, to call our readers' attention to the remarkable improvement that has come in the manufacture of wind instruments of all kinds and to the opportunities which are presented for teaching these instruments. Jazz called the attention of the public to many of these instruments, but their higher possibilities are unlimited, and thousands of students are now studying wind instruments who only a few years ago would never have thought of them.

Charles Wakefield Cadman—Noted American Composer

Candidly, I think too much importance has been placed upon this question of Jazz; too much worry has been given it. It is as silly to stir oneself up over the matter of jazz as it is to get into a fever heat over modern Christianity and Fundamentalism. Attacking jazz can do no good. Championing jazz only makes one ridiculous. I feel the best way to meet this problem is to meet it with the open mind. By that I do not think it is necessary to do any straddling.

---

2. In Norse mythology, Walhalla (or Valhalla) was the name of the hall where the king of the gods entertained warriors who had been killed in battle. As recast by Richard Wagner in his famous quartet of operas, *Der Ring des Nibelungen* (1876), Valhalla is the palace of the gods. [RW]

3. Here the editors show that their familiarity with jazz is limited to the music of white composers, arrangers, and performers. They refer by last names only to songwriters Irving Berlin, Edward "Zez" Confrey, George Gershwin, and George M. Cohan, as well as bandleader Fred Waring. [RW]

4. A reference to the work of horticulturalist Luther Burbank (1849–1926), whose breeding techniques produced more than eight hundred new varieties of plants. [RW]

Simply recognize the fact that jazz is an exotic expression of our present national life. The very fact of its form changing every year shows its impermanence. Its very rhythms and its fantastic effects, which are not without cleverness (because a good musician is usually called in to orchestrate the rather crude piano scores), somehow reflect the restless energy that pulses through the "spirit of the day," a restlessness that has become most patent since the World War. Jazz makes a more popular appeal at this moment than it would make at a more quiescent period of history. It is the craving for excitement on the part of those who can understand only the more popular forms of music, in other words, those who fancy the savage in music because it brings them a "kick."

It is true, indeed, that there are many who never get beyond the appreciation of jazz, but I am inclined to think that there are thousands who grow tired of the ever-recurring agitated forms and soon search for music with a deeper significance. Jazz is not peace-bringing; jazz is not spiritual, nor is jazz very uplifting. Its very lack of thoughtfulness (save in the rhythmic patterns it employs) and a lack of repose, make it *exotic*. Yet, do not let us overlook the fact that many classic tunes which have been pilfered bodily or even in a fragmentary manner and treated jazzily, have led to the understanding and appreciation of the original versions on the part of the most ardent jazzites. I have seen this to be true in cases under my consideration. The fact that the quality of jazz has improved greatly the past few years and that well-trained musicians are able to listen and smile and enjoy the cleverest of it, leads me to feel that we have nothing to be afraid of, and that the problem will take care of itself through natural evolution. Let us accept any "color effects" it has brought us and leave the pathological and psychological aspects to be worked out through the aforesaid evolution, which has ever and *shall* ever find *new* expressions and forms in each succeeding day and generation.

John Alden Carpenter—Distinguished American Composer

Replying to yours of the 2nd, I am afraid that I shall not have time to do justice to the theme; but I should like to be allowed to go on record as deprecating the tendency to drag social problems into a discussion of contemporary popular American music.

All music that has significance must necessarily be the product of its time; and, whether we believe that the world of to-day is headed toward Heaven or Elsewhere, there is no profit in any attempt to induce the creative musician to alter his spontaneous mode of expression in order that he may thus affect the contemporary social conditions. Nor shall we make any better progress by attempting to legislate contemporary American music out of popularity by resolution of clubs or civic bodies.

I am convinced that our contemporary popular music (please note that I avoid labeling it "jazz") is by far the most spontaneous, the most personal, the most characteristic, and, by virtue of these qualities, the most important musical expression that America has achieved. I am strongly inclined to believe that the musical historian of the year two thousand will find the birthday of American music and that of Irving Berlin to have been the same.

Dr. Frank Damrosch—Director of the Institute of Musical Art[5]

Jazz is to real music what the caricature is to the portrait. The caricature may be clever, but it aims at distortion of line and feature in order to make its point; similarly, jazz may be clever but its effects are made by exaggeration, distortion, and vulgarisms.

5. Later known as the Julliard School of Music. [RW]

If jazz originated in the dance rhythms of the negro, it was at least interesting as the self-expression of a primitive race. When jazz was adopted by the "highly civilized" white race, it tended to degenerate it towards primitivity. When a savage distorts his features and paints his face so as to produce startling effects, we smile at his childishness; but when a civilized man imitates him, not as a joke but in all seriousness, we turn away in disgust.

Attempts have been made to "elevate" jazz by stealing phrases from the classic composers and vulgarizing them by the rhythms and devices used in jazz. This is not only an outrage on beautiful music, but also a confession of poverty, of inability to compose music of any value on the part of jazz writers.

We are living in a state of unrest, of social evolution, of transition from a condition of established order to a new objective as yet but dimly visualized. This is reflected in the jazz fad. We can only hope that sanity and the love of the beautiful will help to set the world right again and that music will resume its proper mission of beautifying life instead of burlesquing it.

Franz Drdla—Violinist and Composer of the Famous *Souvenir*

(Drdla, the well known Checo-Slovak composer and violinist, has recently toured America as a star artist in the Keith circuit. Naturally he heard a great deal of Jazz. Since he has appeared repeatedly in Europe with many of the greatest musicians of his time, including Johannes Brahms, his opinions upon jazz given to *The Etude* at this time are most interesting.)

Every time and every age has its characteristic music precisely as it has its characteristic dress. In the Days of the Madrigal, the very character of the words and the text reflect the architecture and the attire of the times. Jazz is the characteristic folk music of modernity because America is the most modern country of the world. It is, however, an expression of the times and it is not surprising that Jazz should rapidly circulate around the globe like the American dollar.

Folk music of this type (if you want to call the artificialities of Jazz folk music) seems to spring into existence after times of great deprivation such as those that accompany great wars. The Waltz, for instance, seemed to spring into international currency just after the French Revolution, as a kind of irrepressible expression of joy and liberty from restriction. Later on came the polka; then, after the Franco Prussian War, seemed to be an outburst of the hilarious *can can* in Paris. The world was putting aside its tragedy for a spree.

At the end of the great war, American ragtime simply went wild and that was Jazz. Like many things it proved very infectious and soon the whole world was inoculated. European nations should not condemn American Jazz as long as its perpetrators seem to enjoy it even more at times than the native Americans.

Much of the Jazz I have heard seems to be in two-four rhythm. It rarely appears in the three-four rhythm. This in itself, with some of the very monotonous background rhythmic figures, makes Jazz very boring at times. It lacks variety in rhythm and meter although it tries to make up for this by introducing all sorts of instrumental color from every imaginable instrument that can be scraped, plucked, blown, or pounded.

Henry F. Gilbert—Distinguished American Composer

Is Jazz a new kind of music? Has it anything to contribute to the art? I find that almost all pieces of so-called Jazz music, when stripped of their instrumentation (i.e., the instruments upon which they are played: saxophones, muted trombones, etc.), have almost nothing new to offer in the way of strictly musical interest.[6] And this is so, even when we consider jazz from a strictly "popular" standpoint.

The amount of purely musical value, and the amount of differentiation of this music from other "popular" music, can be noted by playing a piece of jazz music on the piano. It is true that for several years the rhythmic element in popular music has been growing more insistent and nervous, and it may have reached its culmination in jazz. I rather think it has. So, as far as simple rhythmic forcefulness and iteration are concerned, jazz can claim the proud distinction of being the "worst yet." Technically speaking, however, it must be granted that the popular music of to-day is far richer in contrapuntal devices, in harmony, and in figuration than popular music formerly, in which the interest rested *alone* in the melody.

Another point by which jazz may be distinguished from the popular music of the olden time—say ten years ago—is the large number of cat-calls, clarinet-couacs, smears, glides, trombone-glissandos, and agonizing saxophonic contortions which occur in it. But these things are largely rendered possible by the instruments upon which jazz music is played. Take away these instruments and you take away the jazz quality almost entirely. In fact this jazz quality, far from residing in the music itself, is almost wholly a matter of tone-color, and this tone-color is given to it by the instruments—unusual instruments—and not only unusual instruments but also unusual combinations of instruments. For instance who ever thought of writing for a combination of saxophones, banjos, and muted trombones before? Yet in this, and similar combinations, lies most of the jazz effect in my opinion. Take many a piece of classical music—like some of Grieg's pieces, Dvǒřak's Slavonic Dances, or even some of Mozart's or Beethoven's compositions—and let a good jazz arranger arrange them for the usual jazz orchestra, with all its freak combinations of instruments—and let the arranger not change the original music more than is ordinarily done in transcribing a piano piece for an ordinary orchestra—and I would bet ten to one that it would be received by the majority as a new and authentic piece of jazz music.

In the unusual instruments—their unusual combination—the manner of playing them—the grotesque and burlesque effects which are obtained; in all this lies, for me, the interest in the phenomenon of jazz—*not* in the music. A great deal of my interest in it is purely humorous. By means of these above listed grotesque effects jazz "takes off" or "makes fun of" certain well-known phrases or legitimate methods of procedure in the respectable and established art of music. Jazz rings true in its Americanism in that it insists on laughing and making fun of even the most serious and beautiful things. It is a kind of musical rowdy, and occupies the same relation to the Art of Music that "Burlesque" (on the stage) does to "Legitimate Drama." It can certainly be very funny, and I for one, and I believe many more, have thoroughly appreciated the wit and skill of certain "take-offs." A little musical nonsense now and then is relished by the best of musicians. One night at Ziegfeld's midnight frolic—but the mere recollection of the way the saxophone caricatured a coloratura opera-singer is enough to make me laugh "fit to split," as the saying is.

A word about the saxophone. This instrument may be said to be the principal instrument in the jazz orchestra. It is so much in evidence here, and so little in evidence in the regular symphony orchestra, as to give many persons the idea that it is a special development of jazz. But the saxophone was invented by Adolphe Sax, in Paris, about

6. Gilbert is right, of course: if you strip away all aspects of its performance, reducing the music to notatable melody and harmony, jazz—like all music—loses much of its power and distinctiveness. Compare the excerpt from Sidney Finkelstein's work, included later in this anthology. [RW]

1840.[7] Meyerbeer, Massenet, Bizet, Thomas, and many others have written for it. Bizet has written for this instrument a naive and pastoral melody of much beauty, in his music to Daudet's drama "L'Arlésienne." However, it has never become an integral part of the standard symphony orchestra. It has always remained a special instrument, used on occasion to impart its rich and expressive tone-color to certain isolated phrases or melodies. It has remained for jazz to exploit it. And this has been done in a way to make the angels weep (with laughter). Originally an instrument having a richly pathetic and lyrical tone quality, it has been made to perform all sorts of ridiculous stunts, amounting to an indecent exposure, of all its worst qualities. It is as if a grave and dignified person were forced to play the part of a clown at the circus.

Vincent Lopez

(Mr. Lopez is at the head of the famous orchestra at the Hotel Pennsylvania in New York. The reported action of French authorities in prohibiting Jazz, and thereby making it impossible for certain American players to perform in Paris, has incited Mr. Lopez to wire urgent messages to Secretary of State Hughes, and to Senator Copeland, suggesting that as a reciprocal measure America cut short its hospitality to non-American musicians.)

I have been for a long time making a study both of the word "jazz" and of the kind of music which it represents. The origin of the colloquial word jazz is shrouded in mystery. The story of its beginning that is most frequently told and most generally believed among musicians has to do with a corruption of the name "Charles." In Vicksburg, Miss., during the period when ragtime was at the height of its popularity and "blues" were gaining favor, there was a colored drummer of rather unique ability named "Chas. Washington." As is a very common custom in certain parts of the South he was called "Chaz." "Chaz" could not read music, but he had a gift for "faking" and a marvelous sense of syncopated rhythm. It was a practice to repeat the trio or chorus of popular numbers, and because of the catchiness of "Chaz's" drumming he was called on to do his best on the repeats. At the end of the first chorus the leader would say: "Now, Chaz!"

From this small beginning it soon became a wide-spread habit to distinguish any form of exaggerated syncopation as "Chaz." It was immensely popular from the start, for it had appeal to the physical emotions unobtainable from any other sort of music. "Chaz" himself had learned the effectiveness of this manner of drumming through following the lead of country fiddlers in their spirited playing of "Natchez Under the Hill," "Arkansaw Traveler," "Cotton-Eye'd Joe," and the numerous other similar tunes so dear to the hearts of quadrille dancers.

In my endeavors to place a finger on the exact spot in music that we can "jazz," I found a process of elimination very convenient. There are many movements in the greatest symphonies that are syncopated; yet by no stretch of the imagination can we call them "jazz." The weird music of the North American Indians, based on sing-song vocal melodies with tom-tom accompaniment, is bizarre enough; but it is not "jazz." The Oriental whine of the musette, as used for the dances of the whirling dervishes, cannot be called "jazz." The languid airs of Hawaiian origin are not in that category. A Strauss waltz, a Sousa march, the gayest tune of a Gilbert and Sullivan light opera, an Argentine tango, a minuet, polka, quadrille, bolero, none of these are jazz; and yet any of them can be made into "jazz" by the simple expedient of accentuating that beat which the natural laws of rhythm require to be unaccented.

---

7. Sax patented the instrument in 1846. [RW]

The whole universe is founded on order and rhythm, on regularity and steady tempo. The music of the spheres rushing through space is undoubtedly in strict time; the seasons change on schedule; all astronomical calculations are possible because of the methodical regularity of recurrent events. It is entirely contrary to natural laws to syncopate, and only man does it. The music student has difficulty in acquiring this faculty, for he feels that it is inherently wrong. No wild animal gives a long-drawn cry but that it is in time. When a baby does not cry rhythmically a doctor or a mother immediately realizes that something is seriously the matter with the child. When the wrong beat is accented there is an actual physical effect on the hearer, for a law is being broken.

At the very beginning "jazz" meant "without music" or "contrary to music," but a great change has taken place in it. The "jazz" of war times has very definitely departed; although leaving its indelible mark on music as a whole, it fitted a hysterical period when the times were out of joint and a frenzied world sought surcease from mental agony in a mad outbreak of physical gymnastics. There was a time not long ago when anything odd and fantastical in music was labeled "jazz." The musicians became affected with the glamor of syncopation. The different instrumentalists began to imitate the antics of the drummer. It became a clamor, an uproar. The clarinet whined and whistled; the trombone guffawed grotesquely; the trumpets buzzed and fluttered; the pianist gyrated.

It developed into a contest to attract individual attention. The violinist caught the germ and debased his instrument through the most flagrant musical indecencies. We had for orchestras a bunch of acrobatic maniacs to whom music was entirely secondary and mummery was the word. The cowbell reigned supreme. And that was "jazz."

It is certainly a misdemeanor to call my orchestra, or any other good dance organization, a "jazz band," if taken in the sense of what a "jazz band" used to be. Present day dance music is as different from "jazz" as day from night. Yet the word remains with us; and we do stress syncopation, but we do it musically. It is now combined with the finest arrangements money can buy, the richest chords and modulations that gifted musical minds can conceive and the total elimination of all instruments and effects not of proven musical worth.

Ragtime music was the direct forerunner of "jazz." It was so nicely adapted to a simplified form of dancing that it had an almost universal appeal. It was merely syncopation without any particular emphasis. As the emphasis was added it became "jazz." It is, therefore, sufficiently explicit, so far as the music is concerned, to define "jazz" as emphasized syncopation; but there is another phase of it that includes the dancing in combination with emphasized syncopation.

Because there seems to be something animal-like in the emotional effects of "jazz," we have turned to animal movements to get a name for it. We have had the "turkey trot," the "elephant glide" the "camel walk" and countless other designations; but at last and apparently accepted permanently the "fox trot." Perfection of lithesome, graceful bodily action in faultless rhythm can hardly be better pictured than by the harmonious movement of a fox as he trots. There is an almost imperceptible hesitation as each foot is placed, a perfect timing that is exact balance and the very acme of equilibrium. The name fits both the dance and the music.

Will Earhart—Director of Music, Pittsburgh, PA

I rather welcome the opportunity to express myself on the subject of "Jazz" although nobody believes what anybody else says about it. I don't like "Jazz" and don't approve of it. My reason for not liking it is that it does not come pleasingly to my ears.

Mozart said somewhere—I think in a letter to his father—something to the effect that even in the most terrible situations in opera, music should never cease to be pleasing to the ear. I am willing to concede a place for rough sounds in opera—Alberich's cry is drama if it isn't music[8]—but when music is standing for nothing but sounds and patterns of sounds, I prefer the sounds to be pleasing rather than exciting.

I do not approve of "jazz" because it represents, in its convulsive, twitching, hiccoughing rhythms, the abdication of control by the central nervous system—the brain. This "letting ourselves go" is always a more or less enticing act. Formerly we indulged it in going on an alcoholic spree; but now we indulge it by going (through "jazz") on a neural spree. Just now, the world does not know where to look for some stable principles to cling to, has lost its confidence in the value of ends that it formerly believed in, has been greatly excited, and consequently is not in position to exert the poise and purposeful control that mark the man or the nation that has steadfast ideals, believes in its destiny, and firmly advances toward it. Restlessness, indecision and excitement are characteristic of the interim before we again find compelling aims. "Jazz" is symptomatic of this state.

Since it is a symptom, I am not very much worried about it. It will disappear like all things that are not sound and fundamental always have disappeared, and always will. It is a little irritating—when it is not amusing—to hear it justified because it is dynamic, forceful, energetic. A man in an epileptic fit certainly loosens a large amount of energy; but it is ludicrously foggy thinking to appraise such energy as strength. Energy or force has no value except as it is well controlled and purposefully directed. "Jazz" certainly proves that Americans possess nervous energy. It does not prove that they are safe with it. We have made the mistake before of assuming that fussy, uncontrolled energy meant strength, and we are making it again now.

"Jazz" is defended sometimes because, in its later manifestations, well trained musicians have put some real interest of musical thought and design into it. Such bright spots of the kind that I have noticed are merely intermittent. They usually appear as oases with a desert of drivel before and another following. Their effect, to me, is that of a voo-doo dancer suddenly shouting out some witty epigram and then relapsing to his primitive nature.

Perhaps everything must be judged by the company it keeps—and attracts. Bach fugues, Beethoven symphonies, works by Debussy and Ravel are heard in certain places and received by a certain clientele gathered there. They seem to be appropriate to the places in which they are heard, and to the people who gather to hear them. So does "Jazz."

Lt. Com. John Philip Sousa, U. S. N. RT.— Famous Composer–Conductor

"Jazz, like the poor, are ever with us."

I heard a gentleman remark, "Jazz is an excellent tonic but a poor dominant."

It is unfortunate that the newness of the term has not allowed lexicographers time to define it properly. My Standard Dictionary gives forth, "Jazz:—Ragtime music in discordant tones or the notes for it." This is a most misleading meaning and far from the truth and is as much out of place as defining a symphony when murdered by an inadequate and poor orchestra, "as a combination of sounds largely abhorrent to the ear."

8. A reference to Richard Wagner's operatic cycle, *Der Ring des Nibelungen.* [RW]

Jazz can be as simple as a happy child's musings, or can be of a tonal quality as complex as the most futuristic composition. Many jazz pieces suffer through ridiculous performances, owing to the desire of a performer wishing to create a laugh by any means possible. Sometimes it has as little to do with the composition as the blast of a trombone, or the shrieking of a clarinet in "Traumerei" has to do with the beauties of that composition; it simply makes it vulgar through no fault of its own. Jazz, as far as my observation goes, is simply another word for "Pep" and has a counterpoint in the written drama of "hokum" although that word has not been honored with a line of explanation or definition in either my standard or my slang dictionary.

There is no reason, with its exhilarating rhythm, its melodic ingenuities, why it should not become one of the accepted forms of composition. It lends itself to as many melodic changes as any other musical form. Forms go by cycles. There was a time when the saraband and the minuet occupied the center of the stage, and to-day the fox trot, alias jazz, does, and like the little maiden:

> *"When she was good, she was very, very good*
> *And when she was bad she was horrid."*

Walter R. Spalding—Professor of Music, Harvard University

In reply to your request that I send you a few words concerning the burning jazz question of the hour, it seems to me in this, as in so many other human affairs, that it is a matter out of proportion.

Everyone, I think, feels the excitement and refreshment which has been brought into music by means of the new and stimulating rhythms connected with jazz and ragtime. Some of us only take umbrage when we hear the extreme devotees of Jazz say that is it the greatest modern contribution to music and is destined to supersede all other music. As a matter of fact, Jazz is a development of the rhythmical side of music, which is the most vital factor in music, but which in many ways may be considered somewhat of a negative virtue. It is taken for granted that a normal, healthy man will have a good heart beat; and it is taken for granted that good music will have rhythmic vitality and variety.

But good music must surely have many other qualities, such as melodic outline, deep emotional appeal, sublimity and ideality; and if the best that we can say of Jazz is that it is exciting, it seems to me that many of the highest attributes of music are left out. In this, however, as in many other aspects of music, the good features will gradually be incorporated into the conventional idiom, and extreme mannerisms will be eliminated; for, whatever music is or is not, it is a free experimental art and has always been developed by composers trying all sorts of new possibilities in the way of rhythmic melody and harmonic effects, the possibilities along these lines being boundless.

Booth Tarkington—Famous Novelist and Playwright

I wish I knew enough about jazz to answer your questions with any symptoms of intelligence. I fear, however, that I cannot. I can give you my vague impressions only. I should not think jazz music the outcome of the spirit of unrest of these times. I should not think it the cause of much unrest, either. It might be considered an accompanying phenomenon, perhaps.

I do not think jazz is leading America anywhere.

I do not find myself condemning jazz; that is, not all jazz. I have heard jazz that was mere squeak and boom and holler and bang; and I have also heard jazz that seemed, perhaps, rather sensuous, but it was at least sensuously intelligible. I do not see it as the voice of new America, however. It seems to me to be purely incidental.

Dr. Stephen Wise—Rabbi of the Free Synagogue, New York, N.Y.

I am not sure jazz is leading America. I think that jazz is one of the inevitable expressions of what might be called the jazzy morale or mood of America. If America did not think jazz, feel jazz and dream jazz, jazz would not have taken a dominant place in the music of America.

The substitution of jazz for Beethoven, Bach, Wagner and Handel is no sadder than the substitution of Phillips Oppenheim or Rex Beach for the novels of my youth, George Eliot and Thackeray. Mencken is a sort of literary jazz, though perhaps a little less light-footed than jazz helps folks to be. I would not prohibit jazz or discredit it. The fear of which jazz is an inharmonious symptom is far too deep-seated for censorship or inhibitions or prohibitions. When America regains its soul, jazz will go; not before—that is to say, it will be relegated to the dark and scarlet haunts whence it came and whither unwept it will return, after America's soul is reborn.

Dr. Leopold Stokowski—Distinguished Orchestral Conductor

"Jazz" has come to stay. It is an expression of the times, of the breathless, energetic, super-active times in which we are living, and it is useless to fight against it. Already its vigor, its new vitality, is beginning to manifest itself.

The Negro musicians of America are playing a great part in this change. They have an open mind, and unbiased outlook. They are not hampered by traditions or conventions, and with their new ideas, their constant experiments, they are causing new blood to flow in the veins of music. In America, I think, there lies perhaps the greatest hope in the whole musical world.

In France today there are many clever musicians, most outstanding of whom are Debussy and Ravel. In England a school is growing steadily, and shortly it will burst into bloom like a flower. But though there is much talent, the world is still in the throes of a big unrest, for which it is striving to find expression. There is no great spirit, no great genius, such as Wagner, dominating the world of music at the present time.

With the very complex music of today, an interpreter is a very important factor. The composer creates a work. The interpreter recreates it and breathes life into it and makes it a living pulsating, vibrating thing. He it is who must correlate the instruments, the different kinds of phrasing and the various types of technique and make plain to the public that which, unaided, it could not understand or appreciate.

Art is going to develop in the future, speedily and in multiple forms. There will be no prohibition going on in music. There is going to be greater and greater variety, because it is going to reach more and more persons. Music is going to enter more and more into our lives and become a part of our philosophy.

Clay Smith—Well-Known Chautauqua Performer and Composer of Many Successful Songs[9]

If the truth were known about the origin of the word "Jazz" it would never be mentioned in polite society. I have seen many quotations from active-minded musicians

9. At this time, many lecturers and musicians traveled a circuit of local "Chautauquas," which had developed from nineteenth-century assemblies for general education and popular entertainment in Chautauqua, New York. [RW]

who have guessed at the origin of the term but they are far from the facts. Thousands of men know the truth about the ancestry of "Jazz," and why it has been withheld is hard to tell.

When I was a boy in school, some thirty-five years ago, I played the trombone and it did not take long in those days for me to get the reputation of being a prodigy. At fifteen and sixteen I had already made tours of western towns including the big mining centres when the West was really wild and woolly. Those were hard rough settlements and many of the men were as tough as mankind ever becomes. Like all adolescent boys let loose on the world I naturally received information that was none too good for me and was piloted by ignorant men to dance resorts which were open to the entire town. These dance resorts were known as "Honky-Tonks"—a name which in itself suggests some of the rhythms of jazz. The vulgar word "Jazz" was in general currency in those dance halls thirty years or more ago. Therefore Jazz to me does not seem to be of American negro origin as many suppose.

The primitive music that went with the "Jazz" of those mining-town dance halls is unquestionably the lineal ancestry of much of the Jazz music of today. The highly vulgar dances that accompany some of the modern Jazz are sometimes far too suggestive of the ugly origin of the word.

I know that this will prove shocking to some people but why not tell the truth? "The Truth is mighty and will prevail." "Jazz" was born and christened in the low dance halls of our far west of three decades ago. Present day "Jazz" has gone through many reformations and absorbed many racial colors from our own South, from Africa, the Near East and the Far East. But why stigmatize what is good in the music by the unmentionably low word "Jazz"?

If I were to get upon the platform and merely repeat some of the utterly horrible scenes that were forced upon me at those "Jazz" resorts during those boyhood tours, any respectable audience would be petrified. Do you wonder that the very name "Jazz" is anathema to me!

Having played high-class music with the Smith-Spring-Holmes Company, in some three thousand engagements in Chautauqua and Lyceum, which have taken me to the remotest parts of the country, I have heard so-called modern Jazz of all kinds. Who can help it?

Some of the modern Jazz arrangements are strikingly original and refreshing, with an instrumentation that is often very novel and charming. Music of this kind is far too good and far too clever to slander with the name "Jazz." It is very American in its snap, speed, smartness and cosmopolitan character. Why not call it "Ragtonia" or "Calithumpia" or anything on earth to get away from the term "Jazz"? But, even the best of this entertaining and popular music has no place with the great classics or even with fine concert numbers, except perhaps in a few cases where musicians of the highest standing, such as Stravinsky, Carpenter, Cadman, Guion, Grainger, Huerter, and others with real musical training, have playfully taken "Jazz" idioms and made them into modernistic pieces of the super-jazz type.

14. "The Negro Artist and the Racial Mountain"

POET AND NOVELIST LANGSTON HUGHES (1902–1967) belonged to that extraordinary circle of black writers and musicians whose creative efflorescence in the 1920s became known as the Harlem Renaissance. While all of these "New Negro" intellectuals produced sophisticated, confident work that was meant to displace old stereotypes, Hughes articulated the views of a younger generation that was just as interested in celebrating difference as in proving equality. At a time when most Renaissance thinkers looked to black concert composers such as William Grant Still to "elevate" black music, Hughes insisted that the most important music of the Harlem Renaissance was the blues of Bessie Smith and the jazz of Duke Ellington and Fletcher Henderson.[1] In this essay, he scornfully invokes a "Philadelphia clubwoman" to stand for those in the black community who advocated assimilation to white cultural traditions.

One of the most promising of the young Negro poets said to me once, "I want to be a poet—not a Negro poet," meaning, I believe, "I want to write like a white poet"; meaning subconsciously, "I would like to be a white poet"; meaning behind that, "I would like to be white." And I was sorry the young man said that, for no great poet has ever been afraid of being himself. And I doubted then that, with his desire to run away spiritually from his race, this boy would ever be a great poet. But this is the mountain standing in the way of any true Negro art in America—this urge within the race toward whiteness, the desire to pour racial individuality into the mold of American standardization, and to be as little Negro and as much American as possible.

Certainly there is, for the American Negro artist who can escape the restrictions the more advanced among his own group would put upon him, a great field of unused material ready for his art. Without going outside his race, and even among the better classes with their "white" culture and conscious American manners, but still Negro enough to be different, there is sufficient matter to furnish a black artist with a lifetime of creative work. And when he chooses to touch on the relations between Negroes and whites in this country with their innumerable overtones and undertones, surely, and especially for literature and the drama, there is an inexhaustible

---

Source: Langston Hughes, "The Negro Artist and the Racial Mountain," *The Nation,* June 23, 1926, pp. 692–93. Reprinted by permission of Harold Ober Associates Incorporated.

1. See Samuel A. Floyd, Jr., ed., *Black Music in the Harlem Renaissance: A Collection of Essays* (Knoxville: University of Tennessee Press, 1990).

supply of themes at hand. To these the Negro artist can give his racial individuality, his heritage of rhythm and warmth, and his incongruous humor that so often, as in the Blues, becomes ironic laughter mixed with tears. But let us look at the mountain.

A prominent Negro clubwoman in Philadelphia paid eleven dollars to hear Raquel Meller sing Andalusian popular songs. But she told me a few weeks before she would not think of going to hear "that woman," Clara Smith, a great black artist, sing Negro folksongs. And many an upper-class Negro church, even now, would not dream of employing a spiritual in its services. The drab melodies in white folks' hymnbooks are much to be preferred. "We want to worship the Lord correctly and quietly. We don't believe in 'shouting.' Let's be dull like the Nordics," they say, in effect.

The road for the serious black artist, then, who would produce a racial art is most certainly rocky and the mountain is high. Until recently he received almost no encouragement for his work from either white or colored people. The present vogue in things Negro, although it may do as much harm as good for the budding colored artist, has at least done this: it has brought him forcibly to the attention of his own people among whom for so long, unless the other race had noticed him beforehand, he was a prophet with little honor.

Most of my own poems are racial in theme and treatment, derived from the life I know. In many of them I try to grasp and hold some of the meanings and rhythms of jazz. I am sincere as I know how to be in these poems and yet after every reading I answer questions like these from my own people: Do you think Negroes should always write about Negroes? I wish you wouldn't read some of your poems to white folks. How do you find anything interesting in a place like a cabaret? Why do you write about black people? What makes you do so many jazz poems?

But jazz to me is one of the inherent expressions of Negro life in America: the eternal tom-tom beating in the Negro soul—the tom-tom of revolt against weariness in a white world, a world of subway trains, and work, work, work; the tom-tom of joy and laughter, and pain swallowed in a smile. Yet the Philadelphia clubwoman is ashamed to say that her race created it and she does not like me to write about it. The old subconscious "white is best" runs through her mind. Years of study under white teachers, a lifetime of white books, pictures, and papers, and white manners, morals, and Puritan standards made her dislike the spirituals. And now she turns up her nose at jazz and all its manifestations—likewise almost everything else distinctly racial. She doesn't care for the Winold Reiss portraits of Negroes because they are "too Negro." She does not want a true picture of herself from anybody. She wants the artist to flatter her, to make the white world believe that all Negroes are as smug and as near white in soul as she wants to be. But, to my mind, it is the duty of the younger Negro artists, if he accepts any duties at all from outsiders, to change through the force of his art that old whispering "I want to be white," hidden in the aspirations of his people, to "Why should I want to be white? I am a Negro—and beautiful!"

So I am ashamed for the black poet who says, "I want to be a poet, not a Negro poet," as though his own racial world were not as interesting as any other world. I am ashamed, too, for the colored artist who runs from the painting of Negro faces to the painting of sunsets after the manner of the academicians because he fears the strange un-whiteness of his own features. An artist must be free to choose what he does, certainly, but he must also never be afraid to do what he might choose.

Let the blare of Negro jazz bands and the bellowing voice of Bessie Smith singing Blues penetrate the closed ears of the colored near-intellectuals until they listen and perhaps understand. Let Paul Robeson singing "Water Boy," and Rudolph Fisher writing about the streets of Harlem, and Jean Toomer holding the heart of Georgia in his hands, and Aaron Douglas drawing strange black fantasies cause the smug Negro middle class to turn from their white, respectable, ordinary books and papers to catch a glimmer of their own beauty. We younger Negro artists who create now intend to express our individual dark-skinned selves without fear or shame. If white people are pleased we are glad. If they are not, it doesn't matter. We know we are beautiful. And ugly too. The tom-tom cries and the tom-tom laughs. If colored people are pleased we are glad. If they are not, their displeasure doesn't matter either. We build our temples for tomorrow, strong as we know how, and we stand on top of the mountain, free within ourselves.

15. A Black Journalist Criticizes Jazz

FROM 1925 TO 1929, PIANIST AND BAND leader Dave Peyton (c. 1885–1956) wrote a weekly column, "The Musical Bunch," for the *Chicago Defender*, one of the country's most important black newspapers. Peyton's views on jazz have little in common with those of Langston Hughes; his exhortations combine the pragmatic flexibility of a working musician (leading "Dave Peyton's Symphonic Syncopators") with the disapproving tone of someone who believes in the superiority of European musical practices and worries that some types of jazz might hold back "racial progress." Yet Peyton's warnings also reflect his resentment of how recording companies stereotyped black musicians and confined them to certain ("lower") kinds of music.

"The Musical Bunch," a feature of *The Chicago Defender*, the World's Greatest Weekly, is just two and one-half years old this issue. This writer is proud to know that some good has come out of his advices of the past. Many a musician has been turned around and has followed the straight path that leads to success. At times this writer has been a little severe on some of our brothers, but it was the only way to impress them that they were going the wrong way. They probably were making a mockery out of music—probably were about to make things bad for all of us—and a check had to be put on them, and there is no more sure check than publicity.

Source: Dave Peyton, "The Musical Bunch," *Chicago Defender*, April 28, March 10, and May 12, 1928; all of these columns appeared in part 1, p. 6 of the National Edition.

The trouble with most of our orchestras today is nonversatility. They have adapted themselves on one side of the fence or the other. If they can handle jazz music they fall short when the legitimate score is placed before them and if they are real standard music players they cannot handle the popular variety music. Of course we have superversatile orchestras, but they are few and far between. Bunch, if you are now in a jazz band do not give up proper study on your instrument. You may be called upon to render real service and to play good music. You cannot go wrong by practicing daily scale work. It keeps the mind alert and the fingers flexible. The orchestra today that is versatile gets the preference of best work and secures the best jobs, and the same applies to musicians who can do both kinds of work, standard and jazz.

Jazz Music

Jass music seems to hold a firm grip upon the public today, although there are many who like the standard classics and they always register a large hand when played, but generally jazz music is more overwhelmingly accepted, as it appeals to the popular fancy more than the standards do. This word jazz is a coined word, created by some one, as nobody has yet claimed its creation, and belongs to the slang family of expressions. Ragtime music, which swept the country many years ago, has evolutionized itself into the present-day jazz music. Ragtime music carried in its construction sweet melody flows, accompanied by brilliant harmonic embodiments, the theme or melody always dominating and the development of ragtime music for the orchestra was delightful.

Discordant Jazz

Down on the levees of the Sunny South was the real beginning of jazz music. New Orleans can rightfully claim the birth of jazz After sundown, when the day's work was through, the folks would get together and harmonize. They would select some tune the gang was familiar with and each person would blend in his or her part, producing counterpoints and fugues unconsciously. If they were playing instruments, rich, natural figures would come forth from the instruments. You would at times hear crude overblown tones; you could see the trumpeters with jaws poked out and a look of misery on their faces. Today most of our jazz trumpeters carry this hideous expression while playing. This crude style of jazz playing has developed into the world-famous artistic jazz music.

Popular Jazz

The style of jazz playing today requires musicianship to handle it. There is no faking, every instrument has its part to perform. The expert arrangers, theorists, as a rule put the notes down on paper in partitioned effect for the sections of the orchestra. The players must be musicians to cut the stuff. Many times you run into grand opera figurations which require technical knowledge of the musicians. The melodies, garnished with difficult eccentric figures and propelled by artful rhythms, hold grip on the world today, replacing the mushy, discordant jazz music.

The Trouble with Our Orchestras

We listen to many of the famous white orchestras with their smoothness of playing, their unique attacks, their novelty arrangement of the score and other things that go to make for fine music, and we wonder why most of our own orchestras will fail to deliver music as the Nordic brothers do. There is only one answer, and that is, we must get in line, we are too satisfied with what little we know about music. People pat us on the back and tell how well they like our endeavors and we begin really to think that we are all the berries. We allow these compliments to hinder our progress, we cease to study any longer, we poke out our chests with a feeling of bravado, we loudly sing our own praises and at the same time we continue to stand in a channel of ignorance, unconscious of the fact that we never learn music.

The Individual

Players individually should continue their studies on the various instruments; they should not give up constant daily practice just because they are considered good and a few people rave over them. We can have many advantages these days. Most all music colleges all over the country are open to our students and I mean the best of them. We who are working on steady jobs should make every sacrifice and endeavor to gain more knowledge of music. Use up your idle time at home, working hard to superperfect yourselves. It is surprising to know how little some of our so-called "star" musicians know about music. They really believe that they are good and they have a lot of friends who also will argue this out to a finish, when at the same time if the test is put to them by those who are musically efficient, they would shrink before the onslaught of theoretical interrogation. Let us wash ourselves of this conceit and right now at this moment vow to get into harness, study hard and seek a first class teacher. Things are fast changing in the music game. Jazz is on the wane, and the better class of music is coming back into favor with the critical public. It is much better to be ready when the times comes. If you are now playing in a jazz band for your living, do as I have suggested, use your idle time studying your instrument, your scales, and when you think that you have accomplished some good of your instrument, do not wait, start right away on harmony, counterpoint, and composition. Keep busy, it will only do you good in the long run.

16. "The Caucasian Storms Harlem"

OUR COLLECTIVE MEMORY OF THE ROARING Twenties is the Jazz Age of urban cabarets, indulgence, consumption, and scandalous dancing. Yet the national prohibition of alcoholic beverages from 1919 to 1933 destroyed a number of successful cabaret owners who couldn't survive without profits from booze, opening the way for bootleggers and gangsters to take over. The Cotton Club, perhaps the most famous of the Harlem clubs, reopened for a white clientele in 1923, and by 1925, white audiences were going north to Harlem in substantial numbers, attracted by easier access to alcohol and the "exotic" spectacles black entertainers staged for them.[1] These shows preserved many of the stereotypes of minstrelsy: black characters were depicted as uninhibited, uncivilized, inferior but naturally in touch with a *joie de vivre* white patrons felt was missing from their own lives. Yet black women were presented as glamorous and desirable, and the clubs provided steady work for some of the most talented musicians in the country—Duke Ellington's five-year stay at the Cotton Club (from 1927) furnished him with stable personnel and varied challenges that helped him to develop as a composer.

The unexpected transition of Harlem nightclubs from black to white audiences is the subject of this essay by Rudolph Fisher (1897–1934), a black radiologist, writer, and musician. As a writer, Fisher devoted much thought to the position of the displaced southern Negro in Harlem, though he himself was not from the South. This piece was published in 1927, after Fisher had returned to New York from Washington, D.C., where he had completed his M.D. in 1924. It appeared in the *American Mercury,* which one historian has characterized as "the bible of dissident college youths [and] white musicians who adopted black jazz as a religion."[2] Most of the essay is devoted to Fisher's reminiscences of the summer of 1919: he had just graduated from Brown University and he devoted his summer months to enjoying the Harlem cabarets before the white influx—before anyone had imagined there could ever be one. He closes with some thoughts about just what this cross-cultural attraction might mean and portend.

Source: Rudolph Fisher, "The Caucasian Storms Harlem," *The American Mercury* 11 (1927), pp. 393–98.

1. See Lewis A. Erenberg, *Steppin' Out: New York Nightlife and the Transformation of American Culture, 1890–1930* (Chicago: University of Chicago Press, 1984 [1981]) and David Levering Lewis, *When Harlem Was in Vogue* (New York: Oxford University Press, 1989 [1981]).

2. Grover Sales, *Jazz: America's Classical Music* (New York: Da Capo, 1992 [1984]), p. 94.

It might not have been such a jolt had my five years' absence from Harlem been spent otherwise. But the study of medicine includes no course in cabareting; and, anyway, the Negro cabarets in Washington, where I studied, are all uncompromisingly black. Accordingly I was entirely unprepared for what I found when I returned to Harlem recently.

I remembered one place especially where my own crowd used to hold forth; and, hoping to find some old-timers there still, I sought it out one midnight. The old, familiar plunkety-plunk welcomed me from below as I entered. I descended the same old narrow stairs, came into the same smoke-misty basement, and found myself a chair at one of the ancient white-porcelain, mirror-smooth tables. I drew a deep breath and looked about, seeking familiar faces. "What a lot of 'fays!" I thought, as I noticed the number of white guests. Presently I grew puzzled and began to stare, then I gaped—and gasped. I found myself wondering if this was the right place—if, indeed, this was Harlem at all. I suddenly became aware that, except for the waiters and members of the orchestra, I was the only Negro in the place.

After a while I left it and wandered about in a daze from night-club to night-club. I tried the Nest, Small's, Connie's Inn, the Capitol, Happy's, the Cotton Club. There was no mistake; my discovery was real and was repeatedly confirmed. No wonder my old crowd was not to be found in any of them. The best of Harlem's black cabarets have changed their names and turned white.

Such a discovery renders a moment's recollection irresistible. As irresistible as were the cabarets themselves to me seven or eight years ago. Just out of college in a town where cabarets were something only read about. A year of graduate work ahead. A Summer of rest at hand. Cabarets night after night, and one after another. There was no cover-charge then, and a fifteen-cent bottle of Whistle lasted an hour. It was just after the war—the heroes were home—cabarets were the thing.

How the Lybia prospered in those happy days! It was the gathering place of the swellest Harlem set: if you didn't go to the Lybia, why, my dear, you just didn't belong. The people you saw at church in the morning you met at the Lybia at night. What romance in those war-tinged days and nights! Officers from Camp Upton, with pretty maids from Brooklyn! Gay lieutenants, handsome captains—all whirling the lively onestep. Poor non-coms completely ignored; what sensible girl wanted a corporal or even a sergeant? That white, old-fashioned house, standing alone in 138th street, near the corner of Seventh avenue—doomed to be torn down a few months thence—how it shook with the dancing and laughter of the dark merry crowds!

But the first place really popular with my friends was a Chinese restaurant in 136th street, which had been known as Hayne's Café and then became the Oriental. It occupied an entire house of three stories, and had carpeted floors and a quiet, superior air. There was excellent food and incredibly good tea and two unusual entertainers: a Cuban girl, who could so vary popular airs that they sounded like real music, and a slender little "brown" with a voice of silver and a way of singing a song that made you forget your food. One could dance in the Oriental if one liked, but one danced to a piano only, and wound one's way between linen-clad tables over velvety, noiseless floors.

Here we gathered: Fritz Pollard, All-American halfback, selling Negro stock to prosperous Negro physicians; Henry Creamer and Turner Layton, who had written "After You've Gone" and a dozen more songs, and were going to write "Strut, Miss Lizzie"; Paul Robeson, All-American end, on the point of tackling law, quite unaware that the stage would intervene; Preacher Harry Bragg, Harvard Jimmie MacLendon and half a dozen others. Here at a little table, just inside the door, Bert Williams had supper every night, and afterward sometimes joined us upstairs and sang songs with us and lampooned the Actors' Equity Association, which had barred him because of his color. Never did white guests come to the Oriental except as guests of Negroes. But the manager soon was stricken with a psychosis of some sort, became a black Jew, grew himself a bushy, square-cut beard, donned a skull-cap and abandoned the Oriental. And so we were robbed of our favorite resort, and thereafter became mere rounders.

Such places, those real Negro cabarets that we met in the course of our rounds! There was Edmonds's in Fifth avenue at 130th street. It was a sure-enough honky-tonk, occupying the cellar of a saloon. It was the social center of what was then, and still is, Negro Harlem's kitchen. Here a tall brown-skin girl, unmistakably the one guaranteed in the song to make a preacher lay his Bible down, used to sing and dance her own peculiar numbers, vesting them with her own originality. She was known simply as Ethel, and was a genuine drawing-card. She knew her importance, too. Other girls wore themselves ragged trying to rise above the inattentive din of conversation, and soon, literally, yelled themselves hoarse; eventually they lost whatever music there was in their voices and acquired that throaty roughness which is so frequent among blues singers, and which, though admired as characteristically African, is as a matter of fact nothing but a form of chronic laryngitis. Other girls did these things, but not Ethel. She took it easy. She would stride with great leisure and self-assurance to the center of the floor, stand there with a half-contemptuous nonchalance, and wait. All would become silent at once. Then she'd begin her song, genuine blues, which, for all their humorous lines, emanated tragedy and heartbreak:

Woke up this mawnin'
The day was dawnin'
And I was sad and blue, so blue, Lord—
Didn' have nobody
To tell my troubles to—

It was Ethel who first made popular the song "Tryin' to Teach My Good Man Right from Wrong," in the slow, meditative measure in which she complained:

I'm gettin' sick and tired of my railroad man
I'm gettin' sick and tired of my railroad man—
Can't get him when I want him—
I get him when I can.

It wasn't long before this song-bird escaped her dingy cage. Her name is a vaudeville attraction now, and she uses it all—Ethel Waters. Is there anyone who hasn't heard her sing "Shake That Thing!"?[3]

A second place was Connor's in 135th street near Lenox avenue. It was livelier, less languidly sensuous, and easier to breathe in than Edmonds's. Like the latter, it was in a basement, reached by the typical narrow, headlong stairway. One of the girls there specialized in the Jelly-Roll song, and mad habitués used to fling petitions of greenbacks at her feet—pretty nimble feet they were, too—when she sang that she loved 'em but she had to turn 'em down. Over in a corner a group of 'fays would huddle and grin and think they were having a wild time. Slumming. But they were still very few in those days.

---

3. Ethel Waters (1896–1977) grew up around Philadelphia and developed a lighter singing style than southern blues singers such as Bessie Smith and Ma Rainey. Her theatrical flair helped her to cross over from vaudeville and the nightclubs to the white-dominated mainstream of popular music and a successful acting career. Her early recordings included sexy blues, but "Stormy Weather" became her signature song. [RW]

And there was the Oriental, which borrowed the name that the former Hayne's Café had abandoned. This was beyond Lenox avenue on the south side of 135th street. An upstairs place, it was nevertheless as dingy as any of the cellars, and the music fairly fought its way through the babble and smoke to one's ears, suffering in transit weird and incredible distortion. The prize pet here was a slim, little lad, unbelievably black beneath his high-brown powder, wearing a Mexican bandit costume with a bright-colored head-dress and sash. I see him now, poor kid, in all his glory, shimmying for enraptured women, who marveled at the perfect control of his voluntary abdominal tremors. He used to let the women reach out and put their hands on his sash to palpate those tremors—for a quarter.

Finally, there was the Garden of Joy, an open-air cabaret between 138th and 139th streets in Seventh avenue, occupying a plateau high above the sidewalk—a large, well-laid, smooth wooden floor with tables and chairs and a tinny orchestra, all covered by a propped-up roof, that resembled an enormous lampshade, directing bright light downward and outward. Not far away the Abyssinian Church used to hold its Summer camp-meetings in a great round circus-tent. Night after night there would arise the mingled strains of blues and spirituals, those peculiarly Negro forms of song, the one secular and the other religious, but both born of wretchedness in travail, both with their soarings of exultation and sinkings of despair. I used to wonder if God, hearing them both, found any real distinction.

There were the Lybia, then, and Hayne's, Connor's, the Oriental, Edmonds's and the Garden of Joy, each distinctive, standing for a type, some living up to their names, others living down to them, but all predominantly black. Regularly I made the rounds among these places and saw only incidental white people. I have seen them occasionally in numbers, but such parties were out on a lark. They weren't in their natural habitat and they often weren't any too comfortable.

But what of Barron's, you say? Certainly they were at home there. Yes, I know about Barron's. I have been turned away from Barron's because I was too dark to be welcome. I have been a member of a group that was told, "No more room," when we could see plenty of room. Negroes were never actually wanted in Barron's save to work. Dark skins were always discouraged or barred. In short, the fact about Barron's was this: it simply wasn't a Negro cabaret; it was a cabaret run by Negroes for whites. It wasn't even on the lists of those who lived in Harlem—they'd no more think of going there than of going to the Winter Garden Roof. But these other places were Negro through and through. Negroes supported them, not merely in now-and-then parties, but steadily, night after night.

Now, however, the situation is reversed. It is I who occasionally and white people who go night after night. Time and again, since I've returned to live in Harlem, I've been one of a party of four Negroes who went to this or that Harlem cabaret, and on each occasion we've been the only Negro guests in the place. The managers don't hesitate to say that it is upon these predominant white patrons that they depend for success. These places therefore are no longer mine but theirs. Not that I'm barred, any more than they were seven or eight years ago. Once known, I'm even welcome, just as some of them used to be. But the complexion of the place is theirs, not mine. I? Why, I am actually stared at, I frequently feel uncomfortable and out of place, and when I go out on the floor to dance I am lost in a sea of white faces. As another observer has put it to me since, time was when white people went to Negro cabarets to see how Negroes acted; now Negroes go to these same cabarets to see how white people act.

Some think it's just a fad. White people have always more or less sought Negro entertainment as diversion. . . . But suppose it is a fad—to say that explains nothing. How came the fad? What occasions the focusing of attention on this particular thing—rounds up and gathers these seasonal whims, and centers them about the Negro? Cabarets are peculiar, mind you. They're not like theatres and concert halls. You don't just go to a cabaret and sit back and wait to be entertained. You get out on the floor and join the pow-wow and help entertain yourself. Granted that white people have long enjoyed the Negro entertainment as a diversion, is it not something different, something more, when they bodily throw themselves into Negro entertainment in cabarets? "Now Negroes go to their own cabarets to see how white people act."

And what do we see? Why, we see them actually playing Negro games. I watch them in that epidemic Negroism, the Charleston. I look on and envy them. They camel and fish-tail and turkey, they geche and black-bottom and scronch, they skate and buzzard and mess-around—and they do them all better than I! This interest in the Negro is an active and participating interest. It is almost as if a traveler from the North stood watching an African tribe-dance, then suddenly found himself swept wildly into it, caught in its tidal rhythm.

Willingly would I be an outsider in this if I could know that I read it aright—that out of this change in the old familiar ways some finer thing may come. Is this interest akin to that of the Virginians on the veranda of a plantation's big-house—sitting genuinely spellbound as they hear the lugubrious strains floating up from the Negro quarters? Is it akin to that of the African explorer, Stanley, leaving a village far behind, but halting in spite of himself to catch the boom of its distant drum? Is it significant of basic human responses, the effect of which, once admitted, will extend far beyond cabarets? Maybe these Nordics at last have tuned in on our wave-length. Maybe they are at last learning to speak our language.

17. The Appeal of Jazz Explained

IN THE FIRST BOOK ABOUT JAZZ PUBLISHED in Great Britain (in 1927), R. W. S. Mendl attempted to account for the immense and sudden popularity of jazz. Unlike so many musical journalists of the time, Mendl

---

Source: R. W. S. Mendl. *The Appeal of Jazz* (London: Philip Allan & Co. Ltd., 1927). Pp. 80–85, 92–108, 186–87.

believed that a responsible critic could not simply dismiss a form of music that so many people cared about: it was imperative to understand the music's appeal. Mendl was amazed that jazz had crossed so many national, racial, and class boundaries, but instead of simply proclaiming it "universal," he tried to analyze how jazz was able to produce different meanings for different audiences. While he flirted with "novelty" and "instinct" as contradictory explanations for jazz's success, his primary interest was in locating meanings historically and socially, which led him to reject the highbrow/lowbrow split that many people considered natural.

Jazz has secured and still retains a more widespread vogue among its contemporary listeners than any other form of music ever known. Its general currency among the black people of the American continent, from which it sprang, would alone account for a vast number of jazz lovers. But the interesting feature of its popularity is the way in which it has attracted the white folk of the United States, the masses of the British Isles, the peoples of practically every country in Europe, of Canada, of Australia, of New Zealand and South America. In every quarter of the globe where white races dwell, jazz has obtained a footing: only among more distant Orientals—over whom no Western music can be expected to exert a spell—has it failed to make its mark. But it has penetrated to Turkey, and is now much favored in Constantinople. This syncopated dance music of to-day strikes a chord of which we civilised beings were, previously, but dimly conscious—something elemental, something crude, if you like, but something which once felt, cannot be ignored. It makes our blood tingle, and there is nothing surprising in the fact that some people find it makes their blood boil.

Jazz music has permeated through all "strata" of society. It shows, so to speak, no respect of persons or classes, but exercises its stimulating or disturbing influence over rich and poor alike. Royalty and labourers, aristocrats and clerks, doctors and shorthand typists obey its call with a unanimity which we shall find amusing or disconcerting according to our outlook. Like the Pied Piper of Hamelin, the modern syncopator bids the children of our cities follow in his wake, and lo! they are prone to foot it to his strains.

What are the causes of this amazingly ubiquitous popularity? Why should this bustling intruder from the West have impelled us to rise from our chairs with one accord, to hop or glide or waddle or trip around the room—a thing which some of us, though we have perhaps reached middle age, have never done before or else had long ceased to do?

There is little doubt that on its first appearance syncopated dance music attracted white people by the sheer charm of novelty. Though syncopation was in use in European music, it was almost unknown as a dancing medium, except here and there, as among the Magyars.[1] The very idea of getting your feet to fit in with a tune which was played as it were, out of time, exerted a fascination over those who were new to it. There was an instinctive delight in emphasizing with your feet a beat which was not stressed by the players. We all felt, did we not? that we were playing our little part in the performance. In our heart of hearts, we were rather proud of ourselves for being able to accomplish such a thing. To be able to dance with regular steps to music which was written or played in irregular time—this was indeed an

1. Hungarians. [RW]

achievement. Our ancestors always brought their feet to the ground—or pressed them on the floor—at the same moment as the band placed its emphasis on certain notes. But with the new dance music we were called upon to do nothing of the kind! On the contrary, the orchestra, with a roguery which at first puzzled and then delighted us, was found to be making a point of stressing the unexpected notes and of passing by with a mere nod of the head that sturdy old champion of strict time, the first beat of the bar. What an affront to his dignity! But never mind! It would do him a world of good. How could he expect to monopolize the maximum of attention all his life? It was high time that his hitherto weaker brethren should at last be given a chance, and that his stolid conservatism should receive a gentle dig in the ribs.

Syncopated jazz music marks a striking change. That a form of music which originated among black people should have developed into the most popular music of the white races—nay, the most widely popular form of music in the world's history—is a phenomenon sufficiently remarkable to lead us to probe it still further.

After the long spell of comparative peace which Europe in general, and England in particular, enjoyed during the period which in this country coincided with the reign of Queen Victoria, this twentieth century of ours has been a restless affair indeed. Amid the elemental passions which were aroused by the war and which were awakening in the preceding years of preparation for it, the strong rhythms of a coloured people's music took root and thrived readily. There was in ragtime and there is in jazz a primitive surging force which may at first sight appear to have little or nothing to do with the melancholy story of European strife and jealousy, but which could not be conceived as making an appeal to the restful Victorians or the eighteenth century aristocrats with their powdered wigs and their courtly graces. The violently syncopated strains with their negro origins, the strange, often crude and cacophonous instrumentation of the earlier jazz bands, not merely provided a suitably highly-flavoured relief from the actual horrors of the campaign: they were themselves, in their own way, a reflection of the elemental instincts of war fever.

And in Europe, after the war itself had come to its sudden and dramatic conclusion, it has taken—nay, is taking—many years for these passions to die down; the waters are still turbulent, and the rough music of the negro is still with us. If at last we are now beginning to discover signs that the great ocean of European politics is abating its fury—if a new Europe can be discerned rising from the smouldering ashes which the Great War left behind, do we not also notice a change in the character of this weird jazz music which we have taken to our bosoms? Has not it, too, become more civilized, its rhythms less violent, its orchestration more refined, its performers more disposed to play softly and delicately?

Music, like every other art, is invariably an expression of the times in which it is created. And for the people of Europe jazz music has meant something rather different from that which its original inventors intended or from that which it signified for the people of the United States of America. To the Englishman, the Frenchman, or the German, jazz music has been a curious intruder whose welcome in our midst has been made more genial by the exceptional circumstances in which he has arrived. In America this jazz goblin is no stranger. He is native to the soil. The white people of the United States have the negroes there amongst them. Their attitude towards the negro is correspondingly different from ours. While serious American composers have mostly drawn upon European sources for their musical materials, the American writers of dance music have had recourse to the indigenous product. It was natural that they should do so. These negro rhythms and to some extent also the peculiar instrumentation of the jazz band, at least in its primitive forms, are the only truly American musical products which that great continent possesses. In a sense it is as reasonable for the white American musician to seize upon them and develop them as it was for the German or English composer to build upon the folk songs of his native land.

Jazz music, though it did undoubtedly represent for the young American, when he became engaged in the war, something analogous to that which it meant to the European fighting man, embodies for the white people of America at large a spirit which is characteristic of their nation. The energy, the industry, the hurry and hustle and efficiency of modern American methods, find their counterpart in the swift-moving, bustling, snappy, restless rhythms of syncopated dance music, in the splendid technique of the performers, in the cunning quips and cranks of the jazz orchestra. To some extent, of course, the methods of American industrialism have found their way to Europe and may therefore be held to be in keeping with the European popularity of jazz music. But whereas in the eyes of an Englishman jazz is a popular importation—admittedly inapposite to his traditions, his ancient Gothic cathedrals, and his old Elizabethan and Georgian houses, yet nevertheless welcomed as a stimulating guest—to the American citizen it is a home product expressing something of the life which he has made his own.

In considering the popularity of the syncopated dance music of the twentieth century it is impossible to pass by, without mention, the curious controversy which has taken place in our midst between the advocates of so-called "Classical" music and jazz. For the purposes of this dispute, the assumption is usually made that jazz is the music of the masses, whereas the classics represent the art of the exclusive few. A gulf is established between the two—if only for the sake of argument—and we are encouraged to believe that it is a valley which can with difficulty be bridged. But its importance has been greatly overestimated. There is in truth no definable borderline between jazz music and the classics. Music is one, and the works of Johann Sebastian Bach and Irving Berlin both fall within its ambit. To be frightened of the one is as unnecessary as to be contemptuous of the other. If we are to be fair and catholic in our tastes we must listen to both impartially.

The man who at present only cares for modern dance music is in some respects a more hopeful specimen than that type of musician who can see nothing but evil in jazz. The mere fact that he enjoys jazz shows that, instead of being, like some unfortunate people, utterly indifferent to all music, he is capable of deriving pleasure from certain musical products. The art of tones and rhythms makes some appeal to him, and it is really only a question of environment, of musical acclimatisation, of gradual training, of overcoming his early prejudice against classical music, for him to find that he can get honest enjoyment also from Bach and Schumann and others.

But the cultured musician who has hardened his heart against jazz music is running a graver danger than that in which the untutored jazz lover is involved. He incurs a risk of failing to understand the point of view of the vast majority of his fellow creatures; of being thought, not without some justification, somewhat superior-minded; of being dubbed by that popular and opprobrious epithet of "highbrow," and consequently of having his opinions and advice, which may very probably possess intrinsic value, treated with scant regard, simply because they are tinged with contempt, whether expressed or implied, or by a dash of condescension.

Thus it is that a gulf, which need never have existed, is widened by the faults of both parties. The man who cares only for dance music makes up his mind, quite wrongly, of course, that what he terms popular music and light music are synonymous. He ignores the fact—and will with difficulty be induced to believe it even when it is pointed out to him—that the works of the great masters are chock full of light music; that old Bach wrote stacks of dance tunes which are infinitely more light-hearted than many of the mournful waltzes played in the modern ballroom or even than some of the more sentimental foxtrots of recent times; that the output of Byrd and Morley, of Purcell and Rameau, of Haydn, Mozart, Beethoven, Rossini, Schubert, Brahms, Chopin, Tchaikovsky, and in our own day Richard Strauss, de Falla, Holst, and others, is crowded with light music and often with the most delightful humour. A concerto or an oratorio may, of course, be deadly dull, but so may a one-step or foxtrot or "blues" melody. If they are, they will soon die a natural death. Jazz music has undoubtedly been a revelation to large numbers of people, of their own powers of musical enjoyment. Surely it is misguided to discourage all these new wanderers into the paths of musical pleasure by rubbing it into them that the one form of music in which they have been able to take any live interest is a detestable and worthless product.

Jazz is the product of a restless age: an age in which the fever of war is only now beginning to abate its fury; when men and women, after their efforts in the great struggle, are still too much disturbed to be content with a tranquil existence; when freaks and stunts and sensations are the order—or disorder—of the day; when painters delight in portraying that which is not, and sculptors in twisting the human limbs into strange, fantastic shapes; when America is turning out her merchandise at an unprecedented speed and motor cars are racing along the roads; when aeroplanes are beating successive records and ladies are in so great a hurry that they wear short skirts which enable them to move faster and cut off their hair to save a few precious moments of the day; when the extremes of Bolshevism and Fascismo are pursuing their own ways simultaneously, and the whole world is rushing helter-skelter in unknown directions.

Amid this seething, bubbling turmoil, jazz hurries along its course, riding exultantly on the eddying stream. Nevertheless, the end of civilisation is not yet, and jazz will either be trained and turned to artistic uses or else vanish utterly from our midst as a living force. But even if it disappears altogether it will not have existed in vain. For its record will remain as an interesting human document—the spirit of the age written in the music of the people.

PART 3

The Thirties

18. What Is Swing?

EVEN THOUGH *SWING THAT MUSIC* WAS mostly ghostwritten from his notes and interviews, Louis Armstrong (1901–1971) is usually credited with having authored the first published autobiography of a jazz musician. (Paul Whiteman's *Jazz*, written with M. M. McBride, had appeared ten years earlier, in 1926, so it depends on how one defines "jazz.") Since many musicians and historians hail Armstrong as the first great jazz soloist, he speaks here with considerable authority, and although his voice is highly mediated, the book circulated as his statement.[1] In any case, these excerpts describe well what he actually did as a musician, unlike his other autobiographical writings. Armstrong highlights the tension that exists between the creative freedom of the musician and the authority of the arranger or conductor, insisting that much is lost when jazz is written down. He writes of the successful swing player's "sheer musical instinct," but points out that it takes many years to develop the ability to improvise.

Critics and musicians from Paul Whiteman to Dave Peyton had argued in the 1920s and '30s that written arrangements and complex scoring moved jazz forward along a path of evolutionary improvement. But in these excerpts Armstrong implicitly criticized the smoothly arranged style preferred by so many of the big bands. The famed trumpeter worked to refute the evolutionary view by claiming the popular

---

Source: Louis Armstrong, *Swing That Music* (New York: Longmans, Green, 1936), pp. 30–34, 104–107. Reprinted by permission of Oscar Cohen and The Louis Armstrong Educational Foundation, Inc.

1. For a more extensive evaluation of the provenance and significance of *Swing That Music*, see William H. Kenney III, "Negotiating the Color Line: Louis Armstrong's Autobiographies," in Reginald T. Buckner and Steven Weiland, eds., *Jazz in Mind: Essays on the History and Meanings of Jazz* (Detroit: Wayne State University Press, 1991), pp. 38–59. See also Dan Morgenstern's "Foreword" to Louis Armstrong, *Swing That Music* (New York: Da Capo, 1993), pp. vii–xiii.

> word "swing" (rather than "jazz") for his older New Orleans style of collective improvisation. Creative improvisation linked Armstrong's music, as he saw it, to larger swing bands such as Benny Goodman's, but distanced both from, say, Paul Whiteman's orchestra. The distinction is not one of race but of sensibility: "the 'regular' style music will relax you but the swing is likely to make you feel keen—waiting on edge for the 'hot' variations."[2]

For a man to be a good swing conductor he should have been a swing player himself, for then he knows a player is no good if the leader sets down on him too much and doesn't let him "go to town" when he feels like going. That phrase, "goin' to town," means cuttin' loose and takin' the music with you, whatever the score may call for. Any average player, if he's worth anything at all, can follow through a score, as it's written there in front of him on his instrument rack. But it takes a swing player, and a real good one, to be able to leave that score and to know, or "feel," just when to leave it and when to get back on it. No conductor can tell him, because it all happens in a second and doesn't happen the same way any two times running. It is just that liberty that every individual player must have in a real swing orchestra that makes it most worth listening to. Every time they play there is something new swinging into the music to make it "hot" and interesting. And right here I want to explain that "hot," as swing musicians use the word, does not necessarily mean loud or even fast. It is used when a swing player gets warmed up and "feels" the music taking hold of him so strong that he can break through the set rhythms and the melody and toss them around as he wants without losing his way. That creates new effects and is done whether the music is loud or soft or fast or slow.

You will think that if every man in a big sixteen-piece band had his own way and could play as he wanted, that all you would get would be a lot of jumbled up, crazy noise. This would be and is true with ordinary players, and that is why most bands have to play "regular" and their conductors can't dare let them leave their music as it is scored. The conductor himself may decide on certain variations, an "arrangement" they call it, but the players have to follow that scoring. In that way the conductor or "arranger" may write some "hot" phrasing into an old score and, to those who don't know, the orchestra may seem to be "swinging." But when you've got a real bunch of swing players together in an orchestra, you can turn them loose for the most part. "Give 'em their head," as they say of a race horse. They all play together, picking up and following each other's "swinging," all by ear and sheer musical instinct. It takes a very fine ear and some years of playing to do that. That is why there have been so few really fine swing orchestras in the world. First you have to get a combination of natural swing players and then they've got to learn how to play in and out together as one man. No conductor can *make* them do it, or even show them much how to. His biggest part is to make suggestions and try to get them into a good humor and then let them alone. And I mean alone! If he doesn't, if he starts telling one man just how to play this part and another how to play another part, pretty soon he'll ruin his orchestra and he'll have one that just plods along with the score, playing

2. For an analysis of the controversies over "swing" and "jazz" in the jazz press, see Bernard Gendron, "Moldy Figs and Modernists: Jazz at War (1942–1946)," *Discourse* 15:3 (Spring, 1993), pp. 130–57. [RW]

regular, and all the life will be gone out of the men. Swing players have got to have a good time when they are playing and they can't have a good time, playing and rehearsing as they do twelve and fourteen hours a day, if you just make machines out of them.

No man in my band which you hear over the radio *has* to do anything, except be a good musician and "show" on time and in good shape for rehearsals. If he *can't* play away from the score, I don't want him. He doesn't belong in a real swing band, and, Heaven knows, there are plenty of fine non-swing or "regular" bands in the land which will be glad enough to have him. My men know that—and my knowing it may be the biggest reason why we are out in front today. If I hadn't come up myself as a swing trumpeter, and found out that you've got to be let alone and allowed to play your own way, probably I would be bearing down more on my boys and flattening out their style; and they would not be happy because they all know better.

So if you have been hearing about swing music, but have not known much about the difference, listen closely when you hear one of the big "regular" orchestras playing on the air or in your favorite hotel or club, and then listen carefully to a swing orchestra like Benny Goodman's or Jimmy Dorsey's or the Casa Loma or the Louis Armstrong Band. Pretty soon you will begin to notice that all of the players in the "regular" orchestra are playing almost perfectly together to a regular, set, rhythmic beat, and are smoothly following the melody to the end. No one instrument will be heard standing out at any time during the piece (unless, of course, there happens to be a soloist leading them for a number). Then when you listen to a swing band, you will begin to recognize that all through the playing of the piece, individual instruments will be heard to stand out and then retreat and you will catch new notes and broken-up rhythms you are not at all familiar with. You may have known the melody very well but you will never have heard it played just that way before and will never hear it played just that way again. Because the boys are "swinging" around, and away from, the regular beat and melody you are used to, following the score very loosely and improvising as they go, by ear and free musical feeling. If you pay attention for a little while, you will easily notice the difference. You will probably feel differently, too—the "regular" style music will relax you but the swing is likely to make you feel keen—waiting on edge for the "hot" variations you feel are coming up at any moment. That is because you recognize, maybe without knowing it, that something really creative is happening right before you.

Now I know there are a lot of people who will read this book who will say that "swing" is just a new name for the same old jazz they've been hearing for many years and that I am trying to make it look as though it was something new. Even some of the editors of the publishing house which is publishing this book told me that at first, though of course in a very polite way. But I cannot say too strongly to these people that there is all the difference in the world and if they will just try to understand it they will very soon be singing out when they tune in a band on their radios, "That's swing!" or "That's not swing," and will be able to tell at once.

Now the *basic idea* of swing music is not new. The swing idea of free improvisation by the players was at the core of jazz when it started back there in New Orleans thirty years ago. Those early boys were swing-men, though they didn't know so much about it then as we do today. But they had the *basic idea,* all right. What happened was that this idea got lost when jazz swept over the country. I think the reason it got overlooked and lost was that when the public went crazy over jazz the music publishing companies and the record companies jumped in and had all the songs written down and recorded and they and the theatre producers and northern dance halls paid our boys more money than they'd ever heard of to help write down and play these songs. Popular songs before jazz had always been played the way they were written and that was what made "song hits" for the publishers. So the commercial men wanted the new jazz tunes played the same way so the public would come to learn them easily and sing them. The public liked that, too, because the new tunes were "catchy" and different and people liked to sing them and hear them played that way. Jazz was new to them and they didn't understand it enough to be ready for any "crazy business." So most of the good jazz players and jazz bands which followed the Dixieland Five went down the easiest road where the big money was, and you can hardly blame them when you look back now and see how few people understood what it was really all about anyway.[3] Some of the boys stuck along and just wouldn't follow scoring, it wasn't in 'em, and some of the others that didn't learn to read music went on swinging the way they had learned to love. Very few of them ever made much money, but playing in small clubs and dives they kept swing alive for many years.

Then there was another group of the boys who took a straddle and I think they were the smartest and that they have probably done more to bring swing into its own than anybody. They were the swing-men who went on into the commercial field, joined big conventional bands, played the game as it was dished out to them and made their money, and yet who loved swing so much that they kept it up outside of their regular jobs. They did it through the jam sessions held late at night after their work was done. It makes me think of the way the early Christians would hold their meetings in the catacombs under Rome. With those musicians I guess it was the old saying: "He who fights and runs away will live to fight another day." At any rate, the truth is that most of the best-known swing artists of today are or were the crackshot musicians with big conventional bands (name bands, we call them because they are usually known by the name of their leader) or on big radio programs, but they don't miss their jam sessions where they can cut loose as they please, with or without a leader, feel their own music running through them and really enjoy themselves. These swing-men who have come up to the top because of their musicianship are slowly having an influence on the big bands they play with. Some of them have become so popular with the public that they now have their own bands and can do more what they like to do, like Mr. "Red" Norvo, Mr. Benny Goodman, Mr. Tommy Dorsey, Mr. Jimmy Dorsey, Mr. "Red" Nichols, Mr. Earl Hines, Mr. Chick Webb, Mr. "Fats" Waller, Mr. Teddy Hill, and others.

3. Armstrong refers here to the Original Dixieland Jazz Band, the white group that made the first jazz record in 1917. [RW]

19. Looking Back at "The Jazz Age"

ALAIN LOCKE (1886–1954) WAS ONE OF the leaders of that surge of African-American literary and artistic creativity during the last half of the 1920s, the Harlem Renaissance. Holder of a Harvard Ph.D. in philosophy, Locke exemplified the "Talented Tenth," as W. E. B. Du Bois had called them, the black intellectual elite whose existence countered racism by demonstrating the advancement of the race. Renaissance leaders strove to produce and promote "the New Negro," who would be prepared to enter American society at its highest levels, and Locke edited an influential collection of essays, fiction, and poetry under that title in 1925.

Locke's opinions about jazz are complex and, perhaps, conflicted. Most Harlem Renaissance leaders disliked the "lower forms" of black folk and popular music and looked forward to their eventual "elevation" as art music. Yet in these excerpts from a later book, *The Negro and His Music* (1936), Locke tried to defend jazz against charges of immorality by distinguishing between folk and commercial versions. He considered a number of theories about the meaning and popularity of jazz, pointing to differences in its reception by black and white audiences as crucial to understanding the "Jazz Age" of the 1920s. Locke's defense is perhaps best understood up against the early twentieth-century culture of neurasthenia—the "American nervousness" afflicting that privileged elite who felt most civilized and most affected by modernity.[1] Unlike Du Bois, who had tried to enfranchise blacks culturally by claiming that they, too, were sensitive enough to suffer from neurasthenia, Locke preferred (in his words) the primitive to the decadent, the erotic to the neurotic, the pagan to the commercial. For him, jazz was a complex cultural fusion with multiple, context-dependent meanings.

Jazz and Morals

Calling jazz an epidemic brings out another important aspect of the matter: the connection between jazz and that hectic neurotic period of our cultural life, not yet a completely closed chapter—the "jazz age." The Negro, strictly speaking, never had

---

Source: Alain Locke, *The Negro and His Music* (Washington, D.C.: The Associates in Negro Folk Education, 1936), pp. 86–90.

1. See Tom Lutz, *American Nervousness, 1903: An Anecdotal History* (Ithaca: Cornell University Press, 1991), especially pp. 261–75.

a jazz age; he was born that way, as far as the original jazz response went. But as a modern and particularly as an American also, he became subject to the infections, spiritual and moral, of the jazz age. The erotic side of jazz, in terms of which it is often condemned, is admittedly there. But there is a vast difference between its first healthy and earthy expression in the original peasant paganism out of which it arose and its hectic, artificial and sometimes morally vicious counterpart which was the outcome of the vogue of artificial and commercialized jazz entertainment. The one is primitively erotic; the other, decadently neurotic. Gradually the Negro singers and musicians succumbed to the vogue of the artificial and decadent variety of song, music, dance which their folk-stuff started, and spawned a plague, profitable but profligate, that has done more moral harm than artistic good. The early blues-singers, for instance, were far from elegant, but their deadly effective folk speech was clean and racy by contrast with the mawkish sentimentality and concocted lascivity of the contemporary cabaret songs and dances. When they were "blue," they were really "down-hearted"; when they were revengeful and defiant they

"Had the world in a jug
The stopper in my hand
I'm a goin' to hold it, till
You come under my command."

Ironical, or plain sarcastic, they wailed:

"Some o' you men, don't you make me tired,
Yes, some o' you men, yo' jes' make me tired,
You got a mouthful of 'gimme'—and
A handful o' much-obliged."

The only contemporary blues singer who retains much of this earlier effectiveness and folk flavor is Ethel Waters, and she has been forced by managerial control or suggestion too far out of the line of the original tradition. The older generation sang not for the night clubs and "hot spots" of Harlem and its Broadway imitations that have spread all over the world of commercialized entertainment, but to the folky people for whom this racy idiom was more a safety valve of ribald laughter than a neurotic stimulant and breaker of Puritan inhibitions. Thus jazz is an emotional narcotic in one background and a stimulant in another; healthy paganism in one case, morbid eroticism in the other. As the latter, it is an expression of modern hysteria, common to both black and white sophisticates in our hectic, neurotic civilization of today.

So, even those who violently condemn jazz and its influence are partly right. Its cult does have a direct relationship to the freer sexuality of this age. However, instead of blaming it on jazz, the vogue of jazz should be regarded as the symptom of a profound cultural unrest and change, first a reaction from Puritan repressions and then an escape from the tensions and monotonies of a machine-ridden, extroverted form of civilization. In such dilemmas and their crises, Negro emotional elements have been seized upon, and jazz has become one of the main channels of emotional exhaust and compensation. Its devotees, especially at the height of the craze, rationalized this in a complete creed and cult of primitivism. But it was not original and genuine primitivism; only a sophisticated substitute. We must remember that in the cultural history of England and France such "break-down" periods as the Jacobean Restoration and the Bourbon debacle took place without any Negro inoculation. It is, therefore, unsound to speak of the Negro jazz vogue as the cause of modern eroticism, when in fact, it is mainly a symptom, although it must be admitted, sometimes a compounding factor.

Jazz and the Modern Spirit

For better or worse, jazz is, however, the spiritual child of this age. Phases of it will disappear with the particular phase of civilization which gave birth to it; but some permanent contributions to music and art will have been made. More than that, jazz will always be an important factor in interpreting the subtle spirit of our time, more so after it has passed into history. One naturally wonders why it is that jazz has become so characteristic an expression of the modern spirit.

There are many interpretations, each perhaps with its share of the truth. George Antheil, himself an important modernistic composer, stresses jazz as a gift of "primitive joy and vigor." "Negro music," he says, "appeared suddenly (in Europe) after the greatest war of all time . . . it came upon a bankrupt spirituality. To have continued with Slavic mysticism (Russian music was the great vogue when the World War broke out), would in 1918 have induced us all to commit suicide. We needed the roar of the lion to remind us that life had been going on for a long while and would probably go on a while longer. Weak, miserable, and anemic, we needed the stalwart shoulders of a younger race to hold the cart awhile till we had gotten the wheel back on. . . . The Negro taught us to put our noses to the ground, to follow the scent, to come back to the elementary principles of self-preservation."

Then, there is the theory of emotional escape, seemingly contradicting this first theory of emotional rejuvenation. Jazz, according to these theorists, was a marvelous antidote to Twentieth-Century boredom and nervous exhaustion, a subtle combination of narcotic and stimulant; opium for the mind, a tonic for the feelings and instincts echoing the quick nervous tempo and pace of the hectic civilization of ours, which had originally caused that neurasthenia and disillusionment. It would be a curious fact if jazz really was such a cultural anti-toxin, working against the most morbid symptoms of the very disease of which it itself was a by-product. Many competent observers think it is.

In some important way, jazz has become diluted and tinctured with modernism. Otherwise, as purely a Negro dialect of emotion, it could not have become the dominant recreational vogue of our time, even to date, the most prolonged fad on record. More. importantly, jazz, in its more serious form, has also become the characteristic musical speech of the modern age. Beginning as the primitive rhythms of the Congo, taking on the American Negro's emotional revolt against the hardships and shackles of his life, jazz became more than the Negro's desperate antidote and cure for sorrow. It incorporated the typical American restlessness and unconventionality, embodied its revolt against the drabness of commonplace life, put pagan force behind the revolt against Puritan restraint, and finally became the Western World's life-saving flight from boredom and over-sophistication to the refuge of elemental emotion and primitive vigor. This is the credit side of the jazz ledger, against which the debit side we have already mentioned must be balanced, according to one's judgment and temperament and taste. Both detractors and enthusiasts must admit the power and widespread influence of jazz. It is now part Negro, part American, part modern; a whole period of modern civilization may ultimately be best known and understood as "The Jazz Age."

20. Defining "Hot Jazz"

CRITICS ARGUE—THEIR JOB IS TO WRANGLE over what counts as great and what doesn't, what to buy and what to avoid, what sort of story is unfolding or collapsing. One of the earliest writers who might be called a jazz critic was a Belgian lawyer and poet, Robert Goffin (1898–1984). In this article, his task is to differentiate "hot jazz," exemplified for him by Louis Armstrong, from "melodic jazz," typified by Paul Whiteman. It is a consequential endeavor, for if the distinction was of importance to few people at the time, it underpins all subsequent critical debates (over bebop, free, fusion, and most recently the "smooth jazz" of Kenny G and others).

Goffin inevitably invoked the "noble savage" stereotype when he elevated hot jazz by praising its "untrained," "unconscious," but "brilliant" practitioners. Yet he also argued that the most important musical features of jazz derived from African-American cultural experience. And while he hails Armstrong as "the supreme genius of jazz," he credits white hot musicians with correctly perceiving the grandeur of the music, and with helping to promote "mutual esteem" across the color line.

The English translation of this article first appeared in the context of another attempt to promote respect for black culture: *Negro,* an anthology of writings by and about black artists and authors. Its editor, Nancy Cunard (1896–1965), was the granddaughter of Samuel Cunard, the founder of the ship company, and thus a kind of traitor to her class, for the book was conceived as a way of focusing attention on oppression, lynchings, and racism in the United States. It linked the imperialism of the Western powers in Africa to discrimination and cruelty at home, lauding Soviet Russia as more socially just ("Today in Russia alone is the Negro a free man"). Even though Cunard had convinced some prominent friends—including Ezra Pound, Theodore Dreiser, Langston Hughes, and Samuel Beckett—to contribute to the collection, commercial presses wouldn't touch it, and she published it herself.

Not so long ago André Coeuroy wrote: "improvised jazz is the most potent force in music at the present time; long may it remain so."

Source: Robert Goffin, "Hot Jazz," translated by Samuel Beckett, in Nancy Cunard, ed., *Negro: Anthology Made by Nancy Cunard, 1931–1933* (London: Nancy Cunard at Wishart and Co., 1934), pp. 378–79.

What then exactly is this force that has received the sanction of some of our greatest modem musicians and yet is so little known to others?

It is scarcely necessary to repeat that jazz is Afro-American music, developed in the U.S.A. during the war, and attaining its maximum of expression during the period 1920–1930. In my book *On the Frontiers of Jazz* I have dealt at sufficient length with the various musical, technical and sentimental elements of jazz to make any recapitulation of them here unnecessary. They are common knowledge by now.

Let us therefore confine ourselves to hot jazz, otherwise known as improvised jazz, a type of music that was in existence long before it was formally tabulated. The epithet "hot" is applied to any passage "in which the executant or executants abandon the melodic theme and develop an imaginative structure on the basis of that theme and incorporated with it."[1]

To write the history of this "hot" it would be necessary to trace the whole evolution of jazz in general. For we find its formulae, common enough today, present at every stage of the development of syncopated music. It may be said that jazz would have died a natural death long ago but for this "hot" which has always been its unfailing stimulation, its purest mode of utterance, and to all intents and purposes its *raison d'être.*

The Negro slaves, transplanted from their scorching Africa to the marvellous but inhospitable countries of North America, treasured as their last possession that prodigious sense of rhythm which their traditional dances and their tom-toms beating in the equatorial night had made so ineradicably part of them.

Instinctive and unhappy, highly endowed with the most complete, because the most simple, poetical faculties, they soon began to express their emotions in song; labourers in the cotton plantations, dockers slaving in New Orleans, young Negresses herded together in the markets, fugitives hounded down by mastiffs, they all sang their abominable captivity and the brutal domination of their masters.

The African rhythm had not been lost; they clothed it with simple sentiment, moving expressions of love, biblical cries of celestial yearning, pastoral laments; and thus the Negroes came quite naturally to improvise upon a given rhythmic theme with changes of tone, combinations of voices and unexpected counterpoints—an improvisation that was to culminate in the incomparable harmonies that have bewitched the whole of Europe.

Little by little this habit of improvisation was extended to the brasses and it became customary for groups of musicians to meet and improvise on the themes of spirituals or simply on a given rhythm, each performer weaving his own melody.

Through the cake-walk, rag-time and blues Negro music proceeded 'towards that jazz which was soon to assume such important dimensions and absorb the forms which had gone before it.

"At this time jazz still belonged to the black musicians with their ancient traditions of invention and their unique faculty for improvisation and embellishment according to the dictates of their ingenuous hearts. They were the first teachers of the genuine lovers of jazz, while others in whom the commercial instinct was more highly developed ignored this necessary contact and transposed jazz airs in a way quite foreign to the Negro tradition."

This explains the upgrowth of a school of melodic jazz, exploited for a time with great success by Paul Whiteman, Jack Hylton and other famous leaders, who industrialized jazz to such an extent that nothing remained but a weak dilution devoid of all real musical character.

---

1. Goffin is evidently quoting from his own earlier work. [RW]

Melodic jazz has contributed nothing to music and will only be remembered for its unspeakable insipidness; whereas hot jazz is a creative principle which can scarcely fail to affect the music of the future in the most original and unexpected directions.

Hot jazz has already exploded the automatism of musical composition as practised before the war, when the composer wrote a melody, or a score, on the understanding that its realisation should only vary in accordance with the interpretive ability of successive executants, who generally showed but little initiative in their reading of the work and could only express their own personality in their treatment of detail. It is obvious that the music of Beethoven and Debussy is played today exactly as it was when composed, and as it still will be a century hence.

The most extraordinary achievement of hot jazz has been the dissociation of interpretation from the "stenographical" execution of the work, resulting in a finished musical creation which is as much the work of the performer as of the composer. Up to the time of jazz it is safe to say that the performer was no more than the faithful representative of the composer, an actor whose function was to transmit the least phrase and stimulus of his text.[2] But hot jazz has no patience with stimuli by proxy and requires more of its executants, insisting that each should have ample scope for independence and spontaneity of expression. The task of the performer is to realise, in whatever terms he sees fit, the possibilities of syncopation latent in the generally simple theme written by the composer. He is no longer a conscientious actor reciting his part, but one improvising on the idea or impression of the moment in the Italian *Commedia dell' Arte* tradition.

The admirable achievement of the first orchestras was an unconscious one, ignored at the time and not fully appreciated till twenty years later. We must turn back to these primitive orchestras and listen humbly to the musical inventions of these untrained Negroes before we can realise the brilliant audacity of these musicians who devoted themselves with enthusiasm and in the face of the most fatuous opposition to this new field, later to become the monopoly of the intelligent and cultivated section of the new generation. From this moment every black orchestra played "hot," with occasional discordant abuse of wawas, washboards, and drums, which soon calmed down.[3]

At that time only very few whites were able to appreciate the sublime grandeur of this music of the heart. We must not forget the first white orchestras to play "hot" in an America rotten with colour prejudice; they laid the foundations of a solidarity and a mutual esteem whose benefits came too late for the majority of those most apt to enjoy them. The Cotton Pickers, New Orleans Rhythm Kings, California Ramblers and Original Dixieland will all have an honoured place in the eventual Pantheon of syncopated music.

Already a definite tradition is taking form in the domain of hot jazz and a codification is being gradually developed; such discerning critics as Panassié, Prunières,

---

2. Actually, it's not at all safe to say that. The primacy of the permanent musical work or text and the devaluation of improvisation are nineteenth-century developments. Bach was best known as an improviser, Mozart added his own cadenzas and embellishments to the pieces he composed, etc. This passage reflects a widespread historical amnesia that accepts the practices of early-twentieth-century "classical music" as eternal norms or ideals. [RW]

3. A reference to the wah-wah or plunger mute, used on brass instruments and associated in particular with Duke Ellington's "jungle music." [RW]

Coeuroy, and Sordet concern themselves with the manifestations of hot jazz and keep its development under the strictest observation and control.[4] We are now so familiar with hot jazz, thanks to the countless records made of different orchestras, that we can distinguish the unmistakable note of its lyricism even in the most florid of its vulgarisations.

The talent and genius of certain composers and performers have received their proper recognition. A number of jazz orchestras have conquered the unanimous approval of the public. Finally certain individuals have enriched jazz with contributions of so personal a nature as cannot fail to delight all those who take an interest in the subject, and it is to them that we owe all that is best in modern jazz.

There are many orchestras in both Europe and America whose musical perfection has elicited the admiration of such competent judges as Ravel, Darius Milhaud, and Stravinsky, and in these orchestras some exponents of "hot" whose style, to my mind, has had an enormous influence on the development of jazz in general. Special reference must be made to Louis Armstrong, whom I consider as the supreme genius of jazz. This extraordinary man has not only revolutionised the treatment of brass instruments but also modified almost every branch of musical technique as practised today. Nor should we forget that colossus of jazz, the late Bix Beiderbecke, the pianist Earl Hines, and the tenor saxophonist Coleman Hawkins. There are hundreds of others hardly less important than these four and no less deserving of honour for not being mentioned by name.

Before I conclude this essay I would like to draw attention to the analogy between the acceptance of "hot" and the favour enjoyed throughout Europe by the *Surréaliste* movement.[5] Is it not remarkable that new modes both of sentiment and its exteriorisation should have been discovered independently? What Breton and Aragon did for poetry in 1920, Chirico and Ernst for painting, had been instinctively accomplished as early as 1910 by humble Negro musicians, unaided by the control of that critical intelligence that was to prove such an asset to the later initiators.

Finally, it may be mentioned that hot jazz is regarded today by all the intelligent and cultivated youth of Europe as its staple musical nourishment. As Dominique Sordet says, many young men have derived an almost religious enthusiasm from the contact of this superabundant source of lyricism. For them hot jazz is almost the only form of music that has any meaning for their disrupted generation, and it is my fervent hope that America will not disregard this extraordinary element in its sentimental life and one which is surely of more importance than sky-scrapers and Fordism.

4. The notion that a handful of French critics could control the development of jazz now seems a bit self-indulgent. [RW]

5. A number of writers proposed this analogy between jazz and surrealism, a movement in French art and literature that flourished between the world wars. Because surrealism emphasized dreams and the unconscious as sources of artistic inspiration and insight, the parallel minimized the conscious, learned, and collective aspects of jazz. See, for example, Horace M. Kallen, "Swing as Surrealist Music," *Art and Freedom* 2 (1942), pp. 831–34. [RW]

21. An Experience in Jazz History

CALLED BY LEONARD FEATHER "THE MOST important of all jazz writers," John Hammond (1910–1987) was also the extraordinary record producer who discovered Count Basie, Billie Holiday, George Benson, Aretha Franklin, Bob Dylan, and Bruce Springsteen. Hammond's 1977 autobiography explains why a well-off young man dropped out of Yale to join the jazz world, where he promoted, produced, wrote, worked against racism, and became arguably the most influential nonmusician in jazz history.[1] This address, given by Hammond at a conference at Indiana University in 1969, covers some of the same ground more concisely, giving an insider's view of the record industry in the 1920s and '30s, as recording amplified the impact of jazz worldwide.

I first became interested in jazz in the early 20's. I was born in 1910, so I'd say maybe the first jazz musicians I heard live were from around 1922 and 1923. Ironically, I didn't hear those musicians in New York, because there was no jazz that an eleven- or twelve-year-old kid could hear there. I was on a trip to London in 1923 with my family and there were two things which happened in a place called Lyon's Corner House. They had an American orchestra, and within this was a band called The Georgians which may have been the most outstanding small White jazz band that had been assembled up to that time. Jimmy Dorsey was in it, for example. Every afternoon at five you would have your ice cream sodas or tea, or whatever they served, and listen to a forty-five minute concert of improvised jazz. That was the first time I heard jazz, and it changed my life.

When I first became interested in jazz, there was no such thing as integration. There were very few places where the White public went, where Negro musicians could be heard. We had a completely segregated society in those days, just as segregated in New York as it was in the South. Once in a while those bars were broken. There was a hall in New York called the Roseland Ballroom which would bring in bands like McKinney's Cotton Pickers for the White dancing public, but it was strictly a White public. Negroes were barred as customers. Even the very posh Harlem night clubs and those in Chicago discouraged Negro patronage, even in the heart of the

---

Source: John Hammond, "An Experience in Jazz History," in Dominique-René de Lerma, ed., *Black Music in Our Culture: Curricular Ideas on the Subjects, Materials, and Problems* (Kent State University Press, 1970), pp. 42–53. Reprinted by permission of Dominique-Rene de Lerma.

1. John Hammond with Irving Townsend. *John Hammond On Record* (New York: Ridge Press, 1977).

ghetto. The Cotton Club in New York, where Duke Ellington, Cab Calloway, Jimmie Lunceford and the Blue Rhythm Band made their fame, had an exclusively White audience, although everyone else but the owners was Black. It was very rough for a Negro musician to make even a quarterway decent living in those days.

At an earlier session I brought up the fact that before 1920 the Negro musician was actually better off than after 1920 because the Negro musicians in New York had their own club, the Clef Club, in which James P. Johnson, Clarence Williams and other old timers were the guiding forces. These musicians had a lot of work, although they may have worked for very little, but I know that all the society parties given around World War I in New York were played by what even the square society folks thought were the best musicians, and those best musicians were always Black. When the American Federation of Musicians formed Local 802, the situation changed. I don't know if it was conscious or not, but the White musicians got a lot of the jobs the Blacks held before, and it was very hard for the Black musicians to get back into that market.

The record business really served as one of the principal places of employment for Negro jazz musicians. They didn't accompany the White artists, the Eddie Cantors, the Ted Lewises. They played for innumerable Black singers and comedians. Literally hundreds of Black bands were recorded by the various record companies up until about 1928, when the record business started a very sharp decline. Other places where Black musicians were able to play were in the tent shows and carnivals that toured the South, the Northeast, and the Midwest. There was a Negro theater circuit called the Theater Owners Booking Association which was known in around 48 theaters throughout the country where Negro shows were able to get practically a year's work. The economic and physical conditions in these theaters were pretty frightful. Among Negro performers the TOBA was known as Tough On Black Asses, but this was a very large field where the Black musicians could work.

The big band era didn't actually start until the 30's. There were big bands on records, but they were pretty commercial on the whole. There's an exception to all this in Duke Ellington. He made his first records on an Indiana label in 1926.[2] Those records, Gennett, can no longer be found anywhere. Very soon after that, he recorded for practically every label there was, well over a hundred. Duke is one of the people who really lasted in this business, and there aren't many of them. He was able to get into records because he was the property of a publisher, Irving and Jack Mills. Mills very often paid for these recording sessions because he published all of the tunes, so Duke could write his own ticket with a publisher who was also his manager. He started on records with an eight-piece band called The Washingtonians, a terribly important group in the history of jazz. Around 1928 or '29, it became a twelve-piece band (four rhythms, four reeds, and five brasses). It never swung like Fletcher Henderson's, but Ellington was a genius as a composer, and early things like "Mood Indigo," "Black and Tan Fantasy," "East St. Louis Toodle-oo" are still some of the great works to be found in jazz. If you don't believe they have lasted, go to any of the dives in London or Paris or New York, and you'll find strippers still dancing to a lot of Duke's early music.

The record business was a very important factor in preserving jazz, but in 1928 radio came in and this was the beginning of the end, it looked, for the record business—first the radio, then the 1929 financial collapse. Of about 70 or 80 active labels around 1923 and 1925, by 1931 there were exactly four left. Since jazz was

---

2. Ellington had begun recording in 1924. [RW]

extremely marginal as far as profitability was concerned even in those days, the first kind of records they stopped making was jazz. It might have been a permanent casualty if it hadn't been for the acceptance of jazz in England. It's quite amazing how much England fashions American tastes in music. In 1931, when no jazz was being recorded in this country, the three biggest labels in England all had very active jazz series of the great American jazz artists, both Black and White. They were just screaming for more products, and nobody would give it to them. This is more or less how I came into the record business.

I have a sister now married to Benny Goodman, but in those days she was the wife of a Tory member of the British Parliament. I used to go to England every year or two, and I became very friendly with people in the record business. In 1931, I became the American correspondent for the biggest record magazine in England, *The Gramophone.* I got to know a lot of the English musicians who were fascinated with American jazz. It was obvious to the British, listening to the records that were being put out, that the greatest musicians in the jazz world were the Black-American musicians, yet they couldn't read about what these musicians were doing because none of the U.S. publications—including the Negro press—bothered to write about this. The American trade papers for music rarely even mentioned the Black musicians. They asked me if I would write a regular column for them just detailing what was happening in the Black communities around the country. Since I had sort of an independent income, I decided I would. I used to spend a lot of time in Harlem, in Chicago, and in the deep South. I started writing a column first for *The Gramophone,* and then for *The Melody Maker.* Suddenly, when I went back to England in 1933, the English Columbia Record Company asked me if I would become their American recording director and record jazz for them which would be issued in the U.S. by the American Columbia Company, then in bankruptcy. The year before, I had done a record session for American Columbia of Fletcher Henderson's band. It was my first commercial record session, and I had done some things privately financed in 1931. The band arrived an hour and a half late, being on what we called CPT (Colored People's Time), and we only had 45 minutes to finish the session, but in that 45 minutes we made two marvelous selections: "Honeysuckle Rose," "King Porter Stomp," and a thing I'm sorry to say I let get through called "Underneath the Harlem Moon." W. C. Handy's daughter was singing on it, and she insisted on using the exact words in the lyrics, which included "that's how darkies were born." I had a fit, but Miss Handy said it had to be included.

In Europe, unlike America, the intellectuals in music appreciated the unique role of jazz. One of the most famous music critics of the day, who was also a composer, Constant Lambert, was most enthusiastic. Another supporter was the composer and jazz bass player, Patrick (or "Spike") Hughes. They sort of discovered Armstrong, Ellington, Fats Waller, and all the other people in America who were thought of as entertainers and clowns, and not recognized for the fantastic talent they had. European musicians who came over here were tremendously impressed with the originality and vitality of the Negro jazz musicians. Maurice Ravel would spend hours at the Grand Terrace in Chicago listening to Earl Hines. Walter Gieseking, a really splendid "classical" pianist, was so moved by Negro jazz that he actually wrote a jazz suite which, alas, he never recorded but which I heard him play, and his debt to Earl Hines was just unbelievable.

We had extraordinary Negro jazz musicians in those days. In 1932, I went to Fats Waller's 28th birthday party; Fats would be only 65 if he were alive today. Unfortunately, he died in 1943. At this party, after he had about a fifth of gin, he sat down at the piano and played the entire score of *Petrushka*! Then Reginald Forsythe, a Black English musician, joined him in a four-hand performance of the Delius opera *A Village*

Romeo and Juliet. Fats, who had to be a clown in order to make a living in this country, could actually have been an extraordinary, all-around musician. The American public wasn't ready for that, and certainly the managers who knew how to make a buck out of Fats wanted to have him retain the entertainer image. There were any number of Black musicians frustrated like that.

James P. Johnson was another musician who had a good knowledge of form and arranging. He wrote an opera in 1939 with Langston Hughes, *The Organizer,* which was put on by a reasonably left-wing group in New York, because they were the only people who appreciated the artistry of these two great men. It was a marvelous work, just short of an hour in duration. I don't believe it ever had another performance since 1939, but any educator interested in the contribution of the American Negro to jazz should certainly get hold of the score. I recorded the only tune from that show which was ever recorded, "Hungry Blues." It is in the James P. Johnson album that is now out. This says an awful lot of things about society that just weren't allowed to be said by the White folks and the reactionaries that supervised the record business in those days.

A big year in my life was 1933. I started recording for the British market, hundreds of recordings which were later all released in this country. Early that year I had been in a little place in Harlem called Monette's Place. Monette Moore was a pretty good blues singer of the 20's at a place called the Morocco Club. Some mobster in Harlem decided that he'd back her in her own speakeasy. She asked me to come to opening night, so I went and drank my usual lemonade. She was very busy greeting all the celebrities who were there: Clifton Webb, Carl Van Vechten, and all the Whites who used to spend time in Harlem. But there was a girl singing, just about 17. And her name was Billie Holiday. I was about the first White guy who heard her sing. She had just gotten out of jail. I listened to her, and I couldn't believe what I heard. This was a vocalist who was a horn player, who was everything—I mean she had a complete style of her own. I'd never heard anything like it! I started to talk to Billie and the wonderful pianist with her, a girl called Dot Hill. Billie said, "Maybe, you know my old man, Clarence Holiday." Clarence was the guitar player with Fletcher Henderson's band. I couldn't believe that Clarence would have a talented daughter like this (because I knew immediately she was a star) and wouldn't brag about it! This will give you a small idea of Billie's social background. (Incidentally, we're going to do a movie on her, so I've been digging a lot into her background in Baltimore, before she came to New York.) Anyway, the next day I went to the Congress Ballroom where Fletcher was playing and told Clarence, "I heard your daughter Billie last night. She's the greatest thing I've ever heard!" He frowned at me, so I waited until intermission. Then he told me, "John, for God's sake don't talk about Billie in front of the guys! They'll think I'm old!" He explained to me that he was 14 when she was born, and Billie's mother (whom he married three years later) was 13. Billie was a girl completely outside of the social fabric, and a lot of her desperation and anger and deep feeling came through in her music. I wasn't able to get her recorded immediately because nobody was recording, but I was able to get Benny Goodman to use her on one of his first record sessions in 1933. These were the first records she ever made: "Riffin' the Scotch," and "Your Mother's Son-In-Law." It was a year and a half before I could persuade anybody to get her back into a studio again, but we made up for that with a vengeance in 1935.

While working for the British, I was able to get Benny Goodman's first recording band together. I'll never forget that session because I was trying to get Benny to use Coleman Hawkins and other great jazz musicians who were around. But Benny was worried. "John, you know I worship these guys, but if I play with Negro musicians I'll never get another job on the radio." It was that rough. I believed him, but I didn't stop trying. So the first session we made was with all White folks. We did have some good ones, like Jack Teagarden, Joe Sullivan and Gene Krupa. By the time of the second sessions, Benny decided to take a chance and he added Negro musicians. This was at a time when Black and White musicians could not play together in public. By 1935, he had been recording for two years, originally for the British, and then for Irving Mills. Benny got a band together, first at the Billy Rose Music Hall in New York (all White), and then for the National Biscuit Company (also White). In 1933, I had listened to a radio program and heard a Chicago pianist named Teddy Wilson. I was so excited about Teddy that I sent Benny Carter to bring him to New York, and I got Benny and Teddy Wilson together in the record studio in 1934 for Columbia Records' "Moonglow." Teddy was the first pianist Benny ever heard who could keep up with him technically. He thought it would be wonderful to play with him, and we got a trio together with Gene Krupa which would pave the way through records for these three to play together live. Benny was under contract to Victor, and I got Teddy to sign with Brunswick, and through these arrangements I managed to get Billie Holiday on records again. In June of 1935, I got Billie and Teddy in a band with Cozy Cole (drums), John Kirby (bass), John Trueheart (Chick Webb's guitarist), Roy Eldridge (trumpet), Ben Webster (tenor sax) and Benny Goodman. We made four sides. There have been five or six real highlights for me in the record studio, and this certainly was one. Goodman was in the session because the only way Brunswick would let Teddy record with Benny for Victor was if he would return the favor for Brunswick, which he was doing.

This was the beginning of integration on records. Before this, there were maybe only five or six times the Blacks and Whites had played together on recordings. Fats Waller had played with Ted Lewis in 1931, four of the best sides that miserable band ever made. Eddie Condon, from Chicago, insisted on using Negro musicians. Louis Armstrong once had Joe Sullivan, a White guy, on piano. Milton Mezzrow used to play with Black bands on occasion, but not very well. And Bubber Miley, Duke's great growl trumpet player, used to play with Leo Reisman, a society band leader for Victor, for special effects. All of this was done very secretly because the public wasn't ready to see Black and White together. But then in 1935 the Goodman Trio records came out. If anything, they were more successful than the Goodman band records, although the band records paved the way for the big band era, and Goodman changed American tastes, certainly the relationships between publishers and band leaders, because Benny had Fletcher Henderson do his arrangements. This was part of the deal for the National Biscuit Company radio show. Benny had a budget for eight arrangements a week, and this was how he built his library. Fletcher knew just about how much they could get away with. Benny used a lot of solos, playing only the first chorus pretty straight. The records sold, and Benny could call the tune. After 1936 the publishers could no longer say how to play, and this changed quite a lot of things.

The first time the trio was allowed to appear live was at a concert of the Chicago Hot Jazz Society in 1936, at the Congress Hotel. Everybody was scared. The owner, a nice guy, said, "Gee, I don't know if the public will take it." Of course it was the biggest hit of the concert. Benny was managed by MCA and they felt it would be rough. "We'll never be able to book a band with a Negro performer, you know." But Benny insisted, and they tried it. Out of this came the quartet, and from that the sextet—guys like Tommy Dorsey, Charlie Barnet—and a lot of other big bands soon had one or two Negroes in the band. I think Benny had as many as six. It was a breakthrough, but only a start. The record companies have done more I think than any other part of the amusement business to break down prejudice, but there's a whole lot more to do.

22. On the Road with Count Basie

"I CAN'T STAND TO SING THE SAME SONG the same way two nights in succession, let alone two years or ten years. If you can, then it ain't music, it's close-order drill or exercise or yodeling or something, not music."[1] In an era when many singers emphasized smoothness and consistency, this commitment to improvisation and invention helped make Billie Holiday (1915–1959) perhaps the most acclaimed singer in jazz history. Holiday's musical career began in the early 1930s; she was discovered by John Hammond in 1933, which led to recording sessions with Benny Goodman and touring with the Count Basie band in 1937. In 1938 she became one of the first black singers to join a white band, that of Artie Shaw, and during the 1940s she became a popular star.

In this excerpt from her autobiography, *Lady Sings the Blues* (1956), Holiday describes the Basie tour. She praises the band's musical interaction and creativity—qualities that can be lost when groups rely on written arrangements (as Basie later did). Her account also reveals the hard work and rough reality behind the glamorous image seen by her audiences. Many of the stars of this band became jazz legends, especially tenor saxophonist Lester Young, drummer Jo Jones, and trumpeter Harry "Sweets" Edison. But they developed their music amid the rigors of endless travel to dance halls and hotels across much of the country. Now we know they were making history; at the time, they were mostly trying to make a living.

I joined Count Basie's band to make a little money and see the world. For almost two years I didn't see anything but the inside of a Blue Goose bus, and I never got to send home a quarter.

I had started at the Log Cabin for eighteen dollars a week. By the time I opened at Clark Monroe's Uptown House I was getting thirty-five dollars—when I got it. Half the time Clark would say he was short and come up with fifteen or twenty dollars. When I asked for the rest of my money he would start telling me how much I'd get from this one and that one in tips.

One night a man had given me fifty dollars in the joint for nothing at all, and Clark would remind me of that every time I asked for the rest he owed me. I had

---

Source: Billie Holiday with William F. Dufty, *Lady Sings the Blues* (New York: Doubleday, 1956), pp. 66–74. ©CMG Worldwide. Reprinted with a discography, (New York: Penguin, 1984); this excerpt is from pages 56–62 of that edition.

1. Billie Holiday with William Dufty, *Lady Sings the Blues* (New York: Doubleday, 1956), p. 48.

spent some of my good loot trying to make the joint go. After my record with Teddy Wilson started moving I had a big cardboard sign painted with my picture on it for Clark to put out front, to help bring people in. It began to be a drag—I was getting disgusted.

After I'd closed at the Apollo I was booked into a French joint in Montreal. This was my first date outside New York and I enjoyed it. I tasted champagne there for the first time—hated it and still do. But I like the people. I met a wonderful Canadian boy up there; he always used to tell me scotch would hurt my voice and try to get me on champagne. But I used to drink champagne with him at a table and then sneak into the kitchen for some scotch. He was a fine fellow, but his family caught on to what was going on and they broke it up but quick.

Anyway, John Hammond had brought the Basie band out of Kansas City and was backing their first tour. When they opened in Pittsburgh, in the biggest hotel in town, they died like a dog—flopped. Hammond decided what they needed was a girl vocalist, so he put up some more financing, along with Willard Alexander of MCA, and asked me to join the band—at fourteen dollars a day.

I wasn't even getting my thirty-five dollars a week at the Uptown House, and I guess from one trip to Montreal I thought traveling would be one big romance like that, so fourteen dollars a day sounded real great.

Nobody bothered to tell me that I'd have to travel five hundred to six hundred miles on a hot or cold raggedy-ass Blue Goose bus; that it would cost me two or three bucks a night for a room; that by the time I was through having my hair fixed and gowns pressed—to say nothing of paying for pretty clothes to wear—I'd end up with about a dollar and a half a day. Out of that I had to eat and drink and send home some loot to Mom.

Whenever I had a couple of bucks it was always so little I was ashamed to send it home, so I would give it to Lester Young to invest. I hoped he could shoot enough dice to parley it into a bill big enough I didn't have to feel ashamed to send home.

The first time out we had been riding for three months, and neither Lester nor I had a dime. Both of us were actually hungry. Jimmy Rushing, the blues-singing "Mr. Five by Five," was always the only one who had any loot. We went to him once and asked him real nice for a buck to buy a couple of hamburgers. He wouldn't give us nothing but a lecture on how he saved his money and how we petered ours away.

When we were on the bus coming back to New York from West Virginia, I couldn't stand the thought of coming home to Mom broke. I had four bucks when that crap game started on the bus floor.

"You're not shooting these four," I told Lester. "I'm shooting these myself."

I got on my knees, and the first time up it was a seven. Everybody hollered at me that the bus had swerved and made me shoot it over.

Up came eleven. I picked up the four bucks right there and won the next four pots before someone said something about comfort.

I thought they said, "What do you come for?" I said, "I come for any damn thing you come for." I didn't know the lingo, but I knew Lester did. So I told him I'd do the shooting and he could be the lookout man.

I was on my knees in the bottom of that bus from West Virginia to New York, a few hundred miles and about twelve hours. When we pulled up in front of the Woodside Hotel everybody was broke and crying. I was filthy dirty and had holes in the knees of my stockings, but I had sixteen hundred bucks and some change.

I gave some of the cats in the band enough loot to eat with and some car fare. But not Rushing. I didn't give him back a dime. I took what was left and split on uptown to Mom's. When I walked in she looked at me and like to died, I was so dirty and beat up. I just waited for her to say something, and she did.

"I'll bet you ain't got a dime, either," Mom said.

I took that money, over a thousand dollars, and threw it on the floor. She salted a lot of it away and later it became the nest egg she used to start her own little restaurant, "Mom Holiday's," something she always wanted.

Basie did a wonderful job with the band, but he just wasn't his own boss. He was just out of Kansas City. A big booking agency was backing him and trying to sell the band. We'd play a whole string of riffraff joints, rough Negro dance halls in the South where people were sneaking in corn whisky from across the tracks, and then boom in the middle of this grind we would be booked into some white hotel.

We didn't have the right uniforms, clothes, equipment—the cats in the band didn't even have the right horns they needed—we'd all be beat from traveling thousands of miles with no sleep, no rehearsal, and no preparation—and yet we'd be expected to be real great.

After each crisis on the road we'd end up back in New York. Then there'd be a big strategy meeting, figuring what was wrong with straightening things out.

I was accused of romancing everyone in the band and this was leading to dissension. This was a damn lie and I said so. I wasn't doing anything with anybody in the band except one cat—and not very often with him at that.

The truth was, I was scared of the cats in the band because they were messing with too many chicks on the road.

Living on the road with a band, nobody had time to sleep alone, let alone with somebody. At night, as Lester used to say, we'd pull into a town, pay two to four bucks for a room, shave and take a long look at the bed, go play the gig, come back and look at the bed again, and then get on the bus. We got so fed up with it one time, Lester and me, we threatened to resign and ended up getting a raise. I got raised to fifteen a day and Lester got boosted to eighteen-fifty. I thought this was just too marvelous for words.

For my money Lester was the world's greatest. I loved his music, and some of my favorite recordings are the ones with Lester's pretty solos.

I remember how the late Herschel Evans used to hate me. Whenever Basie had an arranger work out something for me, I'd tell him that I wanted Lester to solo behind me. That always made Herschel salty. It wasn't that I didn't love his playing. It was just that I liked Lester's more.

Lester sings with his horn; you listen to him and can almost hear the words. People think he's too cocky and secure, but you can hurt his feelings in two seconds. I know, because I found out once that I had. We've been hungry together, and I'll always love him and his horn.

I often think about how we used to record in those days. We'd get off a bus after a five-hundred-mile trip, go into the studio with no music, nothing to eat but coffee and sandwiches. Me and Lester would drink what we called top and bottom, half gin and half port wine.

I'd say, "What'll we do, two-bar or four-bar intro?"

Somebody'd say make it four and a chorus—one, one and a half.

Then I'd say, "You play behind me the first eight, Lester," and then Harry Edison would come in or Buck Clayton and take the next eight bars. "Jo, you just brush and don't hit the cymbals too much."

Now with all their damn preparation, complicated arrangements, you've got to kiss everybody's behind to get ten minutes to do eight sides in.[2] When I did "Night and Day" I had never seen that song before in my life. I don't read music, either. I just

2. Here, a "side" means a song. Each 78-rpm record held two songs, and recording sessions (record dates) were scheduled to make a certain number of disks. [RW]

walked in, Teddy Wilson played it for me, and I did it. With artists like Lester, Don Byas, Benny Carter, and Coleman Hawkins, something was always happening. No amount of preparation today is any match for them.

In the old days, if we were one side short on a date, someone would say, "Try the blues in A flat," and tell me, "Go as far as you can go, honey." I'd stand up there and make up my words as I went along. Nowadays you have all this talk and bull and nothing's happening. On a recent date I tried to do it like the old days. I'd never seen the band or the arrangements, and I didn't know the songs they had picked for me, and they wanted me to do eight sides in three hours. We were doing all standards, but nobody could read the stuff; the drummer did nothing but sit there grinning; the music had wrong chords; everybody was squawking. We pushed out about nine sides like they wanted. But not a damn one of them was any good.

You can say what you want about the South, and I've said plenty. But when I've forgotten all the crummy things that happened down there in my days on the road, I'll still remember Fox Theatre in Detroit, Michigan. What Radio City is to New York, the Fox was to Detroit then. A booking there was a big deal. My salary went up automatically to three hundred dollars a week for the run of the show. Everybody was happy.

The show opened and closed with a line of chorus girls doing their barelegged kicks like the Rockettes. In the middle the girls did a big pretty number, with lots of parading around, fancy costumes, lights, and what not.

But Detroit was between race riots then, and after three performances the first day, the theatre management went crazy. They claimed they had so many complaints about all those Negro men up there on the stage with those bare-legged white girls, all hell cut loose backstage.

The next thing we knew, they revamped the whole show. They cut out the girls' middle number. And when the chorus line opened the show, they'd fitted them out with special black masks and mammy dresses. They did both their numbers in blackface and those damn mammy getups.

When he saw what was happening, Basie flipped. But there was nothing he could do. We had signed the contracts to appear, and we had no control over what the panicky theater managers did.

But that wasn't the worst of it. Next they told Basie I was too yellow to sing with all the black men in his band. Somebody might think I was white if the light didn't hit me just right. So they got special dark grease paint and told me to put it on.

It was my turn to flip. I said I wouldn't do it. But they had our name on the contracts, and if I refused it might have played hell with bookings, not just for me, but for the future of all the cats in the band. So I had to be darkened down so the show could go on in dynamic-assed Detroit. It's like they say, there's no damn business like show business. You had to smile to keep from throwing up.

But after a few months with more of the same I quit. Mother almost blew her top. She thought this was the biggest opportunity of my life and I was throwing it over. After a few weeks I began to think she was right. It turned out to be almost six months before I did anything musical after I quit. I didn't even sing. I just ate my damn heart out.

There were a lot of great things about the Basie band, and the experts are just beginning to pick it to pieces after almost twenty years to find out what made it so great. But with the distance of years, you forget all the things that your nose used to be rubbed in, and can add up the score. I still say the greatest thing about the Basie band of those days was that they never used a piece of music, still all sixteen of them could end up sounding like a great big wonderful one sound.

Most of my experience with bands before that had been in hanging out with Benny Goodman. I used to listen to him rehearse with high-paid radio studio bands and his own groups. He always had big arrangements. He would spend a fortune on arrangements for a little dog-assed vocalist.

But with Basie, we had something no expensive arrangements could touch. The cats would come in, somebody would hum a tune. Then someone else would play it over on the piano once or twice. Then Daddy Basie would two-finger it a little. And then things would start to happen.

Half the cats couldn't have read music if they'd had it. They didn't want to be bothered anyway. Maybe sometimes one cat would bring in a written arrangement and the others would run over it. But by the time Jack Wadlin, Skeet Henderson, Buck Clayton, Freddie Green, and Basie were through running over it, taking off, changing it, the arrangement wouldn't be recognizable anyway.

I know that's the way we worked out "Love of My Life" and "Them There Eyes" for me. Everything that happened, happened by ear. For the two years I was with the band we had a book of a hundred songs, and every one of us carried every last damn note of them in our heads.

23. Jazz at Carnegie Hall

THE "FROM SPIRITUALS TO SWING" CONCERT of December 23, 1938, was a landmark in American music history. African-American music had been presented in prestigious Carnegie Hall before—most notably James Reese Europe's Clef Club concerts of 1912–14, a tribute to W. C. Handy in 1928, and Benny Goodman's integrated swing concert earlier in 1938. But "From Spirituals to Swing" was a bold bid to gain recognition and respect for a wide range of music that had largely been dismissed as crude, commercial, or both. The concert was organized by John Hammond, who, as an outspoken advocate of racial equality throughout his career, sought to bring black musicians to the attention of the "sophisticated audience" of Carnegie Hall.[1] The success of the concert led him to produce another the following year, as well as a third in 1967; a recording of the 1938 concert was issued by Columbia.

Funding for the concert came from Eric Bernay, publisher of the Marxist weekly *New Masses*, the leading radical literary journal of the 1930s. Though Hammond claimed to be slightly uneasy about this sponsorship, the alliance made sense: *New Masses* attempted to synthesize artistic and political rebelliousness, and its progressive constituency backed the drive to break down color barriers during that period. Moreover, a year earlier the magazine had published Hammond's exposé of shady business practices and poor working conditions in the record industry.

In their program notes, James Dugan and John Hammond worked to distinguish African-American musical traditions from the huge commercial phenomenon of Swing ("the jitterbug millions"), dominated at this time by white bands. They urged a certain amount of relativism, arguing that different kinds of music use different means of expression. Yet they stressed the idea that jazz and blues share qualities with classical music, hoping to win the audience's respect for these genres. At least some listeners did not get the message: modernist composer Elliott Carter found the concert "fascinating" but came away believing that swing "was really invented by whites" and that jazz in the concert hall "will never interest audiences until a serious composer with artistic perspective" takes over.[2] A list of the performers follows this excerpt from the program notes.

The Music Nobody Knows

The music that will be presented in *New Masses'* "From Spirituals to Swing" program is rarely heard. To be sure, it is not rare, for America is rich with it, but serious audiences have neglected it, and it has had to find its followers among uncritical groups. American Negro music has thrived in an atmosphere of detraction, oppression, distortion, and unreflective enthusiasm. During the nineteenth century it reached the white public in the thoroughly distorted form of the cakewalk, the coon song, and in its most ludicrous caricature, by white men with their faces painted, in minstrel shows.

In this twentieth century it has developed its most stirring forms—blues, boogie woogie piano, and swing—and the misconceptions promptly took new shapes to accommodate the change. George Gershwin, among other white composers, made a sincere attempt to distill from its folk qualities a concert type of music that would be acceptable to prosaic audiences. It is doubtful, however, if this approach did anything more than suppress the genuine thing. White entrepreneurs, recognizing the obvious vitality of Negro rhythm, encouraged certain Negro orchestras to go beyond good jazz into clowning and pyrotechnic displays of virtuosity. But a happy parallel development appeared in the early twenties when groups of white musicians in Chicago and New Orleans began to express their own untutored musical ideas in the Negro spirit. The best of these musicians such as Bix Beiderbecke, cornet genius from Davenport, Iowa; Frank Teschemacher, an inspired and poetic clarinetist of Chicago; Bud Freeman, virtuoso of the tenor saxophone; Jack Teagarden, trombone player and superb blues singer; Eddie Condon, banjo player; and Joe Sullivan and Jess Stacy, two inventive pianists, made their own important contributions to the racially mixed stream of contemporary hot jazz.

In the jazz idiom the Negro people have produced some of the most amazing musicians the world has ever known. We can mention only a few of these artists who have

---

Source: Reprinted in *The Black Perspective in Music* 2:2 (Fall 1974), pp. 191–96.

1. On the "sophisticated audience" and other details, see John Hammond with Irving Townsend, *John Hammond On Record* (New York: Penguin Books, 1981), pp. 199–200. See also Hammond's "An Experience in Jazz History," in this volume.

2. Elliott Carter, "Forecast and Review," *Modern Music* 16:1 (November-December, 1938), pp. 99–100.

made this American music the cultural property of the world: Louis Armstrong, Joe Smith, and Jabbo Smith, who are superlative on the trumpet, natural instrument of jazz; Earl Hines, "Fats" Waller, and Pine Top Smith, pianists; Sidney Bechet and Jimmy Noone, clarinetists; Coleman Hawkins and Leon "Chu" Berry, tenor saxophones; Jimmy Harrison, trombone; John Kirby and Walter Page, bass; and Zutty Singleton, drums. Among the singers Bessie Smith is incomparable and Louis Armstrong has created a unique vocal style which has had many imitators. Duke Ellington, Fletcher Henderson, and Count Basie are the band leaders distinguished for their handling of ensembles.

The music of these hot musicians and their talented colleagues must first be considered as *music;* it is not, as ignorant people contend, a sort of anarchy in music. Good jazz has outlived its highbrow detractors of the twenties and will continue to refute their petty charges. Look to it for the same qualities you expect in the classics: expert instrumentation, a musical structure (even in *ad lib* jazz), and a quality that we must call sincerity. The best hot musicians are men of profound feeling, even if this feeling is inarticulate. It has its special qualities and formal divergencies within this definition. Its melodic instruments are played with a hot intonation, unlike the tone color of usual musicianship; and its rhythmic aspect is of prime importance, characterized by insistent percussion effects, both in slow and fast tempo. It has its own specific style as musical expression.

In this hot jazz style the music is uniquely American, the most important cultural exhibit we have given the world. Playing the biggest role in originating and nurturing it is the American Negro, the oppressed American whose musical qualities have long been recognized in Europe and neglected at home.

It expresses America so clearly that its readiest recognition here has come from the masses, particularly youth. While the intelligentsia has been busy trying to water our scrawny cultural tree with European art and literary movements, this thing has come to maturity unnoticed. One cannot hear Bix Beiderbecke from the tall corn of Iowa without feeling that this is singularly ours and it is about time we wake up to the fact. In a tongue-tied nation, just growing into long pants and consuming its last frontier, art had to be a ready business, too, without highfalutin' airs. And it is an art that no one has had to graft onto the tree; nobody would be more incredulous upon hearing that this is art than the throngs of jitterbugs and the hot musicians themselves. Perhaps this is the spirit of the early Renaissance art movement in Italy, of the stone carvers on Romanesque cathedrals, because it is a thing taken for granted and warmly participated in by the people.

But the jitterbug millions, lurching along on their new Children's Crusade, have scared a lot of people away from hot jazz.[3] Jitterbug taste is not the arbiter of hot music. Equally guilty of planting misconceptions about hot jazz are the cultists who have well nigh segregated jazz from the normal recognition it should have as music. Not the least of the despoilers are the commercial gentlemen, who produce all kinds of ridiculous recorded jazz under the caption "Swing," and who are directly responsible for the stunt music that great men like Armstrong play these days. In this society there are always Breakfast Food people to sell their wares by tying them up with something popular.

In this concert we want to show you what the real thing is by presenting some of its best Negro practitioners. There will be a fair picture of the Negro's many musical forms, but many will be missing, like minstrel music, which has disappeared, and genuine folk songs, which are hard to obtain in their legitimate versions. We have conceded nothing to the misbegotten notions of Negro music obtaining in the North—what you will hear is the most sincere and valid representations our researches could find.

---

3. "Jitterbugs" were swing music fans who danced the jitterbug, or Lindy, an athletic and virtuosic style that became popular around 1936. [RW]

We are dedicating the program to Bessie Smith, who personifies the grandeur and the warmth of Negro music. Bessie Smith was seriously injured in an automobile accident in Virginia fourteen months ago. Taken to a hospital, she was denied admittance because she was a Negro. Before she could be taken to the *proper* hospital she was dead.[4] In this story you have an example of the cruelties Negro musicians share with their fourteen million brothers in America. Bessie Smith will live in the very heart of American music. Her great voice could catapult a triumphant note like a choir of trumpets, or could become as deep and tender as a Southern evening. She invented subtle patterns with the ease of genius. When you hear her singing, say, "Weeping Willow Blues" in front of the quiet trumpet obbligatos of Joe Smith, you can be sure you are hearing something moving and important. She gathered the greatest musicians around her like a queen in a brilliant court. Records exist in which she is accompanied by Fletcher Henderson, Joe Smith, Louis Armstrong, Coleman Hawkins, James P. Johnson, Chu Berry, Benny Goodman, Jack Teagarden, and Frank Newton. Bessie improvised many of her best songs as she sang them; a good example is her beautiful "Back Water Blues" in which James P. Johnson plays an incomparable piano accompaniment, also improvised. Her niece, Ruby Smith, who learned Bessie's songs, will sing some of them at the concert.

Most of the people you will hear are absurdly poor. The greatest of these artists die of privation and neglect and they are often found in the ironic situation of being world music idols and paupers at the same time. Meade "Lux" Lewis, the pianist, works in a Chicago garage; Albert Ammons makes $9 per week for his playing; Big Bill [Broonzy] is a laborer in Chicago; Freddie Green, accomplished guitarist with Count Basie, was earning $1 a week three years ago; Ed Lewis, Basie's first trumpet, played at night and drove a taxi in the daytime; Count Basie's nine-piece band made $175 a week two years ago. The list is endless and shameful.

Jim Crow unions and unscrupulous night club proprietors have denied Negro musicians a living wage and a rightful place in the profession. No radio station in the United States has a Negro in the house band. Although white and Negro musicians have been mingling and playing together on recordings for years, the taboo against mixed orchestras persists. A few manly exceptions to this last situation must be given credit: Nick's in Greenwich Village offers exciting mixed jam sessions, and a similar condition prevailed at the defunct Harlem Uproar House with a mixed orchestra under the direction of the white Milton Mesirow.[5] Benny Goodman has been striving for several years to include Negro musicians in the greatest white jazz orchestra, and for a brief time last month, Lionel Hampton, Negro vibraphone player, pinch hit on the drums in the Waldorf-Astoria Empire Room. *New Masses* hopes to sponsor in the future a program like this one in which the greatest jazz artists, both white and colored, will play an evening of hot jazz.

The producers of this concert ask one indulgence from the audience. Most of the people on the program are making their first appearance before a predominantly white audience; many of them have never visited the North before. They will do their very best if the audience will cooperate with them by creating an atmosphere of informality and interest. The most memorable hot music comes when the performer can feel his audience. May we ask that you forget you are in Carnegie Hall?

---

4. This account of the death of blues singer Bessie Smith (1894–1937) was mistaken, though widely believed; Smith was not directly killed by racist segregation, but the fact that such policies were widespread made the story plausible. Coincidentally, another blues legend, Robert Johnson, had been booked to appear at the concert but died a few months earlier. [RW]

5. Clarinetist Milton Mesirow was better known as Mezz Mezzrow.

The New Masses Presents

AN EVENING OF AMERICAN NEGRO MUSIC

"From Spirituals to Swing"

FRIDAY EVENING, DECEMBER 23, 1938

Carnegie Hall

Conceived and Produced by John Hammond; Directed by Charles Friedman

Note: The following program is not in chronological order

Introduction

AFRICAN TRIBAL MUSIC: From scientific recordings made by the H. E. Tracy Expedition to the West Coast of Africa.

THEME: Count Basie and His Orchestra.

I. Spirituals and Holy Roller Hymns

MITCHELL'S CHRISTIAN SINGERS, *North Carolina*. William Brown, Julius Davis, Louis David, Sam Bryant.

SISTER THARPE, *Florida*. (Courtesy Cotton Club) with guitar accompaniment.

II. Soft Swing

THE KANSAS CITY SIX, *New York City*. Eddie Durham (electric guitar), Freddie Green (guitar), Buck Clayton (trumpet), Lester Young (clarinet and tenor saxophone), Jo Jones (drums), Walter Page (bass).

III. Harmonica Playing

SANFORD TERRY, *Durham, North Carolina*. Washboard playing by artists to be announced at the concert.

IV. Blues

RUBY SMITH, *Norfolk, Virginia*. Accompanied on the piano by JAMES P. JOHNSON, *New York City*.

JOE TURNER, *Kansas City, Missouri*. Accompanied by PETE JOHNSON, *New York City*.

BIG BILL, *Chicago, Illinois*. Accompanied by himself on the guitar.

JAMES RUSHING, *Kansas City, Missouri*. Accompanied by the KANSAS CITY FIVE. Freddie Green (guitar), Buck Clayton (trumpet), Lester Young (clarinet and tenor saxophone), Jo Jones (drums), Walter Page (bass).

HELEN HUMES, *Louisville, Kentucky*. Accompanied by KANSAS CITY FIVE.

V. Boogie-Woogie Piano Playing

ALBERT AMMONS, *Chicago*. MEADE "LUX" LEWIS, *Chicago*. PETE JOHNSON, *Kansas City*. "A Cutting Session."

INTERMISSION

VI. Early New Orleans Jazz

SIDNEY BECHET and his NEW ORLEANS FEET WARMERS. Sidney Bechet (clarinet and soprano saxophone), Tommy Ladnier (trumpet), James P. Johnson (piano), Dan Minor (trombone), Jo Jones (drums).

VII. Swing

COUNT BASIE AND HIS ORCHESTRA. Count Basie (piano), Walter Page (bass), Freddie Green (guitar), Jo Jones (drums), Ed Lewis (first trumpet), Buck Clayton (second trumpet), Shad Collins (third trumpet), Harry Edison (fourth trumpet), Benny Morton (first trombone), Dicky Wells (second trombone), Dan Minor (third trombone), Earl Warren (first alto saxophone), Jack Washington (second alto sax and baritone), Lester Young (third tenor sax and clarinet), James Rushing and Helen Humes (vocalists). Arrangers: Eddie Durham, Count Basie, Albert Gibson, Buck Clayton, etc.

BASIE'S BLUE FIVE. Count Basie, Shad Collins, Walter Page, Jo Jones, Herschel Evans.

THE KANSAS CITY SIX. Eddie Durham, Freddie Green, Buck Clayton, Lester Young, Jo Jones, Walter Page.

24. Duke Ellington Explains Swing

DUKE [EDWARD KENNEDY] ELLINGTON (1899–1974) was one of the most influential composers and bandleaders of the twentieth century. This genial autobiographical statement sketches Ellington's life and career to around 1938, the date of its publication, including a substantial amount of commentary on his music and compositional methods. Like Louis Armstrong in "What Is Swing?", Ellington emphasizes the connections among various musical styles (and like Jelly Roll Morton, he cites the "Spanish syncopations" of early jazz). He defends and defines swing, but points out that he has gone beyond swing with some of his slower compositions. Ellington briefly alludes to the controversial practice of "swinging the classics," but later explains how swing's relationship of composition to performance differs from the typical arrangement in classical music.[1] More important, he describes his process of shared, collective composition, which, by cooperatively incorporating the ideas of his musicians, offered tremendous creative possibilities.[2] This article appeared in an obscure periodical called "TOPS," and Ellington (or perhaps Helen Oakley Dance, from whom Ellington sometimes received writing assistance at this time) obligingly worked that word into the article's original title and closing sentence.

Swing? Well, that's what they're calling it this year; and it's a good enough name. But it all goes back to something just about as old—and as natural—as the circulation of the blood. It belongs to everybody, whether he lives on Lenox, Park, or Second Avenue; whether he plays or dances or just listens. And it hasn't anything at all to do with "highbrow" or "lowbrow"—those terms are out, so far as music is concerned.

Source: Edward Kennedy "Duke" Ellington, "Music Is 'Tops' to You and Me . . . And Swing Is a Part of It," *Tops*, 1938, pp. 14–18.

1. On the consequences of swinging the classics, see, for example, "Puccini Wins Damages for 'Butterfly' Jazz," *New York Times*, November 21, 1923, 21:7.

2. The finished compositions were not collectively copyrighted, however, leading to some resentments among Ellington's band members. See, for example, in the oral history collection of the Institute of Jazz Studies at Rutgers, the transcripts of interviews with Lawrence Brown (reel 4, pp. 32–36) and Barney Bigard (reel 2, p. 14; reel 3, p. 41; reel 5, pp. 3–6).

But here's a funny thing. Take a melody—either your own tune or one people have been singing for years, like "Annie Laurie." Turn it inside out; wrap your own ideas around it; vary the tempos. Now see what happens.

If you're what people usually call a "serious" composer, what you have done is a theme and variations, and you publish it as part of an opus—or a big piece of work. But if you're a swing musician, you may not publish it at all; just play it, making it a little different each time according to the way you feel, letting it grow as you work on it. The people who like it are called alligators; the ones who don't like it say you are desecrating a fine old tune, and try to tune you off the air waves.

That's what happened in Detroit, when Tommy Dorsey was swinging "Comin' Through the Rye." Mr. Leo Fitzpatrick, general manager of WJR, had ordered that the plug be pulled out on all swing arrangements of old tunes. Swing fans howled about it; but there were lots of others who felt that the old songs were being saved from a fate worse than death.

Now what Mr. Fitzpatrick did is too bad, not because it does any harm to swing—you can tune in on Tommy Dorsey over hundreds of other stations—but because it shows a misunderstanding about the real nature of swing and, for that matter, of all music.

Sure, swing is a distinct class of music; and I'm proud to have had some part in its development. Pretty soon we'll try a definition—if you haven't had enough of them already, in a score of magazine and newspaper articles. But let's get this straight: the principles here are the same as those in all really great music. Syncopation? Beethoven was a master of that. Free improvisation? A specialty of any fine concert organist, sticking to the classics. Primarily dance music? Bach composed for the steps of his time; and some of Brahms's Hungarian dances are as frenzied as anything you'll hear in the night clubs.

The truth is, you could take all the swing bands on the earth and drop them into the middle of the Pacific; and, given civilization just as we knew it before, you'd probably have swing music back, going strong, in less than six months. Under another name, maybe; there have been lots of other names. Jazz, for instance. . . .

About the time I was born in Washington, D.C., in 1899, my parents were hearing a great deal of what later came to be called jazz. This had come out of New Orleans where Negro bands, having added solemnity to a funeral by playing dirges en route to the cemetery, marched home at a quickstep touched up with their own variations. Each musician played on his own, spontaneously, yet kept in touch with the original composition. Whatever they called it then, it was something pretty close to swing.

This gets us back into history—history in which the Negro race has played a very important part. Remember that music speaks of the emotions, ranging from grave to gay. Back in the forests and on the plains of Africa the rhythm of nature surrounded the Negro, in the dropping of water from a cliff, in the ominous measured beat of the tom-tom. Transplanted to the fields of the deep South, the Negroes of the slavery period were still moved by these influences; and it is by these influences that their contribution to American music has been shaped. Because they remain so close to nature, they still express their emotions rhythmically.

And so when I came into the world, Southern Negroes were expressing their feelings in rhythmic "blues" in which Spanish syncopations had a part. As I grew to boyhood I lived through the era of rhythmic repetition or ragtime, whose most notable example—Irving Berlin's classic "Alexander's Ragtime Band"—is still going strong. My parents, natural lovers of music, had attached me to a piano keyboard; but it seems I was never destined for a conservatory. Although I liked music, I never got on with practicing lessons. Before I knew it, I would be fashioning a new melody and accompaniment instead of following the score.

Besides, I had other plans—then, I wanted to be an architect, and got as far as earning a scholarship at Pratt Institute. So look what happened: I got a job as soda jerker to make money for college; and instead of going to college I became a musician. There are probably plenty of architects anyway.

It worked out like this. My job was in a place called "The Poodle Dog." The piano player there had a leaning toward accepting free drinks; and when he wasn't able to sit up to the keyboard any longer I filled in, still improvising, composing, or otherwise making free use of some basic melody.

One day while I was playing my original "Soda Fountain Rag," doing it in a different tempo each time I played it, Oliver "Doc" Perry heard me and began coaching me for one of his orchestras. I really studied piano that time. Tussell Wooding was then directing a jazz concert orchestra of sixty pieces in a Washington theater; and—against his better judgment—he gave me a job at one of his five pianos. All went well until I came to a pause. Instead of remaining silent, as the score directed, I broke into a typical Ellington improvisation. Mr. Wooding very properly fired me.

Good "Doc" Perry gave me a job directing one of his orchestras. During 1923 and 1924 I worked with Wilbur Sweatman's band; then I came to New York with five men of my own selection. There followed some mighty hot nights and a few rather hungry dawns; and for a while it looked like no go. But in 1926 we went to work in a Broadway cellar café, The Kentucky Club, where I began to work out a new style of rhythmic playing.

Here we catch up with that history I mentioned a little while back—that trend of American music, in which Negroes have contributed so much. My own early efforts, for example, stemmed from the wild, melancholy trumpet playing of Buddy Bolden, a New Orleans Negro whose improvisations were popular about 1910. In the background, too, was William Christopher Handy's trek from Memphis to the North with his "St. Louis Blues"—and the subsequent frenzied variations by Negro bands which made hectic history and inspired many of the outstanding leaders of jazz bands to imitations.

"King" Oliver, in Chicago, had presented Louis Armstrong to a fascinated public in 1922. That amazing Negro trumpeter, who made free with any and every score offered him, had convinced young Bix Beiderbecke that his white man's trumpeting was corny. Bix adopted the Armstrong technique, became the greatest of white trumpeters, joined Paul Whiteman, and profoundly influenced all other contemporary trumpeters. That's all part of the history.

But swing, as a style, had not been discovered. I was helping to develop it, I suppose—along with lots of others. As far back as 1932—several years before anybody ever heard of jitterbugs or jam sessions—I composed, published, and played a piece entitled "It Don't Mean a Thing If It Ain't Got That Swing." Meanwhile I had built a five-piece combination around my piano, and people were coming around to listen. The music critics and Broadway commentators said it was good music; we were certainly trying hard to make it that.

Then a break came for me in the person of Irving Mills, far-sighted manager of orchestra talent. Mr. Mills professionally adopted me and put me into the Cotton Club, which moved down from Harlem to Broadway not long after that. The rest is recent history: Hollywood, pictures, a tour of Europe, phonograph records, and a lot of radio.

The point of all this? I'm trying to give a rough idea of what music has meant to me, personally. A rough idea, because the rewards go much deeper than publicity and contracts and European tours—pleasant as these all are. Things harder to talk about are the satisfaction of playing because it's the thing you'd rather do than anything else; the regard of many friends whom I have come to know through music.

Just a year ago, when I was celebrating the tenth anniversary of my debut at the Cotton Club, there were messages of congratulation from such men as Ferde Grofé, the composer; André Kostelanetz, of the Columbia Broadcasting System; Irving Mills, who gave me my big chance; Paul Whiteman, Cab Calloway, Chick Webb, Louis Armstrong—and hundreds of others. Things like that keep me going.

For my part, I've tried to make the best contribution I could to native music—and I'm still trying. Nothing else has mattered to me. Naturally my own race is closest to my heart; and it is in the musical idiom of that race that I can find my most natural expression. Just now we're calling it swing—and that brings us to our definition.

In the beginning I pointed out that swing and classical music have principles in common. There is, however, one fundamental difference. In classical music, the composer and conductor are all-important: the score must be interpreted according to the teachings and traditions of the masters. But in swing the musician—the instrumentalist—is all-important: he must add something to the original composition and do it spontaneously—without preparation.

And that's not all. Your good swing man must have very deep feeling. If the feeling is honest, the music is honest. It is not pure showmanship that causes "Pee Wee" Russell, the great white clarinetist, to twist his eyebrows when swinging on a "gobstick" solo. Nor does Satchmo Armstrong, who learned to play a trumpet in a waifs' home, sweat over his swinging trumpet for effect. A good swinger gives everything he's got each time he goes into action.

By now you've probably worked out your own definition. Each player can give you a different one. I like the following because of its brevity: "Swing is an unmechanical but hard-driving and fluid rhythm over which soloists improvise as they play." Starting from there you can lose yourself in a whole new vocabulary used by swingers and their most enthusiastic followers, the jitterbugs.

During the past few years I have produced many samples of swing music. I can score it with a lead pencil on a piece of music paper while riding on a train. But usually I gather the boys around me after a concert, say about three in the morning when most of the world is quiet. I have a central idea which I bring out on the piano. At one stage, Cootie Williams, the trumpeter, will suggest an interpolation, perhaps a "riff" or obbligato for that spot. We try it and, probably, incorporate it. A little later on Juan Tizol, the trombonist, will interrupt with another idea. We try that and maybe adopt it. It generally depends on the majority's opinion.

Thus, after three or four sessions, I will evolve an entirely new composition. But it will not be written out, put on a score, until we have been playing it in public quite a while. And—this is important to remember—no good swing orchestra ever plays any composition, with the same effect, twice. So much depends upon psychological and physical conditions. That's why they have to be good musicians. They must play from intuition or instinct backed by a liberal musical education. If they have had a good academic schooling, so much the better. Most of my boys have gone through high school; many of them have had two or three years in college.

And it's a mistake to think of swing men as a dissolute bunch of fellows. True, the unfortunate finish of the justly famous Bix Beiderbecke, who died of pneumonia in his twenty-seventh year, has been charged up to burning the candle at both ends. After a concert or dance engagement he would gather with a few cronies and a few bottles of gin and jam or jive for riotous hours. From that tragedy has arisen the tradition that all swing musicians must be bottle nurses or marijuana smokers. Well, it doesn't work out that way.

Take the Ellington organization. There's no rule against drinking, "reefing," or smoking. But we work at least twelve hours each day. We can't do our work unless we are in good mental and physical condition.

Even more absurd, I think, is the charge that swing encourages sexual immorality. One critic, a scientist, bases such a warning on comparing swing tempo with the beat of the heart—seventy-two to the minute, in each case. Well, that makes it look bad for the United States Army, where the regulation marching cadence is one hundred and thirty-two beats to the minute. No; there's less of the lascivious in swing, by far, than in the seductively beautiful if more stately waltz. The Shag, the Big Apple, the Suzy Q all call for too much physical energy to leave a great deal more for romantic immoralities. Accept this, if you will, as the belief of a conductor who for many years, from his vantage ground, has seen pretty much all that is going on.

Swing, of course, is only part of the story: the young man with the horn knows something of classical backgrounds, and owes much to them. My own efforts have gone beyond swing in such compositions as "Mood Indigo," "Black and Tan Fantasy," "Sophisticated Lady," "Prelude to a Kiss," and others. I have been encouraged by the generous comments of Percy Grainger, Leopold Stokowski, and others famous in "legitimate" music. Unquestionably I have been greatly helped by studying Stravinski, Debussy, Respighi, and Gershwin.

In my private life I am seldom eccentric. I do order fifteen suits of clothes at a time and then stick to one of them. I hate to go to bed and hate to get up. I'm pretty sure to be late one hour for a scheduled rehearsal. But I haven't changed a mannerism, an ideal, or a friend since I left Washington in 1924. My home is in Harlem, and I expect it to remain there.

It all started in The Poodle Dog; but it all adds up to a lot of satisfaction at the sharing in the achievement of the Negro race. That's why my greatest hope is that I may live to complete the opera in my mind: the story of the Negro's beginning and his migrations, both physically and spiritually. Maybe I'll call it "Boola"—maybe something else; that won't matter. If I can manage to make it worthy of the subject, it'll be the Tops.

25. Jazz and Gender During the War Years

THE ABILITY OF WOMEN TO SUCCEED AS jazz musicians has been much discussed throughout the music's history, but there are special reasons for the prominence of such debates during the 1930s and '40s. The Depression and World War II brought women into the American work force in unprecedented numbers, creating tensions with prevailing notions of gender identities—how men and women were "supposed to" think and act. The ability to succeed in traditionally male domains seemed incompatible with accepted ideas about "femininity," a conflict that was not really redefined until the feminist accomplishments of the 1960s and 1970s. Magazines such as *Down Beat* exploited these issues to attract attention and boost circulation, but they could not have done so in a vacuum. Arguments about popular all-women big bands—the most famous of which was probably the multiracial International Sweethearts of Rhythm—reflected wider controversies concerning the proper social roles of women.[1]

Criticisms of the orchestras varied, as did the defenses offered by the women themselves. Writers on both sides discussed the issue of how women and men might come to perform differently—whether through nature, nurture, or social restrictions. Depending on the writer's agenda, qualities such as intuition, cooperation, and personal attractiveness were made to seem advantageous or crippling. While many jazz critics championed racial equality, gender was different: prejudice and cruel disparagement seem to have been more acceptable for this social category. Despite important changes, these issues are still very much alive; for example, only in 1997 did the Vienna Philharmonic begin to allow female orchestral musicians the opportunity to compete for membership.[2]

"Why Women Musicians Are Inferior"

Why is it that outside of a few sepia females the woman musician was never born, capable of "sending" anyone farther than the nearest exit?[3] It would seem that even though women are the weaker sex they would still be able to bring more out of a poor, defenseless horn than something that sounds like a cry for help. You can forgive them for lacking guts in their playing but even women should be able to play with feeling and expression and *they never do.*

---

1. Even on the subject of female big bands, these debates were not confined to *Down Beat,* from which the items in this selection are drawn. See also, for example, Gypsie Cooper, "Can Women Swing?," *The Metronome,* September 1936, p. 30. Moreover, the debates continued in the same terms at least into the 1950s; see, for example, "Mrs. Cugat Can't See Gals as Tooters; Kills Glamor," *Down Beat,* May 4, 1951, p. 13. For more sympathetic treatments of the topic, see Nat Hentoff, "Cherchez Les Femmes," *Down Beat,* December 3, 1952, p. 5, and Barry Ulanov, "Is There a Place for Women in Jazz Strictly on a Merit Basis?" *Down Beat,* January 9, 1958, pp. 17, 50.

2. Scholarship addressing issues of gender and sexuality in jazz scarcely exists as yet, with a handful of important exceptions; see the articles by Hazel V. Carby's and Sherrie Tucker in this volume, as well as Krin Gabbard, "Signifyin(g) the Phallus: Mo' Better Blues and Representations of the Jazz Trumpet," *Cinema Journal 32:1* (Fall 1992), pp. 43–62 (reprinted in Gabbard, *Representing Jazz* (Durham: Duke University Press, 1995), pp. 104–30), and David Ake, "Re-Masculating Jazz: Ornette Coleman, 'Lonely Woman,' and the New York Jazz Scene in the Late 1950s," *American Music* 16:1 (Spring 1998), pp. 147–66. For historical accounts of women in jazz, see Leslie Gourse, *Madame Jazz: Contemporary Women Instrumentalists* (New York: Oxford University Press, 1995); Sally Placksin, *American Women in Jazz, 1900 to the Present: Their Words, Lives, and Music* (n.p.: Wideview Books, 1982), and Linda Dahl, *Stormy Weather: The Music and Lives of a Century of Jazzwomen* (New York: Pantheon, 1984).

3. Sepia is a brown color originally derived from ink; the term was used by both black and white writers. This author means to exempt a few black women (probably Bessie Smith and other singers) from his criticism. [RW]

Have you ever heard a woman saxophonist who didn't get a quavering tone with absolutely uncontrolled vibrato, or a woman brass player who even though she might have some power, still got a brassy, hard, unfinished quality of tone? Masculine strength is not necessary for brass; diminutive Roy Eldridge who towers little more than five feet on a bicycle has the greatest playing range of any trumpet player and looks as if a strong zephyr would blow him right back to New Orleans. Yet women don't seem to be able to develop a lip, which stymies their taking more than one chorus at a time. The mind may be willing but the flesh is weak!

There are several psychological reasons underlying the apparent futility of women in dance orchestras, especially applicable to wind instruments. In the first place, women are as a whole emotionally unstable, which prevents their being consistent performers on musical instruments.

Another point, though it may seem laughable, is the fact that gals are conscious of the facial contortions so necessary in "blowing it out" and limit their power for fear of appearing silly in the eyes of men. Milady's dimples take an awful beating when reaching for the high ones and dearie, was my face red on that last high note!

One reason which is quite important is the fact that until recently tradition has been against women's playing in dance orchestras. Co-education, too, is comparatively a new idea and though many may deny it, heredity is a prime factor in the development of any artistry and where men have had centuries of musical education behind them women have only within the last few years come into their own as musical entertainers.

If women as a whole were compelled to support themselves, there would doubtless be more capable musicians in the female ranks but where careers are unnecessary except for personal gratification there is little incentive to work for perfection. There was never a musician who didn't have to spend untold hours "woodshedding" his parts and women don't seem to have the time, ambition, or the patience to do this. It may be that they are lazy or it may be that with a few exceptions, all of the girl bands in the country are vaudeville bands where the standard of playing is considerably less than it is in dance bands.[4]

In these show bands, the prime requisite is good looks after which comes playing ability and the art of being able to "hold" three or four other instruments. Witness a certain well known girls' band which features 10 or 12 accordionists. About half the girls actually don't play the instruments but further insult the average musician's intelligence by holding dummy accordions. The other half is made up of two or three who can actually play and a few more who perform the game of "push the button down" on plainly marked bass chords.

Then, the average girl band generally has only a small library, which stagnates their natural ability, if any, and precludes any possibility of versatility.

Women are better performers on strings and piano, which are essentially sympathetic instruments more in keeping with their temperament. They do NOT shine on wind instruments, however, nor do they make good percussionists. If more girl drummers had cradle rocking experience before their musical endeavors they might come closer to getting on the beat.

Source: Unsigned article, "Why Women Musicians Are Inferior," *Down Beat*, February 1938, p. 4. Courtesy *Down Beat* magazine.

IN THE SAME ISSUE, *DOWN BEAT* PRINTED THIS REPLY TO THE PREVIOUS ARTICLE, penned by the leader of one of the most successful white "all-girl" bands.

---

4. "Woodshedding" is rigorous musical practice. [RW]

"Women Musicians Not Inferior Says Rito Rio"

May I submit a rebuttal to my opponent as to why women musicians are not inferior? I should first like permission from the reader to dwell upon points pertaining to the performance expected from a dance orchestra. The first very essential requirement necessary to obtain desired results is endurance. The members of my orchestra have ridden all day and night in a bus and played a five hour dance job, repeated the same the next day and have received compliments from the promoter on their fine performance. They have also rehearsed several hours together while playing five hours at night for many days in succession and haven't complained. How many times one of our fellow musicians has remarked, "Even men won't do that!"

A second and important point is the feeling, tone, and phrasing which good musicians must obtain. This is a quality which girls alone are more likely to possess because of the aesthetic nature of their sex. I think our mutual public will agree that a warm vibrant tone is much more pleasing than the masculine sock so often emphasized by our men bands.

Rhythm in our modern swing generation is also of most important consideration, and I notice girls, because of their feminine tendency, cooperate to make a rhythm section a united unit dependent on each other, rather than the masculine tendency to lead on his own instrument.

As a last rebuke I feel I am rather taking advantage of my opponent in mentioning the fact that either beautiful music or swing music is much more pleasing with a delightful picture than with the trite male band in its uniform tuxedo. Girls find a pleasing picture does not detract from good musicianship or from thoroughness and preciseness which help to comprise the attributes of good musicianship.

In a few paragraphs, I have only touched on a few points offered as reasons why Consolidated Radio Artists find it rather pleasurable to offer promoters their girl orchestras and why there is an increasing demand for girl orchestras.

Signing off with most sincere best wishes to our male competitors.

Rito Rio and her All Girl Orchestra.

Source: Rito Rio, "Women Musicians Not Inferior Says—Rito Rio," *Down Beat*, February, 1938, p. 4. Courtesy *Down Beat* magazine.

THIS FURTHER ATTACK ON FEMALE MUSICIANS APPEARED THE FOLLOWING YEAR. The author offers some interesting arguments about how race and class affect gender. That is, he maintains that the social positions of male jazz musicians within racial and class hierarchies has held back women.

"The Gal Yippers Have No Place in Our Jazz Bands"

There are more swing bands assailing the public with more good jazz than the public can shake a leg at these days. Yet how strange that with this abundance of the right stuff, there is such a dearth of young lovelies who can chirp a tune without causing the boys behind them on the stand (and who knows how many billions sitting beside their radios) to wince as if their ear-teeth were being yanked by the roots.

Various unenlightening theories have been advanced. Some even disagree with the premise and crow gallantly that most of the dolls with these bands are yodeling terrific swing music.[5] But most of the cats will agree that the really hep chirpies are in

5. Not literal yodeling, of course, but this writer's hip slang for "singing." [RW]

the inconspicuous minority. There are also the diehards who will admit the vocal shortcomings of their favorite sparrow, but will explain that she gives the band a little much-needed sex appeal, or that the leader is gone on her, or, pointing out her four foot eight height and big black eyes like saucers, will explain, "You gotta admit she's awful cute."

But nobody seems to have bothered to find out why none of these gals (with the few exceptions, of course) can sing a song that won't react like a monkey-wrench thrown into a smooth-working piece of machinery.

Today's swing music is a product of the environment of America's young musicians, who have recognized, or perhaps rather felt, in the negro's inherent musical expression, something which, when they hear it, gives them a definite satisfaction and a desire to attempt to imitate it, as we always try to imitate that which we recognize as the best.

Not many white musicians have been able to emulate exactly, or even closely, the musical expression of the American Negro. Those who come closest are those who have been under the influence of the negro's music for the longest period of time. They are the men who comprised the New Orleans, Memphis, and Chicago schools. From these, although mostly from the better negro musicians themselves, comes our best swing music today.

America's girls have not had the opportunity to surround themselves with this environment. They've been tending to their knitting preparing themselves either for the kitchen or the career. Grant that those who have been preparing for the career of swing singer have tried to learn from those predecessors who were considered best. Who have they been? Sophie Tucker, Helen Morgan, Ruth Etting, and the rest of that group whose claim to fame lay in their ability to put over a song in a sufficiently novel fashion as to figuratively knock out their listeners. They were soloists and were not attempting to fit their efforts in with any particular idiom as are the gals singing with swing bands today.

The white man started to learn hot jazz by playing it for whatever he could make in the hovels in New Orleans' red light district at the turn of the century. And even up to the present time, while he still tries to learn it, his jazz classroom is the dimly-lighted gin joint in any city where the price he pays for playing the way he wants to play is a salary of maybe one meal a night or whatever the kitty can squeeze out at dawn when work is done.

That has been the heritage of jazz. That has been the background forced upon musicians with wills and souls of their own who wanted to learn and express this new art. So is it any wonder that, excluded (as of course she should have been) from this environment which is the only one which could have given the white girl the insight into what went into making good jazz music, she should be so barren of any appreciation of the finer points of playing jazz on an instrument, let alone trying to interpret it into vocal sounds?

These girls aren't singing jazz. Vocal jazz was originally sounded in the form of the blues, which was (and still is) a purely emotionally-inspired uncultured outpouring of words and vocal sounds expressing a mood.[6] That's the way Bessie Smith sang, and the way Billie Holiday, Jack Teagarden, and a half dozen more are singing today.

Today's girl singers, poor kids, are the victims of a heritage of classic yodeling. Which is all right in its own back yard, the opera and the light classic. But when they

6. By calling such singing "uncultured," the author evokes "authenticity" but trivializes the musical skills involved—obviously, not everyone who feels deeply sings well. Such backhanded compliments often served to dismiss the musical intelligence and craft of black and female musicians. [RW]

try to produce a vocal job in the jazz idiom with that environmental equipment, they're trying to crossbreed the world's classic vocal background with the emotional blues shouting of the southern Negro, and if that doesn't give us a hell of a hybrid, I'll eat my record collection.

No sir. You can take all your female yowlers these days and feed them to the jitterbugs, one by one. Bunny Berigan summed up the entire idea when, auditioning a particularly sad lot of bags recently, he was heard to comment, "I guess this kind of music just wasn't meant to be sung—anyway by a gal." He's right.

Source: Ted Toll, "The Gal Yippers Have No Place in Our Jazz Bands," *Down Beat,* October 15, 1939, p. 16. Courtesy *Down Beat* magazine.

THIS LETTER BY BANDLEADER AND SAXOPHONE PLAYER PEGGY GILBERT IS ACTUALLY a reply to the February 1938 article, "Why Women Musicians are Inferior," but it works well as a rebuttal to Ted Toll's later article because it addresses similar arguments about environment and education. The title was tacked on by a *Down Beat* editor; it doesn't fit Gilbert's letter and she was outraged by it.

"How Can You Blow a Horn With a Brassiere?"

Dear Father Superior:

You get up, make a lot of unintelligible noise, and expect the people to shout, "Bravo!" or echo in reverential tones a deep "Amen." You are like a small boy pulling his sister's pigtails when you think she hasn't a chance to fight back. You are the little boy who yells "Sissy!" from the window on the second floor.

If Gene Krupa were a woman, how long do you suppose he would be an ace drummer in Benny Goodman's band? In evening gown, he might still be sensational even hampered by brassiere straps, girdle, skirt, and high heels—but Mrs. G. K. or Miss Anybody couldn't make a one night stand with bags under her eyes. She could be good, but no matter how good, the public, especially the men, would not tolerate an unattractive, second-hand stage prop. And that's one of the superficial reasons women are inferior to men as musicians *(if they are):* their inability to make a career of music because, for women, as a profession it can last at best only a few years.

Ha! We admit it, you say. You're absolutely right, but your line is as old as time. You think you have put women on the pan. You have. But it has been done for ages, Father Superior—ever since Eve—and far better than you could ever do it. Your weak, illogical, ineffectual argument is hardly resented. It's your attitude we resent, because it expresses the attitude of all professional men musicians toward all professional women musicians. A woman has to be a thousand times more talented, has to have a thousand times more initiative even to be recognized as the peer of the least successful man. Why? Because of that age-old prejudice against women, that time-worn idea that women are the weaker sex, that women are innately inferior to men.

So you actually think that because men have had centuries of musical education behind them that the present masculine generation has inherited that knowledge, that talent? That's not worthy of you, Father. We expect better arguments than that. Knowledge is not hereditary, and whether or not talent is present in the chromosomes is still a matter of conjecture. But even if it were, wouldn't a daughter, being a child also of a talented musician, be just as likely to inherit that characteristic—as a son? If we were ladies, of course, we should ignore that thrust and tactfully help you to forget that you rambled a bit out of your sphere. Now, if you had said environment, perhaps we should have agreed. It's a man's world, admittedly. You would be right without having to prove yourself right. You think what millions of men musicians think—and it may be you are justified. But at least establish a true premise from which to argue (or gripe).

But after all, that's not the issue, is it? Or isn't it? It seems that you, like all the rest, have judged musicians according to sex rather than ability. You have generalized no end to prove your point, always adding in your liberal way "with few exceptions." "Women Musicians Are Inferior"—that's your point, isn't it? You were a bit vague even about that, but the editor kindly clarified the subject in the headline. And why are women musicians inferior *(if they are)*? Since you are not particularly enlightening as to the reasons such a broad statement might be true, we'll hand you a few tips—if you give us an audience and don't rush for the exit because a woman is speaking. We'll use a low, well-modulated voice, and powder our nose and comb our hair.

And then, too, as we have inferred, women are never hired because of their ability as musicians, but as an attraction for the very reason that they are women, and men like to look at attractive women. Consequently, the manager is continually reminding the girls not to take the music so seriously, but to relax, to smile. How can you smile with a horn in your mouth? How can you relax when a girdle is throttling you and the left brassiere strap holds your arm in a vise? If we quaver a little on the high notes, it's because we are asked to do a Houdini—and if we hit an occasional blue note, it's because we play with *too much* feeling, and mascara gets in our eyes. On the other hand, men's orchestras are usually hired because of their ability as musicians. Their good looks, their presentability other than neatness rarely will enter the question. Even the best girl bands in the country have to have an S. A. artist fronting them to captivate the audience while the musicians in the band indulge themselves in that orgy of facial contortions which seems so important to you, Father Superior.[7]

Men have always refused to work with girls, thus not giving them the opportunity to prove their equality. This is especially true of wind instrument players, obviously one of the foci of your attack, Father. Girl violinists and stringed instrument players have had breaks. Descending to the personal for a moment, I wish to add that I have a few girls in my band who could hold first chairs in the best men's bands if given the privilege. But what men's orchestra would consent to such an experiment? A great many men musicians have highly complimented my band saying it was as good or better than their organizations, but if the question of actually giving us an opportunity to establish our equality arose, we should immediately be relegated to an inferior plane and given the form answer A: "It's not being done."

You say that women musicians are inferior because of lack of practice. If that's true, it's because there is no future in music for girl musicians for the reasons previously mentioned. Woodshedding would be fun if we could see there was anything to be gained by it—other than personal gratification. However, even you should agree as an "artist" that that is an admirable motive in itself. Oddly enough, Father, they take just as much pride as men in their work, and they woodshed as much as men and perhaps more, because of the obstacle of prejudice to be overcome and because of the harsh criticism fired at them from all sides such as that in your article. As for the point you noted that women are not compelled to support themselves, we urge you with apologetic banality to go West, young man. Evidently, you haven't

7. "S. A." probably means "sex appeal." [RW]

gone farther in that direction than Chicago. Now, in California, it's different. The women support the men—as well as themselves. Step around a little more, Father, and have a looksee. There are several Misses Prima, Eldridge, Musso, and Trumbauer in circulation—and if you are a fair-minded gentleman, be gallant and respond to their "cries for help."[8]

Very humbly yours,

Peggy Gilbert

Source: Peggy Gilbert, "How Can You Blow a Horn With a Brassiere?," *Down Beat,* April 1938, pp. 3, 17. Courtesy *Down Beat* magazine.

THE LAST OF THE ARTICLES PRESENTED HERE INGENIOUSLY TURNS THE TABLES. In some ways, it anticipates the persecuted tone adopted by male contributors to the 1980s "backlash" against feminism.[9]

"Here's the Lowdown on 'Two Kinds of Women'"

There are two kinds of women, those who don't like jazz music and admit they don't, and those who don't like jazz music but say they do. The latter always have ulterior motives. They are either shining up to a man who likes his music hot, or else they're married to a hot musician and hate to admit to their friends that they have married a musical "failure." Any normal healthy woman can listen to music with you, dig your reaction before you are sure of it yourself, and beat you to your own comment on it; don't get mad at me too soon, because after you marry her you'll find out she had a way of finding out in advance what you would like to have her like.

Of course, no man ever dares say anything against women. If he does, everyone thinks he is letting out on the whole sex a gripe he has against one of them. The man who says the modern girl is "immoral" is the man towards whom no modern girl has shown any immoral tendencies. When a man says women are faithless, he is saying that one woman is being faithful to someone other than himself. So I'm not saying anything against women. . . . But I *am* giving my theory on what's throttling our music, and, since the apple does not fall far from the tree, the theory is simple: Women control the public taste, and women do not like jazz!

First, let's see how women control the public taste. Come along with the argument, save your decision until the whistle blows, and if you are a woman we are serving free transfers from here on out. How does the public at large get to hear most of its music? In movies, over the radio, and at dances.

Movies are made for women, with enough put in for men so they won't refuse to take their women to see them. Start keeping count on the movies that are made up of things that interest women, and bore men—mother love dramas, poor shop girl getting millionaire, girl choosing between two men, life and hard times of a pure hearted

8. These are references to the respected male jazz musicians Louis Prima, Roy Eldridge, Vido Musso, and Frankie Trumbauer. [RW]

9. See Elaine Tyler May, *Homeward Bound: American Families in the Cold War Era* (New York: Basic Books, 1988), and Susan Faludi, *Backlash: the Undeclared War Against American Women* (New York: Doubleday, 1991). "Sending" your audience meant moving them, drawing an enthusiastic response. [RW]

harlot, business girl forced to choose between love and a career, girl becoming stage success, girl reforming man, love triumphant. Love, gush, slush, country girl's idea of New York swank, of women (and the men who think only of love), and for women—that's the movies. How long since you've seen a bang up good outdoor picture? How long since you've seen a picture about a hard working man doing an interesting job of overcoming some of his problems? How long since you have seen a picture for men? You've grown used to the movies for women—but do any of them mean anything to you? Take a look at a handful of movie magazines. Do you see any advertisements for fishing tackle, pipes, guns, or any of the other commercial products that interest men alone?

Now switch on the radio. You'll concede the daytime programs, from about 8:00 A.M. to 6:00 P.M. That leaves about five hours of evening programs for the average man. You listen to them, and you tell me—do you like the advertisements or does the woman like them? Does that smooth sincere announcer sell you, or is his voice working on the women? Of course, they give you a few minutes of good masculine stuff like Fred Allen's burlesques, but just add it up, buddy.

And the same holds for dances. Musicians know they'll go over if they play to the women, and will get a lot of enthusiasm but no jobs if they play for the men. The women decide where they want to go to dance, so you play for them, so you play the music they like.

If you've come this far, draw a total. If movies, radios, and dances cater to women, then the public hears the kind of music women want to hear. If the public never hears jazz it can't ever know what it's about. And we're all against anything we don't understand. So if women won't let jazz be played commercially, jazz will never have an audience.

Do women want jazz to be played commercially, do women like hot music? The answer is, why the hell should they? The stuff comes from march music, doesn't it? It doesn't speak sweetly of love, and relax you like a warm bath. I never heard of women getting excited about a good march. Good jazz is hard masculine music with a whip to it. Women like violins, and jazz deals with drums and trumpets. No fault of women that America is producing no violin music. It is not the fault of women (and of feminine men) that they like only what the classicists call lyric music, while the only music being produced happens to be epic music. But take hot music out of their hands, or they'll starve it to death.

You have heard women say they would like jazz if it wasn't so blary, noisy, rough. If the women are pretty enough that sounds like a good objection. Yet when you think it over—what interest can anyone have in music who worries about such superficialities? If the women who control our music don't care how good it is, but insist that it be genteel, sentimental, soothing, and caressing (and accompanied by words like "how'd you get so divine, you soul stirring angel from heaven"), then the men who are beginning to like their hot music straight had better give up.

The way out is not to try to teach women to like jazz. They never will. The only thing to do is to demand proportionate representation for men. Since men are the only ones who produce any music (or, forgetting Bessie, ever have produced any), it doesn't seem to be an exorbitant demand.[10]

Source: Marvin Freedman, "Here's the Lowdown on 'Two Kinds of Women,'" *Down Beat*, February 1, 1941, p. 9. Courtesy *Down Beat* magazine.

---

10. A reference to blues singer Bessie Smith. [RW]

26. It Don't Mean a Thing if It Ain't in the History Books

THE OLD EXPLANATION FOR THE SCARCITY OF WOMEN in jazz history books was that they just couldn't play well. The newer explanation (for those of us who think that it requires explanation at all) is that a real history of discrimination kept women from doing the things they would have needed to do in order to make it into jazz history. But historian Sherry Tucker (b. 1957) challenges us to acknowledge the activities of hundreds of all-women bands during the swing era, and to recognize their absence from the history books as a reflection of enduring prejudices among those who have written those books.

The challenge is not purely historical: in his ethnography of the current New York jazz scene, Alex Stewart reports that many female musicians still choose to play in all-women big bands rather than endure the discriminatory behavior they would experience in even today's mixed bands.[1]

Most of the women quoted here have passed on, but Tucker began interviewing them early enough to amass a trove of new information about how jazz was lived and breathed—even by women—during this period.

There were hundreds of all-woman bands.

A person can get some pretty interesting responses when she goes around making remarks like that.

Hundreds of all-woman bands? I'll bet.

Well, there were a couple of all-girl bands. I remember Ina Ray Hutton, she was a knockout, and Phil Spitalny, were they ever corny, but hundreds?

Oh yeah, I saw something on the International Sweethearts of Rhythm at a women's film festival. . . . All races of women living together and playing music. There were hundreds of bands like that?

All-woman bands *sounds funny. You should say* all-girl. *We were* all-girl bands *in those days.*

Almost immediately on embarking on this project, I encountered notions that all-girl bands lacked an intangible yet crucial "authenticity" possessed by men's

---

Source: Sherrie Tucker, "Introduction: 'It Don't Mean a Thing If It Ain't in the History Books," in *Swing Shift: "All-Girl" Bands of the 1940s* (Durham and London: Duke University Press, 2000), pp. 1–29. Reprinted by permission of the publisher.

1. See Alexander Stewart, *Making the Scene: Contemporary New York Big Band Jazz* (Berkeley: University of California Press, 2007).

bands. The man who answered my first telephone call to the American Federation of Musicians (AFM) local in San Francisco responded to my request for information by insisting, "Groups of housewives who got together during the war would not be considered *real bands*. They wouldn't have been professional, and they wouldn't have belonged to the union."

Ah, that explains it. All-girl bands are absent from recorded history because they weren't real!

But this opinion about all-girl bands not being professional union bands is not historically accurate. The vast majority of the women I have interviewed belonged to the union and drew wages when they played in the all-girl bands of the 1940s; some, in fact, were life members of the San Francisco local at the time the exchange just reported took place. But the comment does reveal a great deal about attitudes toward women musicians during the war years. It may also yield clues as to what structures need to be dismantled in order to make new narratives in which women musicians are visible.

It might sound odd to speak of a dominant swing discourse, yet a quick trip into the library of nostalgic swing narratives reveals a predictable recurrence of hegemonic riffs. You could almost tap your foot to it. Swing was a music of the 1930s. Benny Goodman was the king of swing. Swing was played by men instrumentalists, although sometimes warbled by women vocalists called *canaries*. All-woman bands seldom appear in dominant swing discourse, and their existence is therefore denied, first-hand reports notwithstanding. Or, in texts where one or two of the hundreds of all-women bands are permitted a type of existence, they are written about in isolation, as if each was a novelty, a gimmick, a dancing dog in the field of real music. In short, we have no good way of talking about all-*women* jazz and swing bands until we find new ways of talking about *all* jazz and swing bands.[2]

The dominant swing texts are not gender neutral (although they pass themselves off as such); they are histories of musical men. In the gender division of jazz and swing labor, the normal configuration is for men to skillfully operate instruments and for women to perform privatized popular versions of femininity with their voices and bodies. As jokes and cartoons in *Down Beat* indicate, stereotypes about "girl singers" highlighted a shortage of musical knowledge and an entertaining excess of sex appeal.[3] "Girl musicians" often inherited the girl singers' stereotype—that they

2. I am grateful to the authors of the growing library of books that attempt to forge new ways of framing jazz and swing histories, ways in which women's bands are not simply mentioned as gimmicks but contextualized historically. Books on women in jazz include Linda Dahl, *Stormy Weather: The Music and Lives of a Century of Jazzwomen* (New York: Limelight, 1989); D. Antoinette Handy, *Black Women in American Bands and Orchestras* (Metuchen, NJ: Scarecrow Press, 1981) and *The International Sweethearts of Rhythm* (Metuchen, NJ: Scarecrow Press, 1983); and Sally Placksin, *American Women in Jazz: 1900 to the Present* (New York: Wideview, 1982). Some new books on jazz and swing allude to women's participation. Among these are recent works that attend to swing in the World War II years, including Lewis Erenberg, *Swinging the Dream: Big Band Jazz and the Rebirth of American Culture* (Chicago: University of Chicago Press, 1998); Burton Peretti, *Jazz in American Culture* (Chicago: Ivan R. Dee, 1997); and David W. Stowe, *Swing Changes: Big Band Jazz in New Deal America* (Cambridge: Harvard University Press, 1994).

3. See the Lou Schurrer cartoons that appeared in *Down Beat*, 15 August 1943, 15 March and 1 July 1944. In the former, two women and a man are seen exiting a stage, arm in arm, as spectators wonder, "Are they his third or fourth wives, or two new members of the brass section?" The March 1944 cartoon is a classic derogatory depiction of a girl singer. The July 1944 cartoon features

were unskilled sex objects. But the women instrumentalists were also seen as freaks in ways that girl singers were not, especially girl musicians who played instruments thought of as masculine: drums, trumpets, saxophones, etc. When girl musicians appeared as a feminine spectacle in an all-girl band, they inherited the sexual objectification accorded dancers in chorus lines. Many women musicians with whom I spoke told stories in which they explicitly differentiated themselves from chorines—not surprising when one considers that the chorus line had been traditionally associated with prostitution since the mid-1800s.[4]

Women musicians were consumed as singers who didn't sing, dancers who didn't dance, cross-dressers who performed entertainment understood as masculine in bodies understood as feminine. Dozens of women trumpet players were dubbed "the female Louis Armstrong," drummers "the female Gene Krupa." A *Down Beat* article in 1937 described the drummer in the all-girl band the Ingenues as "a Gene Krupa in girls' clothes!" Another drummer was described in 1940 as a "skirted Krupa."[5] Like cootch dancers and female Siamese twins, women who produced big band music were viewed as both "like and unlike ordinary women": freaks, gimmicks, spectacles.[6] If they played well, they earned adjectives like *amazing, incredible,* or the ubiquitous *good for girls.*

So even if they enjoyed enthusiastic and loyal audiences, as many all-girl bands did, their popularity, often based on their ability to look like women and play like men, differed from the popularity accorded men's bands. Men simply did not walk into the same set of expectations when they entered the bandstand. Women did not have to play differently to be consumed differently. Jazz and swing musicianship is gendered before anyone blows a note. These are key elements of dominant swing discourse that we miss when we talk only about men's bands.

Producing a separate history of skilled women instrumentalists will not automatically change the structure of gender built into the histories. Rather than selecting a strategy of setting out to prove that gender is meaningless and that women's bands are as real or as skilled as men's bands, I suggest that we look more closely at gender as the feminist historian Joan Scott defines it: "a field in which power is articulated." Scott advocates producing gendered histories by studying how difference between the sexes is constructed in the following areas: representations, normative concepts, politics, and

---

a woman nonmusician unhappily sitting in the saxophone section of a men's band. Why? Her musician boyfriend can't afford to buy her a ticket. These are just some examples of the ways women's bodies were summoned by *Down Beat* to define women on the bandstand as not real musicians and thus mark the boundaries of authentic jazz.

4. The black press tended to treat chorines more respectfully than the white trades or newspapers did. Sympathetic coverage, e.g., of chorines' demands for higher pay and shorter hours at the Apollo Theater, appeared in the *Chicago Defender* (e.g., "'American Guild of Variety Artists' Takes Over," 20 March 1940, p. 20), which also covered the formation of a social organization for chorines in Harlem ("Chorines of Harlem Organize," 27 July 1940, p. 20).

5. "They Have a Gene Krupa in Girls' Clothes," *Down Beat*, April 1937, p. 21. "Anne Wallace Weds, Quits," *Down Beat*, 1 September 1940, p. 8.

6. Alto saxophonist Rosalind Cron recalled her father taking her to see a variety act in which Siamese twins, joined at the back, played saxophones while roller-skating. Her father thought she would enjoy them since the girls were about her age and played her instrument. The impact on Cron was quite the opposite; the act haunted her. Years later, she saw an obituary for these women in a magazine. They had spent their whole lives playing their saxophones, one skating backward, one skating forward (Rosalind Cron, conversation with author, 7 March 1996).

subject formation.[7] This approach might uncover new ways of understanding the gendered spaces of swing.

How was gender difference represented in the spectacles of all-girl band performances? What kinds of masculinities and femininities were represented in men's and women's bands, and how were these effects achieved through sound and image? What versions of femininity were performed, and what versions were not? How were dominant gender constructions affirmed or contested by women musicians? If normative concepts defined women as freaks if they played trumpets, trombones, and drums, what could women musicians do to secure acceptance for themselves on the bandstand? What were the politics of these normative concepts? How were they enforced by labor practices, propaganda, dominant discourses on gender, race, sexuality, and class? What kinds of identities did women develop through their band careers, through producing popular music that women were not thought to be able to play, through their experiences on the road?

In the same way that simply setting out to prove that women played in bands does not dismantle the gender constructions embedded in dominant swing discourse, discussing black women's band participation does not guarantee a departure from the ways in which race discourse operates in jazz and swing histories. The feminized spaces of swing are no more race neutral than the masculinized spaces. The swing gender analyst must diligently pose questions that account for constructions of race difference as well as sex difference. How did race discourse affect which representations were available to black and white women musicians, mixed-race women musicians, and women musicians of color who were not African American? How were concepts of normal womanhood differentiated by race, and how did these affect performance strategies of all-girl bands coded as either black or white? How did the white male subjectivity that shaped dominant jazz and swing histories affect our limited knowledge of all-girl bands? Black women who played in the all-girl bands of the 1940s inherited the same problematic history of representations of black women as "primitive and exotic creatures" that troubled novelists such as Nella Larsen but, as musicians, they also inherited the "alternative form[s] of representation" popularized by powerful blueswomen such as Ma Rainey and Bessie Smith.[8]

Another representational issue affecting the marketability of black women on the stage is colorism. In the 1920s, 1930s, and 1940s, African American women had a better chance of getting jobs in entertainment, particularly as chorines, if they were light skinned. Several members of the International Sweethearts of Rhythm have suggested that the founder of the band preferred to hire light women. According to vocalist Evelyn McGee (Stone), "Dr. Jones seemed to pride himself on getting very

---

7. See Joan Scott, *Gender and the Politics of History* (New York: Columbia University Press, 1998), pp. 42–43.

8. Hazel V. Carby, "It Jus Be's Dat Way Sometime: The Sexual Politics of Women's Blues," in Vicki L. Ruis and Ellen Carol DuBois, eds., *Unequal Sisters: A Multi-Cultural Reader in U. S. Women's History*, 2nd ed. (New York: Routledge, 1994), pp. 332–33 [see also the version reprinted, with the author's corrections, in this volume]. For Carby's analysis of how African American women novelists deconstructed and reconstructed black womanhood through depictions of race women, see her *Reconstructing Womanhood: The Emergence of the Afro-American Woman Novelist* (New York: Oxford University Press, 1987). For a fascinating analysis of how the works of Ma Rainey and Bessie Smith and other blueswomen provided a site for performers and audiences to construct a model for working-class black womanhood, see Angela Y. Davis, *Blues Legacies and Black Feminism: Gertrude "Ma" Rainey, Bessie Smith, and Billie Holiday* (New York: Pantheon, 1998).

light-skinned girls that looked white in the band. And there were some dark ones, because I'm dark. . . . And I was a little shocked. I thought I was with a lot of whites when I first joined [the Sweethearts] in Anderson, South Carolina."[9] I have mentioned that the International Sweethearts of Rhythm rarely figure in the conventional jazz and swing histories, but it is interesting to note that the Darlings of Rhythm, a band that musicians informed me tended to hire darker women, is even more conspicuously absent.[10]

Yet even when bands compliantly reproduced images of idealized white womanhood, enabling them to achieve a modicum of recognition, the resulting historiography still takes the form of mockery. In his history of the big bands, Arthur Jackson wrote, "Obviously all-girl bands would be a natural visual attraction, and if they got by on looks rather than musicianship, well, that was their prerogative."[11] But was it their prerogative? Bandleader Peggy Gilbert (who still played a mean tenor in 1995 at the age of ninety) wrote of the frustration of trying to explain to club owners—almost always men—that replacing a band member because she "doesn't smile enough, or is too fat, or her hair doesn't look just so," was not the way to "maintain a good sounding band."[12] Gilbert put her finger on precisely the dilemma: there was no place in swing discourse for a "good sounding" all-girl band that got by on musicianship rather than looks. The public imagination was not used to such a concept, and the entertainment industry did not promote the idea. In perfect collusion with this construction of common sense, the swing historian George Simon summed up Ina Ray Hutton's Melodears with the preferred verdict of his profession: "Only God can make a tree . . . and only men can play good jazz."[13] Recognition required an unequivocally drawn separate sphere, yet it was precisely this difference that set women's bands, or *all-girl bands*, as they were known, apart from serious consideration for their music.

A college textbook on jazz reports, "Because of the military draft and problems of transportation, the Swing Era came to an abrupt end at the beginning of World War II."[14] Indeed, in many histories, the war marks the demise of the Swing Era, with the draft and enlistment given as primary reasons. And the war did affect the men's bands, to be sure. According to the swing historian Ross Firestone, by August 1942, "it was estimated that every name [male] band had lost between one-quarter to one-half its personnel to the armed forces."[15] But the war affected the women's bands quite differently than it did men. All-woman jazz and swing bands, many of which

---

9. Evelyn McGee Stone, telephone interview with author, 30 November 1996.

10. The Darlings are sometimes mentioned in discussions of bandleader Clarence Love's career, but even these references betray a sense of the band not being "real." Albert McCarthy, in *Big Band Jazz* (New York: Exeter, 1974), offers complete listings of Love's men's territory bands over two decades. However, when it comes to the all-girl band that Love led between 1944 and 1946, McCarthy simply states that Love spent a couple of years "controlling an all-female band called the Darlings of Rhythm" (p. 143). The personnel are not listed, although that information was readily available in issues of the *Chicago Defender*, the *Pittsburgh Courier*, and *International Musician* of the 1940s.

11. Arthur Jackson, *The World of Big Bands* (New York: Arco, 1977), p. 78.

12. Peggy Gilbert, letter to author, 14 November 1990.

13. George T. Simon, *The Big Bands* (London: Macmillan, 1967), p. 261.

14. Paul O. W. Tanner, David W. Megill, and Maurice Gerow, *Jazz*, 7th ed. (Dubuque, Iowa: Wm. C. Brown, 1992), p. 94.

15. Ross Firestone, *Swing, Swing, Swing* (New York: Norton, 1993), p. 315.

existed in the prewar years or had players who had been working professionally since the 1920s or 1930s, were suddenly visible and in demand. New venues were open to the bands; colleges, such as Prairie View College in Texas, started all-woman bands to make up for the shortage of men; military bands, such as the Marine Corps Women's Reserve Band, were formed; civilian all-woman bands, both amateur and professional, new and already established, provided entertainment to the armed forces; the United States Services Organization (USO) featured several all-woman swing bands on its tours. The International Sweethearts of Rhythm played for the black troops in Germany in 1946, the Sharon Rogers All-Girl Band toured the Philippines, Korea, and Japan in 1945–46, and Virgil Whyte's Musical Sweethearts toured bases across the United States in 1945 and 1946.

To end discussion of the Swing Era with U.S. involvement in World War II is to ensure the continued invisibility of all-woman bands. So one of my narrative tactics is to focus on the 1940s, not because there were no all-woman bands in the 1920s and 1930s (there were many), but because the war years form a window of time in which women musicians and women's bands cannot be ignored. If we catch the 1940s in our viewfinder, we will find women.

The Swing Era is an easy deconstructive target once one realizes that, like so many popular music labels, the periodization itself is primarily a commercial construction—it did not have to be historically accurate or inclusive; all it had to do was recruit consumers from the largest affluent demographic group. Swing was an element of music many years before, but the Swing Era was the invention of the white-owned music business, developed as a lucrative way to sell black music as recorded by white artists to white consumers during a particular time period. A common failing of hegemonic American popular music historians (and one that tends to privilege promotion schemes over popular usage and meaning) is to reproduce marketing strategies as historical "epochs" instead of approaching them as advertisements that must be analyzed and problematized. *The Jazz Age, the Swing Era, West Coast Jazz,* all are marketing labels that exemplify what Amiri Baraka (*Blues People,* p. 143) has called the "cultural lag," the way that white artists in the United States have been consistently given credit for, and have often actually had the first opportunities to record, music that had been developed and performed earlier by black artists. Tom Reed has recently pointed out how the era known as *West Coast Jazz* was also a time when many black artists who had been playing jazz on the West Coast for decades were forced to go to New York if they wanted to make a living.[16]

I am not suggesting that we discard these labels, for, like the marketing strategies that constructed all-girl bands as inauthentic, rare, or ridiculous, they tell a great deal about power and ideology in the music business and the audiences that music business executives hoped to reach. David Meltzer (1993) has described the Swing Era's functions as "target[ing] an essentially white middle-class youth market into consuming swing band records, attending dances and concerts, and buying into an identity commensurate with the commercial culture of pop music" (p. 143). I suggest that we reconfigure the Swing Era not only as a youth movement through which a generation of jitterbuggers found expression, identity, and community but also as a splashy ad campaign designed to keep people putting coins in jukeboxes and lining up at dance halls, more akin to Miller Time than to a viable historical time period. Certainly, the idea of a Swing Era was meaningful to people in many other ways as

---

16. Tom Reed, *The Black Music History of Los Angeles: A Classical Pictorial History of Black Music in Los Angeles from the 1920s to 1970* (Los Angeles: Black Accent on LA, 1992), pp. 16–45.

well, but I hope that there is a way of thinking about its cultural, social, and political properties while retaining awareness of its role as an ad campaign.

When women musicians addressed sexuality in conversations with me, the dangers associated with the topic were revealed in often indirect ways. Women came out as straight. Women explained why they were single. Women outed other women (and then asked me please not to write about "that"). Sometimes before the interview began, sometimes even before they had agreed to an interview, women requested that I focus on music rather than on personal lives. When I asked one woman if the all-girl bands were safe places for nontraditional women to earn a living and live their lives, she responded by explaining how important it was not to be taken for a lesbian, whether one was a lesbian or not, because it could hurt one's own career as well as the careers of other band members. All women musicians, she told me, had to be careful not to be seen in public too often in pairs. Women musicians, straight or lesbian, had to pass as straight.

In my cross-generational and often cross-cultural interviews with women musicians, I was frequently reminded that the very strategy of coming out derives its political power within a particular historical moment that had not yet happened in the 1940s. Certainly, there were "out" nontraditional women who loved women before the gay liberation movement, but did visibility mean the same thing then that it does today? Did women who played in all-girl bands identify with such a strategy? Was the closet considered tragic in the 1940s, or was discretion valued by some sexually nontraditional people in a way that is difficult to appreciate from a post-gay liberation viewpoint? Historical reasons for valuing discretion included being blacklisted by talent agencies, losing bookings for the entire band. Indeed, several narrators expressed admiration for lesbians who protected the commercial viability of the band by being discrete. And does *coming out* mean the same thing for African American women and other women of color as it does for white women, who may have very different cultural understandings of what it means to love someone of the same sex and who are not already discriminated against because of race? African American women may have felt that they needed to protect themselves against additional obstacles to housing, jobs, etc.

"There are gays and lesbians in all occupations; why pick on all-girl bands?" one narrator challenged. Although I wanted very badly to present all-girl bands as a site where both sexually traditional and sexually nontraditional women worked together and to find out more about how music may have functioned as an occupation where women who loved women could survive, this comment and the experience of being "picked on" that it revealed made me mindful of other perspectives. Women in all-girl bands were sexualized throughout their careers. Those who played nontraditional instruments like horns aroused suspicions that they must be nontraditional in other ways as well. That the women who played in all-girl bands were stigmatized as lesbians inhibited their success in the swing industry, a realm of very clear sex boundaries that women already crossed by appearing on the bandstand instead of the dance floor and by playing in the band rather than standing in front of it in a gown. What a shock to learn that some women musicians felt that they were also being sexualized by feminist historians.

As I suggested earlier, by and large, the white men who have written the major swing histories have failed to write about women instrumentalists, especially African American women instrumentalists. I argued that this is due, not to lack of available information, but to the power of hegemony. For instance, the oral histories collected by Stanley Dance in *The World of Swing* (1974) opened many opportunities for research that Dance did not pursue. Granted, his approach improved on many jazz histories. Unlike many other chroniclers of the Swing Era, Dance focused on African-American men who were important to the development of the music, although not written about elsewhere, and he constructed his narrative in such a way that it foregrounded the musicians' own words. However, even though many men musicians referred to women musicians in their oral histories, Dance did not provide contextualization for the women so mentioned. In the middle of bandleader Claude Hopkins's narrative we find the following: "And that's how I got my experience, through Caroline Thornton, and also through Marie Lucas, another great pianist, as well as a trombone player and arranger" (Dance 1974: 32). Thanks to later work by Antoinette Handy, we now know that Lucas was a tremendously influential musician who led an African American all-woman orchestra in the Lafayette Theater in New York as early as 1915, yet Dance gives us no information on her or on Thornton.[17] In Dance's oral history of the trumpet player Jonah Jones we find the following: "We had a chance to come down to New York and try out for a job, but we missed it because a girl called Cora La Redd had a band they liked better."[18] There are multiple references to woman instrumentalists, woman bandleaders, yet Dance does nothing with these revelations. Not in his introduction, not in two panel discussions where he serves as interviewer—nowhere does Dance's authorial voice confirm the existence of women instrumentalists, women bandleaders, or all-woman bands. The two women whose oral histories are included in *The World of Swing* are singers, perfectly in keeping with the hegemonic norm.

An additional conquest of the expected story over the opening of new possibilities appears at the end of *The World of Swing*. In the appendix, Dance provides an interpretation of a roster entitled "Bands in Harlem Theatres." "The increasing use of small bands at the Apollo in the '40s is significant," he writes (keeping well within the narrative that says swing died and bop was born in 1941). But what I see dramatized in this stunning list of who played the Apollo during the war years is that the International Sweethearts of Rhythm appeared there in September 1941, January and May 1942, January 1943, February and November 1944, and March 1945—*as often* or *more often* than most men's bands large or small during those years.[19] Yet there is no listing for the Sweethearts in the index of *The World of Swing*. I also see that Eddie Durham's All-Star Girl Orchestra played the famed Apollo in September 1942, February, June, and October 1943, and April 1944. Eddie Durham appears in the index of *The World of Swing*, but his female band does not. These all-woman bands appear only in the appendix, without contextualization of any kind, just the usual directive to notice that small groups replaced the big bands in the 1940s.

Finally, I make interventions whenever possible that work toward explicitly gendering jazz and swing history. In other words, talking in a nongendered, universal way, as so many dominant swing narratives claim to do, is actually to talk about men's history. To press women into these so-called general frames will reliably render them inauthentic. Instead, I will strive toward presenting a history that looks at ways in which women and men were both present and that recognizes swing culture as a field on which specific gender constructions were affirmed, contested, performed, and consumed.

Tap your foot to this narrative. Swing was an African-American musical development in the 1920s, and it is played to the present day. Most of the people who made the most money on swing during the so-called Swing Era were white. Swing was played by both men and women, although usually segregated by gender and race. There were hundreds of all-woman bands.

---

17. Handy, *Black Women in American Bands and Orchestras*, p. 37.

18. Stanley Dance, *The World of Swing* (New York: Da Capo, 1974), p. 167.

19. Dance, *The World of Swing*, p. 404.

PART 4

The Forties

27. "Red Music"

WHY WOULD A GOVERNMENT BOTHER TO control jazz? Why should it be that "the ideological guns and sometimes even the police guns of all dictatorships are aimed at the men with the horns"?[1] Because music teaches us what it is to be human, argues the Czech writer Josef Škvorecký (1924–2012), by contradicting the simplistic divisions of politics and ideology. A critically acclaimed novelist, lecturer, and translator, Škvorecký fled Czechoslovakia after the 1968 Soviet-led invasion, settling in Canada in 1969. "Red Music" was written as a preface to his first English publication after emigrating, a collection of two novellas called *The Bass Saxophone* (1977).

Like much of Škvorecký's fiction, this memoir deals with the desire to escape politics and ideology, born of his experiences living under a series of repressive governments. The excerpt begins with Škvorecký's firsthand experience playing jazz around 1940, during the Nazi occupation of Czechoslovakia, and ends with the continued regulation and suppression of popular music in the postwar years. In fact, the Jazz Section of the Czech Musicians' Union suffered continuous governmental persecution from its formation in 1971, culminating in the trial and imprisonment of its leaders in 1987.[2] Škvorecký's story underscores the importance of the relationships and experiences that jazz offers, and furnishes an example of how the mass mediation of recordings enabled jazz to become vitally important in contexts far removed from the music's origins.

Source: Josef Škvorecký, "Preface: Red Music," in *The Bass Saxophone* (New York: Pocket Books, 1985 [1977]), pp. 3–28.

1. Josef Škvorecký, *The Bass Saxophone* (New York: Pocket Books, 1985 [19771), p. 5.

2. See Josef Škvorecký, "Hipness at Noon," originally published in *The New Republic* (December 17, 1984), reprinted in Škvorecký's *Talkin' Moscow Blues*, ed. Sam Solecki (Toronto: Lester and Orpen Dennys, 1988), pp. 109–30.

In the days when everything in life was fresh—because we were sixteen, seventeen—I used to blow tenor sax. Very poorly. Our band was called Red Music, which in fact was a misnomer, since the name had no political connotations: there was a band in Prague that called itself Blue Music and we, living in the Nazi Protectorate of Bohemia and Moravia, had no idea that in jazz blue is not a color, so we called ours Red. But if the name itself had no political connotations, our sweet, wild music did; for jazz was a sharp thorn in the sides of the power-hungry men, from Hitler to Brezhnev, who successively ruled in my native land.

What sort of political connotations? Leftist? Rightist? Racialist? Classist? Nationalist? The vocabulary of ideologists and mountebanks doesn't have a word for it. At the outset, shortly before the Second World War when my generation experienced its musical revelation, jazz didn't convey even a note of protest. (Whatever shortcomings the liberal republic of T. G. Masaryk may have had, it was a veritable paradise of cultural tolerance.) And no matter what LeRoi Jones says to the contrary, the essence of this music, this "way of making music," is not simply protest. Its essence is something far more elemental: an *élan vital,* a forceful vitality, an explosive creative energy as breathtaking as that of any true art, that may be felt even in the saddest of blues. Its effect is cathartic.

But of course, when the lives of individuals and communities are controlled by powers that themselves remain uncontrolled—slavers, czars, führers, first secretaries, marshals, generals and generalissimos, ideologists of dictatorships at either end of the spectrum—then creative energy becomes a protest. The consumptive clerk of a workingman's insurance company (whose heart had reportedly been moved by the plight of his employer's beleaguered clients) undergoes a sudden metamorphosis to become a threat to closely guarded socialism. Why? Because the visions in his *Castle,* his *Trial,* his *Amerika* are made up of too little paper and too much real life, albeit in the guise of nonrealist literature.[3] That is the way it is. How else explain the fact that so many titles on Senator Joe McCarthy's index of books to be removed from the shelves of U.S. Information Service Libraries abroad are identical to many on the index issued in Prague by the Communist Party early in the seventies? Totalitarian ideologists don't like real life (other people's) because it cannot be totally controlled; they loathe art, the product of a yearning for life, because that, too, evades control—if controlled and legislated, it perishes. But before it perishes—or when it finds refuge in some kind of *samizdat* underground—art, willy-nilly, becomes protest. Popular mass art, like jazz, becomes mass protest. That's why the ideological guns and sometimes even the police guns of all dictatorships are aimed at the men with the horns.

Red Music used to play (badly, but with the enthusiasm of sixteen-year-olds) during the reign of the most Aryan Aryan of them all and his cultural handyman, Dr. Goebbels. It was Goebbels who declared, "Now, I shall speak quite openly on the question of whether German Radio should broadcast so-called jazz music. If by jazz we mean music that is based on rhythm and entirely ignores or even shows contempt for melody, music in which rhythm is indicated primarily by the ugly sounds of whining instruments so insulting to the soul, why then we can only reply to the question entirely in the negative."[4] Which was one reason we whined and wailed, rasped and roared, using all kinds of wawa and hat mutes, some of them manufactured by

3. A reference to the three novels of Franz Kafka. [RW]

4. *Týden rozhlasu,* Prague, March 7, 1942.

ourselves. But even then, protest was one of the lesser reasons. Primarily, we loved that music that we called jazz, and that in fact was swing, the half-white progeny of Chicago and New Orleans, what our nonblowing contemporaries danced to in mountain villages, out of reach of the *Schutzpolizei*, the uniformed Security Service. For even dancing was forbidden then in the Third Reich, which was in mourning for the dead at the Battle of Stalingrad.

The revelation we experienced was one of those that can only come in one's youth, before the soul has acquired a shell from being touched by too many sensations. In my mind I can still hear, very clearly, the sound of the saxes on that old, terribly scratchy Brunswick seventy-eight spinning on a windup phonograph, with the almost illegible label: *"I've Got a Guy," Chick Webb and His Orchestra with Vocal Chorus.* Wildly sweet, soaring, swinging saxophones, the lazy and unknown voice of the unknown vocalist who left us spellbound even though we had no way of knowing that this was the great, then seventeen-year-old Ella Fitzgerald. But the message of her voice, the call of the saxes, the short wailing and weeping saxophone solo between the two vocal choruses, they all came across. Nothing could ever silence them in our hearts.

And despite Hitler and Goebbels the sweet poison of the Judeonegroid music (that was the Nazi epithet for jazz) not only endured, it prevailed—even, for a short time, in the very heart of hell, the ghetto at Terezín. The Ghetto Swingers . . . there is a photograph of them, an amateur snapshot, taken behind the walls of the Nazi-established ghetto during the brief week that they were permitted to perform—for the benefit of Swedish Red Cross officials who were visiting that Potemkin village of Nazism. They are all there, all but one of them already condemned to die, in white shirts and black ties, the slide of the trombone pointing diagonally up to the sky, pretending or maybe really experiencing the joy of rhythm, of music, perhaps a fragment of hopeless escapism.[5]

There was even a swing band in the notorious Buchenwald, made up for the most part of Czech and French prisoners. And since those were not only cruel but also absurd times, people were put behind barbed wire because of the very music that was played inside. In a concentration camp near Wiener Neustadt sat Vicherek, a guitar player who had sung Louis Armstrong's scat chorus in "Tiger Rag" and thus, according to the Nazi judge, "defiled musical culture."[6] Elsewhere in Germany several swingmen met a similar fate and one local Gauleiter issued an extraordinary (really extraordinary? in this world of ours?) set of regulations which were binding for all dance orchestras. I read them, gnashing my teeth, in Czech translation in the film weekly *Filmový Kurýr,* and fifteen years later I paraphrased them—faithfully, I am sure, since they had engraved themselves deeply on my mind—in a short story entitled "I Won't Take Back One Word":

1. Pieces in foxtrot rhythm (so-called swing) are not to exceed 20 percent of the repertoires of light orchestras and dance bands;
2. in this so-called jazz type repertoire, preference is to be given to compositions in a major key and to lyrics expressing joy in life rather than Jewishly gloomy lyrics;
3. as to tempo, preference is also to be given to brisk compositions over slow ones (so-called blues); however, the pace must not exceed a certain degree of allegro, commensurate with the Aryan sense of discipline and moderation.

5. One of the Ghetto Swingers, Eric Vogel, survived; now a music critic in the U.S.A., he wrote about them in an article in *Down Beat.*

6. Dorůžka, I. Poledňák, *Československý jazz,* Prague 1967, p. 71.

On no account will Negroid excesses in tempo (the so-called hot jazz) or in solo performances (so-called breaks) be tolerated;

4. so-called jazz compositions may contain at most 10 percent syncopation; the remainder must consist of a natural legato movement devoid of the hysterical rhythmic reverses characteristic of the music of the barbarian races and conducive to dark instincts alien to the German people (so-called riffs);
5. strictly prohibited is the use of instruments alien to the German spirit (so-called cowbells, flexatone, brushes, etc.) as well as all mutes which turn the noble sound of wind and brass instruments into a Jewish-Freemasonic yowl (so-called wa-wa, hat, etc.);
6. also prohibited are so-called drum breaks longer than half a bar in four-quarter beat (except in stylized military marches);
7. the double bass must be played solely with the bow in so-called jazz compositions;
8. plucking of the strings is prohibited, since it is damaging to the instrument and detrimental to Aryan musicality; if a so-called pizzicato effect is absolutely desirable for the character of the composition, strict care must be taken lest the string be allowed to patter on the fingerboard, which is henceforth forbidden;
9. musicians are likewise forbidden to make vocal improvisations (so-called scat);
10. all light orchestras and dance bands are advised to restrict the use of saxophones of all keys and to substitute for them the violoncello, the viola or possibly a suitable folk instrument.

When this unseemly Decalogue appeared in the story of mine in Czechoslovakia's first jazz almanac (it was in 1958), the censors of an entirely different dictatorship confiscated the entire edition. The workers in the print shop salvaged only a few copies, one of which got into the hands of Milos Forman, then a young graduate of the Film Academy in search of material for his first film. After several years of writing and arguing with the censors, we finally got official approval for our script, whereupon it was personally banned by the man who was at that time the power in the country, President Antonín Novotný. That was the end of our film. Why? Because the decrees of the old Gauleiter were once again in force, this time in the land of the victorious proletariat.

But back in the days of the swastika it was not just that one isolated German in the swing band at Buchenwald, not just the few imprisoned pure-Aryan swingmen—many far more reliable members of the master race were tainted with the sweet poison. How vividly I recall them, in their blue-gray Nazi uniforms, recently arrived from Holland with Jack Bulterman's arrangement of "Lize Likes Nobody," in exchange for copies of which we gave them the sheet music for "Deep Purple" and the next day they were off to Athens, where there were other saxophones swinging, underlined with Kansas riffs. I can see those German soldiers now, sitting in a dim corner of the Port Arthur Tavern, listening hungrily to the glowing sounds of Miloslav Zachoval's Big Band, which was the other, far better swing band in my native town of Náchod. Vainly did I dream of becoming one of Zachoval's swingers. Alas, I was found lacking in skill, and doomed to play with the abominable Red Music.

How naïve we were, how full of love and reverence. Because Dr. Goebbels had decided that the whining Judeonegroid music invented by American capitalists was not to be played in the territory of the Third Reich, we had a ball inventing aliases for legendary tunes so that they might be heard in the territory of the Third Reich after all. We played a fast piece—one of those forbidden "brisk compositions"—called

"The Wild Bull," indistinguishable to the naked ear from "Tiger Rag"; we played a slow tune, "Abendlied" or "Evening Song," and fortunately the Nazi censors had never heard the black voice singing "When the deep purple falls over sleepy garden walls. . . ." And the height of our effrontery, "The Song of Řešetová Lhota," in fact "St. Louis Blues," rang out one misty day in 1943 in eastern Bohemia, sung in Czech by a country girl, the lyrics composed so that they might elaborate on our new title for W. C. Handy's theme song: "Řešetová Lhota . . . is where I go . . . I'm on my way . . . to see my Aryan folk. . . ." In fact, we were fortunate that the local Nazis had never seen Chaplin's *The Great Dictator,* never heard the bullies sing about the "Ary-ary-ary-ary-aryans." Neither had we, of course—"The Song of Řešetová Lhota" was simply an indigenous response to Nazism.[7]

It was, like most of our songs, ostensibly the composition of a certain Mr. Jiři Patočka. You would search for his name in vain in the lists of popular composers of the time since he too was a figment of our imagination. That mythical gentleman's large repertoire also included a tune indistinguishable from "The Casa Loma Stomp." In our ignorance we hadn't the faintest idea that there was a castle of that name in distant Toronto. We believed that Casa Loma was an American band leader, one of the splendid group that included Jimmy Lunceford, Chick Webb, Andy Kirk, the Duke of Ellington (Ellington had been placed among the nobility by a Czech translator who encountered his name in an American novel and decided that this must be a member of the impoverished British aristocracy, eking out a living as a bandleader at the Cotton Club), Count Basie, Louis Armstrong, Tommy Dorsey, Benny Goodman, Glenn Miller—you name them, we knew them all. And yet we knew nothing. The hours we spent racking our brains over song titles we couldn't understand . . . "Struttin' with Some Barbecue"—the definition of the word "barbecue" in our pocket Webster didn't help at all. What on earth could it mean: "walking pompously with a piece of animal carcass roasted whole"? We knew nothing—but we knew the music. It came to us on the waves of Radio Stockholm mostly, since that was the only station that played jazz and that the Nazis didn't jam. Swedish style: four saxes, a trumpet plus rhythm—perhaps the first distinct jazz style we knew, except for big band swing. Curiously there was one film, also of Swedish provenance, that amongst all the Nazi war-propaganda films, the *Pandur Trencks* and *Ohm Kruegers,* escaped the eyes of the watchmen over the purity of Aryan culture. In translation it was entitled *The Whole School Is Dancing.* The original title appealed to us more, even though we understood no Swedish: *Swing it, magistern!* In the territory of the Third Reich, that was the movie of the war. We all fell in love with the swinging, singing Swedish girl called Alice Babs Nielsson, another reassuring indication that though we lacked knowledge we at least had an ear for jazz: much, much later she recorded with Ellington. But that film—I must have seen it at least ten times. I spent one entire Sunday in the movie theater, through the matinee, through the late afternoon show and the evening show, inconsolably sad that there was no midnight mass of *Swing it, magistern!*

"Swing it, magistern, swing it!" became one of the standard pieces played at public concerts in obscure little towns in eastern Bohemia, much to the joy of fans of swing. But of course, enemies of jazz and swing were also to be found amongst our Czech contemporaries. The milder ones were the jazz conservatives to whom swing was an outlandish modern distortion. They would just boo loudly at our concerts. The radicals, the polka buffs, did more than that. They threw apple cores at us, rotten

7. Řešetová Lhota in the title of the Czech version of "St. Louis Blues" is the equivalent of, for example, Hicktown, Backwaterville, or Hillbillyburgh.

eggs, all kinds of filth, and the legendary concerts in the legendary hick towns often ended in a brawl between the polka buffs and the fans of swing. Then the band would have to flee by the back door to save their precious instruments, irreplaceable in wartime, from the wrath of the protectors of the one and only true Czech music: the polka—played, horror of horrors, on an accordion.

The polka buffs never dared throw eggs at our Ella, though. Yes, we even had our own Goddess, our Queen of Swing, Girl Born of Rhythm, Slender Girl with Rhythm at Her Heels, our own Ella. She was white, of course, and her name was Inka Zemánková. She distinguished herself by singing Czech lyrics with an American accent, complete with the nasal twang so alien to the Czech language. My God, how we adored this buggering-up of our lovely language for we felt that all languages were lifeless if not buggered up a little. Inka's theme song was something entitled "I Like to Sing Hot," not one of Jiři Patočka's ostensible compositions but a genuine Czech effort. The lyrics describe a swinging girl strolling down Broadway with "Harlem syncopating in the distance." It contained several bars of scat, and concluded with the singer's assertion, "I like to sing Hot!" This final word, sung in English, alerted the Nazi censors, and on their instructions Inka had to replace it with the equally monosyllabic expression "z not,"—a charmingly absurd revision, for although it rhymes with "hot," the expression means exactly the opposite of singing hot music: it means singing from sheet music, from the notes.

Far from Harlem, from Chicago, from New Orleans, uninformed and naïve, we served the sacrament that verily knows no frontiers. A nucleus existed in Prague that published an underground magazine entitled *O.K.* (not an abbreviation of "Ol Korekt" but of *Okružní Korespondence,* i.e., Circulating Correspondence). Pounded out on a typewriter with about twenty almost illegible carbon copies, this underground publication (really underground, its very possession punishable by a stint in a concentration camp) was our sole source of reliable information. It was distributed through the Protectorate by lovely *krystýnky* on bicycles, the bobby-soxers of those perished times. I can see them in their longish skirts, dancing and "dipping" in the taverns of remote villages, with one fan always standing guard at the door, on the lookout for the German police. When a *Schupo* appeared over the horizon, a signal was given, and all the *krystýnky* and their boyfriends, the "dippers," would scurry to sit down to glasses of green soda-pop, listening piously to the Viennese waltz that the band had smoothly swung into. When the danger had passed, everyone jumped up, the Kansas riffs exploded, and it was swing time once again.

28. "From Somewhere in France"

A PIONEER OF FRENCH JAZZ CRITICISM AND discography, Charles Delaunay (1911–1988) also founded one of the earliest jazz periodicals *(Jazz Hot)*, established a jazz record label, hosted radio programs, and produced jazz concerts, broadcasts, and films. During World War II, he wrote this letter to *Down Beat*, offering a testimonial to the humanity and preciousness of jazz, and complaining that American popularity polls, publicity, and commercialism were trivializing it. Like many critics, he passionately admired some musicians and dismissed others with little explanation.

Delaunay repeats the story that Europeans recognized the importance of jazz before Americans did (historians disagree about whether that was actually the case). This sets up his main argument: that jazz is universal, transcending its American and African-American origins. Emerging as a vigorous cultural fusion, jazz achieved worldwide success because it was simple, direct, and natural—praise that may dangerously minimize the musicians' artistry and artifice. Jazz primitivism was particularly common in France, in part because it participated in a broader tendency in the arts, but also because it supported universalism and opposed American exceptionalism, allowing French critics and fans to participate equally in jazz. Unlike earlier critics who had emphasized the physicality of jazz, placing it on the devalued side of the Cartesian mind/body split, Delaunay's dichotomy is between the mind, which he understood to be shaped by culture, and the emotions, which he saw as natural and unconstructed. Like so many subsequent commentators, he valorized jazz by dehistoricizing it, suggesting that the music's pleasures are deeper than the reach of cultural accountability and hence ineffable. Delaunay's hope for shared human bonds is understandable, particularly amid the horrors of World War II. Yet his faith that all listeners respond alike seems contradicted by the very fact that he thought he had to make these arguments.

These lines are written from "Somewhere in France," where for months in the mud and fog, man seems to have lost all relation to civilized life and appears to be slowly

---

Source: Charles Delaunay. "Delaunay in Trenches, Writes 'Jazz Not American,' " translated from the French by Walter E. Schaap, *Down Beat*, May 1, 1940, pp. 6, 19. Courtesy of *Down Beat* Magazine.

sinking into the primeval ooze. Dear American friends, I hope you shall never know what it is like thus to be deprived of all the things, music for example (for us, specifically, jazz), which had become a part of you in normal life. Such is the present plight of your obedient servant.

For then you will realize the full value of the first musical trickle from an old radio or a hastily-repaired family phonograph. You will learn to cherish the first notes of a solo by Louis Armstrong—a voice seeming to come from a familiar world, now become distant although really it is within you, a world which *was* human. Then, then alone, will you realize the profound meaning which may be attached to such a music as jazz, and you will recognize that it represents a social and artistic phenomenon of universal significance.

For there is something else to jazz besides the pretext for emancipation which permits you to abandon your Anglo-Saxon reserve, to assume the nervous, almost neuropathic, characteristics of the jitterbug (the physical reaction of those who, although still young, lead too sedentary a life). Similarly, by equating jazz to a form of sport, you have created contests, rankings of soloists in which spectacularity (effect, outward appearance) and technique (artificiality) alone seem to count. You have started a competition for high notes and drum solos. You have fertilized the ground for the army of hangers-on, managers and publicity agents, who stage the great meets in the stadia, draw up budgets of thousands of dollars to launch some new orchestra, and bargain in the slave market for musicians who are snatched away from rival orchestras by the promise of easy money.

Competition has its place but it must not be allowed to lead us to such extremes. How remote is this sort of jazz from the true music it was in its beginnings. How many real musicians have let themselves be taken in by the glitter of an artificial and ephemeral success and have sacrificed their talent as well as the future of the music for which they once lived!

I see you smile, my American friends, at the idea that we, poor Europeans without skyscrapers or great orchestras, should proffer our opinions about a music which you have created and which you, rightly enough, should know best of all. However, there is nothing very unusual in one's not noticing the evolution of a phenomenon bound up in his every-day life and his national habits. It is easy to miss the woods for the trees. While this new Art, as we freely admit, was born in the United States, in New Orleans to be exact, it is not altogether surprising that all its originality and promise were first discovered by the intellectuals of "old" Europe, the French artistic *Avant-garde* to be specific. And this discovery took place *more than 10 years before* such enterprising businessmen as Irving Mills appeared on the scene to exploit this new art by urging it to its most improper and mediocre exhibitions.[1]

Jazz is an Art so long as it is created by Artists, so long as its creation is free and sincere. New Music, new Art—jazz was these because it was a symbol of man's emancipation, because it had the instinct to abandon the tics, conventions, and all the draperies of an Art mummified by scholastic routine, because it had the strength to find in itself its inspiration and means of expression. *Jazz is an Art because great artists such as Bechet, Armstrong, Bix, Tesch, Noone, and Harrison* knew how to create an original music from

---

1. Music publisher, impresario, record producer, and musician Irving Mills (1884–1985) managed the Duke Ellington Orchestra from 1926 to 1939 and promoted many other bands. [RW]

improvisation—the simplest, most direct, and most human of musical forms—and *swing*, an entirely new element.[2]

And jazz is not white, nor black, nor Jewish, nor Aryan, nor Chinese, nor American! It was born, so they say, in New Orleans where several hundred civilizations are mingled: *Franco-Spanish culture,* still thriving in Louisiana, from which jazz derives its artistic sensibility and wit; *Anglo-Saxon culture,* which descended the Mississippi, bringing along its spirit of methodical precision and coolness; and the *epic temperament of Negro Africa,* whence jazz draws its youth, vigor, and enthusiasm.

Jazz is much more than an American music—it is the first universal music. It may be termed international because, instead of addressing itself solely *to the mind* (which is dependent on national tradition and culture), it speaks directly *to the hearts* of men (who, when the fictions of "education," "tradition," and "nation" are ignored, are very similar, just as the Lord intended them to be).

We have here an unprecedented revolution. This art has given birth, in all parts of the world, to hundreds of clubs and orchestras of jazz, to countless numbers of collectors (jitterbugs too) and musicians. All of them may not speak the same language, but they understand each other perfectly, and *all beat the same rhythm!*

What an extraordinary contrast in an age when all political efforts seem directed toward fratricidal strife! *Is this to be a vain hope, the spectacle of a world beating the same rhythm?*

But America seems most anxious to kill off this Art which it has sired; jazz is today in the hands of racketeers of music, a commercial market in which Art has no place.

Each season, new values must be created, watered but profitable stock thrown on the market. A new musician is launched or a famous one is bought out; a few front pages, fine photographs, barrages of articles—favorable criticism is bought; some shady deals, several palms scientifically greased, and lo and behold, the new product has made its mark, the new star or orchestra is on its way to the top. The public is easily taken in. It goes around, blindly repeating: "Goodman's reign is menaced," "Killer Diller Doaks is tops," "Watch Zilch, he's sensational." And it votes unthinkingly for the "daily special," the fad of the moment.

But that doesn't make it real jazz; it's often not even music. And without commenting on the latest polls, we are not surprised, on scanning the list of 43 names suggested for leading trumpet, to find that the name of an authentic creator of jazz, the late Tommy Ladnier, is missing. We have to praise the frankness of laureate Harry James, who exclaimed: "But I'm afraid there's been a mistake. Louis Armstrong should have won. He's the greatest horn man that ever lived, and I blush when my ability and his are even mentioned together."

True jazz, the jazz created by Keppard, Dodds, Bechet, Armstrong, Noone, Bix, Tesch, and their like, might eventually have been eclipsed by the artificial glories

2. Among the musicians mentioned in Delaunay's letter are cornetists Bix Beiderbecke and Freddie Keppard, clarinetist and alto saxophonist Frank Teschemacher, clarinetists Sidney Bechet, Jimmie Noone, Benny Goodman, and Artie Shaw, trombonist Jimmy Harrison, trumpeters Louis Armstrong, Tommy Ladnier, Harry James, Bunny Berigan, and Roy Eldridge, alto saxophonist and trumpeter Benny Carter, tenor saxophonist Coleman Hawkins, and pianists Teddy Wilson, Earl Hines, Duke Ellington, and Bob Zurke. "Dodds" is probably clarinetist Johnny Dodds, rather than his brother, drummer Baby Dodds. The Francophone musicians singled out for praise are Belgian guitarist Django Reinhardt, French violinist Stephane Grappelli, and French clarinetists and saxophonists Alix Combelle and André Ekyan. [RW]

of imitators like Harry James, Berigan, Eldridge, Goodman, Shaw, Teddy Wilson, and Zurke, who are not without talent. But when occasion demands, the very same Armstrong, Bechet, Noone, Carter, Hines, and Ellington continue to prove their *indisputable supremacy.*

And so the crucial question arises: *Is Jazz condemned to die with the very persons who created it?*

We trust not, because the worldwide movement which they have aroused has assumed too great proportions for it to die aborning. Even if America should succeed in stifling the spirit of jazz, we would not be surprised to see new and authentic jazz stars appear in the international firmament. Already we can cite as examples, Django Reinhardt, Stephane Grappelli, Alix Combelle, and André Ekyan (the latter two are responsible for the first choruses of Coleman Hawkins' "Crazy Rhythm," Victor 26219). All of these merit honorable mention in the *Down Beat* poll. And the world is wide. . . .

But why waste time with predictions? *Jazz is not dead.* Just listen to Louis Armstrong or Duke Ellington's orchestra today and you'll realize that.

29. Johnny Otis Remembers Lester Young

MOST JAZZ HISTORIANS HAVE WORKED hard to separate a jazz tradition from other kinds of popular music. The career of Johnny Otis (1921–2012) illustrates how genre categories tend to conceal the complexity of musical interactions. As a drummer and vibes player, Otis played with Charlie Parker, Count Basie, and Lester Young; as a bandleader and producer, he discovered and promoted rhythm and blues singers Little Esther Phillips and Big Mama Thornton; he even charted a rock and roll hit in 1958 with "Willie and the Hand Jive." If his musical life confounded the marketing categories that are typically used to organize history, Otis's personal life displayed a parallel devotion to promoting panethnic antiracism in his profession and his community. Born to Greek immigrants, Otis came to feel "Black by persuasion" through his lifelong immersion in and passionate commitment to African-American culture.

Source: Johnny Otis, *Upside Your Head! Rhythm and Blues on Central Avenue* (Hanover, New Hampshire: University Press of New England, 1993), pp. 74–78.

His first book, *Listen to the Lambs* (1968), is an acute account of the Watts riots; his second, from which this excerpt is taken, focuses on the rich jazz/blues/rhythm and blues scene in Los Angeles during the 1940s and '50s.

This brief selection is Otis's tribute to the hipster cool and musical genius of Lester ("Prez") Young (1909–1959), one of the most influential saxophonists in history.[1] Both Young and Otis came up through the "territory bands," which were based in midwestern regional capitals but toured the surrounding areas. Both, as members of black bands, had to cope with the painful legacy of blackface minstrelsy, the nineteenth-century's most popular form of entertainment and the source of seemingly ineradicable racist stereotypes. Both found joy and strength in the music they made, as did their audiences.

Back in the forties, Lester overheard one of my friends call me "Hawk" (as in hawk nose). From that moment on, I was Lady Hawk to him. Nothing negative intended: he called everybody lady something or other. Some years later, as I was getting off the elevator at the Chicago Pershing Hotel, I heard him call out, "Hey Lady Hawk, let me see your machine-o'reenie." Don Robey had just brought me a new portable tape recorder to help me as I scouted talent for his Peacock record label. Even the most portable models weighed a ton in those days, so, I was happy to stop by his room. I would've been delighted anyhow, of course, because to spend time with Prez was to enjoy his "o'reenie, o'roonie" language and to just bask in the glow of his gentle genius.

I'd give my right arm to have the tape Lester and I made that afternoon. Somehow, through the years, it got away from me. Maybe somebody lifted it? I don't know. I wish I had it now so I could transcribe it verbatim. But I've relived it so many times in my mind that I remember a lot of what we chatted about.

LESTER: "So, the Little Esthereenie kittie was a good lick o'reenie for you, huh?"
J. O.: "Yeah, the little chick was a blessing for us. She's raisin' sand all over the country."
LESTER: "Y'all eatin' regular now . . . dig." [chuckle]
J. O.: "Yeah, and payin' the rent too, sometimes."
LESTER: "They'll be tryin' to copy her song, evonce—that's the stuff you gotta' watch, dig."

"Evonce" was another Lester Young secret punctuation word that nobody knew the actual meaning of.

As a kid, Lester was playing in the Young family band. Often this meant minstrel-type performances in the Deep South. The shows featured high-energy showmanship, often in demeaning blackface makeup and outrageous circus costumes. Lester's nephew Jimmy Tolbert explains that young Prez refused to indulge in Big Jay McNeely–style rolling-on-the-floor antics.[2] As the various family members

1. See also Billie Holiday's praise of Young, in this volume. [RW]

2. Big Jay McNeely (b. 1927) pioneered a wild, honking style of tenor sax playing that became popular in the rhythm and blues of the late 1940s. [RW]

were jumping over each other's backs, doing splits and wildly carrying on all over the stage, Lester's idea of flash was to hold his horn sideways and up high, a habit that stayed with him throughout his career.

I remember we had to put on funny hats to amuse the white folks during my time with George Morrison's band in Denver, but that was the early forties, and blackface makeup and overt Uncle Tomming was not something we had to do in Denver during that time. The cutesy hats were degrading enough, however. The older musicians used to tell us about the twenties and thirties when earning a living in the lesser territory bands hinged on one's willingness to swallow pride and act the buffoon.

The white territory bands didn't experience the same degree of humiliation. They were required to don funny hats and clown at times, but it was not racially degrading, as it was in our case. Moving from town to town in our little raggedy school buses, having to go to the back door of restaurants to get something to eat, and being turned away at flea bag hotels and having to sleep in the freezing or sweltering bus—all this was hard to take. But the biggest hardship was the funny hats and having to suffer through some of our bandleader's Uncle Tommish renditions such as "Sonny Boy" or "Shine." George Morrison was a lovely person, but he would whip out his violin at a moment's notion, sit on a stool center-stage, and do a version of "Shine" that would fill the musicians with shame and anger. The white folks loved it, of course, but this only made matters worse. George Morrison rejected the idea that this was kissin' white folk's asses. He referred to it as "Black Diplomacy" and pointed out that without the "Sonny Boy" and "Shine" features, we wouldn't be working. Of course, he had a point.

Lester came up in the twenties and thirties when experiencing what we had to bear in the forties and fifties would've been considered mild. In spite of what he went through, however, I don't hear hardship in Lester's playing. I hear a melancholy power and a lament, but I also hear a joyous celebration of life, the human spirit, and sexuality. But then, I'm a Lester Young freak. To me, Prez is the one figure who stands above the entire field of music as the guiding spirit of African American artistry.

Sweets Edison remembers that Prez "could play anything he thought of." Anyone who plays an instrument and does any improvising, knows that, like reading music, you must be a few bars ahead of yourself at all times. Your brain says, "I'm coming up to the so-and-so part, so I'll play thus and so." But we also have a little monitor sitting up there—I certainly do, because of my technical limitations—and this monitor might tell us, "Yeah, that's a great idea, but don't try it!" So, you either modify the idea or go on to safer ground.

Lester didn't have that problem. He heard something in his head and he played it.

30. A People's Music

JAZZ: A PEOPLE'S MUSIC WAS FIRST PUBLISHED in 1948, just as an anti-Communist campaign was getting under way in the United States, which may help to account for the fact that it has rarely been cited by jazz critics and historians. Yet conservative critic Max Harrison has called the book "the first mature statement of jazz criticism."[1] Its author, Sidney Finkelstein (1909–1974), combined a musicologist's familiarity with Western music history and theory, a humanist's broad knowledge of culture, a jazz fan's enthusiasm, and a Marxist critic's populist commitment. The book's title signals Finkelstein's main argument for the dignity and artistic worth of popular traditions. He saw jazz as a music of protest, born of African Americans' experiences of oppression, but also as a music of triumph, "a gift of the Negro people to America, one that should be a prized cultural treasure." Jazz points the way, Finkelstein predicted, "to a time when the artificial distinction between 'classical' and 'popular' will disappear," when "all forms will be easily accessible to people, and the only questions to be asked will be, is it good music or bad? Is it honest music or dishonest? Does it give us pleasure to know it? Does it help us to know better our fellow human beings and the world which we share with them?"[2]

Source: Sidney Finkelstein, *Jazz: A People's Music* (New York: International Publishers, 1988), pp. 55–58; 21–37; 124–33. Original publication: New York: Citadel Press, 1948. Reprinted by permission of Copyright Clearance Center, Rightslink.

1. Max Harrison, *A Jazz Retrospect* (New York: Crescendo, 1976), p. 146.

2. Sidney Finkelstein, *Jazz: A People's Music* (New York: International Publishers, 1988), pp. 19–20. For an exceedingly different evaluation of jazz by another Marxist musicologist, compare the work of Theodor W. Adorno, who saw jazz as completely contained by and complicit with the dehumanizing "culture industry." See, for example, his "Perennial Fashion—Jazz," in *Prisms*, trans. Samuel Weber and Shierry Weber (Cambridge: MIT Press, 1981 [1953]), pp. 119–32, and Max Horkheimer and Theodor W. Adorno, "The Culture Industry: Enlightenment as Mass Deception," in their *Dialectic of Enlightenment*, trans. John Cumming (New York: Continuum, 1986 [1944]), pp. 120–67. A number of scholars have defended Adorno and jazz from each other by arguing that Adorno based his critique largely on German cabaret music rather than "real" jazz. Yet the "Perennial Fashion" essay mentions Louis Armstrong by name, and more important, there is no sign that Adorno's critique would have been much affected had he heard more jazz than he did. The problem was what he heard when he heard any popular music, given his lack of grounding in its workings and traditions. This, along with the extraordinary insight and sophistication of Adorno's work on Beethoven, Bach, Schoenberg, and other composers of that tradition, makes the whole matter more complicated than that.

In the first excerpt, Finkelstein analyzes the relationship of artistic originality to commodification, suggesting that it is more complex than it is usually taken to be. The second section is his assessment of the music of Duke Ellington. In the third, he treats each of the main instruments of jazz in turn, discussing their histories, performers, techniques, and roles. Finkelstein ends with a characteristic twist: he challenges cultural hierarchy by arguing that an appreciation of the workings of jazz, and of its social significance, can enrich our understanding of classical music as well.

Melody and Originality

Jazz is an art of melody. Much of this melody consists of folk songs taken from the most varied sources, gathered up into the general body of jazz, as the spirituals took to themselves hymn tunes and square dances. In the period of flourishing New Orleans rag, blues, and stomp jazz, new melodies came from fresh sources: old French dances that were still part of the city's living music, Creole songs, minstrel show tunes and dances, songs and dances of Spanish origin, military and parade marches, funeral marches, spirituals and hymns, square dances, even the mock-oriental music often heard in vaudeville. The jazz musician loved melody. He both improvised his own melody, and played a familiar melody with deep affection, adding only the accents and phrasings that any good artist, folk or professional, adds to a work he performs. The jazz musician often added, to a sweet or non-blue melody, blue notes, breaks, and intonations, thus providing us with a fascinating combination of two musical languages in one. When we understand the dual nature of jazz music, the inseparable opposites that make up the unity of the jazz performance, the hot and sweet, the improvisation and the "straight" performance, the solo and the ensemble, the addition of personal "style" to familiar musical material, we can understand many otherwise inexplicable aspects of jazz.

We can see why so many of the great jazz players, noted for their improvisation, like Joe Oliver, Louis Armstrong, Tommy Ladnier, Johnny Dodds, Ellington and his bandsmen, Kid Ory, so often play close to an original melody, with of course the musical taste, the economy where each note makes its own plangent impact, that marks a creative artist.

We can see that jazz is not simply improvisation on "anything"; that sometimes the difference between an exciting performance and a boring one, by the same fine musicians, is simply due to the fact that the first offered to the musicians good melodic material, the second poor. Thus the latter put a strain on their creative artistry which they weren't always up to. We can understand why so many "evergreens"—blues, rags, folk melodies, even pop tunes—come up again and again in the history of jazz, and are still enjoyable today. We can see why, although each jazz player has his own technique and personality, he can also take over bodily and play with affectionate rightness another jazzman's improvisation, as Bechet plays Dodds's "Lonesome Blues" solo, as Williams plays Armstrong's "West End Blues" solo, as Griffin plays Stewart's "Boy Meets Horn," as every jazz clarinet player knows the famous "High Society," "Tiger Rag," "Weary Blues" and "Panama" solos. We can see why the definition of jazz as "pure improvisation" rose only when jazz performances were almost drowned by the flood of hack-created, tin-pan-alley tunes, and the jazz player had to fight his material to make something out of it. We can see why it is possible for a beautiful jazz music to be made out of the popular tune, when the jazz player has assimilated its idioms sufficiently to make it into a strange, free, sinuous and expressive melodic line. Not every popular tune is fit for such treatment, of course, and there is quite a transitional process required. It is the jazz theorist, much more than the player, who has been a "purist."

There is a purity worth fighting for. It is not the purity of a single style or folk material. It is the purity of honest and free musical communication against the manufactured slickness, the repetition and standardization of what were originally living musical ideas, that makes up the vast amount of "popular" music today. However, some theorists lump together as "commercial" everything that appeared in jazz after New Orleans, including in one term the most sensitive and deeply felt creative music and the most uninspired, hack imitations. They frantically attack the musician for "selling out," which is actually the selfish demand that the musician, at the price of poverty, and also the price of giving up his own right to grow, to experiment with whatever new materials and methods please him, provide the critic with the music that the critic has painfully learned to like.

The point I mentioned above, of one musician playing another's solo or composition, brings up the complicated question of "originality." It is important to remember that there are two diametrically opposed processes. One is a process basic to the development of music: of the creative musician, realizing that he is not alone in a musical world, and that he learns only by using, with appreciation, what has gone before. It is an open and honest use of influences, one musician giving credit to another for what he has brought into the musical world. The other is the prevalent tin-pan-alley process, by men with no originality, who take riffs, folk tunes or jazz ideas familiar to every musician, rearrange or embellish them enough to disguise their origin (generally ruining them in the process), and put their name to them as "original compositions."

The entire fetish of originality, which causes the most creative musicians often to be called "unoriginal" and the greatest fakers to call themselves "original" composers, is a product of commercialism. In a folk culture, music is a common language, as it is indeed in all creative music. The old blues singers used a common stock of melodies and even poetic phrases, familiar as well to their hearers. Their originality lay in the variation, embellishment, personality and fresh character they gave to this common language.

With the rise of the market and the music industry, "originality" became a necessary part of a salable commodity, and so every jazz performance as well as every piece of sheet music had to have a composer's name. Yet, if we examine the popular tunes and band performances of New Orleans, we find them a criss-cross of similarities, repetitions of phrase, re-creations of long existing folk and traditional tunes. Such are many of the tunes used by Joe Oliver, W. C. Handy, Clarence and Spencer Williams, Ferdinand [Jelly Roll] Morton, the members of the Original Dixieland Five.

What happened was that with the rise of the market system, musicians began staking out claims on songs they knew and could rearrange into usable form, like a colonist's staking out claims on virgin land. And, as in the case of the true colonist, the explorer (not the real-estate sharper who follows when the ground has been cleared), these first music writers and arrangers were pioneers. Their work has the freshness and life of pioneering exploration. They were men of enough creative ability to demand the utmost respect for their work. It is to their credit that they recognized, re-created, put together and built up into a usable form these fine germ melodies; and the pity is that not enough of it was done. These men used the music they knew as a language in which they could speak. They have nothing in common with the plagiarist, who borrows from one man so that he can disguise what he takes from another.

When Brahms was told that his First Symphony showed similarities to Beethoven's Ninth, he replied, "Any fool can see that." The test of originality, in all cases, is musical quality: the taste, inventiveness, and moving quality of the music that is produced, the something old transformed by the something new. This is entirely different from the claim of some jazz enthusiasts that improvisation is all that matters. Jazz, like all music, is a combination of the individual and the social, the inventive craftsmanship and musical thinking with the common body of musical material, each interpenetrating the other. The reason New Orleans music is still so greatly loved today is its wealth of melody, its fresh creation of a living, malleable body of folk lore. It should be, like the folk music of every country, a part of its musicians' and people's consciousness.

A folk music is not a "pure" music. Music taken from many sources becomes part of people's daily lives, their personal and social thinking. Thus used by them, it takes on new characteristics and a new unity whatever its origins. Through such a language we can see how a people live together, how they react to the world and their fellow human beings.

The Experimental Laboratory and the New Jazz

It was Edward Kennedy "Duke" Ellington who established jazz in the mind of every serious music student as an important music in its own right, needing no "popular" qualifications. After his work became known, jazz became impossible to ignore. In its handling of instrumental sound, in its power of melody, in its rightness of harmony and interweaving of melodic lines, it met every specification of good music within its small scope, and made many products of the conservatories seem, by comparison, mechanical and bloodless. Jazz was music, and the fact that it was also music of dance and song, that it was of the people in idiom and form, only opened up new and challenging ideas as to how good music really came into being.

This does not mean that Ellington's music was better than any jazz that had come before, or was even the best jazz of its time. It does not even mean that Ellington was wholly understood by those who praised him. Ellington's music was not "better" than New Orleans music. It was good for Ellington's time as New Orleans had been for its own time. Ellington used musical materials that were familiar to concert trained ears, making jazz music more listenable to them. These however do not account for his real quality. He even did some harm to jazz, although not of any permanent nature, by falling into the subtle self-deprecation forced upon members of a minority people who rise in the commercial entertainment world. We have already seen this happening in some of Armstrong's performances. Thus the "jungle" titles Ellington gave to some of his earlier works fostered a wrong characterization of both himself and jazz. The works so described were generally mixtures of blues and sweet, like the beautiful "Echoes of the Jungle." Ellington of course has fought his way out of this kind of publicity, and so a later blues work of his, very much like "Echoes of the Jungle," is given the far more meaningful title "Across the Track."

Ellington's work is in the main line of jazz. Comparisons of "better" or "worse," between works of one period and those of another, are meaningless and confusing. The struggle in art is to remain good. The world moves, and art must change. The problem of the creative artist is to do for his own time, for his own audiences, what the best achievements of the past did for their own times. This means the avoidance of meaningless repetitions of old patterns that have served their purpose. It means a constant awareness of new human and musical problems and a struggle to solve them.

This is Ellington's achievement. In his work all the elements of the old music may be found, but each completely changed, because it had to be changed. He may be called a kind of Haydn of jazz, reconstructing all the old materials of jazz in terms of the new sound demanded by his times, as Haydn brought together elements from folk song, comic opera, serenade and street music and infused them into the budding symphony.

His records, taken singly, are not obviously better than other single performances of the time. He produced, however, the most consistent stream of first-rate jazz over a period of more than fifteen years; and this was due to his ability to restore, in terms of the new conditions he had to face, something of the social character of New Orleans music. He gave jazz, in a limited way, a kind of permanent home, in which it could enjoy a degree of security and still continue to experiment. He provided, at least within the confines of his own band, an opportunity for communal music making, and on a higher technical level than had been possible in the past. At the same time, owning a keen musical curiosity and a deep personal integrity, he insisted on the right to change his music whenever he saw fit, regardless of commercial demands. It was an achievement for him to build up so phenomenal a band as he did, and hold its core together over so long a period of time. It was an achievement for him to avoid the morass of tin-pan-alley song plugging, or the blind alley of a successful "style" and remaining holed up in it. Thus he grew as a musician, and gave his fine, creative instrumentalists likewise a chance to grow.

Ellington's accomplishment was to solve the problem of form and content for the large band. He did it not by trying to play a pure New Orleans blues and stomp music, rearranged for large band, as Henderson did, but by re-creating all the elements of New Orleans music in new instrumental and harmonic terms. What emerged was a music that could be traced back to the old roots and yet sounded fresh and new. Many jazz commentators, noticing how different Ellington's music sounded from the old jazz, concluded that he had made a complete break with it. The truth is the opposite. It was because he was faithful to the essential character of the old music that his music sounded different. Experiment is, itself, a characteristic of the old jazz. If present day Dixieland performances reproduce beautifully the actual sound of the old music, Ellington continues its defiance of set patterns, its constant welcoming and absorption of new ideas, its unpredictable twists and turns.

He made the large band, of three trumpets, three trombones, four or five reeds and a four-man rhythm section as flexible, subtle and strong a music instrument as the old seven-piece band, capable of the most delicate shades of tone and the most blasting power. This was an achievement not of mechanical instrumental knowledge, but a knowledge of harmony, and mastery of the musical problem of the relation of harmony to instrumental timbre. What is unique in Ellington's instrumental sense, compared to that of other large band arrangers, is his realization that instrumental timbre is itself a part of harmony, and harmony must be understood in terms of timbre. Such an appreciation of harmony takes into consideration not only the tones directly produced by the instruments, but also the overtones. These overtones, the faintly heard tones that mix with the struck tone to produce the characteristic color or timbre of an instrument, are real tones that have their place in the musical scale. Ellington built his chords on the understanding that when two or three instruments perform together, their overtones also combine, along with the notes directly played, and either strengthen or muddy the resulting harmony. In other words, a chord played by clarinet, trumpet and trombone together, as in "Mood Indigo," is quite different from the same chord sounded on the piano. In "Mood Indigo" Ellington even added to his conscious musical thinking the microphone tone produced by the three combined instruments. Among his recent experiments in timbre has been the use of Kay Davis's wordless singing, in "Minnehaha," and "On a Turquoise Cloud."

Ellington's use of rich chord and sound effects has been assailed by jazz purists as imitating romantic or impressionist composed music. There is something laughable in their easy slinging about of names like Debussy, or Delius, as if comparison to such masters were insulting. There would be some point to the criticism if Ellington had merely borrowed from these composers, as is sometimes done by tin-pan-alley arrangers and song manufacturers. The proof of Ellington's quality lies in the force of the music itself. It sounds exactly like no music written in Europe or anywhere else. It speaks a language of its own. It has been imitated, even by European composers, far more than it has imitated anybody. The real parallel is that Ellington was working independently, and within the harrowing limitations placed upon a band leader in the cut-throat, business entertainment world, upon problems similar to those being worked upon by European composers. His achievements in orchestral sound, timbre and harmonic relations, are an addition to musical knowledge.

Ellington created not only a new sound for the large band, but also a new idiom for it; an idiom drawn partly out of the blues, partly out of popular ballad. The blues are generally the familiar, basic twelve-bar blues, but harmonically more adventurous, adding new, "dissonant" intervals to the familiar, basic, blues chords, and new chromatic notes, but giving the improvising musician the same concentrated, emotional phrases, the same ability to build a musical structure out of them, the same freedom to soar without regard for traditional diatonic harmony, as in the past. In other words, Ellington preserved the harmonic character of the blues, but developed them melodically. What he did with the popular ballad idiom was just as right, and exactly the opposite. He dropped the melodic line, which was generally meaningless, and developed the diatonic and chromatic harmonies that had entered jazz with the popular ballad, creating his own far more sinuous and interesting melody.

Not only did Ellington preserve the melodic curve of the blues, but he also preserved the antiphonal, two-voiced character of the blues, so important in preventing their degeneration into over-sweetness. One rarely hears in his music a single, sustained, melodic line, or a simple, unbroken series of riffs. There is always the antiphony, the statement and answer, found in the interplay of the solo instrument against the full band, of one instrument in dialogue with another, of brass choir against reeds. Even when the solo instrument holds the scene for a series of choruses, its solo lines are of the two-voiced character. Ellington's style and method of construction are generally based on the antiphonal contrast, duet, or "concerto" style, starting within the basic themes themselves and characterizing the entire performance.

This method has enabled Ellington to make the fullest use of the creative talents of his performers, allowing them to grow as individual masters of their instruments and as composers. Ellington's music is fundamentally his own, shaped by his taste and musical thinking. Yet, within these bounds, the complete performance is a kind of collective creation restoring, within the narrow confines of a single band, the social character of New Orleans music. Other large bands depended heavily upon solo improvisations. The Duke, however, evolved a most subtle and inventive musical style, which could set the character of an entire performance, give the soloist short phrases upon which to improvise, and provide a most inventive harmonic and instrumental backing to bring out the best in the solo. The soloist finds complete freedom to develop the possibilities of his instrument, and his creative musical ideas. The performance is relaxed, the soloist only speaking when he has something to say.

The Sound of Jazz

The primary quality which causes jazz to sound different from classical music, or sweet, tin-pan-alley music, is its use of the instrument. The jazz approach to the instrument is the opposite to the one with which we are generally familiar. According to the common conception, the music suggests the instrumentation. In jazz, the instrument creates the outlines of the music.

It is not hard to discover how we get our one-sided conception of the relation between music and the instrument. The tendency of nineteenth-century classical music was to erase from the listener's mind all consciousness of the medium of expression, and instead to arouse in the mind a sense of pictorial color or shifting psychological mood. Whether the music was intended to be thundering or ethereal, the instrumentation had to be of a pervading sweet sensuousness enabling the composer to soothe or captivate the listener. Out of the demands of this music a new kind of performer arose, a virtuoso who had to spend finger-breaking years of training simply to be able to handle the piano so that all trace of percussiveness should be eliminated, or the violin so that there should never be a scratch or harsh tone, or the orchestra so that its massed tone should rise and swell like disembodied sound. This approach to musical sound, seeking to banish from the listener's ear all consciousness of the instrument, produced its own fine, if one-sided instrumental lore. It arrives at its final absurdity in the practise of tin-pan–alley, Broadway and Hollywood, where the "arranger" orchestrates the music supplied by the "composer," as if orchestration and the actual sound of the music were nothing more than the application of some standard rules that anyone could master from a textbook.

But the instrumentation of a music, its final clothing in sound, is as much a part of a composer's thinking as its melodies. And while the science of orchestration, the relation between instrumental timbre and harmony, is an important part of musical knowledge, the fundamental law of musical creation, whether in composed music or jazz, is that the instrument suggests the music. Throughout the history of music it has always been a new instrument that made a new music possible, and this is the basis of jazz instrumentation.

We can understand the logic of this approach better when we analyze what a musical instrument is. It is an extension of the human hand and voice, a tool which adds new powers to the human mind and new subtleties to human senses. Just as the inventions of the hammer and axe opened up to human beings new possibilities of satisfying their wants, so the creation and mastery of musical instruments opened up new possibilities of creating and using the language of organized sound. This relation of the instrument to music was understood by practically all composers up to fairly recent times. It was for his grasp of the possibilities of each instrument that Mozart remains unequaled as an orchestrator, even in these days of grandiose symphony orchestras and seemingly infinite variation of sound.

The jazz treatment of the musical instrument strikes listeners, by contrast, as harsh or strident. Yet this feeling of harshness or roughness is basic to the expressive quality of jazz. When we hear people speak, we are actually listening to what would musically be harsh tones, even in a well modulated voice. Yet we don't get a sensation of harshness. In fact, a person who spoke in an almost musically pitched voice, as some actors do, would annoy us after a few minutes. Sweetness of sound was never, except in some special periods of music, a criterion of artistic quality. Expressiveness and communication is rather the criterion, and expressiveness is a matter of contrasts, of the subtle interplay of opposite timbres and colors. If we call the roughness of jazz sound "primitive," it is only because we are misled by the "old master" mellowness of most concert music heard today.

Jazz then, a product of the Negro and the most exploited people of America, a sign of their imagination, and inventiveness, their struggle to express themselves as human beings in life as well as music, has created a "new sound." Yet part of the fascination of jazz is that it is also an "old sound." It not only reveals to us the immense creative resources that lie deep in the common people. It also teaches us how to listen to music.

For the fact is that a great many classical concert goers, and musicians as well, do not really know how to listen to music. The music they hear is only a fraction of the great world of created music, and even that is often misinterpreted. The art of music, throughout its history, is one of rich improvisation, joy in exploring the possibilities of the instrument, social and communal music making, the song and dance. It is well known that many listeners, who are brought up in the average concert repertory, find contemporary music harsh and baffling, and are also somewhat baffled by the music of the eighteenth, seventeenth and previous centuries, although more respectful toward it.

Listening to jazz, the song-speech of the blues, the many-voiced structure built out of the blues by jazz improvisers, the expressive harshness and sweetness of the instrumentation, and the contrasts and combinations of timbre, listening to its powerful yet elastic rhythmic beat, making us all feel part of the same family and yet intensifying in us our individual sense of the pain and joy of life, we develop new musical ears. We enjoy the song-speech of the Italian, French and English madrigalists; the instrumental exploration of the Bach and Vivaldi concertos, in which the solo passages are so much like jazz "hot solos"; the love of the instrument in its own natural color found in the concertos and chamber music of Mozart and Haydn. We feel a beat, human, powerful, yet elastic, not too distant from jazz, in much old music; Bach in his use of dance patterns for some of his most moving arias; Haydn, in the folkish quality of so many of his symphonic movements.

And our ears become opened as well to modern music, for jazz is also one of the great bodies of modern music. Through jazz we can appreciate better the percussive sonorities of the Prokofiev Seventh Piano Sonata, or his happy use of the most unviolinistic, as well as violinistic tones, in his First Violin Concerto; the rich percussive piano, the use of folkish, violin glissandos, the intricate rhythmic patterns, of the Bartok sonatas and concertos; the song-speech of the Ives songs, and the intricate beat of his barn-dance sonata and symphonic movements; the "parade" spirit of the last movement of the Shostakovich Sixth Symphony, so much like a New Orleans march; the experiment with new scales of the Debussy works, and their fine exploration of new instrumental color combinations; the values of Vaughan Williams's use of English folk song in his symphonic works.

Nor is this re-education in music limited to the periods before and after the nineteenth century, the "concert hall" era. We begin to listen to this music as well with new ears. We find in Beethoven's piano more than a little "barrelhouse," as in the last movements of his "Pastoral" Sonata, Op. 28, and his "Appassionata," Op. 57; and we appreciate better the revolution in our understanding of Beethoven brought by a scholar like Arthur Schnabel. We find in Schubert a wealth of song and dance music. We find in Chopin not only the dreamy "salon" composer, but the Polish national composer, feeling a folk beat not only in his mazurkas and polonaises but in his nocturnes and studies. We see in Liszt not the exhibitionist some pianists make of him, but the artist testing the full range and powers of an instrument. We appreciate better, instead of decrying as "amateur," the bare, economical instrumentation of Musorgsky, the powerful "tuned percussion" of the Clock Scene in "Boris Godunov." We see how great a contribution was made to music by Verdi and Chaikovsky, in restoring to music the strong, athletic line of human song.

Jazz has given us a liberal education.

31. "Bop Is Nowhere"

MANY CONTINUITIES CONNECTED BEBOP with earlier jazz styles, but at the time it was often perceived as a musical revolution. These two excerpts present the negative reactions of a critic and some musicians: a deliberately incendiary *Down Beat* article by one D. Leon Wolff, and a 1948 interview with Louis Armstrong. Wolff heard bebop's new musical possibilities as the abandonment of artistic standards. He covers a lot of ground, disparaging by name many of the leading bop musicians and citing his favorite swing and Dixieland recordings in rebuttal. His claims that bebop is more cliched and less rhythmic than swing, that it is less fluid and more artificial, were tendentious, of course, and provoked an angry response in the next issue.

Ernest Borneman interviewed Armstrong with clarinetists Barney Bigard and Mezz Mezzrow after an international jazz festival in Nice, France. As the musicians reflect on the styles of jazz they've just heard, Armstrong emerges as one of bebop's harshest foes, praising the New Orleans revivalism of French clarinetist Claude Luter and blaming the boppers' competitiveness and "weird chords" for ruining the music business for everyone. Bigard is more tolerant, arguing that music must change as the times change, but Armstrong adamantly defends "nature" over bebop's "science."

Bop cannot continue in its present form. Its list of liabilities is staggering, and there is serious doubt whether its apparent acceptance is authentic. Many of bop's characteristics lead to the suspicion that, as a postwar fad, it will inevitably succumb to a natural reaction.

Bop violates one of the major characteristics of good art—*ease.* The best that is done, written, said, or played ordinarily gives the effect of grace and fluidity. Sam Snead hits a golf ball 280 yards with ease; the duffer nearly bursts an artery to get 200. A comedian who tries too hard usually falls flat. Good jazz, however exciting, rarely gives the impression of pressing for effect. This is true, for example, of Count Basie's early band, the Duke, and Muggsy Spanier's Ragtimers. But bop has carried frantic jazz to the ultimate. In its feverish search for the superkick, it has entered a blind alley. Bop gives itself away. Its considerable reliance on faster tempos, higher registers, and more notes per bar is in itself a strong indication of insecurity and over-compensation. The more frantic jazz gets (any jazz) the more it frustrates itself to the listener.

While not all bop is frantic (Charlie Parker, for example, is usually contained and "thoughtful"), most bop is unbeautiful. Normal standards in music (any music) have been cynically bypassed by shallow bop musicians. The thin, toneless intonation of trumpet and alto adds nothing. Grotesque phrase endings (most of them are terribly banal by now) seem almost deliberately ugly. Strained, elongated phrases add up to unpleasing tension. There is a spendthrift use of notes, often meaningless and placed at random. Clinkers pass easily in bop. Since it is doubtful whether a planned melodic line exists in most solos at up tempo, and since the bizarre is normal, complete fluffs must be greeted by a dubious silence. ("Who knows? Maybe he meant it.") One of the poorest recorded solos in jazz, an almost too-perfect illustration of this point, is Howard McGhee's side on *Jazz at the Philharmonic's Perdido.* Such an aggregation of mistaken notes coupled with the depths of taste is extremely rare, even for bop. McGhee is one of the greatest bop improvisers.

The characteristic *pound* of jazz rhythm has been discarded by bop in favor of a steady uproar. It might almost be said that bop is a-rhythmic. Ross Russell writes in *Record Changer:* "Be-bop drummers no longer try to keep time with the bass pedal . . . the principal objective is to produce a legato sound. . . . To achieve this legato effect the drummer makes almost constant use of the top cymbal." This sounds interesting and perhaps constructive, but the end result is more chaotic and stupefying than it is rhythmically satisfying to the listener. The impact of dynamics, contrasts, and *silences* is gone. In its place is a sustained crash almost without accents. Note, at the other extreme, the terrific rhythmic hypnosis of swing-propelled records such as Roy Eldridge's *Wabash Stomp,* Juan Tizol's *Zanzibar,* and Benny Goodman's *Swingtime in the Rockies.*

More than ever before, the jazz piano has been emasculated by bop into a single-finger toy, utilizing whole tone runs, banal triplets, and slurs in lieu of improvisation. The utter monotony and thinness of bop piano is characterized by Lou Levy. It goes without saying that bop has lost all feeling for the blues. It is now an exercise in "let's see what funny things *you* can do to it." Bop will never produce a blues of genuine emotion like Bob Crosby's *Milk Cow Blues* or Teddy Wilson's *Just a Mood.*

Bop solos, while complex, are in general *predictable.* Standard phrases are repeated incessantly with little or no variation. Triplets and awkward phrase endings are stereotyped. The pattern of most solos is widely spaced ascending notes and rapid whole tone or chromatic descensions. (Serge Chaloff is unusually typical.) The impression is one of emptiness, lack of form, nervousness, and a contempt for beautiful notes and ideas. It is significant that *not one bop musician was ever a well-regarded swing musician.* Thirdraters and unknowns of yesterday are today's geniuses of bop. McGhee was nowhere, as were Parker, Fats Navarro, Thelonious Monk, Max Roach, Tadd Dameron, and Stan Getz. The major figure, Dizzy Gillespie, was a sideman with Jimmie Lunceford chiefly noted for his ability to hit high notes.[1] The greatest swingmen have largely spurned bop. It is inconceivable to assume that their playing and their medium has suddenly become inferior to that of former inferiors.

Bop, essentially, is an aberration in jazz, a frenetic experiment replete with cliches. It is ballyhooed as the "new direction." Some of its innovations, a few of its creators, are not without merit. But whatever path jazz takes, it is doubtful whether this will be it. There is no future in bop, though a very few of its devices may be incorporated in the jazz repertoire. The Mississippi may be deflected a mile or two, but it is not likely to be rerouted due east via Jackrabbit creek.

---

1. Gillespie played not with Jimmie Lunceford but most famously with the big bands of Cab Calloway and Earl Hines. [RW]

Source: D. Leon Wolff, "Bop Nowhere, Armstrong Just a Myth, Says Wolff," *Down Beat,* June 17, 1949, pp. 1, 19. Courtesy of *Down Beat* Magazine.

BORNEMAN: Well, now that it's all over, what do you think the verdict is going to be in the cold light of the morning after?

MEZZROW: If it proves anything, it shows that jazz is the greatest diplomat of them all. Did you dig those young French cats playing like Joe Oliver? Man, that's old Johnny Dodds on clarinet and Baby on woodblocks. And that's thirty years later and in another country. If that's not the great leveller, I don't know what is.

BIGARD: You mean Claude Luter? You must be kidding.

MEZZROW: What do you mean kidding? Those cats sound real good to me.

BIGARD: They're out of tune so bad it hurts your ears.

ARMSTRONG: You're always knocking somebody, pops. I say that little French band plays fine. I could take them youngsters up to the Savoy and bring the walls down with them any day.

BIGARD: That's because you can take any kind of outfit and blow everyone else out of the room.

ARMSTRONG: That's a fine band, pops. That little cornet player sounds just like Mutt Carey to me. I can hear all them pretty little things Mutt used to do when that boy gets up and plays. That's the real music, man.

BIGARD: Real music! Who wants to play like those folks thirty years ago?

ARMSTRONG: You see, pops, that's the kind of talk that's ruining the music. Everybody trying to do something new, no one trying to learn the fundaments first. All them young cats playing them weird chords. And what happens? No one's working.

BIGARD: But Louis, you got to do something different, you got to move along with the times.

ARMSTRONG: I'm doing something different all the time, but I always think of them fine old cats way down in New Orleans—Joe and Bunk and Tio and Buddy Bolden—and when I play my music, that's what I'm listening to. The way they phrased so pretty and always on the melody, and none of that out-of-the-world music, that pipe-dream music, that whole modern malice.

BORNEMAN: What do you mean by that, Louis?

ARMSTRONG: I mean all them young cats along the Street with their horns wrapped in a stocking and they say "Pay me first, pops, and then I'll play a note for you," and you know that's not the way any good music ever got made. You got to like playing pretty things if you're ever going to be any good blowing your horn. These young cats now they want to make money first and the hell with the music. And then they want to carve everyone else because they're full of malice, and all they want to do is show you up, and any old way will do as long as its different from the way you played it before. So you get all them weird chords which don't mean nothing, and first people get curious about it just because it's new, but soon they get tired of it because it's really no good and you got no melody to remember and no beat to dance to. So they're all poor again and nobody is working, and that's what that modern malice done for you.

MEZZROW: Because they're full of a frustration, full of neuroses, and then they blow their top 'cause they don't know where to go from here. All they know is they want to be different, but that's not enough, you can't be negative all the time, you got to be positive about it, you can't just say all the time "That's old, that stinks, let's do something new, let's be different." Different what way? Go where? You can't take no for an answer all the time. You got to have a tradition. They lost it. Now they're like babes in the wood, crying for mammy. Poor little guys, and one after the other blows his top. They ought to see a psycho-analyst before they start playing music. We made a blues about it for King Jazz, and we called it *The Blues and Freud.*

BIGARD: But we're in a new age now, man. It's a nervous age, you got to bring it out in your music.

ARMSTRONG: When they're down, you gotta help them up, not push them in still deeper.

BIGARD: You can say that because you're a genius. I'm just an average clarinet player. . . . It's all so easy for you to talk because you're an exception in everything. We others just got to keep scuffling, and if they want us to play bop, we gotta play bop. It don't matter if we like it or not.

ARMSTRONG: No, that's because I got some respect for the old folks who played trumpet before me. I'm not trying to carve them and do something different. That's the sure way to lose your style. They say to you "I got to be different. I got to develop a style of my own." And then all they do is try and not play like you do. That's not the way to do anything right. That's the sure way you'll never get any style of your own. . . . You see, pops, it's worst with the trumpet players because the trumpet is an instrument full of temptation. All the young cats want to kill papa, so they start forcing their tone. Did you listen to ——— last night? He was trying to do my piece, make fun of me. But did you hear his tone? 'Nuff said. . . .

Pops, I'll tell you what it's all about. Just look at the Street today.[2] Don't let me tell you nothing. Just look at the Street. They've thrown out the bands and put in a lot of chicks taking their clothes off. That's what that bop music has done for the business. And look at them young cats too proud to play their horns if you don't pay them more than the old-timers. 'Cause if they play for fun they aren't king no more. So they're not working but once in a while and then they play one note and nobody knows if it's the right note or just one of them weird things where you can always make like that was just the note you were trying to hit. And that's what they call science. Not play their horns the natural way. Not play the melody. And then they're surprised they get thrown out and have strippers put in their place.

BIGARD: Well, I don't know.

ARMSTRONG: Well, you oughta know, pops, you've been around long enough. Look at the legit composers always going back to folk tunes, the simple things, where it all comes from. So they'll come back to us when all the shouting about bop and science is over, because they can't make up their own tunes, and all they can do is embroider it so much you can't see the design no more.

MEZZROW: But it won't last.

ARMSTRONG: It can't last. They always say "Jazz is dead" and then they always come back to jazz.

Source: "'Bop Will Kill Business Unless It Kills Itself First'—Louis Armstrong," *Down Beat,* April 7, 1948, pp. 2–3. Courtesy of *Down Beat* Magazine.

---

2. 52nd Street in New York, particularly between Fifth and Sixth Avenues, where many of the city's most famous jazz nightclubs flourished from the mid-1930s to the mid-1940s. [RW]

32. To Be or Not . . . to Bop

LIKE RAGTIME, HOT JAZZ, SWING, FREE JAZZ, blues, rock, and rap—or, for that matter, twelfth-century polyphony and Stravinsky's *Rite of Spring*—bebop was initially attacked as unmusical and immoral. Some jazz critics and musicians condemned the new style, but more damaging was the sensationalistic media coverage it received. With his beret, goatee, and horn-rimmed glasses, Dizzy (John Birks) Gillespie (1917–1993) became the genre's icon. Offended by popular conceptions of the music and its subculture, Gillespie devoted a chapter of his 1979 autobiography, *To Be, Or Not . . . To Bop*, to setting the record straight

Gillespie had established himself as a player in the big swing bands of Teddy Hill, Cab Calloway, Earl Hines, Duke Ellington, and others; he later led a big band himself, where he experimented successfully with Afro-Cuban rhythms and percussion instruments. But he is best remembered for his work in small combos, where he and alto saxophonist Charlie Parker set new speed records for instrumental virtuosity and musical imagination. One of the most influential trumpeters in history, Gillespie is usually given chief credit, along with Parker, for developing the genre of bebop during the early 1940s.

In this chapter, Gillespie challenges eleven popular myths about bebop, minimizing the importance of fashions and drugs so that he can underscore the seriousness, artistry, and creativity of the music. Without abandoning the sense of hilarity that won him his nickname, he explains the music's complex social context, where strategies for operating in a racist environment included searching for African roots, converting to Islam, and taking great pride in African-American heroes such as heavyweight boxing champion Joe Louis or singer, actor, and black activist Paul Robeson.

Around 1946, jive-ass stories about "beboppers" circulated and began popping up in the news. Generally, I felt happy for the publicity, but I found it disturbing to have modern jazz musicians and their followers characterized in a way that was often sinister and downright vicious. This image wasn't altogether the fault of the press because many followers, trying to be "in," were actually doing some of the things the press accused beboppers of—and worse. I wondered whether all the "weird"

Source: Dizzy Gillespie with Al Fraser, *To Be, Or Not . . . To Bop* (New York: Doubleday, 1979), excerpted from pp. 278–302 and facing p. 483.

publicity actually drew some of these way-out elements to us and did the music more harm than good. Stereotypes, which exploited whatever our weaknesses might be, emerged. Suable things were said, but nothing about the good we were doing and our contributions to music.

Time magazine, March 25, 1946, remarked: "As such things usually do, it began on Manhattan's 52nd Street. A bandleader named John (Dizzy) Gillespie, looking for a way to emphasize the more beautiful notes in 'Swing,' explained: 'When you hum it, you just naturally say bebop, be-de-bop. . . .'

"Today, the bigwig of bebop is a scat named Harry (the Hipster) Gibson, who in moments of supreme pianistic ecstasy throws his feet on the keyboard. No. 2 man is Bulee (Slim) Gaillard, a skyscraping zooty Negro guitarist. Gibson and Gaillard have recorded such hip numbers as 'Cement Mixer,' which has sold more than 20,000 discs in Los Angeles alone; 'Yeproc Here-say,' Dreisix Cents,' and 'Who Put the Benzedrine in Mrs. Murphy's Ovaltine?' "

The article discussed a ban on radio broadcasts of bebop records in Los Angeles where station KMPC considered it a "degenerative influence on youth" and described how the "nightclub where Gibson and Gaillard played" was "more crowded than ever" with teen-agers who wanted to be bebopped. "What bebop amounts to: hot jazz overheated, with overdone lyrics full of bawdiness, references to narcotics and doubletalk."

Once it got inside the marketplace, our style was subverted by the press and music industry. First, the personalities and weaknesses of the in people started becoming more important, in the public eye, than the music itself. Then they diluted the music. They took what were otherwise blues and pop tunes, added "mop, mop" accents and lyrics about abusing drugs wherever they could and called the noise that resulted bebop. Labeled bebop like our music, this synthetic sound was played heavily on commercial radio everywhere, giving bebop a bad name. No matter how bad the imitation sounded, youngsters and people who were musically untrained liked it, and it sold well because it maintained a very danceable beat. The accusations in the press pointed to me as one of the prime movers behind this. I should've sued, even though the chances of winning in court were slim. It was all bullshit.

Keeping in mind that a well-told lie usually contains a germ of truth, let's examine the charges and see how many of those stereotypes actually applied to me.

Lie number one was that beboppers wore wild clothes and dark glasses at night. Watch the fashions of the forties on the late show, long coats, almost down to your knees and full trousers. I wore drape suits like everyone else and dressed no differently from the average leading man of the day. It was beautiful. I became pretty dandified, I guess, later during the bebop era when my pants were pegged slightly at the bottom, but not unlike the modestly flared bottoms on the slacks of the smart set today.

We had costumes for the stage—uniforms with wide lapels and belts—given to us by a tailor in Chicago who designed them, but we didn't wear them offstage. Later, we removed the wide lapels and sported little tan cashmere jackets with no lapels. This was a trendsetting innovation because it made no sense at all to pay for a wide lapel. *Esquire* magazine, 1943, America's leading influence on men's fashions, considered us elegant, though bold, and printed our photographs.

Perhaps I remembered France and started wearing the beret. But I used it as headgear I could stuff into my pocket and keep moving. I used to lose my hat a lot. I liked to wear a hat like most of the guys then, and the hats I kept losing cost five dollars apiece. At a few recording sessions when I couldn't lay my hands on a mute, I covered the bell of the trumpet with the beret. Since I'd been designated their "leader," cats just picked up the style.

My first pair of eyeglasses, some rimless eyeglasses, came from Maurice Guilden, an optometrist at the Theresa Hotel, but they'd get broken all the time, so I picked up a pair of horn rims. I never wore glasses until 1940. As a child, I had some minor problems with vision. When I'd wake up in the morning, I couldn't open my eyelids—they'd stick together. My mother gave me a piece of cotton; someone told her that urine would help. Every time I urinated, I took a piece of cotton and dabbed my eyes with it. It cured me. I read now without glasses and only use glasses for distance. Someone coming from the night who saw me wearing dark glasses onstage to shield my eyes from the glare of the spotlights might misinterpret their meaning. Wearing dark glasses at night could only worsen my eyesight. I never wore dark glasses at night. I had to be careful about my eyes because I needed them to see music.

Lie number two was that only beboppers wore beards, goatees, and other facial hair and adornments. I used to shave under my lip. That spot prickled and itched with scraping. The hair growing back felt uncomfortable under my mouthpiece, so I let the hair grow into a goatee during my days with Cab Calloway. Now a trademark, that tuft of hair cushions my mouthpiece and is quite useful to me as a player; at least I've always thought it allowed me to play more effectively. Girls like my goatee too.

I used to wear a mustache, thinking you couldn't play well without one. One day I cut it off accidentally and had to play, and I've been playing without a mustache ever since. Some guy called me "weird" because he looked at me and thought he saw only half a mustache. The dark spot above my upper lip is actually a callus that formed because of my embouchure. The right side of my upper lip curls down into the mouthpiece when I form my embouchure to play.

Many modern jazz musicians wore no facial hair at all. Anyway, we weren't the only ones during those days with hair on our faces. What about Clark Gable?

Number three: that beboppers spoke mostly in slang or tried to talk like Negroes is not so untrue. We used a few "pig Latin" words like "ofay." Pig Latin as a way of speaking emerged among blacks long before our time as a secret language for keeping children and the uninitiated from listening to adult conversations. Also, blacks had a lot of words they brought with them from Africa, some of which crept over into general usage, like "yum-yum."

Most bebop language came about because some guy said something and it stuck. Another guy started using it, then another one, and before you knew it, we had a whole language. "Mezz" meant "pot," because Mezz Mezzrow was selling the best pot. When's the "eagle gonna" fly, the American eagle, meant payday. A "razor" implied the draft from a window in winter with cold air coming in, since it cut like a razor. We added some colorful and creative concepts to the English language, but I can't think of any word besides bebop that I actually invented. Daddy-O Daylie, a disc jockey in Chicago, originated much more of the hip language during our era than I did.

We didn't have to try; as black people we just naturally spoke that way. People who wished to communicate with us had to consider our manner of speech, and sometimes they adopted it. As we played with musical notes, bending them into new and different meanings that constantly changed, we played with words.

Number four: that beboppers had a penchant for loose sex and partners racially different from themselves, especially black men who desired white women, was a lie.

It's easy for a white person to become associated with jazz musicians, because most of the places we play are owned and patronized by whites. A good example is Pannonica Koenigswater, the baroness, who is the daughter of a Rothschild. She'll be noticed when she shows up in a jazz club over two or three times. Nica has helped jazz musicians, financially. She saw to it that a lotta guys who had no place to stay had a roof or put some money in their pockets. She's willing to spend a lot to help.

There's not too much difference between black and white women, but you'll find that to gain a point, a white woman will do almost anything to help if it's something that she likes. There's almost nothing, if a white woman sees it's to her advantage, that she won't do because she's been taught that the world is hers to do with as she wants. This shocks the average black musician who realizes that black women wouldn't generally accept giving so much without receiving something definite in return.

A black woman might say: "I'll love him . . . but not my money." But a white woman will give anything, even her money, to show her own strength. She'll be there on the job, every night, sitting there supporting her own goodies. She'll do it for kicks, whatever is her kick. Many white women were great fans and supporters of modem jazz and brought along white males to hear our music. That's a secret of this business: Where a woman goes, the man goes.

"Where you wanna go, baby?"

"I wanna go hear Dizzy."

"O.K., that's where we go." The man may not support you, but the woman does, and he spends his money.[1]

As a patron of the arts in this society, the white woman's role, since white males have been so preoccupied with making money, brought her into close contact with modern jazz musicians and created relationships that were often very helpful to the growth of our art. Some of these relationships became very personal and even sexual but not necessarily so. Often, they were supportive friendships which the musicians and their patrons enjoyed. Personally, I haven't received much help from white female benefactors. All the help I needed, I got from my wife—an outspoken black woman, who will not let me mess with the money—to whom I've been married since 1940. Regarding friendships across racial lines, because white males would sometimes lend their personal support to our music, the bebop era, socially speaking, was a major concrete effort of progressive-thinking black and white males and females to tear down and abolish the ignorance and racial barriers that were stifling the growth of any true culture in modern America.

Number five: that beboppers used and abused drugs and alcohol is not completely a lie either. They used to tell jokes about it. One bebopper walked up to another and said, "Are you gonna flat your fifths tonight?" The other one answered, "No, I'm going to drink mine." That's a typical joke about beboppers.

When I came to New York, in 1937, I didn't drink or smoke marijuana. "You gonna be a square, muthafucka!" Charlie Shavers said and turned me on to smoking pot. Now, certainly, we were not the only ones. Some of the older musicians had been smoking reefers for forty and fifty years. Jazz musicians, the old ones and the young ones, almost all of them that I knew smoked pot, but I wouldn't call that drug abuse.

The first guy I knew to "take off" was Steve, a trumpet player with Jimmie Lunceford, a young college kid who came to New York and got hung up on dope. Everybody talked about him and said, "That guy's a dope addict! Stay away from him because he uses shit." Boy, to say that was really stupid, because how else could you help that kinda guy?

Dope, heroin abuse, really got to be a major problem during the bebop era, especially in the late forties, and a lotta guys died from it. Cats were always getting "busted" with drugs by the police, and they had a saying, "To get the best band, go to KY." That meant the "best band" was in Lexington, Kentucky, at the federal

---

1. Here Gillespie echoes the author of "Here's the Lowdown on 'Two Kinds of Women' "—but without the resentment! See "Jazz and Gender During the War Years," earlier in this volume. [RW]

narcotics hospital. Why did it happen? The style of life moved so fast, and cats were struggling to keep up. It was wartime, everybody was uptight. They probably wanted something to take their minds off all the killing and dying and the cares of this world. The war in Vietnam most likely excited the recent upsurge in heroin abuse, together with federal narcotics control policies which, strangely, at certain points in history, encouraged narcotics abuse, especially among young blacks.

Everybody at one time or another smoked marijuana, and then coke became popular—I did that one too; but I never had any desire to use hard drugs, a drug that would make you a slave. I always shied away from anything powerful enough to make me dependent, because realizing that everything here comes and goes, why be dependent on any one thing? I never even tried hard drugs. One time on Fifty-second Street a guy gave me something I took for coke and it turned out to be horse. I snorted it and puked up in the street. If I had found him, he would have suffered bodily harm, but I never saw him again.

With drugs like benzedrine, we played practical jokes. One record date for Continental, with Rubberlegs Williams, a blues singer, I especially remember. Somebody had this date—Clyde Hart, I believe. He got Charlie Parker, me, Oscar Pettiford, Don Byas, Trummy Young, and Specs Powell. The music didn't work up quite right at first. Now, at that time, we used to break open inhalers and put the stuff into coffee or Coca-Cola; it was a kick then. During a break at this record date, Charlie dropped some into Rubberlegs's coffee. Rubberlegs didn't drink or smoke or anything. He couldn't taste it. So we went on with the record date. Rubberlegs began moaning and crying as he was singing. You should hear those records! But I wouldn't condone doing that now; Rubberlegs might've gotten sick or something. The whole point is that, like most Americans, we were really ignorant about the helpful or deleterious effects of drugs on human beings, and before we concluded anything about drugs or used them and got snagged, we should have understood what we were doing. That holds true for the individual or the society, I believe.

The drug scourge of the forties victimized black musicians first, before hitting any other large segment of the black community. But if a cat had his head together, nothing like that, requiring his own indulgence, could've stopped him. I've always believed that. I knew several guys that were real hip, musically, and hip about life who never got high. Getting high wasn't one of the prerequisites for being hip, and to say it was would be inaccurate.

Number six is really a trick: that beboppers tended to express unpatriotic attitudes regarding segregation, economic injustice, and the American way of life.

We never wished to be restricted to just an American context, for we were creators in an art form which grew from universal roots and which had proved it possessed universal appeal. Damn right! We refused to accept racism, poverty, or economic exploitation, nor would we live out uncreative humdrum lives merely for the sake of survival. But there was nothing unpatriotic about it. If America wouldn't honor its Constitution and respect us as men, we couldn't give a shit about the American way. And they made it damn near un-American to appreciate our music.

Music drew Charlie Parker and me together, but Charlie Parker used to read a lot too. As a great reader, he knew about everything, and we used to discuss politics, philosophy, and life-style. I remember him mentioning Baudelaire—I think he died of syphilis—and Charlie used to talk about him all the time. Charlie was very much interested in the social order, and we'd have these long conversations about it, and music. We discussed local politics, too, people like Vito Marcantonio, and what he'd tried to do for the little man in New York. We liked Marcantonio's ideas because as musicians we weren't paid well at all for what we created.

There were a bunch of musicians more socially minded, who were closely connected with the Communist Party. Those guys stayed busy anywhere labor was concerned. I never got that involved politically. I would picket, if necessary, and remember twice being on a picket line. I can't remember just what it was I was picketing for, but they had me walking around with a sign. Now, I would never cross a picket line.

Paul Robeson became the forerunner of Martin Luther King. I'll always remember Paul Robeson as a politically-committed artist. A few enlightened musicians recognized the importance of Paul Robeson, amongst them Teddy Wilson, Frankie Newton, and Pete Seeger—all of them very outspoken politically. Pete Seeger is so warm; if you meet Pete Seeger, he just melts, he's so warm. He's a great man.

In my religious faith—the Baha'i faith—the Bab is the forerunner of Baha'u'llah, the prophet. "Bab" means gate, and Paul Robeson was the "gate" to Martin Luther King. The people in power made Paul Robeson a martyr, but he didn't die immediately from his persecution. He became a martyr because if you are strangled for your principles, whether it's physical strangulation or mental strangulation or social strangulation, you suffer. The dues that Paul Robeson paid were worse than the dues Martin Luther King paid. Martin Luther only paid his life, quick, for his views, but Paul Robeson had to suffer a very long time.

When the play *Othello* opened in New York with Paul Robeson, Jose Ferrer, and Uta Hagen, I went to the theater to see it. I was sitting way up in the highest balcony. Paul Robeson's voice sounded like we were talking together in a room. That's how strong his voice was coming from the stage, three miles away. Paul Robeson, big as he was, looked about as big as a cigar from where I was sitting. But his voice was right up there next to me.

I dug Paul Robeson right away, from the first words. A lot of black people were against Paul Robeson; he was trying to help them and they were talking against him, like he was a communist. I heard him speak on many occasions and, man, talk about a speaker! He could really speak. And he was fearless! You never hear people speak out like he did with everything arrayed against you and come out like he did. Man, I'll remember Paul Robeson until I die. He was something else.

Paul Robeson became "Mr. Incorruptibility." No one could get to him because that's the rarest quality in man, incorruptibility. Nothing supersedes that because, man, there are so many ways to corrupt a personality. Paul Robeson stands as a hero of mine and he was truly the father of Malcolm X, another dynamic personality who I talked to a lot. Oh, I loved Malcolm, and you couldn't corrupt Malcolm or Paul. We have a lot of leaders that money corrupts, and power. You give them a little money and some power, and they nut. They go nuts with it. Both Malcolm and Paul Robeson, you couldn't get to them. The people in power tried all means at their disposal to get them. So they killed Malcolm X and they destroyed Paul Robeson. But they stood up all the time. Even dying, their heads were up.

One time, on the Rudy Vallee show, I should've acted more politically. Rudy Vallee says, introducing me, "What's in the Ubangi department tonight?"[2] I almost walked off the show. I wanted to sue him but figured there wasn't any money in it, so I just forgot about it and we played. Musicians today would never accept that, but then, somehow, the money and the chance to be heard seemed more important.

We had other fighters, like Joe Louis, who was beautiful. I've known Joe Louis since way, way back when I hung out in Sugar Ray's all the time, playing checkers.

---

2. "Ubangi" is a general name for various groups of people who live in the Congo Basin of Africa. Vallee (and others) used it as a demeaning reference to African Americans. [RW]

Sugar Ray's a good checker player, but dig Joe Louis. He'd come down to hear me play, and people would want Joe Louis to have a ringside seat. He'd be waaay over in a corner someplace, sitting there digging the music. If you announced him, "Ladies and gentlemen, the heavyweight champion of the world, Joe Louis, is sitting over there," he'd stand up to take a bow and wave his hands one time. You look around again, he's gone. Other guys I know would want a ringside seat, want you to announce them and maybe come up on the stage. But Joe Louis was like that. He was always shy, beautiful dude. He had mother wit.

It's very good to know you're a part of something that has directly influenced your own cultural history. But where being black is concerned, it's only what I represent, not me, myself. I pay very little attention to "Dizzy Gillespie," but I'm happy to have made a contribution. To be a "hero" in the black community, all you have to do is make the white folks look up to you and recognize the fact that you've contributed something worthwhile. Laugh, but it's the truth. Black people appreciate my playing in the same way I looked up to Paul Robeson or to Joe Louis. When Joe would knock out someone, I'd say, "Hey . . . !" and feel like I'd scored a knockout. Just because of his prowess in his field and because he's black like me.

Oh, there was a guy in Harlem, up there on the corner all the time preaching. Boy, could he talk about white people! He'd get a little soap box. I don't know his name, but everybody knew him. He wasn't dressed all fancy, or nothing, and then he had a flag, an American flag. Ha! Ha! That's how I became involved with the African movement, standing out there listening to him. An African fellow named Kingsley Azumba Mbadiwe asked me who I was and where I came from. I knew all the right answers. That was pretty hip being from South Carolina and not having been in New York too long. Out friendship grew from there; and I became attached to this African brother. One time, after the Harlem riots, 1945, Mbadiwe told me, "Man, these white people are funny here."

"Whaddayou mean . . . ?"

"Well, they told me to stay outta Harlem," he said.

"Why is that?" I asked.

"They say that it's dangerous for me up here. I might get killed."

"What'd you tell them?"

"Well, I asked them how they gonna distinguish me from anybody else up here? I look just like the rest of them."

Heh, heh, heh. It was at that time I observed that the white people didn't like the "spooks" over here to get too close to the Africans. They didn't want us—the spooks over here—to know anything about Africa. They wanted you to just think you're somebody dangling out there, not like the white Americans who can tell you they're German or French or Italian. They didn't want us to know we have a line so that when you'd ask us, all we could say was we were "colored." It's strange how the white people tried to keep us separate from the Africans and from our heritage. That's why, today, you don't hear in our music, as much as you do in other parts of the world, African heritage, because they took our drums away from us. If you go to Brazil, to Bahia where there is a large black population, you find a lot of African in their music; you go to Cuba, you find they retained their heritage; in the West Indies, you find a lot. In fact, I went to Kenya and heard those cats play and I said, "You guys sound like you're playing calypso from the West Indies."

A guy laughed and he said to me, "Don't forget, we were first!"

But over here, they took our drums away from us, for the simple reason of self-protection when they found out those cats could communicate four or five miles with the drums. They took our language away from us and made us speak English.

In slavery times, if they found out that two slaves could speak the same African language, they sold off one. As far as our heritage goes, a few words creeped in like *buckra*—I used to hear my mother say, "that ole poor buckra"—buckra meant white. But with those few exceptions when they took our drums away, our music developed along a monorhythmic line. It wasn't polyrhythmic like African music. I always knew rhythm or I was interested in it, and it was this interest in rhythm that led me to seize every opportunity to find out about these connections with Africa and African music.

Charlie Parker and I played benefits for the African students in New York and the African Academy of Arts and Research which was headed by Kingsley Azumba Mbadiwe. Eventually, Mbadiwe wound up becoming a minister of state in Nigeria under one of those regimes, but over here, as head of the African Academy, he arranged for us to play some benefit concerts at the Diplomat Hotel which should've been recorded. Just me, Bird, and Max Roach, with African drummers and Cuban drummers; no bass, nothing else. We also played for a dancer they had, named Asadata Dafora.[3] (A-S-A-D-A-T-A D-A-F-O-R-A—if you can say it, you can spell it.) Those concerts for the African Academy of Arts and Research turned out to be tremendous. Through that experience, Charlie Parker and I found the connections between Afro-Cuban and African music and discovered the identity of our music with theirs. Those concerts should definitely have been recorded, because we had a ball, discovering our identity.

Within the society, we did the same thing we did with the music. First we learned the proper way and then we improvised on that. It seemed the natural thing to do because the style or mode of life among black folks went the same way as the direction of the music. Yes, sometimes the music comes first and the life-style reflects the music because music is some very strong stuff, though life in itself is bigger. Artists are always in the vanguard of social change, but we didn't go out and make speeches or say "Let's play eight bars of protest." We just played our music and let it go at that. The music proclaimed our identity; it made every statement we truly wanted to make.

Number seven: that "beboppers" expressed a preference for religions other than Christianity may be considered only a half-truth, because most black musicians, including those from the bebop era, received their initial exposure and influence in music through the black church. And it remained with them throughout their lives. For social and religious reasons, a large number of modern jazz musicians did begin to turn toward Islam during the forties, a movement completely in line with the idea of freedom of religion.

Rudy Powell, from Edgar Hayes's band, became one of the first jazz musicians I knew to accept Islam; he became an Ahmidyah Muslim. Other musicians followed, it seemed to me, for social rather than religious reasons, if you can separate the two.

"Man, if you join the Muslim faith, you ain't colored no more, you'll be white," they'd say. "You get a new name and you don't have to be a nigger no more." So everybody started joining because they considered it a big advantage not to be black during the time of segregation. I thought of joining, but it occurred to me that a lot of

---

3. The first African dancer to present African dance in concert form in the United States. Dafora is called "one of the pioneer exponents of African Negro dance and culture." Born in Sierra Leone in 1890, Mr. Dafora studied and performed as a singer at La Scala before coming in 1929 to the United States where he died in 1965. Dafora also staged the voodoo scene in the Orson Welles production of *Macbeth*.

them spooks were simply trying to be anything other than a spook at that time. They had no idea of black consciousness; all they were trying to do was escape the stigma of being "colored." When these cats found out that Idrees Sulieman, who joined the Muslim faith about that time, could go into these white restaurants and bring out sandwiches to the other guys because he wasn't colored—and he looked like the inside of the chimney—they started enrolling in droves.

Musicians started having it printed on their police cards where it said "race," "W" for white.[4] Kenny Clarke had one and he showed it to me. He said, "See, nigger, I ain't no spook; I'm white, 'W.' " He changed his name to Arabic, Liaquat Ali Salaam. Another cat who had been my roommate at Laurinburg, Oliver Mesheux, got involved in an altercation about race down in Delaware. He went into this restaurant, and they said they didn't serve colored in there. So he said, "I don't blame you. But I don't have to go under the rules of colored because my name is Mustafa Dalil."

Didn't ask him no more questions. "How do you do?" the guy said.

When I first applied for my police card, I knew what the guys were doing, but not being a Muslim, I wouldn't allow the police to type anything in that spot under race. I wouldn't reply to the race question on the application black. When the cop started to type something in there, I asked him, "What are you gonna put down there, C for me?"

"You're colored, ain't you?"

"Colored . . . ? No."

"Well, what are you, white?"

"No, don't put nothing on there," I said. "Just give me the card." They left it open. I wouldn't let them type me in W for white nor C for colored; just made them leave it blank. WC is a toilet in Europe.

As time went on, I kept considering converting to Islam but mostly because of the social reasons. I didn't know very much about the religion, but I could dig the idea that Muhammad was a prophet. I believed that, and there were very few Christians who believed that Muhammad had the word of God with him. The idea of polygamous marriage in Islam, I didn't care for too much. In our society, a man can only take care of one woman. If he does a good job of that, he'll be doing well. Polygamy had its place in the society for which it was intended, as a social custom, but social orders change and each age develops its own mores. Polygamy was acceptable during one part of our development, but most women wouldn't accept that today. People worry about all the women with no husbands, and I don't have any answer for that. Whatever happens, the question should be resolved legitimately and in the way necessary for the advancement of society.

The movement among jazz musicians toward Islam created quite a stir, especially with the surge of the Zionist movement for creation and establishment of the State of Israel. A lot of friction arose between Jews and Muslims, which took the form of a semiboycott in New York of jazz musicians with Muslim names. Maybe a Jewish guy, in a booking agency that Muslim musicians worked from, would throw work another way instead of throwing to the Muslim. Also, many of the agents couldn't pull the same tricks on Muslims that they pulled on the rest of us. The Muslims

---

4. From 1940 to 1967, New York City required everyone who worked in a nightclub, including jazz and other popular musicians, to be fingerprinted and to carry a special "cabaret card." Police could confiscate the cards for drug violations or other offenses, preventing musicians from working in the city. Ostensibly a means of combatting organized crime, the system reflected racism and class prejudice and disrupted the careers of even major stars. [RW]

received knowledge about themselves that we didn't have and that we had no access to; so therefore they tended to act differently toward the people running the entertainment business. Much of the entertainment business was run by Jews. Generally, the Muslims fared well in spite of that, because though we had some who were Muslim in name only, others really had knowledge and were taking care of business.

Near the end of the forties, the newspapers really got worried about whether I'd convert to Islam. In 1948 *Life* magazine published a big picture story, supposedly about the music. They conned me into allowing them to photograph me down on my knees, arms outstretched, supposedly bowing to Mecca. It turned out to be a trick bag. It's of the few things in my whole career I'm ashamed of, because I wasn't a Muslim. They tricked me into committing a sacrilege. The newspapers figured that if the "king of bebop" converted, thousands of beboppers would follow suit, and reporters questioned me about whether I planned to quit and forsake Christianity. But that lesson from *Life* taught me to leave them hanging. I told them that on my trips through the South, the members of my band were denied the right of worshipping in churches of their own faith because colored folks couldn't pray with white folks down there. "Don't say I'm forsaking Christianity," I said, "because Christianity is forsaking me—or better, people who claim to be Christian just ain't. It says in the Bible to love thy brother, but people don't practice what the Bible preaches. In Islam, there is no color line. Everybody is treated like equals."

With one reporter, since I didn't know much about the Muslim faith, I called on our saxophonist, formerly named Bill Evans, who'd recently accepted Islam to give this reporter some accurate information.

"What's your new name?" I asked him.

"Yusef Abdul Lateef," he replied. Yusef Lateef told us how a Muslim missionary, Kahlil Ahmed Nasir, had converted many modern jazz musicians in New York to Islam and how he read the Quran daily and strictly observed the prayer and dietary regulations of the religion. I told the reporter that I'd been studying the Quran myself, and although I hadn't converted yet, I knew one couldn't drink alcohol or eat pork as a Muslim. Also I said I felt quite intrigued by the beautiful sound of the word "Quran," and found it "out of this world," "way out," as we used to say. The guy went back to his paper and reported that Dizzy Gillespie and his "beboppers" were "way out" on the subject of religion. He tried to ridicule me as being too strange, weird, and exotic to merit serious attention.[5] Most of the Muslim guys who were sincere in the beginning went on believing and practicing the faith.

Number eight: that beboppers threatened to destroy pop, blues, and old-time music like Dixieland jazz is almost totally false.

It's true, melodically, harmonically, and rhythmically, we found most pop music too bland and mechanically unexciting to suit our tastes. But we didn't attempt to destroy it—we simply built on top of it by substituting our own melodies, harmonies, and rhythms over the pop music format and then improvised on that. We always substituted; that's why no one could ever charge us with stealing songs or collect any royalties for recording material under copyright. We only utilized the pop song

---

5. Playing on this, sometimes in Europe I'd wear a turban. People would see me on the streets and think of me as an Arab or a Hindu. They didn't know what to think, really, because I'd pretend I didn't speak English and listen to them talk about me. Sometimes Americans would think I was some kind of "Mohommedan" nobleman. You wouldn't believe some of the things they'd say in ignorance. So to know me, study me very closely; give me your attention and above all come to my concert.

format as a take-off point for improvisation, which to us was much more important. Eventually, pop music survived by slowly adopting the changes we made.

Beboppers couldn't destroy the blues without seriously injuring themselves. The modern jazz musicians always remained very close to the blues musician. That was a characteristic of the bopper. He stayed in close contact with his blues counterpart. I always had good friendships with T-Bone Walker, B. B. King, Joe Turner, Cousin Joe, Muddy Waters—all those guys—because we knew where our music came from. Ain't no need of denying your father. That's a fool, and there were few fools in this movement. Technical differences existed between modern jazz and blues musicians. However, modern jazz musicians would have to know the blues.

Another story is that we looked down on guys who couldn't read [music]. Erroll Garner couldn't read and we certainly didn't look down on him, even though he never played our type of music. A modern jazz musician wouldn't necessarily have to read well to be able to create, but you couldn't get a job unless you read music; you had to read music to get in a band.

The bopper knew the blues well. He knew Latin influence and had a built-in sense of time, allowing him to set up his phrases properly. He knew chord changes, intervals, and how to get from one key to another smoothly. He knew the music of Charlie Parker and had to be a consummate musician. In the current age of bebop, a musician would also have to know about the techniques of rock music.

Ever since the days at Minton's we had standards to measure expertise in our music. Some guys couldn't satisfy them. Remember Demon, who used to come to play down at Minton's; he came to play, but he never did, and he would play with anybody, even Coleman Hawkins. Demon'd get up on the stand and play choruses that wouldn't say shit, but he'd be there. We'd get so tired of seeing this muthafucka. But he'd be there, and so we let him play. Everybody had a chance to make a contribution to the music.

The squabble between the boppers and the "moldy figs," who played or listened exclusively to Dixieland jazz, arose because the older musicians insisted on attacking our music and putting it down. Ooooh, they were very much against our music, because it required more than what they were doing. They'd say, "That music ain't shit, man!" They really did, but then you noticed some of the older guys started playing our riffs, a few of them, like Henry "Red" Allen. The others remained hostile to it.

Dave Tough was playing down at Eddie Condon's once, and I went down there to see Dave because he and his wife are good friends of mine. When he looked up and saw me, he says, "You the gamest muthafucka I ever seen in my life."

"Whaddayou mean?" I said.

"Muthafucka, you liable to get lynched down in here!" he said. That was funny. I laughed my ass off. Eddie Condon's and Nick's in the Village were the strongholds of Dixieland jazz.

Louis Armstrong criticized us but not me personally, not for playing the trumpet, never. He always said bad things about the guys who copied me, but I never read where he said that I wasn't a good trumpet player, that I couldn't play my instrument. But when he started talking about bebop, "Aww, that's slop! No melody." Louis Armstrong couldn't hear what we were doing. Pops wasn't schooled enough musically to hear the changes and harmonics we played. Pops's beauty as a melodic player and a "blower" caused all of us to play the way we did, especially trumpet players, but his age wasn't equipped to go as far, musically, as we did. Chronologically, I knew that Louis Armstrong was our progenitor as King Oliver and Buddy Bolden had been his progenitors. I knew how their styles developed and had been knowing it all the time; so Louis's statements about bebop didn't bother me. I knew that I came through Roy Eldridge, a follower of Louis Armstrong. I wouldn't say anything. I wouldn't make any statements about the older guys' playing because I respected them too much.

Time 1/28/47 quoted me: "Louis Armstrong was the one who popularized the trumpet more than anyone else—he sold the trumpet to the public. He sold it, man.

"Nowadays in jazz we know more about chords, progressions—and we try to work out different rhythms and things that they didn't think about when Louis Armstrong blew. In his day all he did was play strictly from the soul, just strictly from his heart he just played. He didn't think about no chords—he didn't know nothing about no chords. Now, what we in the younger generation take from Louis Armstrong . . . is the soul."

I criticized Louis for other things, such as his "plantation image." We didn't appreciate that about Louis Armstrong, and if anybody asked me about a certain public image of him, handkerchief over his head, grinning in the face of white racism, I never hesitated to say I didn't like it. I didn't want the white man to expect me to allow the same things Louis Armstrong did. Hell, I had my own way of "Tomming." Every generation of blacks since slavery has had to develop its own way of Tomming, of accommodating itself to a basically unjust situation. Take the comedians from Step 'n Fetchit days—there are new comedians now who don't want to be bothered with "Ah yassuh, boss. . . ." But that doesn't stop them from cracking a joke about how badly they've been mistreated. Later on, I began to recognize what I had considered Pops's grinning in the face of racism as his absolute refusal to let anything, even anger about racism, steal the joy from his life and erase his fantastic smile. Coming from a younger generation, I misjudged him.

Entrenched artists, or the entrenched society, always attack anything that's new coming in—in religion, in social upheavals, in any field. It has something to do with living and dying and the fear among the old of being replaced by the new. Louis Armstrong never played our music, but that shouldn't have kept him from feeling or understanding it. Pops thought that it was his duty to attack! The leader always attacks first; so as the leader of the old school, Pops felt that it was his duty to attack us. At least he could gain some publicity, even if he were overwhelmed musically.

"It's a buncha trash! They don't know what they're doing, them boys, running off."

Mezz Mezzrow knocked us every time he'd say something to the newspapers over in Europe about bebop. "They'd never play two notes where a hundred notes are due."

Later, when I went to Europe in 1948, they put a knife in my hand, and Mezz Mezzrow was holding his head down like I was gonna chop it off. They printed headlines: DIZZY IS GONNA CARVE MEZZ MEZZROW. . . . Thank goodness this is the age of enlightenment, and we don't have to put down the new anymore; that ferocious competition between the generations has passed.

In our personal lives, Pops and I were actually very good friends. He came to my major concerts and made some nice statements about me in the press. We should've made some albums together, I thought, just to have for the people who came behind us, about twenty albums. It seemed like a good idea some years later, but Pops was so captivated by Joe Glaser, his booking agent, he said, "Speak to Papa Joe." Of course that idea fizzled because Joe Glaser, who also booked me at the time, didn't want anybody encroaching on Louis Armstrong. Pops really had no interest in learning any new music; he was just satisfied to do his thing. And then *Hello Dolly!* came along and catapulted him into super, super fame. Wonder if that's gonna happen to me?

I wonder. Playing all these years, then all of a sudden get one number that makes a big hero out of you. History repeating itself.

Number nine: that beboppers expressed disdain for "squares" is mostly true.

A "square" and a "lame" were synonymous, and they accepted the complete life-style, including the music, dictated by the establishment. They rejected the concept of creative alternatives, and they were just the opposite of "hip," which meant "in the know," "wise," or one with "knowledge" of life and how to live.[6] Musically, a square would chew the cud. He'd spend his money at the Roseland Ballroom to hear a dance band playing standards, rather than extend his ear and spirit to take an odyssey in bebop at the Royal Roost. Oblivious to the changes which replaced old, outmoded expressions with newer, modern ones, squares said "hep" rather than "hip." They were apathetic to, or actively opposed to, almost everything we stood for, like intelligence, sensitivity, creativity, change, wisdom, joy, courage, peace, togetherness, and integrity. To put them down in some small way for the sharp-cornered shape of their boxed-in personalities, what better description than "square"?

Also, in those days, there were supposedly hip guys who really were squares, pseudohip cats. How do you distinguish between the pseudo and the truly hip? Well, first, a really hip guy wouldn't have any racial prejudice, one way or the other, because he would know the hip way to live is with your brother. Every human being, unless he shows differently, is your brother.

Number ten: that beboppers put down as "commercial" people who were trying to make money is 50 percent a lie, only half true. We all wanted to make money, preferably by playing modern jazz. We appreciated people who tried to help us—and they were very few—because we needed all the help we could get. Even during the heyday of bebop, none of us made much money. Many people who pretended to help really were there for a rip-off. New modern jazz nightclubs like the Royal Roost, which had yellow leather seats and a milk bar for teenagers, and the Clique were opening every day, all over the country. Bebop was featured on the Great White Way, Broadway, at both the Paramount and the Strand theaters. We received a lot of publicity but very little money.

People with enough bucks and foresight to invest in bebop made some money. I mean more than just a little bit. All the big money went to the guys who owned the music, not to the guys who played it. The businessmen made much more than the musicians, because without money to invest in producing their own music, and sometimes managing poorly what they earned, the modern jazz musicians fell victim to the forces of the market. Somehow, the jazz businessman always became the owner and got back more than his "fair" share, usually at the player's expense. More was stolen from us during the bebop era than in the entire history of jazz, up to that point. They stole a lot of our music, all kinds of stuff. You'd look up and see somebody else's name on your composition and say, "What'd he have to do with it?" But you couldn't do much about it. Blatant commercialism we disliked because it debased the quality of our music. Our protests against being cheated and ripped off never meant we stood against making money. The question of being politically inclined against commercialism or trying to take over anything never figured too prominently with me. The people who stole couldn't create, so I just kept interested in creating the music, mostly, and tried to make sure my works were protected.

Number eleven: that beboppers acted weird and foolish is a damned lie. They tell stories about people coming to my house at all hours of the day and night,

6. "Hip cat" comes from Wolof, "hipicat"—a man who is aware or has his eyes open.

but they didn't do it. They knew better than to ring my bell at four o'clock in the morning. Monk and Charlie Parker came up there one time and said, "I got something for you."

I say, "O.K., hand it to me through the door!" I've been married all my life and wasn't free to do all that. I could go to most of their houses, anytime, because they were always alone or had some broad. Lorraine never stood for too much fooling. My wife would never allow me to do that.

Beboppers were by no means fools. For a generation of Americans and young people around the world, who reached maturity during the 1940s, bebop symbolized a rebellion against the rigidities of the old order, an outcry for change in almost every field, especially in music. The bopper wanted to impress the world with a new stamp, the uniquely modern design of a new generation coming of age.

Dizzy's Desiderata

Drawing on lessons learned over the course of his career, Gillespie sketched this guide to achieving musical excellence in jazz. *To Be, or Not . . . to Bop* includes a photograph of his handwritten notes.

SOME OF THE PREREQUISITES FOR A SUCCESSFUL JAZZ MUSICIAN

I. Mastery of the Instrument—important because when you think of something to play, you must say it quickly, because you don't have time to figure how—[with] chords changing so quickly.
II. Style—which I think is the most difficult to master—inasmuch as there are not too many truly distinctive styles in all of jazz.
III. Taste—is a process of elimination—some phrases that you play may be technically correct but do not portray the particular *mood* that you are trying for.
IV. Communication—after all, you make your profession jazz first, because you love it, and second, as a means of livelihood. So if there is no direct communication with the audience for whom you are playing—there goes your living.
V. Chord Progressions—as there are rules that govern you biologically and physically, there are rules that govern your taste musically. Therefore it is of prime interest and to one's advantage to learn the keyboard of the piano, as it is the basic instrument for Western music, which jazz is an integral part of.
VI. Rhythm—which includes all of the other attributes, because you may have all of these others and don't have the *rhythmic* sense to put them together; that would negate all of your other accomplishments.

33. The Golden Age, Time Past

A SOMETIME JAZZ MUSICIAN AND FREELANCE photographer before he became a writer, Ralph Ellison (1914–1994) is best known for his novel *Invisible Man* (1952) and for *Shadow and Act* (1964), the collection of essays on literature, music, and cultural politics from which this one is drawn. This essay is about the 1940s, but it could not have been written then; as much as any selection in this volume, it directly addresses the problem of "keeping time." Ellison's purpose is to conjure up vivid images of bebop's early days even as he probes the faultiness of such recollections. With bebop, as with so many innovations, what seemed rebellious and risky now seems historic and pioneering, even to those who remember it firsthand. We have no way to think about the past apart from the present in which it is being thought about, and since the present is complex and conflicted, so are our collective memories. Ellison discusses the varying reception of jazz in terms of clashing sensibilities, concluding with an insightful analysis of the jam session as the jazz musicians' academy, where traditions and innovations meet in a delicate balance of individual competition with communal validation and interdependence.

That which we do is what we are. That which we remember is, more often than not, that which we would like to have been; or that which we hope to be. Thus our memory and our identity are ever at odds; our history ever a tall tale told by inattentive idealists.

It has been a long time now, and not many remember how it was in the old days; not really. Not even those who were there to see and hear as it happened, who were pressed in the crowds beneath the dim rosy lights of the bar in the smoke-veiled room, and who shared, night after night, the mysterious spell created by the talk, the laughter, grease paint, powder, perfume, sweat, alcohol and food—all blended and simmering, like a stew on the restaurant range, and brought to a sustained moment of elusive meaning by the timbres and accents of musical instruments locked in passionate recitative. It has been too long now, some seventeen years.

Above the bandstand there later appeared a mural depicting a group of jazzmen holding a jam session in a narrow Harlem bedroom. While an exhausted girl with shapely legs sleeps on her stomach in a big brass bed, they bend to their music in a quiet concatenation of unheard sound: a trumpeter, a guitarist, a clarinetist, a drummer; their

Source: Ralph Ellison, "The Golden Age, Time Past," *Esquire,* January 1959; reprinted in *Shadow and Act* (New York: Vintage Books, 1972), pp. 199–212.

only audience a small, cock-eared dog. The clarinetist is white. The guitarist strums with an enigmatic smile. The trumpet is muted. The barefooted drummer, beating a folded newspaper with whisk-brooms in lieu of a drum, stirs the eye's ear like a blast of brasses in a midnight street. A bottle of port rests on a dresser, but it, like the girl, is ignored. The artist, Charles Graham, adds mystery to, as well as illumination within, the scene by having them play by the light of a kerosene lamp. The painting, executed in a harsh documentary style reminiscent of W. P. A. art, conveys a feeling of musical effort caught in timeless and unrhetorical suspension, the sad remoteness of a scene observed through a wall of crystal.[1]

Except for the lamp, the room might well have been one in the Hotel Cecil, the building on 118th Street in which Minton's Playhouse is located, and although painted in 1946, some time after the revolutionary doings there had begun, the mural should help recall the old days vividly. But the décor of the place has been changed and now it is covered, most of the time, by draperies. These require a tricky skill of those who would draw them aside. And even then there will still only be the girl who must sleep forever unhearing, and the men who must forever gesture the same soundless tune. Besides, the time it celebrates is dead and gone and perhaps not even those who came when it was still fresh and new remember those days as they were.

Neither do those remember who knew Henry Minton, who gave the place his name. Nor those who shared in the noisy lostness of New York the rediscovered community of the feasts, evocative of home, of South, of good times, the best and most unself-conscious of times, created by the generous portions of Negro American cuisine—the hash, grits, fried chicken, the ham-seasoned vegetables, the hot biscuits and rolls and the free whiskey—with which, each Monday night, Teddy Hill honored the entire cast of current Apollo Theatre shows. They were gathered here from all parts of America and they broke bread together and there was a sense of good feeling and promise, but what shape the fulfilled promise would take they did not know, and few except the more restless of the younger musicians even questioned. Yet it was an exceptional moment and the world was swinging with change.

Most of them, black and white alike, were hardly aware of where they were or what time it was; nor did they wish to be. They thought of Minton's as a sanctuary, where in an atmosphere blended of nostalgia and a music–and-drink-lulled suspension of time they could retreat from the wartime tensions of the town. The meaning of time-present was not their concern; thus when they try to tell it now the meaning escapes them.

For they were caught up in events which made that time exceptional and uniquely *then,* and which brought, among the other changes which have reshaped the world, a momentous modulation into a new key of musical sensibility; in brief, a revolution in culture.

So how *can* they remember? Even in swiftly changing America there are few such moments, and at best Americans give but a limited attention to history. Too much happens too rapidly, and before we can evaluate it, or exhaust its meaning or pleasure, there is something new to concern us. Ours is the tempo of the motion picture, not that of the still camera, and we waste experience as we wasted the forest. During the time it was happening the sociologists were concerned with the riots,

---

1. An important part of Roosevelt's New Deal, the Works Progress Administration (1935–41) included artists and writers among the more than two million workers it employed annually during the last half of the Depression. Ellison himself worked for the W.P.A.'s Federal Writers' Project; here he refers to the murals that were commissioned for Post Offices and other public buildings. [RW]

unemployment and industrial tensions of the time, the historians with the onsweep of the war; and the critics and most serious students of culture found this area of our national life of little interest. So it was left to those who came to Minton's out of the needs of feeling, and when the moment was past no one retained more than a fragment of its happening. Afterward the very effort to put the fragments together transformed them—so that in place of true memory they now summon to mind pieces of legend. They retell the stories as they have been told and written, glamorized, inflated, made neat and smooth, with all incomprehensible details vanished along with most of the wonder—not how it was as they themselves knew it.

When asked how it was back then, back in the forties, they will smile, then, frowning with the puzzlement of one attempting to recall the details of a pleasant but elusive dream, they'll say: "Oh, man, it was a hell of a time! A wailing time! Things were jumping, you couldn't get in here for the people. The place was packed with celebrities. Park Avenue, man! Big people in show business, college professors along with the pimps and their women. And college boys and girls. Everybody came. You know how the old words to the 'Basin Street Blues' used to go before Sinatra got hold of it? *Basin Street is the street where the dark and the light folks meet*—that's what I'm talking about. That was Minton's, man. It was a place where everybody could come to be entertained because it was a place that was jumping with good times."

Or some will tell you that it was here that Dizzy Gillespie found his own trumpet voice; that here Kenny Clarke worked out the patterns of his drumming style; where Charlie Christian played out the last creative and truly satisfying moments of his brief life, his New York home; where Charlie Parker built the monument of his art; where Thelonious Monk formulated his contribution to the chordal progressions and the hide-and-seek melodic methods of modern jazz. And they'll call such famous names as Lester Young and Ben Webster, Coleman Hawkins; or Fats Waller, who came here in the after-hour stillness of the early morning to compose. They'll tell you that Benny Goodman, Art Tatum, Count Basie and Lena Horne would drop in to join in the fun; that it was here that George Shearing played on his first night in the United States; or of Tony Scott's great love of the place; and they'll repeat all the stories of how, when and by whom the word "bebop" was coined here—but, withal, few actually remember, and these leave much unresolved.

Usually music gives resonance to memory (and Minton's was a hotbed of jazz), but not the music then in the making here. It was itself a texture of fragments, repetitive, nervous, not fully formed; its melodic lines underground, secret and taunting; its riffs jeering—"Salt peanuts! Salt peanuts!"[2]; its timbres flat or shrill, with a minimum of thrilling vibrato. Its rhythms were out of stride and seemingly arbitrary, its drummers frozen-faced introverts dedicated to chaos. And in it the steady flow of memory, desire and defined experience summed up by the traditional jazz beat and blues mood seemed swept like a great river from its old, deep bed. We know better now, and recognize the old moods in the new sounds, but what we know is that which was then becoming. For most of those who gathered here, the enduring meaning of the great moment at Minton's took place off to the side, beyond the range of attention, like a death blow glimpsed from the corner of the eye, the revolutionary rumpus sounding like a series of flubbed notes blasting the talk with discord. So that the events which made Minton's *Minton's* arrived in conflict and ran their course—then the heat was gone and all that was left to mark its passage is the controlled fury

2. A reference to Dizzy Gillespie's tune of the same name, which he recorded in 1945. The song's humor (or "jeering") derives from how the catch phrase is sung with syncopated octave leaps. [RW]

of the music itself, sealed pure and irrevocable, banalities and excellencies alike, in the early recordings; or swept along by our restless quest for the new, to be diluted in more recent styles, the best of it absorbed like drops of fully distilled technique, mood and emotions into the great stream of jazz.

Left also to confuse our sense of what happened is the word "bop," hardly more than a nonsense syllable, by which the music synthesized at Minton's came to be known. A most inadequate word which does little, really, to help us remember. A word which throws up its hands in clownish self-deprecation before all the complexity of sound and rhythm and self-assertive passion which it pretends to name; a mask-word for the charged ambiguities of the new sound, hiding the serious face of art.

Nor does it help that so much has come to pass in the meantime. There have been two hot wars and that which continues, called "cold." And the unknown young men who brought a new edge to the sound of jazz and who scrambled the rhythms of those who used the small clear space at Minton's for dancing are no longer so young or unknown; indeed, they are referred to now by nickname in even the remotest of places. And in Paris and Munich and Tokyo they'll tell you the details of how, after years of trying, "Dizzy" (meaning John Birks Gillespie) vanquished "Roy" (meaning Roy Eldridge) during a jam session at Minton's, to become thereby the new king of trumpeters. Or how, later, while jetting over the world on the blasts of his special tilt-belled horn, he jammed with a snake charmer in Pakistan. "Sent the bloody cobra, man," they'll tell you in London's Soho. So their subsequent fame has blurred the sharp, ugly lines of their rebellion even in the memories of those who found them most strange and distasteful.

What's more, our memory of some of the more brilliant young men has been touched by the aura of death, and we feel guilt that the fury of their passing was the price paid for the art they left us to enjoy unscathed: Charlie Christian, burned out by tuberculosis like a guitar consumed in a tenement fire; Fats Navarro, wrecked by the tensions and needling temptations of his orgiastic trade, a big man physically as well as musically, shrunken to nothingness; and, most notably of all, Charlie Parker, called "Bird," now deified, worshipped and studied and, like any fertility god, mangled by his admirers and imitators, who coughed up his life and died—as incredibly as the leopard which Hemingway tells us was found "dried and frozen" near the summit of Mount Kilimanjaro—in the hotel suite of a Baroness. (Nor has anyone explained what a "yardbird" was seeking at the social altitude, though we know that ideally anything is possible within a democracy, and we know quite well that upper-class Europeans were seriously interested in jazz long before Newport became hospitable.) All this is too much for memory; the dry facts are too easily lost in legend and glamour. (With jazz we are yet not in the age of history, but in that of folklore.) We know for certain only that the strange sounds which they and their fellows threw against the hum and buzz of vague signification that seethed in the drinking crowd at Minton's and which, like disgruntled conspirators meeting fatefully to assemble the random parts of a bomb, they joined here and beat and blew into a new jazz style—these sounds we know now to have become the clichés, the technical exercises and the standard of achievement not only for fledgling musicians all over the United States, but for Dutchmen and Swedes, Italians and Frenchmen, Germans and Belgians, and even Japanese. All these, in places which came to mind during the Minton days only as points where the war was in progress and where one might soon be sent to fight and die, are now spotted with young men who study the discs on which the revolution hatched in Minton's is preserved with all the intensity that young American painters bring to the works, say, of Kandinsky, Picasso and Klee. Surely this is an odd swing of the cultural tide. Yet Stravinsky, Webern and Berg notwithstanding, or, more recently, Boulez or Stockhausen—such young men (many of them excellent musicians in the highest European tradition) find in the music made articulate at Minton's some key to a fuller freedom of self-realization. Indeed for many young Europeans the developments which took place here and the careers of those who brought it about have become the latest episodes in the great American epic. They collect the recordings and thrive on the legends as eagerly, perhaps, as young Americans.

Today the bartenders at Minton's will tell you how they come fresh off the ships or planes, bringing their brightly expectant and—in this Harlem atmosphere—startlingly innocent European faces, to buy drinks and stand looking about for the source of the mystery. They try to reconcile the quiet reality of the place with the events which fired, at such long range, their imaginations. They come as to a shrine; as we to the Louvre, Notre Dame or St. Peter's; as young Americans hurry to the Café Flore, the Deux Magots, the Rotonde or the Café du Dìme in Paris. For some years now they have been coming to ask, with all the solemnity of pilgrims inquiring of a sacred relic, to see the nicotine-stained amplifier which Teddy Hill provided for Charlie Christian's guitar. And this is quite proper, for every shrine should have its relic.

Perhaps Minton's has more meaning for European jazz fans than for Americans, even for those who regularly went there. Certainly it has a *different* meaning. For them it is associated with those continental cafés in which great changes, political and artistic, have been plotted; it is to modern jazz what the Café Voltaire in Zurich is to the Dadaist phase of modern literature and painting. Few of those who visited Harlem during the forties would associate it so, but there is a context of meaning in which Minton's and the musical activities which took place there can be meaningfully placed.

Jazz, for all the insistence of the legends, has been far more closely associated with cabarets and dance halls than with brothels, and it was these which provided both the employment for the musicians and an audience initiated and aware of the overtones of the music; which knew the language of riffs, the unstated meanings of the blues idiom, and the dance steps developed from, and complementary to, its rhythms. And in the beginning it was in the Negro dance hall and night club that jazz was most completely a part of a total cultural expression; and in which it was freest and most satisfying, both for the musicians and for those in whose lives it played a major role. As a night club in a Negro community then, Minton's was part of a national pattern.

But in the old days Minton's was far more than this; it was also a rendezvous for musicians. As such, and although it was not formally organized, it goes back historically to the first New York center of Negro musicians, the Clef Club. Organized in 1910, during the start of the great migration of Negroes northward, by James Reese Europe, the director whom Irene Castle credits with having invented the fox trot, the Clef Club was set up on West 53rd Street to serve as a meeting place and booking office for Negro musicians and entertainers. Here wage scales were regulated, musical styles and techniques worked out, and entertainment was supplied for such producers as Florenz Ziegfeld and Oscar Hammerstein. Later, when Harlem evolved into a Negro section, a similar function was served by the Rhythm Club, located then in the old Lafayette Theatre building on 132nd Street and Seventh Avenue. Henry Minton, a former saxophonist and officer of the Rhythm Club, became the first Negro delegate to Local 802 of the American Federation of Musicians and was thus doubly aware of the needs, artistic as well as economic, of jazzmen. He was generous with loans, was fond of food himself and, as an old acquaintance recalled, "loved to put a pot on the range" to share with unemployed friends. Naturally when he opened Minton's Playhouse many musicians made it their own.

Henry Minton also provided, as did the Clef and Rhythm clubs, a necessity more important to jazz musicians than food: a place in which to hold their interminable jam sessions. And it is here that Minton's becomes most important to the development of modern jazz. It is here, too, that it joins up with all the countless rooms, private and public, in which jazzmen have worked out the secrets of their craft. Today jam sessions are offered as entertainment by night clubs and on radio and television, and some are quite exciting; but what is seen and heard is only one aspect of the true jam session: the "cutting session," or contest of improvisational skill and physical endurance between two or more musicians. But the jam session is far more than this, and when carried out by musicians, in the privacy of small rooms (as in the mural at Minton's) or in such places as Halley Richardson's shoeshine parlor in Oklahoma City—where I first heard Lester Young jamming in a shine chair, his head thrown back, his horn even then outthrust, his feet working on the footrests, as he played with and against Lem Johnson, Ben Webster (this was 1929) and other members of the old Blue Devils Orchestra—or during the after hours in Piney Brown's old Sunset Club in Kansas City; in such places as these with only musicians and jazzmen present, then the jam session is revealed as the jazzman's true academy.

It is here that he learns tradition, group techniques and style. For although since the twenties many jazzmen have had conservatory training and were well grounded in formal theory and instrumental technique, when we approach jazz we are entering quite a different sphere of training. Here it is more meaningful to speak, not of courses of study, of grades and degrees, but of apprenticeship, ordeals, initiation ceremonies, of rebirth. For after the jazzman has learned the fundamentals of his instrument and the traditional techniques of jazz—the intonations, the mute work, manipulation of timbre, the body of traditional styles—he must then "find himself," must be reborn, must find, as it were, his soul. All this through achieving that subtle identification between his instrument and his deepest drives which will allow him to express his own unique ideas and his own unique voice. He must achieve, in short, his self-determined identity.

In this his instructors are his fellow musicians, especially the acknowledged masters, and his recognition of manhood depends upon their acceptance of his ability as having reached a standard which is all the more difficult for not having been rigidly codified. This does not depend upon his ability to simply hold a job but upon his power to express an individuality in tone. Nor is his status ever unquestioned, for the health of jazz and the unceasing attraction which it holds for the musicians themselves lies in the ceaseless warfare for mastery and recognition—not among the general public, though commercial success is not spurned, but among their artistic peers. And even the greatest can never rest on past accomplishments, for, as with the fast guns of the old West, there is always someone waiting in a jam session to blow him literally, not only down, but into shame and discouragement.

By making his club hospitable to jam sessions even to the point that customers who were not musicians were crowded out, Henry Minton provided a retreat, a homogeneous community where a collectivity of common experience could find continuity and meaningful expression. Thus the stage was set for the birth of bop.

In 1941 Mr. Minton handed over his management to Teddy Hill, the saxophonist and former band leader, and Hill turned the Playhouse into a musical dueling ground. Not only did he continue Minton's policies, he expanded them. It was Hill who established the Monday Celebrity Nights, the house band which included such members from his own disbanded orchestra as Kenny Clarke, Dizzy Gillespie, along with Thelonious Monk, sometimes with Joe Guy, and, later, Charlie Christian and Charlie Parker; and it was Hill who allowed the musicians free rein to play whatever they liked. Perhaps no other club except Clarke Monroe's Uptown House was so permissive, and with the hospitality extended to musicians of all schools the news spread swiftly. Minton's became the focal point for musicians all over the country.

Herman Pritchard, who presided over the bar in the old days, tells us that every time they came, "Lester Young and Ben Webster used to tie up in battle like dogs in the road. They'd fight on those saxophones until they were tired out, then they'd put in long-distance calls to their mothers, both of whom lived in Kansas City, and tell them about it."

And most of the masters of jazz came either to observe or to participate and be influenced and listen to their own discoveries transformed; and the aspiring stars sought to win their approval, as the younger tenor men tried to win the esteem of Coleman Hawkins. Or they tried to vanquish them in jamming contests as Gillespie is said to have outblown his idol, Roy Eldridge. It was during this period that Eddie "Lockjaw" Davis underwent an ordeal of jeering rejection until finally he came through as an admired tenor man.

In the perspective of time we now see that what was happening at Minton's was a continuing symposium of jazz, a summation of all the styles, personal and traditional, of jazz. Here it was possible to hear its resources of technique, ideas, harmonic structure, melodic phrasing and rhythmical possibilities explored more thoroughly than was ever possible before. It was also possible to hear the first attempts toward a conscious statement of the sensibility of the younger generation of musicians as they worked out the techniques, structures and rhythmical patterns with which to express themselves. Part of this was arbitrary, a revolt of the younger against the established stylists; part of it was inevitable. For jazz had reached a crisis and new paths were certain to be searched for and found. An increasing number of the younger men were formally trained and the post-Depression developments in the country had made for quite a break between their experience and that of the older men. Many were even of a different physical build. Often they were quiet and of a reserve which contrasted sharply with the exuberant and outgoing lyricism of the older men, and they were intensely concerned that their identity as Negroes placed no restriction upon the music they played or the manner in which they used their talent. They were concerned, they said, with art, not entertainment. Especially were they resentful of Louis Armstrong, whom (confusing the spirit of his music with his clowning) they considered an Uncle Tom.

But they too, some of them, had their own myths and misconceptions: That theirs was the only generation of Negro musicians who listened to or enjoyed the classics; that to be truly free they must act exactly the opposite of what white people might believe, rightly or wrongly, a Negro to be; that the performing artist can be completely and absolutely free of the obligations of the entertainer, and that they could play jazz with dignity only by frowning and treating the audience with aggressive contempt; and that to be in control, artistically and personally, one must be so cool as to quench one's own human fire.

Nor should we overlook the despair which must have swept Minton's before the technical mastery, the tonal authenticity, the authority and the fecundity of imagination of such men as Coleman Hawkins, Lester Young, Benny Goodman, Art Tatum, Jack Teagarden, Duke Ellington and Fats Waller. Despair, after all, is ever an important force in revolutions.

They were also responding to the non-musical pressures affecting jazz. It was a time of big bands, and the greatest prestige and economic returns were falling outside the Negro community—often to leaders whose popularity grew from the compositions and arrangements of Negroes—to white instrumentalists whose only originality lay in the enterprise with which they rushed to market with some Negro musician's hard-won style. Still there was no policy of racial discrimination at Minton's. Indeed, it was very much like those Negro cabarets of the twenties and thirties in which a megaphone was placed on the piano so that anyone with the urge could sing a blues. Nevertheless, the inside-dopesters will tell you that the "changes" or chord progressions and the melodic inversions worked out by the creators of bop sprang partially from their desire to create a jazz which could not be so easily imitated and exploited by white musicians to whom the market was more open simply *because* of their whiteness. They wished to receive credit for what they created, and besides, it was easier to "get rid of the trash" who crowded the bandstand with inept playing and thus make room for the real musicians, whether white or black. Nevertheless, white musicians like Tony Scott, Remo Palmieri and Al Haig who were part of the development at Minton's became so by passing a test of musicianship, sincerity and temperament. Later, it is said, the boppers became engrossed in solving the musical problems which they set themselves. Except for a few sympathetic older musicians it was they who best knew the promise of the Minton moment, and it was they, caught like the rest in all the complex forces of American life which come to focus in jazz, who made the most of it. Now the tall tales told as history must feed on the results of their efforts.

34. The Professional Dance Musician and His Audience

MOST JAZZ ISN'T PLAYED BY THE STARS whose names show up in history books, but by working musicians whose pay rarely matches their skills. Taking advantage of his experiences as a Chicago pianist, sociologist Howard S. Becker (b. 1928) interviewed his musical colleagues to gather evidence for this portrait of professional dance musicians during

Source: Howard S. Becker, "The Professional Dance Musician and His Audience," *American Journal of Sociology* 57 (1951–52), pp. 136–44.

the late 1940s, as jazz declined in popularity and began to be regarded as separate from popular or commercial music. Best known for his book *Art Worlds*, a study of how institutions and collective activity produce meanings for art, Becker had earlier studied the social category of "deviance," emphasizing how certain acts are socially defined as deviant and culturally understood by those so labeled. In comparison to some later sociological studies, his pioneering analysis of these musicians is unusually sympathetic and ethnographically grounded.[1]

Since the musicians' union and most venues were racially segregated at the time, most of Becker's interviewees were of various "white" ethnicities; their testimony makes the point that racism was not the only social force or occupational factor to alienate jazz musicians and set them apart from the rest of society. For these musicians, jazz was defined less in terms of musical style than in terms of social autonomy. They saw a conflict between artistic and commercial success, as did, for example, many later rock musicians (but not rap musicians or Mozart). Becker points to the basic tension with his opening gambit, where he categorizes the musician as a worker in "the service occupations." As is often the case in sociology, this analysis doesn't emphasize historical specificity; however, many of the sentiments Becker recorded I heard echoed forty years later, when I was playing similar gigs.

The service occupations are, in general, distinguished by the fact that the worker in them comes into more or less direct and personal contact with the ultimate consumer of the product of his work, the client for whom he performs the service. Consequently, the client is able to direct or attempt to direct the worker at his task and to apply sanctions of various kinds, ranging from informal pressure to the withdrawal of his patronage and the conferring of it on some other of the many people who perform the service.

This contact brings together a person whose full-time activity is centered around the occupation and whose self is to some degree deeply involved in it and another person whose relation to it is much more casual, and it may be inevitable that the two should have widely varying pictures of the way in which the occupational service should be performed. It seems characteristic of such occupations that their members consider the client unable to judge the proper worth of the service and resent bitterly any attempt on his part to exercise control over the work. A good deal of conflict and

1. See Howard S. Becker, *Art Worlds* (Berkeley: University of California Press, 1982) and *Outsiders: Studies in the Sociology of Deviance* (New York: The Free Press, 1963). For a sequel to the article presented here, see Howard S. Becker, "Some Contingencies of the Professional Dance Musician's Career," *Human Organization* 12:1 (Spring 1953), pp. 22–26 (also reprinted in *Outsiders*). Both articles derived from Becker's 1949 M.A. thesis at the University of Chicago. For subsequent studies that were sparked by and responded to Becker's work, see, for example, William Bruce Cameron, "Sociological Notes on the Jam Session," *Social Forces* 33:2 (December 1954), pp. 177–82; Edward Harvey, "Social Change and the Jazz Musician," *Social Forces* 46:1 (September 1967), pp. 34–42; Alan P. Merriam and Raymond W. Mack, "The Jazz Community," *Social Forces* 38:3 (March 1960), pp. 211–22; and Bruce A. MacLeod, *Club Date Musicians: Playing the New York Party Circuit* (Urbana: University of Illinois Press, 1993).

hostility arises as a result, and methods of defense against outside interference become a preoccupation of the members.

The present paper outlines the dimensions of such an occupational dilemma as observed among professional dance musicians in a large American city. This occupation presents an extremely favorable situation for studying such phenomena, since in it the problem is, to a greater degree than in many occupations, frankly faced and openly discussed. Musicians feel that the only music worth playing is what they call "jazz," a term which can be defined only as that music which is produced without reference to the demands of outsiders. Yet they must endure unceasing interference with their playing by employer and audience. The most distressing problem in the career of the average musician is the necessity of choosing between conventional success and his "artistic" standards. In order to achieve success he finds it necessary to "go commercial," that is, to play in accord with the wishes of the nonmusicians for whom he works; in so doing he sacrifices the respect of other musicians and thus, in most cases, his self-respect. If he remains true to his standards, he is doomed to failure in the larger society. Musicians classify themselves according to the degree to which they give in to outsiders; the continuum ranges from the extreme "jazz" musician to the "commercial" musician.

The discussion will center around the following points: (1) the conceptions which musicians have of themselves and of the nonmusicians for whom they work and the conflict they feel to be inherent in this relation, (2) the basic consensus underlying the reactions of both commercial and jazz musicians to this conflict, and (3) feelings of isolation and the segregating of themselves from audience and community. The analysis is based on materials gathered during eighteen months of interviewing and participant observation. My research was disclosed to few people. In general, I was accepted as just another young piano player by most of the men from whom this material was gathered. The bulk of the material comes from younger men, but enough contact was made with other musicians to permit the analysis of basic occupational problems.

I. Musician and "Square"

The whole system of beliefs about what musicians are and what audiences are is summed up in a word used by musicians to refer to outsiders—"square." It is used as a noun and as an adjective, denoting both a kind of person and a quality of behavior and objects. The term refers to the kind of person who is the opposite of all the musician is, or should be, and a way of thinking, feeling, and behaving (with its expression in material objects) which is the opposite of that valued by musicians.

The musician is conceived of by the professional group as an artist who possesses a mysterious artistic gift setting him apart from all other people. Possessing this gift, he should be free from control by outsiders who lack it. The gift is something which cannot be acquired through education; the outsider, therefore, can never become a member of the group. A trombone player said, "You can't teach a guy to have a beat. Either he's got one or he hasn't. If he hasn't got it, you can't teach it to him."

The musician feels that under no circumstances should any outsider be allowed to tell him what to play or how to play it. In fact, the strongest element in the colleague code is the prohibition against a musician criticizing or in any other way trying to put pressure on another musician in the actual playing situation "on the job." Where not even a colleague is permitted to influence the work, it is unthinkable that an outsider should be allowed to do so.

This attitude is generalized into a feeling that musicians are completely different from and better than other kinds of people and accordingly ought not to be subject to the control of outsiders in any branch of life, particularly in their artistic activity. The feeling of being a different kind of person who leads a different kind of life is deep-seated, as the following remarks indicate:

> I'm telling you, musicians are different than other people. They talk different, they act different, they look different. They're just not like other people, that's all. . . . You know it's hard to get out of the music business because you feel so different from others.
>
> Musicians live an exotic life, like in a jungle or something. They start out, they're just ordinary kids from small towns—but once they get into that life they change. It's like a jungle, except that their jungle is a hot, crowded bus. You live that kind of life long enough, you just get to be completely different.
>
> Being a musician was great, I'll never regret it. I'll understand things that squares never will.

An extreme of this view is the belief that only musicians are sensitive and unconventional enough to be able to give real sexual satisfaction to a woman.

Feeling their difference strongly, musicians likewise believe that beings such as they are under no obligation to follow the conventional behavior of the squares. From the idea that no one can tell a musician how to play it follows logically that no one can tell a musician how to do anything. Accordingly, behavior which flouts conventional social norms is greatly admired. Stories reveal this admiration for highly individual, spontaneous, "devil-may-care" activities; many of the most noted jazzmen are renowned as "characters," and their exploits are widely recounted. For example, one well-known jazzman is noted for having jurnped on a policeman's horse standing in front of the night club in which he worked and ridden it away. The ordinary musician likes to tell stories of unconventional things he has done:

> We played the dance and after the job was over we packed up to get back in this old bus and make it back to Detroit. A little way out of town the car just refused to go. There was plenty of gas; it just wouldn't run. These guys all climbed out and stood around griping. All of a sudden, somebody said, "Let's set it on fire!" So someone got some gas out of the tank and sprinkled it around, touching a match to it and whoosh, it just went up in smoke. What an experience! The car burning up and all these guys standing around hollering and clapping their hands. It was really something.

This is more than idiosyncrasy; it is a primary occupational value, as indicated by the following observation of a young musician: "You know, the biggest heroes in the music business are the biggest characters. The crazier a guy acts, the greater he is, the more everyone likes him."

As they do not wish to be forced to live in terms of social conventions, so musicians do not attempt to force these conventions on others. For example, a musician declared that ethnic discrimination is wrong, since every person is entitled to act and believe as he wants to:

> Shit, I don't believe in any discrimination like that. People are people, whether they're Dagos or Jews or Irishmen or Polacks or what. Only big squares care what religion they are. It don't mean a fucking thing to me. Every person's entitled to believe his own way, that's the way I feel about it. Of course, I never go to church myself, but I don't hold it against anybody who does. It's all right if you like that sort of thing.

The same musician classified a friend's sex behavior as wrong, yet defended the individual's right to decide what is right and wrong for himself: "Eddie fucks around too much; he's gonna kill himself or else get killed by some broad. And he's got a nice wife too. He shouldn't treat her like that. But what the fuck, that's his business. If that's the way he wants to live, if he's happy that way, then that's the way he oughta do." Musicians will tolerate quite extraordinary behavior in a fellow-musician without making any attempt to punish or restrain. In the following incident the uncontrolled behavior of a drummer loses a job for an orchestra; yet, angry as they are, they lend him money and refrain from punishing him in any way. It would be a breach of custom were anyone to reprimand him.

JERRY: When we got up there, the first thing that happened was that all his drums didn't show up. So the owner drives all around trying to find some drums for him and then the owner smashes a fender while he was doing it. So I knew right away that we were off to a good start. And Jack! Man, the boss is an old Dago, you know, no bullshit about him, he runs a gambling joint; he don't take any shit from anyone. So he says to Jack, "What are you gonna do without drums?" Jack says, "Be cool, daddio, everything'll be real gone, you know." I thought the old guy would blow his top. What a way to talk to the boss. Boy, he turned around, there was fire in his eye. I knew we wouldn't last after that. He says to me, "Is that drummer all there?" I said, "I don't know, I never saw him before today." And we just got finished telling him we'd been playing together six months. So that helped, too. Of course, when Jack started playing, that was the end. So loud! And he don't play a beat at all. All he uses the bass drum for is accents. What kind of drumming is that? Otherwise, it was a good little outfit. . . . It was a good job. We could have been there forever. . . . Well, after we played a couple of sets, the boss told us we were through.

BECKER: What happened after you got fired?

JERRY: The boss gave us twenty apiece and told us to go home. So it cost us seventeen dollars for transportation up and back, we made three bucks on the job. Of course, we saw plenty of trees. Three bucks, hell, we didn't even make that. We loaned Jack seven or eight.

The musician thus views himself and his colleagues as people with a special gift which makes them different from nonmusicians and not subject to their control, either in musical performance or in ordinary social behavior.

The square, on the other hand, lack this special gift and any understanding of the music or way of life of those who possess it. The square is thought of as an ignorant, intolerant person who is to be feared, since he produces the pressures forcing the musician to play inartistically. The musicians' difficulty lies in the fact that the square is in a position to get his way: if he does not like the kind of music played, he does not pay to hear it a second time.

Not understanding music, the square judges music by standards which are foreign to musicians and not respected by them. A "commercial" saxophonist observed sarcastically:

> It doesn't make any difference what we play, the way we do it. It's so simple that anyone who's been playing longer than a month could handle it. Jack plays a chorus on piano or something, then saxes or something, all unison. It's very easy. But the people don't care. As long as they can hear the drum they're all right. They hear the drum, then they know to put their right foot in front of their left foot and their left foot in front of their right foot. Then if they can hear the melody to whistle to, they're happy. What more could they want?

The following conversation illustrates the same attitude:

JOE: You'd get off the stand and walk down the aisle, somebody'd say, "Young man, I like your orchestra very much." Just because you played soft and the tenorman doubled fiddle or something like that, the squares liked it. . . .

DICK: It was like that when I worked at the M— Club. All the kids that I went to high school with used to come out and dig the band. . . . That was one of the worst bands I ever worked on and they all thought it was wonderful.

JOE: Oh, well, they're just a bunch of squares anyhow.

"Squareness" is felt to penetrate every aspect of the square's behavior just as its opposite, "hipness" is evident in everything the musician does. The square seems to do everything wrong and is laughable and ludicrous. Musicians derive a good deal of amusement from sitting in a corner and watching the squares. Everyone has stories to tell about the laughable antics of squares. One man went so far as to suggest that the musicians should change places with the people sitting at the bar of the tavern he worked in; he claimed that they were funnier and more entertaining than he could possibly be. Every item of dress, speech, and behavior which differs from that of the musician is taken as new evidence of the inherent insensitivity and ignorance of the square. Since musicians have an esoteric culture these evidences are many and serve only to fortify their conviction that musicians and squares are two different kinds of people.

But the square is feared as well, since he is thought of as the ultimate source of "commercial" pressure. It is the square's ignorance of music that compels the musician to play what he considers bad music in order to be successful.

BECKER: How do you feel about the people you play for, the audience?

DAVE: They're a drag.

BECKER: Why do you say that?

DAVE: Well, if you're working on a commercial band, they like it and so you have to play more corn. If you're working on a good band, then they don't like it, and that's a drag. If you're working on a good band and they like it, then that's a drag, too. You hate them anyway, because you know that they don't know what it's all about. They're just a big drag.

This last statement reveals that even those who attempt to avoid being square are still considered so, because they still lack the proper understanding, which only a musician can have—"they don't know what it's all about." The "jazz fan" is thus respected no more than other squares. His liking for jazz is without understanding and he acts just like the other squares; he will request songs and try to influence the musician's playing, just as other squares do.

The musician thus sees himself as a creative artist who should be free from outside control, a person different from and better than those outsiders he calls squares who understand neither his music nor his way of life and yet because of whom he must perform in a manner contrary to his professional ideals.

II. Reactions to the Conflict

We will now consider the attitudes of "commercial" and "jazz" musicians toward the audience, noting both the variation in attitude and the basic consensus underlying the two sets of feelings. Two themes run through this conflict: (1) the desire of the musician to live in terms of the creative principle, and (2) the recognition of many forces influencing him to abandon that principle. The jazzman tends to emphasize the first, the commercial musician the second; but both recognize and feel the force of each of these guiding influences. Common to the attitudes of both kinds of musician is an intense contempt for and dislike of the square audience whose fault it is that musicians must "go commercial" in order to succeed.

The commercial musician, though he conceives of the audience as squares, chooses to sacrifice self-respect and the respect of other musicians (the rewards of artistic behavior) for the more substantial rewards of steady work, higher income, and the prestige enjoyed by the man who "goes commercial." One commercial musician commented:

> They've got a nice class of people out here, too. Of course, they're squares, I'm not trying to deny that. Sure, they're a bunch of fucking squares, but who the fuck pays the bills? They pay 'em, so you gotta play what they want. I mean, what the shit, you can't make a living if you don't play for the squares. How many fucking people you think aren't squares? Out of a hundred people you'd be lucky if 15 percent weren't squares. I mean, maybe professional people—doctors, lawyers, like that—they might not be square, but the average person is just a big fucking square. Of course, show people aren't like that. But outside of show people and professional people, everybody's a fucking square.[2] They don't know anything.
>
> I'll tell you. This is something I learned about three years ago. If you want to make any money you gotta please the squares. They're the ones that pay the bills, and you gotta play for them. A good musician can't get a fucking job. You gotta play a bunch of shit. But what the fuck, let's face it. I want to live good. I want to make some money; I want a car, you know. How long can you fight it? . . .
>
> Don't get me wrong. If you can make money playing jazz, great. But how many guys can do it? . . . If you can play jazz, great, like I said. But if you're on a bad fucking job, there's no sense fighting it, you gotta be commercial. I mean, the squares are paying your salary, so you might as well get used to it, they're the ones you gotta please.

It is to be noted that the speaker admits it is more "respectable" to be independent of the squares, and expresses contempt for the audience, whose squareness is made responsible for the whole situation.

These men phrase the problem primarily in economic terms: "I mean, shit, if you're playing for a bunch of squares you're playing for a bunch of squares. What the fuck are you gonna do? You can't push it down their throats. Well, I suppose you can make 'em eat it, but after all, they *are* paying you."

The jazzman feels the need to satisfy the audience just as strongly, although maintaining that one should not give in to it. Jazzmen, like others, appreciate steady jobs and good jobs and know that they must satisfy the audience to get them, as the following conversation between two young jazzmen illustrates:

CHARLIE: There aren't any jobs where you can blow jazz. You have to play rumbas and pops [popular songs] and everything. You can't get anywhere blowing jazz. Man, I don't want to scuffle all my life.

EDDIE: Well, you want to enjoy yourself, don't you? You won't be happy playing commercial. You know that.

2. Most musicians would not admit these exceptions.

CHARLIE: I guess there's just no way for a cat to be happy. 'Cause it sure is a drag blowing commercial, but it's an awful drag not ever doing anything and playing jazz.

EDDIE: Jesus, why can't you be successful playing jazz? . . . I mean, you could have a great little outfit and still play arrangements, but good ones, you know.

CHARLIE: You could never get a job for a band like that.

EDDIE: Well, you could have a sexy little bitch to stand up in front and sing and shake her ass at the bears [squares]. Then you could get a job. And you could still play great when she wasn't singing.

CHARLIE: Well, wasn't that what Q—'s band was like? Did you enjoy that? Did you like the way she sang?

EDDIE: No, man, but we played jazz, you know.

CHARLIE: Did you like the kind of jazz you were playing? It was kind of commercial, wasn't it?

EDDIE: Yeah, but it could have been great.

CHARLIE: Yeah, if it had been great, you wouldn't have kept on working. I guess we'll always just be unhappy. It's just the way things are. You'll always be drug[3] with yourself. . . . There'll never be any kind of a really great job for a musician.

In addition to the pressure to please the audience which emanates from the musician's desire to maximize salary and income, there are more immediate pressures. It is often difficult to maintain an independent attitude. For example:

> I worked an Italian wedding on the Southwest Side last night with Johnny Ponzi. We played about half an hour, doing the special arrangements they use, which are pretty uncommercial. Then an old Italian fellow (the father-in-law of the groom, as we later found out) began hollering, "Play some polkas, play some Italian music. Ah, you stink, you're lousy." Johnny always tries to avoid the inevitable on these wedding jobs, putting off playing the folk music as long as he can. I said, "Man, why don't we play some of that stuff now and get it over with?" Tom said, "I'm afraid if we start doing that we'll be doing it all night." Johnny said, "Look, Howard, the groom is a real great guy. He told us to play anything we want and not to pay any attention to what the people say, so don't worry about it. . . ."
>
> The old fellow kept hollering and pretty soon the groom came up and said, "Listen, fellows. I know you don't want to play any of that shit and I don't want you to, but that's my father-in-law, see. The only thing is, I don't want to embarrass my wife for him, so play some Dago music to keep him quiet, will yuh?" Johnny looked around at us and made a gesture of resignation.
>
> He said, "All right, let's play the *Beer Barrel Polka.*" Tom said, "Oh shit! Here we go." We played it and then we played an Italian dance, the *Tarantelle.*

Sometimes the employer applies pressure which makes even an uncompromising jazzman give in, at least for the duration of the job:

> I was playing solo for one night over at the Y— on —rd St. What a drag! The second set, I was playing *Sunny Side,* I played the melody for one chorus, then I played a little jazz. All of a sudden the boss leaned over the side of the bar and hollered, "I'll kiss your ass if anybody in this place knows what tune you're playing!" And everybody in the place heard him, too. What a big square! What could I do? I didn't say anything, just kept playing. Sure was a drag.

---

3. Unhappy.

Somewhat inconsistently, the musician wants to feel that he is reaching the audience and that they are getting some enjoyment from his work, and this leads him to give in to audience demands. One man said:

> I enjoy playing more when there's someone to play for. You kind of feel like there isn't much purpose in playing if there's nobody there to hear you. I mean, after all, that's what music's for—for people to hear and get enjoyment from. That's why I don't mind playing corny too much. If anyone enjoys it, then I kind of get a kick out of it. I guess I'm kind of a ham. But I like to make people happy that way.

This statement is somewhat extreme; but most musicians feel it strongly enough to want to avoid the active dislike of the audience: "That's why I like to work with Tommy. At least when you get off the stand, everybody in the place doesn't hate you. It's a drag to work under conditions like that, where everybody in the place just hates the whole band."

III. Isolation and Self-Segregation

Musicians are hostile to their audiences, being afraid that they must sacrifice their artistic standards to the squares. They exhibit certain patterns of behavior and belief which may be viewed as adjustments to this situation; they will be referred to here as "isolation" and "self-segregation" and are expressed in the actual playing situation and in participation in the social intercourse of the larger community. The primary function of this behavior is to protect the musician from the interference of the square audience and, by extension, of the conventional society.

The musician is, as a rule, spatially isolated from the audience, being placed on a platform which, being inaccessible to them, provides a physical barrier that prevents any direct interaction. This isolation is welcomed because the audience, being made up of squares, is felt to be potentially dangerous. The musicians fear that direct contact with the audience can lead only to interference with the musical performance. Therefore, it is safer to be isolated and have nothing to do with them. Once, where such physical isolation was not provided, a player commented:

> Another thing about weddings, man. You're right down on the floor, right in the middle of the people. You can't get away from them. It's different if you're playing a dance or in a bar. In a dancehall you're up on stage where they can't get at you. The same thing in a cocktail lounge, you're up behind the bar. But a wedding—man, you're right in the middle of them.

Musicians, lacking the usually provided physical barriers, often improvise their own and effectively segregate themselves from their audience.

> I had a Jewish wedding job for Sunday night. . . . When I arrived, the rest of the boys were already there. The wedding had taken place late, so that the people were just beginning to eat. We decided, after I had conferred with the groom, to play during dinner. We set up in a far corner of the hall. Jerry pulled the piano around so that it blocked off a small space, which was thus separated from the rest of the people. Tony set up his drums in this space, and Jerry and Johnny stood there while we played. I wanted to move the piano so that the boys could stand out in front of it and be next to the audience, but Jerry said, half-jokingly, "No, man. I have to have some protection from the squares." So we left things as they were. . . .

> Jerry had moved around in front of the piano but, again half-humorously, had put two chairs in front of him, which separated him from the audience. When a couple took the chairs to sit on, Jerry set two more in their place. Johnny said, "Man, why don't we sit on those chairs?" Jerry said, "No, man. Just leave them there. That's my barricade to protect me from the squares."

Many musicians almost reflexively avoid establishing contact with members of the audience. When walking among them, they habitually avoid meeting the eyes of squares for fear that this will establish some relationship on the basis of which the square will then request songs or in some other way attempt to influence the musical performance. Some extend their behavior to their ordinary social activity, outside of professional situations. A certain amount of this is inevitable, since the conditions of work—late hours, great geographic mobility, and so on—make social participation outside of the professional group difficult. If one works while others sleep, it is difficult to have ordinary social intercourse with them. This was cited by a musician who had left the profession, in partial explanation of his action: "And it's great to work regular hours, too, where you can see people instead of having to go to work every night." Some younger musicians complain that the hours of work make it hard for them to establish contacts with "nice" girls, since they preclude the conventional date.

But much of this behavior develops out of the hostility toward squares. The attitude is seen in its extreme among the "X—Avenue Boys," a clique of extreme jazzmen who reject the American culture *in toto*. The quality of their feeling toward the outside world is indicated by one man's private title for his theme song: "If You Don't Like My Queer Ways You Can Kiss My Fucking Ass." The ethnic makeup of the group indicated further that their adoption of these extreme artistic and social attitudes was part of a total rejection of conventional American society. With few exceptions the men came from older, more fully assimilated national groups: Irish, Scandinavian, German, and English. Further, many of them were reputed to come from wealthy families and the higher social classes. In short, their rejection of commercialism in music and squares in social life was part of the casting aside of the total American culture by men who could enjoy privileged status but who were unable to achieve a satisfactory personal adjustment within it.

Every interest of this group emphasized their isolation from the standards and interests of the conventional society. They associated almost exclusively with other musicians and girls who sang or danced in night clubs in the North Clark Street area of Chicago and had little or no contact with the conventional world. They were described politically thus: "They hate this form of government anyway and think it's real bad." They were unremittingly critical of both business and labor, disillusioned with the economic structure, and completely cynical about the political process and contemporary political parties. Religion and marriage were rejected completely, as were American popular and serious culture, and their reading was confined solely to the more esoteric *avant garde* writers and philosophers. In art and symphonic music they were interested also in only the most esoteric developments. In every case they were quick to point out that their interests were not those of the conventional society and that they were thereby differentiated from it. It is reasonable to assume that the primary function of these interests was to make this differentiation unmistakably clear.

Although isolation and self-segregation found their most extreme development among the "X— Avenue Boys," they were manifested by less deviant musicians as well. The feeling of being isolated from the rest of the society was often quite strong;

the following conversation, which took place between two young jazzmen, illustrates two reactions to the sense of isolation.

EDDIE: You know, man, I hate people. I can't stand to be around squares. They drag me so much I just can't stand them.

CHARLIE: You shouldn't be like that, man. Don't let them drag you. Just laugh at them. That's what I do. Just laugh at everything they do. That's the only way you'll be able to stand it.

A young Jewish musician, who definitely identified himself with the Jewish community, nevertheless felt this professional isolation strongly enough to make the following statements.

> You know, a little knowledge is a dangerous thing. That's what happened to me when I first started playing. I just felt like I knew too much. I sort of saw, or felt, that all my friends from the neighborhood were real square and stupid. . . .
>
> You know, it's funny. When you sit on that stand up there, you feel so different from others. Like I can even understand how Gentiles feel toward Jews. You see these people come up and they look Jewish, or they have a little bit of an accent or something, and they ask for a rumba or some damn thing like that, and I just feel, "What damn squares, these Jews," just like I was a *goy* myself. That's what I mean when I say you learn too much being a musician. I mean, you see so many things and get such a broad outlook on life that the average person just doesn't have.

On another occasion the same man remarked:

DICK: You know, since I've been out of work I've actually gotten so that I can talk to some of these guys in the neighborhood.

BECKER: You mean you had trouble talking to them before?

DICK: Well, I'd just stand around and not know what to say. It still sobers me up to talk to those guys. Everything they say seems real silly and uninteresting.

The process of self-segregation is evident in certain symbolic expressions, particularly in the use of an occupational slang which readily identifies the man who can use it properly as someone who is not square and as quickly reveals as an outsider the person who uses it incorrectly or not at all. Some words have grown up to refer to unique professional problems and attitudes of musicians, typical of them being the term "square." Such words enable musicians to discuss problems and activities for which ordinary language provides no adequate terminology. There are, however, many words which are merely substitutes for the more common expressions without adding any new meaning. For example, the following are synonyms for money: "loot," "gold," "geetz," and "bread." Jobs are referred to as "gigs." There are innumerable synonyms for marijuana, the most common being "gauge," "pot," "charge," "tea," and "shit."[4]

4. These words will probably be out of date soon after this is written; some already are. They change as musicians feel that they have gained currency among outsiders.

The function of such behavior is pointed out by a young musician who was quitting the business:

> I'm glad I'm getting out of the business, though. I'm getting sick of being around musicians. There's so much ritual and ceremony junk. They have to talk a special language, dress different, and wear a different kind of glasses. And it just doesn't mean a damn thing except "we're different."

IV. Conclusion

This paper has explored certain dimensions of the relationship between dance musicians and their audience, emphasizing the hostility which arises out of the interaction of professional and layman in the working situation. Attention has also been paid to the way in which musicians feel themselves isolated from the larger society and how they maintain that isolation through various modes of self-segregation.

It may be suggested that similar conflicts are to be found in other service occupations and that research in such areas could profitably focus on such matters as the professional's concept of his client, the manner in which the client impinges on (or, from the professional's point of view, interferes with) his work, the effects of such conflicts on professional organization, with particular reference to the defensive tactics employed by the profession, and the relation of such dilemmas to the individual's participation in the life of the larger society.

PART 5

The Fifties

35. Jazz in the Classroom

"A GENERATION AGO HIGH SCHOOL OR college courses in jazz would be as unthinkable as courses in safecracking," wrote one historian in 1984.[1] In fact, courses in jazz appreciation had occasionally been sponsored by high schools and other institutions since the late 1930s: New York University had hired bandleader Vincent Lopez to teach one in 1937, and the New York City Board of Education asked Benny Goodman, George Gershwin, Duke Ellington, and Rudy Vallee to lecture on jazz in city high schools that same year.[2] But the more rigorously historical and analytical approach of Marshall W. Stearns (1908–1966) had an impact on the growing legitimacy of jazz as a topic for serious study.[3] A professor of

Source: Marshall W. Stearns, "Perspectives in Jazz," syllabus in the files of the Institute of Jazz Studies at Rutgers, the State University of New Jersey, in Newark. Courtesy of the Institute of Jazz Studies, Rutgers, the State University of New Jersey, Newark. Reprinted by permission of Elizabeth Stearns.

1. Grover Sales, *Jazz: America's Classical Music* (New York: Da Capo, 1992 [1984]), p. 209.

2. See "N. Y. U. Will Teach Jazz," *New York Times*, July 15, 1937, p. 16, and David W. Stowe, *Swing Changes: Big Band Jazz in New Deal America* (Cambridge: Harvard University Press, 1994), p. 29. Black journalist and historian Frank Marshall Davis taught secondary-school jazz history classes as early as 1943; see Ronald G. Welburn, *American Jazz Criticism, 1914–1940,* Ph.D. dissertation, New York University, 1983, p. 189. College jazz education is often said to date back to the first jazz performance degree, offered by North Texas State in 1947. But historically black colleges offered instruction in jazz performance long before that. One historian traces jazz education to Len Bowden, who taught jazz at Tuskegee Institute in 1919; see William T. McDaniel, Jr., "The Status of Jazz Education in the 1990s: A Historical Commentary," *International Jazz Archives Journal* 1:1 (1993), pp. 114–39.

3. *Time* magazine reported that the number of colleges offering jazz courses rose from twenty-five in 1965 to over five hundred six years later; see "Jazz Goes to College," *Time,* June 7, 1971, p. 67. The Music Educators National Conference first took notice of jazz in 1956—perhaps not coincidentally, just as rock and roll had begun to make jazz seem less threatening and more respectable. But controversy did continue in the 1950s: while Leonard Bernstein was producing articles and television shows devoted to the appreciation of jazz, his colleague Sir Thomas Beecham publicly condemned the music as "disgusting." See Leonard Bernstein, "The World of Jazz," *Vogue,* March 15, 1956, pp. 103–105, 142–45, and Harry Trimborn, "American Jazz Disgusts Beecham," *Miami Herald,* February 17, 1957.

English literature by day, Stearns was also a contributor to *Down Beat* and the author of *The Story of Jazz,* a widely used history. In 1952, he founded the Institute of Jazz Studies at Rutgers, the State University of New Jersey in Newark, which has developed into what is probably the single most important archive for jazz researchers.

This selection is a slightly condensed version of the syllabus for "Perspectives in Jazz," a course in jazz history taught by Stearns at N. Y. U. in the fall of 1950. Throughout the next decade, Stearns helped organize courses in jazz at several colleges and universities in the New York area.[4] For this one, he shared teaching duties with George Avakian and John Hammond, both influential jazz critics and record producers. Compare the organization and content of this course with modern jazz history courses, and you might notice both similarities and provocative differences in how the story of jazz history has been constructed. Stearns begins with the presumption, for example, that jazz is best examined within a worldwide, cross-cultural, comparative context. Another interesting feature of the syllabus is the astonishing list of guest speakers it promised.

Lecture 1. Jazz Definitions

A. Description of the course.
B. The musics of the world in general and the relationship of jazz to European (classical) music in particular. An exposition of the melodic elaboration of Hindu music, the formal elaboration of Balinese music, and the rhythmic elaboration of African music. The birth of the tempered scale and the exploitation of harmony by European composers. The case for jazz as a separate and distinct art-form to be judged by separate and distinct standards. A word on attitudes toward jazz, and some standards for judgement.
C. Class discussion with Faculty Panel (Avakian, Hammond, and Stearns).

Lecture 2: Jazz Prehistory

A. The general cultural background and the specific musical heritage of the Negro in Africa. Tribal origins on the West coast and the early slave trade. The high level of artistic accomplishment.
B. The African musical heritage in the New World: Haiti, Trinidad, Brazil, Cuba, and Dutch Guiana—half-way stations to the United States. The retention and reinterpretation of African culture patterns depending upon the varying reception in the New World due to social attitudes, prevailing religion, and established musical customs.
C. The African musical heritage in the United States. The socio-economic, religious, and musical background and the varying acceptance and rejection of African patterns according to geographical areas. Various early musical forms and their relationship to jazz. Significant parallels in music.

---

4. Such initiatives have typically come from English and Sociology departments because Music departments, until quite recently, have tended to be narrowly focused on pre-twentieth-century European music, treating popular music as a threat rather than as an area for research and instruction.

Lecture 3: New Orleans *Guest: Edmond Hall*

A. The early history of New Orleans, economic, social, and political, and its variety of Old World cultures. The special role of the slave, the free Negro, and the Creoles of color. Prevailing patterns in the arts.
B. The European musical background and its influence on jazz: Protestant hymns, German marches, Spanish and Cuban rhythms, and Italian, French, Scotch-Irish, and Central European melodies (among others).
C. The process of merging and the evolution of early patterns and forms revealing the imprint of the African musical heritage.

Lecture 4: Jelly Roll Morton *Guest Lecturer: Alan Lomax*

The life and times of Jelly Roll Morton with emphasis upon his early New Orleans environment and the fellow musicians whom he knew and who influenced him. Mr. Lomax will read selections from his forthcoming book on Jelly Roll Morton, illustrate his lecture with recordings from the Library of Congress, and demonstrate various points on his own guitar.

Lecture 5: The Blues

A. The evolution of the blues into the musical archetype of jazz, and the relationship of work-songs, ring-shouts, and shouting spirituals.
B. The blues as a social document, reflecting the life and times of its creators.
C. The blues as literature, folk and otherwise, expressing and communicating a complete artistic experience.

Lecture 6: Ragtime *Guest Lecturer: Rudi Blesh*

The origin, evolution, and influence of ragtime in the world of jazz, and its relationship to barrelhouse piano and boogie-woogie. Mr. Blesh will present material from his forthcoming book on ragtime and illustrate his lecture with rare, unissued recordings which he made himself.

Lecture 7: North to Chicago

A. Early exploratory trips of jazz musicians via showboats and tent-shows, vaudeville tours and pioneer bands from 1890 to 1915.
B. The exodus from Storyville in 1917, combined with post-war restlessness and a general migration North, and the arrival in Chicago. Jazz becomes known from coast to coast.
C. Riverboats and the geography of jazz as charted by Louis Armstrong's successive trips North up the Mississippi, reaching East to Pittsburgh and West to Kansas City.

Lecture 8: Chicago and the Jazz Age *Guest: Louis Armstrong*

Lecturer: George Avakian

A. The background of the "Jazz Age" and the highly-publicized debut of Paul Whiteman in Aeolian Hall (1924).
B. The main stream in Chicago: the history and development of Louis Armstrong on records from accomplishments with the Hot Five to the present day.
C. Latter days in the Windy City and the spread of jazz among a series of followers.

Lecture 9: Big Bands in New York *Guest: Duke Ellington*

Lecturer: Avakian

A. How New York became the center of jazz and the focal point of the music industry: origins and sources in the band field.
B. The history of the big band, culminating in the orchestra of Duke Ellington, with the history of its development on phonograph records.
C. The spread of big bands from Fletcher Henderson to the present day.

Lecture 10: Swing Is King *Guest: Benny Goodman*

Lecturer: Hammond

A. The socio-economic background of the Depression and its effect on jazz.
B. Signs of changing times with isolated jazzmen in big bands and the pioneer jazz bands.
C. Goodman's struggle to the top culminating in the Palomar (1935) and the coast to coast jitterbug craze as the band and its offshoots settled into the groove.

Lecture 11: Kansas City and the Count *Guests: Count Basie, Ralph Ellison*

Lecturer: Hammond

A. The middle South-West as a fertile field of jazz and the various pioneers in this area.
B. Kansas City under the Pendergast machine as a Mecca for all jazz musicians. Local musicians and the local scene.
C. The emergence and popularity of Count Basie in 1936, and an analysis of the factors that made the band outstanding and the most notable ancestor of bop.

Lecture 12: Progressive Jazz and Bebop *Guest: Dizzy Gillespie*

A. The effect of the second World War, the record ban, and the migration North on the jazz of the day.
B. The origin and development of progressive jazz and bop compared and contrasted.
C. The growth of the Afro-Cuban influence and the later commercializations of the idiom.

Lecture 13: New Orleans Revival *Lecturer: William Russell*

A. The beginnings of the revival: the publication of *Jazzmen*, the *New Orleans Memories* album (Morton) of C. E. Smith, and the field recordings of H. H. Broun.
B. The discovery and legend of Bunk Johnson, from his first concert in San Francisco to his untimely death.
C. The growing trend in New Orleans music by amateur and professional groups here and abroad.

Lecture 14: Things to Come *Guests: George Shearing, Lennie Tristano*

Experimental jazz in our day, its aims and accomplishments, with a discussion of the nature of musical progress and the best avenues of approach.

Lecture 15: Standards of Criticism in Jazz *Lecturer: Sidney Finkelstein*

A discussion of the aesthetics of jazz based on a world view of fine art and its place in the total picture, followed by a Panel Discussion (Finkelstein, Hammond, Avakian, and Stearns) with the class participating.

36. A Jazz "Masterpiece"

COMPOSER AND WRITER ANDRÉ HODEIR (1921–2011) studied classical music at the Paris Conservatoire and played violin in a number of French jazz groups. Although he composed many film scores and did some jazz arranging, he is best known as an important pioneer of jazz criticism. In this chapter from his influential book, *Jazz: Its Evolution and Essence* (in French, 1954; in English translation, 1956), Hodeir draws on his classical training to produce what is arguably the first technical, musically specific evaluation of a jazz composition. For his analysis, he chose the 1940 recording of "Concerto for Cootie," which Duke Ellington had written to feature trumpeter Cootie Williams.

As an alternative to conventional jazz criticism—most of which has been written by people who neither perform nor compose—Hodeir's serious treatment of musical structures and details has much to recommend it. Although he considered jazz inferior to European classical music (see p. 190), Hodeir does a good deal to legitimize the music by selectively emphasizing features this piece shares with that tradition. His comments on the relationship of the soloist to the other musicians are insightful, and he specifically defends the Concerto's brevity and the pleasure it gives.

Along with the academic terminology and theoretical concepts, however, came a set of values that is rarely acknowledged openly: Hodeir never explains why formal unity, complex orchestration, and the "test of time" should be valued above improvisation, communicative drama, and timeliness. And despite the technical rigor of the argument,

---

Source: André Hodeir, *Jazz: Its Evolution and Essence,* revised edition (New York: Grove Press, 1980), pp. 77–98. First published as *Hommes et Problèmes du Jazz* (Paris, 1954); first English translation, Grove Press, 1956. Reprinted by permission of Michèle Hodeir.

> some conclusions are simply asserted: how do we really know that Williams's vibrato is "profoundly felt," or that he could not have played this melody any other way? What precisely is meant by "purity" and "authenticity," and why is unity so important? To call a recording a "masterpiece" is a way of gaining prestige for a piece of music and its composer, but that label may also deflect our attention away from the meanings that its performances have had for specific audiences.[1]

I. Ups and Downs of the Concerto

Some pieces of music grow old; others stay young. At times we can hardly believe it possible that once we actually enjoyed listening to a page of music or a chorus that now seems overwhelmingly long on faults and short on merits. To make up for this, some works seem more and more attractive to us as time goes by. For one thing, we are more difficult to please at thirty than we were at twenty. Instead of liking a hundred records, we no longer like more than five or six; but perhaps we like them better. Judging by my own experience, there can be no doubt that the test of time has favored Ellington's "Concerto for Cootie"—more, perhaps, than any other work, and this is a sure sign of merit. It has become clear to me that this piece is one of the high points in Ellington's output, which has been vast and rich in flashes of genius, but unequal and occasionally disappointing. I would even say that it offers a striking epitome of certain essential aspects of his work.

The concerto formula—that is, a composition centered around a single soloist accompanied by large orchestra—is widely used these days. There is almost no repertory that does not include a certain number of arrangements conceived with an eye toward the possibilities, the style, and the ambitions of such and such a popular soloist. In 1940, even though it wasn't exceptional, the concerto was rarer. It was only four years before then that Ellington had recorded his first concertos, one of which, "Echoes of Harlem," had already been designed for Cootie Williams. Admittedly, the appearance of these compositions did not constitute an innovation in the form. Before Ellington, Armstrong had recorded solos that had all the concerto's appearances. But the Ellington style of concerto, from the very beginning, not only introduced a markedly different musical climate but also laid the foundation for an infinitely richer conception. In it, far from merely serving to set off the soloist as in Armstrong's records, the orchestra worked in close collaboration with him. Naturally, it would be impossible to state positively that Duke Ellington and his group grasped from the beginning all the possibilities that this kind of composition offered, but it seems probable all the same. In any case, the fact is that, after several years of varyingly successful experiments (the detestable "Trumpet in Spades," in which Rex Stewart trumpeted to such poor advantage, comes to mind), the orchestra recorded, on March 15, 1940,

1. See Robert Walser, "Deep Jazz: Notes on Interiority, Race, and Criticism," in *Inventing the Psychological: Toward a Cultural History of Emotional Life in America,* ed. Joel Pfister and Nancy Schnog (New Haven: Yale University Press, 1997), pp. 271–96. For arguments that musical analysis of jazz should be grounded in the meanings, priorities, and techniques of African-American culture, see LeRoi Jones and Samuel A. Floyd, Jr. in this volume, as well as Dwight Andrews, "From Black to Blues," in Richard J. Powell, ed., *The Blues Aesthetic: Black Culture and Modernism* (Washington, D.C.: Washington Project for the Arts, 1989), pp. 37–41.

this "Concerto for Cootie," which still strikes us, a decade and a half later, as the masterpiece of jazz concertos and as being, along with "Ko-Ko," the most important composition that Duke Ellington has turned out.

The concerto formula is not faultless; to be more precise, it invites esthetic lapses that the arranger and the soloist do not always manage to avoid, even when they are fully aware of the lurking danger. Fear of monotony engenders an abusive use of effects; the difficulty a soloist has in improvising freely against too melodically and harmonically rich an orchestral background leads to the greatest possible reduction of the orchestra's part. In this way, a kind of by-product of the concerto is produced, with a virtual elimination of all dialogue between the soloist and the orchestra, which is actually the basic reason for the form's existence. On the other hand, the fact that the arranger conceives the concerto in terms of a single soloist—of such and such a special soloist—makes it possible to attain most easily in this form that cardinal virtue of any work of art, unity. Perhaps it will be objected that this is a classical composer's idea, but I think I have had enough experience with jazz to affirm that the notion of unity is just as important in this music as in European music. Is it possible to believe that a record joining the talents of Armstrong and Parker, even at the top of their form, would constitute a composition, in the real sense of the word? Certainly not. We could go further and say that, in actuality, such a confrontation would immediately be recognized as unfruitful. Neither Armstrong nor Parker would really be in top form; it is much more likely neither would be able to play at all. True, I have purposely taken an extreme example; but records have given us many specimens of similar though less extreme confrontations, and I don't remember a single successful one in the lot.

In the light of this, it is easy for me to say in what way "Concerto for Cootie" rates my qualification as a masterpiece. "Concerto for Cootie" is a masterpiece because everything in it is pure; because it doesn't have that slight touch of softness which is enough to make so many other deserving records insipid. "Concerto for Cootie" is a masterpiece because the arranger and the soloist have refused in it any temptation to achieve an easy effect, and because the musical substance of it is so rich that not for one instant does the listener have an impression of monotony. "Concerto for Cootie" is a masterpiece because it shows the game being played for all it is worth, without anything's being held back, and because the game is won. We have here a real concerto in which the orchestra is not a simple background, in which the soloist doesn't waste his time in technical acrobatics or in gratuitous effects. Both have something to say, they say it well, and what they say is beautiful. Finally, "Concerto for Cootie" is a masterpiece because what the orchestra says is the indispensable complement to what the soloist says; because nothing is out of place or superfluous in it; and because the composition thus attains unity.

2. Structure of "Concerto for Cootie"

"Concerto for Cootie" should not be considered as an ordinary arrangement. Its unusual structure, the polish of its composition, the liberties with certain well-established rules that are taken in it, the refusal to improvise—these characteristics are enough to place it rather on the level of original composition as this term is understood by artists of classical training. "Concerto for Cootie" is not derived from any earlier melody. True, "Do Nothin' Till You Hear From Me" uses the same melodic figure; but this song, composed by Ellington, is several years later than the orchestral work. There can be no doubt that it was adapted from it. "Do Nothin'" is in a way the commercial version of the guiding idea behind "Concerto for Cootie." Indeed, it retains only the initial phrase. We wouldn't even have mentioned the song here but for the fact that this phrase had to be revised to conform to the traditional framework of the thirty-two bar song. We shall be able to appreciate the original better by comparing it with this popularized version.

This initial phrase, which constitutes the principal theme of the "Concerto," undergoes numerous transformations in the course of the composition. We shall call it theme A at its first exposition, A', A", and A"' in what follows. Figure B, which comes between the second and third exposition of A, serves merely as an episode; actually, it comes where the bridge would have if "Do Nothin'" had preceded the "Concerto."[2] On the contrary, theme C is extremely important. Played in a new key—and one that is not even neighboring—it completely changes the lighting and atmosphere of the composition. The lyricism of its lines, its range spread over a whole octave, and its being diatonic form a perfect contrast with the restraint of the first theme, which is static, chromatic, and confined within the limits of a fourth except for its last phrase. Finally, the re-exposition of A is immediately followed by a final coda that borrows its components from Ellington's "Moon Glow," put out in 1934 by Brunswick. Here, in outline form, is how these various elements are joined together:

PLAN OF "CONCERTO FOR COOTIE"

Introduction	8 bars
I. Exposition (F major)	
Theme A	10 bars
followed by A'	10 bars
followed by B	8 bars
followed by A"	10 bars
followed by a modulatory transition	2 bars
II. Middle section (D-flat major)	
Theme C	16 bars
followed by a modulatory transition	2 bars
III. Re-exposition and coda (F major)	
A"'	6 bars
Coda	10 bars

For a number of reasons, this construction is the furthest thing from being customary in jazz. The notion of variation scarcely subsists in it at all. As for the concept of chorus, it has disappeared without a trace. For that matter, since improvisation doesn't play any active role here, there would have been no reason for Ellington to preserve the traditional division in choruses. It was logical to adopt a more flexible structure, one more closely related to the "composed" nature of the piece. The mold chosen calls to mind the da capo form of the eighteenth-century Italians, although the recurrence of A after the middle section C is hardly more than suggested.

Another surprising thing is the use of ten-bar phrases, an unprecedented practice in the history of jazz arrangements. This innovation is even bolder than it seems at first encounter. The initial phrase, as it appears in the printed edition of "Do Nothin'," does indeed comprise eight bars. The two extra bars of A and A' could therefore be considered as little orchestral codas added as an afterthought, constituting a kind of rebound of the phrase played by the soloist, even though they fit in—it would not be enough to say merely that they follow—so perfectly that the ear is

2. Many jazz compositions have a contrasting middle section that is often called a "bridge." [RW]

aware of no break. But a closer analysis of the phrase's articulation reveals that its final turn in the "Do Nothin'" version is completely different from the original ending. The new turn is, for that matter, pretty weak, and there can be no doubt that it was added in order to reestablish a rhythmic equilibrium of the conventional kind that the "Concerto," a free composition, deliberately ignored. Notice (Ex. 1) that in "Concerto for Cootie" the final note comes one bar sooner than is customary. Ending a phrase like this on a weak measure was, in 1939, absolutely revolutionary, and yet no one seems to have noticed it, because the band takes up the phrase right away and goes ahead with it as naturally as can be. The listener who hasn't been forewarned is not aware that the real phrase ends in the sixth measure, and the forewarned listener doesn't react much differently. It would almost seem as though seven-bar melodies had been heard since the beginning of jazz.

The second exposition of A—that is, A'—fits in with the traditional rules; the twofold repetition, in the sixth measure, of a group of four eighth notes is enough to create anew the usual symmetry. The little orchestral coda remains, though, making

the section cover ten bars. A'', on paper, differs from A only in these last two measures, which prepare the transition to C. However, the performance gives the phrase quite a different aspect. In addition to the question of sonority, which we shall consider later, it must be noticed that Cootie here gives back to the notes their rhythmic values, which he had deliberately distorted during the first exposition of the theme. Finally, A''' is a merely suggested restatement of A. After four bars, which include a melodic variant, there is a sudden branching out to the coda—a conclusion for which the way has been prepared by the changing harmonies that underline this restatement.

3. Simplicity and Subtlety of the Harmony

The harmonic language of "Concerto for Cootie" is, on the whole, extremely simple. Apart from the introduction, the general climate of the piece is as resolutely consonant as "Ko-Ko," Ellington's other masterpiece of that period, was the opposite. In the "Concerto," dissonance plays a secondary role; it does not constitute the foundation of the harmony. It does not serve to create a feeling of tension, but operates as a means of adding color. Nonetheless, the many dissonanes to be found in the work are not there for nothing: there can be no doubt that their suppression would weaken it considerably. It is they, certainly, that by contrast make the consonances sound so bright and fresh. This over-all harmonic simplicity doesn't rule out subtlety of detail. Certain passages have presented problems to the best-trained ears. The little phrase in contrary motion in the seventh and eighth measures of the coda, which is harmonically a real gem, would provide a test in musical dictation for the greatest specialists in this ticklish sport; but I want to call attention merely to its musical beauty, which I like to think any listener will appreciate.

Another exceptional passage is the measure just before the exposition of theme C. I doubt that there are many examples of modulations more striking than this one, not only in jazz but in all music. On paper, it seems extremely simple, and no doubt it actually is. Listening to it, one has to admire the abruptness and rigor of this turning; and its effect is all the more astonishing because Ellington has put before it a two-beat rest that constitutes—taking into consideration the completely inconclusive phrase just preceding it—the most effective break you could ask for between one part of a piece and another that you would have expected to follow without any break at all. To call this a stroke of genius is, for once, not to misuse the phrase.

It would be possible to mention a number of other harmonic finds. In spite of its ambiguous character and a certain acidity that does not lack charm, the introduction is not the most successful part of the composition. I prefer certain details in the purely accompanying part: the saxes' dissonances behind phrase A' or a complementary phrase like the one in the eighth measure of C, which has a melodic, harmonic, and instrumental savor that is truly penetrating. Atttention should also be called to the occasional use of blue notes in some of the trombones' punctuation of phrases A and A'. Although, basically, "Concerto for Cootie" has no more connection with the blues than Hawkins's "Body and Soul," these blue notes are by no means out of place; the faint touch of the blues that they introduce fits into the atmosphere of the piece perfectly.

There remains the added-sixth chord, which is put to considerable use here. This harmonic combination, which generally raises my hackles, fills me with joy in the "Concerto." It is true that Ellington sometimes uses it in a regrettably Gershwin-like way, but that certainly is not the case here. Why? I couldn't say for sure; that sort of thing is more easily felt than explained. Perhaps the consonant climate of the piece accounts for a large part of it; perhaps the general feeling and the orchestration itself play a decisive role. What must be remembered is that no chord, however flaccid, is inherently ugly; the only thing that counts is the use made of it.

4. The Orchestra at the Soloist's Service

There is no point in dwelling on the orchestra's role in "Concerto for Cootie." What we have already said is enough to define it. In this piece, as in most jazz concertos, the orchestra never dominates the soloist; it introduces him, supports him, continues where he leaves off, provides a connection between two of his phrases—in a word, it is at his service. Notice that the orchestra states no theme; when it happens to sketch one of the main motifs, it does so as a reply, not as a statement. The soloist always takes the initiative. Like a good servant, the orchestra is satisfied with approving. Even the admirable modulation that precedes the entry of C is not, from a structural point of view, anything but the opening of a door; once the guest of honor is shown in, the servant fades away into the background.

Still, this servant, though he may not obtrude, says exactly what must be said, and his clothes may not be sumptuous but they are exceptionally elegant. The orchestra's bearing is equaled in sobriety only by the orchestration. In both respects, "Concerto for Cootie" is a model of discretion and authenticity. It displays an economy of means that is the sign of real classicism. To me, the little syncopated figure that is given alternately to the saxes and the brasses to punctuate each exposition of A is infinitely more valuable than the overloaded backgrounds that the big modern band does not always know how to do without; it achieves a maximum of effectiveness without using more than two chords, although it is true that these are renewed each time. Judged by the same standards, the orchestral background of B is possibly even more successful. And what is there to say about the countermelody of C, where the saxes, in their chromatic movement, support Cootie's lyric flight so majestically?

Another cause for admiring astonishment is the incomparable coordination between the harmony and the orchestration. In order to express the nuances of a clear harmony in which there are nonetheless plenty of half-tints, the composer has everywhere hit upon just the instrumentation called for. Orchestral color and harmonic color blend in a way that delights the amateur in me as I observe what this combination brings to the piece and that impresses the professional in me as I remember how rare such a combination is. Actually, this blending is the principal virtue of an orchestration that doesn't offer any sensational innovations but that can still boast some captivating details. I shall mention only the orchestra's big descent at the end of A' (cf. Ex. 1), in which the principal motif, taken by the clarinet, does not emerge clearly from the cloud of enveloping chromatic lines but is delicately suggested; the imitation of the theme is guessed at rather than actually heard.

If I have stressed the lesson in simplicity that the "Concerto" presents in both its harmony and its orchestration, it is because that is precisely what the piece has to teach. However, it is all too easy to confuse what is simple with what is merely simplified. "Concerto for Cootie" demonstrates the possibility of achieving a real orchestral language while observing the strictest economy of means. It constitutes, indeed, a summit that few musicians have reached. In this respect, Duke Ellington here makes one think of Mozart. I don't know whether the jazz fan will appreciate the significance of such a comparison, but I feel safe in making it because this composition deserves to be considered not merely as a specimen of jazz, which is only one kind of music, but as a specimen of music, period.

5. Strong and Weak Points of the Performance

We have just considered the orchestral part of the "Concerto" in its conception. But we must not forget that the conception of a work of jazz cannot be separated from its execution. When Ellington wrote the trumpet part, he wasn't thinking of anyone but Cootie, and similarly he didn't design the work as a whole for any orchestra but his own. Whether the "Concerto" was composed by one man or by a whole group is a good question. It has been and will continue to be asked, although the answer can be provided only by those who were present when the piece was created, either as participants or witnesses. The only thing we can be sure of is that the whole band, then in its great period, took part in the performance. Wallace Jones and Rex Stewart were on trumpet, Joe Nanton, Juan Tizol, and Lawrence Brown on trombone, Barney Bigard on clarinet, Otto Hardwicke, Johnny Hodges, Ben Webster, and Harry Carney on sax, Duke Ellington at the piano, Fred Guy on guitar, Jimmy Blanton on bass, and Sonny Greer on drums; and we mustn't forget, of course, Cootie Williams on solo trumpet. Listing these names and remembering that we are now going to talk about performance brings us right to the heart of jazz. Let us accordingly abandon the very general approach we adopted when talking about the problems offered by the harmonic and orchestral aspects of the piece.

I don't know exactly when the "Concerto" was composed or when it began to be performed, so it would be hard for me to prove that it was not completely broken in when it was recorded, but this seems likely. If so, perhaps the record would have been the better for being put off until after enough performances to correct the occasional lack of preciseness of which the band is guilty. But it is not certain that the result would have been very different. Even at that time the Ellington orchestra was frequently somewhat easygoing in its performance as a group; it rarely had Lunceford's kind of precision. On the other hand, there is no way of knowing whether Cootie would have played his part with the same spirit after another twenty run-throughs; his fire might have died down along the way, and it must be admitted that this would have been completely regrettable. For that matter, the flaws I have referred to are notably few; they are venial and easily overlooked. If they cause regrets in spite of this, it is because they are the only thing to be criticized in a record that otherwise calls only for praise. But you would have to be particularly narrow-minded to let the beauties of this piece be obscured by paying too much attention to the fact that the saxes, for example, scurry after one another in the scale leading to the coda. Alongside these slight defects, the playing in "Concerto for Cootie" actually has many solid virtues. The balance among the players and their fine sound in both loud and muted passages are highlighted by excellent recording technique. Nuances are performed with sensitivity and taste. The band seems to be one man following or, even better, anticipating the leader's wishes.

The tempo of "Concerto for Cootie" is "slow moderato," a difficult one to keep to, but just right for the piece. There are few records in which the rhythm section of the band plays in quite such a relaxed way, and by the same token there are few in which the band phrases with as much swing. Naturally, this is not a torrid record like Hampton's "Air Mail Special." That kind of exaltation, which has its own appeal, is only rarely Duke Ellington's line. But "Concerto for Cootie" is a perfect example of a performance that is full of swing in a gentle climate.

The rhythmic success of the performance is based largely on Jimmy Blanton's playing, of which this is certainly one of the best recorded examples. It is fascinating to follow the bass's admirable part, curiously aired out as it is with whole bars of silence. At each exposition of theme A, Blanton stops playing, only to put in a discreet but effective reappearance at the fifth bar. Such details might constitute the whole attraction of an ordinary record. Here, they almost pass unobserved. I remember that, when I once put Pierre Gérardot on the spot by asking whether the tempo of "Concerto for Cootie" was slow or medium, he had to stop and think a moment before being able to answer. If I had asked him such a question about some run-of-the-mill record that had just appeared, he would doubtless have replied right off; but the "Concerto," for him as for me, was in a world apart from the jazz of every day.

6. An Authentic Composition and the Interpreter's Part in It

The time has come to turn to the soloist's part and ask questions about it just as we did about the orchestra's role. We have just seen that one of the essential characteristics of "Concerto for Cootie" is the elimination of improvisation. There is nothing arbitrary about this; it was imposed upon Ellington by circumstances. As we have already said, partly because it is a kind of concert music but even more because of its very form, the jazz concerto (at least when the orchestra plays more than a merely passive role) seems to require of the soloist greater circumspection than he usually shows in a simple chorus-after-chorus performance. It is appropriate to mention that most of the concertos that came before this one were already notable for the extent to which they had been worked out. No one would believe, for instance that Barney Bigard's part in "Clarinet Lament" was spontaneously improvised from one end to the other in the studio. Nevertheless, a large part was surely left to the moment's inspiration. "Concerto for Cootie" has every appearance of being the first jazz record with an important solo part in which improvisation does not figure at all.

Does that mean that we have here a European-style concerto, a composition worked out in private, then written down, and finally rehearsed and performed? Yes and no. Undoubtedly Ellington realized that such a piece had to be thought out from the first to the last, right up to and including the solo part. Whether this part was put down in black and white or memorized makes little difference. The only thing that counts is its character, which, as far as the melody is concerned, is that of something fixed and final. There seems nothing unwarranted in saying that one performance must have differed from another only in minor expressive details that are left to the interpreter in other kinds of music as well. It remains to be determined whether the trumpet part, of which at least the actual notes were decided on before the recording, is the work of Cootie, of Duke, or of several hands. The question is not easy for anyone who wasn't there when the composition was created. It is hard to believe that a piece of music so perfectly unified as to be almost without parallel in the whole jazz repertory should not be the work of a single man; and that man would have to be Duke Ellington. True, anyone who is familiar with the way that famous band works would have to think twice before positively rejecting the possibility of a collective effort; but, all things considered, this kind of gestation seems unlikely. Pending definite information to the contrary, we shall regard "Concerto for Cootie" as a real *composition* as European musicians understand this word.

However, if the notes of this trumpet part were decided on before the recording, it was still only the notes that were. This feature is what takes us far away from European conceptions. Ernest Ansermet had the right idea when he observed, more than thirty years ago, that even though the work of jazz may be written down, it is not fixed. Unlike the European concerto, in which the composer's intention dominates the interpreter's, the jazz concerto makes the soloist a kind of second creator, often more important than the first, even when the part he has to play doesn't leave him any melodic initiative. Perhaps Cootie had nothing to do with the melody of the

"Concerto"; he probably doesn't stray from it an inch; and still it would be impossible to imagine "Concerto for Cootie" without him.

We here touch upon one of those mysteries of jazz that classical musicians have so much trouble in recognizing but that are basically simplicity itself. For the European musician, sound is a means of expression that is distinct from the creation of a work; for the jazz musician, it is an essential part of this creation. That difference is enough to create a gulf between two conceptions that in other respects seem to work together in the piece we are talking about. No interpreter of European music, whatever his genius, will tell us as much about himself as Cootie does in these three minutes. It is the expressionist conception of jazz that allows the interpreter to substitute himself for the composer, to express his personality completely, to make himself a creator. Some people condemn expressionism of any kind, regarding it as a debasement. To do so is to condemn almost all jazz. Although many soloists may have abused the possibilities offered them, the greatest have managed to stay within certain limits; but these limits themselves are broader than some ears, convinced of the absolute superiority of European art, can tolerate in a musical manifestation that is judged, a priori, to be inferior.

Don't misunderstand me: I don't in the least claim, like most specialized critics, that jazz is *the* music of our time. On the contrary, I wish very much to stress, even though I were to be accused of "racial prejudice," that, to me, the riches of jazz, however precious, cannot for a moment match the riches of contemporary European music. But it is perhaps worthwhile to recall that several centuries had passed before the mind of a genius, Arnold Schoenberg, gave birth to the idea of a "melody of timbres" *(Klangfarbenmelodie)*— that is, a musical sequence in which each sound is expressed by a different timbre. Isn't that, in a different way, what jazz musicians accomplish spontaneously by giving to the sonority of one instrument the most varied possible aspects?

7. A Bouquet of Sonorities

Few records do more than the "Concerto" to make possible an appreciation of how great a role sonorities can play in the creation of jazz. The trumpet part is a true bouquet of sonorities. The phrases given to it by Ellington, which have a melodic beauty of their own that should not be overlooked, are completely taken over by Cootie. He makes them shine forth in dazzling colors, then plunges them in the shade, plays around with them, makes them glitter or delicately tones them down; and each time what he shows us is something new. Even if he had had to put up with a less charming melody, his art would have been enough to make us forget its banality. But it mustn't be thought that this gamut of sonority is merely decorative, artificial, gratuitous. The sonorities he imposes on the melody were conceived in terms of the melody itself. A different melody would have been treated differently; but this particular one, under his fingers, could not have been treated in any other way.

It is interesting to note that there is a different sonority corresponding to each of the three themes. The reason is easy to understand. It is appropriate that theme A, which we have already described as static, should be handled in subdued colors; that theme B, which is savagely harsh, should invite free use of the muted wa-wa's stridencies, which here have an extra brutality; and the lyricism of theme C can be fully expressed only in the upper register of the trumpet, played open. But there are other, more subtle details. Why is there such a diversity of expression in the different expositions of A? (Only A' and A''' are played in the same spirit.) Why does the trumpet have such a violent vibrato in A, whereas A' is played with an even sonority that almost prefigures the way modern trumpets sound? Why, in A", is there that sound held like a thread, which is so disconcerting that it is rather hard to believe it is a muted trumpet rather than a violin? To ask such questions, which come naturally to the classically trained listener, would show ignorance of the fact that "Concerto for Cootie," like many works of jazz, owes its vitality to the contrast of sonorities—a contrast that does not in the least affect its basic unity.

Furthermore, with what taste, with what sense of proportion Cootie uses his amazing technique for producing different timbres! How admirably he knows how to bring to bear on expressive detail the resources of an art that, used with less discipline, would risk being nothing more than an advanced exercise—far from ordinary to be sure, but without special significance! Unreserved admiration is the only possible reaction to his discreet and sensitive use of the glissando, which is scarcely noticeable in the various versions of A, is more developed in B, and becomes in C an essential part of the lyricism. This judicious use of sonorities is perfectly paralleled by the intelligence of his phrasing. We have already noted that Cootie deliberately twisted the rhythmic values of theme A. It is not easy to bring off that sort of treatment. Even when the melody lends itself to it—and this one does—there is the constant danger of being corny in the worst possible way. Cootie's performance does not for a moment seem in the least bit mannered. From the very first, the listener cannot doubt that the kind of vibrato he uses is profoundly felt.

8. How the Piece Stands

Let's try to place the "Concerto" now, first of all among the trumpeter's performances. The job is not so simple as it might seem at first. The "Concerto" seems to represent a synthesis. Nowhere else has Cootie appeared under more varying aspects; nowhere else has he succeeded in bringing into such radical opposition serenity and passion, lyricism and simple tenderness. Nonetheless, what traces are to be found here of the magical, incantatory Cootie of "Echoes of Harlem," of the mocking Cootie of "Moon Glow," of the hell-bent-for-leather Cootie of "It's a Glory," and of all other Cooties that there isn't room to mention? At the most there is, from time to time, an intonation or the fragment of a phrase to serve as a furtive reminder that it is, after all, the same artist. And yet, who could make any mistake? What soloist leaves a more indelible imprint on his work than this disconcerting Cootie? In a way, he is one of those who constantly show the public a different face. Someone like Louis Armstrong is always more or less himself. It is his incomparable inventive gift that saves him from being repetitious; it doesn't take any time to recognize his triumphal accent, his straightforward phrasing. Cootie covers a wider range; he seems always to be discovering something. For all that, he doesn't lose his identity. This man of a thousand sonorities is still one whose particular sonority you would recognize in a thousand.

In any case, the "Concerto" is certainly one of the most successful records Cootie has made. It can be said that he completely lives up to the music that Duke Ellington wrote for him and surrounded him with. He attains real greatness here, both in feeling and in taste; there is nothing in this music that is not authentic. I don't know of many soloists who rate such praise.

Before concluding, it might be appropriate to try to refute two objections that will surely occur to those who, taking advantage of the similarities we have more than once indicated, would like to place this work in relation to the classical concerto. These objections are not unimportant; it is simply that they don't apply to the scale of values by which jazz is to be judged.

The first objection would be that "Concerto for Cootie" is a sample of "easy" music; in other words, a work without depth, one of those that reveal all their secrets at a single hearing, and to any kind of listener, without requiring any effort. That may be. By comparison with the great pages of contemporary music, the "Concerto" is not a complex work, and it is even less a revolutionary work. Neither its harmonic system nor its perfectly tonal melody can offer the slightest problem to a trained person. The classical critic, accustomed to judging modern music by certain criteria, will naturally be disappointed at failing to find here, apart from effects of sonority, anything that can't be grasped immediately.

But, in an age when creators have got so far ahead of the public that the bridges threaten to be cut off for some time, is it not fortunate that a composer can resume contact with a more accessible kind of music and give us a well-balanced work that is simple in idiom, sound and not bare of nobility in thought, admittedly easy to understand but individual, even original, and savorful in a way that withstands repeated listening? Isn't there room, alongside Schoenberg's *Suite for Seven Instruments* and Webern's *Chamber Symphony,* for an art designed to please without making any concessions to vulgarity or bombast? Doesn't the "Concerto" satisfy this definition just as do certain pieces by Haydn and Mozart that are not scholarly music but have nonetheless withstood the test of almost two centuries of listening?

The other objection is less important. It has to do with the piece's proportions, "Concerto for Cootie" takes only one side of a ten-inch seventyeight—three minutes. Judged by the standards of European music, by which a symphonic idea of no great significance may well be stretched over more than a quarter of an hour, that is not very much. But what is such a criterion worth? It is to be feared that attaching so much importance to size is one of the prejudices of the European mind, which is under the influence of several grandiose achievements. The *St. Matthew Passion* is not a masterpiece because it lasts almost four hours; it is a masterpiece because it is the *St. Matthew Passion.* For that matter, this prejudice has been gravely breached even in Europe. Didn't Schoenberg, in reaction to the bombast of post-Romanticism, say he would like to see a novel expressed "in a single sigh"? Didn't Webern make some of his compositions incredibly brief? Speaking little makes no difference if a great deal is said. Though it is no miracle of condensation, "Concerto for Cootie" says more in three minutes than such a long and uneven fresco as the *Liberian Suite.*[3]

All that remains is to place "Concerto for Cootie" as jazz. Almost twenty years of experience were required before orchestral jazz produced, within a few days of each other, its two most important works. The first is "Ko-Ko." It has less freshness and serenity, but perhaps more breadth and grandeur. The second is the "Concerto." In the perfection of its form and the quality of its ideas, the "Concerto," which combines classicism and innovation, stands head and shoulders above other pieces played by big bands. It has almost all the good features found in the best jazz, and others besides that are not generally found in Negro music. It makes up for the elements it doesn't use by the admirable way in which it exploits those that constitute its real substance. Isn't that exactly what a masterpiece is supposed to do?

---

3. A much longer Ellington composition of 1947. [RW]

37. Sonny Rollins and the Challenge of Thematic Improvisation

IF ANDRÉ HODIER CREATED THE FIRST detailed formalist account of a jazz composition, it fell to composer and conductor Gunther Schuller (b. 1925) to do the same for an improvisation. A historian as well as a musician (he is the composer most prominently associated with the idea of "third-stream" blendings of jazz and academic modernism), Schuller has made important contributions to jazz scholarship, particularly his book *Early Jazz* and this influential article, written for the first issue of *The Jazz Review* (November 1958).[1] For his analysis, Schuller chose the 1956 recording of "Blue 7" by tenor saxophonist Sonny Rollins (b. 1930). Schuller argued that Rollins's extensive use of thematic development marked a new level of musical "evolution"; like Hodeir, Schuller celebrated structural unity as a sign of progress in jazz.[2]

Schuller's analysis was an important milestone for jazz scholarship in that it dealt specifically and rigorously with the details of an improvised solo. Yet its lack of cultural context meant that it illuminated only his own delight in the music, without necessarily explaining why other listeners might have enjoyed Rollins's performance (such as the bohemian intellectuals who heard him, around the same time, at the Five Spot in New York). Moreover, it is a reminder that what is useful to historians need not be helpful to musicians: after coming across this article, Rollins resolved to stop reading reviews of his playing.[3]

Source: Gunther Schuller, "Sonny Rollins and the Challenge of Thematic Improvisation," in *Musings: The Musical Worlds of Gunther Schuller* (New York: Oxford University Press, 1986), pp. 86–97. Reprinted from *The Jazz Review*, November 1958. Reprinted by permission of Gunther Schuller.

1. See Gunther Schuller, *Early Jazz: Its Roots and Musical Development* (New York: Oxford University Press, 1968); *The Swing Era: The Development of Jazz, 1930–1945* (New York: Oxford University Press, 1989); and *Musings: The Musical Worlds of Gunther Schuller* (New York: Oxford University Press, 1986), in which the Rollins analysis was reprinted.

2. In fact, it is striking how similar their two analyses look, even though one piece was swing composed for a big band, the other hard bop improvised by a small combo. Analyses always reflect values: both Hodeir and Schuller studied in an analytical tradition that prized organic unity, and both found what they had been trained to look for. For a comparable and nearly contemporary celebration of the Modern Jazz Quartet, see Martin Williams, "The Pleasures of Form," *The Griffin* 9:12 (December 1960), pp. 9–16. For further analysis of Rollins's improvisation and Schuller's treatment of it, see Robert Walser, "Deep Jazz: Notes on Interiority, Race, and Criticism," in *Inventing the Psychological: Toward a Cultural History of Emotional Life in America*, ed. Joel Pfister and Nancy Schnog (New Haven: Yale University Press, 1997), pp. 271–96.

3. See Francis Davis, *In the Moment: Jazz in the 1980s* (New York: Oxford University Press, 1986), pp. 124–25.

Since the days when pure collective improvisation gave way to the improvised solo, jazz improvisation has traveled a long road of development. The forward strides that characterized each particular link in this evolution were instigated by the titans of jazz history of the last forty-odd years: Louis Armstrong; Coleman Hawkins; Lester Young; Charlie Parker and Dizzy Gillespie; Miles Davis; collectively the MJQ under John Lewis's aegis; and some others in varying but lesser degrees. Today we have reached another juncture in the constantly unfolding evolution of improvisation, and the central figure of this present renewal is Sonny Rollins.

Each of the above jazz greats brought to improvisation a particular ingredient it did not possess before, and with Rollins thematic and structural unity have at last achieved the importance in pure improvisation that elements such as swing, melodic conception, and originality of expression have already enjoyed for many years.

Improvisatory procedures can be divided roughly into two broad and sometimes overlapping categories which have been called paraphrase and chorus improvisation. The former consists mostly of an embellishment or ornamentation technique, while the latter suggests that the soloist has departed completely from a given theme or melody and is improvising freely on nothing but a chord structure. (It is interesting to note that this separation in improvisational techniques existed also in classical music in the sixteenth to eighteenth centuries, when composers and performers differentiated between ornamentation (*elaboratio*) and free variation (*inventio*).) Most improvisation in the modern jazz era belongs to this second category, and it is with developments in this area that this article shall concern itself.

In short, jazz improvisation became through the years a more or less unfettered, melodic-rhythmic extemporaneous composing process in which the sole organizing determinant was the underlying chord pattern. In this respect it is important to note that what we all at times loosely call "variation" is in the strictest sense no variation at all, since it does not proceed from the basis of varying a given thematic material but simply reflects a player's rumination on an *unvarying* chord progression. It is thus more "passacaglia" than "variation." As André Hodeir put it in his book *Jazz: Its Evolution and Essence*, "Freed from all melodic and structural obligation, the chorus improvisation is a simple emanation inspired by a given harmonic sequence."

Simple or not, this kind of extemporization has led to a critical situation: to a very great extent, improvised solos—even those that are in all other respects very imaginative—have suffered from a general lack of over-all cohesiveness and direction—the lack of a unifying force. There are exceptions to this, of course. Some of the great solos of the past (Armstrong's "Muggles," Hawkins's "Body and Soul" (second chorus), Parker's "Ko-Ko," etc.) have held together as perfect compositions by virtue of the improviser's genial intuitive talents. (Genius does not *necessarily* need organization, especially in a strict academic sense, since it makes its own laws and sets its own standards, thereby creating its own kind of organization.) But such successful exceptions have only served to emphasize the relative failure of less inspired improvisations. These have been the victims of one or perhaps all of the following symptoms: (1) the average improvisation is mostly a stringing together of unrelated ideas; (2) because of the *independently* spontaneous character of most improvisation, a series of solos by different players within a single piece have very little chance of bearing any relation to each other (as a matter of fact, the stronger the individual personality of each player, the less uniformity the total piece is likely to achieve); (3) in those cases where composing (or arranging) is involved, the body of interspersed solos generally has no relation to these nonimprovised sections; (4) otherwise interesting solos are often marred by a sudden quotation from some completely irrelevant material.

I have already said that this is not altogether deplorable (I wish to emphasize this), and we have seen that it is possible to create pure improvisations which are meaningful realizations of a well-sustained over-all feeling. Indeed, the majority of players are perhaps not temperamentally or intellectually suited to do more than that. In any case, there is now a tendency among a number of jazz musicians to bring thematic (or motivic) and structural unity into improvisation. Some do this by combining composition and improvisation, for instance the Modern Jazz Quartet and the Giuffre Three; others, like Sonny Rollins, prefer to work solely by means of extemporization.

Several of the latter's recordings offer remarkable instances of this approach. The most important and perhaps most accessible of these is his "Blue 7" (Prestige LP 7079). It is at the same time a striking example of how *two* great soloists (Sonny and Max Roach) can integrate their improvisations into a unified entity.

I realize fully that music is meant to be listened to, and that words are not adequate in describing a piece of music. However, since laymen, and even many musicians, are perhaps more interested in knowing exactly how such structural solos are achieved than in blindly accepting at face value remarks such as those above, I shall try to go into some detail and with the help of short musical examples give an account of the ideational thread running through Rollins's improvisation that makes this particular recording so distinguished and satisfying.

Doug Watkins starts with a restrained walking bass-line and is soon joined by Max Roach, quietly and simply keeping time. The noncommittal character of this introductory setting gives no hint of the striking theme with which Rollins is about to enter. It is made up of three primary notes: D, A flat, and E (Ex. 1).[4] The chord progression underlying the entire piece is that of the blues in the key of B flat. The primary notes of the theme (D, A flat, E) which, taken by themselves, make up the essential notes of an E-seventh chord thus reveal themselves as performing a double function: the D is the third of B flat and at the same time the seventh of E; the A flat is the seventh of B flat and also (enharmonically as G sharp) the third of E; the E is the flatted fifth of B flat and the tonic of E. The result is that the three tones create a bitonal complex of notes in which the "blue notes" predominate.[5]

At the same time, speaking strictly melodically, the intervals D to A flat (tritone) and A flat to E (major third) are among the most beautiful and most potent intervals in the Western musical scale. (That Rollins, whose music I find both beautiful and potent, chose these intervals could be interpreted as an unconscious expression of affinity for these attributes, but this brings us into the realm of the psychological and subconscious nature of inspiration and thus quite beyond the intent of this article.)[6]

---

4. The notes C, D flat, and A in bar 5 are simply a transposition of motive *a* to accommodate the change to E flat in that measure, and all other notes are nonessential alterations and passing tones.

5. Bitonality implies the simultaneous presence of two tonal centers or keys. This particular combination of keys (E and B flat—a tritone relationship), although used occasionally by earlier composers, notably Franz Liszt in his *Malediction Concerto,* did not become prominent as a distinct musical device until Stravinsky's famous "Petrushka chord" (F sharp and C) in 1911.

6. It should also be pointed out in passing that "Blue 7" does not represent Rollins's first encounter with these particular harmonic-melodic tendencies. He tackled them almost a year earlier in "Vierd Blues" (Prestige LP 7044, Miles Davis Collector's Items). As a matter of fact, the numerous similarities between Rollins's solos on "Blue 7" and "Vierd Blues" are so striking that the earlier one must be considered a study or forerunner of the other. Both, however, are strongly influenced, I believe, by Thelonious Monk's explorations in this area in the late forties, especially such pieces as "Misterioso" (Blue Note LP 1511, Thelonious Monk, Vol. 1).

Ex. 1

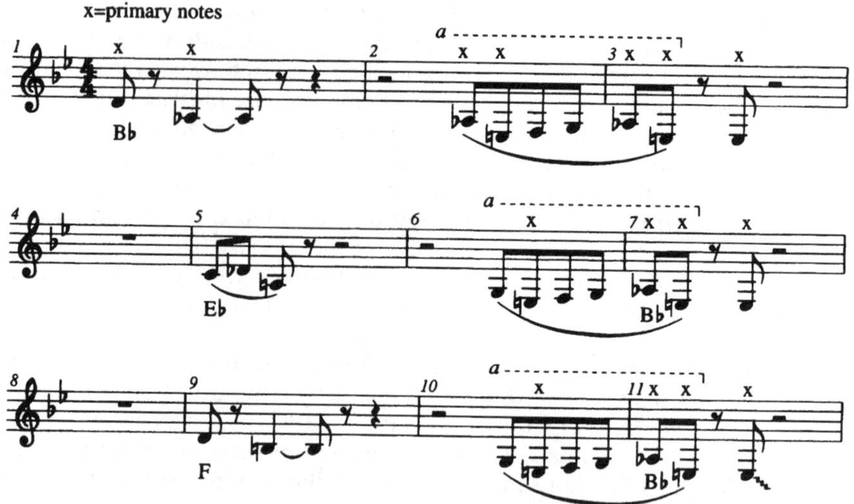

This theme then—with its bitonal implications (purposely kept pure and free by the omission of the piano), with its melodic line in which the number and choice of notes is kept at an almost rock-bottom minimum, with its rhythmic simplicity and segmentation—is the fountainhead from which issues most of what is to follow. Rollins simply extends and develops all that the theme implies.

As an adjunct to this twelve-bar theme, Rollins adds three bars which in the course of the improvisation undergo considerable treatment. This phrase is made up of two motives. It appears in the twelfth to fourteenth bars of Rollins's solo, (Ex. 2) and at first seems gratuitous. But when eight choruses later (eight counting only Rollins's solos) it suddenly reappears transposed, and still further on in Rollins's eleventh and thirteenth choruses (the latter about ten minutes after the original statement of the phrase) Rollins gives it further vigorous treatment, it becomes apparent that it was not at all gratuitous or a mere chance result, but part of an over-all plan.

A close analysis of Rollins's three solos on "Blue 7" reveals many subtle relationships to the main theme and its three-bar sequel. The original segmentation is preserved throughout. Rollins's phrases are mostly short, and extended rests (generally from three to five beats) separate all the phrases—an excellent example of how well-timed silence can become a part of a musical phrase. There are intermittent allusions to the motive fragments of his opening statement. At one point he introduces new material, which, however, is also varied and developed in the ensuing improvisation. This occurs four bars *before* Max Roach's extended solo. A partial repetition of these bars *after* Max has finished serves to build a kind of frame around the drum solo.

Ex. 2

In this, Rollins's second full solo, thematic variation becomes more continuous than in his first time around. After a brief restatement of part of the original theme, Rollins gradually evolves a short sixteenth-note run (Ex. 3) which is based on our Ex. 1, motive *a*. He reworks this motive at half the rhythmic value, a musical device called diminution. It also provides a good example of how a phrase upon repetition can be shifted to different beats of the measure thus showing the phrase always in a new light. In this case Rollins plays the run six times: as is shown in Ex. 3 the phrase starts once on the third beat, once on the second, once on the fourth, and three times on the first beat.[7]

Ex. 3

Another device Rollins uses is the combining and overlapping of two motives. In his eighth chorus, Rollins, after reiterating Ex. 2, motive *a*, continues with motive *b*, but without notice suddenly converts it into another short motive (Ex. 4) originally stated in the second chorus. (In Ex. 5 the small cue-sized notes indicate where Rollins would have gone had he been satisfied with an exact transposition of the phrase; the large notes show what he did play.)

7. It is also apparent that Rollins had some fingering problems with the passage, and his original impulse in repeating it seems to have been to iron these out. However, after six attempts to clean up the phrase, Rollins capitulates and goes on to the next idea. Incidentally, he has experimented with this particular phrase in a number of pieces and it threatens to become a cliché with him.

Ex. 6

Example 6: *a* is derived from our Ex. 2, motive *a*; *b* from Ex. 2, motive *b*; *c* from Ex. 1; *d* from Ex. 4; *f* from Ex. 1, motive *a*; and *g* comes from the same, using only the last two notes of motive *a*; *e* is derived from the new material used in the "frame" passage around Max's solo. Bar 26 in this example is an approximation; Rollins delays each repetition by a fraction of a beat in such a way that it cannot be notated exactly.

But the crowning achievement of Rollins's solo is his eleventh, twelfth, and thirteenth choruses (Ex. 6) in which, out of twenty-eight measures, all but six are directly derived from the opening and two further measures are related to the four-bar section introducing Max's drum solo. Such structural cohesiveness—without sacrificing expressiveness and rhythmic drive or swing—one has come to expect from the composer who spends days or weeks writing a given passage. It is another matter to achieve this in an on-the-spur-of-the-moment extemporization.

The final Rollins touch occurs in the last twelve bars in which the theme, already reduced to an almost bare-bones minimum, is drained of all excess notes, and the rests in the original are filled out by long held notes. The result is pure melodic essence (Ex. 7). What more perfect way to end and sum up all that came before!

This then is an example of a real variation technique. The improvisation is based not only on a harmonic sequence but on melodic/motivic ideas as well.[8] It should also be pointed out that Rollins differs from lesser soloists who are theme-conscious to a certain extent, but who in practice do not rise above the level of exact repetition when the chords permit, and when they don't, mere sequential treatment. Sequences are often an easy way out for the improviser, but easily become boring to the listener. (In fact, in baroque music, one of the prime functions of embellishment techniques was to camouflage harmonically sequential progressions.) In this respect Rollins is masterful since in such cases he almost always avoids the obvious and finds some imaginative way out, a quality he has in common with other great soloists of the past, e.g., Prez, Parker, etc.

On an equally high level of structural cohesiveness is Max Roach's aforementioned solo. It is built entirely on two clearly discernible ideas: (1) a triplet figure which goes through a number of permutations in both fast and slow triplets, and (2) a roll on the snare drum. The ingenuity with which he alternates between these two ideas gives not only an indication of the capacity of Max Roach as a thinking musician, but also shows again that exciting drum solos need not be just an unthinking burst of energy—they can be interesting and meaningful compositions. Behind Rollins Max is a fine accompanist, occasionally brilliantly complementing Sonny's work, for example eleven bars after his drum solo, when he returns with a three-bar run of triplets followed a second later by a roll on the snare drum—the basic material of his solo used in an accompanimental capacity.[9]

Ex. 7

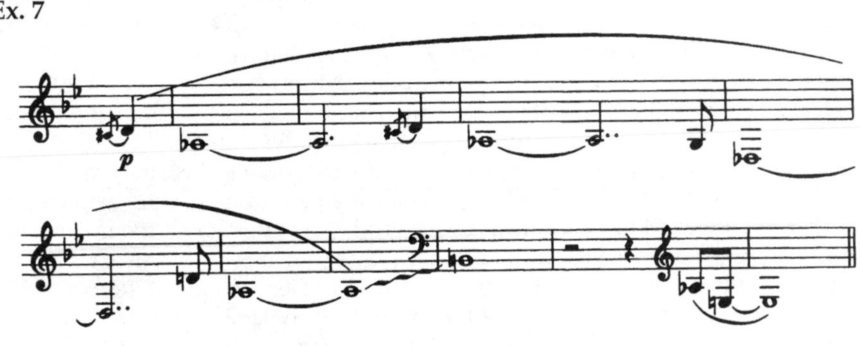

8. In this Rollins has only a handful of predecessors, notably Jelly Roll Morton, Earl Hines, Fats Waller, and Thelonious Monk, aside from the already mentioned Lewis and Giuffre.

9. A similarly captivating instance of solo thematic material being used for accompanimental purposes occurs in the first four bars of John Lewis's background to Milt Jackson's solo in "Django" (Prestige LP 7057).

Such methods of musical procedure as employed here by Sonny and Max are symptomatic of the growing concern by an increasing number of jazz musicians for a certain degree of intellectuality. Needless to say, intellectualism here does not mean a cold mathematical or unemotional approach. It does mean, as by definition, the power of reason and comprehension as distinguished from *purely* intuitive emotional outpouring. Of course, purists or anti-intellectualists (by no means do I wish to *equate* purists with anti-intellectuals, however) deplore the inroads made into jazz by intellectual processes. Even the rather reasonable requisite of technical proficiency is found to be suspect in some quarters. Yet the entire history of the arts shows that intellectual enlightenment goes more or less hand in hand with emotional enrichment, or vice versa. Indeed the great masterpieces of art—any art—are those in which emotional *and* intellectual qualities are well balanced and completely integrated—in Mozart, Shakespeare, Rembrandt. . . .

Jazz too, evolving from humble beginnings that were sometimes hardly more than sociological manifestations of a particular American milieu, has developed as an art form that not only possesses a unique capacity for individual and collective expression, but in the process of maturing has gradually acquired certain intellectual properties. Its strength has been such that it has attracted interest in all strata of intellectual and creative activity. It is natural and inevitable that, in this ever broadening process, jazz will attract the hearts and minds of all manner of people with all manner of predilections and temperaments—even those who will want to bring to jazz a roughly five-hundred-year-old musical idea: the notion of thematic and structural unity.

And indeed I can think of no better and more irrefutable proof of the fact that discipline and thought do not necessarily result in cold or unswinging music than a typical Rollins performance. No one swings more (hard or gentle) and is more passionate in his musical expression than Sonny Rollins. It ultimately boils down to how much talent an artist has; the greater the demands of his art—both emotionally and intellectually—the greater the talent necessary.

A close look at a Rollins solo also reveals other unusual facets of his style: his harmonic language, for instance. Considering the astounding richness of his musical thinking, it comes as a surprise to realize that his chord-repertoire does not exceed the normal eleventh or thirteenth chord and the flatted-fifth chords. He does not seem to require more and one never feels any harmonic paucity, because within this limited language Rollins is apt to use only the choicest notes, both harmonically and melodically, as witness the theme of "Blue 7." Another characteristic of Rollins's style is a penchant for anticipating the harmony of a next measure by one or two beats. This is a dangerous practice, since in the hands of a lesser artist it can lead to lots of wrong notes. Rollins's ear in this respect is remarkably dependable.

Dynamically, too, Rollins is a master of contrast and coloring. Listening to "Blue 7" from this point of view is very interesting. There is a natural connection between the character of a given phrase and its dynamic level (in contrast to all too many well-known players who seem not to realize that to play seven or eight choruses resolutely at the same dynamic level is the best way to put an audience to sleep). Rollins's consummate instrumental control allows him a range of dynamics from the explosive outbursts with which he slashes about, for instance, after Max's solo (or later when he initiates the "fours") to the low B natural three bars from the end, a low note which Sonny floats out with a breathy, smoky tone that should make the average saxophonist envious. Rollins can honk, blurt, cajole, scoop, shrill—whatever the phrase demands without succumbing to the vulgar or obnoxious. And this is due largely to the fact that Sonny Rollins is one of those rather rare individuals who has both taste and a sense of humor, the latter with a slight turn toward the sardonic.

Rhythmically, Rollins is as imaginative and strong as in his melodic concepts. And why not? The two are really inseparable, or at least should be. In his recordings as well as during several evenings at Birdland recently Rollins indicated that he can probably take any rhythmic formation and make it swing. This ability enables him to run the gamut of extremes—from almost a whole chorus of nonsyncopated quarter notes (which in other hands might be just naive and square but through Rollins's sense of humor and superb timing are transformed into a swinging line) to asymmetrical groupings of fives and sevens or between-the-beat rhythms that defy notation.

As for his imagination, it is (as already indicated) prodigiously fertile. It can evidently cope with all manner of material, ranging from Kurt Weill's "Moritat" and the cowboy material of his *Way Out West* LP (Contemporary 3530) to the more familiar area of ballads and blues. But to date his most successful and structurally unified efforts have been based on the blues. ("Sumphin'," for instance, made with Dizzy Gillespie (Verve 8260) is almost on the level of "Blue 7"; it falls short, comparatively, only in terms of originality, but is also notable for a beautifully organized Gillespie solo.) This is not to say that Rollins is incapable of achieving thematic variations in non-blues material. Pieces such as "St. Thomas" or "Way Out West" indicate more than a casual concern with this problem; and in a recent in-the-flesh rendition of "Yesterdays," a lengthy solo cadenza dealt almost exclusively with the melodic line of this tune. His vivid imagination not only permits him the luxury of seemingly endless variants and permutations of a given motive, but even enables him to emulate ideas not indigenous to his instrument, as for instance in "Way Out West" when Rollins, returning for his second solo, imitates Shelly Manne's closing snare drum roll on the saxophone!

Lest I seem to be overstating the case for Rollins, let me add that both his live and recorded performances do include average and less coherent achievements—even an occasional wrong note, as in "You Don't Know What Love Is" (Prestige LP 7079)—which only proves that (fortunately) Rollins is human and fallible. Such minor blemishes are dwarfed into insignificance by the enormity of his talent and the positive values of his great performances. In these and especially "Blue 7," what Sonny Rollins has added conclusively to the scope of jazz improvisation is the idea of developing and varying a *main* theme, and not just a secondary motive or phrase which the player happens to hit upon in the course of his improvisation and which in itself is unrelated to the "head" of the composition. This is not to say that a thematically related improvisation is *necessarily* better than a free harmonically based one. Obviously any generalization to this effect would be unsound: only the quality of a specific musician in a specific performance can be the ultimate basis for judgment. The point is not—as some may think I am implying—that, since Rollins does a true thematic variation, he therefore is superior to Parker or Young in a nonthematic improvisation. I am emphasizing primarily a *difference* of approach, even though, speaking quite subjectively, I may feel the Rollins position to be ultimately the more important one. Certainly it is an approach that inherently has an important future.

The history of classical music provides us with a telling historical precedent for such a prognosis: after largely non-thematic beginnings (in the early Middle Ages), music over a period of centuries developed to a stage where (with the great classical masters) thematic relationships, either in a sonata or various variational forms, became the prime building element of music, later to be carried even further to the level of continuous and complete variation as implied by Schoenberg's twelve-tone technique: in short, an over-all lineage from free almost anarchical beginnings to a relatively confined and therefore more challenging state. The history of jazz gives every indication of following a parallel course, although in an extraordinarily condensed form. In any case, the essential point is not that, with thematically related solos, jazz improvisation can now discard the great tradition established by the Youngs and Parkers, but rather that by building *on* this tradition and enriching it with the new element of thematic relationships, jazz is simply adding a new dimension. And I think we might all agree that renewal through tradition is the best assurance of a flourishing musical future.

38. Beneath the Underdog

"IN OTHER WORDS I AM THREE. . . . THE man who watches and waits, the man who attacks because he's afraid, and the man who wants to trust and love but retreats each time he finds himself betrayed."[1] Using multiple narrative voices to dramatize his conflicts and contradictions, Charles Mingus (1922–1979) wrote one of the most vivid and passionate autobiographies in jazz. Besides being a technically advanced and imaginative double bass player, Mingus was a highly innovative band leader and composer. Drawing on his expertise in a wide range of musical styles, he blurred the lines between improvisation and composition, orally dictating parts to musicians, planning complicated forms and contrasts, but fostering musical dialogue and collective improvisation. Written over many years and finally published in 1971, Mingus's book reflects his awareness of race as an omnipresent social category that affected every aspect of his experience.

In the first excerpt presented here, Mingus recalls his friendship with virtuosic bebop trumpeter Fats Navarro (1923–1950), whom he met while both were playing with Lionel Hampton's band during 1947–48. The second section recounts his experiences playing with the Red Norvo Trio (with Norvo playing vibraphone and Tal Farlow on guitar), 1950–51, as well as his brief tenure with Duke Ellington. The third

---

Source: Charles Mingus, *Beneath the Underdog* (New York: Alfred A. Knopf, 1971), chapters 21, 33, and 39.

1. Charles Mingus, *Beneath the Underdog* (New York: Alfred A. Knopf, 1971), p. 7. [RW]

recreates the night in 1960 when Mingus met Judy Starkey, who would become his third wife, incorporating an explanation of his rhythmic concept of "rotary perception."

There was a man named Fats Navarro who was born in Key West, Florida, in 1923. He was a jazz trumpet player, one of the best in the world. He and my boy met for the first time on a cold winter night in 1947 in Grand Central Station in New York City.[2] Lionel Hampton's band had just got off the train from Chicago and Benny Bailey gaily said good-bye and split: he was leaving for Paris, France. The guys all stood around in their overcoats by the clock, waiting for the new man joining the band. A big, fat fellow walked up carrying a trumpet case and asked in the oddest high squeaky voice "This the Hampton crew?" and Britt Woodman introduced Fats Navarro.

Charles felt embarrassed as the band walked out. There were strangers, women and children, all around, and the guys were laughing too loudly and joking and words like motherfucker and cocksucker echoed through the station. They took the shuttle to Times Square and another subway to Pennsylvania Station and boarded the train for Washington, D.C. It was my boy's first trip to the Apple, but all he saw of it was underground.

Next day they rehearsed in the Palace Theatre in Washington. Hampton had a nine-brass book. The trumpets were Wendell Cully, Duke Garrett, Walter Williams and the high-note player they all called "Whistler."[3] Navarro just sat there placidly with his horn on his lap waiting for his solos while the rest of the band played arrangements. When Hamp pointed to him, Fats stood up and played, and played, and played! played! played! One of the other trumpet players became resentful of this new star in their midst and started muttering, "Schitt, this guy can't even read!" Fats laughed, grabbed the musician's part, eyed it and said, "Schitt, you ain't got nothin' to read here!" And he sight-read from the score impeccably for the entire last show.

Fats was featured all that week in Washington and then they went on the road. The trumpet player whose part Fats had read with such scornful ease couldn't forget what had happened. He was a man who carried a gun and he was convinced he had been insulted. He was lipping a lot about how he would kill Fats one of these days.

They travelled by bus. The small instruments were in the luggage racks, the basses lay cushioned in the back row. Seats were assigned by seniority and the one next to my boy was vacant and was given to Fats Navarro. Mingus and he hadn't talked much up to now. The first night out the whole band was tired and they settled down to rest as the bus headed west. Later Mingus woke up feeling uneasy. It was past twelve midnight and everything was still, the men were sleeping, but the seat beside Mingus was empty. He heard a voice in the dark, someone pleading. "No . . . nooo . . . noooo . . ." Then a familiar little high-pitched squeaked, "Don't *ever* say you gonna cut or shoot somebody 'less you do it, hear? Now if you don't be quiet I might cut you too deep so hold still while I makes you bleed a little 'cause when Theodore Navarro says *he's* gonna cut you that's what he's gonna do." My boy felt the others waking and listening too but nobody made a sound.

---

2. "My boy" is Mingus referring to himself in the third person. [RW]

3. Leo "The Whistler" Sheppard. [RW]

Later Fats came quietly back to his seat. After a silence he said, "That wasn't no way to treat a new member, that was old-fashioned jealousy schitt. Me and Miles and Dizzy and little Benny Harris played together and didn't never have no old-fashioned jealousy schitt. Why should any old member of the band be so uncourteous as to uncourteously threaten a new member?"

Nothing was said afterwards about the cat who got scratched and nothing more was heard from him about shooting Fats.

The band played thirty or forty one-nighters in a row, usually arriving in town just in time to check into their dingy hotel rooms and wash up. Fats and my boy liked to talk to each other and began to room together. It was cheaper that way anyhow.

So this bus rolled on and on across the country, sometimes by day and sometimes at night. And in the crummy hotel rooms with big old-fashioned brass beds that sagged under Fats's enormous weight like hammocks they began a dialogue that continued off and on until the time it had to end.

"You like all kinds of music, Mingus? I was born in Key West, Florida. My family's Cuban. You play Cuban music?"

"I'm not hip to that, Fats. I know some Mexican tunes."

"Hang out with me and I'll take you to some of the joints. You can sit in, blow some. Do you play any other than bass?"

"I try my best not to but I get my chops up on piano sometimes when I'm scoring long enough. I love to hear it on piano."

"Who'd you work with before, Mingus?"

"Illinois Jacquet . . . Alvino Rey . . ."

"Yeah? I played with Jacquet too. You play with Diz or Bird when they was in California? See, I knowed of you before you knowed of me. Talk to Jacquet or someone else—you ain't so undiscovered. Miles played once with you. He used to tell about the band you guys had."

"He did? He hardly said a word except with his horn. How cool can you get when a cat don't even say hello. That's the system, Fats, the system that keeps the blacks apart."

"I see what you mean—so busy worrying how to make a dime with your horn, ain't got time to make a race. Gotta go downtown and see the man, ain't got time to shake your hand. So we play jazz in its place."

"Where's the place, Fats?"

"Right in their faces. They know we know where it's at. Aw, they own us, Mingus. If they don't own us, they push us off the scene. Jazz is big business to the white man and you can't move without him. We just work-ants. He owns the magazines, agencies, record companies and all the joints that sell jazz to the public. If you won't sell out and you try to fight they won't hire you and they give a bad picture of you with that false publicity."

"Sell out, Fats? To who? Look at Ellington, Armstrong, Basie—look at Hamp. All big famous band-leaders. You can't tell me that agents and bookers own guys like that!"

"Mingus, you a nice guy from California, I don't want to disillusion you. But I been through all that schitt and I had to learn to do some other things to get along. I learned better than to try to make it just with my music out on these dirty gang-mob streets 'cause I still love playing better than money. Jazz ain't supposed to make nobody no millions but that's where it's at. Them that shouldn't is raking it in but the purest are out in the street with me and Bird and it rains all over us, man. I was better off when nobody knew my name except musicians. You can bet it ain't jazz no more when the underworld moves in and runs it strictly for geetz and even close out the coloured agents.[4] They shut you up and cheat you on the count of your record sales and if you go along they tell the world you a real genius. But if you don't play they put out the word you're a trouble-maker, like they did me. Then if some honest club owner tries to get hold of you to book you, they tell you're not available or you don't draw or you'll tear up the joint like you was a gorilla. And you won't hear nothin' about it except by accident. But if you behave, boy, you'll get booked—except for less than the white cats that copy your playing and likely either the agent or the owner'll pocket the difference."

"But Fats, I know a lot of guys with managers taking a fair cut—fifteen, twenty, maybe thirty per cent."

"Who told you that? Mingus, *King Spook* don't even own fifty per cent of himself! His agent gets fifty-one, forty-nine goes to a corporation set up in his name that he don't control and he draws five hundred a week and don't say *nothing—but* he's famous, Mingus, hear, he's famous!"[5]

"Nobody didn't hold no gun on King Spook to sign no contract like that."

"You sure about that? One time he got uppity and they kicked him out of the syndicate joints. He had to break up his band out in California. He tried to buck it on his own with nobody but his old lady to help him beat the system. Mingus, that's the biggest gun in the world to stick in a man's ribs—*hunger.* So he sold out again. Now he's got a club named after him but it ain't his. Oh, it's a hard wrinkle, Mingus. Haw haw! I'm thinking when Peggy Lee be appearing in some east side club. Her biggest applause come when she says, 'Now I'm going to do the great Billie Holiday,' and Billie be out on the street and they all be saying she's a junkie. They had Billie so hung up they wouldn't pay the right way, they just put a little money in her hand every night after work, just enough so she come back tomorrow. They drives ya to it, Mingus. They got you down and they don't let you up."

"If you're right, why don't some of the big Negro businessmen step into the picture?"

"'Cause they ain't caught on it's a diamond mine and they too busy scufflin' in their own corn patch and maybe scared. You breaking into Whitey's private vault when you start telling Negroes to wake up and move in where they belong and it ain't safe, Mingus. When the day comes the black man says I want mine, then hide your family and get yourself some guns. 'Cause there ain't no better business for Whitey to be in than Jim Crow business."

"I guess you got something here, Fats. I notice you and me staying in hotels like this one for twice what the white man pays."

"Well, if things don't change, Cholly, do like I tell you, get yourself some heat, guns, cannons, and be willing to die like *they* was. That's all I heared when I was a kid, how bad they was and not afraid to die—to arms, to arms, and all that schitt, give me liberty or give me death! Show me where that atomic power button is and I'll give them cocksuckers some liberty!"

"You said money shouldn't matter to musicians, Fats. What if we all gave up on fame and fortune and played 'cause we love to, like the jazzmen before us—at private sessions for people that listened and respected the players? Then people would know that jazz musicians play for love."

"I thought you had some children, Mingus. Don't they need no ends out there in California?"

---

4. "Geetz" is a slang term for money. [RW]

5. "King Spook" is probably a private nickname for Louis Armstrong. [RW]

"I'm going to write a book and when I sell it I'm not gonna play any more for money. I'll compose and now and then rent a ballroom and throw a party and pay some great musicians to play a couple of things and improvise all night long. That's what jazz originally was, getting away from the usual tiddy, the hime, the gig."

"But Mingus, how about them crumb-crushers of yours when their little stomachs get to poppin' and there ain't nothin' in their jaws but their gums, teeth and tongue, what you gonna do? Play for money or be a pimp?"

"I tried being a pimp, Fats. I didn't like it."

"Then you gonna play for money."

The tour continued and Fats began to complain that he didn't feel good, he hurt all over and he wanted out. My boy thought it was just an excuse because they were all tired of the strenuous one-nighters. One day on the bus Fats began coughing up blood. When they got to Chicago he quit the band and left for New York. But my boy and he were to meet and talk again many times before the day in July of 1950 when Fats Navarro died in New York City of tuberculosis and narcotics addiction. He was twenty-six years old.

So now you've got a job again, boy, in a trio, boy, with a famous name. The leader has red hair, boy, and the guitar player is a white man too, from North Carolina. You're playing in San Francisco and making records and the critics are writing good things. Boy! Boy! Boy!

Then you go out on the road. How does it feel to drive through the South as a member of an otherwise all-white trio and in addition to that you've got a white girl travelling with you? How do you do it? I'll tell you. First you straighten your hair. That's before you start. You're travelling in two cars and your girl rides with you on the road. But before you get to another town, out on the empty highway your girl changes cars and pretends to be the wife of one of the white men so you can check into hotels. You trade rooms that night and again in the morning so she can walk out with her "husband."

How do you go into restaurants? Your girl and her "husband" go in first, then the leader of the band takes you in, big white-man style. You've got straight hair and your skin isn't too dark and you're in the company of a famous guy. But the bouncer looks right at you, looks at you hard, slamming his fist into his palm again and again. He doesn't say anything but you know what he's thinking and he wants you to know.

How does it feel on your last overnight stop in the South when you find in the morning the two other white guys have checked out and you're left there in that hotel, boy, alone with a white woman? It feels very dangerous, that's how it feels. You pack and go downstairs separately not knowing what's going to happen. But thank God nobody says anything, they just *look* at you funny. You get out as fast as you can, get in your car and drive out of that town, and down the road a piece in front of a restaurant you see your leader's car and inside are the two dumb white boys having breakfast.

The trip is almost over so you don't quit. You drive straight through to New York in two cars and go in with this trio to a famous jazz club on the Upper East Side. You want to work and the critics are making it worthwhile—if the bread's low, they at least boost your ego.

How does it feel when the Redhead's trio is asked to do an important, special television show in *colour?* If feels great. At night you're playing this first-class club and daytimes you're rehearsing in the studio. One day during a break you're tuning the bass and you see this producer or somebody talking to the Redhead across the room and they're both looking at you. You feel something is wrong but you don't know what. In a few minutes some guy calls out: "That's all for today, tomorrow at ten," and everyone leaves. While you're packing up, the Redhead comes over and says something like this: "Charlie, I'm sorry to tell you but I have to get another bassist for this show. We'll continue at the club but I can't use you here." What do you say? You ask the name of the new bassist, of course. He tells you. The bassist is white. Now what do you do, curse him out? Probably. You don't remember what you said. He goes away fast. That night he doesn't come to the club, he sends word he's sick. After that somehow you never get a chance to talk to him, he comes late and cuts out early. You have to find out. You start going by where he's staying, at a residential hotel on Broadway. But the desk always says he's not in, they won't even ring. You never get a chance to discuss it with him. Schitt, he can't talk anyway—can't talk about anything real, only about what chick you're going with and like that. You can't talk to the guitarist about it, either, he never says anything. Two dumb white boys that can't talk to you. So you quit the trio. How can you play with guys you can't talk to? You wonder and wonder why he didn't tell you face to face or why he didn't walk off the TV job—some leaders would have. He wanted the money too bad. If he had hired Red Mitchell or somebody like that to replace you, you might have even believed it was something to do with your playing. But what's good in a club is good anywhere else, wouldn't you think? It didn't take much to figure it out. The way television was in those days, they had sponsors who worried about "the Southern market" and "mixing" was taboo.

Yeah, there are certain things in this life that nobody likes to talk about. Nobody white, that is.

So what do you do after that? Maybe you get a job with the Duke himself. This is The Hero, and this is the band you don't quit, but this time you're asked to leave because of an incident with a trombone player and arranger named Juan Tizol. Tizol wants you to play a solo he's written where bowing is required. You raise the solo an octave, where the bass isn't too muddy. He doesn't like that and he comes to the room under the stage where you're practicing at intermission and comments that you're like the rest of the niggers in the band, you can't read. You ask Juan how he's different from the other niggers and he states that one of the ways he's different is that HE IS WHITE.[6] So you run his ass upstairs. You leave the rehearsal room, proceed toward the stage with your bass and take your place and at the moment Duke brings down the baton for "A-Train" and the curtain of the Apollo Theatre goes up, a yelling, whooping Tizol rushes out and lunges at you with a bolo knife. The rest you remember mostly from the Duke's own words in his dressing room as he changes after the show.

"Now, Charles," he says, looking amused, putting Cartier links into the cuffs of his beautiful hand-made shirt, "you could have forewarned me—you left me out of the act entirely! At least you could have let me cue in a few chords as you ran through that Nijinsky routine. I congratulate you on your performance, but why didn't you and Juan inform me about the adagio you planned so that we could score it? I must say I never saw a large man so agile—I never saw *anybody* make such tremendous leaps! The gambado over the piano carrying your bass was colossal. When you exited

6. Tizol was Puerto Rican; when Ellington's band appeared in films of 1929 and 1930, Tizol was forced to blacken his face so that audiences would not think a white musician was performing with a black group. [RW]

after that I thought, 'That man's really afraid of Juan's knife and at the speed he's going he's probably home in bed by now.' But no, back you came through the same door with your bass still intact. For a moment I was hopeful you'd decided to sit down and play but instead you slashed Juan's chair in two with a fire axe! Really, Charles, that's destructive. Everybody knows Juan has a knife but nobody ever took it seriously—he likes to pull it out and show it to people, you understand. So I'm afraid, Charles—I've never fired anybody—you'll have to quit my band. I don't need any new problems. Juan's an old problem, I can cope with that, but you seem to have a whole bag of new tricks. I must ask you to be kind enough to give me your notice, Mingus."

The charming way he says it, it's like he's paying you a compliment. Feeling honoured, you shake hands and resign.

What do you do after that? You start with the gigs again. Maybe you go down to Boston and play a tiddy at Storyville. And in Boston you meet a very sensitive cat named Nat Hentoff who interviews you on his radio show and turned out to be one of the few white guys you could really talk to in your life. Afterwards you get in the habit of writing to him from time to time when you're feeling the pain in the middle of the night and the larger questions that seem to have no answers loom up before your eyes but Hentoff always digs the meaning of the question and replies, all in caps on yellow paper like a story off the wires.

> CHARLIE, THIS IS WHAT I THINK: LOVE, THE DIFFICULTIES OF REAL COMMUNICATION, THE REASON FOR WANTING TO HAVE A REASON FOR STAYING ALIVE, THESE HAVE CONCERNED ME TOO EVER SINCE I CAN REMEMBER. I LAY NO CLAIM TO HAVING ACHIEVED ANY ROCK-LIKE EQUILIBRIUM NOR TO HAVE ANSWERED THE QUESTIONS FOR ANYONE BUT MYSELF. BUT SO FAR THIS IS WHAT I'VE FOUND. THE REASON FOR HATING OTHERS IS HATE OF ONESELF, FEELING THE SELF IS INADEQUATE IN SOME VAGUE OR SPECIFIC WAY, AND PROJECTING THAT TO OTHER OBJECTS. HATE IS A DESTRUCTIVE EMOTION INCAPABLE OF DOING ANY GOOD OR CREATING ANYTHING AND DESTROYS THE MAN WHO HATES MORE PAINFULLY AND THOROUGHLY THAN THE MAN HE HATES. THE MAN WHO HATES DOESN'T REALIZE EVERYONE ELSE IS AS COMPLEX AS HE KNOWS HIMSELF TO BE. NOT THAT THERE AREN'T MANY PEOPLE WHO DO EVIL THINGS AND IN THAT RESPECT ARE EVIL. . . . BUT WHAT MADE THEM THAT WAY? NO ONE IS BORN TO DESTROY. THIS IS SOUNDING MORALISTIC, A TONE I TRY TO AVOID, BUT BECAUSE WE KNOW EACH OTHER SO WELL IF MAINLY THROUGH LETTERS I'LL GO ON. AT THE POINT A GUY BEGINS TO REALIZE THE AMAZING EXTENT OF HIS OWN POTENTIALITY HE BEGINS TO KNOW HE S BEEN WASTING PAIN AND ENERGY IN BLAMING HIMSELF AND HATING OTHERS FOR THINGS THAT HAVE BEEN, THAT WERE DONE, THAT WERE NOT DONE, TO HIMSELF, TO A RACE, TO A UNIVERSE. AT THAT POINT HE SEES THAT LIFE, AS CHAPLIN SAYS, IS A DESIRE NOT A MEANING, WHICH IS WHY A ROSE OR A BIRD HAS TO BE. AFTER ACCEPTING THE SHEER PLEASURE OF WALKING AND BREATHING AND SEEING A SKY, THEN THE QUESTION OF MEANING ARISES.
>
> FOR ME A MAN'S MEANING, THE REASON HE HAS TO KEEP ON LIVING, IS THAT WERE HE TO LIVE THOUSANDS OF YEARS HE WOULD NEVER FULFILL ALL HIS POSSIBILITIES, NEVER COMMUNICATE OR CREATE ALL HE IS CAPABLE OF. SO HE MUST USE WHAT TIME HE HAS CREATING NOW FOR THE FUTURE AND UTILIZE THE PAST ONLY TO HELP THE FUTURE, NOT AS A RAZOR STROP FOR GUILTS AND FEARS THAT INHIBIT HIS VERY BEING. OR LIKE IT SAID AT THE END OF A LABOR UNION SONG I LIKED A LOT WHEN I WAS A KID: WHAT I MEAN IS, TAKE IT EASY, BUT TAKE IT.

I DON T KNOW IF THIS HAS MADE SENSE OR IS OF ANY USE BUT IT S WHAT I THINK.
NAT.

The Fast Buck is packed as usual and several cars with chauffeurs are waiting outside, parked against the mountains of snow piled up in the dark streets, with motors running to keep the drivers warm. My boy is back playing in a small club deep in the warehouse district on the Lower West Side of Manhattan. Bellevue seems far in the past, Dr. Wallach is again in charge of his head and women are his escape from reality.[7]

The club is definitely the place this season for society and college girls from New York and out-of-town who want to have a fling at life via the bandstand or the single male customers who press around the bar and it's nothing wild to walk in on a crowded night and find Mingus at a table with half a dozen girls huddled around him or sitting on his knees or him perching on theirs. The owner, Mr. Caligari, calls him son and his two sons call my boy brother and they've given him a contract saying he can always return with his group anytime he chooses no matter who's playing there. These days Charles feels wholly free and not only as good as any white people but better than most and he's found a musical home, a place to play for people who really seem to want to hear.

But there's lumps in everything in this life. My boy can't help having a hunch that the Police Deparment really enjoys harassing any club where a healthy integrated feeling is a little too out in the open—like the night he sees through a crack from a cubicle in the men's room a uniformed policeman remove and pocket a bar of soap from the washbasin. As soon as the cop walks out my boy finds himself a sliver, quickly lathers his face and runs out to face Mr. Blue writing up a no-soap-in-the-mens'-room citation. Perhaps he suspects it the night another cop walks up outside the big street window, pulls out his penis and pisses right in front of the customers, or when still another one is seen unobtrusively dropping a cigarette butt on the floor, "discovering" it and then writing out a ticket for violation. Perhaps it's the presents of money in brown paper bags going out of the place as "sandwiches" to cops on the beat, and what he sees written all over fuzz faces when he's making what some folks call free with the white ladies. Maybe it doesn't go down well either when he talks about these things and doesn't care who hears.

Tonight the tall, blue-eyed student nurse with short blonde hair and the kind of bony face he's always liked is sitting at Table Four with her two girlfriends. They've come all the way in from White Plains to hear Mingus and they're in high spirits. When he joins them between sets there's much laughter over very little. She's in her twenties, her father is a milkman, she loves jazz, her name is Judy. My boy asks if he can drive her home. All the way to *Westchester?*—groovy, but he'll have to take Roxanne and Mary Lou home too, okay? And she flirts and asks him a lot of fresh questions. He loves her jovial attitude. But she becomes quiet and listens with interest when the English critic comes over and asks for an interview. "Do excuse me,

7. "Dr. Wallach" is Mingus's pseudonymn for Dr. Edmund Pollock, the analyst who treated him after his release from Bellevue Hospital, to which he had voluntarily committed himself in 1958. "The Fast Buck" is a disguise for the Half Note Café, whose owner, Mike Canterino, appears as "Mr. Caligari" in the autobiography. [RW]

Mr. Mingus, but may I ask a question or two for my paper? For instance, what do you feel about jazz?" "Man, just listen, it's all there." "No, actually, they'd like to know what you think in England, just a few words?" "Well . . . I can tell you how I feel tonight anyway. Up to now, I don't think *nobody* has given *nothing* important since Bird died except his contemporaries who were overlooked at the time—Monk, Max, Rollins, Bud, others, maybe even me. Bird was playing then what they're calling avant-garde today—putting major sevenths with minor sevenths, playing a fourth away from the key, things like that, and people would say he squeaked. Well, now they hear what those squeaks meant. All this free-form business isn't new—dropping bar lines and all. I was doing it and Duke before me and Jelly Roll before that. I wrote "What Love" back in '42 and played it with Buddy Collette and Britt Woodman and just recently some horn men looked at it and said it couldn't be played—too freaky, too hard."

"How would you characterize the kind of music you play now?"

"There once was a word used—swing. Swing went in one direction, it was linear, and everything had to be played with an obvious pulse and that's very restrictive. But I use the term 'rotary perception.' If you get a mental picture of the beat existing within a circle you're more free to improvise. People used to think the notes had to fall on the centre of the beats in the bar at intervals like a metronome, with three or four men in the rhythm section accenting the same pulse. That's like parade music or dance music. But imagine a circle surrounding each beat—each guy can play his notes anywhere in that circle and it gives him a feeling he has more space. The notes fall anywhere inside the circle but the original feeling for the beat isn't changed. If one in the group loses confidence, somebody hits the beat again. The pulse is inside you. When you're playing with musicians who think this way you can do anything. Anybody can stop and let the others go on. It's called strolling. In the old days when we got arrogant players on the stand we'd do that—just stop playing and a bad musician would be thrown."

"What about the Mingus extended forms?"

"I've been using extended forms and prolonged chords for years and I wasn't the first with that either. I got ideas from Spanish and Arab music. And much more can be done with pedal points—you know, notes sustained underneath changing harmonies but above these notes the keys can be varied so you get all kinds of effects." My boy put his foot against Judy's under the table. "Is that all?" he asked the Englishman.

"What about British jazz? Have we got the feeling?"

"If you're talking about technique, musicianship, I guess the British can be as good as anybody else. But what do they need to play jazz for? It's the American Negro's tradition; it's his music. White people don't have a right to play it, it's coloured folk music. When I was learning bass with Rheinschagen he was teaching me to play classical music. He said I was close but I'd never really get it. So I took Paul Robeson and Marian Anderson records to my next lesson and asked him if he thought *those* artists had got it. He said they were *Negroes trying* to sing music that was foreign to them. Solid, so white society has its own traditions, let 'em leave ours to us. You had your Shakespeare and Marx and Freud and Einstein and Jesus Christ and Guy Lombardo but we came up with *jazz,* don't forget it, and all the pop music in the world today is from that primary cause. British cats listen to our records and copy them, why don't they develop something of their own? White cats take our music and make more money out of it than we ever did or do now! My friend Max Roach has been voted best drummer in many polls but he's offered less than half of what Buddy Rich gets to play the same places—what kind of schitt is that? The commercial people are so busy selling what's hot commercially they're choking to death the goose that's laid all them golden eggs. They killed Lester and Bird and Fats Navarro and they'll kill more, probably me. I'll never make money and I'll always suffer 'cause I shoot off my mouth about agents and crooks and that's all I feel like saying tonight!"

My boy gets up thinking now what did I get into that for? He doesn't like to talk on serious subjects when he's working, it interrupts the natural mood that should sustain itself between sets, so he goes back to the bandstand angry, calls the first number—"Hellview of Bellevue!"—and stomps off a furiously fast tempo. The musicians respond with a great burst of power, the horns run unbelievable frantic phrases leaping up and down octaves, tied to whole-note end phrases. It's an insane set.

At closing time the student nurse and her friends are still waiting. He drives the other girls home first because this Judy laughs a lot and makes him laugh and besides, she's exciting. But she cries a little and touches his heart when she tells him she's just broken up with her boyfriend, whose name was Charles too. They agree that much as they need the opposite gender neither of them will *ever* be in love again and that the ideal life is a peaceful, friendly relationship with plenty of sex. By dawn, still riding around near the student nurses' quarters, they're saying they're obviously the kind of people who should be married to each other.

"What would you do," Judy asks my boy, "if you had your life to live all over again?"

"That's easy," Mingus says. "I'd become a pimp, bigger and better than my cousin Billy Bones out in San Francisco. I wouldn't get involved with music or women at all, other than what they could do for me. My main motive for living would be getting money to buy my way out of a decaying society, that's destroying itself while it tries to figure out what to do with the new kind of 'black' it produced. But I'd have nothing to do with black or white, I'd be a member of the raceless people of this earth. When one part of this uncivilized society got around to blowing up the others I'd be in some other country eating caviar and reading the news for the sole purpose of finding out where to move next to keep one jump ahead of the assholes who want to fight. But I'd keep me a loaded forty-five in event of any personal affront and my whores would be non-racist and agree fully with me and they'd carry forty-five automatics too. I state forty-fives because that means business. I wouldn't be carrying a gun to bluff—if I had to use it I'd want it to make a full-size hole that couldn't be patched. I'd live to enjoy life, not to lecture or preach. I wouldn't believe in any bullschitt like 'love' and I wouldn't get involved with any woman who talked it—any woman in my company would have to admit that what she loved was money. I'd play music as a hobby and only for close friends in the raceless set. I'd study bass for kicks, I wouldn't get involved in commercial competition. I might even become a junkie if my bank roll could stand it and I felt like that scene. That's what I'd do if I had my life to live all over again."

The girl Judy laughs. She's entertained and amused and she doesn't believe a word of it, otherwise she never would have married him and borne his two youngest children, would she?

39. Psychoanalyzing Jazz

JAZZ, ACCORDING TO THIS 1958 ARTICLE by Miles D. Miller, M.D., offers a variety of pleasures, including cathartic release, a gratifying sense of play, or a reassuring sense of order. It is the first of these that most interested Miller, and using the example of the trombone, he offers a psychoanalytic explanation of how some jazz produces pleasure by satisfying repressed impulses. Like many psychoanalytic interpretations of culture, this essay is quite ahistorical: characters and desires are formed in infancy, and where or in what century a child lives is made to seem inconsequential. Psychosexual development proceeds, presumably, in a "normal" pattern of development that has little to do with larger issues of culture or history. In particular, more knowledge of jazz history would have caused Miller to rein in a few interpretive flights of fancy, such as his explanation of "tailgate" trombone. (Humorless or prudish readers should probably skip this entire item.)

However, those who would wholly dismiss psychoanalytic approaches have yet to produce completely illuminating accounts of how musical pleasures are created; some of Miller's observations are certainly plausible and suggestive. And in remarking that what he calls "anal aggression" occurs more typically in New Orleans jazz than in "Modern" jazz, Miller points us toward a much needed exploration of jazz styles as embodiments of different sensibilities rather than sets of formal features.

Any attempt at studying the pleasure produced by an aesthetic experience is hampered by the complexity of the multiple, abstract, and illogical factors involved. Enjoyment of art is similar to primary process thinking and is not mastered by translation into the logical language of secondary process. Psychoanalysis has contributed much toward better understanding of artistic enjoyment in the fields of painting and literature but the study of music has been somewhat neglected. Freud himself is said to have been tone deaf and had very little appreciation for music. Only during the past fifteen years have analysts become interested in examining the process of musical enjoyment.[1]

Source: Miles D. Miller, M.D., "Jazz and Aggression," *Psychiatric Communications*, 1958, pp. 7–10.

1. H. Kohut and S. Levarie, "On the Enjoyment of Listening to Music," *Psychoanalytic Quarterly* 19 (1950), pp. 64–87; H. Kohut, "The Psychological Significance of Musical Activity," *Music Therapy* 1 (1951), pp. 151–58; H. Kohut, "The Psychological Functions of Music," *American Psychoanalytic Association* 5 (1957), pp. 389–407; I. Coriat., "Some Aspects of a Psychoanalytic Interpretation of Music," *Psychoanalytic Review* 32 (1945), pp. 408–18. See also R. Sterba, "Toward the Problem of the Musical Process," *Psychoanalytic Review* 33 (1946), pp. 37–43; N. Margolis, "A Theory of the Psychology of Jazz," *American Imago* 11 (1954), pp. 263–90; A. Esman, "Jazz—A Study in Cultural Conflict," *American Imago* 8 (1951), pp. 219–26.

If the enjoyment of music is defined as a tension release similar to any other form of pleasure, it is then possible to begin a study of how this kind of release is brought about. Kohut has shown that music is able to discharge tensions arising at each of the three structural levels of the Psyche: id, ego, and super ego.[2] On the id level, music is an emotional experience that allows catharsis of repressed primitive impulses. On the ego level, music is a form of "play" which constitutes an exercise in repetitive mastery of the threatening noises in the environment. On the super ego level, music is an enjoyable submission to the aesthetic set of rules demanded by the culture. Although all aspects of musical enjoyment are important only the catharsis of aggressive id impulses through music will be considered in this paper.

The most widely recognized and well understood aspect of music is that related to the gratification of the sexual impulses. Music has always been associated with love and most people are aware of the sensual stimulations produced by melodious and rhythmic musical forms. However, the expression of aggressive impulses in music has been little discussed probably due, in part, to the strong cultural repression placed on aggressive activity.

This paper is an attempt to show how jazz music is also used as a sublimated means of releasing tension associated with repressed hostile and aggressive impulses. These impulses will be studied in four basic areas. Using jazz music we will examine the aggressive aspects found in: the musical sounds, the act of playing an instrument, the musical style of the musician, and the musical kinesics of the musician.

In the examination of each of these areas, examples will be given from observations made on jazz slide-trombone players, but they can be applied to other wind instruments as well. The slide-trombone is chosen for discussion because it is one of the familiar instruments in which aggressivity is easily illustrated, while at the same time not limited to the production of only rhythmic sounds as are the drums.

I. Aggression in the Musical Sounds

The sounds produced by the trombone are in a low pitched range with considerable vibratory quality. After a period of listening, it is striking how closely some of the musical sounds resemble the normal noises produced by the human body such as belching, intestinal rumbling, and flatus. Physiologically, belching and passing flatus are explosive releasing of gas from the gastrointestinal tract usually associated with pleasurable sensations. This pleasure results not only from a release of visceral tension but also includes remnants of the pleasurable sense of mastery and power first felt in childhood after attaining control over the anal musculature. The child often used this mastery to obtain sadistic pleasure by using his feces to control, dominate, and punish his parents.

In adults some of this sadistic pleasure remains connected to these body sounds. In addition to the sounds themselves, imitations of flatus produced by the mouth (Bronx cheer and razzberry) are often used to convey hostile disapproval. These sounds also seem to give aggressive pleasure. Society, which strictly regulates toilet habits, associates these body noises with uncouth crudeness and demands that they be suppressed in public. Intentional breaking of these cultural taboos results in guilt and fear of retaliation which usually outweighs the pleasure associated with their free expression.

In jazz music, these forbidden noises subtly camouflaged in a musical form can give the same pleasurable sensations without the guilt resulting from transgression of cultural codes. The low pitch of the trombone is especially well suited for expression of these anal sounds and this may be a contributing factor to its enjoyment.

2. Kohut, "The Psychological Functions of Music."

People listening to a trombone solo seem to get a pleasurable sensation when an especially low pitched note is played. Often a titter is heard through the crowd and sly pleasant smiles are seen on most faces. It is not uncommon during a concert to have the audience burst into applause when a low note is sounded, especially when the musician appears to be straining to reach the note.

The pleasure connected with this sublimated anality is derived not only from a throwing off of super ego taboos, but also comes about through a sudden momentary release of the energy needed to repress the aggressive impulses. This release of energy is similar to the energy suddenly released in laughter at aggressive jokes.

II. Aggression in the Act of Playing an Instrument

In addition to the symbolic gratification derived from the individual sounds of jazz music, the act of playing an instrument also has many sublimated aspects which have their roots in primitive gratifications. It is known through dream symbolism that the playing of any instrument can be an unconscious symbol of masturbatory movements and is closely associated with auto-erotic genital stimulation. The act of playing also shows components of gratification associated with earlier levels of psychosexual development.

The trombone is played by forcing air out through tightly held lips pressed into a mouthpiece. The sound, produced by the vibration of the lips, is controlled by motion of the tongue and variation of the lip tension. In its simplest form the playing of a trombone resembles a combination of the acts of spitting and protrusion of the tongue, both of which are forceful ejaculations from the mouth. Spitting and tongue protruding are first used by the infant to expel unwanted or distasteful substances and then as the child grows older they become methods of conveying disgust or disapproval toward an object or person. In our adult society the acts of spitting and protruding the tongue are forbidden by strict taboos.

A musician, however, in the act of playing a horn, can experience the same oral aggressive pleasure without the associated guilt. In a sublimated way he is literally spitting through his horn and "spraying" the notes over the crowd. Instead of becoming incensed at the effrontery of his aggression, the audience seems to gain some of these same pleasures through unconscious identification with the musician in the same manner that they identify with the aggressor in any other conflict.

Anal expulsive components also enter into the act of playing. In skillfully controlling the ejection of air, the musician uses his mouth as an oral sphincter with the same pleasurable sensations as are connected with anal sphincter control. Both musical and anal control are associated with breath holding, grimacing, and tensing of the abdominal muscles. Expression of this anal aggression in jazz music is able to give sadistic pleasure without the usual guilt because the aggressive content is masked from consciousness by the musical form which allows the ego to attribute the pleasures received to harmless infantile regression.

III. Aggression in the Musical Style of the Musician

The style or technique used by the musician also contains many sublimated aggressive elements. Trombone players can, by varying the tone, produce a guttural growl-like sound resembling the snarl of an animal or angry person. In musical slang this style is called "gut-bucket-growl" indicating some unconscious perception of its oral and anal aggressive roots.

Another common technique used by trombone players is the sliding from one note to another up or down the scale. The musical term for this is glissando but the slang terms call it "smearing" or "tailgate" which again seem unconsciously to refer to anality and sphincter control. Other aggressive techniques include driving rhythm, loud playing (shouting), high notes (shrieking), and sounds resembling ripping or tearing.

IV. Aggression in the Musical Kinesics of the Musician

The body motions of jazz musicians while playing help to communicate the conscious and unconscious meanings of the music. Rhythmic swaying, closed eyes and instrument manipulation serve to accentuate the erotic stimulation. Here too, elements of aggressive discharge are seen in the exaggerated gesticulating with the musical instrument, rhythmic clapping, tapping of feet, and shouting. The construction of the trombone necessitates constant protrusion of the sliding portion of the tubing to almost double its original length. This becomes a real and phantasied means of bumping, striking, intruding into, and penetrating the environment in an aggressive, phallic way.

Anal aggression is also unconsciously communicated by the body motion of the trombone players. When straining for a difficult note they often squat slightly or raise one leg. The crowd usually responds at these times by shouting, laughing, and clapping. These pleasures arise from unconscious expressions of anal sadistic aggression but are consciously attributed to the simple pleasures of the musical form.

It is interesting that the anal aggressive sounds seem to appear more often in Dixieland or New Orleans Jazz than in Modern Jazz. Possibly this apparent lack of restraint in Dixieland may be permitted by the humorous atmosphere and care-free, relaxed attitude present in its musical form. Modern Jazz, with its concentration on a more serious mood and on technical perfection, may need to be more sublimated and restrained. In this way individual preference for listening to a particular type of jazz may be predetermined by character patterns which control the method of handling aggressive and sexual impulses. It is also possible that a character pattern which has a strong need to repress any expression of these impulses may play a part in that individual's dislike for this type of music.

Summary

Observations are given on the hypothesis that the sublimated release of repressed aggressive impulses while listening to jazz music is a factor in the enjoyment or dislike of the music.

40. An Appeal to the Vatican

"WHAT MUSIC IS RELIGIOUS? WHAT MUSIC is not?" asked French composer Gabriel Fauré. As a source of ecstasy and a promoter of community, music has been vital to many religious traditions. But when sacred music is adapted from secular sources, there is always the question of what sort of ecstasy is experienced, what sort of community called into being. Martin Luther's argument that popular music could be the Church's strongest ally in winning souls for God—"Why should the Devil have all the good tunes?"—makes no sense to those who regard the religious sphere as higher and purer than the music of everyday life.

This *New York Times* article points to the decline in jazz's popularity after World War II and shows why it has sometimes been in the interest of fans to try to disassociate jazz from other musical styles. It also raises the issue of whether politicians (in this case, the Italian Fascist government of c. 1925–43) should be in the business of regulating musical pleasure.

The request for a ruling on jazz predated by only a few years the Second Vatican Council, which from 1962 to 1965 worked to liberalize the Catholic liturgy, eventually permitting the use of vernacular musics and sparking the creation of folk masses, rock masses, rhythm and blues masses, polka masses, mariachi masses, and jazz masses.[1] Perhaps because of the changes to come, the Vatican apparently never responded to the appeal. But the request was not without precedent; reportedly, the Vatican had in 1914 officially condemned the turkey trot.[2]

Italian "cats" are seeking a Vatican ruling on the moral aspects of jazz. They contend that the "lift" they get out of jam sessions is a valuable spiritual experience. They

---

Source: Paul Hofmann, "Vatican Is Asked to Rule on Jazz," *New York Times*, April 30, 1957, p. 33.

1. See Robert Walser, "The Polka Mass: Music of Postmodern Ethnicity," *American Music* 10:2 (Summer 1992), 183–202.

2. See Charles Hamm, *Music in the New World* (New York: W. W. Norton, 1983), p. 400. Moreover, jazz is still not immune to such criticism; see Marc Fisher, "Jazz? Church Won't Hear of It," *The Washington Post*, May 13, 1997, pp. Cl, C2.

3. Here the Italian "cats" try to move jazz up the ladder of cultural prestige by pointing to rock and roll, now occupying a lower rung. [RW]

warn that the recent invasion of juke boxes and rock'n'roll should not be used as an argument for indicting "pure" jazz.[3]

A public appeal to the highest Roman Catholic authority was made today to counter criticism of all jazz music voiced recently in church quarters. The latest and harshest attack came from Catholic Action, a militant lay organization that has about 4,000,000 members in Italy. *Noi Uomini,* the newspaper of the men's branch of the Italian Catholic Action, described jazz as "Music of materialistic and Dionysiac orientation." The reference to Dionysus, Greek god of wine and ecstasy, evidently was meant to suggest that jazz was pagan and orgiastic. "From the Christian viewpoint the judgment on jazz music can and must be severe," wrote *Noi Uomini,* branding it as a "triumph of sensuality."

The Italian Jazz Federation, which says it speaks for "several thousand" persons, today issued a statement to rebut these accusations. It said a great many young Roman Catholics "who listen and play jazz with passion and with absolutely pure intent" were distressed at such condemnations as pronounced by *Noi Uomini.* Jazz enjoys "enormous popularity" among young Catholics throughout the world, the statement asserted. It explained that jazz derived from Negro spirituals, "which even today move us with their profound religious feeling."

Fear was expressed that the attack by Catholic Action might result in further curtailment of radio time devoted to "serious" jazz. The Italian State Broadcasting System is the most powerful institution here in the field of contemporary music and jazz lovers complain that it is neglecting them. No immediate reaction to the request of the Jazz Federation for an authoritative Roman Catholic pronouncement could be elicited in the Vatican or from Catholic Action today.

An organized jazz movement started in Italy twenty years ago with the foundation in Milan of a "hot jazz club." It went underground when the Fascists declared jazz "degenerate." Since then Italian jazz tastes have gone from "hot" to "cool." United States soldiers who occupied Italy in the last stages of World War II propagandized jazz. Louis Armstrong's first tour here in 1949 marked the peak of the music's popularity. In the last few years jazz has again become a matter for dedicated enthusiasts. The number of Italians who take an interest not only in dancing to syncopated rhythms but in "pure" jazz is placed at 50,000, not impressive for a nation approaching 50,000,000.

41. America's "Secret Sonic Weapon"

FOR SOME U.S. OFFICIALS, JAZZ WAS A diplomatic asset during the Cold War. According to a State Department estimate, Willis Conover's jazz program on the Voice of America, broadcast primarily to Communist countries, was reaching 80 million listeners during the late 1950s. Musicians such as Duke Ellington, Dizzy Gillespie, and Louis Armstrong presented a dynamic, creative, and racially harmonious image to the world as they toured with government subsidies, defusing foreign criticism of American racism and promoting, as one State Department report put it, "Mutual Understanding in the Nuclear Age."

Political use of jazz was not without opposition: the Senate Appropriations Committee objected to such frivolous expense in 1956, arguing that the country was better served by dignified presentations of choral singing. But one year earlier, this news report of an Armstrong concert in Geneva, Switzerland took the opposite view, praising jazz's popularity and performing some important spin control on the music's politics. It followed the government's Cold War rhetoric, equating jazz with total freedom and appropriating the music as a representation of "our way of life." If jazz has become "universal," it implies, it is because America has become universal. Minimizing the cooperative, collaborative, and cultural aspects of jazz, this short article manages to include the words "individual" or "individuality" no fewer than five times.

America's secret weapon is a blue note in a minor key. Right now its most effective ambassador is Louis (Satchmo) Armstrong. A telling propaganda line is the hopped-up tempo of a Dixieland band heard on the Voice of America in far-off Tangier. This is not a pipedream from a back room jam session. It is the studied conclusion of a handful of thoughtful Americans from Moscow to Madrid. Somewhere in the official files of one of Washington's myriad agencies all this has been spelled out. Because nothing has been done about it, more than one observant American traveling the Continent has remarked: "We don't know our own strength."

Cash customers were turned away in droves tonight because Victoria Hall here could not accommodate the crowd that wanted to hear "Ole Satchmo" do tricks with his trumpet. The disappointed customers were not Swiss "hep cats" but sober adults willing to pay almost $4 to hear musical individuality. All Europe now seems to find

---

Source: Felix Belair, Jr., "United States Has Secret Sonic Weapon—Jazz," *New York Times*, November 6, 1955, pp. 1, 42.

American jazz as necessary as the seasons. Yet Europeans don't bounce to the syncopated rhythm of Stan Kenton or Duke Ellington and their bands or the still popular recordings of Benny Goodman's quartet. They can swing and sway with Sammy Kaye, but for the most part they find in jazz a subject for serious study. Theirs is what most Americans would call a "long-haired approach." They like to contemplate it, dissect it, take it apart to see what makes it what it is. They like to ponder the strength of its individuality and speculate on the qualities that differentiate it from the folk music of any other country. Somewhere along the line they get curious about the kind of people that first contrived it.

The popularity of jazz and the market for it is a phenomenon that strikes Americans returned to the continent after a long absence. Men actually have risked their lives to smuggle recordings of it behind the Iron Curtain and by methods that the profit motive cannot explain. A German Swiss of Zurich came closest to the explanation the other day after he had heard Hoagy Carmichael's "Stardust" from the keyboard of Art Tatum. "Jazz is not just an art," he said. "It is a way of life."

Whatever the essence of the matter, the remark helps explain why the police states give up the attempt to outlaw jazz as the product of a decadent capitalist nation. In the satellite countries particularly, authorities learned the hard way that it was only the promise of a ragtime band later on that kept the radios tuned to their Communist preachments. Something of the same strength of musical Americana caused uninhibited Moscow children to ask visiting American news men a year ago what they knew of Bing Crosby and Frank Sinatra. More ponderous explanations of the attraction of American jazz are available from those in Europe who have given it a lot of thought. One is that the contest between musical discipline and individual expression comes close to symbolizing the conditions under which people of the atomic age live.

Whatever the exactions of musical discipline, there can be little question of the appreciation throughout Europe of the individuality of expression involved. Thus, it is not surprising to switch on a radio and hear a jazz band doing a syncopated adaptation of the César Franck symphony or a piece of sacred music heard as written only at the Christmas season. Tiny Switzerland boasts about a hundred amateur jazz bands, and about sixty of these specialize in the Dixieland variety. The radio station of every good-sized city has its "jazz specialist."

What many thoughtful Europeans cannot understand is why the United States government, with all the money it spends for so-called propaganda to promote democracy, does not use more of it to subsidize the continental travels of jazz bands and the best exponents of the music. The average European tour of a musician like Louis Armstrong and his band is about six weeks. On a profit and loss basis he can play only to the biggest audiences. Small houses mean deficits that not even devotees like Satchmo can long endure. With a small Government subsidy, he might play the smaller intermediate towns and [have] his tour stretched to six months by train instead of six weeks by bus.

American jazz has now become a universal language. It knows no national boundaries, but everybody knows where it comes from and where to look for more. Individual Americans will continue to pack them in and the reasons for this are clear. The New York Philharmonic-Symphony, London's Symphony and the Boston Pops are no strangers to any European capital. They are appreciated for their versatility as much as for their faithful renditions of the classics associated with European composers over the centuries. But there is not a wide difference between the best symphony orchestras of the United States and Europe—not where the masses of the people are concerned.

But nobody plays jazz like an American.

42. The White Negro

CHARLIE PARKER AND DIZZY GILLESPIE were among the "Secret Heroes" of the Beat writers; the members of that postwar literary movement—Allen Ginsberg, Jack Kerouac, Lawrence Ferlinghetti, William Burroughs, many others—even took their name from slang used by jazz musicians. Though not a Beat writer himself, Norman Mailer (b. 1923) shared their passionate resistance to accepted social norms. After the success of his first novel, *The Naked and the Dead* (1948), Mailer became an outspoken critic of dominant American values, which he denounced as racist, sexually repressive, and stiflingly conformist.

The word "hip" was also used as a synonym for "beat" in the mid-1950s, and in this famous essay Mailer traces the attitudes of the hipster to origins in African-American experience. For Mailer, American society had become a totalitarian nightmare still haunted by the memory of concentration camps and atomic bombings; for learning how to cope within such a world, who could be better teachers than black Americans, who had survived generations of racist horrors? "The White Negro" offended some readers by attributing to African-Americans greater physicality and psychopathy (a survival skill, Mailer maintained), and the author later retreated from some of its arguments. These excerpts offer insights about how jazz has been used and understood by different audiences, how its importance and meanings have varied according to what people have needed from it and thought they found in it. For the hipster, jazz seemed to enable violent rebellion at the same time that it marked membership in a community; Mailer saw it as both private orgasm and artful communication.

Probably, we will never be able to determine the psychic havoc of the concentration camps and the atom bomb upon the unconscious mind of almost everyone alive in these years. For the first time in civilized history, perhaps for the first time in all of history, we have been forced to live with the suppressed knowledge that the smallest facets of our personality or the most minor projection of our ideas, or indeed the absence of ideas and the absence of personality could mean equally well that we might still be doomed to die as a cipher in some vast statistical operation in which our teeth would be counted, and our hair would be saved, but our death itself would

---

Source: Norman Mailer, "The White Negro: Superficial Reflections on the Hipster," *Dissent* 4:3 (Summer, 1957), pp. 276–93.

be unknown, unhonored, and unremarked, a death which could not follow with dignity as a possible consequence to serious actions we had chosen, but rather a death by ***deus ex machina*** in a gas chamber or a radioactive city; and so if in the midst of civilization—that civilization founded upon the Faustian urge to dominate nature by mastering time, mastering the links of social cause and effect—in the middle of an economic civilization founded upon the confidence that time could indeed be subjected to our will, our psyche was subjected itself to the intolerable anxiety that death being causeless, life was causeless as well, and time deprived of cause and effect had come to a stop.

It is on this bleak scene that a phenomenon has appeared: the American existentialist—the hipster, the man who knows that if our collective condition is to live with instant death by atomic war, relatively quick death by the State as *l'univers concentrationnaire,* or with a slow death by conformity with every creative and rebellious instinct stifled (at what damage to the mind and the heart and the liver and the nerves no research foundation for cancer will discover in a hurry), if the fate of twentieth century man is to live with death from adolescence to premature senescence, why then the only life-giving answer is to accept the terms of death, to live with death as immediate danger, to divorce oneself from society, to exist without roots, to set out on that uncharted journey into the rebellious imperatives of the self. In short, whether the life is criminal or not, the decision is to encourage the psychopath in oneself, to explore that domain of experience where security is boredom and therefore sickness, and one exists in the present, in that enormous present which is without past or future, memory or planned intention, the life where a man must go until he is beat, where he must gamble with his energies through all those small or large crises of courage and unforeseen situations which beset his day, where he must be with it or doomed not to swing. The unstated essence of Hip, its psychopathic brilliance, quivers with the knowledge that new kinds of victories increase one's power for new kinds of perception; and defeats, the wrong kind of defeats, attack the body and imprison one's energy until one is jailed in the prison air of other people's habits, other people's defeats, boredom, quiet desperation, and muted icy self-destroying rage. One is Hip or one is Square (the alternative which each new generation coming into American life is beginning to feel), one is a rebel or one conforms, one is a frontiersman in the Wild West of American night life, or else a Square cell, trapped in the totalitarian tissues of American society, doomed willy-nilly to conform if one is to succeed.

A totalitarian society makes enormous demands on the courage of men, and a partially totalitarian society makes even greater demands for the general anxiety is greater. Indeed if one is to be a man, almost any kind of unconventional action often takes disproportionate courage. So it is no accident that the source of Hip is the Negro for he has been living on the margin between totalitarianism and democracy for two centuries. But the presence of Hip as a working philosophy in the sub-worlds of American life is probably due to jazz, and its knife-like entry into culture, its subtle but so penetrating influence on an avant-garde generation—that post-war generation of adventurers who (some consciously, some by osmosis) had absorbed the lessons of disillusionment and disgust of the Twenties, the Depression, and the War. Sharing a collective disbelief in the words of men who had too much money and controlled too many things, they knew almost as powerful a disbelief in the socially monolithic ideas of the single mate, the solid family and the respectable love life.

So no wonder that in certain cities of America, in New York of course, and New Orleans, in Chicago and San Francisco and Los Angeles, in such American cities as Paris and Mexico, D. F., this particular part of a generation was attracted to what the

Negro had to offer.[1] In such places as Greenwich Village, a ménage-à-trois was completed—the bohemian and the juvenile delinquent came face-to-face with the Negro, and the hipster was a fact in American life. If marijuana was the wedding ring, the child was the language of Hip for its argot gave expression to abstract states of feeling which all could share, at least all who were Hip. And in this wedding of the white and the black it was the Negro who brought the cultural dowry. Any Negro who wishes to live must live with danger from his first day, and no experience can ever be casual to him, no Negro can saunter down a street with any real certainty that violence will not visit him on his walk. The cameos of security for the average white: mother and the home, job and the family, are not even a mockery to millions of Negroes; they are impossible. The Negro has the simplest of alternatives: live a life of constant humility or ever-threatening danger. In such a pass where paranoia is as vital to survival as blood, the Negro had stayed alive and begun to grow by following the need of his body where he could. Knowing in the cells of his existence that life was war, nothing but war, the Negro (all exceptions admitted) could rarely afford the sophisticated inhibitions of civilization, and so he kept for his survival the art of the primitive, he lived in the enormous present, he subsisted for his Saturday night kicks, relinquishing the pleasures of the mind for the more obligatory pleasures of the body, and in his music he gave voice to the character and quality of his existence, to his rage and the infinite variations of joy, lust, languor, growl, cramp, pinch, scream and despair of his orgasm. For jazz is orgasm, it is the music of orgasm, good orgasm and bad, and so it spoke across a nation, it had the communication of art even where it was watered, perverted, corrupted, and almost killed, it spoke in no matter what laundered popular way of instantaneous existential states to which some whites could respond, it was indeed a communication by art because it said, "I feel this, and now you do too."

So there was a new breed of adventurers, urban adventurers who drifted out at night looking for action with a black man's code to fit their facts. The hipster had absorbed the existentialist synapses of the Negro, and for practical purposes could be considered a white Negro.

The only Hip morality (but of course it is an ever-present morality) is to do what one feels whenever and wherever it is possible, and—this is how the war of the Hip and the Square begins—to be engaged in one primal battle: to open the limits of the possible for oneself, for oneself alone because that is one's need. Yet in widening the arena of the possible, one widens it reciprocally for others as well, so that the nihilistic fulfillment of each man's desire contains its antithesis of human cooperation.

If the ethic reduces to Know Thyself and Be Thyself, what makes it radically different from Socratic moderation with its stern conservative respect for the experience of the past, is that the Hip ethic is immoderation, childlike in its adoration of the present (and indeed to respect the past means that one must also respect such ugly consequences of the past as the collective murders of the State). It is this adoration of the present which contains the affirmation of Hip, because its ultimate logic surpasses even the unforgettable solution of the Marquis de Sade to sex, private property, and the family, that all men and women have absolute but temporary rights over the bodies of all other men and women—the nihilism of Hip proposes as its final

1. D. F. is the abbreviation for Distrito Federal, the area around Mexico City. [RW]

tendency that every social restraint and category be removed, and the affirmation implicit in the proposal is that man would then prove to be more creative than murderous and so would not destroy himself. Which is exactly what separates Hip from the authoritarian philosophies which now appeal to the conservative and liberal temper—what haunts the middle of the Twentieth Century is that faith in man has been lost, and the appeal of authority has been that it would restrain us from ourselves. Hip, which would return us to ourselves, at no matter what price in individual violence, is the affirmation of the barbarian for it requires a primitive passion about human nature to believe that individual acts of violence are always to be preferred to the collective violence of the State; it takes literal faith in the creative possibilities of the human being to envisage acts of violence as the catharsis which prepares growth.

What makes Hip a special language is that it cannot really be taught—if one shares none of the experiences of elation and exhaustion which it is equipped to describe, then it seems merely arch or vulgar or irritating. It is a pictorial language, but pictorial like non-objective art, imbued with the dialectic of small but intense change, a language for the microcosm, in this case, man, for it takes the immediate experiences of any passing man and magnifies the dynamic of his movements, not specifically but abstractly so that he is seen more as a vector in a network of forces than as a static character in a crystallized field. (Which, latter, is the practical view of the snob.) For example, there is real difficulty in trying to find a Hip substitute for "stubborn." The best possibility I can come up with is: "That cat will never come off his groove, dad." But groove implies movement, narrow movement but motion nonetheless. There is really no way to describe someone who does not move at all. Even a creep does move—if at a pace exasperatingly more slow than the pace of the cool cats.

Therefore one finds words like go, and make it, and with it, and swing: "Go" with its sense that after hours or days or months or years of monotony, boredom, and depression one has finally had one's chance, one has amassed enough energy to meet an exciting opportunity with all one's present talents for the flip (up or down) and so one is ready to go, ready to gamble. Movement is always to be preferred to inaction. In motion a man has a chance, his body is warm, his instincts are quick, and when the crisis comes, whether of love or violence, he can make it, he can win, he can release a little more energy for himself since he hates himself a little less, he can make a little better nervous system, make it a little more possible to go again, to go faster next time and so make more and thus find more people with whom he can swing. For to swing is to communicate, is to convey the rhythms of one's own being to a lover, a friend, or an audience, and—equally necessary—be able to feel the rhythms of their response. To swing with the rhythms of another is to enrich oneself—the conception of the learning process as dug by Hip is that one cannot really learn until one contains within oneself the implicit rhythm of the subject or the person.

43. Louis Armstrong on Music and Politics

BY THE MID-1950S, LOUIS ARMSTRONG HAD become much more than a great jazz trumpeter and popular singer—his recordings, concerts, and appearances in nearly fifty movies had made him one of the best-known entertainers in the world. Fame made his opinions news, and although he toured internationally with U.S. State Department sponsorship, Armstrong did not shrink from commenting on the civil rights struggles of the time, which often pitted grass-roots activists and community leaders such as Martin Luther King, Jr. against local, state, and federal officials. One such clash came in 1957, when Arkansas governor Orval Faubus defied the Supreme Court's 1954 ban on racial segregation in public schools, ordering the Arkansas National Guard to block integration of Little Rock Central High School. President Eisenhower dispatched federal troops to enforce the Court's order, but not before he received strong criticism for having delayed.

This set of newspaper clippings traces some of Armstrong's participation in the public debates of the time, showing too how his charges generated angry rebuttals.[1] Although he had been dismissed as an Uncle Tom by some critics earlier in his career (see the comments by Dizzy Gillespie in this volume), Armstrong now was being attacked for being too militant. His cosmopolitan perspective, born of frequent world travel, made him painfully aware of the contradictions between his status as a "jazz ambassador" and the struggles of African-Americans for basic civil rights. Note in the fourth excerpt how one paper chose to transcribe Armstrong's accent (and imagine the effect if journalists were to do the same for white politicians such as Jimmy Carter or Ted Kennedy). The first excerpt, from a joint interview of Armstrong and bassist Pops Foster, upsets any assumption that racial injustice diminishes through gradual and inevitable progress.

INTERVIEWER: Was there race segregation among the musicians in New Orleans?

FOSTER: I played in mixed bands for years. We played all the hotels, all over New Orleans. It wasn't like today.

INTERVIEWER: Do you run into many race-conscious musicians?

1. These clippings were found in the Armstrong file at the Institute of Jazz Studies at Rutgers, the State University of New Jersey. Some details of their source citations were missing. [RW]

ARMSTRONG: No. Anybody that knows his horns don't pay much attention to color. What you got to realize about restrictions and things, such as in New Orleans now—

INTERVIEWER: Wait a minute, what do you mean, "such as in New Orleans now"?

ARMSTRONG: Since 1954, in New Orleans, they don't want white and Negro musicians playing together. The people who made those laws don't know anything about music. Because in music, it doesn't make any difference. I don't run into much trouble with segregation, 'cause I don't go where I'm not wanted. And—please don't take this out, I'm going to tell this straight—I don't go to New Orleans no more.

Source: Interview conducted in San Francisco by Albert M. Colegrove, published as "Jazz Grew Up 'On the Wagon,'" *San Francisco News,* September 25, 1958, p. 13.

Louis (Satchmo) Armstrong charged today that President Eisenhower was a "two-faced" man with "no guts" who was letting Gov. Faubus of Arkansas run the federal government. Explaining in Grand Forks, N. D., why he canceled a good-will concert trip to Russia, Armstrong said: "The people over there ask me what's wrong with my country. What am I supposed to say?" He added, "It's getting almost so bad a colored man hasn't got any country."

Source: New York Post, September 19, 1957.

Louis "Satchmo" Armstrong, justly famous Negro trumpet player and jazz singer, plays what the boys in the trade call a "gang o' horn." But in politics, it is evident now, he blows sour.

In the past "Ambassador Satch," as he enjoys being dubbed, has gained a lot of good will for the United States on his jazz tours abroad. He made a grievous error, however, when he put his horn down and blasted President Eisenhower, "the government," and various other persons and places for their handling of the Negro problem in the United States.

Thoughtful, responsible folk in both the South and the North, at every level of government and in all fields of endeavor, know that the exercise of the most painstaking statemanship is needed to meet the difficulties linked with school segregation and all phases of civil rights. They know that the settlement of these issues, no matter how troublesome, must be achieved through the orderly processes of government acting under law. They want no violence. They reject the use of force on any side.

Obviously, from the tenor and content of the President's meeting at Newport with Gov. Orval Faubus of Arkansas, this is the path—law and order—that Mr. Eisenhower wishes to tread. And the governor has said he agrees. The dispute in Little Rock is to be resolved in the courts.

For Armstrong to charge the President with "no guts" because he has taken the orderly road is to indulge in pointless insult.

Source: Redlands [California Facts] September 23, 1957.

The new, subdued Louis Armstrong granted a brief backstage interview last night. He had just played a concert to an almost-packed Massey Hall and there was nothing subdued about the music. It's just about the same as ever. The step-easy policy appears to have taken over in the opinion department.

Pencils hovering, reporters asked:
"How is the race situation going in the South?"
"Ooooh, dear."
"Your manager says you don't talk about things like that anymore. Is that so?"
"Yaah, ya might say."
"Why?"
"Well, talkin' about it don' do no good."
"Have you tried talking about it?"
"Man, have Ah eveh. Papahs all ustah be fulla me talkin'."
"So what do you talk about now?"
"Music."
"What's new with music?"
"Pretty well the same ol' thing."
"Did rock 'n' roll ever cut into your audience when it was at its height?"
"Nah. It nevah came close."
"Why not?"
" 'Cause Ah play good music."
"How much longer are you going to play?"
"Ah've been at it 'bout fohty-se'm yeahs now. Go on fo-evah, Ah guess."

Source: "Satchmo Silent on Racial Crisis," source unknown, April 27, 1960.

Jazz trumpeter Louis Armstrong, on his way to a concert tour of Africa, today said he didn't care whether he plays in South Africa or not. "I don't know nothing about politics," he said. "I just play."

A ban on the 60-year-old Negro artist and his six "All Stars" was imposed by South African authorities several weeks ago. Armstrong, beginning a 45-concert tour of African countries, said he did not know about the South African ban. "If they book us into South Africa, we're looking forward to playing for them cats," he said.

First stop on the tour will be Saturday at Accra, where all 50,000 seats in the Ghanaian capital's open-air sports stadium have been sold. Armstrong described the trip as "the most important event of my life." It is sponsored by the U. S. State Dept. and an American soft drink firm.

Source: "Satchmo Is Real Cool About S. Africa Ban," *New York Post,* October 12, 1960.

Louis "Satchmo" Armstrong, famed jazz trumpeter, said last night he "got sick" after watching television films of racial violence in Selma, Ala. Armstrong said he didn't take part in freedom marches because: "They'd only smash my face so that I couldn't use my trumpet." When a newsman expressed surprise that anyone would "beat up" someone like "Satchmo," Armstrong said of the white segregationists: "They would even beat Jesus if He was black and marched."

Something must be done about the intolerable circumstances in Alabama, he said. "How is it possible that human beings can still treat each other that way?" He is in Denmark on his way to jazz concerts behind the Iron Curtain. "My mission is music," he said.

Source: Toronto Telegram, March 11, 1965.

PART 6

The Sixties

44. Critical Reception of Free Jazz

THE JANUARY 18, 1962 ISSUE OF *DOWN BEAT* contained the magazine's first double review of an album: *Free Jazz,* which had been recorded in 1960 by alto saxophonist and composer Ornette Coleman (b. 1930). Like many jazz musicians of the 1950s and 1960s, Coleman had come up through rhythm and blues bands—but unlike most, he had been fired from such bands and even beat up on account of his unorthodox playing. The *Free Jazz* album appeared in the wake of *The Shape of Jazz to Come* (1959) and Coleman's extended engagement at the Five Spot in New York (beginning in November 1959) with Don Cherry on trumpet, Charlie Haden on bass, and Billy Higgins on drums. *Free Jazz* featured a double quartet of these musicians plus drummer Ed Blackwell, bassist Scott LaFaro, trumpeter Freddie Hubbard, and Eric Dolphy on bass clarinet. Coleman would later add to the critical controversy by performing on trumpet and violin; he went electric in 1975 with a sextet called Prime Time.

The double review was a good tactic for dealing with this album, for its repudiation of preset harmonic patterns and song structures, along with its fluid sense of pitch and motivic association, helped make it the most influential avant-garde recording of the decade and Coleman the most controversial musician in jazz. Coleman advanced a theory of "harmolodics" to justify his practices; though his explanations are enigmatic, he certainly emphasizes melodic gestures and shapes over harmony and form. But what some musicians and critics heard as progress toward greater improvisatory freedom others heard as the incoherent fumblings of someone who hadn't paid his dues and either wouldn't or couldn't play real jazz. Musicians and critics such as John Hammond, Miles Davis, Charles Mingus, and Roy Eldridge denounced Coleman as

---

Source: Pete Welding and John A. Tynan, "Double View of a Double Quartet," *Down Beat,* January 18, 1962, p. 28. Courtesy of *Down Beat* magazine.

a fake, while Gunther Schuller, Martin Williams, Nat Hentoff, Leonard Bernstein, and John Lewis hailed him as a genius, even a new Charlie Parker. The *Down Beat* reviewers, who differed absolutely in their judgments, rated the album on the magazine's usual five-star scale before proceeding to justify their evaluations.[1]

Review by Pete Welding

RATING: * * * * *

In this most recent Atlantic recording, iconoclast alto saxist Coleman carries to their logical (though some listeners will dispute this term) conclusion the esthetic principles present to a lesser degree—quantitatively at least—in his previous recordings.

The entire LP—both sides—is given over to a collective improvisation by a double quartet (Dolphy, Hubbard, LaFaro, and Higgins make up the second quartet) that lasts 36½ minutes. Using only the sketchiest of outlines to guide them, the players have fashioned a forceful, impassioned work that might stand as the ultimate manifesto of the new wave of young jazz expressionists. The results are never dull.

In first hearing, *Free Jazz* strikes one as a sprawling, discursive, chaotic jumble of jagged rhythms and pointless cacophonies, among which however are interlarded a number of striking solo segments (particularly those of the two bassists). The force, intensity, and biting passion that motivate it also come across.

On repeated listening, however, the form of the work gradually reveals itself, and it is seen that the piece is far less unconventional than it might at first appear. It does not break with jazz tradition; rather it restores to currency an element that has been absent in most jazz since the onset of the swing orchestra—spontaneous group improvisation. Yet Coleman has restored it with a vengeance; here we have better than half an hour's worth, with only a minimal amount of it predetermined to any degree.

In *Free Jazz* the soloist is free to explore any area in his improvisation that his musical esthetic takes him to; he is not bound by a harmonic, tonal, or rhythmic framework to which he must adhere rigidly. The performance (and his role in it) is completely fluid: rhythm usually follows the soloist's lead (though he may occasionally take his cue from it), and the remaining three horns contribute as they see fit—from complex contrapuntal patterns arrived at spontaneously and independently to accidental "harmonic" riffs of a sort.

A very exciting—but equally dangerous—proposition, to be sure, and one that requires executants of an extraordinary sensitivity and ability. On these grounds, this work is not always successful.

The piece is begun by a brief polyphonic ensemble in which the horn men seek to establish the emotional climate of the piece. This determined, a short "arranged" passage leads to a gripping five minute exploration by Dolphy in his most waspish, acerbic manner; Hubbard's graceful solo follows and is of equal length; Coleman's searing solo is next in line and consumes a full 10 minutes. It is by all odds the most successful improvisation of the lot, despite its length, and provokes the other three

1. See also *Down Beat's* 1992 reevaluation of this album, which appears later in this volume. [RW]

horns to some of their most complex and interesting contrapuntal interplay on the disc. After a terse unison figure, Cherry's flatulent, meandering solo sputters on for five minutes. It is succeeded by powerful bass statements by both Haden and LaFaro, and finally the drummers have the field before all come together for the close.

All things considered, the disc is largely successful—it certainly lives up to Coleman's dicta, at least. It *is* a powerful and challenging work of real conviction and honest emotion: it poses questions and provides its own answers to them; it is restless in its re-examination of the role of collective improvisation, and this is, in many respects, where the work is most successful.

Needless to say, there is nothing of smugness or complacency about it. And it is almost a total improvisation, a sort of seamless whole in which the over-all organic structure takes precedence over its constituent elements (selection of notes, etc.). As a result, Cherry's faltering solo makes little real difference in terms of the larger work—enough momentum has been established by this time to carry it right through.

Some salient points:

It seems to me that experiments ought to be presented as such—and not as finished works. This piece does have more than its share of inevitable rough spots; but how much of this results from this group having been brought together in the studio just for the purposes of recording this piece? A much fuller rapport would appear to be necessary before the maximum results could be achieved from this method and approach. Still, Coleman has made his point with this disc, and this cannot be denied him. I, for one, have been completely won over. I look forward to more pieces of this nature—but of a less ambitious scheme.

Review by John A. Tynan

RATING: NO STARS

This friendly get-together is subtitled "a collective improvisation by the Ornette Coleman Double Quartet." One might expect a "collective improvisation" by Coleman's usual crew of four to be a merry event. But here we shoot the moon. It's every man-jack for himself in an eight-man emotional regurgitation. Rules? Forget 'em.

Where does neurosis end and psychosis begin? The answer must lie somewhere within this maelstrom.

If nothing else, this witch's brew is the logical end product of a bankrupt philosophy of ultraindividualism in music. "Collective improvisation"? Nonsense. The only semblance of collectivity lies in the fact that these eight nihilists were collected together in one studio at one time and with one common cause: to destroy the music that gave them birth. Give them top marks for the attempt.

45. "Jazz and the White Critic"

SINCE THE EARLY 1960S, LEROI JONES (1934–2014) has been recognized as a preeminent African-American poet, playwright, and critic. He is best known for his play *Dutchman* (1964) and his book *Blues People* (1963), the first major study of jazz by a black writer. In 1968, he changed his name to Amiri Baraka, explaining that he no longer wished to bear his "slave name."

This essay appeared in *Down Beat* in 1963, and was reprinted in Jones's book *Black Music* (1967). Baraka begins with the question of why the most influential jazz musicians have been black and the most influential critics white. Yet this is merely an introduction to his important plea on behalf of *understanding*, rather than "appreciating," jazz. The difference between these approaches lies in what he calls the "why" of the music, which requires attention to the philosophical and political matrices that frame the production and reception of jazz. Jones/Baraka has always been controversial and provocative, but his ideas about race are central to his passionate but nuanced view of the cultural history of jazz, and his concerns are still highly relevant to jazz criticism and education.

Most jazz critics have been white Americans, but most important jazz musicians have not been. This might seem a simple enough reality to most people, or at least a reality which can be readily explained in terms of the social and cultural history of American society. And it is obvious why there are only two or three fingers' worth of Negro critics or writers on jazz, say, if one understands that until relatively recently those Negroes who *could* become critics, who would largely have to come from the black middle class, have simply not been interested in the music. Or at least jazz, for the black middle class, has only comparatively recently lost some of its stigma (though by no means is it yet as popular among them as any vapid musical product that comes sanctioned by the taste of the white majority). Jazz was collected among the numerous skeletons the middle-class black man kept locked in the closet of his psyche, along with watermelons and gin, and whose rattling caused him no end of misery and self-hatred. As one Howard University philosophy professor said to me when I was an undergraduate, "It's fantastic how much bad taste the blues contain!" But it is just this "bad taste" that this Uncle spoke of that has been the one factor that has kept the best of Negro music from slipping sterilely into the echo chambers of

---

Source: LeRoi Jones, "Jazz and the White Critic," *Down Beat*, August 15, 1963, pp. 16–17, 34; reprinted in LeRoi Jones, *Black Music* (New York: Quill, 1967), pp. 11–20. Courtesy of *Down Beat* magazine.

middle-brow American culture. And to a great extent such "bad taste" was kept extant in the music, blues or jazz, because the Negroes who were responsible for the best of the music were always aware of their identities as black Americans and really did not, themselves, desire to become vague, featureless, Americans as is usually the case with the Negro middle class. (This is certainly not to say that there have not been very important Negro musicians from the middle class. Since the Henderson era, their number has increased enormously in jazz.)[1]

Negroes played jazz as they had sung blues or, even earlier, as they had shouted and hollered in those anonymous fields, because it was one of the few areas of human expression available to them. Negroes who felt the blues, later jazz, impulse, as a specific means of expression, went naturally into the music itself. There were fewer social or extra-expressive considerations that could possibly disqualify any prospective Negro jazz musician than existed, say, for a Negro who thought he might like to become a writer (or even an elevator operator, for that matter). Any Negro who had some ambition towards literature, in the earlier part of this century, was likely to have developed so powerful an allegiance to the sacraments of middle-class American culture that he would be horrified by the very idea of writing about jazz.

There were few "jazz critics" in America at all until the '30s and then they were influenced to a large extent by what Richard Hadlock has called "the carefully documented gee-whiz attitude" of the first serious European jazz critics. They were also, as a matter of course, influenced more deeply by the social and cultural mores of their own society. And it is only natural that their criticism, whatever its intention, should be a product of that society, or should reflect at least some of the attitudes and thinking of that society, even if not directly related to the subject they were writing about, Negro music.

Jazz, as a Negro music, existed, up until the time of the big bands, on the same socio-cultural level as the sub-culture from which it was issued. The music and its sources were *secret* as far as the rest of America was concerned, in much the same sense that the actual life of the black man in America was secret to the white American. The first white critics were men who sought, whether consciously or not, to understand this secret, just as the first serious white jazz musicians (Original Dixieland Jazz Band, Bix, etc.) sought not only to understand the phenomenon of Negro music but to appropriate it as a means of expression which they themselves might utilize. The success of this "appropriation" signaled the existence of an American music, where before there was a Negro music. But the white jazz musician had an advantage the white critic seldom had. The white musician's commitment to jazz, the *ultimate concern*, proposed that the sub-cultural attitudes that produced the music as a profound expression of human feelings, could be *learned* and need not be passed on as a secret blood rite. And Negro music is essentially the expression of an attitude, or a collection of attitudes, about the world, and only secondarily an attitude about the way music is made. The white jazz musician came to understand this attitude as a way of making music, and the intensity of his understanding produced the "great" white jazz musicians, and is producing them now.

Usually the critic's commitment was first to his *appreciation* of the music rather than to his understanding of the attitude which produced it. This difference meant that the potential critic of jazz had only to appreciate the music, or what he thought

1. Jones refers to the 1920s, when Fletcher Henderson, Duke Ellington, Don Redman, Jimmie Lunceford, and Luis Russell—all middle-class black men born near the turn of the century—were the primary shapers of the emerging big band style. [RW]

was the music, and that he did not need to understand or even be concerned with the attitudes which produced it, except perhaps as a purely sociological consideration. This last idea is certainly what produced the reverse patronization that is known as Crow Jim. The disparaging "all you folks got rhythm" is no less a stereotype, simply because it is proposed as a positive trait. But this Crow Jim attitude has not been as menacing or as evident a flaw in critical writing about jazz as has another manifestation of the white critic's failure to concentrate on the blues and jazz attitude rather that his conditioned appreciation of the music. The major flaw in this approach to Negro music is that it strips the music too ingenuously of its social and cultural intent. It seeks to define jazz as an art (or a folk art) that has come out of no intelligent body of socio-cultural philosophy.

We take for granted the social and cultural milieu and philosophy that produced Mozart. As Western people, the socio-cultural thinking of eighteenth-century Europe comes to us as a history legacy that is a continuous and organic part of the twentieth-century West. The socio-cultural philosophy of the Negro in America (as a continuous historical phenomenon) is no less specific and no less important for any intelligent critical speculation about the music that came out of it. And again, this is not a plea for narrow sociological analysis of jazz, but rather that this music cannot be completely understood (in critical terms) without some attention to the attitudes which produced it. It is the philosophy of Negro music that is most important, and this philosophy is only partially the result of the sociological disposition of Negroes in America. There is, of course, much more to it than that.

Strict musicological analysis of jazz, which has come into favor recently, is also as limited as a means of jazz criticism as a strict sociological approach. The notator of any jazz solo, or blues, has no chance of capturing what in effect are the most important elements of the music. (Most transcriptions of blues lyrics are just as frustrating.) A printed musical example of an Armstrong solo, or of a Thelonious Monk solo, tells us almost nothing except the futility of formal musicology when dealing with jazz. Not only are the various jazz effects almost impossible to notate, but each note *means something* quite in addition to musical notation. The notes of a jazz solo exist in a notation strictly for musical reasons. The notes of a jazz solo, as they are coming into existence, exist as they do for reasons that are only concomitantly musical. Coltrane's cries are not "musical," but they *are* music and quite moving music. Ornette Coleman's screams and rants are only musical once one understands the music his emotional attitude seeks to create. This attitude is real, and perhaps the most singularly important aspect of his music. Mississippi Joe Williams, Snooks Eaglin, Lightnin' Hopkins have different emotional attitudes than Ornette Coleman, but all of these attitudes are continuous parts of the historical and cultural biography of the Negro as it has existed and developed since there was a Negro in America, and a music that could be associated with him that did not exist anywhere else in the world. The notes *mean something;* and the something is, regardless of its stylistic considerations, part of the black psyche as it dictates the various forms of Negro culture.

Another hopeless flaw in a great deal of the writing done about jazz that has been done over the years is that in most cases the writers, the jazz critics, have been anything but intellectuals (in the most complete sense of that world). Most jazz critics began as hobbyists or boyishly brash members of the American petit bourgeoisie, whose only claim to any understanding about the music was that they knew it was *different;* or else they had once been brave enough to make a trip into a Negro slum to hear their favorite instrumentalist defame Western musical tradition. Most jazz critics were (and are) not only white middle-class Americans, but middle-brows as well. The irony here is that because the majority of jazz critics are white middle-brows, most jazz criticism tends to enforce white middle-brow standards of excellence as criteria for performance of a music that in its most profound manifestations is completely antithetical to such standards; in fact, quite often is in direct reaction against them. (As an analogy, suppose the great majority of the critics of Western formal music were poor, "uneducated" Negroes?) A man can speak of the "heresy of bebop" for instance, only if he is completely unaware of the psychological catalysts that made that music the exact registration of the social and cultural thinking of a whole generation of black Americans. The blues and jazz aesthetic, to be fully understood, must be seen in as nearly its complete human context as possible. People made bebop. The question the critic must ask is: *why?* But it is just this *why* of Negro music that has been consistently ignored or misunderstood; and it is a question that cannot be adequately answered without first understanding the necessity of asking it. Contemporary jazz during the last few years has begun to take on again some of the anarchy and excitement of the bebop years. The cool and hard bop/funk movements since the '40s seem pitifully tame, even decadent, when compared to the music men like Ornette Coleman, Sonny Rollins, John Coltrane, Cecil Taylor and some others have been making recently. And of the bop pioneers, only Thelonious Monk has managed to maintain without question the vicious creativity with which he first entered the jazz scene back in the '40s. The music has changed again, for many of the same basic reasons it changed twenty years ago. Bop was, at a certain level of consideration, a reaction by young musicians against the sterility and formality of Swing as it moved to become a formal part of the mainstream American culture. The New Thing, as recent jazz has been called, is, to a large degree, a reaction to the hard bop-funk-groove-soul camp, which itself seemed to come into being in protest against the squelching of most of the blues elements in cool and progressive jazz. Funk (groove, soul) has become as formal and clichéd as cool or swing, and opportunities for imaginative expression within that form have dwindled almost to nothing.

The attitudes and emotional philosophy contained in "the new music" must be isolated and understood by critics before any consideration of the *worth* of the music can be legitimately broached. Later on, of course, it becomes relatively easy to characterize the emotional penchants that informed earlier aesthetic statements. After the fact, is a much simpler way to work and think. For example, a writer who wrote liner notes for a John Coltrane record mentioned how difficult it had been for him to appreciate Coltrane earlier, just as it had been difficult for him to appreciate Charlie Parker when he first appeared. To quote: "I wish I were one of those sages who can say, 'Man, I dug Bird the first time I heard him.' I didn't. The first time I heard Charlie Parker, I thought he was ridiculous. . . ." Well, that's a noble confession and all, but the responsibility is still the writer's and in no way involves Charlie Parker or what he was trying to do. When that writer first heard Charlie Parker he simply did not understand *why* Bird should play the way he did, nor could it have been very important to him. But now, of course, it becomes almost a form of reverse snobbery to say that one did not think Parker's music was worth much at first hearing, etc., etc. The point is, it seems to me, that if the music is worth something now, it must have been worth something then. Critics are supposed to be people in a position to tell what is of value and what is not, and, hopefully, at the time it first appears. If they are consistently mistaken, what is their value?

Jazz criticism, certainly as it has existed in the United States, has served in a great many instances merely to obfuscate what has actually been happening with the music itself—the pitiful harangues that raged during the '40s between two "schools" of critics as to which was the "real jazz," the new or the traditional, provide some very ugly examples. A critic who praises Bunk Johnson at Dizzy Gillespie's expense is no critic at all; but then neither is a man who turns it around and knocks Bunk to swell Dizzy. If such critics would (or could) reorganize their thinking so that they begin their concern for these musicians by trying to understand why each played the way he did, and in terms of the constantly evolving and redefined philosophy which has informed the most profound examples of Negro music throughout its history, then such thinking would be impossible.

It has never ceased to amaze and infuriate me that in the '40s a European critic could be arrogant and unthinking enough to inform serious young American musicians that what they were feeling (a consideration that exists before, and without, the music) was false. What had happened was that even though the white middle-brow critic had known about Negro music for only about three decades, he was already trying to formalize and finally institutionalize it. It is a hideous idea. The music was already in danger of being forced into that junk pile of admirable objects and data the West knows as *culture.*

Recently, the same attitudes have become more apparent in the face of a fresh redefinition of the form and content of Negro music. Such phrases as "anti-jazz" have been used to describe musicians who are making the most exciting music produced in this country. But as critic A. B. Spellman asked, "What does anti-jazz mean and who are these ofays who've appointed themselves guardians of last year's blues?" It is that simple, really. What does anti-jazz mean? And who coined the phrase? What is the definition of jazz? And who was authorized to make one?

Reading a great deal of old jazz criticism is usually like boning up on the social and cultural malaise that characterizes and delineates the bourgeois philistine in America. Even rereading someone as intelligent as Roger Pryor Dodge in the old *Record Changer* ("Jazz: its rise and decline," 1955) usually makes me either very angry or very near hysterical. Here is a sample: ". . . let us say flatly that there is no future in preparation for jazz through Bop . . . ," or "The Boppists, Cools, and Progressives are surely stimulating a dissolution within the vagaries of a non-jazz world. The Revivalists, on the other hand have made a start in the right direction." It sounds almost like political theory. Here is Don C. Haynes in the April 22, 1946 issue of *Down Beat,* reviewing Charlie Parker's *Billie's Bounce* and *Now's The Time:* "These two sides are bad taste and ill-advised fanaticism. . . ." and, "This is the sort of stuff that has thrown innumerable impressionable young musicians out of stride, that has harmed many of them irreparably. This can be as harmful to jazz as Sammy Kaye." It makes you blush.

Of course there have been a few very fine white writers on jazz, even as there are today. Most of them have been historians. But the majority of popular jazz criticism has been on about the same level as the quoted examples. Nostalgia, lack of understanding or failure to see the validity of redefined emotional statements which reflect the changing psyche of the Negro in opposition to what the critic might think the Negro ought to feel; all of these unfortunate failures have been built many times into a kind of critical stance or aesthetic. An aesthetic whose standards and measure are connected irrevocably to the continuous gloss most white Americans have always made over Negro life in America. Failure to understand, for instance, that Paul Desmond and John Coltrane represent not only two very divergent ways of thinking about music, but more importantly two very different ways of viewing the world, is at the seat of most of the established misconceptions that are daily palmed off as intelligent commentary on jazz or jazz criticism. The catalysts and necessity of Coltrane's music must be understood as they exist even before they are expressed as music. The music is the result of the attitude, the stance. Just as Negroes made blues and other people did not because of the Negro's peculiar way of looking at the world. Once this attitude is delineated as a continuous though constantly evolving social philosophy directly attributable to the way the Negro responds to the psychological landscape that is his Western environment, criticism of Negro music will move closer to developing as consistent and valid an aesthetic as criticism in other fields of Western art.

There have been so far only two American playwrights, Eugene O'Neill and Tennessee Williams, who are as profound or as important to the history of ideas as Louis Armstrong, Bessie Smith, Duke Ellington, Charlie Parker or Ornette Coleman, yet there is a more valid and consistent body of dramatic criticism written in America than there is a body of criticism about Negro music. And this is simply because there is an intelligent tradition and body of dramatic criticism, though it has largely come from Europe, that any intelligent American drama critic can draw on. In jazz criticism, no reliance on European tradition or theory will help at all. Negro music, like the Negro himself, is strictly an American phenomenon, and we have got to set up standards of judgment and aesthetic excellence that depend on our native knowledge and understanding of the underlying philosophies and local cultural references that produced blues and jazz in order to produce valid critical writing or commentary about it. It might be that there is still time to start.

46. A Jazz Summit Meeting

WHEN THE FIRST ISSUE OF *PLAYBOY* hit newsstands in 1953, readers were offered not only the now-famous centerfold of Marilyn Monroe, but also a critique of marriage and a utopian vision of the good life for men: if he could manage to escape the bread-winner role, a man's aspirations might shift from the family barbecue to evenings with "a female acquaintance," for "a quiet discussion of Picasso, Nietzsche, jazz, sex." According to historians such as Barbara Ehrenreich, *Playboy* helped break down the rigid gender roles of the 1950s, but it did so by promoting a "fraternity of male rebels" whose self-absorbed devotion to luxury items replaced an earlier masculine ideology of family support.[1] Even the magazine's first issue included jazz among the trappings of the good life for single white men, marking a significant shift from the music's earlier associations with, for example, social dance or exotic spectacles.

Source: "The Playboy Panel: Jazz—Today and Tomorrow," *Playboy*, February, 1964, pp. 29–31, 34–38, 56, 58, 139–41. Reprinted by permission of Nat Hentoff.

1. Barbara Ehrenreich, *The Hearts of Men: American Dreams and the Flight From Commitment* (New York: Anchor Press, 1983), especially chapter 4; the quotations are from pages 43 and 44.

Playboy's interest in jazz led to, among other things, this extraordinary multiple interview of 1964. Many of the foremost musicians and critics of the time were assembled to address a host of issues: performing in clubs vs. formal concerts, playing on TV and for the State Department overseas, the meaning of the word "jazz" and its relationship to other popular music, the future of avant-garde jazz and "third stream" fusions with classical music, and, in this tense year before the Watts riots, the crucial topic of race. It is a long interview, but the stature of the panelists and the quality of their discussion, which includes productive disagreements, make it an important document. Since it is no longer easily accessible, it is reprinted here in its entirety.

The article begins by introducing the participants, but it leaves out the interviewer. The voice identified as "Playboy" was that of Nat Hentoff (b. 1925), an associate editor of *Down Beat* in the 1950s and an influential jazz critic and essayist on civil liberties through subsequent decades. Pictures of the panelists (except Hentoff) were provided, discreetly ensuring that the reader knew that four of the musicians—Cannonball Adderley, Dizzy Gillespie, Charles Mingus, and George Russell—were African-American. Both critics—Ralph Gleason and Nat Hentoff—were white, along with musicians Dave Brubeck, Stan Kenton, and Gerry Mulligan, and composer Gunther Schuller.

The Panelists

Julian "Cannonball" Adderley is an urbane alto saxophonist and leader who has achieved sizable popular success during the past five years. He is also a recording director and has helped many musicians get their first chance at national exposure. Adderley has termed his music "modern traditional," indicating his knowledge and respect for the jazz past as well as his interest in continuing to add to the music. Through his lucid, witty introductions at concerts, festivals, and night clubs, Adderley has become a model of how to make an audience feel closer to the jazz experience.

Dave Brubeck, the rugged, candid pianist, leader, and composer, has won an unusually large audience to the extent of even having had a number of hit single records. Instead of coasting in a familiar groove, however, he has continued to experiment; in recent years he has turned to time signatures comparatively new to jazz. Although Brubeck is characteristically friendly and guileless, he is a fierce defender of his musical position and does not suffer critics casually.

John "Dizzy" Gillespie is now recognized throughout the world as the most prodigious trumpet player in modern jazz. He is also the leading humorist in jazz and he has demonstrated that a jazz musician can be a brilliant entertainer without sacrificing any of his musical integrity. He is now leading one of the most stimulating groups of his career, and is also engaged in several ambitious recording projects.

Ralph J. Gleason, one of the few jazz critics widely respected by musicians, is a syndicated columnist who is based at the *San Francisco Chronicle.* He has edited the book *Jam Session;* has contributed to a wide variety of periodicals, in America and abroad; and is in charge of *Jazz Casual,* an unprecedentedly superior series of jazz television shows, distributed by the National Education Television Network. As a critic, Gleason is clear, sometimes blunt, and passionately involved with the music.

Stan Kenton is a leader of extraordinary stamina and determination. He has created a distinctive orchestral style and, in the process, has given many composers an opportunity to experiment with ideas and devices which very few other bands would have permitted. The list of Kenton alumni is long and distinguished. In a period during which the band business has been erratic at best, Kenton is proving again that a forceful personality and unmistakably individual sound and style can draw enthusiastic audiences.

Charles Mingus, a virtuoso bassist, is one of the most original and emotionally compelling composers in jazz history. His groups create a surging excitement in producing some of the most startling experiences jazz has to offer. He is also an author, and has completed a long, explosive autobiography, *Beneath the Underdog*. An uncommonly open man, Mingus invariably says what he feels, and continuously looks for, but seldom finds, equal honesty in the society around him.

Gerry Mulligan has proved to be one of the most durable figures in modern jazz. In addition to his supple playing of the baritone saxophone, he has led a series of intriguingly inventive quartets and sextets as well as a large orchestra which is one of the most refreshing and resourceful units in contemporary jazz. Mulligan also has acted in films and is now writing a Broadway musical. He has a quality of natural leadership which is manifested not only in the way all of his groups clearly reflect his musical personality, but also in the fact that whenever jam sessions begin at jazz festivals, Mulligan is usually in charge.

George Russell has emerged during the past decade as a jazz composer of exceptional imagination and originality. He has recorded a series of albums with his own group, and these represent one of the most impressive bodies of work in modern jazz. He is also a teacher, and among his students in New York are a number of renowned jazzmen. A pipe-smoking, soft-voiced inhabitant of Greenwich Village, Russell is not one of the more prosperous jazzmen, despite his stature among musicians, but he refuses to compromise his music in any way.

Gunther Schuller is a major force in contemporary music—both classical and jazz. He is one of the most frequently performed American composers, has been awarded many commissions here and abroad (his most recent honor, a Guggenheim fellowship), and is also an accomplished conductor. For ten years, Schuller was first French horn with the Metropolitan Opera Orchestra, but now devotes his full time to composing, conducting, and writing about music. He has had extensive experience in jazz and is largely responsible for the concept of "third-stream music." He is currently working on an analytical musical history of jazz for Oxford University Press. A man of seemingly limitless energy, Schuller is expert in many areas of music as well as in literature and several of the other arts.

PLAYBOY: There appears to be a paradox in the current jazz situation. The international stature of the music has never been higher, and jazz is receiving more and more attention in print. Yet musicians are complaining that work is becoming harder and harder to find. Is jazz declining economically, and if it is, how do you reconcile that decline with all the publicity it is receiving?

BRUBECK: I don't think there's much of a connection between how much is written in newspapers and magazines about jazz and the growth of its audience. After all, if this were important, classical music would have a much larger audience than pop music. Yet you can't compare the record sales of even the most popular classical artists, such as Leonard Bernstein, with those of Johnny Mathis. Now let's carry this over to jazz; certainly there's more being written today about jazz musicians, but I don't think it will affect the popularity of the jazz musician much, or his record sales, or the amount of work he gets.

As for work being harder and harder to find, I think this is true. Not true for the accepted jazz musicians, the ones who have been around for a while. I'd say the pianists I feel are my contemporaries—Erroll Garner, George Shearing, Oscar Peterson—are certainly working as much as they want to work. I am, too. You couldn't say we're complaining. But a young pianist coming up today might have a harder time than we did.

GLEASON: While it is true that several night clubs have gone out of business—night clubs that have been associated with jazz over the years—I don't think jazz is in any economic decline. The sales of jazz records and the presence of jazz singles on the hit parade indicate it isn't. The box-office grosses of the Newport Jazz Festival and the Monterey Jazz Festival indicate it isn't. The proven drawing ability of groups like those led by Miles Davis, Count Basie, John Coltrane—and from this panel, Brubeck, Dizzy, and Cannonball Adderley—show that there is a very substantial market for jazz in this country.

But there is *not* a market for second-rate jazz, and at certain times in the past, we have had an economy that has supported second-rate jazz as well as first-rate jazz. I think that those fringe groups are now finding work difficult to get. On the other hand, all the jazz night clubs complain consistently that it's hard to find top-caliber acts to fill out a 52-weeks-a-year schedule. Jazz is, of course, receiving a great deal of publicity these days, in *Playboy* as well as elsewhere, but I don't think this fact is related to anything at all except the growing awareness on the part of the American public that jazz is something worthy of its interest.

MULLIGAN: I think this all has to be seen in perspective. During the big upsurge of jazz in the early 1950s, we saw a tremendous increase in the number of clubs. Now we start wailing the blues and we say, look how terrible times are when these clubs start to close. But we forget that what has happened is that the business has settled back to normal. I'd imagine that there are probably more jazz clubs today than there were in the 1930s. I think you'd find that there were many fewer units in the Thirties and probably none of them was making the money that even some relatively unknown groups are making today.

RUSSELL: I can't agree with the optimism that has been expressed so far. I think economic conditions are bad for all but the established groups, and the reason goes to the basic structure of American life. During the swing era, anti-Negro prejudice was at a vicious level. So the young Negro rebels, intellectuals and gang members alike, shared a reverence for jazz because it expressed the feelings of revolt that they needed. It seemed that they had to feel that at least something in their culture was a dynamic, growing thing. The creative jazz musician was one of the most respected members of the Negro community. Then bop came along and was generally accepted by the culturally unbiased dissidents and rejected by those committed to status goals—in either case, irrespective of race.

Another conflict was added to jazz which also transcended race—between the innovator who creates the art (seeking what he can give to it), and the imitator who dilutes and who is mostly interested in what art can give to him.

There is, to be sure, a revolution going on in America. People want an equal chance to compete for status goals that compromise rather than enhance a meaningful life. What I would like to see is a renaissance. Shouldn't a social revolution be armed with a violent drive not only to elevate the individual, but to elevate and enrich the culture as well? If we continue to cater to the tyranny of the majority, we shall all be clapping our hands to *Dixie* on one and three.

MINGUS: You have to go further than that. No matter how many places jazz is written up, the fact is that the musicians themselves don't have any power. Tastes are *created* by the business interests. How else can you explain the popularity of an Al Hirt? But it's the musicians' fault for having allowed the booking agents to get this power. It's the musicians' fault for having allowed themselves to be discriminated against.

SCHULLER: I'll go along with George and Charles that there are serious economic problems in jazz today, but the basic answer is very simple. It's not a comforting answer economically, but I believe that jazz in its most advanced stages has now arrived precisely at the point where classical European music arrived between 1915 and 1920. At that time, classical music moved into an area of what we can roughly call total freedom, which is marked by such things as atonality, or free rhythm, or new forms, new kinds of continuity, all these things. So the audience was suddenly left without a tradition, without specific style, without, in other words, the specifics of a language which they thought they knew very well. By also moving into this area—and I believe the move was inevitable—jazz has removed itself from its audience.

ADDERLEY: I don't know about that. There is an audience out there now, a sizable audience. But you have to play *for* it. When we go to work, we play for that audience because the audience is the reason we're able to be there. Of course, we play what we want to and in the way we want to, but the music is directed at the audience. We don't play for ourselves and ignore the people. I don't think that's the proper approach, and I've discovered that most of the guys who are making a buck play for audiences. One way or another.

PLAYBOY: Can you be more specific?

ADDERLEY: Well, I think the audience feels quite detached from most jazz groups. And it works the other way around, too. Jazz musicians have a tendency to keep themselves detached from the audience. But *I* speak to the audience. I don't see that it's harmful to advise an audience that you're going to play such and such a thing and tell them something about it. Nor is it harmful to tell something about the man you're going to feature and something about why his sound is different. Or, if somebody requests a song we've recorded with some measure of success, we'll program it.

GILLESPIE: Yes, I think some jazz artists are forgetting that jazz is entertainment, too. If you don't take your audience into consideration and put on some kind of a show, they'd just as soon sit at home and listen to your records instead of coming to see you in person.

PLAYBOY: A number of musicians—Erroll Garner, the Modern Jazz Quartet, and Dave Brubeck here, among them—have either stopped playing night clubs entirely or are curtailing their night-club engagements drastically. Do you think the future of jazz lies largely in the concert field rather than in night clubs? And, trends aside, do you prefer to play the clubs or at a concert?

KENTON: For big bands, there does seem to be a trend away from the clubs, because so many of the clubs have had such problems trying to keep alive. We might finally be left with only concert halls—where you can book spotty dates. But personally, I really don't see a lot of difference between clubs and concerts so long as you can play jazz for listening. I don't think most of us mind whether people are drinking while they listen or whether they're just sitting in a concert hall. I'd just as soon play in either context.

GLEASON: I don't think the future of jazz lies largely in the concert field. I think that it lies *partially* in the concert field and *partially* in the night clubs. The fact that Brubeck and Erroll Garner and the Modern Jazz Quartet have all reached a level of economic independence where they can function outside the night club most of the time is an indication of their success, not necessarily an indication of the future of jazz.

All the jazz groups I've ever heard have something different to offer when they're in night clubs than they do when they're on the concert stage. I recently heard the Brubeck quartet, for instance, play the first night-club engagement on the West Coast that it's played in probably six or seven years. I came to that night-club engagement after having heard them in two concert appearances, and the thing that happened in the night club was much more interesting and much more exciting than it was in the concert hall. And all four musicians commented on how great they felt and how well the group played in the night-club appearance.

MINGUS: I wish I'd *never* have to play in night clubs again. I don't mind the drinking, but the night-club environment is such that it doesn't call for a musician to even care whether he's communicating. Most customers, by the time the musicians reach the second set, are to some extent inebriated. They don't care what you play anyway. So the environment in a night club is not conducive to good creation. It's conducive to *re*-creation, to the playing of what they're used to. In a club, you could never elevate to free form as well as the way you could, say, in a concert hall.

BRUBECK: I can understand that feeling. The reason we got away from night clubs has nothing to do with the people who go to night clubs, or night clubs themselves, or night-club operators. It has to do with the way people *behave* in night clubs. The same person who will be very attentive at a concert will often not be so attentive in a night club. But I must also say that there are some types of jazz I've played in groups which would not come across well in a concert-stage atmosphere. And to tell you the truth, I'm usually happiest playing jazz in a dance hall, because there I don't feel I'm imposing my music and myself on my audience. They can stand up close to the bandstand and listen to us, or they can dance, or they can be way in the back of the hall holding a conversation.

GILLESPIE: Maybe so, but for myself, the atmosphere in a night club lends itself to more creativity on the part of the audience as well as the musician. One reason is that the musician has closer contact with the people and, therefore, can build better rapport. On the other hand, I also like the idea of concerts, because, for one thing: the kids who aren't allowed into night clubs can hear you at concerts and can then buy your records. But to return to the advantages of clubs, when you're on the road a lot, the club—at least one where you can stay a comparatively long period of time—does give you a kind of simulated home atmosphere. There's a place for both clubs and concerts.

ADDERLEY: Yes, I like to play them both, too. And I like festivals. I like television shows—any kind of way we get a chance to play consistently. I like to *do.* But unlike Charles, a joint has my favorite atmosphere. It's true that some people can get noisy, but that's part of it. It seems to me that I feel a little better when people seem to be having a good time before you even begin. And it gives me something to play on. In a concert, sometimes, we don't have enough time to warm up and if the first number is a little bit below our standards, we never quite recover. At least in a club you have sets, and if one set doesn't go well, you have a chance to review what you've done and approach it another way the second time around.

My own preferences aside, however, I think that the night-club business in general is on an unfortunate decline. In a short while, the night club will be a relic, because night clubs are too expensive for most people to really support in the way they should be supported. Just recently, I was talking to a guy who has a club in Columbus, Ohio. Several years ago, he played Art Blakey and the Jazz Messengers, Horace Silver, Miles Davis, Kai Winding, the Oscar Peterson Trio, and my band. He said he didn't pay over $2200 a week for anybody. But now groups that used to cost him $1250 cost $2500, and the same way up the line. But he has no more seats than he had before, and the people are unwilling to pay double for drinks even though the bands cost the owner double. Yet, at the same time, the musicians' cost of living has also gone up. It's a rough circle to break.

PLAYBOY: Are you saying, then, that the future of jazz is going to be largely in the concert hall?

ADDERLEY: Not particularly. I think there'll be other things. There'll be theaters. I think festivals are going to come back in a different way. The George Wein type of festival of today stands a good chance.[1] In the purest sense, his are not jazz festivals the way Newport was in the beginning. But if Wein presents somebody like Gloria Lynne at a festival today, whether or not she is a jazz singer isn't the point. The fact is she is going to draw a certain number of people. So Wein, thereby, can also present Roland Kirk and he can call it a jazz festival. Most people are not going to quibble over whether Gloria Lynne is a jazz singer; they'll come to hear her at a jazz festival.

MULLIGAN: Well, I want to try whatever outlets for playing we have. I don't want to do the same thing all the time. As for clubs, at any given time, there are maybe only three to five clubs in the country that I really enjoy playing. And when you figure two to three weeks in each of five clubs, about 15 weeks of the year are already taken care of. Fortunately, in New York, there is more than one club in which we can work, so that we can stay there longer. We need that time, because otherwise we'd never get any new material.

There are advantages and disadvantages on both sides. I find clubs very wearying in a way in which concerts aren't. The hours themselves—working from nine to two or nine to four, whatever it is. It plays hell with your days. I know guys who are able to get work done in the daytime when they're playing clubs. Maybe they're better disciplined than I am, but I find I'm drained by clubs. So that's what concerts can mean to me—a chance to work during the day. But I also need clubs because we need that kind of atmosphere for the band—an atmosphere in which you just play and play and play. The hard work of it—playing hour after hour, night after night, in the same circumstances—is good for a band. Concerts, however, are also good for the big band, because they allow me to do a greater variety of things. And economically, there are very few clubs into which I can take the big band—because of transportation costs and the problems of working out some kind of consecutive tour. So, I have to think in terms of both concerts and clubs. So far as I'm concerned, I don't see my future as exclusively in one or the other direction.

MINGUS: I'll tell you where I'd like more of *my* future work to be. I'd like some Governmental agency to let me take my band out in the streets during the summer so that I could play in the parks or on the backs of trucks for kids, old

1. George Wein (b. 1925) was the important promoter and producer who founded the Newport Jazz Festival, the New Orleans Jazz and the Heritage Festival, and the Playboy Jazz Festival in Los Angeles. [RW]

people, anyone. In delinquent neighborhoods in the North. All through the South. Anywhere. I'd like to see the Government pay me and other bands who'd like to play for the people. I'm not concerned with the promoters who want to make money for themselves out of jazz. I'd much rather play for kids.

PLAYBOY: Perhaps more important than the question of where jazz is going to be played is that of *what* will be played. We seem to be in a period similar to the early 1940s—when Dizzy Gillespie, Charlie Parker, Thelonious Monk, and others began to change the jazz language. In other words, a new generation of young musicians is insisting on greater freedom—melodically, harmonically, and rhythmically. Do you think that it is indeed time for another expansion of the jazz language? Has the music of the established players become too predictable, too "safe"?

SCHULLER: It's not entirely accurate to relate what's happening now to what took place in the 1940s. The language of "bop" at that time remained largely tonal, and even a comparative novice could connect it with what had gone before in jazz. This is no longer true. The music of the jazz avant-garde has gone across that borderline which is the same borderline which the music of Schoenberg passed in 1908 and 1909. At that time, it was the most radical step in some 700 years of classical music. In jazz, nothing so radical as what has been going on during the past five years took place in the previous 40 or 50 years of jazz history. Everything previously, even the bop "revolution," was more of a step-by-step evolution. What's happening now is a giant step, a radical step. Because of the radical nature of the advance, there is a much greater gap between player and audience now than there was in the 1940s.

KENTON: I agree about the gap, but I also feel that a lot of the modern experimenters are taking jazz too fast. Sometimes they're doing things just to gain attention—being different for the sake of being different. They're also running the risk of losing their audience entirely. After all, if a music doesn't communicate to the public, I don't care how sophisticated a listener may be, eventually he'll lose interest and walk off if there's no communication. The listener might kid himself for a while if he thinks there's something new and different in the music, but if there's no validity to the music, I'm afraid the jazz artist might lose the listener entirely.

GLEASON: First of all, I don't think that the jazz of the established players has become too predictable or too safe. What's predictable or safe about the way Miles Davis or Dizzy Gillespie plays, or John Coltrane? Secondly, jazz musicians are by nature experimental. Every new generation of jazz musicians will try to do something new. And in trying to do something new, they may do a lot of foolish things and a lot of dull things. They may do a lot of things that will have no interest for other musicians, now or in the future. But this won't stop them from experimenting.

BRUBECK: We are certainly in a period during which musicians are starting to branch out into very individualistic directions, and that's very healthy. It's also healthy because we're not codified. It doesn't all have to be bop or swing or New Orleans or Chicago style. We can all be working at the same time in our own individual ways. We are now in the healthiest period in the history of jazz. As for the new generation of young musicians insisting on greater freedom—melodically, harmonically, and rhythmically—they certainly should. This is their role—to expand, to create new things. But it's also their role to build on the old, on the past; and when you have all these new, wild things going on, there are some of the wild experimenters who aren't qualified yet. They haven't the roots to shoot out the new branches. They will die.

GILLESPIE: That's right. You have to know what's gone before. And another thing, I don't agree that the established players have become too "safe." It takes you 20 to 25 years to find out what *not* to play, to find out what's in bad taste. Taste is something—like wine—that requires aging. But I'd also agree that jazz, like any art form, is constantly evolving. It has to if it's a dynamic art. And unfortunately, many artists do not evolve and thus remain static. As for me, I'm stimulated by experimentation and unpredictability. Jazz shouldn't be boxed in. If it were, it would become decadent.

MINGUS: Any musician who comes up and tries changing the *whole* pattern is taking too much in his hands if he thinks he can cut Charlie Parker, Louis Armstrong, King Oliver, and Dizzy all in one "new thing." You see, there's a danger of those experimenters getting boxed in themselves in their own devices. As for now, I don't hear any great change in jazz. Twenty years ago, I was playing simple music that was involved with a lot of things these musicians are doing now. And I'm still playing the same simple music. I haven't even begun to play what I call way-out music. I have some music that will make these cats sound like babies, but this is not the time to play that kind of music.

ADDERLEY: I'd agree with what the question implies—we've had a certain amount of lethargy in recent years. Everybody knew how to do the same thing. So, I'd like to say thank God for Ornette Coleman and such players because, whether or not you're an Ornette Coleman fan, his stimulus has done much for all of us. I know it caused me to develop. It caused Coltrane to develop even further, because he felt he had exhausted chord patterns and so forth. However, there has also been a focusing on another area—one Dizzy mentioned. I heard a new record by Illinois Jacquet the other day and it made me realize again that as certain guys get older, they develop a tendency to get more out of less. Illinois gets more out of his sound, more out of a little vibrato in the right place than he used to. Therefore, don't discount the maturity that has come with experience and discipline. As I say, many of us have been stimulated by what's going on, but we're also aware that often emotion is missing in all this emphasis on freedom. Too many of the newer players are interested in just being different. I don't think it's necessary to be different so much as to be right. To be felt. To be beautiful.

MULLIGAN: Yes, the concept of freedom has been overworked a great deal. In the course of "freeing" themselves, as Mingus said, a lot of the guys have become even more rigidly entrenched in a stylized approach.

PLAYBOY: In regard to the casting off of old jazz forms, what is your reaction to the concept of "third stream" music—a music which will draw from both jazz and classical heritages but which is intended to have an identity of its own?

GLEASON: My reaction? Hooray! Let's have third-stream music and fourth-stream music and fifth-stream music and sixth-stream and whatever. Let's just have more music. There's nothing inherently good or bad in the idea of a new kind of music which will draw from various musical heritages. This may turn out to be a very good thing. Some of it has already turned out to be quite interesting.

KENTON: I'd agree that music is music, but as for "third stream," I think it's just a kind of merchandising idea. I've been interested in the development, but I don't think there's anything new there.

ADDERLEY: Well, I'm the last person to discourage anyone's interest in trying to do something different. However, as much as I respect and admire the willingness of the third-stream people to work hard, their music misses me most of the time. I listen to a lot of classical music and it seems to me that most of what they're doing with the third stream has already been developed further by the more venturesome classical composers. Besides, Duke Ellington has shown us how to develop jazz from *within* to do practically anything. On the other hand, we know how ridiculous Stravinsky's *Ebony Concerto* is.

MULLIGAN: As Dizzy said, we already use certain devices that can be traced to some kind of classical influence. But this idea of an autonomous music—separate from both jazz and classical music—I don't see any need for it. That's not to say I wouldn't like to write things for, or play with, a symphony, but whether a third stream should come along and have its own niche is something else. It seems to me it's going to have to be absorbed into one or the other main stream.

RUSSELL: A third stream isn't necessary. In fact, jazz itself may be the main stream of music to come. I mean that, to me, jazz is an evolving classical music. In my own work, I don't draw that heavily on traditional classical standards. I have been influenced by composers like Bartok, Stravinsky, and Berg, but if those influences go into my music, it's unconscious. A *conscious* attempt to combine the two is not my way of doing things. You see, I think jazz itself is the classical music of America, and eventually it will transcend even that role and become, in every profound musical sense, an international classical music.

BRUBECK: When *wasn't* jazz what you describe as third-stream music? Melodically, from the beginning, jazz has been mostly European. Harmonically, it's been mostly European. The forms used have been mostly European. In fact, the first written jazz form was the rag and that was a copy of the European march. I think it's time we realize that we couldn't have had jazz without the merging of the African culture with the European culture. But in the beginning it was primarily a European music transformed to fulfill the expression of the American Negro. Once having acknowledged that, we ought to forget about who did what and when and we ought to forget whether jazz is African or European. Jazz now is an *American* art form and it's being played all over the world.

PLAYBOY: To get back to the idea of the "third stream," Gunther, as the man most closely identified with the concept, do you still think it is a viable approach?

SCHULLER: Absolutely, and this is confirmed for me almost every day of my life—especially this past summer at Tanglewood, where I was very much in touch with what you could call a cross section of the young American musical generation. Tanglewood draws its 200 students from all over the country; and even in this citadel of nonjazz music, at least 30 to 40 percent of the young musicians there were in some sense involved with jazz or could play it. And some of them played it extremely well. Now, these musicians epitomized what I feel about third-stream music, and that is the elimination of a radical barrier or difference between jazz and classical music. To the kids, there is no such big difference. It's all either good or not-so-good music. And the question of jazz style or nonjazz is not a fundamental issue with them. They deal with much more fundamental musical criteria—is a piece, in whatever style, good or bad? This means that the third-stream movement, whether the critics or certain musicians happen to like it or not, is developing by itself—without any special efforts on anybody's part.

ADDERLEY: My feeling, though, is that when you deal with something like third stream, which mixes jazz with classical music, you're going to weaken the basic identity of jazz.

SCHULLER: It's true that many people worry about the guts being taken out of jazz as it evolves. They worry about it becoming "whitened." However, jazz has indeed basically changed into something different from what it started as. It started as folk music, as a very earthy, almost plainly social expression of a downtrodden people. It then became a dance music, an entertainment music—still with roots in the very essence and heart of life. It was not an art music. Now, as it becomes an art music—and there's no question that it already has in the hands of certain people—it will change its character. The process is inevitable.

PLAYBOY: In some of your statements so far, the term "art music" has been used in connection with jazz. The French critic André Hodeir would agree that jazz is becoming more and more of an art music. He also says, however, that jazz was never really a popular music anyway—although jazz-influenced bands did draw large audiences in the 1930s. In any case, he claims that now, as jazz is inevitably evolving into an art music, its audiences are going to be small and select—similar, in a way, to the audiences for chamber music and poetry. Do you agree?

KENTON: Yes. Jazz, to start with, is not a popular music at all. It's true that a lot of the bands in the Golden Era of bands were kind of jazz oriented and did quite well playing dance music and swing, but real jazz has no greater following throughout the world today than has classical music. I think we might as well make up our minds that that's the way it's going to be.

GLEASON: I don't agree that jazz audiences are going to become smaller and more select. If Count Basie's band and Duke Ellington's band weren't jazz bands, and aren't jazz bands, then I don't know what are. Woody Herman's also. And these bands at various times have had very large audiences. Benny Goodman's biggest successes were scored with bands that were really jazz bands, not just jazz-influenced bands.

BRUBECK: That's right. In the late 1930s and the beginning of the 1940s, I saw some tremendous jazz bands with some very large audiences in the interior of California, a place called Stockton, where I was going to college. It's pretty much off the beaten path, so if you could draw large audiences there at that time, you could draw large audiences anyplace in the United States. Duke Ellington was there for a week and he had a full house every night. Jimmie Lunceford was there. Stan Kenton came through. Woody Herman. Count Basie. Now, I wouldn't call those bands jazz influenced. They were *influencing* jazz. I think Hodeir is referring to some other bands that may have been more popular, but I hardly think they were that much more popular. The bands then were set up to be more entertaining than we are today—but they were also playing great music. I do agree with Hodeir that jazz is becoming much more of an art music. In other words, we aren't putting on a show and good jazz at the same time. We're each of us putting on our own individual brand of jazz, and it's not meant to be entertaining in the sense that it's a show. But it's entertaining in the sense that it's good music, sincere music that we hope reaches an audience. Maybe this absence of a "show" does put jazz into the art-music category, but I for one wouldn't mind seeing jazz go back to the days of the 1930s when you had more entertaining bands, such as Ellington's. And don't forget that Ellington, while he was entertaining, was also able to create a *Black, Brown, and Beige.*

SCHULLER: But jazz is not going to go back to the 1930s. And I maintain that, to the extent that jazz ever has been a really popular music, it has been the result of a certain commercialization of jazz elements. Even with the best of the jazz bands, like Fletcher Henderson's, their style wasn't popular. What became popular was a certain simplification of that style as it was used by Benny Goodman.

ADDERLEY: I don't agree with Hodeir. I don't think jazz ever will cease to be important to the layman, simply because the layman has always looked to jazz for some kind of escape from the crap in popular culture. Anybody who ever heard the original form of *Stardust* can hardly believe what has happened to it through the efforts primarily of jazz musicians. Listen to the music on television. Even guys who think in terms of Delius and Ravel and orchestrate for television shows draw from jazz. The jazz audience has always existed, and it always will.

RUSSELL: I think there'll be a schism in the forms of jazz. There definitely will be an art jazz and a popular jazz. As a matter of fact, that situation exists today.

GILLESPIE: I'm optimistic. Yes, the audience will become select, but it won't be small. Let me put it another way: The audience will become larger but it will be more selective in what it likes.

SCHULLER: I don't see how. The people who are going to become involved with jazz, as it's developing now, are going to become *very much* involved. You just can't take it passively as you could, for instance, the dance music of the bands in the 1930s. You could be comparatively passive about them. But if you're going to be involved with Ornette Coleman at all, you've got to be involved very deeply, or else it goes right past you.

We must expect a smaller audience from now on, and there's nothing wrong in that. A sensitive audience is a good audience. Because of what's happened to the music, we can no longer expect the kind of mass appeal that certain very simplified traditions of jazz were able to garner for a while.

MINGUS: None of you has dealt with another aspect of this. This talk of small, select audiences will just continue the brainwashing of jazz musicians. I think of Cecil Taylor, who is a great musician. He told me one time, "Charlie, I don't want to make any money. I don't expect to. I'm an artist." Who told people that artists aren't supposed to feed their families beans and greens? I mean, just because somebody didn't make money hundreds of years ago because he was an artist doesn't mean that a musician should not be able to make money today and still be an artist. Sure, when you sell yourself as a whore in your music you can make a lot of money. But there are some honest ears left out there. If musicians could get some economic power, they could make money and be artists at the same time.

PLAYBOY: Let's discuss the changing jazz horizons even further. You, Dizzy, Miles Davis, and John Coltrane, among others, have been studying folk cultures of other parts of the world—North Africa, India, Spain, etc.—and have been incorporating some of these idioms into jazz. Is there any limitation to the variety of materials which can be included in jazz without jazz losing its own identity?

ADDERLEY: No, I don't think so. I think that you can play practically anything so long as your concept is one of bringing it into jazz. We have some Japanese folk music in our repertory which Yusef Lateef has reorganized, and we're working on a suite of Japanese folk themes.

GLEASON: There's no limitation to the variety of materials which can be included in jazz without jazz losing its own identity—provided the player is a good jazz musician. We've already had the example of all sorts of Latin and African rhythms brought into jazz. We have bossa nova, which is an amalgam of jazz and Afro-Brazilian music, and we will have others. In fact, I think that the bringing into jazz music of elements of the musical heritage of other cultures is a very good thing, and something that should be encouraged.

MINGUS: It's not that easy. Sure, you can pick up on the gimmick things. But I don't think they can take the true essence of the folk music they borrow from, add to it, and then say it's sincere. I'm skeptical, because what they probably borrow are the simple things they hear on top. Like the first thing a guy will borrow from Max Roach is a particular rhythmic device, but that's not what Max Roach is saying from his heart. His heart plays another pulse. What I'm trying to say is that you can bring in all these folk elements, but I think it's going to sound affected.

BRUBECK: I don't agree that it necessarily has to sound that way. This is something that has concerned me for a long time. About 15 years ago, I wrote an article for *Down Beat*—the first article I ever did—and I said jazz was like a sponge. It would absorb the music of the world. And I've been working in this area. In 1958, I did an album, *Jazz Impressions of Eurasia,* in which I used Indian music, Middle Eastern music, and music influenced by certain countries in Europe. I certainly think jazz will become a universal musical language. It's the only music that has that capability, because it is so close to the folk music of the world—the folk music of any country.

RUSSELL: I still have my doubts about this approach. When I say I think jazz can become a universal kind of music, I mean it in the sense of pure classical music. I don't mean by consciously melting the music of one culture with another. I mean that jazz through its own kind of melodic and harmonic and rhythmic growth will become a universal music. Furthermore, I find that American folk music in itself is rich enough to be utilized in terms of this new way of thinking. But as for going into Indian or Near Eastern cultures, it's not necessary for me. Oh, I can see its value as a hypnotic device—you know, inducing a sort of hypnotic effect upon an audience. But many times that doesn't really measure up musically. It doesn't produce a music of lasting universal value. And I think jazz is capable of producing a music that is as universal and as artistic as Bach's.

GILLESPIE: I'm with Ralph Gleason on this. So long as you have a creative jazz musician doing the incorporating of other cultures, it can work. Jazz is so robust and has such boundless energy that it can completely absorb many different cultures, and what will come out will be jazz.

PLAYBOY: We're beginning to hear the language of jazz spoken in many tongues; more and more jazzmen of ability are making themselves heard all over the world—Russia, Japan, Thailand, almost everywhere. John Lewis of the Modern Jazz Quartet claims that it will soon no longer be the rule that all important jazz innovations—and innovators—start in America. Instead, the most influential jazz player of the next decade may suddenly arise in Hong Kong. Do you think this prediction is accurate, or will a jazzman still need seasoning in America before he has the capacity to contribute importantly to the music?

GILLESPIE: The prediction may be true, but as of now, jazz is still inherently American. It comes out of an American experience. It's possible that jazzmen of other cultures can use jazz through a vicarious knowledge of its roots here or maybe they can improvise their native themes and their own emotional experiences in the context of jazz. It's also possible that one day American jazz will become really, fundamentally, international. In fact, I think that the cultural integration of all national art forms is inevitable for the future. And when that happens, a new type of jazz will emerge. But it hasn't happened yet.

KENTON: I think it's altogether possible. And it would be very good for the American ego if an outstanding player did come from left field somewhere.

ADDERLEY: I don't think there ever will be an important, serious jazz musician from anywhere but the United States, if only because jazz musicians themselves are not going to allow jazz to escape from where it was developed. I'm talking about real jazz.

SCHULLER: No, I don't agree. It's not at all inconceivable that in the next five or ten years, an innovator could come from Europe. Of course, it depends on where you choose to draw your limitations as to what jazz is. If you mean Cannonball's kind of jazz, which is certainly in the main stream of jazz development, then I'd agree with you. But jazz can no longer be defined in only that way. Jazz has grown in such a way as to include what even ten years ago would have been considered outside of jazz or very much on its periphery. The music has grown to such an extent that these things are now part of the world of jazz; and as jazz reaches out and expands and goes farther into these outer areas, jazz will of necessity include players who do not have this main stream kind of orientation. So that, in this larger sense—and I know this is the sense in which John Lewis's statement is to be taken—it's entirely possible to have important innovations come from outside this country. A genius can crop up anywhere.

RUSSELL: Perhaps, but there has not been a precedent yet for any major contributor coming from any but our country, or more specifically, from any other city but New York. I mean, he's had to have worked in New York at one time or another. I suppose the reason for the importance of New York is the interchange that goes on among musicians in this city, even when they're not in contact. Also, there's a feeling of panic and urgency in New York which provides the trial by fire that seems to make it happen. In New York, you always get a nucleus of people who haven't settled into a formula, who haven't yet sold out for comfort or for other reasons. The nucleus of that kind of musician seems to gather here, and they inspire one another.

MULLIGAN: There's a catch in the question. When you say "important innovation," that implies something different from talking about a great player who will be influential on his instrument. After all, guys have already come out of other countries who have influenced people here. Django Reinhardt is a perfect example. As Gunther says, there's no telling where genius is going to come from. But whether any major innovations in jazz are going to come from abroad—something which will radically change what went before—George is probably right, though I don't know about the New York part of what he says. What seems important to me—and I've noticed this often—is that the biggest problem jazz musicians from other countries have is that they have grown up in an entirely different kind of musical background. Most of us in this country are raised with not only jazz, but all the popular music of whatever particular time we're growing up in. But foreign players don't have that kind of ingrown background. Yet, it's also a little more complicated than that. The reason I wouldn't be surprised to see great players coming out of other countries, and conceivably creating something different on their instruments, is that fellows who don't speak English wind up phrasing differently. Many times, I hear players who speak Swedish or French imitate the phrasing of an American jazz player, but it's not quite right, because the very phrasing of an American jazz player reflects his mode of speech, the accent of his language, even his regional accents. Perhaps, when foreign horn men begin reflecting *their* natural phrasing, we will get significantly different approaches.

KENTON: What we have to remember is that while it's true that a foreign player has to be exposed to American jazz before he can grasp the dimension and the character of the music, that doesn't mean he can't eventually contribute without even visiting the States. American jazz musicians now are traveling so much around the world that foreign players can stay at home and be exposed to enough American jazz so that they can become part of the music.

MINGUS: I don't see it that way. Not the way the world and this country is now. Jazz is still an ethnic music, fundamentally. Duke Ellington used to explain that this was a Negro music. He told that to me and Max Roach, as a matter of fact, and we felt good. When the society is straight, when people really are integrated, when they *feel* integrated, maybe you can have innovations coming from someplace else. But as of now, jazz is still our music, and we're still the ones who make the major changes in it.

PLAYBOY: Do you believe there is any political gain in the flow of jazz "ambassadors" overseas, or are we conning ourselves when we think the enthusiastic acceptance of a jazz unit in a foreign country is a political advantage for us?

GILLESPIE: Well, mine was the first band that the State Department sent in an ambassadorial role, and I have no doubts that jazz can be an enormous political plus. When a jazz group goes abroad to entertain, it represents a culture and creates an atmosphere for pleasure, asking nothing in return but attentiveness, appreciation and acceptance—with no strings attached. Obviously, this has to be a political advantage.

GLEASON: I'm in favor of sending more jazz musicians overseas everywhere. Now, whether this turns out to be a political gain or not, I don't know. I do think it's a humanitarian and an artistic gain. I don't think we are totally conning ourselves as the United States of America when we consider the enthusiastic reception of a jazz unit in a foreign country to be a political plus. As Tony Lopes, the president of the Hong Kong Jazz Club, remarked recently, "You can't be anti-American and like jazz." But I don't think that any amount of jazz exported to Portugal, for instance, will ever make the attitude of the American Government toward the government of Portugal accepted by the Portuguese people as a good thing. Same thing for Spain and the rest of the world. But no one has yet seen a sign: AMERICAN JAZZMAN, GO HOME!

ADDERLEY: Sure, I think having a jazz musician travel under the auspices of the State Department is a good thing. It can signify to the audience for which it is intended that the United States Government thinks that jazz is our thing, we're happy with it, and we want you to hear some of it because we think it's beautiful.

RUSSELL: But there's an element of hypocrisy there. The very people who send jazz overseas are not really fans of jazz, and the country in whose name jazz is traveling as an "ambassador" completely ignores its own art form at home. It's not going to hurt the musician who goes, however, because music traditionally is known for its ability to unite at least some of the people. At least, the people in power do recognize the capacity jazz has to unite people.

ADDERLEY: Yes, it can unite people, but politically, I don't think jazz does a damn thing. I don't think it influences anybody that way. I think the Benny Goodman tour had nothing to do with helping create a democratic attitude in a Communist country.

BRUBECK: There are other kinds of political effects. I certainly think that when the Moiseyev Dancers were here, there was kind of a friendship toward Russia which was communicated through almost every TV set tuned to those people. The effect was like saying, "Well, the Russians can't be too bad if they've got great, happy people like these dancers, singers and entertainers. They must be very much like us. In fact, they might be better dancers." And communication from jazz groups going overseas is the same thing in reverse. After all, when we were in India during the Little Rock crisis, it made the headlines in the Indian newspapers seem maybe not quite so believable to an Indian audience that had just seen us. Our group was integrated, and the headlines were making it sound as if integration was impossible in the United States. But right before their eyes, they saw four Americans who seemed to have no problems on that score. And I think there are other assets as well.

SCHULLER: I was able to get an idea of the impact of jazz in Poland and Yugoslavia a few months ago. It's hard for anyone who hasn't been there to realize the extent to which people abroad, especially in Iron Curtain countries now, admire jazz and what it stands for. I mean the freedom and individuality it represents. However, in many cases, they don't even think of it as a particularly American product. They regard it simply as the music of the young or the music of freedom.

One thing that does concern me about sending jazz overseas is the occasional lack of care in selecting the musicians who go. The countries where many of these musicians have been sent have been much more hip than our State Department.

MINGUS: I wish the Government was more hip at home. They send jazz all over the world as an art, but why doesn't the Government give us employment here? Why don't they subsidize jazz the way Russia has subsidized its native arts? As I said before, rather than go on a State Department tour overseas, I'd prefer to play for people here. The working people. The kids.

PLAYBOY: Whether abroad or at home, has the scope of jazz widened to the point at which the term "jazz" itself is too confining?

KENTON: I feel the same way about the word jazz as some other musicians do. The word has been abused. I think it was Duke Ellington who said a couple of years ago that we should do away with the word completely, but if you do, another word will take its place. I don't think the situation would be changed at all.

BRUBECK: Yes, Duke has spoken of dropping the word jazz. I agree with him. Just call it contemporary American music, and I'd be very happy. But if you keep calling it jazz, it doesn't make me unhappy.

ADDERLEY: The word doesn't bug me in the least. In fact, I'm very happy to associate myself with the term, because I think it has a very definite meaning to most people. It means something different, something unique. Furthermore, I like to be identified with all that "jazz" represents. All the evil and all the good. All the drinking, loose women, the narcotics, everything they like to drop on us. Why? Because when I get before people, I talk to them and they get to know how I feel about life and they can ascertain that there is some warmth or maybe some morality in the music that they never knew existed.

RUSSELL: The term isn't at all burdensome to me. I like to accept the challenge of what "jazz" means in terms of the language we inherited and in terms of trying to broaden it. The word and what it connotes play a part in my musical thinking. It forces me sometimes to restrict an idea so that it will come out with more rhythmic vitality. In other words, occasionally I'll sacrifice tonal beauty for rhythmic vitality.

GLEASON: Once again, I'm not sure what the question means. In one sense, jazz covers the whole spectrum of popular music in the country. There are aspects of jazz in rhythm and blues, rock 'n' roll, Van Alexander's dance band, the Three Suns. So I don't know whether it can expand too far or not. Everybody means what *he* means when he says jazz. He doesn't always mean what you or I mean. And I don't think there's any reason to sit around looking for a new word, because we're not going to *invent* a new word. When the time comes—if it ever does—for a new word, it will arrive. *Down Beat* conducted a rather silly contest some years ago to select a new word for jazz, and came up with "crewcut." That word had a vogue which lasted for precisely one issue of *Down Beat.*

MINGUS: Well, the word jazz bothers me. It bothers me because, as long as I've been publicly identified with it, I've made less money and had more trouble than when I wasn't. Years ago, I had a very good job in California writing for Dinah Washington and several blues singers, and I also had a lot of record dates. Then by some chance I got a write-up in a "jazz" magazine, and my name got into one of those "jazz" books. As I started watching my "jazz" reputation grow, my pocketbook got emptier. I got more write-ups and came to New York to stay. So I was really in "jazz," and I found it carries you anywhere from a nut house to poverty. And the people think you're making it because you get write-ups. And you sit and starve and try to be independent of the crooked managers and agencies. You try to make it by yourself. No, I don't get any good feeling from the word jazz.

PLAYBOY: Some critics have remarked on the scarcity of significant jazz singers in recent years. Is this a correct assumption, or have the critics too narrowly defined what they consider "authentic" jazz singing? Do you feel there will be an important place of singing in the jazz of the future, and what changes are we likely to have in the concept of jazz singing?

KENTON: Well, I don't know as we've ever had a great raft of jazz singers. There have been singers who border on jazz and whose styles have a jazz flavor, but there haven't been many out-and-out jazz singers. I mean somebody like Billie Holiday who was 100 percent jazz. You could even hear it in her speaking voice. No, I don't think we're any shorter of *that* kind of jazz singer than we were 20 years ago.

GLEASON: Agreed. There has always been a scarcity of significant jazz singers. And there will always be an important place for singing in jazz. I don't see any changes, however, that we're likely to have in the concept of jazz singing. The things that were done by Ran Blake and Jeanne Lee seem to me to have almost nothing to do with the possibilities of expanding the scope of jazz singing. Carmen McRae is the best jazz singer alive today and what she's doing is really simple, in one sense. And because of that simplicity, it's exquisitely difficult.

ADDERLEY: The question is a hard one for me, because I don't know just what a jazz singer is. What does the term mean? We've had our Billie Holidays, Ella Fitzgeralds, and Mildred Baileys and Sarah Vaughans, but they've been largely jazz *oriented* and jazz *associated.* Any real creative jazz innovation has been done by an instrumentalist. In other words, to me jazz is instrumental music, so that, although I'll go along with a term like jazz oriented, I don't recognize a jazz singer as such.

MULLIGAN: I agree with that. I've always thought of jazz as instrumental music. To be sure, there have been singers who were influenced by the horn players—and a lot of them wound up being excellent singers who learned things about phrasing that they would never have learned otherwise. But fundamentally, the whole thing of improvising with a rhythm on a song, or improvising on a progression, is instrumental. It always bugs me when I hear singers trying to do the *same* things the horns do. The voice is so much more flexible than the horn, it seems unnecessary for a singer to try to restrict himself and make himself as rigid in his motion as a horn. To answer the question, I'd say singers do have a function in jazz, but as Cannonball says, it's more accurate to refer to them as *jazz-oriented* singers.

RUSSELL: I agree that superior jazz singers are rare, but I think it's possible—as in the case of Sheila Jordan—for a good vocal improviser to give you the same experience you get from listening to instrumental jazz. I mean a singer who is musical enough to take a song and make his or her own composition out of it.

SCHULLER: It's a difficult subject—jazz singing. I don't think there ever were any criteria for jazz singing. If you look at the few great jazz singers, you'll find they made their own criteria, but those criteria couldn't be valid for anybody else, because they were too individual. What Louis Armstrong and Bessie Smith and

Billie Holiday and Sarah Vaughan—especially the early Sarah Vaughan—did was so individual it couldn't be used by anyone else.

There's another problem here, too. A matter of economics. Singers with jazz capacity are usually drawn toward the big-money market that exists on the periphery of jazz. Often it's simply a matter of survival, because it's economically very difficult for a singer to survive in jazz. So they move to the periphery and their work becomes diluted. I've said this before, and I can't say it often enough, that so many people are worried about the possible dilution of jazz through third-stream music, but no one seems to be concerned about the constant, daily, minute-by-minute dilution of jazz by the commercial elements in our music industry.

PLAYBOY: As jazz composition, which is making the singer's role more difficult, becomes more and more important, is there also a possibility—as composer Bill Russo once suggested—that a time may come when all jazz is notated with no room left for the improviser? Or do you expect improvisation to remain at the core of jazz performance, whether traditional or avant-garde?

GILLESPIE: Improvisation is the meat of jazz. Rhythm is the bone. The jazz composer's ideas have always come from the instrumentalist. And a lot of the things the composer hears the instrumentalist play cannot be notated. I don't think there'll ever be a situation in which all of jazz will be written down with no room for the individual improviser.

GLEASON: If Bill Russo has suggested that a time may come when all jazz is notated with no room left for the improviser, I think he's out of his mind. This is not foreseeable. There will always be guys playing jazz who can't read music. There will always be guys playing jazz who just want to improvise, and don't want to read and yet who can read. And there may be a great deal of jazz composed in the future that will be played and well played, and good jazz. But it will not be exclusively compositional jazz. Improvisation, and the quality and feeling of improvisation—or the implication of improvisation—seem to me to be characteristic of good jazz, and I think always will be.

KENTON: Both composition and improvisation will continue to be important to jazz. The problem today is that good improvisers are so rare. There are many people who can make sense out of their improvisations, but very few people are really *saying* anything.

SCHULLER: I do think it's possible to have jazz which is totally notated, but I would deplore the possibility of eventually eliminating improvisation from jazz. Improvisation is the fundamental and vital element which makes jazz different from other music. Taking improvisation away from jazz is almost inconceivable.

RUSSELL: I don't think the question takes into account what is really happening in terms of jazz composition. Notation in the old sense is becoming less important. I think the jazz composer's role will not necessarily be that of notating the music, but of designing situations, blueprinting them—and then leaving it to the improviser to make the blueprints come alive. But this won't be happening in terms of actual musical notation as we've known it. As Dizzy says, some ideas just can't be notated. I know that Ornette Coleman thinks the music of the future is going to be entirely improvised. I don't think that's necessarily true either, but I think there is a middle ground.

PLAYBOY: With avant-garde jazz becoming more musically complex, and with jazz used increasingly as social protest, has the music become too somber? Has the fun gone out of jazz? Is there no place left for the happy sound?

GLEASON: The fun hasn't gone out of jazz for me, baby. And when it does, you won't find me sitting around in night clubs or concerts listening to jazz musicians. And I don't think the fun has gone out of jazz for Miles Davis, no matter how much he may complain, nor for Dizzy Gillespie, nor for anybody else who is really playing anything worth listening to. The fun certainly hasn't gone out of jazz for Duke Ellington or even Louis Armstrong.

And what do you mean "the happy sound"? The happy sound is still here. Listen to Basie. Listen to Miles Davis playing *Stella by Starlight* or *Walkin'*. Happy sound? John Coltrane's *My Favorite Things* is a happy record, a beautiful record. The happy sound is never going to go out of jazz. Jazz expresses a variety of emotions, all kinds of moods, and not exclusively one emotion any more than exclusively one style or one rhythm section, or one anything else. I don't think jazz has become too solemn. I think some of it has become boring, but I don't think all of it has.

KENTON: Yes, but so much of the jazz heard today is full of negative emotions and ugly feelings. I, for one, wish the happy sound would return. Its absence is one of the things that have killed jazz commercially. People don't want to subject themselves to these terrible experiences. After all, jazz shouldn't be all education. It's a thing you should enjoy. If you have to fight it, I don't think the music's any good.

BRUBECK: I think we ought to look at this historically. To some extent, jazz was a music of protest when it began. It expressed the feeling of Negroes that they must achieve freedom. And at other times in the history of jazz, the music has again been used as a form of protest. That's the way it's being used by some today. But jazz isn't only a music of protest. It was and is also a music of great joy. Let's bring the joy back into jazz. Jazz should express all the emotions of all men.

GILLESPIE: It seems to me that the answer is simple. Today's jazz, yesterday's jazz, tomorrow's jazz—they all are based on all of the component parts of human experience. An artist can be comic and satirical and still be just as serious about his music as an artist who is always somber or tragic. In any case, the members of an audience seek out those artists who fill their particular needs—whether beauty, hilarious comedy, irony, or pathos. It's always been that way. Furthermore, moods change from day to day, so that a listener may find one of his needs being met by a particular artist one night and a quite different need being fulfilled by a quite different artist the next night.

RUSSELL: As Dizzy says, a satirist can be very serious about his music. And I find a good deal of wit and satire in what's called the "new thing" in jazz. It all depends on what level your own wit is. Some people who think the fun has gone out of jazz simply don't have the capacity to appreciate a more profound level of humor. Now, if jazz is becoming an art music, you have to expect it to search for deeper emotions and meanings in all categories. To me, jazz has never been more expressive on every level than it is getting to be now, and it certainly doesn't lack wit.

MINGUS: Now look, when the world is happy and there's something to be happy about, I'll cut everybody playing happy. But as it is now, I'll play what's happening. And anybody who wants to escape what's really going on and wants to play happy, Uncle Tom music, is not being honest. I'll tell you something else. The old-timers didn't think jazz was just a happy music. I was discussing this with Henry "Red" Allen recently, and he told me he doesn't play happiness. He plays what he feels. So do I. And I'm not all that happy.

SCHULLER: How can anyone expect this music to be happy, or any music to be entirely happy, in these ridiculously unhappy times in which we live? I mean, one has to manufacture one's own happiness, almost, in order to survive. And the music cannot help but reflect the time in which we live. Besides, as jazz changes from an entertainment music to an art music, it will lose a lot of that superficially happy quality it used to have, because if you're entertaining, your job is to make people happy. Sometimes I'm sorry about this change, but you just can't turn back the clock. I like to listen to happy jazz. Sometimes, I hear good Dixieland and I think, "It's true. That was a happy music. It was fun and there weren't all these psychological overtones and undertones." But what can you do about it? Many of the musicians in jazz today do not live in this kind of happy-go-lucky situation. They don't live that way and they don't feel that way.

MULLIGAN: Nonetheless, I do think those who lament the passing of the "happy sound" do have a legitimate complaint. Playing music is fun. That's not to say that everything is necessarily humorous. But humor is not the only thing that's lacking these days. There are a lot of guys who appear to take themselves too seriously. They're too deadly serious about their music. It's one thing to be deeply involved in what you're doing, but it's not necessary to have that terrible striving feeling about art—with capital letters. I find this very disheartening when it happens. It's as a result of self-consciousness that a lot of the fun goes out of jazz.

PLAYBOY: Aside from whether jazz is becoming too serious, is there also a tendency toward Dadaism in some experimental jazz? When Don Ellis, for example, appeared on an educational television program last year, each of his musicians took a card at random from a deck before the performance started and that card helped determine the shape of the music to come. Is the introduction of "the music of chance" into jazz—and even some John Cage–like uses of silence—indicative of the music becoming so anarchic as to be noncommunicable? Have some jazz musicians reached the point where they have no desire to communicate?

RUSSELL: Well, the last refuge of the untalented is the avant-garde. Yes, there certainly are musicians who jump on the band wagon—like a few critics. There are musicians who say, "Since there's freedom, we can do anything and make a buck at it, too." But as the standards of the new jazz become clearer and more substantial, these people will be weeded out. They can't possibly survive.

GILLESPIE: It all depends on who's doing it. If a man really has something to say, the devices themselves aren't important. It's what comes out.

MINGUS: Yes, anything can be used honestly and anything can be used dishonestly. Like, if a man is writing or playing, he's entitled to put a couple of cuspidors in there if that's the sound he hears. But this isn't new. Duke Ellington has used playing cards to rip across the piano strings. He's used clothespins and he's had his trombonists use toilet plungers.

GLEASON: When you have experimentally minded musicians, you're going to have experimental music of all kinds. And I don't see anything being done in jazz today that I've heard in person or on records that can be described as Dada in a pejorative sense. I don't think that jazz musicians have reached the point where they have no desire to communicate. I don't think any artist that I've ever heard of has reached that point. It may be that the terms they select in which to communicate, the vehicles that they use, and the devices that they use, and the language, may, by definition, limit the potential auditors for their communications. But they still *want* to communicate.

KENTON: I don't know whether they don't have any desire to communicate or whether they're just desperate for ideas to such an extent that they're going to try any sort of thing in order to gain attention. I do think that if this stuff is allowed to go on too long, it's going to ruin the interest in jazz altogether.

SCHULLER: My concern with the sort of thing you describe is that it takes away and makes unnecessary most of the fundamental artistic disciplines. I don't even mean specific musical disciplines. I'm putting it on a broader, more fundamental level than that. I mean the old challenge of a seemingly insurmountable object which makes you rise above your normal situation to overcome. In the music of John Cage and some of Stockhausen—and Don Ellis, in so far as he uses a similar approach—this critical element which has been at the base of art for centuries is eliminated. In fact, some of them want to eliminate the personality of the player. They want to make music in which the Beethoven concept of the creative individual is totally eliminated and the music is *instigated* by someone, but not *created* by him. They talk about finding pure chance—which is really a mathematical abstraction which cannot be found by habit-prone human beings—and they try to involve as much chance as is possible in a given situation so as to eliminate this question of the individual personality. This to me is a radically new way of looking at art. It completely overthrows any previous conceptions of what art is, or has been, and at this point, I stop short.

PLAYBOY: The experimentalists have attracted attention in one way. It has often seemed, too, that for a jazz figure to make it in a big way, he has had to have a singularly prominent personality trait—droll like Dizzy, aggressively distant like Miles, aggressive like Mingus, comical like Louis, etc. To what extent has the "cult of personality" had too great an influence on jazz?

BRUBECK: Well, early in my career, I realized that I could reach the audience with one thing only, and that was music. This is something it seems most groups have forgotten—that the primary reason they are there is to reach the audience through the music. And I was so aware that I could reach an audience that way I made it almost a rule to never speak over the microphone. This lasted for years. We didn't dress in any way that was beyond the average business suit, and we didn't wear funny hats or goatees or beards or berets. In other words, we just let the music do what the music should do—and that is get to an audience.

Years later, I decided it would be permissible to announce a few tunes and, as the years go by, I can even be funny once in a while and it doesn't bother me. Who knows? I may show up sometime with a beard. But I think that the main thing for any jazz group to remember is that if you'll stick to music, you don't have to get up and dance around or think a great chorus without playing it. Just get in there and play, have something to say and say it, and forget all those other things.

GLEASON: I don't think the cult of personality holds too great a sway over the world of jazz. Dave has made it big in jazz, for instance, and aside from what he's already said, if you apply the cult of personality to Dave, you've got a guy who doesn't drink or smoke, who has been married to one woman for over 23 or 24 years, and has a houseful of children, likes horses, and wants to stay home in the country. I don't think that Dizzy is droll, by the way. I think he is wildly hilarious. And I don't think that Miles is aggressively distant, either. And I don't think Mingus is aggressive. And I don't find Louis comical, any more than I find Miles aggressively distant. I think if you look at Louis and have a comic image in your mind, you're doing the man a great injustice. And I also think you're indicating something about yourself. The cult of personality doesn't seem to me to have anything to do with jazz musicians at all, and if it exists, it only has something to do with the jazz audience.

ADDERLEY: It depends on what you mean by personality. Some people—Yusef Lateef, Mingus, Dizzy—have strong personalities which they are able to project. They play *at* people. Yusef, for instance, plays through the horn, not just into the horn. People who don't have this, who cannot project, will never be successful even if they play beautifully. For example, as a group, the Benny Golson–Art Farmer Jazztet lacked a strong enough personality, and it failed. The Modern Jazz Quartet has several strong personalities. They even go in different directions. Everybody in that group is strong, and the group's collective identity is also strong. Dave Brubeck has a strong personality in the sense that he has a definite identity. It's not a wishy-washy kind of thing.

MULLIGAN: Any public performer has to have a strong personality to be unusually successful. There are more things possible for somebody who is accepted as a personality, aside from being a musician, than there are for the straight musician who doesn't project.

SCHULLER: Yet I would suspect that those who didn't make it to the top in the sense of a fairly broad acceptance must have had something missing beyond just the matter of personality.

MULLIGAN: Yes, if a man can blow, it doesn't matter if he's old, if he's blue, or if he's got a personality. As long as people like him. If he can blow.

SCHULLER: What I mean is that the matter of coming on with a fantastic getup or a goatee or other "quirks" of personality are all in the realm of fandom. But the more serious listeners to jazz, after all, are very sensitive to the subtle degrees of projection which a player has or doesn't have. A man can be a very fine musician, but there can be a certain kind of depressing or negative quality in his music that will hold him back in terms of acceptance. It may be that you can't fault his music in any way technically, but it doesn't have this way of going out there into the 20th row. And if that's the case, then I think there's nothing terribly wrong in the fact that such a man does not become the star that, say, Charlie Parker was.

MINGUS: You're underestimating the fact that jazz is still treated by most people as if it were show business. The question has some validity. Take Thelonious Monk. His music is pretty solid most of the time, but because of what's been written about him, he's one of those people who'd get through even if he played the worst piano in the world. Stories go with musicians, and that again is the fault of the critics—and of the jazz audience, too. There are many ways of being successful. Like going to Bellevue. After I went there on my own, and the news got out, I drew more people. In fact, I even used to bounce people out of the clubs to get a little more attention, because I used to think that if you didn't get a write-up, you wouldn't attract as many people as you would with a lot of publicity. But now I see what harm that kind of write-up has done to me, and I'm trying to undo it.

GILLESPIE: I don't know about this cult-of-personality thing. A musician must be who and what he is. If his personality is singular, and if he lets it come through his art naturally, he'll reach an audience. But I don't think you can force it.

PLAYBOY: While we're talking about popularity, is there a meeting ground somewhere for the multimillion-viewer audience required by TV and the more specialized attractions of jazz? Most efforts in the past have been either financial or artistic failures, or both.

GLEASON: As far as I'm concerned, there's a place for jazz on TV, because I'm involved with doing a jazz show on television. It's on educational television, so we aren't hung up with commercials, we aren't hung up with having to play somebody's tune or allowing somebody to sit in with the group. And we aren't hung up with all the restrictions of commercial television as to length and selection of material. We have a multimillion-viewer audience, and the musicians do whatever they want to. In fact, the musical director of each one of the programs on *Jazz Casual* is the leader who's on the program that week. *He* selects the music. Sometimes he lets us know in advance what it will be and sometimes we find out when he plays it. And I don't think jazz's attraction is specialized. Let's just say all jazz programs in the past have been failures—I'll buy that—with the exception of the one show they did on Miles Davis, and that CBS show, *The Sound of Jazz.*

PLAYBOY: To give credit where it's due, both of those programs were produced by Robert Herridge.

GLEASON: With the exception of those (and *Jazz Casual),* almost everything I've seen on television on jazz has been a failure. And the reason for it is that television has never been willing to accept the music on its own terms, but always wanted to *adapt* the music to television's requirements. Under the assumption that you had to produce a product that was palatable to some guy walking down the streets of Laredo, I guess, I don't know. Jazz will get along on television if they'll leave jazz musicians alone, and let them play naturally.

GILLESPIE: Exactly. TV, of all media, is ideally suited to the uniqueness of jazz, because you can hear and see it while it's being created. I think the big mistake in most of the jazz formats in the past has been their lack of spontaneity. Maybe jazz could be done on TV by means of a candid-camera technique.

KENTON: If you're talking about the major networks, I'd say there's no place on television for jazz at this time at all, because television has to appeal to the masses, and jazz has no part of appealing to the masses. It's not a case of how well it's presented—whether by candid camera or some other device. It's just that jazz is a minority music, it appeals to a minority, and that minority is not large enough to support any part of commercial television.

RUSSELL: I'm almost as pessimistic. It won't happen so long as the tyranny of the majority is working. No producer in his right mind is going to have the courage to buck the majority and come up with something tasteful. Yet, if one of the powers in the industry *did* have enough courage to put on something very tastefully conceived, and if he did it often enough, I think jazz would eventually get through.

ADDERLEY: Well, so far all of you have been talking about jazz as a separate thing on television. I don't really see why jazz has to be shunted off to be a thing alone. I don't see why it's not possible to present Dave Brubeck as Dave Brubeck, jazz musician, on the same program with Della Reese. We in the community of jazz seem to feel that we need our own little corner because we have something different that is superior to anything else that's going. But it's all relative, and there's a kind of pomposity involved in that kind of attitude when you check it. I think that I could very easily be a guest artist on the Ed Sullivan show or the *Tonight* show along with the other people they have. Like Allan Sherman. Let me do my thing, and there's a good chance I might communicate to the same mass audience that he does. The same thing is true of Miles Davis or Dizzy or anyone else. I think there's a place for us on television—once we get admitted to the circle.

MULLIGAN: I still think it would be possible to produce a reasonably popular jazz show, but it would have to start on a small scale. I think a musician—whether it's me or whoever—should be master of ceremonies if the show is going to have the aura of jazz. And this musician would have to be able to produce a musical show with enough variety to be able to sustain itself. If I were doing it, and I'd like nothing better than to try, I'd prefer to do it as a local show which could be taped for possible use on networks. That way we could keep expenses down while we tried to prove what kind of audience we could attract.

Now, Cannonball talks about being part of the circle of guest attractions on the major shows. Well, our group has been on some of them, and I don't know whether it really does us any good or not. Being on that kind of show does give you a kind of prestige value with people who have no awareness of jazz. But I wonder whether seeing and hearing jazz groups in that sort of surrounding gives TV viewers any increased sensitivity to jazz. I think not. It just makes them think of me—or any of the other jazz musicians who make those shows—as being bigger names, as being bigger stars in relation to stars as they think of them. But it doesn't really help create a larger audience for jazz itself. I'll keep on doing those appearances as long as they're offered to me, but what I'd really like to try is that local show. I think we could build a really good presentation which people would go for. But nobody's made an offer yet.

MINGUS: Let's face it. Television is Jim Crow. Oh, for background scores, the white arrangers steal from the latest jazz records. But as for putting our music on television in our own way and having us play it, no. Not until the whole thing, the whole society changes.

PLAYBOY: Which brings us right into the sensitive area of jazz and race. A significant number of Negro musicians have expressed their conviction that, with a few exceptions, Negro jazzmen are more "authentic" and tend to be more original and creative than their white counterparts. They say this is not a genetically determined condition, but results from environment—the kind of music the Negro child hears and the kind of experiences a Negro in America has. Do you agree with this contention? Also, some have termed this feeling of superiority among some Negroes "Crow Jim." Do you think that term is valid in so far as it connotes a form of reverse prejudice in jazz?

GLEASON: I agree that Negro jazzmen are more authentic and tend to be more original and creative than their white counterparts. I also agree that this is not a genetically determined condition, but results basically from environment.

SCHULLER: I'd agree, too, but I'd add the point that because of this kind of background, a majority of musicians among Negroes will *turn* to jazz while a majority of white musicians—because they don't have as much access to this music in their formative years—will not. But, of course, the picture is changing all the time. And this has never meant that white musicians cannot—by some fluke or some fortuitous set of circumstances—have the kind of background that Negro musicians have.

BRUBECK: I don't agree with anything that says being white, black, purple or green makes you a better jazz musician. I think that your inner core, your philosophy, is the important thing. The depth of your convictions and your ability to get these convictions across is what counts. To me, it's ridiculous to say that a Negro expresses jazz better than a white person, or the other way around. You mention environment. Let me say that if I were going to pick saxophone players, I would not pick them on the basis of what their childhood environment had been, but on the basis of what they say as *adults.* And I would pick *individuals.* There would certainly be a Paul Desmond who can probably express a melodic line better than any other Negro or white player and who has an emotional quality that is individually his own. There would be a Stan Getz. There would be a Gerry

Mulligan. There would be a Charlie Parker. There would be a Sonny Rollins. When I think of these men, I'm not going to think about color.

ADDERLEY: Although I pretty much agree that Negro jazz musicians, because of their environment, tend to be more authentic, I think that basically it's a matter of sincerity and of really being in love with the music. Anyone can have a passion for jazz. I think Zoot Sims is just as creative as anyone else. He's passionately involved with the real, pure, unadulterated jazz. So is my pianist, Joe Zawinul, an Austrian. When Joe plays on a record, I defy a layman to determine his race. I've always contended that environment *and* exposure determine the way a guy performs. I'm sure no one could tell whether Al Haig was white or Negro.

Certainly jazz is a synthesis of various Negro forms of music, but recently, it has added colors and developments from European "serious" music (and I'm not implying jazz isn't serious). So today, it is less a Negro music than an American music, because everybody is contributing in his own way. Eventually jazz will be "colorless."

However, as of now, jazz is still quite colored. It's true you can't tell Joe Zawinul's color from listening to a record, but you can certainly tell Stan Getz is white, as contrasted with, say, John Coltrane. You simply can't deny, if you know anything about the medium, that you can tell the color of people by the way they play. As time goes on, though, this will probably be less and less true.

RUSSELL: I would say that, so far, the important innovators have been Negroes, but this doesn't mean that every Negro jazz musician is as good as a lot of white musicians. There are some excellent white musicians around. I'll hire for my band the best people available. Sometimes the band is integrated straight down the middle and other times it may be four-fifths Negro.

PLAYBOY: What about the charge that Crow Jim exists in jazz?

MINGUS: Well, until we start lynching white people, there is no word that can mean the same as Jim Crow means. Until we own Bethlehem Steel and RCA Victor, plus Columbia Records and several other industries, the term Crow Jim has no meaning. And to use that term about those of us who say that this music is essentially Negro is inaccurate and unfeeling. Aren't you white men asking too much when you ask me to stop saying this is my music? Especially when you don't give me anything else?

Sure, we have pride in the music. People who called themselves civilized brought the black man over here and he appeared primitive to them. But think about what we've done. We've picked up your instruments and created a music, and many of us don't even know the notes on the horn yet. This shows me that maybe African civilization was far superior to this civilization. We've sent great white classical trumpet players into the woodshed to practice and try to play some of the things we've created, and they still haven't been able to. If you wrote it down for a classical trumpet player, he'd never even get started.

GILLESPIE: That phrase Crow Jim doesn't make sense. There is and always has been a kind of aristocracy of art. Those who feel what they're capable of and are proud of what they can do. Even haughty. But I refuse to abide by color boundaries. Just name the top jazz artists. Obviously they're not all Negroes. The good white jazz musicians are as well recognized by the Negro jazz musicians as they are by the white musicians.

GLEASON: I don't term the feeling of superiority among Negro jazz musicians as Crow Jim. If there's a definition of Crow Jim, it seems to me, it is when you adopt the position that no white musician can play jazz at all. And no Negro jazz musician of any major status adopts this position, as far as I know. I think you might adopt the term Crow Jim to describe the feeling of some fans who will pay attention only to Negro jazz musicians—who will not listen to any white jazz musician.

But I think that the position of the white jazz musician who feels himself slighted these days, or who feels a draft from the Negro jazz musician, is a very real position. And I think the only road out of this situation is the one that Jon Hendricks describes: "When you enter the house of jazz you should enter it with respect." And I think that white jazz musicians, many of them in the past, who have tried to do the impossible in their music, which is to cross over the color line in reverse, have made a mistake. I think what they have to do is to bring into it their own feeling and their own originality. As Dizzy Gillespie said at a student press conference, "We aren't the only ones that swing, baby," and then he went on to explain about many musicians in all countries in the world who could swing. But that doesn't change the fact that jazz is a Negro music and was invented and created by Negroes. But it also does not mean that it can't be played by non-Negroes. Now it's simply a fact that at least one jazz night club I know of does not want to book jazz musicians who are not Negroes, because, in the club owner's experience, white jazz groups have not made money in his club for him, and Negro jazz groups have. On the other hand, it's quite obvious that he would book Dave Brubeck if he could.

RUSSELL: Yes, I do think club owners have fallen into this kind of thinking, but they perpetuate it much more than the musicians do. I don't think the true jazz musician can be Crow Jim, because the very nature of the art demands honesty. And I don't see how, if the only player around who is going to do it for you is a white player, you can honestly hire anyone of any other color who is an inferior player. Miles, all the leaders, now have integrated bands. The important people don't think in Crow Jim terms.

ADDERLEY: While I do feel that practically all Negro musicians in jazz feel superior to practically all white musicians in jazz, it can be explained by the fact that this was one thing Negroes have had to grasp for a long time. The feeling is that since we have this, and it is now considered something worthwhile, we can take pride in the fact that we know we can play jazz better than anybody else. But I won't accept this on the basis of *ethnic* superiority. *We have* played this music from its beginning and we have been exposed to it more than the whites. But anyone with a passion for the music and with exposure and with artistry and a chance to play it can develop into a good jazz musician. There's another point: If a Negro says he can play better jazz than a white, that gives whites license to say, "Well, you can't play in our symphony orchestras, because we, as whites, can play classical music better than you do." And I think that's ridiculous, too.

MULLIGAN: Questions like this are not important to me. People get themselves all worked up over things like this, but I don't give a damn if a man is green or blue. If he can blow, let him blow. If he can't blow, let him do something else.

KENTON: But you do have to face the facts about color in jazz today. It is much more difficult today for white musicians and colored musicians to play together than it ever was before. I realize that the civil-rights problem had to arise and I think the Government is doing just exactly what it should do and had to do about it. But before the Government started demanding integration, we had many places around America where we could play together. We called them black-and-tan clubs and all sorts of things, where the white and colored musicians met and played together, and white and colored clientele came to the place. But when the Government started pushing integration, this did away with almost every one of those places. And it made the white and colored musicians kind of stand at a distance, even though they were always very close before, because there's the problem of civil rights that's like a barrier between them and that, somehow, is not easily surmountable. The civil-rights issue has to be solved in this country. The barrier now is such that people even forget what has happened in the past. Like, a man recently accosted me and wanted to know why I'd never had any colored musicians in my band, and I finally had to sit down and write out about two dozen names of Negroes who had played in my band for long periods of time. But because of the mere fact that I have no colored musicians in my present band and that I have received some unfavorable publicity regarding this, that man believed I was Jim Crow and that, of course, is impossible.

You ask about Crow Jim. Well, I think that colored audiences started boycotting white jazz as long as ten years back. And there are colored musicians who do feel today that jazz is *their* music and they don't want white musicians infringing on their art. It's only natural that they feel that way, but they're wrong, because the Negro would not have had jazz without the white man. If this weren't true, we'd have jazz going in parts of the world where Africans live. To discount the white man's position in jazz is doing the white jazz musician a great injustice.

PLAYBOY: Do you think there are still elements of Jim Crow in jazz in bookings, in the general way in which Negro jazz musicians are treated as contrasted with the way white jazzmen are treated?

GILLESPIE: There's no doubt that Jim Crow exists in jazz bookings, as flagrantly as ever. Today, however, it's been developed into refined refusals.

SCHULLER: Dizzy is right; there is still a lot of Jim Crow going on, but it's become more subtle. The businessmen in jazz still apply all kinds of old criteria to the Negro musician. They treat him as an entertainer and as someone below their own level.

ADDERLEY: In practically 200 percent of the cases, Negroes are always treated as Negroes. Even if you're treated as a very special Negro. It's that old paternalism. Whites, all whites, regardless of how liberal, need to have somebody to feel superior to. It makes no difference how big a Negro gets in terms of money, so-called social position, and so forth. As long as the Negro wears the badge, the lowest white man feels, "Well, at least I'm not a Negro." In jazz, it sometimes works in another way. Somebody will say, "Your music is really good. I'd like you to come to my house for dinner. You know, I wouldn't let just anybody come to my house for dinner, but you come to my house for dinner, because you play very well." You understand what I mean? It works the same way all the time. You're always conscious of the fact that you're Negro.

PLAYBOY: But is there specific Jim Crow in the business end of jazz? Some Negro musicians have complained that some of the booking offices consider the Negro jazzman as part of their plantation. And that some club owners also act that way.

ADDERLEY: No, I've never really felt that. I have felt this: We've played clubs where a club owner will very frankly say, "You draw a lot of white business. You know, most Negro groups don't draw a lot of white business. So I can afford to pay you more because you draw Negroes and whites." Color consciousness again. But I've never had the feeling that I was entertainment for the white folks.

BRUBECK: I've always figured that the charge of Jim Crow in jazz was a fairy tale, because I played for years during which one Negro soloist would be making more than my entire quartet. Anybody who says that certain Negroes have not been paid as much as certain white musicians doesn't really know the whole story. Think of Nat Cole. He's been well paid, and he deserved to be well paid. Don't tell me Charlie Parker wasn't well paid, because I know he was. I was there. I can't think of any jazz musician who, if he was determined to make it and behave and show up on time, didn't get paid what he was worth. I would say, however, that there have been discriminatory practices in television. But on TV, it's been harder for the man with a mixed group, such as mine, than for the all-Negro or the all-white group. I know that I lost the highest paying job I was ever offered in my life because my group was mixed. An all-Negro group took it. And that was on nationwide television. Within jazz, and within society, the mixed groups will meet with more problems and will solve more problems.

GLEASON: There certainly are Jim Crow elements in jazz, just as there are Jim Crow elements in the rest of this society. I know that there are bookings that Negro jazz musicians do not get because of prejudice. This is considerably less than it was in the past years, but I think it's still true today. The situation has changed a great deal, and it's a great deal better than it was. This does not mean that it's good. And the elimination of Jim Crow is long overdue. There's a residual Jim Crow in a lot of areas. Jazz musicians encounter this, and if they're Negro jazz musicians, they encounter it sometimes very strongly.

Ray Charles, for instance, has had a great deal of this on one-nighter tours in smaller towns, where it's OK for them to play, but they want to get 'em out of town as soon as possible. And Negro jazz musicians are treated like all other Negroes in many parts of the country, where they can't stay in many motels and hotels. But the way in which the major booking agencies function, as far as I can tell from where I stand, is not Jim Crow. All *they're* interested in doing is making money, and they're not interested any more than any other money-making machine is in the color of the person who makes the money for them.

PLAYBOY: Thank you, gentlemen. This conversation has demonstrated that, as in the music they play, compose, and write about, there is spirited diversity in the opinions of jazzmen. We have, however, reached a consensus in a number of areas. Jazz, for one thing, is far from a dying form; it is instead in a period of unusual growth and creativity. Jazz is also clearly evolving into an art music, but is retaining its roots in improvisation. While there are elements of prejudice in jazz, as in the rest of society, there is a strong feeling among most musicians that it is a man's passion for the music and his ability—not his color—that determines his worth as a jazzman. And, as all of you have shown, the jazz musician is deeply committed to his music and proud of its traditions. Furthermore, the impact of jazz throughout the world is becoming broader and deeper. It is a remarkable tribute to this music's vitality and capacity for expansion that jazz, which was created in this country from Afro-American folk sources, is now an important international language whose future is challengingly unpredictable—and limitless.

This discussion has also proved, to those for whom such proof is still necessary, that the vintage myth that jazz musicians are inarticulate is hardly true. While jazz is still primarily a music of the emotions, there is a great deal of thought and discipline involved in its conception and execution. The quality of that thought, as you have shown, is both penetrating and persistently independent.

PART 7

The Seventies

47. The Scale Syllabus

HOW WE PRACTICE SAYS A LOT about how we think about music. Arguably, no one has had a greater influence on how aspiring jazz musicians practice than Jamey Aebersold (b. 1939), saxophonist, theorist, and jazz education entrepreneur. Through his clinics, jazz camps, and publications, Aebersold has affected an unprecedentedly large group of aspiring jazz musicians from the 1960s into the new millennium. And particularly through his series of play-along recordings, the first issued in 1967 and now numbering over one hundred, he has enabled two generations of musicians to work on their improvisatory skills in a virtual ensemble, without the complications of convening live groups.

The "Scale Syllabus" is included with most of the play-alongs, and it means to organize theoretically how accomplished jazz musicians choose certain pitches to play with certain chords, so that learners can work practically on improving that aspect of their playing. Aebersold accomplished a kind of revolution in jazz pedagogy, convincing many that it was not a matter of one simply being able to improvise or not, but that improvisation was a skill that could be taught and learned systematically.

Like all theoretical tools, the Scale Syllabus illuminates certain aspects of music and marginalizes others: there is no rhythm syllabus, timbre syllabus, or interaction syllabus, and perhaps there couldn't be. This way of approaching jazz is concerned with correct pitch choices. It can certainly be helpful to aspiring players, yet it is worth noticing its inevitable limitations, such as the way that it implies that all correct pitches have basically the same significance—being correct—and doesn't go into the ways in which each pitch matters differently over the

---

Source: Jamey Aebersold, "Introduction to the Scale Syllabus" and "Scale Syllabus," included on most volumes of his Play-A-Long Book and Recording Sets, for example *Volume 63: Tom Harrell* (New Albany, IN: Jamey Aebersold Jazz, Inc., 1994). Earlier versions appeared in volumes published during the 1970s. The Scale Syllabus is now available as a free download from jazzbooks.com. Reprinted by permission of jazzbooks.com.

THE SCALE SYLLABUS

LEGEND: H = Half Step, W = Whole Step.; Δ = Major 7th; + or ♯ = raise H; ♭ or - = lower H; Ø = Half-diminished; –3 = 3H (Minor Third)

CHORD/SCALE SYMBOL		SCALE NAME	WHOLE & HALF STEP CONSTRUCTION	SCALE IN KEY OF C	BASIC CHORD IN KEY OF C
C	FIVE BASIC CATEGORIES	Major	W W H W W W H	C D E F G A B C	C E G B D
C7		Dominant 7th (Mixolydian)	W W H W W H W	C D E F G A B♭ C	C E G B♭ D
C–		Minor (Dorian)	W H W W W H W	C D E♭ F G A B♭ C	C E♭ G B♭ D
CØ		Half Diminished (Locrian)	H W W H W W W	C D♭ E♭ F G♭ A♭ B♭ C	C E♭ G♭ B♭
C°		Diminished (8 tone scale)	W H W H W H W H	C D E♭ F G♭ A♭ A B C	C E♭ G♭ A (B♭♭)
1. MAJOR SCALE CHOICES		**SCALE NAME**	**W & H CONSTRUCTION**	**SCALE IN KEY OF C**	**BASIC CHORD IN KEY OF C**
CΔ (Can be written C)		Major (don't emphasize the 4th)	W W H W W W H	C D E F G A B C	C E G B D
C		Major Pentatonic	W W –3 W –3	C D E G A C	C E G B
CΔ+4		Lydian (major scale with +4)	W W W H W W H	C D E F♯ G A B C	C E G B D
CΔ		Bebop (Major)	W W H W H H W H	C D E F G G♯ A B C	C E G B D
CΔ♭6		Harmonic Major	W W H W H –3 H	C D E F G A♭ B C	C E G B D
CΔ+5, +4		Lydian Augmented	W W W W H W H	C D E F♯ G♯ A B C	C E G♯ B D
C		Augmented	–3 H –3 H –3 H	C D♯ E G A♭ B C	C E G B D
C		6th Mode of Harmonic Minor	–3 H W H W W H	C D♯ E F♯ G A B C	C E G B D
C		Diminished (begin with H step)	H W H W H W H W	C D♭ D♯ E F♯ G A B♭ C	C E G B D
C		Blues Scale	–3 W H H –3 W	C E♭ F F♯ G B♭ C	C E G B D
2. DOMINANT 7th SCALE CHOICES		**SCALE NAME**	**W & H CONSTRUCTION**	**SCALE IN KEY OF C**	**BASIC CHORD IN KEY OF C**
C7		Dominant 7th	W W H W W H W	C D E F G A B♭ C	C E G B♭ D
C7		Major Pentatonic	W W –3 W –3	C D E G A C	C E G B♭ D
C7		Bebop (Dominant)	W W H W W H H H	C D E F G A B♭ B C	C E G B♭ D
C7♭9		Spanish or Jewish scale	H –3 H W H W W	C D♭ E F G A♭ B♭ C	C E G B♭ (D♭)
C7+4		Lydian Dominant	W W W H W H W	C D E F♯ G A B♭ C	C E G B♭ D
C7♭6		Hindu	W W H W H W W	C D E F G A♭ B♭ C	C E G B♭ D
C7+ (has ♯4 & ♯5)		Whole Tone (6 tone scale)	W W W W W W	C D E F♯ G♯ B♭ C	C E G♯ B♭ D
C7♭9 (also has ♯9 & ♯4)		Diminished (begin with H step)	H W H W H W H W	C D♭ D♯ E F♯ G A B♭ C	C E G B♭ D♭ (D♯)
C7+9 (also has ♭9, ♯4, ♯5)		Diminished Whole Tone	H W H W W W W	C D♭ D♯ E F♯ G♯ B♭ C	C E G♯ B♭ D♯ (D♭)
C7		Blues Scale	–3 W H H –3 W	C E♭ F F♯ G B♭ C	C E G B♭ D (D♯)
DOMINANT 7th SUSPENDED 4th					
C7 sus 4	MAY BE WRITTEN G-/C	Dom. 7th scale but don't emphasize the third	W W H W W H W	C D E F G A B♭ C	C F G B♭ D
C7 sus 4		Major Pentatonic built on ♭7	W W –3 W –3	B♭ C D F G B♭	C F G B♭ D
C7 sus 4		Bebop Scale	W W H W W H H H	C D E F G A B♭ B C	C F G B♭ D
3. MINOR SCALE CHOICES*		**SCALE NAME**	**W & H CONSTRUCTION**	**SCALE IN KEY OF C**	**BASIC CHORD IN KEY Of C**
C– or C–7		Minor (Dorian)	W H W W W H W	C D E♭ F G A B♭ C	C E♭ G B♭ D
C– or C–7		Pentatonic (Minor Pentatonic)	–3 W W –3 W	C E♭ F G B♭ C	C E♭ G B♭ D
C– or C–7		Bebop (Minor)	W H H H W W H W	C D E♭ E F G A B♭ C	C E♭ G B♭ D
C–Δ (maj. 7th)		Melodic Minor (ascending)	W H W W W W H	C D E♭ F G A B C	C E♭ G B D
C– or C–6 or C–		Bebop Minor No. 2	W H W W H H W H	C D E♭ F G G♯ A B C	C E♭ G B D
C– or C–7		Blues Scale	–3 W H H –3 W	C E♭ F F♯ G B♭ C	C E♭ G B♭ D
C–Δ (♭6 & maj. 7th)		Harmonic Minor	W H W W H –3 H	C D E♭ F G A♭ B C	C E♭ G B D
C– or C–7		Diminished (begin with W step)	W H W H W H W H	C D E♭ F F♯ G♯ A B C	C E♭ G B D
C– or C–♭9♭6		Phrygian	H W W W H W W	C D♭ E♭ F G A♭ B♭ C	C E♭ G B♭
C– or C–♭6		Pure or Natural Minor, Aeolian	W H W W H W W	C D E♭ F G A♭ B♭ C	C E♭ G B♭ D
4. HALF DIMINISHED SCALE CHOICES		**SCALE NAME**	**W & H CONSTRUCTION**	**SCALE IN KEY OF C**	**BASIC CHORD IN KEY OF C**
CØ		Half Diminished (Locrian)	H W W H W W W	C D♭ E♭ F G♭ A♭ B♭ C	C E♭ G♭ B♭
CØ♯2 (CØ9)		Half Diminished #2 (Locrian #2)	W H W H W W W	C D E♭ F G♭ A♭ B♭ C	C E♭ G♭ B♭ D
CØ (with or without ♯2)		Bebop Scale	H W W H H H W W	C D♭ E♭ F G♭ G A♭ B♭ C	C E♭ G♭ B♭
5. DIMINISHED SCALE CHOICES		**SCALE NAME**	**W & H CONSTRUCTION**	**SCALE IN KEY OF C**	**BASIC CHORD IN KEY OF C**
C°		Diminished (8 tone scale)	W H W H W H W H	C D E♭ F G♭ A♭ A B C	C E♭ G♭ A

NOTES: 1) The above chord symbol guide is my system of notation. I feel it best represents the sounds I hear in jazz. Players should be aware that each chord symbol represents a series of tones called a scale. **2)** Even though a C7+9 would appear to have only a raised 9th, it also has a ♭9, +4 and +5. The entire C7+9 scale looks like: Root, ♭9, +9, 3rd, +4, +5, ♭7 & root (C, D♭, D♯, E, F♯, G♯, B♭, C). My chord symbol C7+9 is therefore an abbreviation, while the complete name of this scale is Diminished Whole Tone (sometimes called Super Locrian or Altered Scale). Similarly, C7♭9 also appears to have only one altered tone (♭9) but it actually has three: ♭9, +9 and +4. The entire scale looks like: Root, ♭9, +9, 3rd, +4, 5th, 6th, ♭7 & root (C, D♭, D♯, E, F♯, G, A, B♭, C). This is called a Diminished scale and my chord symbol abbreviation is C7♭9. **3)** All scales under the Dominant 7th category are scales that embellish the basic Dominant 7th sound. Some scales provide much more tension than the basic dominant 7th sound and require practice and patience to grasp the essence of their meaning. I encourage you to work with ***Volume 3 "The 11-V7-1 Progression"*** since it emphasizes Diminished and Diminished Whole Tone scales and chords. **4)** In category #3, MINOR SCALE CHOICES, the PURE MINOR scale choice is not used very often. I have found the order of preference to be Dorian, Bebop, Melodic, Blues, Pentatonic, and then any of the remaining Minor scale choices.

chord, differs rhetorically from all other pitches. Following is Aebersold's basic introduction to the "Scale Syllabus" and the syllabus itself.

Each chord/scale symbol represents a series of tones which the improviser can use when improvising or soloing. These series of tones have traditionally been called scales. The scales listed here are the ones I most often hear musicians play. I have listed the Scale Syllabus in the key of C Concert so you can have a frame of reference and can compare the similarities and differences between the various chords/scales.

The scale syllabus is intended to give the improviser a variety of scale choices which may be used over any chord—major, minor, dominant 7th, half-diminished, diminished, and suspended 4. Each category begins with the scale most closely resembling the chord/scale symbol given to the left. The scales are arranged according to the degree of dissonance they produce in relation to the basic chord/scale sound. Scales near the top of each category will sound mild or consonant. Scale choices further down the list will become increasingly tense or dissonant. Each player is urged to start with the scales at the top and with practice and experimentation gradually work his or her way down the list to the most dissonant or tension-producing scales.

Scales and chords are the backbone of our music, and the better you equip yourself, the more fun you will have playing music.

48. Beyond Categories

ONE OF THE ORIGINAL INNOVATORS OF BEBOP, Max Roach (1924–2007) had a long and varied career as a drummer, composer, lecturer on jazz, and—especially during the tumult of the 1960s and early '70s—an outspoken critic of American racism.[1] Like Duke Ellington, Roach felt frustration with genre categories that serve record companies and pundits more than audiences and artists; here, he argues against using the very word "jazz." In this 1972 essay for *The Black Scholar*, Roach also offers some insightful commentary on modes and processes of learning as aspects of different cultural traditions.

Source: Max Roach, "What 'Jazz' Means to Me," *The Black Scholar*, Summer 1972, pp. 3–6.

1. For other musicians' contemporary statements on this topic, see the interviews conducted by Arthur Taylor in *Notes and Tones: Musician to Musician Interviews*, expanded edition (New York: Da Capo, 1993), especially those with Freddie Hubbard and Sonny Rollins.

While it is apparent to many of us that a transformation in black consciousness is taking place throughout the political, social, and cultural framework of the United States, it is not always clear what relationship black music has to that transformation. Nor is it clear what impact this transformation of black consciousness has had on black musicians, and on the black man's perception of his music.

What I shall do here is attempt to make those relationships more clear, drawing upon my own lifetime of experience in the black music industry. Since the essence of black consciousness is the recognition of a distinct black identity, it is essential for us to recognize the black nature of our music, and develop the appropriate terms and nomenclature for that music and the things which relate to it.

Let us first eliminate the term "jazz." It is not a term or a name that we, as black musicians, ever gave to the art which we created. It is a name which was given to the Afro-American's art form by white America, and which therefore inherits all the racist and prurient attitudes which have been directed to all other aspects of the black experience in this country.

If we check out the etymology of the word "jazz," we find that it has its roots in 19th century Afro-American slang. "Jazz" was a term referring to the act of sexual intercourse and other aspects of the sexual experience. According to Webster's New World Dictionary, College Edition, jazz has the following origins: "Creole patois *jass,* sexual term applied to the Congo dances (New Orleans); present use from Chicago, c. 1914 but ? from earlier similar use in the vice district of New Orleans." The history of the word "jazz" tells us much about the entry of this Afro-American music into the white American experience, and the attitudes toward it.

From the etymology just outlined, we see that the term "jazz" first entered the vocabulary of white America in 1914, and it carried with it loose, free-swinging, bawdy-house connotations. It's not surprising, therefore, that a period of permissive behavior thereafter came to be known as The Jazz Age—the 1920's. It was a period of self-avowed irresponsibility, related morality and gay behavior. Black musicians, presumably as some kind of sexual totem, were sought out, courted and listened to in the black bowels of Harlem and Chicago, New Orleans and other cities, by the swinging white set of that era.

Furthermore, when "jazz" did become acceptable and assimilated throughout white America on a mass basis, it was taken over by white production-recording and managing industries. This became the period of the big bands in the '30s, promoting white musicians such as Bix Beiderbecke, Benny Goodman, the Dorsey brothers and others.

It is of course a crowning irony that Paul Whiteman became named as "the King of Jazz." And, during the same period, the foremost black musician was labelled "the Duke"—Duke Ellington. It is sufficient to point out here that Duke Ellington has continued into the 1970s as a vital force in black music, and that his Twenties and Thirties compositions are still alive—*Caravan, Black, Brown and Beige, Mood Indigo*— and still played. Whereas, there's not a single Paul Whiteman tune or arrangement still alive.[2]

The point is not to debate the relationship of black and white musicians throughout the history of black music. But, instead, to delineate a clear line of black musical

2. To be fair, there are many reasons why music survives, vanishes, or is revived. In 1940, all of Bessie Smith's recordings were out of print, along with everything recorded by Louis Armstrong's Hot Fives and by Jelly Roll Morton's Red Hot Peppers. Musical "quality" was not the issue. [RW]

development from Duke (and before Duke) on into the present, to indicate that black music was and still is locked in the jaws of racism and exploitation.

What "jazz" means to me is the worst kind of working conditions, the worst in cultural prejudice. I could go down a list of club names throughout the country which are a disgrace to somebody who has been in the business as long as I have and who has attained "the kind of status" in the black music world that I have, who has been called "one of the giants," one of the founders of this, that and the other. Club conditions and expenses are such—especially transportation costs—that increasingly fewer musicians are making night club tours. The musician has to have at least four weeks at a club, as well as a concert or two, to defray the cost of transportation—especially if he takes his whole group, four or five men, with him. Typically, the clubs are owned by persons who have no cultural or musical appreciation of black music. The prevailing attitude is, "Play 40 minutes on the bandstand, come off and take 20 minutes," then back on the set—which is impossible to do.

So jazz to me has meant small dingy places, the worst kinds of salaries and conditions that one can imagine. With the leading clubs, it takes years to develop a reputation before you can demand more than "the union scale." Take for instance in Harlem, the Village of Harlem. There, the union wages for a black musician who doesn't have the stature of a Miles Davis or Dizzy Gillespie or Duke Ellington, or a record album—the scale is so low I hesitate to mention it. It is $90 a week. A man who might have majored in music and has decided to pursue black music as his life work and to take care of his family until he achieves stature, is subject to these dismal wages and treatment. The same situation prevails the length and breadth of this country, of course.

Furthermore, clubs in the black areas of town of course pay lower than in the white sections of the city. The argument is that the poverty of black people as an audience keeps the club from making money. However, of course, people come from all over the area to these clubs when some musician of stature works there. Whereas, in the downtown area a man can have a club half the size of the club in the black area and his scale goes up to $175 to $200 a week.

The term "jazz" has come to mean the abuse and exploitation of black musicians; it has come to mean cultural prejudice and condescension. It has come to mean all of these things, and that is why I am presently writing a book, *I Hate Jazz*. It's not my name and it means my oppression as a man and musician.

Of course I do not hate black music, of which I am a part, which is a part of me, and which expresses the vision of black people here in America. My point is that we must decolonize our minds and re-name and re-define ourselves. What is "jazz"? It is the cultural expression of Africans who are dispersed on this North American continent. It derives in a continuing line from the musical and cultural traditions of Africa. We must recognize what those traditions are, what it is we are doing musically, how we learn our music, how it pleases and has meaning, and what its significance is.

First of all, the "jazz musician" spends as much time developing his craft as any musician in the world. It is a 24 hour thing with us. We learn it mostly from mouth to mouth in rap sessions, in practice and improvisation with each other. We do not learn our craft by going to schools or academies, complete with blackboards, text books and rigid homework assignments. But there is tremendous "homework" and discipline going on.

We have to listen to records. The kid who plays like John Coltrane today can't read Coltrane in a book. He gets it from records. He has to listen, to learn by his ears, which constantly sharpens his rhythm, timing, tone and musicality.

I remember myself, one day I asked Sidney Cabot, who is a great innovator and also a great musician, "How could I develop my left hand? I've got to get a fast left hand." So he said to me, which was really a very fine technique, "The simple things you do with your right hand, do with your left hand. If you open the house door with the key in your right hand, put your key in your left hand pocket." He did not tell me to go home and practice with my left hand for 20 hours a day. His approach gave my left hand more sense of belonging to me than going home and practicing with the drumsticks. Consequently, over a period of time, I found myself doing things I ordinarily would not have done—musically and personally, with this new dexterity.

By contrast, some years ago in the '40s, I had been playing on 52nd Street and had a little loot. So I enrolled in a conservatory, with a percussion major. I went the first day to my percussion teacher and he asked me to play something for him. Well, the first thing he said to me was *that I held the sticks wrong.* Now I was on 52nd Street working with Charlie Parker, Coleman Hawkins, making more money than he was making. He said, "You are holding the sticks wrong." Well, his point of reference was how to drum in a symphony orchestra. Whereas, my thing was down close to everything, settled into the drums so that any of them could be reached instantly. So I said, "Man, if I change the way I hold the sticks and everything, I wouldn't be able to pay my tuition to this place."

Or let us take singing, for example. To develop the kind of quality Mahalia Jackson developed as a singer takes a lot of time and training. Black people come up in the church at 5, 6, 7, 8 years old. Instead of playing or singing a piece at graduation to show what you have learned the four years you have been in the conservatory, there is, instead, the way a Mahalia Jackson or an Aretha Franklin has developed and demonstrates ability. It is a much stronger form because they have to sing before a group of people and either make somebody cry or jump up and shout for joy.

Now that, to me, is what an artist is all about. No matter how much technique you have got, if you don't create some kind of emotion or some kind of electricity between yourself and somebody else, it doesn't mean a damned thing—whether you are a writer, a painter, a musician, what have you. We have come from that school as black people, that when somebody doesn't get something from you, then you don't have anything anyway.

I am often asked, "Can whites play your kind of music?" My answer is "Yes, anybody can play something that's already been set out there. If a painter paints a certain thing, I can imitate it. But no whites have ever contributed to the creative or innovative aspects of black music." White musicians have not contributed for the same reason that no blacks have come to the stature of Debussy and Schoenberg and others in Western European music. For society has forbidden either musician to be fully engaged in the other's culture. And all of our art forms grow out of culture. Our way of life is a culture—the way we eat, the way we look at our women, the way we swagger when we walk, the way black women have big fannies—this is all part of the culture, nor is the value of that culture sufficiently appreciated. Nobody has ever bestowed a doctorate upon musicians like Charlie Parker or Duke Ellington, yet both are past masters of creativity.[3]

But beyond recognizing the esthetics and the learning processes involved in black music, we must cleanse our minds of false categories which are not basic to us and which divide us rather than unite us. They are misnomers: jazz music, rhythm and blues, rock and roll, gospel, spirituals, blues, folk music. Regardless of what they are called, they are various expressions of black music, black culture itself, the

3. Actually, Ellington had already received honorary doctorates from Howard University (1963) and Yale (1967). But a great improviser such as Parker is less easily assimilated by the academy; Ellington seems more closely to match its dominant ideal, the classical composer. [RW]

expression of Africans in the diaspora. Yet black musicians are placed in these categories, their works are merchandised and they face financial success or failure depending upon the popularity of their classification at a given time. Take Ray Charles, for example. He's a black musician—and he does everything. He sings everything, plays piano and alto saxophone, composes, writes, arranges in the complete range of black music. Once it's boiled down, he is a black musician playing black music. Period. Nor is he unique, unusual, or an exception. He is typical.

The categories and misnomers extend beyond music, as well. Take the term "civil rights." What do you mean, I don't have my civil rights. When I tumbled out of my mother's womb, I had my rights to everything that everybody else has. It was never a matter of my getting my civil rights; it was a matter of my regaining something wrongfully taken from me. Yet, in its context, "civil rights" was a shadow which someone else placed before me, saying, "Well, your problem is that you don't have civil rights." So, I fought for this shadow called civil rights, at that time. And there are other terms: "black power, black studies, revolutionary, ghetto, slums, avant garde, black experience, militant, integration, non-violence, etc." I often wonder when I hear black people talking and using these terms constantly, if they ever realize that this terminology did not come from black people to describe the black condition, but instead came overwhelmingly from white media, academia, and politicians?

In all respects, culturally, politically, socially, we must re-define ourselves and our lives, in our own terms. As we continue this process, we will more accurately see indeed what we are, and what power we do have. The power is there. Music is a 20 billion dollar a year industry and it has been built and sustained by the talents of black people. We must see this fact as a prime example of the power and capability black people possess. And we must learn to translate this new vision into effective management and practice, to control our lives, to liberate the basic black creativity and ingenuity that have allowed us to survive, and move beyond survival to power and dominion.

49. The Musician's Heroic Craft

AT VARIOUS TIMES AN AIR FORCE MAJOR and a college teacher, Albert Murray (1916–2013) became one of the most important African-American intellectuals of his generation through his several books of criticism and fiction. He is best known for *The Omni-Americans:*

Source: Albert Murray, *Stomping the Blues* (New York: Vintage Books, 1982 [originally published in New York by McGraw-Hill, 1976]), pp. 87, 90, 98–99, 245, 250–54.

New Perspectives on Black Experience and American Culture (1970) and *Stomping the Blues* (1976), both of which have been very influential, particularly in their insistence that the blues affirm life rather than express sorrow.

These excerpts from the latter book tackle issues of musical meaning and communication. Contradicting those who have understood the blues as "authentic expression" of individual artists' feelings, Murray argues that in "blues-idiom music," which includes jazz, performing artists are rhetoricians who deliberately move audiences by drawing skillfully upon a tradition of signification. These passages also sketch one of Murray's favorite themes, the heroism of the blues or jazz musician.

Blues musicians play music not only in the theatrical sense that actors play or stage a performance, but also in the general sense of playing for recreation, as when participating in games of skill. They also play in the sense of gamboling, in the sense that is to say, of fooling around or kidding around with, toying with, or otherwise having fun with. Sometimes they also improvise and in the process they elaborate, extend, and refine. But what they do in all instances involves the technical skill, imagination, talent, and eventually the taste that adds up to artifice. And of course such is the overall nature of play, which is so often a form of reenactment to begin with, that sometimes it also amounts to ritual.

By the same token, to the extent that references to singing the blues have come to suggest crying over misfortune, there is also likely to be the implication that blues music does not require artifice but is rather a species of direct emotional expression in the raw, the natural outpouring of personal anxiety and anguish, which in addition to reinforcing the old confusion of blues music with a case of blues as such, also ignores what a blues performance so obviously is. It is precisely an artful contrivance, designed for entertainment and aesthetic gratification; and its effectiveness depends on the mastery by one means or another of the fundamentals of the craft of music in general and a special sensitivity to the nuances of the idiom in particular.

When working musicians (whether they execute by ear or by score) announce that they are about to play the blues, what they most often mean is either that the next number on the program is composed in the traditional twelve-bar blues-chorus form, or that they are about to use the traditional twelve-bar chorus or stanza as the basis for improvisation. They do not mean that they are about to display their own raw emotions. They are not really going to be crying, grieving, groaning, moaning, or shouting and screaming. They mean that they are about to proceed in terms of a very specific technology of stylization.

Nothing is likely to seem more spontaneous than call-and-response passages, especially in live performances, where they almost always seem to grow directly out of the excitement of the moment, as if the musicians were possessed by some secular equivalent of the Holy Ghost. But as is no less the practice in the Sunday Morning Service, the responses are not only stylized (and stylized in terms of a specific idiom, to boot), but are almost always led by those who have a special competence in such devices. After all, no matter how deeply moved a musician may be, whether by personal, social, or even aesthetic circumstances, he must always play notes that fulfill the requirements of the context, a feat which presupposes far more skill and taste than raw emotion.

Obviously, such skill and taste are matters of background, experience, and idiomatic orientation. What they represent is not natural impulse but the refinement of habit, custom, and tradition become second nature, so to speak. Indeed on close inspection what was assumed to have been unpremeditated art is likely to be largely a matter of conditioned reflex, which is nothing other than the end product of discipline, or in a word, training. In any case practice is as indispensable to blues musicians as to any other kind. As a very great trumpet player, whose soulfulness was never in question, used to say, "Man, if you ain't got the chops for the dots, ain't nothing happening."

That musicians whose sense of incantation and percussion was conditioned by the blues idiom in the first place are likely to handle its peculiarities with greater ease and assurance than outsiders of comparable or even superior conventional skill should surprise no one. But that does not mean, as is so often implied, if not stated outright, that their expression is less a matter of artifice, but rather that they have had more practice with the technical peculiarities involved and have also in the normal course of things acquired what is tantamount to a more refined sensitivity to the inherent nuances.

All of which makes what is only a performance seem like a direct display of natural reflexes, because it obscures the technical effort. But blues performances are based on a mastery of a very specific technology of stylization by one means or another nonetheless. And besides, effective make-believe is the whole point of all the aesthetic technique and all the rehearsals from the outset. Nor does the authenticity of any performance of blues music depend upon the musician being true to his own private feelings. It depends upon his idiomatic ease and consistency.

Back during the time when the so-called bop and so-called cool movements were being publicized as the living (which is to say ultimate) end of all blues stylization and hence the only possible route to true hipness or inness, some used to dress the part of being appropriately *modern* and *progressive* by wearing a beret and heavy-frame glasses like Dizzy Gillespie, the then current pacesetter on trumpet. Many, perhaps many more, used to act the part by aping the self-centered bandstand mannerisms of Charlie Parker, the veritable touchstone of the movement, who seems to have struck them as being so totally wrapped up in the esoteric ramifications of what he was expressing with such overwhelming elegance that nothing else in the world mattered anymore, not even the paying customers.

Which of course was not the case at all with Parker himself, who, true to his Kansas City upbringing, was, with all his individuality and in spite of all his personal problems, nothing if not a sensational crowd pleaser. Nevertheless such was the primacy of role playing among some of his self-styled followers that sometimes it was as if the only audience beyond themselves that counted was other musicians, whom they were not nearly so interested in entertaining as impressing and being one-up on. Not that they really wanted to be left alone. No blues-idiom musicians were ever so recital oriented. They wanted audiences that would give them their undivided attention, not dancers out to have their own good time.

But thus did they become involved in another ritual altogether. For the ceremony they are concerned with is not a matter of dance-beat-oriented incantation leading to celebration. They proceed as if playing music were a sacred act of self-expression that can only be defiled by such Dionysian revelry as characterizes the Saturday Night Function, and thus should be restricted to Amen Corner witnesses, and to journalists who (despite their own incurable squareness) will give it maximum publicity in the national and international media and thus reemphasize its exclusiveness and gain new converts at the same time.

What it all represents is an attitude toward the nature of human experience (and the alternatives of human adjustment) that is both elemental and comprehensive. It is a statement about confronting the complexities inherent in the human situation and about improvising or experimenting or riffing or otherwise playing with (or even gambling with) such possibilities as are also inherent in the obstacles, the disjunctures, and the jeopardy. It is also a statement about perseverance and about resilience and thus also about the maintenance of equilibrium despite precarious circumstances and about achieving elegance in the very process of coping with the rudiments of subsistence.

It is thus the musical equivalent of the epic, which Kenneth Burke in *Attitudes toward History* categorizes as a Frame of Acceptance as opposed to a Frame of Rejection. Burke is discussing poetic statements in terms of whether they represent a disposition to accept the universe with all its problems or to protest against it, and in the category of Acceptance he also includes tragedy, comedy, humor, and the ode. What is accepted, of course, is not the status quo nor any notion of being without potentiality nor even the spirit of the time; what is accepted is the all too obvious fact that human existence is almost always a matter of endeavor and hence also a matter of heroic action.

In the category of Rejection, which he characterizes as representing a negative emphasis while also pointing out that the differentiation cannot be absolute, Burke places the plaint or elegy, satire, burlesque (plus such related forms as polemic and caricature), the grotesque (which he says "focuses in mysticism"), and the didactic, which today is usually called propaganda. At bottom, what is rejected by such statements of lamentation, protestation, and exaggeration is the very existence of the circumstances that make heroic endeavor necessary. Not that most of the lamentation and protestation may not be in interest of better times, but what is featured all the same almost always turns out to be the despicable, the forlorn, the dissipated, and the down and out.

The trouble, however, is that when you get down to details, rituals of self-expression are beyond criticism. Anything goes because it is all a matter of the innermost truth of the performer's being. Thus if his musicianship seems lacking in any way, it is not because he is working in an idiom with which the listener is unfamiliar but which has a different set of requirements, but rather because it is the best of all possible ways to express what the musician in question is all about! The self-portrait (and/or the personal signature) that emerges from the music of Jelly Roll Morton, King Oliver, Bessie Smith, Louis Armstrong, Duke Ellington, Lester Young, and Charlie Parker is not primarily a matter of such egotistical self-documentation but rather of the distinction with which they fulfilled inherited roles in the traditional ritual of blues confrontation and purgation, and of life affirmation and continuity through improvisation. Incidentally, the revolutionary nature of their innovations and syntheses was not nearly so much a matter of a quest for newness for the sake of change as of the modifications necessary in order to maintain the definitive essentials of the idiom.

In one sense Charlie Parker's widely imitated innovations did indeed represent a radical counterstatement of certain aspects of the blues convention that had been so overworked that he had come to regard them as the same old thing. But for all that, Parker, unlike so many of his so-called progressive but often only pretentious followers, was not looking for ways to stop blues from swinging; he was looking for ways to make it swing even more, and sometimes when he really got going he achieved an effect that was both flippantly humorous and soulfully lyrical at the same time. On balance, Parker, it is true, must be considered as having been more of a jam-session musician than a dance-hall musician as such; but for him the jam session was not primarily an experimental workshop; it was to remain essentially the same old multidimensional good-time after-hours gathering it had always been. The experimental innovations were mainly a matter of having something special to strut your stuff with when your turn came to solo on the riff-solo-riff merry-go-round.

Nor should the overall personal and social implications of the blues statement be confused with the flamboyant costumes and overstylized mannerisms of the so-called hipsters (erstwhile hip cats and hep cats), the dandies, fops, and swells of the idiom. After all, the hipster's behavior is the same as that of the dilettante, who lives the "literary life" but only dabbles in literature as such. He knows all the right names, and like the *flâneur* of the art galleries he is also nothing if not up to date on what is in vogue as of tomorrow. In a sense he is also like the sedentary spectator whose concerns are completely circumscribed by the world of his favorite sport. Costuming himself and sounding off as if he belongs are about the extent of his involvement.

In any case the hipster's application of the disposition to riff with elegance is usually limited to jiving and woofing on his street-corner hangout and to shucking and stuffing along the mainstem, as if the night club, the ballroom, the music hall, and the bars that the performers, gamblers, and the sporting crowd frequent were what life itself were all about. Indeed some hipsters, not unlike some churchgoers, are so preoccupied with the trappings and procedures of the ceremonial occasion per se that their involvement amounts to idolatry. They misconstrue the symbol and the ritual reenactment as the thing itself.

There are those who regard blues music as a statement of rejection because to them it represents the very opposite of heroism. To many it represents only the anguished outcry of the victim, displaying his or her wounds and saying that it is all a lowdown dirty shame. To some, such purification as is involved is not of the atmosphere (which is indeed a matter of epic heroism) but of the individual, whose action is an effort not to contend but to "let it all hang out"; which, however, removes blues music from the realm of ritual and art and makes it a form of psychological therapy (although there is a literary analogy even so: the tear-jerker, the penny dreadful, the pulp confession story, which is almost always the sad saga of a victim). But thus also is blues music mistaken for that of the torch singer.

Blues music, however, is neither negative nor sentimental. It counterstates the torch singer's sob story, sometimes as if with the snap of two fingers! What the customary blues-idiom dance movement reflects is a disposition to encounter obstacle after obstacle as a matter of course. Such jive expressions as *getting with it* and *taking care of business* are references to heroic action. Indeed the improvisation on the break, which is required of blues-idiom musicians and dancers alike, is precisely what epic heroism is based on. In all events, such blues-idiom dance gesture is in effect an exercise in heroic action, and each selection on a dance program is, in a sense, a rehearsal for another of a never-ending sequence of escapades *as is suggested by the very fact that each not so much begins and ends as continues: And one and two and three and four and another one and a two and a three and a four and also and also and also* from vamp to outchorus to the next vamp.

50. Creative Music and the AACM

FOUNDED IN 1965 AND BASED IN CHICAGO, the Association for the Advancement of Creative Musicians (AACM) is a nonprofit musicians' co-operative devoted to African-American avant-garde music. Its first president was pianist Muhal Richard Abrams (b. 1930), and other active and prominent members have included reed players Roscoe Mitchell, Joseph Jarman, and Anthony Braxton, trumpeter Lester Bowie, violinist Leroy Jenkins, and trombonist George Lewis. Like the early twentieth-century societies founded by modernist composers such as Arnold Schoenberg, Paul Hindemith, and Edgard Varèse, the AACM was formed to encourage and promote musical activities that had relatively little market value and sometimes even met with hostile responses. In addition, the Association was meant to serve as a training ground for younger musicians. Its emphasis on collaboration, with all participants making equal contributions, prompted one writer to credit the group with having achieved "musical socialism."[1]

Trumpeter Leo Smith (b. 1941, now Wadada Leo Smith) joined the AACM in 1967. Raised in the heart of the Mississippi Delta, his father a friend of B. B. King, Smith never abandoned the musical gestures of the blues but always resisted the restrictions of chords, scales, and standard intonation. In these excerpts from a pamphlet self-published in 1973, Smith explains his musical philosophy, leading off with a brief mission statement for the AACM before turning to his ideas about "creative music" and improvisation (note that he nowhere uses the word "jazz"). Smith relates his music to African-American predecessors, defining not only connections but fundamental differences, one of them being that creative music cannot be criticized. A favorite topic is the poor fit between creative music and values of the larger capitalist context. Since Smith's essay is nothing if not a challenge to conventional assumptions, his idiosyncratic typography has been preserved (with his approval).

Source: Leo Smith, *notes (8 pieces) source a new world music: creative music* (Connecticut, 1973), n. p. Reprinted by permission of the author.

1. Valerie Wilmer, *As Serious as Your Life: The Story of the New Jazz*, revised ed. (Westport, Conn.: Lawrence Hill & Co., 1980), p. 115.

The AACM: Association for the Advancement of Creative Musicians

The AACM is a cooperative of artists (musicians, dancers, painters, and poets) which established itself to present and sustain creative music through the promotion of original works of black artists. It proposed to develop an awareness of creative black music, and to create an environment in which the black community could receive and appreciate the works of their black artists on a regular basis. For the first time in the history of black music and other areas of BLACK ART, black artists were able to sit down and talk about the presentation and promotion of their art and to address themselves to particular problems of creative music (improvisation), theater, dance, environmental projects, and how to integrate all the known properties of the performing arts into a total expression as indicated in the historical roots of the black man. As a result of their interchange, these black artists were able to combine their energies and present programs in the black community.

A few years after establishing itself as a functioning organization, the AACM set up a free training-program to cover elementary and advanced areas of music which adults and young children of the black community could attend regularly once a week. This training program consisted of lectures and practical workshop-classes on elementary-traditional and advanced theory dealing with improvisation, and provided private lessons on all levels covering the great body of black traditional music as well as the creative contemporary black music of our time.

The inspiration leading to the establishment of the AACM originated with the Experimental Orchestra, a group of musicians who had come together a few years earlier to rehearse and perform creative music. Its identity as an absolute entity is a composite of the individual concepts of each member of the orchestra. The orchestra offers every member the opportunity to develop his craft in improvisation, to direct the orchestra through rehearsal and performance of his music, and to gain experience in performing in an orchestra situation.

The contribution of the AACM to creative music is in evidence throughout the musical world.

Creative Music

in the art of music (rhythm-sound), there are but two types of disciplines; improvisation (improvisors) and composition (interpreters)—improvisation means that the music is created at the moment it is performed, whether it is developing a given theme or is improvisation on a given rhythm or sound (structures) or, in the purest form, when the improvisor creates without any of these conditions, but creates at that moment, through his or her wit and imagination, an arrangement of silence and sound and rhythm that has never before been heard and will never again be heard; composition means that the music must first be composed and then interpreted later, with the emphasis during performance being that it should sound the same (the mechanics of it) each time it is performed, as in euro-american music.

creative music is dedicated to developing a heightened awareness of improvisation as an art form—i feel that the creative music of afro-america, india, bali and pan-islam has done much along these lines, and is also creating a balance in the arena of world music (africa, aria, europe, euro-america, afro-america) and that this music will eventually eliminate the political dominance of euro-america in this world—when this is achieved, i feel that only then will we make meaningful political reforms in the world: culture being the way of our lives; politics, the way our lives are handled.

Thoughts of an Improvisor

time has ripened for a new creative improvisor who is able to perform creative music in all its aspects (solo, ensemble, and orchestra) without any prepared planning or setting up of conditions (as far as the improvisation is concerned), but with the creative expressive ability to technically deliver a performance of music on a creative level which we have not as yet experienced or dealt with on such a broad scale—this would call for a heightened consciousness in all of our lives as well as among the musicians who participate directly or not at all in this next level of music creation—the new creative musician in most cases would be multi-instrumentalist, but for other creative musicians this would not be necessary, for the instrument is only part of a larger consciousness that transcends the mere means of an instrument or instruments—what is required is that the new creative improvisor must have the absolute ability to instantaneously organize sound, silence, and rhythm with the whole of his or her creative intelligence—the improvisor's total life experience is drawn from, including faculties of rightreasoning and the make-up of his or her psychological and physiological existence—all of these factors determine what is actually being expressed at the moment of conception and creation—thus, at each instance, this new creative improvisor's creations include the entire spectrum of space and cycle of time—this new musician is termed creative musician, a sensitive being who feels a higher calling and responds by seeking to enter into proper attunement with mind and body: it prevails in all space and unifies the wholeness of creation—the creative musician can learn and utilize this great law involving mind, for music is mental, as it is conceived in the mind

if we are to achieve this next music level, we must first cut-connection with this factory of death, and that is creatively speaking (commercial business-production-journalism and the likes of the powerMAN)—now that could mean many things, like for instance getting control of our music, i.e. freeing ourselves from the "powerMAN"—that depends on where we are standing, and rarely if ever are we standing on the "powerMAN"—freedom means the sharing of power, equally—and that is proportionately among all involved, and if that is not achieved, then it is not possible to be dealt a fair hand at the table of business—so, we should do the business ourselves—secondly, we as creative musicians must realize that it is not just one of us, but rather that all are responsible for an improvisation—now that's true in the absolute sense, but on the other levels, consideration must be given to what this improvisation means—there are many forms of improvisation, and of the various forms, if there are elements that are structured by one individual, then that person has scored an improvisation—but it goes much further than that—if whoever is performing in an improvisation form contributes a solo or any substantial amount of improvising in the piece, then he or she too should be given credit for the solo—(in countries that have barbaric type laws pertaining to the registering of creations, like the u. s. and some european countries, only the "leader" is allowed official registration, and so total credit is given to one person only—if the types of laws requiring registration of creations persist, and it seems that they will, then every improvisor should be able to copyright and protect the material that they contribute to the total improvisation, and they should share too in the profit of its sale by being assured of contractual royalties)—thirdly, as improvisors, we must forever have our instrument or instruments and mind and body in a state of readiness—impeccable strength in these areas is the least that is required

the creation is of all, and once we all have realized this truth, the more will we as creative improvisors be able to draw from that great endless source of inspiration—it is apparent that man-made laws concerning creation have retarded many an improvisor by channeling them into the areas of composition; but there are a few who have continued along the path of master improvisor, and it is these few who will bring about the needed change of consciousness in the masses and the deliverance of creative music

now to the point of this piece (exposition): can creative music (an improvisational music) be criticized, as was musical composition? as in all cases of something that comes into existence with absolutely no mate to-it anywhere in the world, it naturally brings its own rules of understanding, of interpretation, and technique of expression. so it was with the coming of the twentieth century when we entered a new dimension of art, a dimension of art-music that never before existed: creative music, the improvisors. and so, the answer is *no*, creative music cannot be criticized. it does not require that form of journalism. creative music is totally determined by the improvisor, and everything in the environment affects it—the improvisor, the listener, and even the contours and shape of the environment in which the music is being performed (like the temperature and the different elements of air and the so-forths). so from the standpoint of these facts, it becomes impossible to criticize it. secondly, in this age of improvisation, critique, as we know it, is invalid in the sense of explaining what the artist has said or what is to be said. creative music-new rules. what is required is creation: to create. if you hear creative music, and the improvisor and you reach that level of creative communication, then that is what is required: an understanding of a true level of realization in-self. it can go no further than you-inside-you. it is not a music that allows one to use it and still refer to it. if someone uses the music—for example, tries to write about how it has "succeeded" or "failed" or how it was "not quite there" and how the audience "reacted" to it—they fail (lose) in just that slight moment trying to bring outside something that is inside *(for* the inside: soul). this great creative music is of a feeling. feeling and intelligent communion happens inside of each being and is sparked by each being. the result of this creative exchange immediately revitalizes the essence of the individual of all. that is, philosophically speaking, it takes the human, earth-being, feeling, being, in absoluteness. this creates within the contemporary maze of confusion a balance of understanding: first point love. creative music brings the conscious level of earth-beings' awareness to its highest stage of development so far as travel during this cycle.

(sources) a new
world
music: creative music
the
improvisors & improvisation

with the coming of the twentieth century, a new creative black music emerged in north america—a music whose form of expression is improvisation. this new creative music forecast the end of european music (composition) as the dominant form of expression, and lifted the boundaries from its performers (improvisors), giving them a part in the creation of the music.

at the turn of the century, european instrumental and vocal music had reached a dead-lock as far as its pitch system was concerned because of the continued exclusive use of the chromatic scale in composition. here in north america, new generating sources of rhythm and sound became evident in afro-american music—ragtime and "stride" (solo piano), vocal music, ensemble and orchestra music (collective creative improvisation). the creative artists responsible for these new sources brought to music a new technique in instrumental and vocal performing. they did not confine themselves to a limiting chromatic scale, but instead projected their improvisation through the use of the entire spectrum of sound. their rhythm was conceived as units: each improvisor became a complete entity and so moved away from reference to time in unison with a group.

what is improvisation? improvisation is an art form used by creative musicians to deliver an expression or musical thought at the very instant that their idea is conceived. the improvisor must have an ability to instantaneously organize sound, silence and rhythm with the whole of his or her creative intelligence. his total life experience is drawn from, including his faculties of rightreasoning and the make-up of his psychological and physiological existence. all of these factors determine what is actually being expressed at that moment of conception and creation. thus, at each instant, the improvisor's creation includes the entire spectrum of space and cycle of time (past, present and future). his music is not, like composition, one that is conceived as one idea at one instant, only to be funneled at a later time through a standard system of notation onto paper as merely a related idea, and finally interpreted and performed sometime in the future as an idea removed at least three times from the original.

although an improvisor may create and notate certain types of symbols and forms in which to retain creative music, this process is not composition, for any elements of improvisation that are notated are but mere forms to be exploited by creative improvisors. the method and symbols used by the improvisor in retaining an improvisation have never been (and must never be) standardized.

likewise, technique for the improvisor is not an arbitrary consumption of an abstract standardized method, but rather a direct attunement with the mental, spiritual and mechanical energy necessary to express a full creative impulse. in other words, to improvise, a display of flawless standardized technique is not enough: an improvisor must be creative. from the very moment of the improvisor's acquaintance with technique, it is the all-out goal to respond to the solo creative impulse from within which makes for the uniqueness of originality among all creative performers. the improvisor realizes that the natural course of his music is to respond to his own impulses, which by their very nature are original and individual.

creative music, throughout its history in black america, has developed a classical art music, both in the instrumental and vocal idioms: spiritual, ragtime, blues, bebop and free music.

spiritual music is a vocal-religious music, the history and development of which has been explored quite thoroughly in the music literature already written by black americans. since this piece is to deal only with instrumental music, further explanation of spiritual music will not be made.

ragtime, initially, was not a completely composed music, but was a very free and vital rhythmic vehicle for creative improvisation; but, eventually, because of the imbalance inherent in the racist society in which it developed where composed music was unduly thought to be of a higher order than improvised music, the improvisors of ragtime were swayed toward composition. ragtime is solo piano music that usually consists of several different sections with the first and last sections usually having the same key center, and one or more changes of key center usually occurring during the middle sections. (shortly after the decline of ragtime in popularity, an improvisation piano music—"stride"—developed in harlem using basically the same form as ragtime, excepting that it was improvisation built off of themes.)

it has been commonly mistaken that the blues is pitch oriented (chords) and relies upon a rigid structure (12 bars). rather, the blues is determined by its sound and its rhythm, and not by its harmonic function. blues can consist of 8 bars, 12 bars,

16 bars, modern (any blues functioning in an uneven structure that is recurring), or free blues (no given amount of bars, not does the sound function in relation to a progression). the blues is a most unique music in that it has several forms within it: e.g. it is a vocal as well as an instrumental music, and there is a distinct form of blues music for piano, guitar, ensemble, and orchestra. inherent in the vocal blues form is the history of a people, "the seventh son", the newest of earth-beings. truly, there is the making of a new being, spiritually. this explains why we are the only ones who have created a new and different culture as a whole new-art-music, without going the route of the "universal orchestra" or european-way (composition). the blues form was the first music to assert this.

bebop, or bop, as it has been called, is a music that has had several periods of change, i.e. hard bop, funk, and extension bop. each of these periods has brought significant changes in the musical structure and the philosophical attitudes of its creators. originally, bop was as complex as the earlier black music—the collective improvisational orchestras in which each improvisor created a different line. the complexities of bop were similarly exhibited in the improvised solo-line. most of the "musical analysts" who have allegedly transcribed the solo-lines of the great masters, however, have misrepresented them by not transcribing the whole of the line, but by singling out, instead, only one element of the line. in the evaluation of this music, the opinion has been that the solo-line is the creation of a "soloist", and that the other improvisors involved are mere accompaniment. this is an invalid evaluation. the solo-line, in fact, is created by all improvisors contributing to it (any combination of reeds, brass, drums, and piano): all the component parts become the solo-line. a "solo" alone can only be created by one improvisor.

bebop unfolded toward a lesser complex music. hard bop addresses itself to more simple lines and harmonic function. funk leaned even further toward simplicity. some improvisors of funk were interested in simulating the human voice with their instruments, and this form leaned closely toward the sound of the black church.

extension bop was, again, as complex as the original bop, and innovated the music by incorporating more advanced harmonic structures and extending rhythms (i.e. the grouping of rhythms together became compound). the bop extensionists employed far advanced harmonic structures and incorporated modality into the music as a completely new level of sound; but the basic music form did not essentially change because the use of the song form and the blues continued to hold this new music within. these bop extensionists would create improvisations by superimposing several different chords on one chord that had been dictated in the harmonic structure. because of this superimposition and grouping of chords, the rhythm became of mixed levels—that is, the grouping together of uneven figures (single-line runs, chords, and multi-rhythms).

the emergence and innovations of bop, then, marked the third and final stage in the evolution of the solo-line and brought the first period of our music to its completion—a period that had begun when the collective improvisational orchestras with their many lines gave way to the expression of the essence of the music through one line, which was then extended by the addition of advanced and complex harmonic, melodic (and the added level of sound through the exclusive use of modes) and rhythmic structures.

the second period of creative music began with the inception of free form, the elements of which parallel the blues form in almost every aspect as a music of many levels. the improvisor could build improvisations of great length and was again offered a chance to return to a very free and open structure, thus leading back to the original intention of all great music: to create and express original ideas without being inhibited by certain prescribed forms. in free-music we have many forms: structured forms that supply a beginning leading into improvisations; link form, whereby several different predetermined elements are linked together to form improvisations; and, at its highest level, improvisation created entirely within the improvisor at the moment of improvisation without any prior structuring.

there is another form that is not particularly an outgrowth of the evolution in free form. this form is called solo-form. here the solo refers to the improvisor who performs a complete improvisation as a soloist. the instruments that have thus far been liberated exclusively by creative music in this area have been: reeds (tenor, alto, clarinet, bass clarinet); brass (trumpet and flugelhorn); drums (trap set). (the voice, piano, balophone, and keyboard types of instruments, zither, guitar, and string instruments using a bow have been omitted here because the solo elements of these instruments have been exploited in composition as well as in ancient art music.) a new dimension of the solo form which *is* particular to free-music is provided by the multi-instrumentalist improvisor. here one improvisor creates a complete improvisation with more than one instrument and of mixed character (e.g. trumpet, flugelhorn, percussion instruments, and flute).

in free-music there are many new additional forms being created, and the few that have been outlined here only represent the first fifteen years or so of its development.

in conclusion, it must have become apparent to anyone reading this piece that creative music (black music) is a music with a set of principles that apply exclusively to itself. its image and procreators have been persecuted since its inception in this country (u. s. a.) because the music critics and those who set the standards and regulations for registering music have insisted on confining their evaluation of improvisation to a rigid set of principles that apply only to composition (e.g. it has only been in 1972 that creative music can be registered in the library of congress in the form of a sound recording; and it is still impossible to register any scored improvisation unless it has been merely notated after the fact of creation as though it were a composition. it is a vital art form with a future as absolute as the mind. creative improvisors must not be discouraged by the obvious elements trying to destroy them (i.e. recording companies, booking agents, trade magazines, lack of proper performing places, lack of government recognition in the form of proper subsidies—all necessitating periodic exoduses abroad). these artists must hold true to the pureness of their calling. listeners, too, must not be discouraged or misled. it is time for them to move to a higher lever of consciousness in terms of their music and to protect it by making certain that more adequate conditions be provided from creative musicians in this country. first we can start with a conscientious cultural program that is financed through the tax program of this country which would enable all segments of these united states to become fully aware of and experience this great classical art music of afro-america. (it is time to realize that the classical art music of europe is *not* that of all america.) furthermore, it is high time that we begin to help and set up cultural ties with the other more than three-fourths of these americas (north, central, and south). finally, we must seek out other cultures that have improvisation as their classical art music (india, pan-islam, the orient, bali, and africa) and make lasting cultural commitments with them. for the days are set in time that this vast world of ours can only survive unless we, as humans, become earth-beings committed in our cultural and political aspects to a pan-world future.

51. Jazz Pop—A "Failed Art Music" Makes Good

WRITING IN 1977, CRITIC ROBERT PALMER (1945–1997) anticipated later debates over "smooth jazz" by analyzing "jazz pop," an almost equally controversial antecedent. Palmer was chief popular music critic for the *New York Times* in the 1980s and is perhaps best known for his insightful book *Deep Blues*. In this piece, he analyzes the perspectives of two of jazz pop's major figures, guitarist George Benson (b. 1943) and saxophonist Grover Washington Jr. (1943–1999). Along the way, he also offers a definition of the fundamental difference between rock and pop, and by extension jazz rock and jazz pop, in terms of the social organization of the groups in each camp.

"Sure I still love to play jazz," says George Benson, a guitarist with jazz roots and a jazz-derived style whose last album sold almost two million copies. "I feel good *when* I'm playing it, and I feel good *after* I've played it. I just wish there was an audience for it. The fact is, the people who like regular jazz won't come out and patronize it, and they won't buy a lot of records. And anyway, when I do make a regular jazz record, the companies put it on the shelf. I did a date with Benny Goodman more than a year ago and we were *swinging*. All that material will come out sometime, but probably not in time to do *me* any good."

Benson's new album, "In Flight," is jazz pop. It is heavily produced, with lush orchestral arrangements by Claus Ogerman, swirling overlays of electronic keyboards, fashionable disco rhythms, and material originally recorded by Stevie Wonder and War, the black rock group. It may equal or even surpass the sales of "Breezin'," Benson's most recent record, because it is even more commercial. "Breezin'" lodged firmly in the national top ten because its one vocal, "This Masquerade," picked up enough airplay to become a hit single. "In Flight" has six selections, and four of them feature Benson's vocals. He is an accomplished soul singer but not an exceptional one, and he is the most gifted jazz guitarist of his generation. But Benson is no longer making records for a relative handful of jazz aficionados. He is aiming his music at a broad pop audience, and if that audience wants more vocals, he gives them more vocals.

Grover Washington Jr., a saxophonist, has to his credit two albums which sold in the millions and several hit singles, and his new LP, "A Secret Place," sounds like it may be his biggest yet. As jazz, his music is not very interesting. He is a capable but rather anonymous-sounding player with an undistinguished sound on the tenor,

---

Source: Robert Palmer, "Jazz Pop—A 'Failed Art Music' Makes Good," *New York Times*, February 13, 1977, p. D20. Reprinted by permission of Augusta Palmer.

occasional intonation problems on the soprano, and a determinedly low-key approach. But Creed Taylor, who pioneered contemporary jazz pop when he was producing Wes Montgomery for Verve, likes to put records together around Washington's dependable improvising, and at present the saxophonist is the best-selling artist on Taylor's CTI label.

"A Secret Place," like Washington's previous releases, is a glossy affair that glides along at a mellow medium tempo. Jazz fans may object to it as jazz-tinged Muzak, but when it is coming over a car radio in the evening or percolating pleasantly behind a low-keyed conversation, it is hard to fault. And although George Benson might legitimately be criticized for prostituting his considerable talents, it is difficult to imagine Washington making more satisfying records away from Creed Taylor's tutelage.

The best way to listen to jazz pop is to forget that many jazz fans consider it a failed art music. In essence it is pure pop with jazz instrumentalists featured up front, and it is often superior pop. As such, it must be distinguished from jazz rock. The difference between pop and rock may be a subtle one in some instances, but in the case of jazz-related musics it is absolutely fundamental.

Rock is primarily a group music, and although it has its dominant personalities, they often allow themselves to be upstaged by their backing groups. Mick Jagger of the Rolling Stones needs Keith Richards as a counterbalance. Bob Dylan has never been afraid to use musicians with strong personalities, from the Band to his gypsy violinist, Scarlet Rivera. Even Elvis Presley depends on his band to put across out-and-out rock numbers.

Similarly, jazz rock is a group music. The most successful jazz rock players have always depended on a band sound and on group chemistry, from the exchanges between John McLaughlin and Billy Cobham in Manavishnu Orchestra to Chick Corea's empathy with Stanley Clarke in Return to Forever.

In pop, the featured artist is the undisputed star; musical backdrops are often slick, but they are never distinctive enough to upstage the front man. Jazz rocker Herbie Hancock's band, the Headhunters, would be instantly recognizable no matter who they were backing up, but a Claus Ogerman arrangement for George Benson would serve Grover Washington Jr. equally well.

This may put jazz pop stars in something of a musical straightjacket on records, but in person they often enjoy more improvisational freedom than their jazz-rocking brethren. Live, a jazz rocker is limited because he has to help project a familiar band sound. When George Benson or Grover Washington Jr. perform, their well-rehearsed backup groups simply cook along in an amiably serviceable manner, and the stars get to play as long as they want to, with all of the complexity of which they are capable.

In fact, jazz pop may prove the least compromising way for a jazz player to attain mass acceptance. George Benson, for example, recorded "In Flight" with a hand-picked mixture of top session players and members of his regular performing unit. He insisted on recording everything but the orchestral arrangements and his vocals "live" in the studio, and as a result his performances on the album generate some of the heat of a personal appearance.

The guitarist was not always so fortunate. "When I recorded for CTI," he recalls, "Creed Taylor wanted to put records together piecemeal, track by track. I would play by myself in the studio, trying to get into the groove of what I was hearing on ear-phones. I was always uncomfortable on my records, and I sounded like it, but try telling that to him." Even a casual comparison will confirm Benson's judgment. Nothing in his CTI catalogue attains the urgency of his long solos on "The World Is a Ghetto" from "In Flight."

Nevertheless, Taylor must be given his due. He may be an autocrat, but his records have an admirable consistency and maintain high standards of musicianship. The albums by Grover Washington Jr. are particularly successful because of their even dynamic levels. Benson's "In Flight" balances lyrical interludes against peaks of intensity, vocals against instrumental solos, pounding rhythms against out-of-tempo passages. Washington's "A Secret Place" has no real climaxes; both the saxophonist's solos and David Matthews's brass arrangements contribute to a static quality which turns out to be quite effective. You can dance to it, you can daydream to it, you can put it on and ignore it. If you want to focus your attention on something relaxing, you can listen to it.

When he works with musicians whose styles are more distinctive, Taylor adjusts his productions accordingly. Hank Crawford, who used to play alto saxophone with Ray Charles, has a stinging, bittersweet sound and a personal manner of phrasing, and his new CTI album, "Hank Crawford's Back," includes plenty of the sort of expressive hills and valleys "A Secret Place" lacks. Washington is the principal soloist on his album; indeed, he is featured most of the way through. Crawford shares solo space with two equally original musicians, Jeremy Steig on flute and Fred Wesley on trombone. He is saddled with hopeless material—"Canadian Sunset," "I Can't Stop Loving You"—but the soloists' aggressively personal sounds and original ideas are adequate compensation.

A number of developments from within the pop mainstream have paved the way for the success of jazz pop. Disco renditions of standard tunes, the sophisticated production techniques of record makers like Philadelphia's Gamble and Huff, the popularity of longer and longer album cuts and maxi-singles for dancing, the infiltration of jazz musicians and jazz ideas into rock, and the "crossover" to pop acceptance by jazz rock groups like Mahavishnu Orchestra and Herbie Hancock's Headhunters have all been important stimuli.

At the present time, jazz rock is somewhat stagnant, and jazz musicians who allow themselves to be produced and packaged like pop singers are selling records in unprecedented quantities. Whether Benson will be able to educate his listeners to accept records which are worthy of his talents, and whether Grover Washington Jr. will develop a strong musical personality independent of the CTI production machine, remain to be seen.

PART 8

The Eighties

52. "America's Classical Music"

DURING THE 1940S, PIANIST WILLIAM "BILLY" TAYLOR (1921–2010) worked with many of the founders of bebop, including Dizzy Gillespie and Charlie Parker; after 1952, he performed primarily with his own trio. Taylor's dissertation on the history of jazz piano earned him a doctoral degree in 1975, and he was long an influential advocate for jazz education. In this article, Taylor sums up several strands of thought that had been explored by many others.[1] He argues for the dignity and importance of jazz, displaying an understandable resentment of prejudicial treatment for European classical music. While he properly credits black musicians like himself as the main developers of jazz, he insists that the music is equally available to anyone, regardless of ethnic background. Although he points out that jazz should be evaluated according to its own standards, he works to legitimate it as a "classical music." To this end, he emphasizes the individuality of jazz performance rather than its cooperative aspects, and its appeal across many cultural boundaries rather than its specific cultural meanings.

Both the diversity of American society and the success of jazz abroad would seem to complicate Taylor's claim that jazz expresses "uniquely American feelings and thoughts." More interesting, though, are the implications of the main argument, particularly when we realize that "classical music" is primarily a twentieth-century category that lumps together music from many countries, many centuries, many social settings. In fact, it is a cultural category that achieved prestige in part by obscuring diverse meanings and purposes. Classical music is now firmly

---

Source: William "Billy" Taylor, "Jazz: America's Classical Music," *The Black Perspective in Music* 14:1 (Winter 1986), pp. 21–25. Reprinted by permission of the Billy Taylor Estate.

1. Many musicians and critics had argued for understanding jazz as "America's classical music"; perhaps the best-known earlier usage of that phrase is Grover Sales's 1984 book, *Jazz: America's Classical Music* (New York: Da Capo, 1992 [1984]).

associated with written scores and institutional training, even though J. S. Bach, for example, never went to college and was known primarily as an improviser.[2] To "classicize" music is to blur its history: what is gained and what is lost if we think of jazz as classical music?

Jazz is America's Classical Music. It is both a way of spontaneously composing music and a repertoire, which has resulted from the musical language developed by improvising artists. Though it is often fun to play, jazz is *very serious* music. As an important musical language, it has developed steadily from a single expression of the consciousness of *black* people into a *national* music that expresses American ideals and attitudes to Americans and to people from other cultures all around the world.

As a classical music, jazz has served as a model for other kinds of music; its influence is international in scope. It is studied, analyzed, documented, and imitated in India, Thailand, Finland, Sweden, Denmark, Holland, France, Belgium, Great Britain, Cuba and Japan. It is even studied and performed in Russia, Poland, Hungary, and other Iron Curtain countries. This last fact is most important because it is an indication of how jazz is used as a political statement—in a typical jazz performance each individual performer contributes his or her personal musical perspective and thereby graphically demonstrates the democratic process at work. There is no conductor directing the musical flow, but rather, the interaction of individuals combining their talents to make a unique musical statement.

Jazz is simple, complex, relaxed, and intense. It embodies a bold tradition of constantly emerging musical forms and directions. Jazz has developed its own standards of form, complexity, literacy, and excellence. It has also developed a repertoire, which codifies and defines its many varied styles—and its styles are really varied. There is a style of jazz which sounds like European classical music (i.e., the Modern Jazz Quartet); there is a style of jazz that sounds like Latin American Music (i.e., Eddie Palmieri, Machito, and Mongo Santamaria); there is a style of jazz which sounds like East Indian classical music (i.e., Mahavishnu, John Mayer/Joe Harriott). There are styles of jazz which sound like various other kinds of music heard in this country and elsewhere in the world.

Americans of African descent, in producing music which expressed themselves, not only developed a new musical vocabulary, they created a *classical* music—an authentic *American* music which articulated uniquely American feelings and thoughts, which eventually came to transcend ethnic boundaries.

This classical music defines the national character and the national culture. In one sense it serves as a musical mirror, reflecting who and what Americans were in

---

2. On the development of hierarchical thinking about culture in the late nineteenth century, see Lawrence W. Levine, *Highbrow/Lowbrow: The Emergence of Cultural Hierarchy in America* (Cambridge: Harvard University Press, 1988); Paul DiMaggio, "Cultural Entrepeneurship in Nineteenth-Century Boston: The Creation of an Organizational Base for High Culture in America," *Media, Culture, and Society* 4 (1982), 33–50; Paul DiMaggio, "Cultural Entrepreneurship in Nineteenth-Century Boston, Part II: The Classification and Framing of American Art," *Media, Culture, and Society* 4 (1982), 303–22; and Robert Walser, "Highbrow, Lowbrow, and Voodoo Aesthetics," in *Microphone Fiends: Youth Music and Youth Culture,* ed. Tricia Rose and Andrew Ross (New York: Routledge, 1994), pp. 235–49. On some of the ideological implications of "classical music," see Christopher Small, *Music, Society, Education* (Hanover, N.H.: Wesleyan University Press, 1996 [1977]). [RW]

their own view at different points in their development. Thoughts of the 1920s, for example, evoke memories of people dancing to the tune "Charleston," composed by jazz pianist James P. Johnson, *and* of folks from downtown going uptown to the Cotton Club in Harlem to hear Duke Ellington play "It Don't Mean a Thing if It Ain't Got That Swing." And thoughts of the 1930's remind us of the way Americans and others danced to the music of the great swing bands. You can pick your favorites—mine were Chick Webb, Benny Goodman, Artie Shaw, Jimmy Lunceford, and of course Count Basie. No matter when or where it is composed or performed, from the "good old days" to the present, jazz, our ubiquitous American music, speaks to and for each generation—especially the generation that creates it.

The jazz of today certainly underscores this point—it speaks to and for the contemporary generation. The work of Wynton Marsalis, Stanley Jordan, Paquito D'Rivera, Emily Remler, Jane Ira Bloom, Tiger Okoshi, Chico Freeman, Branford Marsalis, and Kenny Kirkland provide excellent examples of what I am speaking of in this regard. Their music and the music of many older musicians like Chick Corea, Herbie Hancock, Freddie Hubbard, Toshiko Akiyoshi, Bobby Hutcherson, and Kenny Barron are relevant to the moods and tempo of today's life. Their music expresses—in its melodies, rhythms and harmonies—feelings and emotions which people, regardless of their cultural and ethnic backgrounds, can understand and appreciate. Jazz, America's classical music, has indeed become multi-ethnic and multi-national in usage.

Let's examine this unique American phenomenon a little more closely. Black-American music, from the very beginning of its development in this country, incorporated elements from other musical traditions, yet it has retained its own identity throughout its history. Though jazz has utilized and restructured materials from many other musical traditions, its basic elements were derived from traditions and aesthetics which were non-European in origin and concept. It is an indigenous *American* music whose roots and value systems are *African.* Its basic rhythmic traditions are found throughout the African continent.

In the African tradition there were *no onlookers;* everyone was a participant in creating rhythm and responding to it. This adherence to African rhythmic practices made it easier for people to participate on their own level. They could play an instrument, dance, sing, clap their hands, stomp their feet, or combine these with other rhythmic methods of self-expression such as shaking or rattling makeshift instruments. Rhythm was fundamental in the African musical tradition and has remained so in jazz. It is interesting to note that when the use of African drums was banned by the slaveholders, all of those drums-inspired rhythms were incorporated into melodies which projected similar feelings and other rhythmic devices were substituted (i.e., Hambone, pattin' juba, etc.).

The basic elements of jazz can be found in the work songs, spirituals and other early forms of music created by slaves. When the blacks were brought to this country, they were forced to quickly adapt to new languages, strange new customs, new religious practices, and the cultural preferences of the slave owners. They were only allowed to retain those cultural traditions which in the opinion of the slave masters made them *better* slaves. Since African culture was considered inferior to European culture, it was systematically and deliberately destroyed by Americans engaged in the slave trade. Tribes and families were broken up on the auction block, and many slaves found themselves living and working with people whose language and customs they did not understand.

Since music had always played such an important part in the daily life of so many Africans, despite the fact that they belonged to different nations and had different backgrounds, it was quickly seized upon as a tool by the slaves to be used for communication and as relief from both physical and spiritual burdens. In the African societies they had come from, there was music for working, playing, hunting, and most daily activities. There was also music for important events, such as births, initiation rites, marriages, and much, much more. For those Africans, music had many uses; its rhythms and melodies were an integral part of whatever they did.

People who came to this country as free people brought with them the songs, customs, and attitudes of the various places of their origin. They also brought musical instruments and other artifacts with them. They were transplanted people, free to express themselves in ways which were traditional to them, so they were able to sustain and maintain their musical heritage without external need to change.

The transplanted Africans who were enslaved did not have the same freedom to maintain their cultural identity, so their musical traditions had to change. As they endured slavery, they were obliged to reshape and redefine work songs, religious music, leisure songs, dance music and other traditional African music to make that music useful in new situations. They also created new forms of musical expression when some of the old forms no longer satisfied their needs. In Africa, music had been used to accompany and define all the activities of life, so the slaves used well-established techniques to restructure the music they needed for survival tools in the hostile atmosphere of the "land of the free."

African-Americans endured indescribable hardships while they were surviving slavery and other forms of racism in America, but by retaining the cultural supports that worked and by restructuring or discarding those that did not, black Americans created something of beauty from the ugliest of situations—human bondage. They created a new idiom—Afro-American music. This new music was the trunk of the tree from which another truly American music would grow—a classical music in every sense of the word—jazz.

Classical music must be time tested, it must serve as a standard or model, it must have established value, and it must be indigenous to the culture for which it speaks. Jazz meets the criteria by which classical music is judged.

The syntax, semantics, and kinesthetics of jazz are American, and its attitudes reflect prevalent American viewpoints. The gradual changes which that syntax has undergone show a consistent process of developing a unique musical expression. This can be examined and analyzed in the same manner that one can examine and analyze the syntax and forms of other classical styles of music. One can study both the written scores and phonograph recordings of the jazz repertoire and the work of the artists who epitomize the chronological and historically-important styles of the music.

The semantics of jazz convey thoughts, impressions, and feelings which are relevant to generations of Americans through implicit and connotative musical symbols. Americans share an understanding of the emotional connotations of jazz which is based on an Afro-American value system, but the *interpretation* of the musical symbols varies a great deal because the music has transcended ethnic boundaries and reflects and defines the national character as well as the national culture. Pianists Chick Corea and Herbie Hancock have different priorities when they write and play jazz, yet their playing is very compatible when they improvise together in a twin-piano setting.

The kinesthetics or physical movements of jazz are important, but often underestimated, factors in the production of the music. Since jazz is a way of playing music as well as a repertoire, these factors must be considered in any discussion of its characteristics. The physiological aspects of jazz rhythms and tone production supply the music with many of its unique qualities. Because American cultural practices have determined *where* jazz could be played, those cultural practices have had an influence on *how* jazz would be played. In many cases the kinesthetics of jazz have been directly related to the place where the performance occurred and to the response of the audience. A night club, a park, or a riverboat might encourage dancing, hand-clapping, whistling, or stomping, while a church, a concert hall, a school auditorium, or a small classroom might produce a more subdued interaction between the jazz musicians and the audience.

When the syntax, semantics, and kinesthetics of jazz are carefully and impartially examined and when the chronological development of the music is studied, it becomes apparent that jazz has emerged as America's classical music. About western-European classical music, Charles Rosen writes:

> The classical style appears inevitable only after the event. Looking back today we can see its creation as a natural one, not an outgrowth of the preceding style (in relation to which it seems more like a leap or a revolutionary break), but a step in the progressive realization of the musical language as it had existed and developed. . . .

Although written about western-European classical music, that statement can be applied to jazz and to music from other non-European aesthetic traditions—for example, the classical music of India. Robert E. Brown points out the classical elements in the music from India:

> The Indian musician inherits an oral tradition which provides an impressively rich vocabulary for him to use and he works with a degree of freedom which belies the usual conception of what we like to refer to as tradition-bound cultures. The more intensive his training and the more he gives to his art, the more he is enabled to bring his own personality into play, to communicate, to create. He accepts certain conventions of musical language in order to be able to speak, but these, though relatively precise, are simply *foundations* full of potential, for weaving more elaborate and more personal interpretations.

Jazz is America's classical music, yet many Americans have been consistent in their bias against it. They believe that western-European classical music is superior to any other in the world and therefore the only music that warrants serious and intensive study. This belief has resulted in the systematic exclusion of jazz from much of the American cultural experience. For the most part, jazz has not received serious or consistent attention from educators, media programmers, music critics, symphony orchestras, concert performers, managers or presentors, funding agencies, or *the black community*. Therefore, the general public has been deprived of appropriate exposure to jazz and receives too little accurate and up-to-date information about it.

Those of us who belong to the ethnic group which created jazz should be concerned about the fact that jazz is being studied, analyzed, documented, defined, and supported in white schools and communities, while being virtually ignored in black schools, that the comprehensive training in jazz a student receives at North Texas State, Indiana University, and the Berklee School of Music cannot be obtained in a black institution. Those of us who are attending this *seminar* should be doing more to change that situation.[3] We should be studying it, teaching it, presenting it, defining it, recording it, filming it, documenting it, performing it, publishing it, and most of all *supporting* it.

---

3. Apparently, Taylor's article was originally delivered as a conference paper. [RW]

53. "A Rare National Treasure"

OFFICIAL ARBITERS OF CULTURE IGNORED or dismissed jazz for much of its history, but by the 1980s, jazz had risen so far up the ladder of cultural prestige that many people forgot it had ever been controversial. A watershed moment came in 1987, when Congress passed a resolution designating jazz "a rare and valuable national American treasure." During House debate of the resolution, its chief sponsor, Representative John Conyers, Jr. of Michigan, pointed out that jazz musicians have been highly effective ambassadors, "bringing disparate groups of people and countries together," yet "the Congress had never once spoken on this subject of its appreciation to these unique artists who have promulgated this unique art form." Conyers was right: the State Department had been eager to use jazz musicians to polish the country's image since the start of the Cold War, but official approval of the music had been withheld. In particular, government arts funding flowed overwhelmingly to classical music organizations, particularly symphony orchestras. With this resolution, however, the U.S. government officially expressed its approval of jazz and asserted that it is an important part of the cultural heritage of American youth—a statement with at least potential ramifications for public music education and arts funding.

Despite the air of celebration during discussion of the resolution, undercurrents of disagreement swirled in the House. The wording of the resolution embraces conflicting interpretations: jazz is both a music of the people *and* an art form; it enacts both individual expression *and* democratic cooperation. Both Conyers and Representative Mervyn Dymally, of California, expressed concern about the greater prestige and popularity jazz has found in other countries, particularly Japan. "I have been in countries throughout Europe in which many people thought that the art form [jazz] was their art form," remarked Conyers; one motive for the resolution appears to have been a patriotic urge to set the record straight. In contrast, Representative Constance Morella of Maryland discounted the political significance of the music, insisting that "jazz belongs to the world." And while Representative Conyers emphasized the Afro-American roots of jazz, Representative Henry

Source: Congressional Record—House, September 23, 1987, H7825–27.

Gonzalez of Texas stressed the ethnic and racial diversity of the musicians who have played it throughout the century. No one talked about the broader framework of cultural hierarchy and legitimation, however: if jazz is singled out as worthy of study and support, does that open the door for other American popular musics—rap, rock, rhythm and blues, country—or close it?

H. Con. Res. 57

Whereas, jazz has achieved preeminence throughout the world as an indigenous American music and art form, bringing to this country and the world a uniquely American musical synthesis and culture through the African-American experience and—

1. makes evident to the world an outstanding artistic model of individual expression and democratic cooperation within the creative process, thus fulfilling the highest ideals and aspirations of our republic,
2. is a unifying force, bridging cultural, religious, ethnic, and age differences in our diverse society,
3. is a true music of the people, finding its inspiration in the cultures and most personal experiences of the diverse peoples that constitute our Nation,
4. has evolved into a multifaceted art form which continues to birth and nurture new stylistic idioms and cultural fusions,
5. has had a historic, pervasive, and continuing influence on other genres of music both here and abroad, and
6. has become a true international language adopted by musicians around the world as a music best able to express contemporary realities from a personal perspective; and

Whereas, this great American musical art form has not yet been properly recognized nor accorded the institutional status commensurate with its value and importance;

Whereas, it is important for the youth of America to recognize and understand jazz as a significant part of their cultural and intellectual heritage;

Whereas, in as much as there exists no effective national infrastructure to support and preserve jazz;

Whereas, documentation and archival support required by such a great art form has yet to be systematically applied to the jazz field; and

Whereas, it is in the best interest of the national welfare and all of our citizens to preserve and celebrate this unique art form: Now, therefore be it

Resolved by the House of Representatives (the Senate concurring), That it is the sense of the Congress that jazz is hereby designated as a rare and valuable national American treasure to which we should devote our attention, support, and resources to make certain it is preserved, understood, and promulgated.

54. Soul, Craft, and Cultural Hierarchy

ENERGETIC, ARTICULATE, AND MUSICALLY impressive, Wynton Marsalis (b. 1961) brings considerable weight to the contention that jazz is superior to other popular musical genres, and to a restrictive view of the jazz tradition. As forcefully opinionated as he usually is, though, Marsalis was brought up short a few times during this joint interview with keyboardist Herbie Hancock (b. 1940). For Marsalis, free jazz, electric instruments, and pop influences blur that tradition's boundaries and dilute its artistic force. For Hancock, these are all vital resources for the creative musician. But despite Hancock's interest in other genres, his credentials as a virtuosic bebopper are beyond reproach, making arguments about the musical limitations of pop musicians tricky for Marsalis. Moreover, years earlier, handing the young trumpeter one of his first big breaks, Hancock had invited Marsalis to tour with him, bassist Ron Carter, and drummer Tony Williams—the legendary rhythm section that had backed Miles Davis in the 1960s. So Marsalis is in a bind: while he does not respect what Hancock respects, he cannot help respecting Hancock.

In this interview for *Musician* magazine (moderated by journalists Rafi Zabor and Vic Garbarini), each musician reveals much about his values, goals, and musical training. Their disagreements are instructive, reminding us of the many consequences of how we think about jazz's past and future. Both musicians are principled and passionate. For Marsalis, "black music is being broken down"; for Hancock, the more walls come down, the better.

MUSICIAN: We don't want to get you guys into an argument.
HANCOCK: Oh, we won't, we never argue.
MARSALIS: I would never argue with Herbie.
MUSICIAN: I'll tell what we want to start with. Is there a necessity for any young player, no matter how brilliant he is, to work his way through a tradition?
MARSALIS: That's a hard question to answer. When we deal with anything that's European, the definitions are clear cut. But with our stuff it all comes from blues, so "it's all the same." So that'll imply that if I write an arrangement, then my

---

Source: Rafi Zabor and Vic Garbarini, "Wynton Vs. Herbie: The Purist and the Crossbreeder Duke It Out," *Musician 77* (March 1985), pp. 52–64. Reprinted by permission of Vic Gabarini and Rafi Zabor.

arrangement is on the same level as Duke Ellington. But to me it's *not* the same. So what I'm trying to determine is this terminology. What is rock 'n' roll? What does jazz mean, or R&B? Used to be R&B was just somebody who was black, in pop music they are white. Now we know the whole development of American music is so steeped in racist tradition that it defines what we're talking about.

***MUSICIAN*:** Well there's the Berklee School of Music approach, where you learn technique. And some people would say, "Well, as long as it's coming from the heart, it doesn't matter about technique."

MARSALIS: That is the biggest crock of bullshit in the history of music, that stuff about coming from the heart. If you are trying to create art, the *first thing* is to look around and find out what's meaningful to you. Art tries to make life meaningful, so automatically that implies a certain amount of emotion. Anybody can say "I have emotion." I mean, a thousand trumpet players had soul and emotion when they picked up trumpets. But they weren't all Louis Armstrong. Why?

HANCOCK: He was a better human being.

MARSALIS: Because Louis Armstrong's technique was better.

***MUSICIAN*:** Is that the only thing, though?

MARSALIS: Who's to say that his soul was greater than anybody else's? How can you measure soul? Have any women left him, did he eat some chicken on Saturday night? That's a whole social viewpoint of what payin' dues is. So Duke Ellington shouldn't have been great because by definition of dues he didn't really go through as much as Louis Armstrong, so naturally his piano playing didn't have the same level of soul. Or Herbie wasn't soulful, either. Because when he was coming up, black people didn't have to eat out of frying pans on Friday nights.

***MUSICIAN*:** Well, one of the ways of judging soulfulness, as you say, is suffering. But it's not the only way.

MARSALIS: I read a book [by James Lincoln Collier] where a cat said that "in 1920-something we notice that Louis Armstrong's playing took on a deeper depth of emotion. Maybe that's because his mother died." What brings about soulfulness is realization. That's *all.* You can realize it and be the richest man in the world. You can be someone living in the heart of Harlem in the most deprived situation with no soul at all. But the social scientists . . . oh, soul. That's all they can hear, you know. Soul is part of technique. Emotion is part of technique. Music is a craft, man.

HANCOCK: External environment brings fortune or misfortune. Both of them are means to grow. And that's what soul is about: the growth or, as Wynton said, realization. To realize how to take that experience and to find the depth of that experience in your life. If you're able to do that, then everything becomes fortune.

MARSALIS: The thing that makes me most disgusted is that a lot of guys who write about the music don't understand the musicians. People have the feeling that jazz is an expression of depression. What about Louis Armstrong? To me, his thing is an expression of joy. A celebration of the human condition.

HANCOCK: Or the other concept is somebody who, out of his ignorance and stupidity, dances and slaps his sides. No concept of intelligence, focus, concentration . . . and the study, the concern. Even the self-doubt and conflict that goes into the art of playing jazz.

Look, I didn't start off playing jazz. I hated jazz when I first heard it. It sounded like noise to me. I was studying classical music, and at the same time, going to an all-black grammar school. I heard groups like the Ravens. But I really didn't have many R&B records. I was like a little nerd in school.

MARSALIS: Well, I don't know about *that.*

HANCOCK: Jazz finally made an impression on me when I saw a guy who was my age improvising. I thought that would be impossible for somebody my age, thirteen or fourteen, to be able to create some music out of his head.

I was a classical player, so I had to learn jazz the way any classical player would. When it came to learning what one feels and hears as soulful nuances in the music, I actually had to learn that technically.

MARSALIS: That's interesting, because I did it the opposite way. When you put out *Headhunters* and *Thrust,* Branford [Marsalis] and I listened to those albums, but we didn't think it was jazz. My daddy would play jazz, but I was like, Hey, man, I don't want to hear this shit. I grew up in New Orleans—Kenner, Louisiana, actually, a country town. All I ever did was play "When the Saints" and stuff. I couldn't really play, I had no technique. So when I came to high school, everybody else could play the trumpet and I was the saddest one. The first record I heard was [John Coltrane's] *Giant Steps.* My daddy had all those records, but I never would listen to them. Why listen to jazz, man?

HANCOCK: None of your friends were playing it?

MARSALIS: None of the people I knew. You couldn't get no women playing jazz! Nobody had a philosophy about what life was supposed to be about. We didn't have a continuum. I never listened to Miles or Herbie. I didn't even know you played with Miles, until I was sixteen. Then when I started listening to jazz, I would only listen to a certain type. Only bebop. So I can relate to starting from a fan-type approach. But when you play music, you're going to play the way you are.

***MUSICIAN*:** What about your statement at the Grammys?

MARSALIS: It was very obvious what I was saying.

HANCOCK: I have to congratulate you on that. You implied that there was good music and music that was in bad taste. Everybody wondered, "What music is he referring to?"

MARSALIS: Listen, the only statement I made was that we're trying to elevate pop music to the level of art. Not just in music. Pop culture. Pop anything. I have nothing against pop music. I listen to the radio. I'm not saying people should listen to jazz or buy jazz records, or even know the music. Just *understand* what the music is about, because the purpose and the function of pop music is totally different from jazz.

HANCOCK: A few people that have interviewed me have asked me if the statement that he made was directed against what I was doing. That never dawned on me.

MARSALIS: I wasn't even thinking about that.

***MUSICIAN*:** A lot of people do think that.

MARSALIS: People think I'm trying to say jazz is greater than pop music. I don't have to say that, that's *obvious.* But I don't even think about it that way. The two musics say totally different things. Jazz is *not* pop music, that's all. Not that it's greater. . . . I didn't mean it was obvious.

HANCOCK: That's your opinion, which is fine. Now you're making a statement of fact.

***MUSICIAN*:** So is classical music "greater" than jazz?

MARSALIS: Hell no, classical music is a European idiom. America has a new cultural identity. And the ultimate achievement for any culture is the creation of an art form. Now, the basic element of our art form is the blues, because an art form makes life meaningful. Incidentally, I would like to say—and I hope you will print this—classical music is *not* white music. When Beethoven was writing music, he wasn't thinking white or black. Those terms became necessary in

America when they had to take white artists and make them number one because they couldn't accept black artists. We constantly have historical redefinitions to take the artistic contributions out of the hands of people who were designated black. The root of the colloquial stuff throughout the whole world now comes out of the U.S. Negro's lifestyle.

***MUSICIAN*:** Is there something in some of the rootforms of this music that has a certain inner strength?

MARSALIS: People don't know what I'm doing basically, because they don't understand music. All they're doing is reacting to what they think it remotely sounds like.

We don't have to go *back* to the sixties. Beethoven didn't have to go *back* to Haydn. We never hear that. What they say is, Well, Beethoven is an extension of Haydn. Everybody has to do that—Stravinsky, Bartok. But in European music people have a cultural continuum. And our music is just, "Well, what is the next new Negro gonna think up out of the blue sky that's gonna be innovative?" Ornette Coleman sounds like Bird; he was playing rhythm changes on "The Shape of Jazz to Come." Have I ever read that by anybody reviewing those albums? No. Why? Because they don't know what rhythm changes sound like. So they're gonna write a review on what I'm doing and I'm supposed to say, "That's cool."

HANCOCK: When you first asked the question, I heard it as sensitively as he heard it. 'Cause I said to myself, "He's saying Wynton is going back to play the sixties-style of music in 1984."

***MUSICIAN*:** We all agreed apparently at one point that jazz was more meaningful, in some sense, than pop music. Since you work in the two idioms, what do you feel is different?

HANCOCK: Wait a minute. I *don't* agree. Let me address myself to that. When we have life, we have music. Music can be manifest in many different forms, and as long as they all have purpose, they shouldn't be pitted against each other as one being more important than the other. That's stupid. That's like apples and oranges.

***MUSICIAN*:** All right, you're doing both. What's the difference in the quality of the experience with each kind of music?

HANCOCK: Let me tell you how I started getting my feet wet with pop music. When I got into high school and started getting into jazz, I didn't want to hear anything else but classical music and jazz. No R&B, nothing, until I heard James Brown's "Papa's Got a Brand New Bag." Later on, when I heard [Sly and the Family Stone's] "Thank You Falettinme Be Mice Elf Agin," it just went to my core. I didn't know *what* he was doing, I mean, I heard the chorus but, how could he *think* of that? I was afraid that that was something I couldn't do. And here I am, I call myself a musician. It bothered me. Then at a certain point I decided to try my hand at funk, when I did *Headhunters*. I was not trying to make a jazz record. And it came out sounding different from anything I could think of at the time. But I still wasn't satisfied because in the back of my head I wanted to make a funk record.

I had gotten to the point where I was so directed toward always playing something different that I was ignoring the validity of playing something that was familiar. Visually I symbolize it as: There's the space from the earth up to somewhere in the sky, then I was going from the sky up to somewhere further up in the sky. And this other thing from the earth up to the sky I was kind of ignoring. And so one thing about pop music that I've discovered is that playing something that's familiar or playing the same solo you played before has no negative connotations whatsoever. What's negative is if it doesn't sound, each time, like it's the first time you played it. Now, that's really difficult for me to do. Take Wah Wah Watson, for example. He's not a solo player, he's a rhythm player. But he used to play a little solo on one tune and it would be the same solo every night. And every night he would get a bigger hand than I would. And every night it was the same notes but it sounded fresh. So my lesson was to try to learn to play something without change, and have it sound fresh and meaningful.

MARSALIS: I look at music different from Herbie. I played in a funk band. I played the same horn parts every night all through high school. We played real funk tunes like Parliament Funkadelic, authentic funk. It wasn't this junk they're trying to do now to get their music played on white radio stations. Now, to play the Haydn Trumpet Concerto is a lot different from playing "Give Up the Funk" or "Mothership Connection." I dig "Mothership Connection," but to me what pop music is trying to do is totally different. It's really geared to a whole base type of sexual thing. I listen to the radio. I know tunes that they have out now: here's people squirming on the ground, fingering themselves. It's low-level realizations of sex. Now, to me, music to stimulate you is the music that has all the root in the world in it, but is trying to elevate that, to elevate the people to a certain level rather than go down.

HANCOCK: It's not like that, Wynton. If it were, it would just stay the same. Why would the music change?

MARSALIS: Because they get new computers. You tell me, what's the newest thing out that you've heard?

HANCOCK: Okay, Prince, let's take that.

MARSALIS: What is the tune "Purple Rain"? Part of it is like a little blues. I've got the record, I listen to it all the time. The guitar solo is a rehash of some white rock.

***MUSICIAN*:** It's a rehash of Hendrix, too.

MARSALIS: Well, I'm not gonna put that on his head because he can do stuff Hendrix never thought of doing, which a lot of people want to overlook just to cut him down and say he sounds like Hendrix. You can print that if you talk about him. But there's no way you can get new in that type of music because the message will always be the same.

HANCOCK: There are songs that have a lot of musical episodes. I saw Rick Springfield's video. I don't care if he's got a bad reputation. I heard some harmonic things that were really nice.

MARSALIS: You can get the newest synthesizers, but that music'll only go to a certain level. I'm not saying that's negative.

***MUSICIAN*:** In a sense you're describing what Herbie's doing.

MARSALIS: He knows what he's doing, right? [laughs]

HANCOCK: It's *not* true because I know. You mention drum machines. There are examples of pop music today using drum machines specifically in a very automated way. Automation doesn't imply sex to me at all. It's the opposite of sex.

MARSALIS: But that's not what we're talking about.

HANCOCK: You said the music is about one thing, and it's about sex. And I'm saying it's not just about that.

MARSALIS: We don't even want to waste our time discussing that because we *know* that that's what it's about.

HANCOCK: If you name specific things, I would certainly agree with you. If you say dancing is about sex, I would agree with you, too. But I think you're using some false ammunition.

MUSICIAN: In most of the world's traditions sex is both connected with the highest creative aspects and then can be taken to the lowest basic—

MARSALIS: That's what I'm saying. What direction you want to go with it and which level it's marketed on. When I see stuff like videos with women looking like tigers roaming through the jungle, you know, women playing with themselves, which is cool, man, but to me that's the high school point of view. The problem I have is when people look at that and start using terms like "new video art with such daring concepts."

A lot of stuff in our society is racially oriented, too. I read a quote from Herbie. He said, "I heard that people from MTV were racist oriented and I didn't want to take any chances, so when I did my video I made sure they didn't focus on me and that some of the robots' faces were white." That somebody like him would have to make a statement like that. . . .

MUSICIAN: That is a heavy statement.

MARSALIS: But what he's saying is true. Maybe they wouldn't have played his video. And what pisses me off is the arrogance of people whose whole thing is just a blatant imitation of the negroidal tradition. Blatant. And even the major exponents of this type of music have said that themselves. And they'll have the arrogance and the audacity to say, "Well, we just gonna play white people's videos." How am I supposed to relate to that?

MUSICIAN: On the other hand, "Rockit" won five video awards. It partly broke open MTV; there are now more black acts on. And now kids in the heartland who have never heard black music are beginning to hear it. It's probably because of what you did.

MARSALIS: They're still not hearing it. Black music is being broken down. It's no longer black music. This is not a discussion or argument. You get the Parliament records and the EW&F [Earth, Wind & Fire] and the James Brown, the Marvin Gaye, and you listen. What I hear now is just obvious rock 'n' roll elements like Led Zeppelin. If people want to do that, fine. If they want to sell more records, great. What I'm saying is, that's reaffirmation of prejudice to me. If bending over is what's happening, I'm going to bend over.

MUSICIAN: Is there another side? What do you think, Herbie?

HANCOCK: Well, Wynton is not an exponent of the idea that blending of musical cultures is a good thing.

MARSALIS: Because it's an *imitation* of the root. It loses roots because it's *not* a blending. It's like having sex with your daughter.

HANCOCK: Okay, let me say this because this is something that I know. Up until recently a black artist, even if he felt rock 'n' roll like Mick Jagger, couldn't make a rock 'n' roll record. Because the media actually has set up these compartments that the racists fit things into. You can hear elements of rock from black artists.

MARSALIS: You don't just hear elements. What I hear in them is blatant, to the point of cynicism.

HANCOCK: Okay, okay. I'm not disagreeing. I know that there have been black artists that have wanted to do different kinds of music than what the R&B stations would play. That to me is more important, the fact that we can't do what we want to.

MARSALIS: I'm agreeing with you, everybody should do what they want to do. But what's happening is, our vibe is being lost. I see that in movies. I see it on television. What you have now is white guys standing up imitating black guys, and black guys sitting back and looking at an imitation of us saying, "Ohhh . . ." with awe in their faces. You have black children growing up with Jehri curls trying to wear dresses, thinking about playing music that doesn't sound like our culture.

MUSICIAN: Does Herbie "hear" what he's doing?

MARSALIS: Herbie hears what Herbie plays. But a lot of that music Herbie is not writing. And when Herbie is playing, he's gonna make the stuff sound like Herbie playin' it.

HANCOCK: Let me explain something about "Rockit." If you're a black artist doing some forms of pop music, which "Rockit" is, you have to get on black radio and become a hit. And if you get in the top twenty in black radio—or urban contemporary they call it now [laughter]—anyway, if it's considered crossover material, then at that point the record company will try to get the rock stations to play it. And so I said to myself, "How can I get this record exposed as quickly to the white kids as to the black kids?" So the video was a means to an end.

MUSICIAN: Did it bother you, having to make that decision?

HANCOCK: I didn't care about being in the video. I don't care about being on the album cover of my record. It's not important to me. Why should I have to be in my own video? [Marsalis winces]

MUSICIAN: But why *shouldn't* you? I mean, it's your video.

HANCOCK: That was not an issue with me. I'm not on the cover of most of my records. What I care about is whether the cover looks good or not. I wanted the video to be good. That's the first thing. The second thing I said: Now, how am I gonna get on there, because I want to get my record heard by these kids?

MUSICIAN: Can't you see this strategy is a way of breaking something in?

MARSALIS: If you cheese enough, they'll make you President.

HANCOCK: I wasn't cheesing. I was trying to get heard.

MUSICIAN: He broke open the medium, partially.

MARSALIS: Michael Jackson broke the medium open. Let's get that straight. What's amazing to me is that [Herbie's] thing was used by all the cats that were doing break dancing.

HANCOCK: There were three things against it. First of all, no vocals. Secondly, that kind of music wasn't even getting any airplay at that time. Third thing is my name.

MARSALIS: Right. But the only thing that I hate, the only thing that disgusts me about that is I've seen Herbie's thing on *Solid Gold* as "New Electronic" type of jazz or something. I mean, it's a *pop* tune, man. Our whole music is just going to continue to be misunderstood. You have to understand that people who hear about me, they don't listen to the music I play. If I have girlfriends, they don't listen to what I'm playing. They don't care. They only know Wynton as an image. Or Wynton, he's on the Grammys, he has a suit on. So their whole thing is media oriented. I'm not around a lot of people who listen to jazz or classical music, forget that! I did a concert and people gave me a standing ovation before I walked onto the stage. But in the middle of the first piece they were like [nods off] . . . so that lets you know right there what's happening.

MUSICIAN: Is this a black audience?

MARSALIS: Black people. Yeah, this is a media thing, you understand. I'm talking to people who are in the street.

HANCOCK: I understand what you're talking about, about black artists with Jehri curls and now with the long hair. And I don't mean the Rastas, either. . . .

MARSALIS: Well, check it out. Even deeper than that, Herbie, is when I see brothers and sisters on the TV. I see black athletes, straining to conform to a type of personality that will allow them to get some more endorsements. What disturbs me is it's the best people. When somebody is good, they don't have to do that. I was so happy when Stevie's album came out. I said, Damn, finally we got a groove and not somebody just trying to cross over into some rock 'n' roll.

HANCOCK: I understand what you mean about a certain type of groove, like this is the real R&B, and so forth. But I can't agree that there's only one way we're supposed to be playing. I have faith in the strength of the black contribution to music, and that strength is always going back to the groove, anyway. After a while certain things get weeded out. And the music begins to evolve again.

MARSALIS: Now, check out what I'm saying—

HANCOCK: No, 'cause you've talked a lot—

MARSALIS: Okay, I'm sorry. I'm sorry, man.

HANCOCK: [laughter] Give me a break! I've never been on an interview with you, so I didn't know how it was. Wowww! I understand what you're saying, but I have faith that whatever's happening now is not a waste of time. It's a part of growth. It may be a transition, but transition is part of growth, too. And it doesn't bother me one bit that you hear more rock 'n' roll in black players, unless it's just not good. The idea of doing rock 'n' roll that comes out of Led Zeppelin doesn't bother me. I understand it's third-hand information that came from black people to begin with, but if a guy likes it, play it. When Tony Williams and I first left Miles, we did two different things. My orientation was from a funk thing. What Tony responded to was rock 'n' roll. That's why his sound had more of a rock influence than *Headhunters.* I can't say that's negative.

MARSALIS: I agree with what Herb has said. If somebody wants to go out with a dress on, a skirt, panties—that's their business. But what happens is not that one or two people do that. Everybody has to do that. It doesn't bother me that [black] comedians can be in film, I think that's great. And the films are funny. What bothers me is that *only* comedians can be in films.

I think since the sixties, with people on TV always cursing white people but not presenting any intellectual viewpoint, that any black person who tries to exhibit any kind of intellect is considered as trying not to be black. We have allowed social scientists to redefine what type of people we are. I play some European [music] to pay respect to a great, great music which had nothing to do with racial situations. Beethoven wasn't thinking about the social conditions in America when he wrote something, he was thinking about why did he have to get off the street for the princes. So his music has the same type of freedom and struggle for abolition of the class system, as Louis Armstrong's music is a celebration of that abolition. See, Beethoven's music has that struggle in it. Louis Armstrong is the resolution of that. This gigantic cultural achievement is just going to be redefined unless I take an active part in saying what I think is correct.

HANCOCK: Now that you've voiced all—not all, but *many* of your objections—what do you do about it? How do we make it better? If all we do is complain. . . .

MARSALIS: We're not complaining. We're providing people with information.

HANCOCK: Well, there's two ways to provide people with information. One way is to point your finger at them or intimidate them by pulling at their collars. But many times what that does is it makes the person feel uncomfortable, and then if he starts to get on the defensive, you've lost more ground than you've gained. So I've found from my own life that I can get more accomplished by getting a person inspired to do something. Inspiration, not intimidation.

MARSALIS: 'Cept intimidation is good, too.

HANCOCK: This is where you and I differ. I haven't said much before because I'm not like that.

MUSICIAN: You've really defined your point of view in terms of this interview, and Herbie hasn't yet.

MARSALIS: I was talking too much. Sorry I was being uncool.

HANCOCK: No, no, no. It was cool. It's all right. I'll come back another day when you're not here. . . . [general laughter]

MARSALIS: The problem is in the educational system. I've had conversations with people about you. Musicians have no idea who you are. They have no understanding or respect for being able to play. It's just like they think they're you or something. The first question I hear everywhere is, "How do you get over? How did you get your break with Herbie?" I said, "When I was with Herbie and them, I was just fortunate to be on the bandstand. Just to be learning from Herbie. . . ." No, seriously, man, I'm not saying it to kiss your ass. You know it's true.

HANCOCK: That's what I feel about him. He came in with one trumpet, nineteen years old playing with me, Ron, and Tony.

MARSALIS: I was scared.

HANCOCK: When I heard him play, then I had to call up Ron and Tony and say—

MARSALIS: Hey, this mother is sad. [laughs]

HANCOCK: Look, it's gonna work. What he did was so phenomenal. You remember that tour. That tour was bad.

MARSALIS: I learned so much on that tour, man.

HANCOCK: So did I, man. You taught me a lot. You made me play. Plus you made me get some new clothes. [laughs]

MARSALIS: I can get publicity until I'm a hundred. That's not gonna make me be on the level with cats like Miles or Clifford [Brown], or know the stuff that you know. Even "Rockit" has elements that I can relate to. But in general you made funk cats musicians. And that has been overlooked.

MUSICIAN: In the end, were the compromises involved in doing the video worth it?

HANCOCK: I had a choice. And I'm proud of the choice that I made. But as a result, what happened? Between Michael Jackson's video and my video, the impact opened the thing up. Now, I'm sure Michael can take more credit for that. Anyway, if it was true that MTV was racist—

MARSALIS: It was true. You don't have to say "if."

HANCOCK: I have never claimed that to be true.

MARSALIS: I'll say it.

HANCOCK: I've only claimed that this is what I observe. But now you see plenty of videos with black artists. It doesn't even look like there's any difference anymore. Even though I wasn't even looking for that as a solution, if this additional thing was accomplished, I feel really good about that. And I feel good about getting five awards on MTV. They were trying to copy something before. Now they realize they have something that's more powerful than what they were trying to copy.

MARSALIS: The sound of Michael Jackson's music, the sound of Prince's music, the sound of "Rockit"—that sound is *not* black. People are consciously trying to be crossovers. I've read interviews where people say, "We take this type of music and we try to get this type of sound to appeal to this type of market to sell these many records."

MUSICIAN: Do you think Michael did that?

MARSALIS: Of course he did. But the thing that separates Michael Jackson from all other pop artists is the level of sincerity in his music.

MUSICIAN: You're saying he's got sincerity, and yet at the same time he contoured his sound?

MARSALIS: He's a special person. He's not contrived. What I don't understand is why he did that cut with Mick Jagger.

HANCOCK: I'll tell ya, I just did a record with Mick Jagger and, man, Mick Jagger's *bad.*

MARSALIS: Yeah, well. . . .

HANCOCK: I didn't know that. And you don't know that, either.

MARSALIS: I'm not doubting that he's bad. . . .

HANCOCK: Wynton, you *don't* know that.

MARSALIS: I'm not doubting that he's bad, Herbie. Check it out. But a lot of pop music is geared toward children. It's not something that I can really have a serious discussion about.

HANCOCK: You're right. It's geared toward teens and the preteens. So what it's doing is stimulating my own youth and allowing me to express my own youth. Because it's not like I'm doing my daughter's music. This is *my* music. And we both happen to like it because we both feel that youthful element. People tell me I look younger now than I did five years ago. And I do . . . except in the morning. [laughs] I would venture to say that a lot of it has to do with the music I'm playing now. Electric music, you know. I'm finding a door that hasn't been opened. That's exciting me, and I'm given the opportunity to use some elements from the "farthest out" jazz stuff in this music, and have it be unique.

***MUSICIAN*:** How do you get human feeling in automated, computerized music like that?

HANCOCK: First we create the music. Afterwards I sit back and listen, and sometimes I discover things that I wasn't really thinking about when I was doing them. I hear the elements that have warmth. Sometimes it's a particular synthesizer sound. But it could be how it's played.

MARSALIS: I'm coming off negative and that's not what I'm intending. . . . The purpose of pop music is to sell records that appeal to people on a level that they want to accept it on. If you put out a record and it doesn't sell, then your next response is, Why didn't the record sell? Let's try to do this or that to make the record sell.

***MUSICIAN*:** That's terribly condescending toward pop. . .

HANCOCK: Why are we asking him about pop music? What does *he* know about pop music?

MARSALIS: I know a lot about pop music.

HANCOCK: No, you don't.

MARSALIS: I played in pop—

HANCOCK: Wynton, you don't. You *think* you know.

MARSALIS: I don't want to mess with you.

HANCOCK: The very statement that you just made makes it obvious that you don't know.

MARSALIS: That's cool. I'm not going to get into it. I've had conversations with you, where you told me, "Man we're trying to get this kind of market." It's not like I don't know pop musicians. It's not like I don't listen to music.

HANCOCK: Then there's some things you misunderstand about it. Because I *never* use the word *sell.*

MARSALIS: I don't know. Remember what you told me before? "Yeah, man, my record just went gold, man. I need to get me some more records like that." We had long conversations about that. We shouldn't be arguing about this in the press, man. We have to be cool. We've talked about this already.

HANCOCK: Do you think I'd object if my records sold millions?

MARSALIS: Don't say you don't think about that.
HANCOCK: Of course I would.
MARSALIS: Because you do. You *do* think about that.
MUSICIAN: To think about it and have it as your aim are two different things.
HANCOCK: Thank you.
MARSALIS: I'm getting tired now. You said the opposite of what I wanted to hear.
HANCOCK: Look, I'd like to have a Rolls-Royce, too. But I'm not purposefully trying to set myself up to get a Rolls-Royce.
MARSALIS: Pop music is something that you don't really have to know too much to know about.
HANCOCK: [long silence] . . . Okay, next!
MUSICIAN: When you play pop music, do you feel as musically fulfilled as when you're playing jazz?
MARSALIS: Don't lie, Herbie.
HANCOCK: Okay. I only feel musically fulfilled when I can do both. If I don't play any jazz this year or half of next year, I'm gonna still be doing fine. But at a certain point I'm gonna want to play some. Now, what I wanted to say was when I did "Rockit," when I did *Light Me Up* . . . I'm not sitting down and saying, "What can I put in this music to make it sell?" That's what I *don't* do. When I'm sitting and actually making the music, I know my frame of mind. And you can't tell me—
MARSALIS: I can't tell you anything. . . .
HANCOCK: No, I'm being honest. Let's say you want to do cartoons, or make a comic book, and you're Gauguin. If Gauguin were to do a comic book, I would respect him if he had the same kind of attitude of trying to make something happen with the cartoon, and learn from dealing with a medium that's more popular than the one he's accustomed to.
MUSICIAN: What he's also saying is there's this evolutionary sweep that takes all these things in its stride. . . .
HANCOCK: I'm not looking at these things that you're objecting to as the end. I look at them more as an interim.
MARSALIS: It's just ignorance being celebrated to the highest level. If somebody wants to say anything that has any kernel of intellect, immediately the word elitist is brought out and brandished across the page to whip them back down into ignorance. Especially black artists and athletes. We are constantly called upon to have nothing to say. I'm just trying to stimulate . . . some kind of intellectual realization. I'm just trying to raise questions about why we as musicians have to constantly take into account some bullshit to produce what we want to produce as music, what Herbie is saying about evolution. Frankly, I never thought about it that way. But he brought out something interesting. All I can say is, I hope he's right.

55. A Music of Survival and Celebration

FEW PEOPLE LISTEN TO ONLY ONE KIND OF music, but scholars who cross musical boundaries are rare. One such is Christopher Small (1927–2011), whose brilliant meditations on musical meaning have been published as a trio of books: *Music-Society-Education* (1977), *Music of the Common Tongue: Survival and Celebration in Afro-American Music* (1987), and *Musicking: The Meanings of Performing and Listening* (1998). After earning music and science degrees in his native New Zealand, Small studied composition in London, where he then taught for some years. After retiring to Spain, he was able to devote more time to writing, while continuing to compose and perform.

Small's work reintroduced the gerund "musicking" to the modern world, as a way of urging us to think about music less as a product or a thing and more as a human activity. In this excerpt from his second book, jazz is the focus of a wide-ranging inquiry, its arguments supported by references to J. S. Bach, Balinese gamelans, and heavy metal. Small's central insight is that music is a matter of relationships and values. Musical activities, he argues, create particular kinds of relationships among the participants, providing opportunities for performers and audiences to explore and affirm identities. This perspective enables Small to illuminate cultural tensions—around black and white participation in jazz, for example, or between the opposite pulls of classical notation and blues orality—by analyzing the values that are sought and celebrated by those involved. In contrast to many portrayals of jazz as individualistic, Small highlights the communal aspects of the music, showing how individual experiences are inseparable from the social environments in which people live, develop, create, and relate.

Of all the styles of Afro-American music, in so far as they can be separated out from one another, that which is known as jazz is the one with which white intellectuals and classical musicians today feel most at ease. They manage to assimilate the values and the aesthetic of jazz to those with which they were brought up, and they feel able to accord to its artists a status and a respectability denied to other Afro-American musicians, and not far beneath that accorded to classical artists. This almost classical status is illustrated neatly by the fact that the British Broadcasting Corporation devotes

---

Source: Christopher Small, *Music of the Common Tongue: Survival and Celebration in Afro-American Music* (New York: Riverrun, 1987), pp. 311–20, 329–30, 332–35, 338–39. Reprinted courtesy the author.

about four hours of a total weekly airtime of some 120 hours on its classical-music channel to jazz. Among intellectuals and classical musicians the names, and the work, of Brubeck, Basie, and Beiderbecke are almost as familiar as those of Boulez, Beckett, and Bergman, and there exists a literary tradition of jazz scholarship, criticism, and exegesis, not shared by any other Afro-American style, going back fully fifty years to the pioneering writings of André Hodeir and Hugues Panassié. All this suggests that jazz has affinities with classical music that other Afro-American styles do not have.

Of all Afro-American musicians jazzmen, and jazzwomen, have always been the most eclectic; everything they hear, from blues to symphonic music to Anglo-Celtic folksong, from gospel to opera arias to the post-war avant garde, is grist to their mill. It may even be possible to propose a definition of jazz as that aspect of Afro-American musicking that has closest links with classical music. It is not a satisfactory definition, but it does have the merit of drawing attention to the fact that a major source of creative energy for the artist in jazz has come from the tensions between European, or Euro-American, and Afro-American values.

These tensions can be perceived in a number of ways. We can see them as between, on the one hand, the literate culture of western industrial society, with all its tendency towards centralization and standardization, and on the other the orality and decentralization of black American culture. In musical terms this can be heard as, on the one hand, composition through notation, the separation of composer from performer and the authority of the written text, and, on the other, improvisation, non-literate composition and the autonomy of the performer. As we have seen, the composition-improvisation antithesis has important implications for the kinds of relationship that are brought into being by a musical performance—how close to or distant from one another the participants are, how active or passive the listeners, and so on. We have seen, too, how the classical tradition has abandoned improvisation, and it is interesting to see how whenever that tradition has become dominant in jazz the space for improvisation has become curtailed; one could use the extent to which the musicians are obliged to rely on notation as a yardstick for determining which of the two cultures is dominant at any point in the history of jazz performance.

It is important to bear in mind that these two tendencies, or orientations, are not mutually exclusive, but exist side by side in most western people, white and black. We have seen that even the most literate of western people still acquire some of their most important cultural attitudes and assumptions through the oral-aural mode, from parents, elders and peers, even if in our society the superiority of the literate mode is assumed without discussion. Conversely, it should not need to be pointed out that black Americans are just as much at home in the literate mode as are their white compatriots—but they continue to place a higher value on orality, and tend to be more proficient and imaginative with the spoken word, than whites. The fact that a literate society is a centralized and hierarchical one, which Africans and Afro-Americans have traditionally resisted, is also important.

If the fundamental concern of all music is human relationships, the problem in group music making of all kinds, from symphony orchestras to Balinese gamelans to heavy-metal bands, is the establishment of workable relationships between the participants, which will allow room for the individual player to make full use of his or her musical skills and imagination to explore, affirm and celebrate an identity, while preserving that over-all order which is essential if the musicking is to generate any meaning either for performers themselves or for whoever is listening. Those relationships incarnate ideal human relationships as imagined by the participants, and both the technical problems encountered and the techniques used to solve them are metaphors for the problems, and the methods, of maintaining an acceptable social order.

In a symphony orchestra those problems have been solved, once and for all, by the evolution of a hierarchical structure and centralized authority vested partly in a composer and partly in a conductor, each of whose authority in his own area is absolute—an uneasy combination at best, at least when the composer is around to make his views known. Those who have worked in or with professional symphony orchestras know that while an orchestra's power structure may, in theory, be precisely defined and static, the actual day-to-day relationships are as edgy as those in any other industrial organization, with the players constantly challenging the conductor's authority and subjecting each new piece to the most merciless scrutiny. But, grumble and smoulder as they may, they make no serious attempt to depose either authority from his (it is rarely her) position, not surprisingly since without a conductor and a score they would be at a complete loss for anything to play or for how to play it. In a symphony orchestra, then, as in other kinds of classical performance today, the question of order has been settled in the way most contemporary governments would like to be able to settle it. The performances that are made possible by this centralized and authoritarian order can be of an indubitable splendour and brilliance, but they are bought at the price of the players' autonomy and of creative satisfactions that ought to be commensurate with the skills and the musicality that are demanded of them. The players are rewarded for this sacrifice in other ways, with a social status and a degree of financial security that is denied to their colleagues in vernacular musicking.

That there is necessarily an antithesis between individual freedom and social order is a notion that Europeans, and those who have absorbed European and Euro-American culture, have interiorized so completely that they scarcely even notice that they are thinking in that way, still less consider the possibility of alternatives. The notion is implicit in the activities of all contemporary governments, who take it for granted that considerable sacrifices of individual freedom are necessary to preserve a social order in which it is possible to live free from the fear of rape, pillage and robbery—and of conquest by the forces of other, like-minded governments. It is implicit in the writings of some of the greatest of European thinkers; the whole line of thought that is descended from Thomas Hobbes's *Leviathan* is based on it, while even Freud, in his last writings, mused despairingly on the repression that seems to be necessary if civilization is to exist at all. It is noticeable also in the whole organizational structure and the teachings of the Christian church, even if it is less in evidence in the recorded words of its founder. But in traditional African culture such an antinomy is by no means self-evident. As the Ewe proverb has it, "Man is man because of other men"; individual and society live, not in antagonism but in mutual dependency, the individual coming to fullest development only within the social framework, and the society flourishing only on the basis of fully realized individuals whose individuality is necessary for social health. The elaborate rituals of traditional African societies, the musicking, the dancing, the masking, the cult ceremonies, are all designed ultimately to mediate social and individual necessity, to bring them into harmony rather than merely to effect compromises between antagonists. We have seen how the Africans brought their social attitudes with them on the Middle Passage and how those attitudes became a powerful factor for survival in the terrible conditions of slavery and its aftermath, and I have suggested that Afro-American musical performances in this century, especially in blues and gospel, have been rituals that have continued to affirm and to celebrate the mutual support of individual and community.

To play jazz, for a black musician, is to go beyond such rituals into a more complex and even dangerous task; it is to move out from one's base in the community (that is, from blues and gospel music) and to engage oneself with the values and the assumptions of white society, going to meet them and to play with them, and trying on roles in symbolic fashion in relation to that culture and society through its musicking, discovering what is of use for oneself and for the community. Black jazz musicians are thus no less the ritual representatives of the community than are bluesmen and gospel singers, and their task is in many ways even more important. Conversely, when white musicians play jazz, they are in almost a complementary situation in exploring the values of the black culture. How deeply they are able to do this will depend on the extent to which they are able to submit to the social and musical values they find there; it is in a sense even more difficult for them than for their black confrères, since as members of the socially dominant culture they have more to unlearn, and more intellectual baggage to dispose of, before they can enter fully into the engagement.

But both are also engaging with that most pressing of twentieth-century problems: that of the relationship between freedom and social order, and they are empowered to do so by a style of musicking which does not assume that there is any necessary antithesis between the two. In jazz a soloist appears at his or her best (which is not the same as "most virtuosic") when collaborating with equals, the composer realizes his or her compositions most fully when they are taken up and developed by fellow musicians, the individual realizes his or her gifts best in the company of a committed group. Thus the notion found in many histories and other studies of jazz, of the great individual artist-hero—Charlie Parker, John Coltrane, Miles Davis for instance—creating out of his own nature and genius, has to be treated with great caution.

Of course, there have been many outstanding artists over the history of jazz, but we should beware of treating them as great isolated originators, as the classical tradition today treats Beethoven, Mozart, and J. S. Bach (it is strongly arguable that the way they are treated is a gross distortion of the real nature and achievement of those artists also) or indeed, as the world of commercial entertainment—showbiz—treats its stars. In so far as the jazz musician's world perforce overlaps with and partakes of the nature of both those worlds it is understandable that this should happen—and of course it does pay the musicians, who after all have a living to make in that world, to go along with it as far as they can—but it should never be forgotten that those who stand out as the "great names" in histories and other studies of jazz are no more than first among equals, and owe at least a part of their eminence to the labours of many other musicians. To say this is not in any way to detract from their gifts or their achievements, but simply to point out that the nature of jazz performance requires that performers, whether famous or obscure, function in skilled and close collaboration, and that they depend on one another in everything they do.

The words "composer" and "composition" therefore have a very different significance in jazz from classical musicking; in jazz as in the great age of classical music, to be a musician is primarily to be a performer, and those who compose regard composition simply as the creation of material for themselves and their colleagues to play. It is rare, though not unknown, for what is created to be a fully worked-out composition; more usually it is a springboard, which may or may not be notated, from which all the musicians may take off into collaborative creation. Many of these "compositions," such as Thelonious Monk's "Round About Midnight," Charles Mingus's "Goodbye Pork Pie Hat" and Charlie Parker's "Parker's Mood" are beautiful in themselves, but they reveal, and are meant to reveal, their full character only when the composer and his colleagues have played with them, in all seriousness and all fun (the two are not incompatible). The composer's gesture to his fellow musicians is one of love and trust in giving them a part of himself to make of it what they will, and it calls from those musicians a greater sense of responsibility and involvement than does the realization of a fully notated score. And in so far as there can be as many versions of the "piece" as there are occasions of its performance, the place and the listeners also make their contribution, just as in African musicking.

All too often, of course, the place is a sleazy nightclub with a minuscule bandstand, a tinny beat-up piano and a dressing room that is no more than a cupboard next to the gents' toilet, while the listeners are a crowd of drunken businessmen and their wives on a night out, but the musicians' loyalty to one another and to their musicking can still make the performance transcend the limitations of the occasion. And when the place is suitable (not necessarily either grand or luxurious), the listeners committed and the dancing skilled (for does not dancing reveal a deeper involvement with the musicking than just sitting still and listening?) the performance, for as long as it lasts, can transform the participants into a society of mutual love and responsibility, of deep and multi-valent relationships, that reveals the poverty of the affluent European society of a concert hall.

For a jazz performance is not as much about the *rejection* of European values as about *transcending* them, and about the incorporation of the oppositions of classical music into more realistic unities. Jazz musicians have always been concerned with classical music, not as representatives of an inferior culture trying to latch on to the superior, but as natural heirs who are claiming it as their birthright—or, rather, as a part of their birthright—and building it into their own synthesis. It is a dangerous game; the musician is constantly on both a musical and a social tightrope in attempting to reconcile the two sets of values. It is for this reason that, for all the excitement that can be generated by a jazz performance, the quality most valued by the musicians themselves is "cool"—that coolness of mind and clarity of musical judgement which together enable them to keep their balance while on the tightrope. The history of jazz is littered with, on the one hand, fine and even great musicians for whom the responsibility was too great, and, on the other, with musicians who have given in to the pull of one or the other culture.

There is a stereotype of a black jazz musician who, brilliant as he or she may be as performer, is nonetheless inadequate or worse in everyday relationships and the business of life, who is killed by drugs, alcohol and the appurtenances of high living; Charlie Parker and Billie Holiday are two often-quoted examples. They could not, we are led to believe, live out the ideal relationships which they brought into being with their music. This dissonance between the actual world and its relationships, and the ideal world which they have not just imagined but actually experienced, has always placed highly creative musicians in danger; Mozart, who died only two years older than Parker, was clearly overwhelmed by it, while even the archetypal artist-hero, Ludwig van Beethoven, managed somehow to survive twenty years more without ever coming to terms with the world in which he lived, or even being able to form a mature relationship with another human being. In the case of black artists the dissonance is intensified, only they know how deeply, by the racism of the society which they are obliged to inhabit, and for which they are creating their model of a community held together, not by coercion, but by love. The marvel is not that some succumb, but that so many survive, and survive triumphantly, with that ideal still alive, if not unscarred by their experiences. And that even those who, like Parker and Holiday, did succumb, continued to affirm their "philosophies of beauty and ethics" for as long as they were physically able.

The relative pulls of the two cultures spanned by jazz are not symmetrical, owing to the far higher social and financial rewards which the classical culture is able to offer to most musicians. A musician who accedes to the pull of the Afro-American culture will be found playing blues or gospel, in a musical ritual of a community that remains largely isolated from the mainstream of American society, and which continues to find within itself the resources for survival. For black musicians such a step is to move back into the maternal culture, a recharging of the batteries perhaps, which many, if not most, seem to do from time to time, while for white musicians, on the other hand, it is a venture not merely into a culture that still remains exotic and mysterious, not merely an adventure, but almost also a homecoming, an acknowledgement of one's real ancestors. For the musician playing jazz, it is the pull of the European classical culture that represents the greater threat, since as the dominant and socially superior culture it has more to offer. It can co-opt musicians almost without their realizing what is happening to them—a not infrequent happening in the history of Afro-American music as a whole. For the black musician it tends to be a no-win situation, as the guardians of the classical culture are liable to pat him on the head and make it clear to him that he is getting ideas above his station. Every so often there appears on the scene a young lion who is intent in storming the classical music citadel; I cannot help wondering whether what is in that citadel—the approbation of white middle-class audiences and critics—is really worth his effort.

The history of jazz can be seen as a struggle between the two sets of values, expressed in musical terms as a to-and-fro between solutions to the problem of freedom and order. Unlike the situation in classical music, the struggle presents us with no final solution, only with a constantly changing series of accommodations; perhaps the only conclusion to be drawn is that no conclusion is possible—something with which Africans would no doubt concur. It should, of course, not be assumed from this that relations between white and black musicians within jazz have been of hostility or even of opposition; the history of the art abounds with shining examples of amicable, even loving collaboration. But it is easy to understand that because a black musician is staking more on his musicking than a white one, it has been black musicians who have been mostly the leaders and innovators, since genuine musical innovation, as we have seen, is a matter not just of new sounds or techniques but of new forms of relationship. This has been a more urgent quest for blacks than for whites—though, God knows, the white majority is in more desperate and urgent need than it knows of what it can learn from its black compatriots. Albert Murray expresses it memorably when, writing in praise of certain white musicians, he says that they "eagerly embrace certain Negroes not only as kindred spirits but as ancestor figures indispensable to their sense of romance, sophistication and elegance as well. Negroes like Duke Ellington, Louis Armstrong, Bessie Smith, Billie Holiday, Chick Webb, Coleman Hawkins, and others too numerous to mention inspire white Americans like Woody Herman, Gerry Mulligan, and countless others to their richest sense of selfhood and their highest levels of achievement."[1]

"Ancestor figures," we notice—that is to say, models not only of music but also of values and conduct—and it can be said, not only that the most creative periods in the development of jazz have been those in which black musicians moved to throw off white domination of their art, but also that those same musicians have at those times quite consciously and deliberately chosen to re-assert the traditional social as well as musical values of their culture. At such key moments, it has been to the sources of black music, much of it outside the experience of whites, that they have turned for renewal; if, as is sometimes said, jazz should be called "Afro-American classical music," it is in the sense that Haydn, who was well in touch with the

1. Quoted in Geoff Wills, "Under Pressure," *International Musician*, October 1984, p. 46.

vernacular sources of his art, would have understood, while Boulez or Cage, to whom such nourishment seems to be inaccessible, would probably not. Murray does in fact, in his book *Stomping the Blues,* refer to the major figures of such moments—Louis Armstrong, Ornette Coleman, Charlie Parker and others—as bluesmen *tout court,* which is fair enough in a way, and does enable us to recognize the vernacular roots of their art but at the same time it ignores the important factor of cultural tension, which is far stronger in jazz than in blues and is not only a principal source of its creative energy but also a key to its human importance in our time.

The tendency to drift into easy solutions, based on imposed authority, to the problem of musical order was to recur frequently, and, indeed, is still with us. The temptation to do so grew greater over the 1920s as the size of bands increased in response to the need for bigger sounds to fill the ever-larger ballrooms without the aid of electronic amplification, and to the desire for a greater range and variety of instrumental colour. We see it occurring to various degrees in the big white, and some black, swing bands from Benny Goodman and Fletcher Henderson to Artie Shaw, and culminating in the relentlessly rehearsed arrangements of the Glenn Miller Band, whose ideals of instrumental blend are remarkably similar to those of the symphony orchestra, and whose working practices allowed no room for the uncertainties of improvised solos.

Jazz became during the 1930s and 1940s a popular music for the first and last time; the big bands appeared regularly in Hollywood films, and bandleaders were stars whose activities, and especially their sex lives, were reported and commented on as avidly as those of film stars—or, indeed, of rock and pop stars today. Jazz and jazz musicians had been co-opted to serve the values of white society, and its challenge had been defused.

This kind of jazz survives today, in showbands and backing bands, its style changed remarkably little since the 1940s. It survives also, interestingly, in educational institutions, whose "Jazz Ensemble," "Jazz Band" or "Show-band," usually under the baton of the Director of Music, can form a showpiece for the school's or college's progressive image. Such ensembles, however, are generally dependent on scores, usually commercial arrangements, which leave little room for either individual or group improvisation (they sometimes include fully notated "improvised" solos) and leave the conductor firmly in charge of everything that takes place. There is no conflict here with the values of the school, or of the centralized industrial state whose interests, as we have already noted, the school is designed to serve.

That such a solution is not inevitable even when a large number of musicians is involved can be seen from the history of jazz in the midwest and southwestern United States, especially in those blues-based bands, climaxing in the long-lived band of Count Basie, which sheltered from the Great Depression in the relative prosperity of the corrupt but freehanded Pendergast administration in Kansas City. The Basie band consisted of individuals each of whom was in his or her own right a musician of superb skill and musical intelligence, who realized those qualities to their fullest by placing them at the service of the common enterprise. It was a remarkable social, no less than musical, achievement, not the least of which lay in the realization that the problems can never be solved once and for all but must be solved again and again every day and require constant vigilance and diplomacy to keep the need for order and the need for freedom in harmony with each other. But the rewards were commensurate with the effort; judging from theirs recordings, I do not know of any of the major bands of the time, not even that of Duke Ellington himself, that could play with such power and such delicacy and with such evocation of the spirit of joy and of love as the Count Basie Orchestra. Those fifteen or so musicians, constantly free to create something new, must have felt most fully themselves when building their commonwealth of the spirit in collaboration with their listeners and dancers (we recall that it was Lester Young, the band's great tenor saxophonist of its peak years, who liked to play for dancers because "the rhythm of the dancers comes back to you"). Even if a large proportion of those listeners were just the proverbial tired businessmen on a night out, all but the most insensitive must have perceived, however faintly, the outlines of that commonwealth and have been touched, if not fully knowing why, by its values. In its later years, it is true, the band succumbed to some extent to pressures for a more smoothly complete product and became more dependent on written arrangements, with a consequent loss of the players' improvisatory freedom, but it remained a powerful and beautiful group right up to Basie's death in 1984.

The group which perhaps shows most clearly how delicate is the balance between improvisatory freedom and audible order is that of Duke Ellington. When the orchestra began playing, in 1923, it was a co-operative group, of which Ellington gradually assumed command, more, it seems, through a talent for leadership than through his musical skills, which were at that time somewhat sketchy. The orchestra's performances initially evolved on a collaborative basis, with all the musicians making creative contributions, and as Ellington began to take control it became simply a matter of his having a veto over those suggestions and ideas as they were tried out. The conditions under which they worked from 1927 to 1933, at Harlem's Cotton Club, where they were required to provide music not just for the patrons to dance to, but also for the lavish and often fantastic floor shows, demanded a type of composition that could be co-ordinated with choreography and repeated on successive nights—which meant using notation. It was under these conditions that they developed a way of working in which ideas presented by the leader, or by one of the sidemen, were tried over, added to and placed within a framework in such a way as to allow a considerable degree of improvising freedom to the various brilliant soloists in the orchestra. Only after this process had been gone through would the arrangement come into being and be written down—and even then it was possible for it to go on developing as it was performed.

That jazz served well enough the spirit of revolt in the 1920s is clear from the electric effect that bands, both black and white, had on the young (black bands did not get to record until 1923 and did not until much later gain the amount of exposure offered to white bands, while racially mixed bands were unthinkable until the 1930s),[2] especially on young middle-class whites and, perhaps even more explosively, on young middle-class blacks such as Edward Ellington in Washington, D.C., Fletcher Henderson in Georgia, and James Lunceford in Fulton, Missouri. As the carrier (one might say, the embodiment, since the values were embodied in the ways in which the music was played and responded to) of values which called into question those of white American culture of past and present, jazz was the natural medium of rebellion against the standards of prosperous middle-class America which had given the young everything except what they really needed: communality, warmth and emotional honesty.

What is implied here is that what attracted the young white musicians, and their equally young audiences, to jazz was not just new sounds and rhythms, but new relationships, those of the hitherto inaccessible culture. It does not matter too much that the whites' perceptions of black culture were coloured by a great deal of

2. The year was actually 1922, when Kid Ory first recorded. [RW]

romanticism and wishful thinking (we must remember that the society that was brought into existence in a jazz performance was, for blacks no less than for whites, an ideal, a potential rather than an actual society); what people believe affects what they do no less than what actually is, and the important thing was the view that jazz seemed to offer of an alternative set of values and relationships. Their elders, who remained apparently satisfied with white America as it was, felt otherwise, and social leaders—politicians, clergymen, teachers and medical men—thundered about the mental, physical and moral damage inflicted by jazz (the fulminations against rock 'n' roll in the 1950s had a familiar ring to those who had lived through the 1920s). The vehemence of the denunciations suggests an appreciation, even if it was not fully conscious, of the challenge offered to conventional assumptions about the nature of human societies by the music and the manner of its performance, but, given the preoccupations of white culture at the time, it is not surprising that most of the alleged dangers of jazz boiled down to the usual brew of sexual and racial fears. As in the 1950s, the outrage at the flouting of familiar values was compounded by fear disguised as contempt for the mysterious foreigners in their midst, who seemed to have access to pleasures and to sources of power denied to themselves.

None of this, I hope, should suggest that jazz as a way of musicking, or the issues that it raises, concerns black Americans only. For generations now there have been white musicians for whom jazz is a natural way of playing, who are motivated by nothing more or less than a need to affirm, explore, and celebrate values to which they feel closer than to the official ones of western society as embodied in classical music, and more profoundly than popular music permits. On the other hand, jazz will in all probability never again be a popular music; it is too uncomfortable for that. But those who are prepared to allow themselves to go with the tensions generated by that way of musicking can be rewarded with some of the most heartening musical experiences possible in western society today. Players and listeners are taking part in a process which at any point can end in disaster; the musicians have chosen to place themselves in the most delicate, subtle and dangerous relationship with their listeners, while the listeners have the responsibility of feeding back to the players the energy which they have received from them, so that when the performance is going well it resonates back and forth, to create a community in which at the same time all can feel fully realized as individuals. Contrary to what is often said, the excitement generated by a good jazz performance is not just physical, although the part played by bodily response and bodily movement must not be denied; it is the exhilaration of finding oneself, to use Albert Murray's words once more, raised "to the richest sense of selfhood and to the highest level of achievement." There is no product, no final solution to the problems, only the unending process of exploration, affirmation and celebration. The magic does not happen with every performance, even with the finest and most devoted performers and the most sympathetic of audiences and the most skilled of dancers; there are too many workaday pressures which militate against it, not least of which are the pressures on the musicians to produce a saleable and consistent product and to ease tension by submitting to routine. But the ideal remains, and is realized sufficiently often to make the enterprise worth while for both players and their listeners ("Once a year, if I'm lucky," said Dizzy Gillespie).[3]

---

3. Albert Murray, *The Omni-Americans: New Perspectives on Black Experience and American Culture* (New York: Outerbridge and Dienstfrey, 1970), p. 102.

PART 9

The Nineties

56. Who Listens to Jazz?

IN 1956, CRITIC LEONARD FEATHER DREW upon a *Down Beat* readers' poll to analyze "the jazz fan." Within that sample, he found ages clustered between 15 and 24, peaking at 20; there was little overlap with the audience for classical music, and most jazz fans hated rock and roll and rhythm and blues. Feather recorded more about what fans did (how many records they bought, whether they danced) than who they were, but previous attempts to find out who listened to jazz had been far less rigorous and more impressionistic.[1] In the 1980s and '90s, the National Endowment for the Arts commissioned a series of studies of American audiences for various arts, and solid data on the jazz fan of at least this period became available. The results, if not always surprising, are instructive in the context of the changing reception of jazz.

The survey data are analyzed here by musicologist Scott DeVeaux, whose thoughtful conclusion highlights the importance of the institutions that support and promote jazz.[2] If jazz does become accepted as "America's classical music," will it inherit classical music's wealthy, aging, and shrinking audience? Or will popular artists like Kenny G eventually be accepted as part of the stream of jazz history, as swing was? DeVeaux's findings remind us that what we think of the state of jazz depends on how we define it—and vice versa.

Source: Scott DeVeaux, "Jazz in America: Who's Listening?" *Research Division Report #31,* National Endowment for the Arts (Carson, California: Seven Locks Press, 1995), pp. 1–4, 36–37, 56–57.

1. Leonard Feather, "The Jazz Fan," in *The Encyclopedia Yearbook of Jazz* (New York: Horizon Press, 1956), pp. 27–48. See also, for example, Rudi Blesh, "The Jazz Audience," *New York Herald Tribune,* February 27, 1947, section V, p. 7:1; Leonard Feather, "Big Boom," *Redbook,* November, 1953, pp. 49–51, 109–12.

2. See also the excerpt from DeVeaux's "Constructing the Jazz Tradition," later in this volume.

Introduction/Executive Summary

In 1992, the National Endowment for the Arts (NEA) funded a broad-based statistical investigation into the audiences for various art forms in the United States. The Survey of Public Participation in the Arts (SPPA) for 1992 was the third such survey over the past decade. As in the two earlier surveys (conducted in 1982 and 1985), the 1992 survey listed jazz as one of seven "benchmark" arts activities. It gathered detailed information on the size and demographic characteristics of the jazz audience: those adult Americans who attend jazz events, participate in jazz through the media, perform jazz, or simply say they like the idiom.

This monograph examines the data from the 1992 survey and provides a context for interpretation. Many items are compared with the findings from the 1982 SPPA.[3] The information provided by the SPPAs, it must be emphasized, does not distinguish between potentially conflicting definitions of jazz—between, for example, the conventional definition of the "jazz tradition" favored by educators, critics, and the arts establishment, and the recent pop-oriented styles often referred to as "contemporary jazz." (Traditional jazz is nothing if not contemporary, with artists creating new music and charting new territory every year.) The SPPA figures should be understood as reliable data regarding the aggregate audience for jazz in all of its current manifestations. The respondents defined jazz as they saw fit.

The Potential Jazz Audience

The potential audience of jazz has grown significantly. About one-third of American adults (up from 26 percent in 1982) reported that they "liked jazz," and about 5 percent (up from 3 percent in 1982) reported that they liked jazz "best of all" musical genres. In 1992, 25 percent of adult Americans expressed a desire to attend jazz performances more often than they do now, compared with 18 percent in 1982.

Only half of those who preferred jazz to any other musical form attended a jazz event during the previous year. Supply may have been a limitation, but there are few data on changes in the number of opportunities to participate in jazz. Anecdotal evidence indicates a gradual shift from private commercial venues, such as night clubs, to public sites, such as civic auditoriums and colleges. Record companies have greatly expanded their jazz output, focusing, surprisingly, on the "authentic" kind of jazz as well as on its easily marketed "accessible" counterpart. Commercial and public radio have expanded jazz programming, and there are a few all-jazz stations.

Size of the Jazz Audience

In 1992, approximately 10 percent of adult Americans (19.7 million) attended a jazz performance during the previous year, and 20 percent listened to a jazz recording. These figures are approximately the same as those reported for 1982. But 22 percent watched jazz on television in some form (broadcast or videotape), up from 18 percent in 1982; and 28 percent listened to jazz radio, a dramatic increase over the 18 percent a

3. These findings are summarized in Harold Horowitz, "The American Jazz Audience," pp. 1–8 in David N. Baker, ed., *New Perspectives on Jazz* (Washington: Smithsonian Institution Press, 1990). [RW]

decade earlier. The growth in jazz radio is attributable in part to the spread of new pop-jazz formats (e.g., New Adult Contemporary) on commercial radio and to the increased popularity of more traditional forms of jazz on public broadcasting.

Cross-tabulations of the 1992 SPPA data show that most of those who attend jazz performances also participate in jazz through the media at a rate three times that of the population as a whole. Of those who attend jazz performances, 76 percent listen to jazz on the radio, 67 percent listen to jazz recordings, and 61 percent watch jazz on some form of television. About a third of those who listen to jazz recordings also attend concerts.

The 1992 survey provides, for the first time, data on the frequency of attendance. Those who attended a jazz performance during the previous year did so an average of 2.9 times—higher than comparable rates for any of the other benchmark performing arts. But a large majority of those attending jazz events did so less frequently than this average: 44 percent attended only once, while an additional 26 percent attended only twice. Thus, a small percentage of the jazz audience forms a disproportionately large share of the total number of attendees. Even so, the total number of attendances at jazz events was nearly as large as that for classical music.

Demographic Characteristics of the Jazz Audience

The overall profile reveals an audience base that is affluent, well educated, youthful, and ethnically diverse. The frequency-of-attendance data show that the audience that frequently participates in jazz is strikingly male, well educated, well off, and black, in comparison with the general adult population. These findings are consistent with readership surveys by jazz magazines.

Participation in jazz correlates strongly with education and income. Nearly half of those attending jazz performances, for example, are college graduates; over three-quarters have had some college education. Those earning more than $50,000 a year are more than twice as likely to attend performances as those earning less than $25,000. In this respect, the audience profile for jazz resembles that of the other benchmark arts activities, for which the highest rates of participation are found among the most affluent and highly educated.

The jazz audience is predominantly youthful, especially when compared with the audiences for the other benchmark arts activities. Over two-thirds of those attending jazz performances are under 45, with a peak in the age group of 25 to 34. But comparison with the 1982 figures shows a distinct greying trend, with decreases in nearly all forms of jazz participation or preference in the 18-to-24 age group compensated by increases in groups over age 34. The 1992 SPPA data show a striking increase in the participation in jazz through the media by respondents 75 and older. A possible explanation is that by 1992 this group had long been exposed to jazz during the years when musical tastes are likely to be formed.

The demographic profile of the audience with respect to gender and race reveals other qualities unique to jazz. Participation rates are consistently higher for men than for women; although men make up only 48 percent of the adult population in the United States, the audience for most forms of participation in jazz is 52 to 54 percent male. In contrast, *in all other benchmark arts activities,* participation rates are higher for women than for men. Similarly, participation rates for African Americans are consistently higher than for white Americans; although blacks make up 11 percent of the adult population, between 16 and 20 percent of the audience for various forms of participation in jazz is black. Jazz is unique among the benchmark activities in being derived from African American traditions.

The statistics on frequency of attendance and on those who prefer jazz to all other musical genres provide a way of focusing on the characteristics of the most loyal and intense sector of the jazz audience. Within this small but influential group, the findings with regard to race and gender, noted above for the jazz audience as a whole, become sharper, with males and African Americans showing strikingly high rates of involvement. Nearly a quarter of those who attend as many as nine jazz performances per year are black, and three-fifths are male. Approximately a third of those who report liking jazz "best of all" are black, and two-thirds are male. These findings are corroborated by demographic surveys conducted by major jazz specialty magazines, which find men and African Americans disproportionately represented among their readership.

Other Findings

- In 1992, approximately 1.7 percent of adult Americans reported "performing or rehearsing" jazz over the previous year. Less than half this number (0.8 percent) performed jazz in public—roughly the same percentage reported in the 1982 SPPA. Performers are predominantly male, white (although blacks and Asians are somewhat more likely to perform jazz than whites), and youthful (71 percent under the age of 45). Ninety-three percent of the jazz performers have had some formal musical education.
- Although jazz retains a multiracial audience, it enjoys particular support in the black community. More than half (54 percent) of the adult African American population reports liking jazz, compared with only a third (32 percent) of whites. Roughly 16 percent of African Americans like jazz "best of all"—only religious music captured a larger percentage—compared with 4 percent of whites.
- The audiences for jazz and classical music overlap to a considerable extent: roughly a third of those who attend performances of one genre also attend performances of the other.
- Those who attend jazz performances are more likely than the population as a whole to participate in a wide range of leisure activities, such as movies, exercise, sports, or charity work.

Preference for Jazz in Relation to Other Musical Genres

The detailed demographic information on those expressing preference for the other 19 musical genres surveyed in the SPPA provides an intriguing and highly useful way of situating the taste for jazz in a broader social context.

Where does jazz fall in this broad spectrum of musical taste? All 20 musical genres are included in the discussions of music liked "best of all." Unfortunately the data are flawed for those who "like" the four categories of new age, mood/easy, choral/glee, and gospel/hymns. These genres are therefore omitted from the following discussions of music "liked." Of the 16 other genres, jazz ranks fifth, between big bands and classical/chamber music. Country and western is the most popular genre, as it was in 1982 and 1985. It is the only musical genre that more than half of adult Americans say they like, while jazz and classical music are liked by about one-third of them. Table 1 shows the percentages of respondents who said they "liked" the 10 genres that were most popular.

The position of jazz is approximately the same when the question is which genre is preferred above all others. Several genres—blues, bluegrass, and show tunes—prove to have wide but shallow appeal and drop in rank. Others, such as jazz and classical,

TABLE 1 Percentages of Respondents Who Liked the 10 Most Popular Musical Genres

Genre	Percentage
1. Country/western	52
2. Rock	44
3. Blues/R & B	40
4. Big band	35
5. Jazz	34
6. Classical/chamber	33
7. Bluegrass	29
8. Show tunes/operettas	28
9. Soul	24
10. Folk	23

have a more dedicated following and rise in the standings, which now include mood and gospel. Country and rock, the dominant genres of popular music, lead the list (followed by the 13 percent who declined to name a favorite genre). Religious and mood music follow, with the two dominant "art music" genres, jazz and classical, not far behind. (Opera reports a much smaller audience.) Table 2 shows the percentages of respondents who reported liking 1 of 10 musical genres "best of all."

TABLE 2 Percentages of Respondents Who Liked a Musical Genre Best of All*

Genre	Percentage
1. Country	21
2. Rock	14
3. Hymns/gospel	9
4. Mood/easy	9
5. Classical	6
6. Jazz	5
7. Big band	4
8. Ethnic	3
9. Latin	3
10. Blues	3

*13% of the respondents indicated they preferred "no one type."

Conclusions

The decade from 1982 to 1992 has seen a crucial generational shift in jazz. Many of the giants from the formative years of swing and modern jazz passed from the scene during this period, among them Thelonious Monk (1982), Count Basie (1984), Benny Goodman (1986), Miles Davis (1991), and Dizzy Gillespie (1993). Their deaths symbolize the end of an era and have caused some longtime observers of the jazz scene to wonder whether the links between contemporary forms of music making and the jazz tradition have become attenuated. "Jazz has always lived not by the hipness of the public," writes Eric Hobsbawm, "but by what Cornel West calls 'the network of apprenticeship,' the 'transmission of skills and sensibilities to new practitioners.' The cords of this network are fraying. Some of them have snapped."[4]

4. Eric Hobsbawm, *The Jazz Tradition* (New York: Pantheon, 1993), p. xxii.

And yet the contemporary image of jazz—as exemplified by the new generation of performers led by Wynton Marsalis, if not by Kenny G—is not only young, black, and hip, but fiercely committed to ideals of tradition, artistic discipline, and education. Jazz is undergoing a historic transition from a music embedded in popular culture (though carving out an ironic stance to it) to an official, if belatedly recognized, part of the art establishment. "Straight-ahead jazz almost died in the 1970's," wrote a correspondent for *Time* in 1990, "as record companies embraced the electronically enhanced jazz-pop amalgam known as fusion. Now a whole generation of prodigiously talented young musicians is going back to the roots, using acoustic instruments, playing recognizable tunes and studying the styles of earlier jazzmen."[5] These two assessments—one pessimistic and elegiac, the other optimistic and celebratory—sum up the ambiguous position of jazz as it approaches the end of the century. Compared with other "official" arts, jazz still retains traces of its origins in popular culture: the relative youthfulness of its audience and the associations with old (blues) and new (rap, reggae) forms of African American music. But contemporary audiences are increasingly likely to encounter jazz in settings carefully sealed off from the marketplace: college classrooms, PBS specials, concert halls. As the new century nears, jazz will continue to compete with the European "classical" tradition as the music of choice for the training of young musicians. And knowledge of jazz, its history, and its major performers will increasingly be seen as a desirable outcome of education, a crucial component of American "cultural capital."

This presents advocates of jazz—those who wish to see it thrive as an American art form—with a peculiar challenge: to marshal the prestige and financial resources of the arts and educational establishment on its behalf without endangering its appeal to a youthful, pop-oriented audience. Whether the current audience profile for jazz will persist into the future is a key question. Will jazz become even more the special province of the affluent, the educated, and the middle-aged; or will it continue to be, as it is now, the favored music of the 25-to-44 age group, delicately balanced between the adolescent enthusiasm for pop music and the considerably older audience for most other official arts? Will the African American audience continue to embrace jazz—perhaps as its *own* officially sanctioned art—or will jazz be displaced by newer forms of vernacular African American music that speak more directly to current concerns and tastes? As jazz becomes more integrated into existing arts networks and less associated with the insular, intense world of enthusiasts, will the imbalance in participation between men and women gradually disappear?

These questions cannot be answered by the current survey; the information it contains can only provide fuel for speculation. And yet for those who cherish jazz as a uniquely American form of artistic expression and who have some sense of the extraordinary path it has taken over the past century, these figures cannot help but encourage a feeling of optimism. The audience for jazz is modest, but diverse and expanding; in the language of market research, it "reaches all demographics." For the foreseeable future, the music will continue to be heard.

5. Thomas Sancton, "Horns of Plenty," *Time*, 22 October 1990, p. 66.

57. *Free Jazz* Revisited

THIRTY YEARS AFTER *DOWN BEAT* PUBLISHED its dual reviews of ornette Coleman's *Free Jazz*, the magazine invited two prominent critics to reconsider that influential album and evaluate its legacy. Artistic judgments inevitably change over time, but like the original reviews, the first of this pair, by John McDonough, could not be more different from the second, by John Litweiler. Before turning it over to the critics, *Down Beat* asked bassist Charlie Haden (b. 1937), who played on the album, to describe the 1960 recording session and its impact. All three writers are doing much more than commenting on the worth of a single album; each reveals a great deal about his sense of what jazz is and what its history has been.

The Making of *Free Jazz*, by Charlie Haden

When I first met Ornette Coleman in 1957, he told me the way that he was hearing music was to improvise on the feeling and the inspiration of a song rather than on the chord structure. I told him that I had been hearing the same thing before I met him, but every time I tried to do that people would become very upset with me. And he said, "They used to throw me off bandstands. If they would just listen to what's happening, they would understand that we are actually playing the song."

There are so many different ways to improvise. It's all about honesty and beauty and communicating beautiful music. And how you go about it is what's inside you. As Ornette told me, you can take any standard song, your inspiration from that song, and play from that inspiration and spontaneously create a new chord structure as you're playing.

When we arrived in New York in November of '59, we went into rehearsal at the Five Spot. Ornette had been writing some music for a double quartet: he wanted to use two drummers, two bass players, two trumpets, and two saxophones. He was already thinking about who to use as horn players, including [cornetist/trumpeter] Don Cherry, [drummers Ed] Blackwell and Billy [Higgins], having played with them before, and [the late bassist] Scotty LaFaro, my closest friend in life. Sometimes Scotty would go to rehearsals that I did with Ornette and listen; although, he told me on the side, "I don't know if I can play this music or not because I love playing chord changes." And I said, "That's what we're doin'!" And he said, "No you're not!" And I said, "Yes we are!" Sometimes when I wasn't available, Scotty would play for me.

Source: "Pro and Con," *Down Beat*, January, 1992, 30–31. Courtesy of *Down Beat* magazine.

Ornette told me that he had called Freddie Hubbard and Eric Dolphy to do the other horns. It wasn't a surprise that he would call Eric, but it was a surprise to me that he would call Freddie Hubbard, because Freddie was really a bebop trumpet player. He had spoken to Freddie and heard him play and he thought that he was one of the only other trumpet players that was open-minded enough to do this thing that Ornette wanted to do.

If I remember correctly, I don't think we actually had a formal rehearsal for the *Free Jazz* session until we got to the recording studio at Atlantic Records. Their old studio was real small; I remember we went in and went over the music one time and then recorded it. We did two takes of everything, and the best take was released as the Double Quartet record *Free Jazz* on Atlantic with the Jackson Pollock painting [on the cover]. Later, about 15 or 20 years later, they issued the second take on another album.

Ornette's reasoning behind the Double Quartet doing this kind of album was that with more horns things could open up even more than with just the Quartet, and become even freer if the horns were playing the right music; as far as the composition was concerned, that would give them a takeoff point for improvisation. And he thought it through with that instrumentation, including whatever instrument Eric chose to play. Eric ended up bringing just his bass clarinet and didn't play alto. As it was, everyone was open to discovery, experimenting, and playing free. There was a discussion where Ornette said, "Just listen, and your roles will come to you. Somebody will have a certain role, and then that role will be taken by somebody else and you'll have a different role. And the double instrumentation can free each player up to do what they want to do at different times."

The impact of what is called avant garde jazz and free jazz was very very strong when we came to New York and opened at the Five Spot. It was more than a controversy because a lot of people became angry, including the press, and a lot of musicians were very upset, saying things they took back later on after they discovered that the music was really valid. The impact in that time period was tremendous, similar to the impact that Bird and Diz brought to 52nd Street, the same kind of feeling.

In the wake of *Free Jazz,* there have been a number of new groups, like the Jazz Composers Orchestra, Archie Shepp's band, the AACM, Art Ensemble of Chicago, Cecil Taylor, the direction John Coltrane eventually went—including a date with Don, Eddie, and myself, Sonny Rollins hiring Don Cherry and Billy Higgins. There's John Scofield; Pat Metheny; and Keith Jarrett, in the late '60s and '70s, when he hired Dewey Redman and me, writing some tunes by and for Ornette; Old And New Dreams; Geri Allen; the Liberation Music Orchestra; Lincoln Center presenting the music of Dewey Redman and Ornette this past November. Ornette has influenced almost every musician who's making any kind of contribution to the art form.

In essence, the ongoing spirit of the music is to play and improvise with an energy that's different from the traditional jazz energy, to create something that's never been before in a way that's going to change the world and is something that you do with your whole life's energy, that you do on another level, a level above chord changes. Actually, any great musician that's made any kind of impact on the art form, like Coleman Hawkins, Sonny Rollins, or Bud Powell, that's the way they approached improvisation. Bird's approach to improvisation, risking his life with every note he played, was to create something that's never been before, on a level that's way above the normal level of life. That's what Ornette's music is about, that lasting way of improvising, that desperation to create something that's never been before.

Ornette and I used to talk about when you look at music, play it as if you never heard music before, creating it for the first time. As for the audience, they know they are going to be challenged, and that they're going to have an experience they'll never forget.

Failed Experiment, by John McDonough

When Ornette Coleman's *Free Jazz* came out in 1961, swing had been over for about a decade. But I think those memories of the '40s influenced the critical response to free music, generally, and to *Free Jazz* in particular. By stonewalling bop, only to see it become the dominant voice in jazz, conservatism as a critical position destroyed its credibility. And this, among other factors, predisposed the next generation of critics, I think, toward a sloppy, anything-goes, open-mindedness.

You can't get more open-minded (or empty-headed) than Bill Mathieu, who wrote this about Albert Ayler's "Ghost": "To an astonishing degree it commands the suspension of critical judgment and [presents] itself . . . to the listener on a level above quality, above personal like or dislike. It simply is what it is." He gave it five stars and never had the vaguest idea why. Free jazz apparently meant freedom from critics as well.

No critic wants to be caught on the wrong side of history. And many who were obliged to stand up and be counted on free jazz knew well that to oppose a new idea that ultimately prevails is to reserve space for oneself in the next edition of Nicolas Slonimsky's *Lexicon of Musical Invective,* that famous collection of contemporary but distinctly unprophetic snipes against the likes of Beethoven, Tchaikovsky, and Chopin. But what to make of free jazz? Were Ornette Coleman, Cecil Taylor, and all the others charlatans or geniuses? Jazz had never produced a music in which fakes could move so easily and undetected among real musicians.

In trying to find a reference point where none existed, some artists made radicalism itself an esthetic in the '60s. The problem was critics jumped the gun and gave the resulting music the benefit of much doubt too easily. They honored its raw, unprocessed "energy" and "passion" as if these elements constituted artistic achievements. They proclaimed its importance before the "experiment" was done. Their writing reflected a romantic faith in the concept of progress. Jazz was said to have "progressed" from swing to bop with a branch into cool, then through hard-bop and modes, and ultimately to "freedom," the implication being that each step produced something more "advanced" than the one before, as if jazz were a metaphor for the American dream.

But free jazz contained a more subversive metaphor, namely that even progress has limits and that beyond those limits looms an abyss of disintegration. The irony is that jazz did not *progress* into freedom. It *retrogressed* into it. It was not an advancement of musical law. It was a rejection of it. Total freedom cast jazz backward into a primal lawlessness, an emotional state of nature; and in so doing reminded us that all progression is not necessarily progress.

I first heard *Free Jazz* around 1965 and thought it was a gag. When I realized it wasn't, I listened with bewildered fascination, trying to find some point in the experiment. Over the years I came back to it from time to time, thinking that fusion or what little rock I had heard might make it sound suddenly accessible or even conservative. I'm listening to it now as I write. And still it seems without cohesion, even hostile. Thirty years have passed now. *Free Jazz* is now itself history. Has history repeated itself? Has free jazz prevailed as bop did? I think not.

The systems of free jazz, if they existed, were too insubstantial to sustain a critical mass, like those of the Woodstock Nation and other social experiments in freedom of the period. By disposing with form, the freedom movement took its cue from Milton Babbitt: "Who cares if you listen?" Free ensembles like the AACM and the Globe Unity Orchestra were not jazz bands; they were and remain research and development labs. I have no problems with experimentation—as long as the process is not confused with the result.

In 30 years, the trajectory of free jazz as a whole seems to have jumped only from the Five Spot to the Knitting Factory without ever escaping the smell of sawdust or the crutch of subsidy. I say this because there comes a point in the life of every *avant garde* when it must either put up or shut up. Free jazz has not made that leap. It led up to a dead end because, ultimately, it was more ideology than music. It may be that any genre as self-defined and unaccountable as free jazz lies beyond the reach of critical affirmation or reproach. I'm not sure about that. But I do know that lasting artistic value is not given down by the gods. It rises up through an informed cultural consensus involving musicians, critics, and the public. And no amount of critical affirmative action on behalf of free jazz has made this happen. I don't know how big the free jazz audience is today, nor would I guess. Besides, to argue over numbers would be to submit art to a kind of plebiscite.

Whatever its size, though, it remains a counterculture, separate and apart from the main body of jazz activity. This is why it has not had a major impact in music education programs or on the generation of musicians who are now inheriting the assets of jazz history. Bop and hard-bop remain the axis on which modernism still spins in jazz and people listen. Free jazz, with its ideological subtexts of black liberation, third world primitivism, and spiritualism, continues to exist in the outer world of 20th century eccentrics.

Thank You, Ornette! by John Litweiler

We all know that you intended the name *Free Jazz* for one of your compositions, not for the new jazz idiom you created. And we all know that you had no intention of starting a revolution in jazz when you first recorded in 1958, and said, "I believe music is really a free thing . . ." any more than Louis Armstrong intended to start a revolution in 1926. Nevertheless, those revolutions happened, and jazz is so much the richer for them.

Why did your music have such an impact? Why did the last revolution in jazz begin with you, rather than with, for instance, Lennie Tristano or Bob Graettinger or others a few years earlier? Because you *had* to create music your way—based on melodic lines rather than on chord changes—in order to express what you had to express. "I believe jazz should try to express more kinds of feeling than it has up to now," you said, and the rare breadth and depth of emotion and insight that you offered were the best possible demonstration. Jazz's uniqueness, above all its other features, lies in its implicit insistence that each jazz artist must, as Von Freeman says, "Express yourself"—not someone else's ideas, not what a code or rule book or tradition demands, but *yourself.* What was most immediately useful about your vision was the freedom of choice it gave other musicians. Now they realized they had the option of playing outside chord changes, if they chose.

Of course, none of this was the least bit experimental—as Don Cherry pointed out, your teachings were "a profound system," and the young Chicago musicians who discovered their own voices within Muhal Richard Abrams's bands learned from your and John Coltrane's and Albert Ayler's discoveries. These Chicagoans were a humanizing force in free jazz—they brought back blues, the sounds of traditional jazz and swing, long-ignored instruments such as the violin and clarinet, and self-invented and found instruments. At least as important, they were creating new extended forms and even restructuring the jazz ensemble. Rhythm section-less wind groups and unaccompanied horn solos appeared. Meanwhile, after you and some friends toured Europe, a generation of musicians in England, Germany, exiled South Africans, and others discovered they could join their own native musical heritages with the jazz tradition. Why, free jazz even inspired much that occurred in the final development of bop—that is, modal jazz and fusion music.

You certainly altered the mainstream of jazz. There is a main line, or mainstream, of jazz development that stretches from Buddy Bolden and James Reese Europe down to the very latest works by Edward Wilkerson and Dennis Gonzales. Before you came along, Ornette, a very few individuals (most obviously, Armstrong and Parker) and idioms (early jazz, swing, bop, and their extensions) dominated jazz. Even though you and some others have exerted a very wide influence indeed, so many separate idioms have appeared—yours, Cecil Taylor's, Ayler's, the Art Ensemble of Chicago's, free improvisation, and on and on—that no single individual or idiom dominates; it's as if the mainstream of jazz has become a delta, like the mainstreams of the other Westem arts near the end of the 20th century.

It's no accident that in your wake, jazz has begun to receive its appropriate respect as a fine art, often with the same kind of foundation and government support that symphonic composers and orchestras receive. After all, you received the first Guggenheim fellowship for jazz composition, and you led the way in bringing jazz into the concert halls and rooms, large and small, of today, just as bop took jazz out of dance venues and put it into nightclubs.

And now in 1992, there is a wonderful wealth of music to be heard, from the throb of your electric rhythm tribe Prime Time and the free fusion of Ronald Shannon Jackson and Blood Ulmer to the down-home romps of Henry Threadgill's Very Very Circus, to the bawdy humor of Lester Bowie and Ray Anderson and George Lewis to the wild humor of Hal Russell's NRG Ensemble and the quirky humor of John Zorn, to the intense thematic investigations of Roscoe Mitchell and the freewheeling blowing of the Rova and World Saxophone quartets, to the post-Monk evolution of Steve Lacy and Mal Waldron, to the intense, spiky interplay of the Evan Parker Trio and goofy satire of William Breuker, to the operas of Anthony Davis and Leo Smith, the symphonic works of yourself and Anthony Braxton—like you, he touches all bases—and the dense sonatas-upon-sonatas of Cecil Taylor, to the lyricism of Bobby Bradford and the fire of Paul Smoker, to the Latin American folk jazz of Charlie Haden's Liberation Music Orchestra and the West African jazz of Pierre Dørge's New Jungle Orchestra, to the compositional mastery of Carla Bley and Muhal Richard Abrams and blues-stomping Edward Wilkerson with his 8 Bold Souls, to the pastoral harmonies of Pat Metheny and the thoroughly urban harmonies of McCoy Tyner, to the grand scope of the Art Ensemble of Chicago, the grand ambitions of Keith Jarrett, and many other, different directions.

When Claude Debussy, at the tum of the last century, said, "There are no more schools of music, and the main business of the musician today is to avoid any kind of outside influences," he was prophesying jazz today. None of this would have happened if you hadn't had your own vision, Ornette, and if you hadn't taught those young Los Angeles musicians in the 1950s how to create a kind of music that hadn't been played before. After the breath of life you gave it, jazz has been a living, changing, and, yes, growing music for the last 30 years and more. For all these free musics, then, a mighty large chorus of voices thanks you, Ornette Coleman.

58. Ring Shout, Signifyin(g), and Jazz Analysis

MOST CLOSE ANALYSIS OF JAZZ MUSIC HAS been carried out by people trained in methods developed for European classical music.[1] In this complex and provocative article, Samuel A. Floyd, Jr. (b. 1937) draws upon the work of literary critics and historians to argue that jazz critics and scholars should begin using analytical methods that are more closely related to the music they study. Former Director of the Center for Black Music Research at Columbia College in Chicago, Floyd is the author of several books, including *The Power of Black Music: Interpreting Its History From Africa to the United States* (1995). In this article, he demonstrates that music scholars have much to learn from those who deal with other aspects of culture—and that they can also give something back—through his analysis of Jelly Roll Morton's 1926 recording of "Black Bottom Stomp."[2]

Floyd turns to the "ring shout" dances of slave times, myths of the African deity Esu-Elegbara, and the rhythmic, rhymed "toasts" of black oral traditions to show how the cultural history of African Americans, including its African roots, informs the practices of jazz musicians and audiences. He uses Sterling Stuckey's study of the ring shout and Henry Louis Gates, Jr.'s theory of "Signifyin(g)" as models of how to deal with cultural difference on its own terms, instead of maintaining, for example, that jazz is worthy of study because it is just like classical music.[3]

Source: Samuel A. Floyd, Jr., "Ring Shout! Literary Studies, Historical Studies, and Black Music Inquiry," *Black Music Research Journal* 11:2 (Fall, 1991), pp. 265–87. Reprinted with the permission of The Center for Black Music Research.

1. See, for example, the articles by André Hodeir and Gunther Schuller in this volume.

2. This excerpt from the original article omits an opening discussion of Gates's and Stuckey's work as well as a closing analytical section devoted to William Grant Still's *Afro-American Symphony* (1931).

3. Sterling Stuckey, *Slave Culture: Nationalist Theory and the Foundations of Black America* (New York: Oxford University Press, 1987). Henry Louis Gates, Jr., *The Signifying Monkey: A Theory of African-American Literary Criticism* (New York: Oxford University Press, 1988). For other applications of Gates's theory to musical analysis, see Gary Tomlinson, "Cultural Dialogics and Jazz: A White Historian Signifies," in Katherine Bergeron and Philip V. Bohlman, eds., *Disciplining Music: Musicology and Its Canons*, pp. 64–94 (Chicago: University of Chicago Press, 1992), and Robert Walser, "Out of Notes: Signification, Interpretation, and the Problem of Miles Davis," *Musical Quarterly* 77:2 (Summer, 1993), pp. 343–65 (also reprinted in this volume). Although it has not escaped criticism, Gates's theory has enabled useful scholarship in a number of fields.

Gates's notion of Signifyin(g) codifies a set of ideas about processes of signification—of how meanings are produced—and offers a bag of new conceptual tools for musical analysis. In contrast to dictionary definitions, where meanings seem clear and fixed, Signifyin(g) works through reference, gesture, and interaction to suggest multiple meanings through association; in this mode of artistic activity, performance, negotiation, and dialogue with past and present are central. Gates does not claim that Signifyin(g) is unique to African-American culture, but rather that it has best been developed and theorized there. Similarly, Floyd emphasizes that culture is learned, not inherent in the social category of race; thus, he argues, knowledge of African-American cultural traditions is essential for anyone who would discuss the meanings of jazz.

Over the past ten years, black scholars in the field of English literature have identified a black literary tradition and developed critical strategies for studying that tradition from within black culture. And black historians have also been writing black history and American history from a black perspective. In the field of history, their works include Sterling Stuckey's *Slave Culture: Nationalist Theory and the Foundations of Black America* (1987) and Mary Frances Berry's and John Blassingame's *Long Memory: The Black Experience in America* (1982), and in literary criticism, Houston Baker's *Blues, Ideology, and Afro-American Literature: A Vernacular Theory* (1984) and *Modernism and the Harlem Renaissance* (1987) and Henry Louis Gates, Jr.'s *The Signifying Monkey: A Theory of African-American Literary Criticism* (1988).[4] By taking an insider's view of black cultural and literary traditions, these books offer insights that cannot be achieved through more conventional means. The success of an Afrocentric perspective in these fields invites black music scholarship to move beyond the standard approaches of musicology and ethnomusicology, by learning from the theoretical insights of black historians and literary scholars and applying that knowledge to the study of black music.

On Criticism of the Music

Gates and Stuckey in their work have identified black vernacular traditions that can be effectively examined for their analytical and interpretive implications. And Gates, together with others, has identified a canon—a tradition—of black literature. Through their works, these scholars and those from other disciplines invite us to "step outside the white hermeneutical circle into the black"[5] and to invent other modes of inquiry that reveal the distinctive qualities of the black music tradition.

Explanations of musical works and performances as realizations of "ideal form," achievements of "organic unity," or as functional artifacts are insufficient for black music inquiry because they all separate the works from their cultural and aesthetic

4. Houston Baker, *Blues, Ideology, and Afro-American Literature: A Vernacular Theory* (Chicago: University of Chicago Press, 1984); Houston Baker, *Modernism and the Harlem Renaissance* (Chicago: University of Chicago Press, 1987); Mary Frances Berry and John Blassingame, *Long Memory: The Black Experience in America* (New York: Oxford University Press, 1982).

5. Gates, *Signifying Monkey*, p. 258.

foundations. And conventional musical analysis is in itself inadequate for the demands of black music scholarship and criticism. In its concern for recognizing previously sanctioned and favored harmonic progressions, melodic contours, rhythmic conventions, formal structures and their implications and deviations (recognitions that merely stand and substitute for musical evaluation and judgment), traditional musicology has given little attention to the development of judgmental criteria and has ignored fundamental cultural concerns, having found both areas of concern to be subjective and speculative, and the latter to be "social, not musical." Therefore, it is imperative that music scholarship develop criteria for the aesthetic evaluation of works and for the fundamental cultural concerns of every repertory.

The key to effective criticism lies in understanding the tropings and Signifyin(g)s of black music-making, for such practices *are* criticism—perceptive and evaluative acts and expressions of approval and disapproval, validation and invalidation through the respectful, ironic, satirizing imitation, manipulation, extension, and elaboration of previously created and presented tropes and new ideas. For our purposes, therefore, criticism may be seen as the act of discovering, distinguishing, and explaining cultural and musical value in works of black music through the identification of the elements that captivate our attention and mediate our perceptions and reactions. Attention to this task implies the responsibility of explaining how well or, indeed, *whether* composers and performers have *succeeded* in capturing and mediating our perception.

As culture-based and culture-wise observers respond to poorly done oral-verbal Signifyin(g) with such disapproving comments as "That's phoney," and "That's lame" and to well-done Signifyin(g) with positive comments and expressions[6]—recognizing the effectiveness of the intended witty put-downs and other poetic constructions of oral Signifyin(g) artists—such observers of black music-making respond similarly to musical Signifyin(g) tropes. Whether in verbal or musical arts, this responding customarily often takes place *during* rather than after performances, creating as a counterpoint to them a variety of call-and-response events. In this way, the black-music experience is, to a large degree, self-criticizing and self-validating, with criticism taking place as the experience progresses. Comments such as "Oh yeah," "Say it," "He's cookin'," and "That's bad" (in response to Signifyin(g) musical events) show approval of those events and, as Murray would say, their extensions, elaborations, and refinements. Musical Signifyin(g) by the performers elicits response and interaction from a knowledgeable and sensitive audience, which participates by responding either vigorously or calmly to the performance. The musical "toasting" that is improvisation is particularly noted by black-music audiences. To paraphrase Mitchell-Kernan, a Signifyin(g) act that surpasses another in an excellent performance is particularly treasured, while incompetent performances are "likely to involve confusion, annoyance, boredom, and . . . indifference."[7] Those who know the culture know when the notes and the rhythms do not fit the context and when the idiomatic orientation is wrong. So must critics. If they are to be taken seriously within the tradition they are criticizing, they must recognize their duty "to increase the

6. Claudia Mitchell-Kernan, "Signifying," in Alan Dundes, ed., *Mother Wit from the Laughing Barrel: Readings in the Interpretation of Afro-American Folklore* (New York: Garland, 1981 [1979]), p. 324.

7. Mitchell-Kernan, "Signifying," p. 325; quote from Albert Murray, *The Hero and the Blues* (Columbia, Missouri: University of Missouri Press, 1973), p. 87.

accessibility of aesthetic presentation. . . . [It is] primarily a matter of coming to terms with such special peculiarities as may be involved in a given process of stylization."[8]

(The self-criticizing process operates spontaneously where performers sing and play in contact with their cultural base. But it cannot function the same way when, for example, blues, jazz, or gospel music are performed for audiences whose behavior is governed by the customs of the European concert hall.)

All of this implies that Signifyin(g) tropes must be decoded before they can be appreciated and explained.[9] Indeed, decoding and explaining are what I have tried to do below in my analysis of the Morton piece. Such decoding and explanations are the stuff of interpretation, and they will vary somewhat from critic to critic. Therefore, we must not eschew differing interpretations of a particular work; but we can insist that they result in warrantably assertible statements of value-perception.

"Call-Response": The Musical Trope of Tropes

The musical practices present in the ring are all musical tropes that can be subsumed under the master musical trope of Call-Response, a concept embracing all the other musical tropes (as the black concept of Signifyin(g) embraces the rhetorical tropes of the dozens, rapping, loud-talking, etc.).[10] The term Call-Response is used here to convey the dialogical, conversational character of black music. Its processes include the Signifyin(g), troping practices of the early calls, cries, whoops, and hollers of early Afro-American culture, which themselves were tropes from which evolved—through extension, elaboration, and refinement—varieties of the subtropes: call-and-response, elision, multimeter, pendular and blue thirds, and all the rest, including interlocking rhythms, monosyllabic melodic expressions, instrumental imitations of vocal qualities, parlando, and other processes that have a kind of implicative musical, as well as semantic, value.

The lyrics of a work of black music obviously have semantic value—value whose meaning can easily be understood by informed auditors. And for those familiar with

8. Albert Murray, *Stomping the Blues* (New York: Doubleday, 1978), p. 196.

9. Mitchell-Kernan, "Signifying," p. 327.

10. The term trope, originally a literary expression, "denotes any rhetorical or figurative device" (J. A. Cuddon, *A Dictionary of Literary Terms*, rev. ed. [New York: Penguin Books, 1979], p. 725); it was later used to refer to "a newly composed addition . . . to one of the antiphonal chants," usually as a preface to or interpolation to a chant (Donald J. Grout and Claude Palisca, *A History of Western Music*, 3rd ed. [New York: W. W. Norton, 1980], pp. 52–53). The term is used here in its original meaning, but it is applied in this instance to a purely musical device. Musical troping, as I have used the term here, is more properly understood as a rhetorical or figurative musical device—a Signifyin(g) musical event.

Call-Response must not be confused with call-and-response. The latter is a musical *device*, but Call-Response is meant here to name a musical *principle*—a dialogical musical rhetoric under which are subsumed all the musical tropological devices, including call-and-response.

I am grateful to Bruce Tucker for putting me onto this idea early in the development of my ideas, when he stated to me that something like the Afro-American musical process of call-and-response, metaphorically speaking, might be considered as the musical trope of tropes. Call-and-response seemed to be too limited a concept to embody all of the black musical tropes, but Bruce's statement carried the necessity of a dialogic and descriptive terminology for this all-important, all-encompassing concept. So, in trying to remain as close as possible to the spirit of Bruce's statement and to the dialogic nature of the music, I coined the term Call-Response.

black musical culture, the semantic value of instrumental music is equally evident. Such non-verbal semantic value is explained by Albert Murray in *The Hero and the Blues,* where he contends that the musician is concerned with "achieving a *telling effect.*" Murray describes how the solo instruments in Ellington's band, for example, state, assert, allege, quest, request, and imply, while others mock, concur, groan, "or signify misgivings and even suspicions."[11] But this semantic meaning, this telling effect, is not external to the music. In one sense, at least, Murray's "telling effect" is synonymous with Gates's "semantic relations"[12]; and both concepts can account for and intellectualize what black vernacular musicians feel and assume as they nonchalantly claim that when they play they are "telling a story." Another aspect of semantic value is the exhortative potential of such instrumental music: the tropes, Signifyin(g)s, and other constructions can exhort soloists to create ever more exciting improvisations and riffs, these exhortations carrying the semantic values of urging, beseeching, and daring. What is being asserted, implied, mocked, exhorted—indeed, Signified—here are the musical tropes of Call-Response: tropes that carry with them the values, sensibilities, and cultural derivatives of the ring.

Call-Response—this master trope, this musical trope of tropes—functions in black music as Signifyin(g) functions in black literature and can therefore be said to Signify. It implies the presence within it of Signifyin(g) figures (Calls) and Signifyin(g) revisions (Responses, in various guises) that can be one or the other, depending on their context. For example, when pendular thirds are used in an original melodic statement, they may constitute a "Call"; when they are used to comment upon, or "trope," a pre-existing use of such thirds, they can be said to constitute a "Response," or Signifyin(g) revision. This concept of Call-Response, although suggested by Gates's rhetorical trope of Signifyin(g), is implied by and derived from the musical processes of Stuckey's ring; it is subject to the hermeneutical strategies of Gates's Esu.[13]

The theory implied here assumes that works of music are not just objects, but cultural transactions between human beings and organized sound—transactions that take place in specific idiomatic cultural contexts, that are fraught with the values of the original contexts from which they spring, that require some translation by auditors in pursuit of the understanding and aesthetic substance they can offer. With this in mind, I turn now to the application of this approach to a recorded performance, building on Gunther Schuller's analysis of Jelly Roll Morton's "Black Bottom Stomp."

"Black Bottom Stomp"

The performers in "Black Bottom Stomp" are Morton, piano; George Mitchell, trumpet; Kid Ory, trombone; Omer Simeon, clarinet; Johnny St. Cyr, banjo; John Lindsay, bass; and Andrew Hillaire, drums. Together they form the typical New Orleans ensemble: trumpet, clarinet, and trombone fronting a rhythm section. The recording was made on September 15, 1926, as Victor 20221.[14] Gunther Schuller's analysis, illustrated on a chart in his *Early Jazz,* divides the performance into thirteen "structural divisions" in which he notes the instrumentation and number of bars in each and

11. Emphasis mine; Murray, *The Hero and the Blues,* p. 10; p. 86.

12. Gates, *Signifying Monkey,* p. 48.

13. See the editor's introduction to the excerpt. [RW]

14. Jelly Roll Morton's Red Hot Peppers, "Black Bottom Stomp," Victor 20221. For my analysis here, I used the Smithsonian Institution's reissue in the *Smithsonian Collection of Classic Jazz* set.

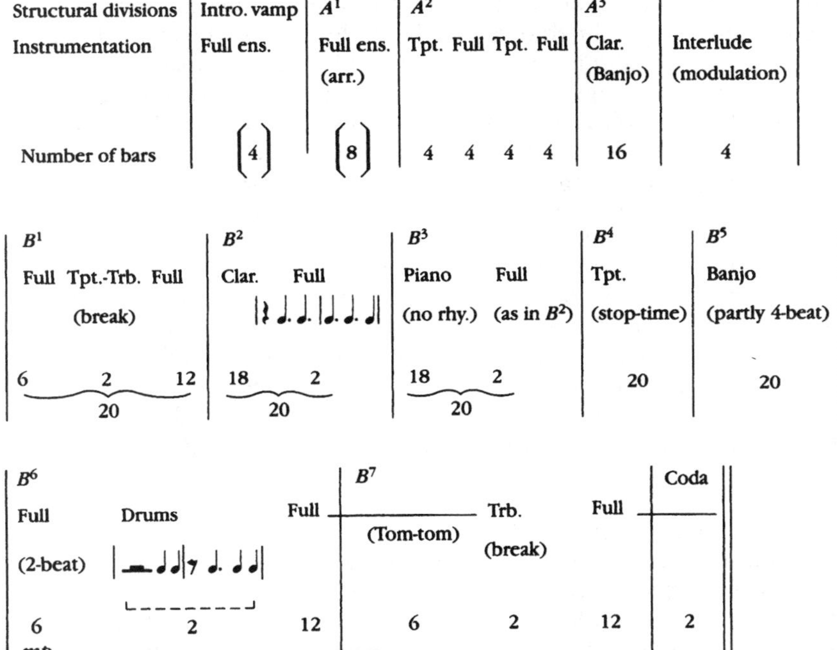

FIGURE 1 *Black Bottom* Stomp—Scheme

points out other matters of structural interest such as "breaks," "stop-time" events, and modulations [see Figure 1]. Schuller's narrative reveals "at least four different themes and one variant," "a brilliantly stomping Trio," the usual key relationships and chord progressions, the appearances of solos, varieties of rhythm, metric fragments, and use of instruments.[15] Schuller's analysis, as usual, is perceptive, revealing, and informative. I would like now to expand upon it from the perspective established in the preceding pages.

In "Black Bottom Stomp" the "exuberance and vitality," the "unique forward momentum," and what constitutes those "Morton ingredients," all mentioned but not explained by Schuller, are the very derivations from the ring that are basic to Afro-American music. The performance is governed by the Call-Response principle, relying upon the Signifyin(g) elisions, responses to calls, improvisations (in fact or in style), continuous rhythmic drive, and timbral and pitch distortions that I have identified as retentions from the ring. At every point, "Black Bottom Stomp" Signifies on black dance rhythms. Underlying it all is the time-line concept of African music: as rhythmic foundation for the entire piece, but kept in the background for the most part and sometimes only implied, there is a continuous rhythm that subdivides Morton's two beats per bar into an underlying rhythm of eight pulses. This continuous, implied, and sometimes-sounded pulse serves the function of a time-line over which the foreground two-beat metric pattern has been placed, and it serves as the reference

15. Gunther Schuller, *Early Jazz: Its Roots and Musical Development* (New York: Oxford University Press, 1968), pp. 155–61.

pulse for the two-beat and four-beat metric structures and the cross-rhythms and additive rhythms that occur throughout the performance. The clarinet and the banjo frequently emphasize this time-line with added volume, thereby bringing it into the foreground as a Signifyin(g) trope, as in, especially, the sections Schuller labels B^2 and B^5, respectively, but also throughout the performance. At B^2 the clarinet revises and emphasizes the "stomp" rhythm introduced in A^3, as well as the time-line, with cross-rhythms derived from African performance practices; in B^5 the banjo does the same. This is accomplished by these instruments' filling in the quarter-note values and the eighth-note rest of the A^3 pattern with repeated eighth notes in which the accents expected on beat three of each measure are anticipated by a half beat. It is against and around the time-line that all other rhythmic organization and activity take place. The four-beat rhythm that occurs in B^1, B^3, and B^5, the breaks that occur in B^1 and B^7 and the stop-time of B^4, the accented cross-rhythm of the drummer in B^2 and B^6, the "stomp" rhythm highlighted in A^3 (clarinet) and B^7, and the after-beats on the tom-toms in B^7 all signify on and serve as enhancements of the time-line. The activity in B^5 that Schuller calls "partly 4-beat" is particularly effective, and the breaks serve effectively as goal-delay devices that Signify on the goal-directedness of the piece's melodic, harmonic, and rhythmic structures.

It is within this rhythmic and structural frame that improvisation takes place—improvisation that Signifies on (1) the structure of the piece itself, (2) the current Signifyin(g)s of the other players in the group, and (3) the players' own and others' Signifyin(g)s in previous performances. These Signifyin(g)s take place at the same time the performers are placing within the frame and including within their improvisations timbral and melodic derivations from the ring—the trombone's smears (elisions) in A^1, the trombone's Signifyin(g) smear on the clarinet's note in B^1, the muted trumpet with its elided phrase endings in B^4, the cymbal break in B^5, the trombone smears (cries) and the new tom-tom timbre in B^7. Highlighting the entire structure is the string of solos that occur between B^1 and B^5 and then the out-chorus (B^7). Like Martin Williams and unlike Schuller, I hear the exchange between the trumpet and the full band in A^2 as a call-and-response structure, albeit composed (the calls change, the response remains the same), as I do the exchanges in the modulatory interlude following A^3—revising tropes that extend and elaborate, or update, the call-and-response device, which operates on many different structural levels.[16] I also hear the trombone's held-notes in the out-chorus (B^7) as evocative "shouts" that Signify black religious shouting and its counterpart expression in secular life—calls, cries, and hollers—and I hear Morton's solo in B^3 as Signifyin(g) on ragtime, which itself Signifies on the foot-patting, hand-clapping after-beats of the shout (with a "pretty" and embroidered version of the style) and on the stomp rhythm by playing on the time-line while introducing a four-beat rhythm (i.e., the bass player or drummer plays on every beat instead of every other one). The banjo's strummed solo (B^5) does not repeat the melody that preceded it but Signifies on it and on the accompanying harmony. And the out-chorus Signifies on all that has gone before it. The entire performance, of course, Signifies on the stomp rhythm first heard in A^3, a troping that validates the title of the piece.

Throughout the performance, the breaks, riffs, four-beat tropings, and trombone smears serve as exhortations to the soloists, exciting and inciting them to create more inspired solos, as for example, in B^1 (four-beat), B^2 (additive accents), B^4 (stop-time and

16. See Martin Williams, *Jelly Roll Morton*, Kings of Jazz Series (New York: A. S. Barnes & Co., 1963).

turn-around), B^6 (four-beat and additive accents), and B^7 (trombone smears and break). And the performance swings—exhibiting that essential quality of products of the ring—with the normal tropings of the time-line throughout the performance. This quality is pronounced at points where off-beats, back-beats, cross-rhythms, and four-beat rhythms occur—sometimes subtle, sometimes pronounced—such as in the interlude; at B^1, B^4, and B^5, where the bass and the drums trope the time-line and the banjo's phrasings; and in the last three measures of B^3. The back-beats of the out-chorus (B^7) are particularly effective in this regard. Related to this quality is the constant filling of the musical space by the banjo as it tropes the time-line by sounding all its notes, when the other instruments lay out, except in stop-time passages, as at A^3. Swing is particularly pronounced in the sections for full band, where several instruments trope the time-line together, in different ways, and at different points.

The elisions (smears), call-and-response devices, meter changes, accented cross-rhythms, after-beats, breaks, stop-time tropes—indeed, all the shuckin' and jivin' Signifyin(g) figures in the piece (particularly those of the clarinet and piano)—are rhetorical Call-Response figures that Signify on the musical values and expressions of the ring and its musical derivations; each improvisation Signifies on Morton's melodies and on the inventions of some of the other musicians; and the structure of the piece Signifies, most immediately, on ragtime and, though perhaps indirectly, on European social dance music (which, by the way, includes the compositions of the black composer Frank Johnson who, a century earlier, also improvised on and added inventions to the form with rhetorical tropes, as in his *Voice Quadrilles* and some of his marches).

"Black Bottom Stomp" is fraught with the referentiality that Gates describes as "semantic value," exemplifying (1) how performers contribute to the success of a performance with musical statements, assertions, allegations, questings, requestings, implications, mockings, and concurrences that result in the "telling effect" Murray has described and (2) what black performers mean when they say that they "tell a story" when they improvise.

Much more could be said about this piece along similar lines, but my goal in discussing it has been simply to suggest that, heard in this way, the Morton band's performance of "Black Bottom Stomp" is fraught with funded meanings from the Afro-American musical tradition, and its grounding in the ring is unmistakably evident. The expression and communication of the performance, in other words, is fully and deeply rooted in black culture. Like the descendants of Esu—the tricksters of Afro-American culture—its performers combine the ritual teasing and critical insinuations of Signifyin(g) with self-empowering wit, cunning, and guile.

Summary and Conclusions

"Analysis" is an activity that emerged and matured as a way of examining chiefly European works of music, and it can shed some light on works from the African-American tradition also, as evidenced by Schuller's treatment of "Black Bottom Stomp." But there are many elements of African-American music that it will not uncover. For those, an Afrocentric approach is indispensable—an approach that must be based on the following elements: (1) a system of referencing, here called Signifyin(g), drawn from Afro-American folk music; (2) a tendency to make performances occasions in which the audience participates, in reaction to what performers do, which leads in turn to (3) a framework of continuous self-criticism that accompanies performance in its indigenous cultural context; (4) an emphasis on competitive values that keep performers on their mettle; and (5) the complete intertwining of black music and dance. All these elements combine to create, foster, and define what I have called here Call-Response.

Perhaps continuing application of this theory, together with its refinement and additional research, will tell us more about its efficacy and its limits. But my preliminary analyses suggest that the mode of inquiry introduced here can be applied successfully to music as diverse as Bessie Smith's "Empty Bed Blues," Thomas A. Dorsey's "Precious Lord, Take My Hand," Olly Wilson's *Akwan*, and T. J. Anderson's *Variations on a Theme by M. B. Tolson*.

The relationship of black music and dance is evident in the very existence and character of "Black Bottom Stomp," which is unadulterated Signifyin(g) black dance music. Our awareness of this interdependence, which had its genesis in the ring, will enhance our understanding of the nature and character of the music and its Signifyin(g) revisions. And our critical interpretations should take into account this relationship, as I have tried to do in the case of the Morton piece.

The approach offered here is intended to address directly these issues in a way that will allow students of the music to recognize, explain, and judge the drama of the progression, juxtaposition, and Signification of the idiomatic tropes of black music-making. Perhaps this beginning will lead to increasing refinement of this mode of inquiry, with the expectation that it will increasingly illuminate black music as a much more complex and richly textured art than has been made clear by more traditional and inappropriate analytical procedures.

59. Ferociously Harmonizing with Reality

"FEROCIOUSNESS" IS THE WORD PIANIST Keith Jarrett (b. 1945) uses to describe Miles Davis's playing, but it clearly applies to his own approach as well. Groans, grunts, and gyrations often punctuate Jarrett's intensely physical performances (prompting much criticism), and his stylistic eclecticism parallels Davis's musical restlessness. Jarrett came to wide attention playing with Charles Lloyd and then with Miles Davis during 1970–71, just after the latter had popularized jazz-rock fusion. In 1972, Jarrett began performing solo concerts made up of extended

Source: Keith Jarrett, interviewed by Kimihiko Yamashita. "In Search of Folk Roots." *Anteus* 71/72 (Autumn 1993), pp. 109–15. Courtesy of Stephen Cloud Productions.

improvisations, which brought him great popularity even as he broke new ground in improvisational scope.

Jarrett's lively eclecticism takes many forms: he also performs on soprano sax, composes for orchestra, records classical music, and draws upon many musical genres in his improvisations and compositions. A frequent solo improviser, he is also fascinated by the different kinds of time musicians bring together as they interact (as he discusses in this interview). A voracious student of musical styles and instruments, he nonetheless draws the line at synthesizers. In rebuttal to the classicizing impulse, Jarrett amplifies Davis's assertion that jazz ought to be regarded as a kind of folk music, yet he plays almost exclusively in concert halls and admonishes the audience if they are not silent. Jarrett closes with some thoughts on cultural identity and the preciousness of diversity.

Originally part of a lengthy work published in Japanese, this excerpt appeared in the literary journal *Antaeus* in 1993; Jarrett was interviewed by Kimihiko Yamashita, whose portions of the dialogue have been set in italics.

Miles said that many people misunderstood what John Coltrane was doing.

> I don't understand this talk about Coltrane being difficult to understand. What he does, for example, is to play five notes of a chord and then change it around, trying to see how many different ways it can sound. It's like explaining something five different ways. And that sound of his is connected with what he's doing with the chords at any time.
> —Miles Davis

Miles is never wrong. But there's always more to say about it.

> I think a movement in Jazz is beginning away from the conventional string of chords, and a return to emphasis on melodic rather than harmonic variation. There will be fewer chords but infinite possibilities as to what to do with them. Classical composers—some of them—have been writing this way for years, but jazz musicians seldom have.
> —Miles Davis

Miles talked about Ahmad Jamal's use of space. Is this the same thing you've talked about—space and melody?

No, this is space with tempo. I'm talking about space with space. Ahmad plays with a rhythm section so the space he uses is taken up by the rhythm section. That's not space the way I was talking about it.

> Listen to the way that Jamal uses space. He lets it go so that you can feel the rhythm section and the rhythm section can feel you. It's not crowded . . . Ahmad is one of my favorites.
> —Miles Davis

I was talking about the kind of space when there is no sound and no pulse. This space can have a pulse anyway. It depends on what came before it and what comes next. The spaces can start having their own melodic position.

> Miles was intrigued by Monk's masterful and idiosyncratic manipulation of mysterious-sounding chord progressions, but he was especially fascinated by Monk's use of space in his solos.
> —Eric Nisenson

> Monk's concept of space alone was one of the most important things he taught Coltrane; when to lay out and let somebody else fill up that space, or just leave the space open. I think John was already going in that direction, but working with Monk helped him reach his goal that much faster.
> —McCoy Tyner

Did you have something special in mind you wanted to accomplish with Miles's band?

I had heard his band just before I started to play with it. I heard it with Tony Williams and Wayne Shorter, and Herbie Hancock or Chick Corea.

And everybody sounded like they were playing alone, they didn't sound like they were playing in a band. They were only hearing themselves and it sounded so much like an ego trip.

Then when Miles played it sounded so refreshing. He would play these short solos and go off the stage and the rest of the band sounded like, "Let's try to be me," "I'm going to be me now." I didn't think Miles deserved this kind of thing, so that night I thought, "Well, there's gonna come a time when I'll work with him for a while." That was a little before the time I actually started to play with him.

So, after you joined his band, what did you feel?

That's a big, big, question. I mean, what did I feel about what? Everything in the world [he laughs]?

What you were trying to do in the band.

He asked for me, so he had already heard me—many times. I didn't think I was there to be pretending I was someone else. He knew who he was getting. He knew who he had heard play, so I didn't have to do anything special except stay myself there.

> Bill Evans and Keith Jarrett were different. Chick Corea is different. Chick knocks me out at that tempo [Miles taps out a medium up tempo]. Then you get Herbie; Herbie can do anything. He and Keith, I think they must have drunk the same dye [he laughs].
> —Miles Davis

He was not so happy . . . he wanted more funk in the band; so I knew I could be a part of that. I think that's one thing he didn't believe Chick could do.

> Miles is trying to get further out (more abstract) and yet more basic (funkier) at the same time.
> —Tony Williams

Jack DeJohnette was in the band and Jack and I had played together . . . we knew each other very well and we knew we could play together and have a good time . . . But I was temporary, I knew I was temporary.

> Keith played so nice I had to give him two pianos. He'd go like this [Miles imitates Jarrett in a pianistic frenzy]. I'd say, "Keith, how does it feel to be a genius?"
> —Miles Davis

> The music that Miles had wouldn't have worked with acoustic piano. You couldn't play chords (functional harmony)—it wasn't chordal at all. It was just . . . sounds . . . I thought the band was the most egocentric organization I had heard musically . . . except for Miles. Miles was still playing nice, beautiful things, and the rest of the band was in boxes. So in a way . . . I just wanted to do something a little bit to change the feeling. And I knew Jack DeJohnette was there, so we play well together.
> —Keith Jarrett

I didn't want to play electric keyboard but that's the way it was. I could have played electric typewriter, that would have bean o.k., too. Same thing.

I have this funny vision of people pulling electric keyboards away from keyboard players while they're playing and putting different ones in front of them; they all feel the same and the last one is a typewriter but they're so into it they don't know it's a typewriter.

I collect watches because I'm very interested in time. Now with every-one wearing a digital watch, it says time goes in a straight line . . . one, two, three, four, five, six. Time does not move like that. It's never perfect either.

Digital time is like record production. In record production we have the bass, then you say now we add the vocalist, now we have the conga drums, we go this way—one, two, three, four.[1] Real music, when people play together, is like this: you come together, you go away, you come together. There are no edges, no sharp edges.

Even when people talk they are not spontaneous, they prepare. You prepare, like putting a frame—I'm going to say this first, and I'm going to say this second, and then I'm going to say this.

But if you're spontaneous you talk about everything—on a good day you talk about everything all the time. So for me a watch is a symbol.

There are many kinds of time altogether.

Time is subjective. See, music can tell you many things, if you listen well. Different drummers can prove that time is subjective because none of them plays the same tempo, at the same tempo. They find their own time. If time was the same for everyone, every drummer would play the same. But there are many kinds of time.

When I hear Miles play with his new band, the new band is like a digital watch. Miles comes and Miles is round, he is alive. He just plays one note.

Someone could say, "Oh, anyone can play like Miles." He has a trumpet sound that is almost like a student has when a student is learning trumpet. You get that same sound—almost—for a while and then you get more brassy and then you play more and more and you lose this "innocent" sound that Miles has. So the whole world can say, "anybody can get that sound," but nobody can get it.

And the reason Miles gets that sound and no one else gets it is because Miles wants the sound more than they do, he wants that sound. He wants it with this ferociousness, so he gets it.

I don't know what other word to use . . . ferociousness is just . . . I can't think of a better word. . . . It's not enough to say Miles wants the sound, because everybody can say they want things, but Miles wants it with all his energy.

The ferociousness can't be egotistical; that's why I used that word. An animal doesn't have an ego like we do and animals can be ferocious. They need to eat, they

---

1. Jarrett is referring to the methods of multitrack recording, where each instrument is recorded separately and the musicians might never even meet each other. [RW]

are ferocious. They don't let anything get in their way. But they are not doing it for an ego, they're doing it to survive or for something to survive . . . maybe their kids . . . their little baby lions.

I'm using that word because a poet was talking about one of my favorite writers, who's Persian, and he, this poet, said something about how no one understands how ferocious this writer is. If they understood that, they would see more about what he's saying. And that was the first time I heard someone say the right word for this, so I'm using it because it's true.

I'm trying to get out of this thing where "want" means something like "desire." I don't mean desire. Ferocious is too fast for desire. Desire is "I'd love to do this." The kind of want that would make me play the note I hear isn't ego. That's not ego, that's a sort of harmonizing with reality in a powerful way.

Miles can play soft and it's powerful, other trumpet players play soft and it's weak. There is ferociousness even in the soft note.

But it's not anger or ego, it's the whole note—"I *want* this note. Not for me but for the air." The thing that makes it ferocious is what happens before he plays the note. He has to be ready for the note, for his own note, not someone else's note. Not the note on paper, not the note somewhere in the air above him, but *his* note. He has to be ready for this. And that's very difficult.

> Underneath his lyricism, Miles swings. He'll take care of the lyricism, but the rest of the band must complement him with an intense drive. And it's not that they supply a drive he himself lacks. Actually, they have to come up to him. As subtle as he is in his time and phrasing and his courage to wait, to use space, he's very forceful. There is a feeling of unhurriedness in his work and yet there's intensity underneath and through it all.
> —Gil Evans

> Miles's conception of time has led to greater rhythmic freedom for other players. His feeling, for another thing, is so intense that he catapults the drummer, bassist, and pianist together, forcing them to play at the top of their technical ability and forcing them with his own emotional strength to be as emotional as possible.
> —Cecil Taylor

Miles said something in one of his interviews about your playing . . .
About Irish melody?
Yes, how did you feel about that?
I kind of knew what he meant.
Can you explain it?
No [he laughs].

> Years later Miles would say that Jarrett was "the best pianist I ever had." Jarrett's technique was awesome, but his imagination was often annoyingly eclectic. Left to his own devices, he would show off all the styles that he had mastered. He could play bebop one moment, then switch to a Bill Evans romanticism, and then suddenly leap into a frantic, "outside" Cecil Taylor pandemonium. He could also be extraordinarily lyrical, playing what Miles called "those beautiful Irish melodies."
> —Eric Nisenson

That's just what he heard in some of the things I played. I remember though that when I wrote compositions like "Metamorphosis" and other things on *In the Light*, I remember always thinking that there was a section of each piece that sounded Irish.

> I also think of it ["Metamorphosis"] as Universal Folk Music.
> —Keith Jarrett

> Jazz is getting too far from its folk roots.
> —Miles Davis

> Jazz today is closer to classical music than it is to folklore music, and I'd rather stay closer to folklore music.
> —Miles Davis

> Miles saw vital connections between rock and jazz, and expressed the opinion that rock wouldn't fade away, because, like jazz, it's folk music.
> —Ian Carr

Miles lamented back in the seventies that jazz was getting further and further away from its folk roots. How do you feel about that?

Well, now he went pretty far from it too. Now he has pop roots [he laughs]. Maybe he lost the way back to the folk roots, you know. But it's true, jazz did that.

So you think jazz relates to folk roots?

Jazz is folk music. Now it doesn't seem like it is, but the thing that I would call jazz is still a tribal language. A local thing.

Many people think that the world should speak the same language eventually, every country would speak the same language, and many people think that would be a really good thing to happen. But I don't agree. If that was the way the earth was two hundred years ago, we would have no jazz. We would have no folk music to listen to from anywhere else. We would only have one thing, it would be like New Age music forever. So to me something local is very important. Something that's only in a certain geography.

Nobody would play anything that anyone else would learn from. Everyone would hear the same thing and play the same thing.

Because language, the way we talk, is connected strongly to how we hear—so if everyone spoke the same way, the same words, they would be all hearing the same sounds.

Geography makes the language. I don't think people just come up with some imaginary language from nothing. I think the sound of the language comes from the colors in the sky and the landscape.

If you go to beaches in Belgium, it's very gray all the time. There's not much color in the sky and there's not much color in the ocean. The shells don't have much color. If you go to the South Pacific where the ocean is very blue then the shells are very colorful. People aren't immune to that. People are affected by the geography. So if we are all forced to speak the same language we won't even see our own geography anymore.

So when the indigenous people of each country—the Indians of North America, African natives—when they become civilized they lose what they can give to us. I can see that very clearly here in the United States.

If I see a black man and I hear him talk like a Wall Street executive who is white, there is something he cannot give me anymore. He's traded. He gives himself, and he gets this Wall Street image, but he can never get back his local sound again.

So maybe the trio with Jack DeJohnette and Gary Peacock needs to exist for one important reason that is not musical. We are keeping this language alive. We are not saying, "Well now, it's modem day, we move to fusion or we have to change our language." We are keeping this language no matter what the pressures are around us.

There is a funny story from when I was with Miles and Gary Bartz was with the band. Gary is black and I'm white. Gary and I went into a coffee shop to have some food before we played and the man comes up with the sandwiches and says, "So you're musicians." We said, "Yes." He said, "What kind of music do you play?" And Gary said, "We play black music." I said, "Wait a minute, no, no, no, wait a minute. Gary plays black music and I play Hungarian music" [laughs]. I said, "Let's be fair. We have to be fair."

60. Constructing the Jazz Tradition

CHRISTOPHER SMALL HAS CRITICIZED THE concept of "classical music" by pointing out how that category flattens out Gregorian chant, Renaissance dances, Lutheran cantatas, serial operas, and aleatoric electronic music into a group of interchangeable pieces that have lost their historical meanings.[1] In the same spirit we might ask: in what sense are New Orleans collective improvisation, big band swing, bebop, free jazz, and fusion variants of the same thing? Or in what ways do they exemplify distinct historical moments and sensibilities? We use cultural categories and historical narratives to create coherence and define relationships, but the complexity of culture renders all such abstractions incomplete. The stories we tell both orient and blinker us, so that to accept as natural any narrative of jazz history is to acquiesce to an array of arguments about the value and meanings of many kinds of music.

As jazz has gained a foothold in the academy, jazz scholarship has begun to reflect the influence of intellectual currents that have animated the humanities in recent decades. For example, drawing on Hayden White's influential work on narrativity and the philosophy of history, musicologist Scott DeVeaux (b. 1954) produced the sophisticated essay on jazz historiography from which this excerpt is taken. The author of *The*

Source: Scott DeVeaux, "Constructing the Jazz Tradition: Jazz Historiography," *Black American Literature Forum* 25:3 (Fall, 1991), pp. 525–60. Reprinted by permission of Scott DeVeaux.

1. See Christopher Small, *Music-Society-Education* (Hanover, N.H.: Wesleyan University Press, 1996 [1977]).

Birth of Bebop: A Social and Musical History (1997) and several insightful articles, DeVeaux surveyed a number of different (and contradictory) ways of telling the story of jazz.[2] Jazz history is organized around values, he argues, such as the celebration of an ethnicity or the rejection of capitalism. Writers often depend on what Hayden White called modes of narration, such as the "Tragic" mode of self-destructive musicians like Buddy Bolden or Bix Beiderbecke, or the "Romance" of Louis Armstrong or Benny Goodman, who prevailed against many disadvantages to become virtuosos and stars. DeVeaux criticizes the widespread use of metaphors of growth and evolution in jazz history, which minimize the contestation and uncertainty that have accompanied musical changes.[3] Yet he is sensitive to the practical problems of teaching jazz history without undermining the useful aspects of narrative explanations. Throughout, DeVeaux emphasizes the constructedness and interestedness of traditions, and how they can distract us from history—from the meanings jazz has had at particular times and places.

"I don't know where jazz is going. Maybe it's going to hell. You can't make anything go anywhere. It just happens."
—Thelonious Monk

To judge from textbooks aimed at the college market, something like an official history of jazz has taken hold in recent years. On these pages, for all its chaotic diversity of style and expression and for all the complexity of its social origins, jazz is presented as a coherent whole, and its history as a skillfully contrived and easily comprehended narrative. After an obligatory nod to African origins and ragtime antecedents, the music is shown to move through a succession of styles or periods, each with a conveniently distinctive label and time period: New Orleans jazz up through the 1920s, swing in the 1930s, bebop in the 1940s, cool jazz and hard bop in the 1950s, free jazz and fusion in the 1960s. Details of emphasis vary. But from textbook to textbook, there is substantive agreement on the defining features of each style, the pantheon of great innovators, and the canon of recorded masterpieces.

This official version of jazz history continues to gain ground through the burgeoning of jazz appreciation classes at universities and colleges. It is both symptom and cause of the gradual acceptance of jazz, within the academy and in the society at large, as an art music—"America's classical music," in a frequently invoked phrase.[4] Such acceptance, most advocates of jazz agree, is long overdue. If at one time jazz

2. See Scott DeVeaux, *The Birth of Bebop: A Social and Musical History* (Berkeley: University of California Press, 1997), "Constructing the Jazz Tradition: Jazz Historiography," *Black American Literature Forum* 25:3 (Fall 1991), pp. 525–60, and "What Did We Do to Be So Black and Blue?," *Musical Quarterly* 80:1 (Fall 1996), pp. 392–430.

3. See also Gary Tomlinson, "Cultural Dialogics and Jazz: A White Historian Signifies," in Katherine Bergeron and Philip V. Bohlman, eds., *Disciplining Music: Musicology and Its Canons*, pp. 64–94 (Chicago: University of Chicago Press, 1992), and Krin Gabbard, "The Jazz Canon and Its Consequences," *Annual Review of Jazz Studies* 6 (1993), pp. 65–98.

4. See Grover Sales, *Jazz: America's Classical Music* (New York: Da Capo, 1992 [1984]), and Billy Taylor's "Jazz—America's Classical Music," in this volume. [RW]

could be supported by the marketplace, or attributed to a nebulous (and idealized) vision of folk creativity, that time has long passed. Only by acquiring the prestige, the "cultural capital" (in Pierre Bourdieu's phrase) of an artistic tradition can the music hope to be heard, and its practitioners receive the support commensurate with their training and accomplishments. The accepted historical narrative for jazz serves this purpose. It is a pedigree, showing contemporary jazz to be not a fad or a mere popular music, subject to the whims of fashion, but an autonomous art of some substance, the culmination of a long process of maturation that has in its own way recapitulated the evolutionary progress of Western art.

The added twist is that this new American classical music openly acknowledges its debt not to Europe, but to Africa. There is a sense of triumphant reversal as the music of a formerly enslaved people is designated a "rare and valuable national American treasure" by the Congress, and beamed overseas as a weapon of the Cold War. The story of jazz, therefore, has an important political dimension, one that unfolds naturally in its telling. Louis Armstrong, Duke Ellington, and John Coltrane provide powerful examples of black achievement and genius. Their exacting discipline cannot be easily marginalized, *pace* Adorno, as "mere" popular entertainment, or as the shadowy replication of European forms.[5] The depth of tradition, reaching back in an unbroken continuum to the beginning of the century, belies attempts to portray African Americans as people without a past—hence the appeal of an unambiguous and convincing historical narrative: If the achievements that jazz represents are to be impressed on present and future generations, the story must be told, and told well.

For all its pedagogical utility, though, the conventional narrative of jazz history is a simplification that begs as many questions as it answers. For one thing, the story that moves so confidently at the outset from style to style falters as it approaches the present. From the origins of jazz to bebop there is a straight line; but after bebop, the evolutionary lineage begins to dissolve into the inconclusive coexistence of many different, and in some cases mutually hostile, styles. "At the century's halfway mark," complains one textbook, "the historical strand that linked contemporary jazz to its roots suddenly began to fray. The cohesive thread had been pulled apart in the '40s by the bebop musicians, and now every fiber was bent at a slightly different angle" (Tirro 1977, p. 291). Beginning with the 1950s and 1960s, the student of jazz history is confronted with a morass of terms—*cool jazz, hard bop, modal jazz, Third Stream, New Thing*—none of which convincingly represents a consensus.[6] For the

5. See, for example, Theodor W. Adorno, "Perennial Fashion—Jazz," in *Prisms,* trans. Samuel Weber and Shierry Weber (Cambridge: MIT Press, 1981 [1953]), pp. 119–32, or Max Horkheimer and Theodor W. Adorno, "The Culture Industry: Enlightenment as Mass Deception," in their *Dialectic of Enlightenment,* trans. John Cumming (New York: Continuum, 1986 [1944]), pp. 120–67. [RW]

6. A sampling from recent jazz textbooks gives some of the flavor of this loss of direction. Tanner and Gerow's *A Study of Jazz* follows neatly defined chapters on "Early New Orleans Dixieland (1900–1920)," "Chicago Style Dixieland (the 1920s)," "Swing (1932–1942)," "Bop (1940–1950)," "Cool (1949–1955)," and "Funky (c. 1954–1963)," with a "period" of over forty years called the "Eclectic Era," a "pot-pourri of some eighty years of continuous development" (119). The "Chronology of Jazz Styles Chart" in Mark Gridley's *Jazz Styles* begins with comfortingly concise periods for "Early Jazz (1920s)," "Swing (1930s)," "Bop (1940s)," and "West Coast (1950s)," but soon degenerates into "Coexistence of Hard Bop, Free Jazz, and Modal Jazz (1960s)," "Transition to Jazz-Rock (late 1960s)," and "Coexistence of AACM, Jazz-Rock, and Modal Jazz (1970s)" (356–57). Billy Taylor's last chapter in *Jazz Piano* (after the terse chapters "Bebop," and "Cool") is entitled "Abstract Jazz, Mainstream Jazz, Modal Jazz, Electronic Jazz, Fusion" (187).

most recent decades, the most that writers of textbooks can manage is to sketch out the contrasting directions pointed to by free jazz and jazz/rock fusion, implying to the impressionable student that an informed view embraces both, as it embraces all preceding styles, and that the future of jazz is bound up with a pluralism that somehow reconciles these apparently irreconcilable trends (the persistence of earlier styles of jazz is sometimes counted as yet another direction). No one, apparently, has thought to ask whether the earlier "cohesive thread" of narrative might mask similarly conflicting interpretations.

At the same time that jazz educators have struggled to bring order to jazz history, a controversy over the current state and future direction of jazz has become noisily evident in the popular media. The terms of this debate pit so-called *neoclassicists,* who insist on the priority of tradition and draw their inspiration and identity from a sense of connectedness with the historical past, against both the continuous revolution of the *avant-garde* and the commercial orientation of *fusion*. At stake, if the rhetoric is taken at face value, is nothing less than the music's survival. Some have argued, for example, that the neoclassicist movement, led by youthful celebrity Wynton Marsalis, has rescued jazz from extinction. "Largely under his influence," proclaimed a *Time* author in a recent cover story,

> a jazz renaissance is flowering on what was once barren soil. Straight-ahead jazz music almost died in the 1970s as record companies embraced the electronically enhanced jazz-pop amalgam known as fusion. Now a whole generation of prodigiously talented young musicians is going back to the roots, using acoustic instruments, playing recognizable tunes and studying the styles of earlier jazzmen. (Sancton 1990, p. 66)

Other critics counter that the triumph of a retrospective aesthetic is in fact all the evidence one might need that jazz is dead; all that is left to the current generation is the custodial function of preserving and periodically reviving glorious moments from the past (Martin 1986, p. 204; Kart 1990).

The neoclassicists' nostalgia for a Golden Age located ambiguously somewhere between the swing era and 1960s hard bop resonates curiously with issues that go back to the earliest days of jazz historiography. Marsalis and his followers have been called "latter-day moldy figs" (Santoro 1988, p. 17), a term that links them to critics of the 1930s and '40s who, by insisting on the priority of New Orleans-style jazz, earned themselves the reputation as defenders of an outdated and artificially static notion of what jazz is and can be. The countercharge that either (or both) avant-garde or fusion constitutes a "wrong turn," or a "dead end," in the development of jazz represents the opposing argument, of the same vintage: Any change that fails to preserve the essence of the music is a corruption that no longer deserves to be considered jazz.[7]

The difference in tone between these assessments—the rancor of the journalistic debate, and the platitudinous certainty of the classroom—disguises the extent to which certain underlying assumptions are shared. With the possible exception of those in the fusion camp (who are more often the targets of the debate rather than active participants in it), no one disputes the official version of the history. Its basic narrative shape and its value for a music that is routinely denied respect and institutional support are accepted virtually without question. The struggle is over *possession* of the history, and the legitimacy that it confers. More precisely, the struggle is over

7. See the debate between Wynton Marsalis and Herbie Hancock, in this volume. [RW]

the act of definition that is presumed to lie at the history's core; for it is an article of faith that some central essence named *jazz* remains constant throughout all the dramatic transformations that have resulted in modern-day jazz.

That essence is ordinarily defined very vaguely; there is ample evidence from jazz folklore to suggest that musicians take a certain stubborn pride in the resistance of their art to critical exegesis. (To the question *What is jazz?* the apocryphal answer is: "If you have to ask, you'll never know.") But in the heat of debate, definition is a powerful weapon; and more often than not, such definitions define through exclusion. Much as the concept of purity is made more concrete by the threat of contamination, what jazz is *not* is far more vivid rhetorically than what it is. Thus fusion is "not jazz" because, in its pursuit of commercial success, it has embraced certain musical traits—the use of electric instruments, modern production techniques, and a rock- or funk-oriented rhythmic feeling—that violate the essential nature of jazz. The avant-garde, whatever its genetic connection to the modernism of 1940s bebop, is not jazz—or no longer jazz—because, in its pursuit of novelty, it has recklessly abandoned the basics of form and structure, even African-American principles like "swing." And the neoclassicist stance is irrelevant, and potentially harmful, to the growth of jazz because it makes a fetish of the past, failing to recognize that the essence of jazz is the process of change itself.

Defining jazz is a notoriously difficult proposition, but the task is easier if one bypasses the usual inventory of musical qualities or techniques, like improvisation or swing (since the more specific or comprehensive such a list attempts to be, the more likely it is that exceptions will overwhelm the rule). More relevant are the boundaries within which historians, critics, and musicians have consistently situated the music. One such boundary, certainly, is ethnicity. Jazz is strongly identified with African-American culture, both in the narrow sense that its particular techniques ultimately derive from black American folk traditions, and in the broader sense that it is expressive of, and uniquely rooted in, the experience of black Americans. This raises important questions at the edges—e.g., how the contributions of white musicians are to be treated and, at the other end of the spectrum, where the boundary between jazz and other African-American genres (such as blues, gospel, and R&B) ought to be drawn. But on the whole, ethnicity provides a core, a center of gravity for the narrative of jazz, and is one element that unites the several different kinds of narratives in use today.

An equally pervasive, if divisive, theme is economics—specifically, the relationship of jazz to capitalism. Here, the definition is negative: Whether conceived of as art music or folk music, jazz is consistently seen as something separate from the popular music industry. The stigmatizing of "commercialism" as a disruptive or corrupting influence, and in any case as something external to the tradition, has a long history in writings on jazz. In the words of Rudi Blesh (writing in 1946),

> Commercialism [is] a cheapening and deteriorative force, a species of murder perpetrated on a wonderful music by whites and by those misguided negroes who, for one or another reason, choose to be accomplices to the deed. . . . Commercialism is a thing not only hostile, but fatal to [jazz]. (pp. 11–12)

Such language was particularly popular with defenders of New Orleans-style jazz who, like Blesh, narrowly identified the music with a romanticized notion of folk culture. But the same condemnatory fervor would be heard from proponents of bebop in the 1940s:

> The story of bop, like that of swing before it, like the stories of jazz and ragtime before that, has been one of constant struggle against the restrictions imposed on all

progressive thought in an art that has been commercialized to the point of prostitution. (Feather 1949, p. 45)

Bebop is the music of revolt: revolt against big bands, arrangers . . . Tin Pan Alley—against commercialized music in general. It reasserts the individuality of the jazz musician. . . . (Russell 1959, p. 202)

These attitudes survive with undiminished force in recent attacks on fusion, which imply a conception of jazz as a music independent of commercial demands that is in continuous conflict with the economic imperatives of twentieth-century America. *Agoraphobia,* fear of the marketplace, is problematic enough in artistic genres that have actually achieved, or inherited, some degree of economic autonomy. It is all the more remarkable for jazz—a music that has developed largely within the framework of modern mass market capitalism—to be construed within the inflexible dialectic of "commercial" versus "artistic," with all virtue centered in the latter. The virulence with which these opinions are expressed gives a good idea how much energy was required to formulate this position in the first place, and how difficult it is to maintain. This is not to say that there is not an exploitative aspect to the relationship between capitalist institutions and jazz musicians, especially when the effects of racial discrimination on the ability of black musicians to compete fairly are factored in. But jazz is kept separate from the marketplace only by demonizing the economic system that allows musicians to survive—and from this demon there is no escape. Wynton Marsalis may pride himself on his refusal to "sell out," but that aura of artistic purity is an indisputable component of his commercial appeal.

Issues of ethnicity and economics define jazz as an oppositional discourse: the music of an oppressed minority culture, tainted by its association with commercial entertainment in a society that reserves its greatest respect for art that is carefully removed from daily life. The escape from marginalization comes only from a self-definition that emphasizes its universality and its autonomy. The "jazz tradition" reifies the music, insisting that there *is* an overarching category called *jazz,* encompassing musics of divergent styles and sensibilities. These musics must be understood not as isolated expressions of particular times or places, but in an organic relationship, as branches of a tree to the trunk. The essence of jazz, in other words, lies not in any one style, or any one cultural or historical context, but in that which links all these things together into a seamless continuum. Jazz is what it is because it is a culmination of all that has come before. Without the sense of depth that only a narrative can provide, jazz would be literally rootless, indistinguishable from a variety of other "popular" genres that combine virtuosity and craftsmanship with dance rhythms. Its claim to being not only distinct, but elevated above other indigenous forms ("America's classical music"), is in large part dependent on the idea of an evolutionary progression reaching back to the beginning of the century. Again and again, present-day musicians, whether neoclassicist or avant-garde, invoke the past, keeping before the public's eye the idea that musics as diverse as those of King Oliver and the Art Ensemble of Chicago are in some fundamental sense *the same music.*[8]

Those who subscribe to an essentialist notion of jazz history (and there are few who do not) take all this for granted. But even a glance at jazz historiography makes

---

8. The Art Ensemble of Chicago makes a point of avoiding the term *jazz* as too limiting (although this deters no one from claiming them as part of a narrative of jazz). As their motto "Great Black Music—Ancient to Modern" makes clear, that is not because they are uninterested in issues of ethnicity and historical tradition, but because they wish to situate their music within an even more ambitious narrative.

it clear that the idea of the "jazz tradition" is a construction of relatively recent vintage, an overarching narrative that has crowded out other possible interpretations of the complicated and variegated cultural phenomena that we cluster under the umbrella *jazz.* Nor is this simply an academic complaint: The crisis of the current jazz scene is less a function of the state of the music (jazz has, in many ways, never been better supported or appreciated) than of an anxiety arising from the inadequacy of existing historical frameworks to explain it.

The question *Where is jazz going?* is usually asked with an anxious undertone—as if, in Monk's words, "Maybe it's going to hell." And Monk's dismissive response is on target. Whether jazz will "survive" depends not on what musicians choose to do. They will continue to make music, and whether that music is called jazz is a matter of relative inconsequence. The question is rather of the uses to which the jazz tradition is to be put: whether as an alternative conservatory style for the training of young musicians; as an artistic heritage to be held up as an exemplar of American or African-American culture; or as a convenient marketing tool for recording companies and concert promoters, a kind of brand name guaranteeing quality and a degree of homogeneity.

As an educator and scholar, I inevitably find myself allied with the first two of these projects, especially the second. My courses in jazz history are designed to inculcate a feeling of pride in a racially mixed university for an African-American musical tradition that manages, against all odds, to triumph over obstacles of racism and indifference. For this, the narrative of jazz history as Romance is a powerful tool, and I have invested a good deal into making it a reality in my students' minds through all the eloquence and emotion I can muster.

And yet I am increasingly aware of this narrative's limitations, especially its tendency to impose a kind of deadening uniformity of cultural meaning on the music, and jazz history's patent inability to explain current trends in an cogent form. There is a revolution underway in jazz that lies not in any internal crisis of style, but in the debate over the looming new orthodoxy: jazz as "America's classical music." As jazz acquires degree programs, piano competitions, repertory ensembles, institutes, and archives, it inevitably becomes a different kind of music—gaining a certain solidity and political clout, but no longer participating in the ongoing formulation of meaning; no longer a *popular* music in the best sense of the word. The histories we construct for jazz also have this effect: Each new textbook dulls our sensibilities, "retells the stories as they have been told and written, . . . made neat and smooth, with all incomprehensible details vanished along with most of the wonder" (Ellison 1946, p. 200).

Meanwhile, music continues to change: the explosion in new technologies, the increased pace of global interaction, the continued erosion of European art music as the measure of all things. The narratives we have inherited to describe the history of jazz retain the patterns of outmoded forms of thought, especially the assumption that the progress of jazz as art necessitates increased distance from the popular. If we, as historians, critics, and educators, are to adapt to these new realities, we must be willing to construct new narratives to explain them. These alternative explanations need not displace the jazz tradition (it hardly seems fair, in any case, to deconstruct a narrative that has only recently been constructed, especially one that serves such important purposes). But the time has come for an approach that is less invested in the ideology of jazz as aesthetic object and more responsive to issues of historical particularity. Only in this way can the study of jazz break free from its self-imposed isolation, and participate with other disciplines in the exploration of meaning in American culture.

References

Blesh, Rudi. *Shining Trumpets: A History of Jazz.* New York: Knopf, 1946.
Ellison, Ralph. *Shadow and Act.* New York: NAL, 1946.
Feather, Leonard. *Inside Be-Bop.* New York: Robbins, 1949.
Gridley, Mark. *Jazz Styles: History and Analysis,* third ed. Englewood Cliffs: Prentice Hall, 1988.
Kart, Larry. "Provocative Opinion: The Death of Jazz?" *Black Music Research Journal* 10:1 (1990), pp. 76–81.
Martin, Henry. *Enjoying Jazz.* New York: Schirmer, 1986.
Russell, Ross. "Bebop." In Martin Williams, ed., *The Art of Jazz,* pp. 187–214. New York: Oxford University Press, 1959.
Sancton, Thomas. "Horns of Plenty." *Time,* 22 October 1990, pp. 64–71.
Santoro, Gene. "Miles Davis the Enabler: Part II." *Down Beat,* November 1988, pp. 16–19.
Taylor, Billy. *Jazz Piano: History and Development.* Dubuque: Brown, 1982.
Tirro, Frank. *Jazz: A History.* New York: W. W. Norton, 1977.

61. Local Jazz

JAMES LINCOLN COLLIER (B. 1928) IS A PROLIFIC AUTHOR whose works include full-scale biographies of such major stars as Benny Goodman, Duke Ellington, and Louis Armstrong. But here he points out that the vast majority of jazz is played by people whose names virtually no one has ever heard. Such music doesn't show up in the history books or the daily newspaper reviews, yet it amounts to most of the live jazz that is played and heard. Collier tries to account for why so many musicians continue to participate in jazz performance, despite poor pay, long travel, and other obstacles that would seem likely to discourage professionals and amateurs alike. But somehow they don't. And debates over which direction jazz is going or should go usually overlook the steady march of what might be called local jazz, which goes wherever the people who play it want to take it.

Source: James Lincoln Collier, "Local Jazz," in *Jazz: The American Theme Song* (New York: Oxford University Press, 1993), pp. 263–75.

Jazz criticism and jazz history have always concentrated on the big names, the stars, and the famous clubs and dance halls where they worked. In fact, jazz history is usually written around a chain of major figures—Oliver, to Armstrong, to Beiderbecke, to Ellington, to Goodman, to Parker, to Davis, to Coltrane, to Coleman—to the point where it might appear to the outsider that these great players *were* jazz history.

But, in fact, perhaps 90 percent of the music has always been made by unknown players working in local bars and clubs for audiences drawn from the surrounding neighborhood, town, and country. Right from the beginning, all over the United States, there have been thousands of jazz bands manned by people who, in the main, play the music only part-time. Some of these are outright amateurs offering a very rough version of the music for the amusement of their friends at tailgate parties, anniversaries, or fraternity beer busts. Others are semi-professionals who play for money on a more or less regular basis in restaurants, bars, lake cruises, clubhouses, campus lounges, community centers—almost anywhere that it is possible to make music. Many are high school teachers. Still others are professional musicians who make the bulk of their living playing club dates in their area, but keep together trios and quartets that find jazz work two or three times a month. Finally, a fairly considerable number of full-time professional jazz musicians dip into the local jazz scene from time to time when they have nothing else booked, in order to "keep their chops up," as a favor, or because they would rather be out playing than sitting home watching television. I have seen notables like Al Haig, Max Kaminsky, Wild Bill Davison, and Eddie Gomez playing with semi-pros, and even Armstrong, Goodman, and Parker have been known to sit in with such groups on occasion.

It should be borne in mind that this "local" jazz scene exists in big cities as well as small towns and suburban communities. New York, Chicago, Boston, Philadelphia, San Francisco, and other cities have their contingents of part-time players who find bars and restaurants where they can work regularly for modest sums.

It is difficult to calculate how extensive this local jazz scene is. The Horowitz survey gives us some clues, however.[1] It reports that about .8 percent of Americans play jazz in public from time to time—about 1.3 million adults. There are about 144,500 members of the American Federation of Musicians, which most full-time professional jazz musicians belong to; and as many of these people are not jazz players, it is clear that, as Horowitz says, the 1.3 million jazz players aforementioned are "largely amateur performers."

My own experience suggests that there is some sort of regular local jazz activity in most cities with populations of 50,000 and above. There are about 500 such cities in the United States, and as the larger cities will have several—even dozens of regularly constituted jazz bands working part-time—the total number of such bands must run into the thousands, and the players in them to the tens of thousands.

But it is not just in the cities, large or small, that these local jazz bands are found. Startling numbers of them are to be found in suburban restaurants, and even roadhouses in rural areas. I have repeatedly been astonished to find in a local barroom in a rural backwash a jazz musician of the first quality playing for an audience of working people out for a little fun. (It often turns out that such players were once "on the road with Woody.")

To this must be added the 20,000 college, high school, and even junior high school stage bands and jazz units that rehearse regularly and give occasional concerts. Admittedly, the audience for most of these student groups is artificial, consisting of

1. See "Who Listens to Jazz?" in this volume. [RW]

parents and fellow students dragged out two or three times a year to dutifully applaud the carefully rehearsed version of "Little Darlin'." Nonetheless, it is a jazz experience for everyone involved.

Thus, even though we can only put rough numbers to this local jazz scene, we can be sure that in bulk it vastly outweighs the big-time professional arena in any terms we wish to use—numbers of musicians involved, numbers of gigs played, the size of the live audience. At this moment *The New Yorker* lists nine well-known jazz clubs in New York City that usually feature name jazz musicians. I can think offhand of at least twice that many clubs in Manhattan alone that use semi-professional jazz bands several nights a week. And this is in the heart of the supposed jazz capital of the world, where every night the unsung must compete with the likes of Phil Woods, Barney Kessel, and Gerry Mulligan, all of whom are playing in Manhattan as I write. In most small cities and suburban towns, there are *no* locations that regularly hire big-name jazz musicians: the Mulligans and Kessels appear at such places only for occasional concerts. Here the locals dominate by a factor of at least ten to one, and perhaps many times that: there are thousands of towns in which the appearance of a star jazz musician is a rare event, but which offer local jazz bands on a weekly basis.

This is especially true of Dixieland. With the recent deaths of the last of the Dixieland veterans, like Wild Bill Davison, there are virtually no professionals left playing in this style. There are a few exceptions, like the Jim Cullum Happy Jazz Band, but almost all of the some one hundred bands that show up at the Sacramento Dixieland Festival each year are manned, in the main, by part-timers. It is one of the paradoxes of jazz that this basic form has virtually disappeared from the repertory of the professionals: it is kept alive by the local players.

These local players come from everywhere in the society and include every class and ethnic group. Nonetheless, a disproportionate number of them are middle-class, both black and white, many of them from the higher end of the socioeconomic spectrum. We would not be surprised to find among them a fair number of writers, painters, or college professors, for whom jazz is part and parcel of the intellectual or semi-bohemian lifestyle many of them adopt. It is more surprising to find in the group a large number of doctors, lawyers, dentists, and captains of industry, many of them political conservatives, a strain not generally thought to be widespread in jazz. This phenomenon is important to note, for it contradicts the stereotype of the jazz player as outsider or political radical. It is simply true that there are plenty of skilled, sensitive jazz players around who vote for conservative candidates, oppose gun control, and believe that welfare cheats are responsible for the present federal budget deficit.

Part of the explanation for the disproportionate number of upper-middle-class professionals in the ranks of the part-time players is that there were paths open to them other than music. Most of them, black and white, came from middle-class homes where it was taken for granted that they would go on to college and have professional careers. Despite that, many of them considered careers in music, some even trained at it, and a fair number actually tried it for a few months or even years. But most quickly began asking themselves why they should settle for the risky, even marginal lives most musicians lead, when they could be doctors, lawyers, government officials, and upper-level corporate executives, with the prestige and money that go along with such careers. For these people, the critical decision to give up music usually followed the realization that they would be spending the bulk of their lives in music playing club dates, or if they were lucky, working in the studios or in pit orchestras. For a kid from a working-class home who may have dropped out of high school to go out on the road, a lifetime of club dates sounds a good deal better than thirty years in the canning plant or the post office. To the young adult with a college degree, there are other alternatives: if you are not going to be playing jazz in any case, why not aim for a professional career and play jazz on the side?

But it is hardly the case that the part-timers among the local players are all surgeons with half-million-dollar annual incomes. The local scene is very democratic. Any local jazz band is likely to include a high school music teacher, a mail carrier or cab driver, one or two full-time club date musicians, as well as a doctor, lawyer, or college professor. They frequently include a retiree who finally has the time to work at his music. Most revealingly, the pecking order on the bandstand forms up along musical, rather than occupational, lines. The clarinet-playing bank president will take his cues from the club-date pianist who earns a fraction of the banker's income but knows Bird's changes to the bridge to "Cherokee."

One factor that keeps the local jazz scene in good health is the fact that the players come cheap. To a few the money is important; some bands of part-timers develop local reputations and can work a hundred or more gigs a year, often for seventy-five, a hundred, or more dollars a man, and for some players the extra five thousand dollars a year is significant. But most of the gigs local bands of this kind work pay twenty-five to fifty dollars a man, and many are what the musicians call "freebies." For many local players, the earnings do not cover their expenses—travel costs, reeds and strings, and instrument repair, to say nothing of the between-set beers, which may not always be on the house.

What matters to these people is the chance to play jazz, and especially to play it in public, and that is as true of the working club-date musician as it is of the rank amateur. There are many busy professional musicians who will give up a Sunday afternoon and travel an hour or more each way to play a jazz gig with agreeable companions for nominal money. Exactly why it is important for them to play in front of a real audience is difficult to know; obviously, the experience of playing, of itself, is no different in a basement den or a rehearsal hall from what it is in a club. But it does matter to the local players to work before an audience. For the part-time musician this is to some extent a matter of credentials: a player who is working in public for a fee, however small, can savor the idea that he is a jazz musician, in the same way that a schoolteacher who occasionally places a short story with a little magazine can think of himself as a writer.

But I think there is more to it than that. Ordinary local jazz players, whether they work in jazz full-time or not, lead the same sort of daily life that most Americans do: a routine job, marriage, and family life with the normal ups and downs; births, deaths, commuting trains, vacation trips, the flu, office parties. The experience of playing jazz in the local gin mill, however seedy, is the plus, the added factor that lifts them out of their daily lives and enables them to accept more easily the graying hair, the children's failures, the grind of the job. It heals the battered ego, provides a sense of being on the inside of something, a feeling of doing something wholly worthwhile for a change.

Beyond this, the experience of playing regularly with the same people is like belonging to a bowling league. There is a genuine camaraderie among people who play jazz together frequently. This sense of good fellowship is an important aspect of their gig, especially where the musicians have been working together for a period of time, as is likely to be the case with local groups, who do not have the vast pool of first-rate jazz musicians to call on that exists in big cities. A sense of good feeling on the bandstand is an attraction for audiences, too, who notice the players kidding each other about mistakes, cheering each other on, and indulging in a certain amount of good-natured banter. Good spirits like these are infectious. It is common to hear audiences say, "You all seem to have such a good time playing."

Having a good spirit on the bandstand is more important to local players, who are not doing it for money or prestige, than it is for professionals who more frequently have something to prove—a reputation to uphold, a leader to impress. As a consequence, big egos and domineering personalities are not well tolerated among the locals, and such people are likely to find themselves excluded, no matter how good they are, in favor of less adequate musicians who are more personable, more willing to play the supporting roles that a jazz band, like a football team, requires. Most jazz musicians—and that includes professionals as well—feel a *responsibility* for the music. You don't cheat, you don't look for the showy effect, you don't push yourself forward at the expense of others. You remain humble in the face of the difficulty of playing jazz well, and the example of the great players who manage to do so consistently. Local players generally have little use for musicians who lack this humility.

It is probably here that the line between the full-time jazz player and the part-timer is most clearly drawn. Professionals are working in a very tight market and are perforce more competitive than those who are not dependent on jazz for their living or, just as important, a place in the world. They are more likely to endure the abrasive but gifted player who draws audiences, and to tailor their playing to the demands of the market in order to keep the gig. Local jazz players—and once again we remember that they include a lot of professional club-date musicians—are not immune to commercial pressures, because they, too, want to keep their gigs. But their attitude is more likely to be, "I'm not doing this for the money; why am I driving all the way over here just to play this stuff?" The nonprofessional has the luxury of principle, which the professionals do not always have.

Jazz critics have usually looked down on the nonprofessionals with, at best, amused condescension and, at worst, outright scorn. They have written virtually nothing about the local jazz scene, one exception being John S. Wilson of *The New York Times*, who occasionally reports on clubs where the unsung groups play. To the average critic, this local jazz scene, with its tens of thousands of players and its huge audience, does not exist.

Nonetheless, these local, part-time jazz players are a far more important part of jazz than has been generally recognized. For one thing, anyone sufficiently devoted to music to endure the often painful struggle to play it as well as they can in constrained circumstances, is bound to care for jazz with something of the fervor of an acolyte. These tens of thousands of local players constitute an important audience for jazz. They listen regularly to the jazz radio programs; they buy tapes and CDs; they tape scores and even hundreds of hours of music for their personal jazz libraries; they go to clubs and concerts when their favorites are appearing.

Moreover, they are an extremely knowledgeable audience. They can hear, to one degree or another, what is going on in the jazz they listen to. They know how So-and-so's version of a tune differs from the standard way of playing it, because they have played it a hundred times themselves. They know which technical stunts are easier to bring off than they sound, and which lazy passages are actually very difficult to play. They are more appreciative of the *musicianship* required of a particular performance, even where the jazz content is not very important. Their experience over the years of playing from time to time with solid professionals, even big-name players, gives them a very clear idea of what goes into a first-rate jazz performance. They are likely to be better critics of the music than many of the well-known jazz writers whose pieces they frequently read. In sum, they make up the best kind of audience jazz musicians have, because they know what is going on in a performance, they approach their art with humility, and they respect those who can do it well.

For another thing, they make available to the public a tremendous amount of live music that otherwise would not exist. In fact, these local players provide a lot of free music, for they are frequently asked to play concerts for retired people on small incomes, the weddings and anniversaries of friends and relatives, school concerts meant to educate children about jazz, political rallies, and, inevitably, memorial services for other musicians. In some cases, a well-known jazz band will be seen as a community resource, and will find itself being asked to provide free music at community functions—the opening of the new library, the Christmas party for the indigent, the block association's annual fundraiser. As such, these local groups are integrating jazz into the community in a more real and personal way than the professionals do, who by and large resent being asked to perform for nothing on the reasonable grounds that they ought not be required to compete with themselves.

Jazz stopped being a folk music long before it escaped New Orleans. But in the hands of the local players, jazz remains, in a certain sense, folk music. They are providing for nominal sums, or indeed for nothing, functional music to people who share this aspect of a common culture. And this is why these players are so important to the music: they are not playing jazz for fame and money, but sheerly because they love the music. They are the pure in heart, and they should be condescended to by critics no more than we condescend to the club tennis player who gets onto the court every Sunday for the love of the game.

These local players are essential in jazz. They are the foot soldiers in the army, and in the end it is the foot soldiers, not the generals, who win wars. If the record companies suddenly stopped recording jazz, the radio stations stopped playing it, the jazz clubs switched to hip-hop, and the name players disappeared into the studio, jazz would endure, because their foot soldiers, the local musicians, would go on playing it in neighborhood taverns, high school auditoriums, tailgate parties, or if need be, in their own basement game rooms. As long as these, the true acolytes, go marching on, the music will live.

62. "Out of Notes": The Problem of Miles Davis

THE EDITOR OF THIS VOLUME (b. 1958) IS, among other things, a trumpet player, and this study of a performance by Miles Davis draws on that experience to analyze how and why Davis expanded the normal techniques

---

Source: Robert Walser, "'Out of Notes': Signification, Interpretation, and the Problem of Miles Davis," *Musical Quarterly* 77:2 (Summer, 1993), pp. 343–65. © The Musical Quarterly. Reprinted by permission of Copyright Clearance Center, Rightslink.

and vocabulary of the instrument to create a new sensibility in jazz. This article was first published in 1993 and has been often anthologized since then. It appears here, in slightly abbreviated form, at the request of a number of reviewers.

I played "My Funny Valentine" for a long time—and didn't like it—and all of a sudden it meant something.
—Miles Davis (Hentoff 1979: 162)

A flurry of posthumous tributes to Miles Davis almost managed to conceal the fact that jazz critics and historians have rarely been able to explain the power and appeal of his playing. Of course, there has been no lack of writing about Davis, and no shortage of praise for his accomplishments. For example, *Musician* magazine, which includes jazz but is not primarily devoted to it, launched a cover story with the extraordinary statement, "In the entire recording age, no one has meant more to music than Miles Davis."[1] But histories of jazz, biographies of Davis, and jazz journalism often beg the question of *why* he ought to be so highly regarded: there is a curious absence of engagement with Davis's music, and especially with his trumpet playing.

Miles Davis has always been difficult to deal with critically: along with his controversial personal life, and his even more controversial decision to "go electric" around 1969, Davis has long been infamous for missing more notes than any other major trumpet player. While nearly everyone acknowledges his historical importance as a bandleader and a musical innovator, and although large audiences flocked to his concerts for decades, critics have always been made uncomfortable by his "mistakes," the cracked and missed notes common in his performances. "The problem of Miles Davis" is the problem Davis presents to critics and historians: how are we to account for such glaring defects in the performances of someone who is indisputably one of the most important musicians in the history of jazz?

Often, critics simply ignore the mistakes. In his history of jazz, Frank Tirro (1977) delicately avoids any mention of the controversies surrounding Davis, whether missed notes, drug use, or electric instruments. Joachim Berendt, in *The Jazz Book* (1982) regretfully mentions Davis's "clams" but quickly passes on, and the widely used jazz appreciation text by Mark Gridley (1991), like that of Donald D. Megill and Richard S. Demory (1989), similarly whitewashes Davis's career.[2] When Howard Brofsky (1983) and Bill Cole (1974) independently transcribed and published the trumpet solo of Davis's 1964 recording of "My Funny Valentine," both chose to leave out the cracks, slips, and spleeahs, enabling them to produce nice, clean texts and to avoid many problematic aspects of the performance.[3]

---

1. *Musician* , December 1991, p. 5. Other important tributes appeared in *Down Beat* (December 1991) and *Rolling Stone* (November 14, 1991).

2. Tirro does mention fusion, but without any hint that it was controversial, that it was anything other than natural evolution.

3. *My Funny Valentine: Miles Davis in Concert* (Columbia CS 9106). This is a live recording of a performance at Philharmonic Hall in New York City, February 12, 1964. Davis performed with George Coleman, Herbie Hancock, Ron Carter, and Tony Williams. Ian Carr's (*Miles Davis*, 1982: 306) transcription is much better in this respect. While most critics refer to "missed notes" or "cracked notes," trumpet players themselves tend to prefer more colorful, onomatopoeic terms, such as "spleeah," "clam," or "frack."

Critics sometimes apologize for Davis's flaws or try to explain them away. Bill Cole acknowledges that Davis had what he calls "mechanical problems," but asserts that Davis "used them well to his advantage," building a style out of his weaknesses, forging "his mistakes into a positive result" (1974: 127, 129). Gary Giddins similarly credits Davis with "a thoroughly original style built on the acknowledgment of technical limitations." Giddins comments: "By the time of 'My Funny Valentine,' which contains one of the most notorious fluffs ever released, one got the feeling that his every crackle and splutter was to be embraced as evidence of his spontaneous soul" (1985: 79, 84). But Giddins himself does not seem convinced by this argument, and he remains unable either to embrace the fluffs or to excuse them. The best that can be said of Miles Davis in this light is that he was a good musician but a bad trumpet player.

James Lincoln Collier, as usual, is bolder than most other critics:

> But if his influence was profound, the ultimate value of his work is another matter. Miles Davis is not, in comparison with other men of major influence in jazz, a great improvisor. His lines are often composed of unrelated fragments and generally lack coherence. His sound is interesting, but too often it is weakened by the petulant whine of his half-valving. He has never produced the melodic lines of a Parker or Beiderbecke, or the dramatic structure of Armstrong or Ellington. And although certainly an adequate instrumentalist—we should not overstress his technical inadequacies—he is not a great one. Perhaps more important, he has not really been the innovator he is sometimes credited with being. Most of the fresh concepts he incorporated into his music originated with other men, ironically, in view of his black militancy, many of them white. . . . He has to be seen, then, not as an innovator, but as a popularizer of new ideas. (1978: 435)

Collier's complaint is that Davis lacks originality, formal regularity, timbral purity and consistency, and technical facility. But would Davis's playing really be better if his sound were more pure and uniform, or his phrases more regular? By claiming that Davis failed to measure up to presumably objective musical standards, Collier suggests that Davis was not a good trumpet player *or* a good musician, despite the popularity and respect he has earned from fans and musicians. Though he is more blunt in his denunciation of Davis than are most other jazz critics, Collier's assessment is not unique. But when critical judgments become so out of synch with the actual reception of the music they address, it may be time to reexamine some basic premises. Perhaps there are other methods and criteria to use in analyzing and evaluating jazz; perhaps there is a way of theorizing Davis's playing that would account for its power to affect deeply many listeners.

Miles Davis may be the most important and challenging figure for jazz criticism at the present moment, because he can't be denied a place in the canon of great jazz musicians, yet the accepted criteria for greatness do not fit him well. (The complexity of Duke Ellington's scoring or the virtuosity of Charlie Parker's improvisation, for example, seem to be much easier to explain and to legitimate than Davis's performances.) The uneasiness many critics display toward Miles Davis's "mistakes," and their failure to explain the power of his playing, suggest that there are important gaps in the paradigms of musical analysis and interpretation that dominate jazz studies. Understanding Davis's missed notes and accounting for his success as a performer may require rethinking some of our assumptions about what and how music means.

Some useful ways of doing so are implicit in the theory of signification presented by Henry Louis Gates Jr. in his book *The Signifying Monkey: A Theory of African-American Literary Criticism* (1988). I am not the first to notice that this book has much to offer music scholars; John P. Murphy (1990) has drawn upon Gates's work in his discussion of dialogue among jazz improvisers, Gary Tomlinson (1992) has used Gates's ideas in his excellent essay on jazz canons and Miles Davis's fusion period, and Samuel Floyd (1991) has deployed Gates's theory in his insightful analysis of the dialogue of rhythmic relationships and formal conventions in Jelly Roll Morton's "Black Bottom Stomp."[4] But I will argue that Gates's theory of signifying might yet be applied at a finer level of musical analysis, to illuminate the significance of specific musical details and the rhetoric of performance.

At the core of his theory is Gates's delineation of two different ways of thinking about how meanings are produced. Gates distinguishes between two cultural traditions, white "signifying" and black "Signifyin(g)"; I find the latter a rather precious and unwieldy alteration of the vernacular term, and I will refer to these as "signification" and "signifyin'," respectively ("Signification" also has the advantage of preserving the static, foundationalist character of the theories of meaning to which Gates refers, while "signifyin'" retains the vernacular focus on agency). The two modes contrast sharply. Signification is logical, rational, limited; from this perspective, meanings are denotative, fixed, exact, and exclusive. Signifyin', conversely, works through reference, gesture, and dialogue to suggest multiple meanings through association. If signification assumes that meanings can be absolute, permanent, and objectively specified, signifyin' respects contingency, improvisation, relativity—the social production and negotiation of meanings. We might compare the way a dictionary prescribes meanings with the ways in which words constantly change meaning in actual usage by communities of language users. The difference is like that between semantics and rhetoric: signification assumes that meaning can be communicated abstractly and individually, apart from the circumstances of exchange; signifyin' celebrates performance and dialogic engagement.

As Gates himself insists, signifyin' is not exclusive to African-American culture, though it is in that culture that signifyin' has been most fully articulated theoretically, not only by scholars but also in folklore and song lyrics. In fact, the concept could be compared to literary critic Mikhail Bakhtin's (1981) ideas about dialogue in the novel, or to a variety of other twentieth-century interrogations of the nature of language and meaning, from Wittgenstein to the American pragmatists to the French post-structuralists.[5] But Gates, while certainly influenced by these critics and theorists, means to illuminate African-American literature by taking seriously the modes of signifyin' developed within black vernacular traditions.

Henry Louis Gates Jr.'s theory is useful precisely because his goal was to create the means to deal with cultural difference on its own terms, as an antidote to theoretical assimilation by more prestigious projects. Gates does not shy away from questions of value and analysis, yet his work unmasks the shallowness of attempts to show that African literature is worthy of study because it is fundamentally the same as European literature, or that jazz is worthy of study because it is just like classical music (Gates 1988: xx). Gates's notion of signifyin' codifies a set of ideas about processes

---

4. Floyd's fine essay actually appeared long after its publication date, when my article had largely been completed; his reading of Gates and his analytical focus differ somewhat from mine, but our goals are quite similar. See also Gabbard (1992).

5. It might seem that semiotics would be highly relevant to musical signifyin'. But scholars working in the area of musical semiotics have typically assumed that the production of musical meaning is a matter of semantics, following older models developed by structuralist linguistics, or they remain tied to a foundationalist epistemology that is unable to cope with the social and contested production of meanings. See, for example, Nattiez 1990.

of signification, offers us a bag of new conceptual tools for musical analysis, and challenges us to rethink not only the tactics but also the goals of such work. I want to illustrate the productive potential of these ideas through a detailed analysis of Miles Davis's 1964 recording of "My Funny Valentine." But since audiences hear Davis's recording up against a long history of other performances of the song, I will begin with the issue of intertextuality.

Consider a pop vocalist's treatment of the song, such as Tony Bennett's 1959 recording.[6] Bennett's voice is warm, with constant vibrato throughout; like many singers, he uses vibrato as a component of the vocal sound rather than as an ornament, so that it projects sincerity and expressivity evenly over the course of the entire song. Bennett follows the original printed version of the song closely, but he often slightly alters the rhythm of the melody to make his delivery of the text seem more natural and intimate; he also changes a note here and there, to suggest even more personal earnestness. A few deft appoggiaturas serve to underline his casual control of the music, and to complete his modest customizing. Bennett's warm voice presents the singer as an ostensibly benevolent patriarch, for when the song is sung by a man to a woman (the opposite of the original context in the Broadway musical *Babes in Arms*), the text's enumeration of faults ("Is your figure less than Greek? Is your mouth a little weak?") becomes somewhat condescending and insulting, however well masked by the tender music. The pianist's nod to "Greensleeves" at the very end completes the atmosphere of poignant sincerity Bennett has worked to create.

"My Funny Valentine" was composed by Rodgers and Hart in 1937. By the time of Bennett's recording, Davis had already recorded the song twice himself, in 1956 and 1958; his live recording was made five years after Bennett's. Now can we say that Davis is signifyin' on—commenting on, in dialogue with, deconstructing—Bennett's version? The question is made more complex by the idea that as a performer Davis is signifyin' on all of the versions of the song he has heard; but for his audience, Davis is signifyin' on all of the versions each listener has heard. What is played is played up against Davis's intertextual experience, and what is heard is heard up against the listeners' experiences. Moreover, Davis is no doubt engaging with the many Bennett-like performances of "My Funny Valentine" he must have heard, but he is also signifyin' on many jazz versions, including his own past performances.[7] This chain of signifyin' spins out indefinitely, though most fundamentally Davis is in dialogue with the basic features of the song itself, as jazz musicians would understand them, and as listeners would recognize them. The whole point of a jazz musician like Davis playing a Tin Pan Alley pop song could be understood as his opportunity to signify on the melodic possibilities, formal conventions (such as the AABA plan of the 32-measure chorus), harmonic potentials, and previously performed versions of the original song.[8]

---

6. First issued on Columbia CS-8242, this recording also appears in the Smithsonian Collection *American Popular Song* (Smithsonian Institution and CBS, RD-031). Most of the comments that follow could apply just as well to Frank Sinatra's recording on *Songs for Young Lovers* (Capitol, 1954).

7. See Brofsky, 1983, for a comparison of three different performances by Davis of "My Funny Valentine."

8. We might say that the early bebop musicians were signifyin' on Tin Pan Alley popular songs when they stripped away the melody, doubled the tempo, and explored the harmonic possibilities they found in such tunes as "I Got Rhythm" and "Cherokee." But bebop practice would have been to give "My Funny Valentine" a new melody and not acknowledge that the tune had any connection with popular song. Davis, when he used Tin Pan Alley songs, always said so, making the signifyin' less private and esoteric, more explicit and popular. See Lhamon 1990: 172–73.

Davis signifies from the very beginning of his 1964 performance; after Herbie Hancock's piano introduction, Davis understates the first two phrases of the melody (see Figure 1).[9] His is tone is soft and without vibrato, and he has clipped the long notes of the song, making his statement seem idiosyncratic yet restrained. Without a constant vibrato such as Bennett uses, there is no warm surface to hide behind; Davis's statement seems stark and vulnerable. After each phrase, he pauses, and the empty time creates a sense of dramatic engagement as we wait for the continuation we know must occur. On the third phrase (m. 5), Davis deceives us; he begins on the proper note, but instead of ascending to follow the melody, he descends into the lowest register of the trumpet before seeming to gain momentum that shoots him up to almost an octave higher than where he should be, if he were still following the tune. The melody of "My Funny Valentine" was so familiar to his audience that Davis did not need to state it before signifyin' on it; two brief phrases serve to establish the tune. The third phrase not only deceives, but contrasts sharply with the first two (mm. 1 and 3): during this eruption Davis plays loudly for the first time, and adds some vibrato while he holds the final high note. Unlike Tony Bennett, Davis uses vibrato selectively so that its presence or absence is significant; here he uses it to intensify the end of this outburst before he retreats back to a soft note in his middle range.

9. My transcription is provided as a guide to the analysis that follows. The analysis, though, is based on the sounds of the performance, not the sight of the transcription. It should be clear that I have no illusions about the capacity of musical notation to represent musical performances completely or accurately. I have tried, however, to furnish a transcription that acknowledges its own limitations, one that records the existence of aspects of the performance that are not notatable or that are usually overlooked by analysis. Even so, an enormous amount of important musical information is left out, especially nuances of pitch and timbre. Note the key to special symbols that appears at the end of the transcription.

19 Eb△ F-7 G-7 F-7 Eb△ G7 C– Bb-7 A7 Ab△
p
0-3-0
false fingering
a''
24 D∅ G7b9 C– C-△ C-7 C-6
29 Ab△ D∅ G7b9 C– Bb-7 A7 Ab△
ff
squeeze
34 F-7 Bb7 Eb6 D∅ G7b9
IIa
37 C– C-△ C-7
40 C-6 Ab△ F-7 D∅
bend
waver
a'
44 G7b9 C– C-△
p
47 C-7 C-6 Ab△
false fingering
b
50 F-7 Ab-6 Bb7b9 Eb△ F-7 G-7 F-7
Latin
squeeze
bend
55 Eb△ F-7 G-7 F-7 Eb△ G7
splatter
squeeze
58 C– Bb-7 A7 Ab△ D∅ G7b9
a''
61 C– C-△ C-7 C-6
Swing
f

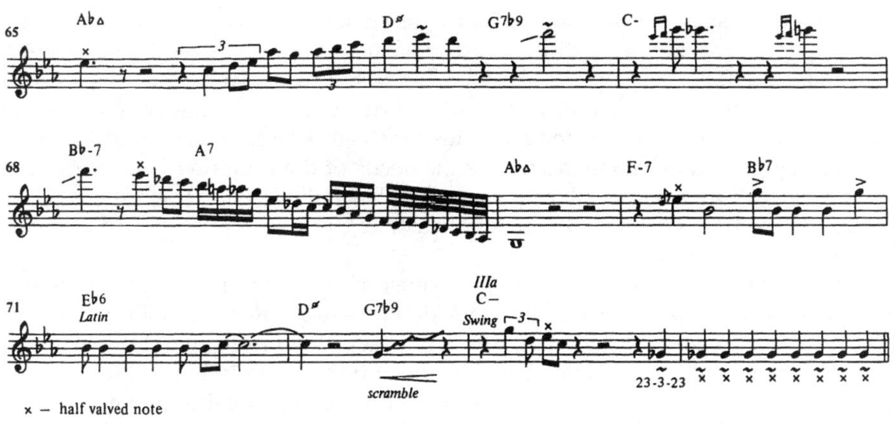

That next note, in the last measure of the first A section (m. 8), is rich in signifyin'. Davis plays an Ab in the normal way, with the trumpet's first valve depressed.[10] He then slides down to a G without changing valves. This is a technique that, on the trumpet, is difficult, risky, and relatively rare. Acoustically, the trumpet should not be able to play any notes between Ab and Eb with only the first valve depressed; Davis must bend the note with his lips without letting it crack down to the next harmonic.[11] The result is a fuzzy sound, not quite in tune. There is no conceivable situation in classical trumpet playing where such a sound would be desirable. Yet in this solo, it is the audible sign of Davis's effort and risk, articulating a moment of strain that contributes to the affect of his interpretation. If we explain this measure in terms of quarter tones or, as Howard Brofsky does, transcribe it as simply two notes, an Ab and a G, we gain a neater description but miss the point of the music. Davis deliberately risks cracking that note because it is the only way to achieve that sense of strain. Here, he manages to hold onto the note; at other moments in the solo such wagers are not won. However, it is crucial to appreciate the extraordinary lengths to which Davis goes to make playing the trumpet even more difficult and risky than it already is, and to understand the musical results of his doing so.

The trumpet, like most wind instruments, underwent a continual process of "improvement" throughout the nineteenth century and, to a lesser extent, the twentieth. In particular, instrument makers sought to adapt the trumpet to the needs of the expanding nineteenth-century orchestra by striving for a smooth, even timbre across the whole range of the instrument, one that would be consistent at all dynamic levels. In contrast, the eighteenth-century trumpet parts of J. S. Bach make use of the inconsistencies of the instrument as Bach knew it. On the trumpets of that time, every note had a different timbre and a different degree of stability. Bach carefully exploited

10. Pitches are given at concert pitch, so as to match the transcription. A trumpet player would think of this note as a Bb.

11. Acoustical facts permit a valveless brass instrument, such as a bugle, to play only the notes (or harmonics) of an overtone series, such as Ab, Eb, Ab, C, Eb, Gb, Ab, Bb, etc. The trumpet's valves allow it to switch quickly among various series. Without them, there would be gaps in place of notes that the instrument could not produce.

these characteristics, using weaker or fuzzier notes in harmonically strained passages, and returning to cadence with the most gloriously solid notes on the instrument. Players of the time developed a very flexible technique as well, practicing a great variety of articulations, working to make their lines uneven and musically subtle (see Walser 1988). All of this was undone in the nineteenth century, as both instruments and pedagogy became standardized for the needs of the symphony orchestra. As a consequence, jazz trumpet players like Miles Davis have had to wrestle with an instrument that was literally designed to frustrate their attempts to produce a wide variety of timbres.[12]

Throughout the solo, Davis uses another risky technique; he half-valves—depresses a valve only part of the way down, which creates a split, unfocused airstream—to create a variety of timbres and effects. In mm. 10 and 11, half-valving is combined with dissonant pitches and halting, fragmented rhythms to create a temporary sense of dislocation. Another half-valved slide blurs the beginning of a reference to the original melody in m. 12. After his unnerving silence during the major seventh chord in the next measure—an important point of arrival in the song—Davis uses a grace note and a slight half-valve to make the high point of the phrase seem delicately virtuosic (m. 14). A quick reprise of the risky bend finishes off the phrase, and we must wait almost two measures for another utterance from Davis.

When it comes, the next phrase contrasts sharply with the previous statement, for its climb is loud and brash, featuring no fewer than three cracked notes in two measures. I suspect that the last of these was done deliberately, to make the other two seem thematic in retrospect. This is not uncommon among jazz musicians, who are free to signify on the music they have played just seconds before. Improvisers can comment on what they have just played by spontaneously repeating, embellishing, and developing their best ideas. But jazz musicians can also engage with their most infelicitous phrases; though they cannot be unplayed, they can be resituated and reinterpreted by subsequent statements. Thelonious Monk was particularly adept at using musical accidents as material for development and elaboration. But of course jazz musicians vary greatly in their attitudes about such things. Many abhor technical imperfections and strive to avoid uncontrolled noises. Some, like Monk or Davis, play in ways that create such unforeseen sounds, though Monk seemed to find them fascinating while Davis simply accepted them as consequences of the way he played.

I don't mean to suggest that Davis wanted to make mistakes, or that he was not bothered by them. He had absorbed a dislike of technical failings from many sources, including his first trumpet hero, Harry James, who was famous for his stylish phrasing and flawless technique. And when Davis had to choose among various takes after a recording session, he is said to have invariably picked the one with the fewest mistakes.[13] Yet Davis has also been quoted as saying: "When they make records with all

---

12. Davis is certainly not the only trumpet player to wrestle with the instrument in this way. For example, Charles Schlueter, former Principal Trumpet of the Boston Symphony Orchestra (and for four years my trumpet teacher), has throughout his career struggled to produce a great range of timbres. Schlueter's experiments with equipment and his risky playing techniques and interpretations made him perhaps the most controversial trumpet player in American orchestral circles. Like Davis, he has missed more notes than many think he should, but his risks have also paid off in unsurpassedly rich and beautiful performances. On the controversies surrounding Schlueter, see Vigeland 1991.

13. Berendt (1982: 84) cites unnamed "recording directors" who agree on this point. On Davis's admiration for Harry James, see Davis 1989: 32.

the mistakes in, as well as the rest, then they'll really make jazz records. If the mistakes aren't there, too, it ain't none of you."[14] Despite his dislike of failure, Davis constantly and consistently put himself at risk in his trumpet playing, by using a loose, flexible embouchure that helped him to produce a great variety of tone colors and articulations, by striving for dramatic gestures rather than consistent demonstration of mastery, and by experimenting with unconventional techniques. Ideally, he would always play on the edge and never miss; in practice, he played closer to the edge than anyone else and simply accepted the inevitable missteps, never retreating to a safer, more consistent performing style.

After the glaring "clams" of mm. 17 and 18, Davis returns with a soft nod to the original melody of "My Funny Valentine" in the following two bars. The next lick again goes beyond the classical boundaries of trumpet technique by using an alternate fingering to produce a different timbre and slightly low pitch. Davis plays a lazy triplet of D's, the first and last with the normal fingering of open, but the middle one with the third valve. Another curt nod to the melody sets up a tremendous silence, a charged gap of almost three full measures. Henry Louis Gates Jr., in one of his few explicit comments on African-American music, explains how such a pause can be understood as signifyin':

> [A] great musician often tries to make musical phrases that are elastic in their formal properties. These elastic phrases stretch the form rather than articulate the form. Because the form is self-evident to the musician, both he and his well-trained audience are playing and listening with expectation. Signifyin(g) disappoints these expectations; caesuras, or breaks, achieve the same function. This form of disappointment creates a dialogue between what the listener expects and what the artist plays. Whereas younger, less mature musicians accentuate the beat, more accomplished musicians do not have to do so. They feel free to imply it. (Gates 1988: 123)

To create a pause of such length, during one of the most tense harmonic moments of the song, is, among other things, Davis's confident assertion of his stature as a soloist. Would an audience wait eagerly through such a gap for a lesser musician? Would a lesser musician dare to find out? Davis indulges in that sort of manipulation that is the prerogative of the virtuoso and at the same time illustrates his freedom from having to articulate all of the chords; rather, the chords are there as a field upon which he signifies.

In a deviation from the standard 32-bar form, Rodgers and Hart extended the final A section of "My Funny Valentine" with an extra four measures (beyond the usual eight). In the ninth bar of this section (m. 33), we can hear Davis signal, with a single pair of notes, a doubling of the tempo, which is immediately picked up by the other musicians. A high rip, solidly on the downbeat, gets their attention, and the subtle swing of two eighth-notes on the second beat is enough to cue the band to shift tempo. The eighth-notes are signifyin' on the previous rhythmic feel and cannot be contained within it, prompting the change.[15] By starting the new rhythmic feel four measures before the start of a new chorus, Davis cuts against the regularity of the song's formal plan, building momentum at what should be the most predictable point in the song, the turnaround into the next chorus, where the melody relaxes.

---

14. Ralph J. Gleason, *Celebrating the Duke* (Boston: Little, Brown, and Co., 1975), p. 134.

15. It is quite possible that this tempo change was planned, or that it was at least an option that had been taken in previous performances. But it is made to feel spontaneous, to seem musically cued by Davis.

That he succeeds in sparking increased engagement with the audience is clear from their spontaneous applause here, in the middle of his solo.

Davis begins the second chorus of his solo with a striking contrast, a splattered high note followed by one that is neatly and precisely placed (m. 37). The first note comes across as a scream, particularly since it is on the tense ninth degree (D over C minor); the second note not only resolves harmonically to the tonic but also resolves the gesture of wildness with a demonstration of control. Precise placement of even more dissonant notes in the following measure emphasize Davis's willfulness and strength, as he clashes deliberately with the harmonic context.

The third measure of this chorus (m. 39) is a mess. Clear, distinctly pitched notes are almost wholly absent; what we hear is a raucous, complex ascending gesture. Davis keeps his embouchure very loose and uses breath accents on the higher notes to shape the line. What results is indeterminate in pitch but rhetorically clear. It is a chaotic, almost frantic climb that briefly shoots past the tonic to the flat ninth degree, then spins back to the tonic and down an octave by way of a deft flip into bluesier terrain. Again, Davis is less interested in articulating pitches than in signifyin'; the two halves of this phrase are in dialogue, the messy scramble upward answered by the casual, simple return. Their juxtaposition furthers our sense of Davis's playful, adventurous, multifaceted, sometimes strained but ultimately capable character.[16] Davis doesn't present his audiences with a product, polished and inviting admiration; we hear a dramatic process of creation from Davis as from few others. And as we listen, we can experience these feelings of playfulness, complexity, struggle, and competence as our own.

For the next seven measures, Davis works primarily with rhythm; his phrases are simple and exquisitely swung, and he places substantial pauses in between them so that the rhythm section can be heard swinging in response. Skipping ahead, we hear him doing something similar at the start of the last A section (m. 61), creating a space for dialogue just before he ascends into a series of stratospheric screeches that must have surprised those critics who have insisted that Davis is a weak trumpet player with a limited range. The solo ends (m. 74) with a series of fading quarter notes on the beat, pitched in Davis's midrange, a dissonant tritone away from the tonic; an appoggiatura both blurs and emphasizes each note, making the end of his solo seem enigmatic and inconclusive.

Characterizing Davis's style as "prideful loneliness," Nat Hentoff has argued that Davis's power as a soloist was due to his

> relentless probing of the song, of himself and of the resources of his horn. There is also the constant drawing of melodic and emotional lines as taut as possible before the tension is released only to build up again. And there is the unabashed sensuality of tone, together with the acute pleasure of surprising oneself in music.[17]

Hentoff's comments are certainly evocative of what I have called signifyin' in Davis's music. And Ben Sidran's book about orality in African-American music similarly directs our attention toward the dialogic aspects of jazz, as do LeRoi Jones's *Blues*

---

16. Krin Gabbard (1992: 60) cites this solo as a perfect example of how Davis alternated strongly phallic gestures with moments of post-phallic vulnerability.

17. Nat Hentoff, "Liner Notes for Miles Davis's *My Funny Valentine*" (Columbia, 1964). "Prideful loneliness" is from *Jazz Is*, p. 141.

People and Christopher Small's *Music of the Common Tongue: Survival and Celebration in Afro-American Music.*[18]

Such arguments, however, seem not to have been very influential upon jazz scholarship; with the exception of Hentoff, these writers are not often cited in jazz bibliographies.[19] The reason for this, I think, has been the lack of attention within jazz scholarship and criticism to articulating links among the impressions of listeners, the techniques of musicians, and the actual sounds that result. Bill Cole remarked of this solo that Davis "holds his listeners' interest by playing every note as if it were the most important note he would ever play. It is this intensity that is so persuasive in his playing."[20] This argument is itself persuasive, but how do we actually hear an abstract quality like "intensity"? Gary Tomlinson has nicely described "the technical revolution brought to the trumpet by black Americans, a revolution that toppled the prim Arban methods and military precision of Victorian cornet virtuosos and broke wide open the expressive range of the instrument." Tomlinson goes on to say specifically of Miles Davis: "the power of his vision was such that he could make even his famous cracked and fluffed notes a convincing expressive aspect of it."[21] Like Gary Giddins, Tomlinson is trying to valorize aspects of Davis's performances that escape conventional accounts; like Giddins's attempt, though, it appeals to a fairly misty notion of "vision." But most important, none of these comments is very specific musically; jazz criticism has lacked detailed analyses of specific performances that articulate links among reactions, theories, performance choices, and technical details.

My analysis of "My Funny Valentine" is certainly not exhaustive; it focuses selectively on certain aspects of one solo, in order to make a number of methodological and analytical points. I have presented it as an example of a kind of analysis that takes us into the notes but acknowledges the centrality of rhetoric, that leads us into the trees but also sees the forest. The value of a theory of signifyin' is that it can help direct our attention to aspects of jazz performance and reception that have not been cogently addressed, and it helps provide a language for doing so. And by grounding his theory in African-American practices, but not limiting its applicability to African-American culture, Gates helps us to gain a new perspective on many different cultural practices.

Prevalent methods of jazz analysis, borrowed from the toolbox of musicology, provide excellent means for *legitimating* jazz in the academy. But they are clearly inadequate to the task of helping us to *understand* jazz, and to account for its power to affect many people deeply—issues that ought to be central for critical scholarship of jazz. They offer only a kind of mystified, ahistorical, text-based legitimacy, within which rhetoric and signifyin' are invisible. Such methods cannot cope with the problem of Miles Davis: the missed notes, the charged gaps, the technical risk-taking, the whole challenge of explaining how this powerful music works and means.

---

18. Ben Sidran, *Black Talk* (New York: Da Capo, 1983 [1971]); LeRoi Jones, *Blues People* (New York: William Morrow, 1963); Christopher Small, *Music of the Common Tongue: Survival and Celebration in Afro-American Music* (New York: Riverrun Press, 1987). See also Amiri Baraka [formerly LeRoi Jones], "Miles Davis: One of the Great Mother Fuckers," in Amiri and Amina Baraka, *The Music: Reflections on Jazz and Blues* , pp. 290–301 (New York: William Morrow, 1987).

19. For example, Martin Williams's bibliography for the *Smithsonian Collection of Classic Jazz* , rev. ed. (1987) ignores Sidran and Jones, as does the entry on "Jazz" in the *New Grove Dictionary of Music and Musicians* (1980).

20. Cole, *Miles Davis*, p. 156.

21. Tomlinson, "Cultural Dialogics" (1992), pp. 90–91.

Why must it be explained? Because it will be, somehow, unavoidably. Artistic experiences are never unmediated by theoretical assumptions, whether positivist or formalist, mystifying or signifyin'. And how we think about Davis's solo on "My Funny Valentine" has implications far beyond our response to this particular performance. The work of Miles Davis seems to repudiate conventional notions of aesthetic distance and to insist that music is less a thing than an activity; his music itself provides the most eloquent argument for analysis to open itself up to issues of gesture and performativity. The problem of Miles Davis is that if technical perfection is assumed to be a universal and primary goal, the deliberate efforts of musicians like Davis to take chances are invisible, and their successes are inaudible. If individuality and originality are fetishized, signifyin' is lost, for it is fundamentally dialogic and depends upon the interaction among musicians, their audiences, and the experiences and texts they exchange.

For example, one of Davis's biographers asserted that the "My Funny Valentine" solo demonstrates "no readily apparent logic," while another waxed enthusiastic about the "dramatic inner logic" of the same solo. Each critic found it a powerfully moving performance, but both lacked an analytical vocabulary that could do justice to their perceptions.[22] Pianist Chick Corea muses: "Miles's solos are really interesting to look at on music paper, because there's nothing to them. On a Trane solo or Charlie Parker solo, you can string the notes out and see all these phrases and harmonic ideas, patterns, all kinds of things. Miles doesn't use patterns. He doesn't string notes out. It's weird. Without the expression, and without the feeling he puts into it, there's nothing there."[23] Corea's comments dramatize the problems of accounting for the rhetorical power of aspects of Davis's performances that escape conventional notation and theorization.

Miles Davis once said, "Sometimes you run out of notes. The notes just disappear and you have to play a sound."[24] The title of this essay takes as a motto Davis's insistence that musical creativity need not be limited by abstractions such as notes and it signals a call for critics and scholars not to allow such concepts to constrain *their* work. Musical analysts need to confront the challenges of signifyin', the real-life dialogic flux of meaning, never groundable in a foundationalist epistemology, but always grounded in a web of social practices, histories, and desires. Modernism and classicism can't take us into notes, where choices and details signify; nor out of notes, onto that risky rhetorical terrain Miles Davis never stopped exploring.[25]

---

22. See Eric Nisenson, *Round About Midnight: A Portrait of Miles Davis* (New York: The Dial Press, 1982), p. 187; and Carr, *Miles Davis*, p. 175. The other important biography of Davis (besides Cole's, mentioned previously) is Jack Chambers's *Milestones: The Music and Times of Miles Davis* (New York: Quill, 1985), a tremendous compilation of facts and quotes, but a book that offers little analysis of the music and its meanings. Barry Kernfeld's *Adderly, Coltrane, and Davis at the Twilight of Bebop: The Search for Melodic Coherence (1958–59)* (Ph.D. dissertation, Cornell University, 1981) uses traditional musicological tools to generate detailed descriptions of Davis's music.

23. Howard Mandel, "Sketches of Miles," *Down Beat* , December 1991, pp. 18–20.

24. Khephra Burns, liner notes for Miles Davis, *Aura* (CBS, 1989 [rec. 1984]).

25. Earlier versions of this paper were performed as lecture-demonstrations at the African-American Music Forum, University of Michigan, April 26, 1990; the IASPM conference in New Orleans, May 1, 1990; McGill University, January 31, 1992; and the University of California–Riverside, March 11, 1992. This article has benefited from the comments and questions of the audiences at those presentations, and from correspondence with Krin Gabbard, George Lipsitz, and Christopher Small. I am grateful for the corrections and challenges issued by the anonymous reviewer, and to John Puterbaugh for setting my transcription.

Other Works Cited

Bakhtin, M. M. *The Dialogic Imagination*. Trans. Caryl Emerson and Michael Holquist. Austin: University of Texas Press, 1981.

Berendt, Joachim E. *The Jazz Book: From Ragtime to Fusion and Beyond*. Westport, CT: Lawrence Hill, 1982.

Brofsky, Howard. "Miles Davis and *My Funny Valentine:* the Evolution of a Solo." *Black Music Research Journal* (1983): 23–45.

Carr, Ian. *Miles Davis: A Critical Biography*. London: Paladin, 1982.

Cole, Bill. *Miles Davis: A Musical Biography*. New York: William Morrow, 1974.

Collier, James Lincoln. *The Making of Jazz*. New York: Dell, 1978.

Davis, Miles, with Quincy Troupe. *Miles: The Autobiography*. New York: Simon & Schuster, 1989.

Floyd, Samuel A., Jr. "Ring Shout! Literary Studies, Historical Studies, and Black Music Inquiry," *Black Music Research Journal* 11:2 (Fall 1991): 265–87.

Gabbard, Krin. Signifyin(g) the Phallus: *Mo' Better Blues* and Representations of the Jazz Trumpet." *Cinema Journal* 32:1 (Fall 1992): 43–62. Reprinted in *Representing Jazz*. Ed. Krin Gabbard. Durham: Duke University Press, 1995: 104–30.

Gates, Henry Louis, Jr. *The Signifying Monkey: A Theory of African-American Literary Criticism*. New York: Oxford University Press, 1988.

Giddins, Gary. *Rhythm-a-ning: Jazz Tradition and Innovation in the '80s*. New York: Oxford University Press, 1988.

Gridley, Mark C. *Jazz Styles: History and Analysis*. 4th ed. Englewood Cliffs, NJ: Prentice-Hall, 1991.

Hentoff, Nat. *Jazz Is*. New York: Random House, 1976.

———. "An Afternoon with Miles Davis." *Jazz Panorama*. Ed. Martin Williams. New York: Da Capo, 1979. 161–68.

Llamon, W. T., Jr. *Deliberate Speed: The Origins of a Cultural Style in the American 1950s*. Washington: Smithsonian Institution Press, 1990.

Megill, Donald D., and Richard S. Demory. *Introduction to Jazz History*. Englewood Cliffs, NJ: Prentice-Hall, 1989.

Murphy, John P. "Jazz Improvisation: The Joy of Influence," *The Black Perspective in Music* 18, nos. 1–2 (1990): 7–19.

Nattiez, Jean-Jacques. *Music and Discourse: Toward a Semiology of Music*. Princeton: Princeton University Press, 1990.

Tirro, Frank. *Jazz: A History*. New York: Norton, 1977.

Tomlinson, Gary. "Cultural Dialogics and Jazz: A White Historian Signifies." *Disciplining Music: Musicology and Its Canons*. Ed. Katherine Bergeron and Philip V. Bohlman. Chicago: University of Chicago Press, 1992. 64–94.

Vigeland, Carl A. *In Concert: Onstage and Offstage with the Boston Symphony Orchestra*. Amherst: University of Massachusetts Press, 1991.

Walser, Robert. "Musical Imagery and Performance Practice in J. S Bach's Arias with Trumpet," *International Trumpet Guild Journal* 13, no. 1 (Sept. 1988): 62–77.

Williams, Martin. "Suggestions for Further Reading." *Smithsonian Collection of Classic Jazz*. Rev. ed. CBS Special Products, 1987. 118–19.

63. A Revolutionary Music?

THE POLITICAL SIGNIFICANCE OF JAZZ has been debated throughout its history. Did the new musical freedoms jazz offered express new social freedoms, or desires for them? What, then, of the new discipline that jazz demanded, balancing individual liberties with obligations to the group? And whose freedoms? Is jazz available to anyone who wants such experiences, or does the history of racial segregation impose limits on non-African Americans?

Jazz is inherently revolutionary, argues baritone saxophonist and composer Fred Ho (b. 1957), containing the necessary ingredients to be put to political use by any oppressed peoples. Of Chinese descent himself, Ho believes that since Asian Americans have experienced racial discrimination, too, the music is available to articulate their protests and dreams. In his own compositions, Ho often fuses Asian and African-American elements as a means of building solidarity between those peoples and traditions, and his purposes are openly political. In addition to founding groups such as the Afro Asian Music Ensemble, he has also established nonmusical civic organizations, following the lead of the black civil rights movement, dedicated to Asian American empowerment.

I do not use the term "jazz," as I do not use such terms as *Negro, Oriental,* or *Hispanic*. Oppressed peoples suffer when their history, identity, and culture are defined, (mis) represented, and explicated by our oppressors. The struggle to redefine and reimage our existence involves the struggle to reject the stereotyping, distortions, and devaluation embodied in the classifications of conquerors and racists. The struggle over how to describe past and present reality is the struggle to change reality, and the continued usage of the term "jazz" persists in marginalizing, obfuscating, and denying the fact that this music is quintessentially American music. However, it is the music of an American oppressed nationality and not the music of the dominant, American, white, European heritage. It is white-supremacist racism that will not properly and justly accept both the music and its creators in a position of equality.[1]

Source: Fred Wei-han Ho, "What Makes 'Jazz' the Revolutionary Music of the 20th Century, and Will It Be for the 21st Century?," *African American Review* 29:2 (Summer, 1995), pp. 283–90. Reprinted in *Wicked Theory, Naked Practice: A Fred Ho Reader* (University of Minnesota Press). Courtesy the author.

1. Several etymologies have been asserted for the word "jazz." The less credible ones assert an African derivation, but these words are from languages not spoken south of the Sahara and therefore were not commonly used among the West and Central African, sub-Saharan peoples enslaved and brought to the Americas. More likely, "jazz" comes from either *jass* or *jizz*, which means "semen" (the original piano music was common to houses of prostitution). Another

As a result of the movement of oppressed peoples that exploded in the 1960s, we have replaced terms such as *Negro* with *Black* or *African American*, and *Oriental* with *Asian* or *Asian American*. More problematical are *Hispanic* (literally, of or belonging to Spain) and *Latino* (emphasizing, again, the Latin or European)—I personally use "Spanish-speaking oppressed nationalities" when referring to Puerto Ricans, Dominicans, Chicanos, Central and South Americans, and Caribbean peoples in the United States whose only commonality is that they speak Spanish (and even that Spanish has national peculiarities). However, a satisfactory replacement for "jazz" has yet to emerge, and continues to be part of the ongoing struggle to dismantle white supremacy and Eurocentrism in American culture and society. At times, certain descriptors have gained some currency, such as Rahsaan Roland Kirk's "Great Black Music," or Archie Shepp's "African American Instrumental Music," or Max Roach's preference: "the music of Louis Armstrong, the music of Charles Parker, etc." Billy Taylor simply said "twentieth-century American music." Some might argue that "jazz" should be reclaimed and that its meaning should be transformed from a pejorative term and usage to a statement of celebratory "in-your-face" defiance—as militant gays and lesbians have reappropriated the once-derogatory and insulting *queer* and *fag*. *Black* was once a term loaded with negativity that the Black Liberation Movement transformed to symbolize pride and self-respect.

Yet as the twentieth century comes to an end, we find a curious phenomenon: "jazz" has become accepted into the halls of American (white, mainstream) cultural citadels. We find "Classical Jazz at Lincoln Center." We find a black artistic director criticizing other black musicians for not playing "black music." We find the internecine war over what is and what isn't "jazz" and who should define it. I argue in this essay that, ironically, it is those most bent on defining and essentializing "jazz" that are indeed its greatest enemies, because they contradict the revolutionary essence of the music.

Defining and representing "jazz" is highly and inescapably political, and it seems to me that the politics of music must be understood both sociologically and musicologically—in a dialectical, interdependent, and interactive manner. Yet much of the literature has focused on socio-history (e.g., LeRoi Jones's *Blues People*, which argues that black music changed as black people changed), ideology (e.g., Frank Kofsky's *Black Nationalism and the Revolution in Music*, which assess the music's sociopolitical content via the consciousness/attitudes of the musicians), or political economy (a lot of writing on the profiteering and exploitation of black music and artists). Only the work of Christopher Small (*Music of the Common Tongue*) systematically attempts to examine "jazz" or African American music primarily from a musical/aesthetical perspective.

As a young Chinese (Asian) American growing up in the 1970s, I was profoundly drawn to and inspired by African American music as the expression of an oppressed nationality, because of its social role as protest and resistance to national oppression, and for its musical energy and revolutionary aesthetic qualities. I identified with its pro-oppressed, anti-oppressor character: with the militancy the musicians displayed, with its social history of rebellion and revolt, and with its musical defiance to not kow-tow to, but challenge and contest, Western European "classical" music and co-opted, diluted, eviscerated commercialized forms that became American pop music.

---

explanation is that "jazz" comes from the French verb—New Orleans, the birthplace of the music, was a French colonial territory—*jasser* , meaning "to chatter nonsensically." In either case, "jazz" has a pejorative context, as do many terms from the legacy of colonialism and exploitation.

"Jazz," or African American music, is the revolutionary music of the twentieth century—not just for America, but for the planet as well. It is the music that embodies and expresses the contradiction of the century, fundamentally rooted to the world's division between oppressor, imperialist nations and the struggle of the oppressed nationals and nationalities. Its historical emergence and development parallel the rise and development of imperialism—the globalization of finance capital—at the turn of the century. Its musical and stylistic innovations reflect the changes in the twentieth-century life of the African American oppressed nationality.

"Jazz" is the music of the emerging African American proletariat or urban, industrial working class. Its predecessor, blues, was the music of post-Reconstruction. Just as old socioeconomic formations persist while new ones supplant them, so also do musical forms overlap. One exception is the persistence of pre-twentieth-century Western European "classical" music today—a result of the continual institutional/cultural expression of white settler-colonialism in North America.

"Jazz" emerged as formerly rural African-American laborers traveled north to urban industrial and commercial centers of Chicago, Kansas City, Detroit, St. Louis, New York, and Philadelphia. A new music arose with a new class of urban workers grafting the rich and unique African American music of formerly enslaved plantation laborers, rural tenant farmers, and migratory workers onto a sophisticated, cosmopolitan, industrial, and multiethnic urban culture of growing capitalist America.

No longer Southern, blues, or field songs, the music draws on all these cultural precedents and transforms them. All of the characteristics of African American music that are distinctive and transformative of Western European concert music are retained but intensified. The Western European concert tradition of metronomic sense of time and general singularity of rhythm vis-à-vis the grafting of West African multiple and layered rhythms produces the polyrhythmicality of African-American twentieth-century music; the fixed pitch and fixed diatonic temperament of Western European concert music vis-à-vis West and Central African oral tradition produces a revolutionary unity of composition and improvisation for twentieth-century African American music; and the primacy of the conductor and composer for Western European concert music vis-à-vis call and response/soloist-leader and group leads to the player-as-leader-as-soloist-as-virtuoso improviser/performer/composer.

For the most part, "jazz" has never looked back to the past as "classical" music has—fixated upon finer and finer degrees of perfection in the interpretation of past, "classic" treasures. Rather, "jazz" has been about the present ("Now Is the Time") and the future ("Space Is the Place"). Its entire history has been the freeing of time, pitch, and harmony from fixed, regulated, predictable standards. Every major innovation in the history of the music has been from the struggle of musicians to attain greater and greater levels of expressive freedom through liberating the two basic fundamentals of music: time (meter) and sound (pitch/temperament/harmony).

Indeed, every feature of the music is an expression of revolutionary dialectics. Demarcations are dissolved between soloist and ensemble; among the elements of melody, time, and harmony; between composition and improvisation; between "traditional" and "avant-garde"; between "artist" and "audience"; between "art" and "politics"; between "Western" and "Eastern"; etc. If there is any "tradition," it is the continual exploding of time and pitch in quest of greater human expressiveness and a deeper spiritualizing of the music that is fundamentally rooted in the struggle to end all forms of exploitation and oppression and to seek a basic "oneness" with life and nature.[2]

---

2. Musicians' various ideological/spiritual pronouncements reflect this quest and struggle.

Finally, let me address the issue of composition/notation and improvisation. Some have argued that once the composition is heavily notated and improvisation is necessarily diminished, the music becomes more "European" and less "African American." Initially, Western European music also relied on improvisation; player/composers under economic pressure were required to come up quickly with new works to entertain and satisfy their aristocratic employers. Though these musicians were "literate," improvisation satisfied both economic expediency and their own creative desire to avoid the repetitive boredom of performing the same hits the same way all the time. As solo and small-group works expanded to large ensembles and extended compositions, and as paying audiences began to demand faithful replication of their favorites, notation assumed increasingly greater dominance.

African American music has never, until recently, had to face the prospect of institutionalization, canonization, standardization and codification by a ruling class (presently, bourgeois). Paradoxically, the music of an oppressed nationality was free to be free. Duke Ellington's orchestra could play the same show every night for years and still retain spontaneity and freshness, no matter how much notation, choreography and staging was set. As "jazz" became more of an "art" music (i.e., primarily listened to and not danced to), and the "jazz" composer (who could still be a player/leader) began to pen extended works such as suites, ballets, theater and film scores, etc., the best and strongest writing always allowed for an enhanced spontaneity and for improvised contributions from the players. Ideally these written compositions are memorized and internalized until the written page is no longer looked at and the players play from understanding and interaction. The essence of African American music is a whole, which is greater than the sum of its inseparable and mutually dependent parts—player and composer, notation and performance, composition and improvisation.

Notation is not the enslaver, the oppressor of spontaneity and improvisation. Calcification, de-African Americanization, co-optation is not caused by musical deviations and practices, but, in my view, by ethical violations. Clearly, in Ellington's large-scale works, the essence of African American spontaneity is reflected in a highly composed music. And there are players who play "correct jazz" which is sterile and reactionary.

As a non-African American, but a person of color (oppressed nationality in the U.S.), I was drawn to and inspired and revolutionized by the music's musical and—possibly more profoundly—extramusical qualities. Many years later, after becoming a professional musician, I came across a statement by V. I. Lenin, which crystallizes this confluence: "Ethics will be the aesthetics of the future." Twentieth-century African-American music is part of an extramusical ethical/spiritual/sociopolitical revolution—the commitment, attitude, resistance, perseverance, celebration, love and joy opposing oppression, brutality, poverty, persecution, and exclusion. Archie Shepp expressed it in poetic language: "Jazz is the lily in spite of the swamp." It is the triumph of the human spirit, of spirituality and ethicality in the midst of cannibalistic and corrupting capitalism.

The carrier of the music (the musician) must not violate the ethical bond between the music and the people (i.e., a bond of merit, of excellence, of meaning, of purpose, of significance in the people's aspirations and efforts to be free). The musician bears a responsibility that transcends careers, critical praise, conservatory training, and cash to affirm the music's fundamental celebration of humanity and to remain committed to the liberation of an oppressed nationality—African Americans—in an age of internationalized commodity production and exchange.

"Jazz" was born amidst the contradictions of our epoch. The music changes just as the people, the society, and the world change. African Americans in the twentieth century have been the largest and leading oppressed nationality of U.S.

society. Their political, social, and cultural impact has been revolutionary. By the twenty-first century, Spanish-speaking oppressed nationalities will become numerically the largest group of oppressed nationalities. Asian/Pacific Islanders are proportionally the fastest growing oppressed nationalities. And indigenous peoples facing the most extreme and desperate conditions are resorting increasingly to armed struggle (cf. Chiapas, Mexico) to defend their land and way of life. In the years to come—it has already begun—a new music will arise, rooted in all that has come before, yet moving with greater volatility, altering and exploding time and sound, and thereby changing music itself.

The petty machinations which attempt to "institutionalize jazz," the reactionary "back to the tradition" (tradition is not something one can or should go back to, but move from), the business-suited corporate and government recognition which legitimizes "jazz" and makes it acceptable—all of these violate the spirit, the sacred bond between culture and people, the ethics of the aesthetics. The appropriation of oppressed peoples' culture and history for the service of Yankee imperialism is antithetical and inimical to creative development. Whether "jazz" comes to be the vital, transformative, revolutionary music of the twenty-first century that it has been in the twentieth century depends on how this struggle plays out. A new "jazz"—maybe something that won't use this term because it has become so co-opted and reactionary—will affirm and attest to the revolutionary heritage that began in the twentieth century: that the music of all oppressed peoples fighting imperialism is indeed *Jazz*.

An Ethical Mandate among the Music, the Musician and the People

1. **Speak to the People.** The music has to and will embody messages, either explicitly (in the form of lyrics and/or song titles) or implicitly (in the sound and in its spirit). Some examples have been, but are certainly not limited to, "Strange Fruit" (composed by Lewis Allen and popularized by Billie Holiday), "A Tone Parallel to Harlem" (Duke Ellington), "A Love Supreme" (John Coltrane), "Things Have Got to Change" (composed by Calvin Massey and performed by Archie Shepp), "Remember Rockefeller at Attica" (Charles Mingus), etc.
2. **Go to the People.** The music must be performed where people can enjoy it. Rather than expect the people to come to the music (an approach which depends more on marketing hype and advertisement dollars than on artistry or quality), bring the music to the people. Often, artists have very little control over how their music is distributed, promoted, and presented. In many ways, the musician and the music have both left the community in which both were spawned. The parallel to "underdevelopment" is striking: a people's cultural and natural resources are drained off for the benefit of corporate plunderers and not the people. Activists, managers, cultural presenters and producers, and artists need to work together to build a community base to support the music.
3. **Involve the People.** Just as we need environmentally sustainable development for natural resources, we need culturally sustainable development for the arts. We need to bridge the separation between artist and audience, between professional and amateur. The essence of cultural democracy is true popular culture—culture and the arts created by and for the common people and not by and for an elite. The rationalization of corporate entertainment is

to "give the people what they want." Unfortunately, the truth is really "give the people what the corporations want them to want."

4. **Change the People.** Ultimately, the music and culture of oppressed peoples, if it is to have value and meaning, must revolutionize the consciousness, values, aesthetics, and actions of the people. This is the music's "spiritualizing" quality: to fortify and prepare us to continue the struggle until liberation.

64. Improvised Music After 1950: Afrological and Eurological Perspectives

COMPOSER, TROMBONIST, AND SCHOLAR GEORGE LEWIS (b. 1952) has ranged from playing with the Count Basie band to developing a computer program that creates interactive music. As an African-American performer who spans the worlds of jazz and avant-garde "classical" performance, Lewis has a particular interest in their interrelationship. Here he discusses two major figures of twentieth-century music, Charlie Parker (1920–1955) and John Cage (1912–1992), arguing that the former's influence on the latter is perhaps as profound as it is unremarked. His theorization of "Afrological" and "Eurological" should not be understood as racially inherent or essential, but rather as the result of historical experiences that are specific to the contexts he discusses. Indeed, Lewis, as much a scholar as a performer, argues that it is such apparently neutral terms as "experimental," "art," "serious," and "contemporary" that actually carry racially coded meanings that are linked to cultural prestige and access to the resources that support certain artistic activities rather than others.

After a gap of nearly one hundred and fifty years, during which real-time generation of musical structure had been nearly eliminated from the musical activity of the Western or "pan-European" tradition, the postwar putative heirs to this tradition

---

Source: George E. Lewis, "Improvised Music after 1950: Afrological and Eurological Perspectives," *Black Music Research Journal* 16 (1996), pp. 91–122. Reprinted by permission of Copyright Clearance Center, Rightslink. For the author's later comments on these ideas, see George Lewis, "Afterword to 'Improvised Music After 1950': The Changing Same," in Daniel Fischlin and Ajay Heble, eds., *The Other Side of Nowhere: Jazz, Improvisation, and Communities in Dialogue* (Middletown: Wesleyan University Press, 2004), pp. 163–72.

have promulgated renewed investigation of real-time forms of musicality, including a direct confrontation with the role of improvisation. This ongoing reappraisal of improvisation may be due in no small measure to musical and social events taking place in quite a different sector of the overall musical landscape. In particular, the anointing, since the early 1950s, of various forms of "jazz," the African-American musical constellation most commonly associated with the exploration of improvisation in both Europe and America, as a form of "art" has in all likelihood been a salient stimulating factor in this reevaluation of the possibilities of improvisation.

Already active in the 1940s, a group of radical young black American improvisers, for the most part lacking access to economic and political resources often taken for granted in high-culture musical circles, nonetheless posed potent challenges to Western notions of structure, form, communication, and expression. These improvisers, while cognizant of Western musical tradition, located and centered their modes of musical expression within a stream emanating largely from African and African-American cultural and social history. The international influence and dissemination of their music, dubbed "bebop," as well as the strong influences coming from later forms of "jazz," have resulted in the emergence of new sites for transnational, transcultural, improvisative musical activity.

In particular, a strong circumstantial case can be made for the proposition that the emergence of these new, vigorous, and highly influential improvisative forms provided an impetus for musical workers in other traditions, particularly European and American composers active in the construction of a transnational European-based tradition, to come to grips with some of the implications of musical improvisation. This confrontation, however, took place amid an ongoing narrative of dismissal, on the part of many of these composers, of the tenets of African-American improvisative forms.

Moreover, texts documenting the musical products of the American version of the move to incorporate real-time music-making into composition often present this activity as a part of "American music since 1945," a construct almost invariably theorized as emanating almost exclusively from a generally venerated stream of European cultural, social and intellectual history—the "Western tradition." In such texts, an attempted erasure or denial of the impact of African-American forms on the real-time work of European and Euro-American composers is commonly asserted.

This denial itself, however, drew the outlines of a space where improvisation as a theoretical construct could clearly be viewed as a site not only for music-theoretical contention but for social and cultural competition between musicians representing improvisative and compositional modes of musical discourse. The theoretical and practical positions taken with regard to improvisation in this post-1950 Euro-American tradition exhibit broad areas of both confluence and contrast with those emerging from musical art worlds influenced by African-American improvisative musics.

This essay attempts to historically and philosophically deconstruct aspects of the musical belief systems that ground African-American and European (including European-American) real-time music-making, analyzing the articulation and resolution of both musical and what were once called "extramusical" issues. This analysis adopts as critical tools two complementary connotative adjectives, "Afrological" and "Eurological." These terms refer metaphorically to musical belief systems and behavior which, in my view, exemplify particular kinds of musical "logic." At the same time, these terms are intended to historicize the particularity of perspective characteristic of two systems that have evolved in such divergent cultural environments.

Improvisative musical utterance, like any music, may be interpreted with reference to historical and cultural contexts. The history of sanctions, segregation, and slavery, imposed upon African Americans by the dominant white American culture, has undoubtedly influenced the evolution of a sociomusical belief system that differs in critical respects from that which has emerged from the dominant culture itself. Commentary on improvisation since 1950 has often centered around several key issues, the articulation of which differs markedly according to the cultural background of the commentators—even when two informants, each grounded in a different system of belief, are ostensibly discussing the same music.

Thus my construction of "Afrological" and "Eurological" systems of improvisative musicality refers to social and cultural location and is theorized here as historically emergent rather than ethnically essential, thereby accounting for the reality of transcultural and transracial communication among improvisers. For example, African-American music, like any music, can be performed by a person of any "race" without losing its character as historically Afrological, just as a performance of Hindustani vocal music by Terry Riley does not transform the raga into a Eurological music form. My constructions make no attempt to delineate ethnicity or race, although they are designed to ensure that the reality of the ethnic or racial component of a historically emergent sociomusical group must be faced squarely and honestly.

In developing a hermeneutics of improvisative music, the study of two major American postwar real-time traditions is key. These traditions are exemplified by the two towering figures of 1950s American experimental musics—Charlie "Bird" Parker and John Cage. The work of these two crucially important music makers has had important implications not only within their respective traditions but intertraditionally as well. The compositions of both artists are widely influential, but I would submit that it is their real-time work that has had the widest impact upon world musical culture. The musics made by these two artists, and by their successors, may be seen as exemplifying two very different conceptions of real-time music making. These differences encompass not only music but areas once thought of as "extramusical," including race and ethnicity, class, and social and political philosophy.

Bird

In the musical domain, improvisation is neither a style of music nor a body of musical techniques. Structure, meaning, and context in musical improvisation arise from the domain-specific analysis, generation, manipulation, and transformation of sonic symbols. Jazz, a largely improvisative musical form, has long been explicitly and fundamentally concerned with these and other structural issues. For African-American improvisers, however, sonic symbolism is often constructed with a view toward social instrumentality as well as form. New improvisative and compositional styles are often identified with ideals of race advancement and, more importantly, as resistive ripostes to perceived opposition to black social expression and economic advancement by the dominant white American culture.

Ebullient, incisive, and transgressive, the so-called "bebop" movement brought this theme of resistance to international attention. Influencing musicality worldwide, the movement posed both implicit and explicit challenges to Western notions of structure, form, and expression. In the United States, the challenge of bop, as exemplified by the work of Charlie "Bird" Parker, Dizzy Gillespie, Thelonious Monk, Bud Powell, and Kenny "Klook" Clarke, obliged the dominant European-American culture to come to grips, if not to terms, with Afrological aesthetics.

Bop improvisers, like earlier generations of jazz improvisers, used "heads," or precomposed melodic material, as starting points for a piece. Bop heads, however, as Gridley (1994: 165) points out, "resembled little or nothing that the average listener had heard before." In a further abstraction, bebop improvisers felt no obligation to use the melodic material of the "head" as material for improvisational transformation. Instead, the underlying harmonic sequence, usually subjected to extensive reworking by the improvisers, became the basis for improvisation. Often this harmonic material was appropriated from the popular show tunes of the day, linking this music with earlier jazz styles. The musicians often "signified on" the tunes, replacing the melodic line with another, then naming the new piece in an ironic signifying riff on Tin Pan Alley as well as upon the dominant culture that produced it.

Bebop raised the stakes in the game of cultural thrust and parry to a new level of intensity, providing models of both individual and collective creativity that were adopted and extended during later periods in improvised music. The outlines of this model are well described by Walton (1972: 95), who characterizes bebop as requiring "concentrated listening, allowing an expansion of self through identification with the symbolic communication of the performer." Moreover, through extensive improvisation, each performance of a given bebop "piece" could become unique, different in many respects from the last. Even in many strains of Afrological improvisative practice today, the generative and interactional aspects of how the roles of both improviser and listener are constructed carries distinct traces of the attitudes promulgated by bebop improvisers.

Bebop's challenge to the dominant culture was not limited to musical concerns; in fact, bebop musicians challenged traditional notions of intra- and extramusicality. The composer and improviser Anthony Braxton (1985: 124) comments that "bebop had to do with understanding the realness of black people's actual position in America." Frank Kofsky (1970: 270–71) quotes Langston Hughes's blues signifyin' on bebop's origins in "the police beating Negroes' heads . . . that old club says, 'BOP! BOP! . . . BE-BOP! . . . That's where Be-Bop came from, beaten right out of some Negro's head into them horns."

In *Blues People* , Amiri Baraka (then LeRoi Jones) asserts that bebop "had more than an accidental implication of social upheaval associated with it" (Jones 1963: 188). For the bebop musicians this upheaval had a great deal to do with the assertion of self-determination with regard to their role as musical artists. While jazz has always existed in the interstices between Western definitions of concert music and entertainment, between the commercial and the experimental, challenging the assigned role of the jazz musician as entertainer created new possibilities for the construction of an African-American improvisative musicality that could define itself as explicitly experimental.

This radical redefinition was viewed as a direct challenge, by extension, to the entire social order as it applied to blacks in 1940s apartheid America: "The young Negro musician of the forties began to realize that merely by being a Negro in America, one *was* a nonconformist" (Jones 1963: 188). Indeed, the musicians were often called "crazy"—an appellation often assigned to oppositional forces, either by the dominant order itself or by members of an oppressed group who, however onerous their present situation, are fearful of the consequences of change.

Cage

Like Bird, Cage and his associates, such as Christian Wolff, David Tudor, Morton Feldman, and Earle Brown, had profound and wide-ranging influence not only in the musical, literary, and visual domains but socially and culturally as well. The musical and theoretical work of these composers can be credited with radically reconstructing Eurological composition; the trenchancy of this reconstruction involved in large measure the resurrection of Eurological modes of real-time musical discourse, often approaching an explicitly improvisative sensibility.

Along with his associates, Cage was responsible for the entrance into musical history of the term "indeterminacy." Cage's essay on indeterminacy from *Silence* (Cage 1961: 35–40) presents examples of "indeterminate" elements in European music from the last two centuries, from Karlheinz Stockhausen's *Klavierstück XI* to J. S. Bach's *Art of the Fugue*. According to Cage, Bach's nonspecification of timbre and amplitude characteristics identifies these elements not as absent but simply as non-determined but necessary material, to be realized by a performer. The construction as indeterminate of nonspecified elements in the Bach work allows "the possibility of a unique overtone structure and decibel range for each performance" (35). The performer's function in this case is "comparable to that of someone filling in color where outlines are given" (35).

Another of Cage's lasting contributions to both compositional and improvisative method is the radical use of these "chance operations." The 1951 *Music of Changes* was composed by Cage using the ancient Chinese oracular method known as the *I Ching*, or *Book of Changes*, to generate musical material within parameters chosen by the composer. The object of the use of the *I Ching*, as described by the composer himself in explaining his compositional process for the *Music of Changes*, is the creation of "a musical composition the continuity of which is free of individual taste and memory (psychology) and also of the literature and 'traditions' of the art" (Cage 1961: 59). In this regard, Cage consistently maintains that "sounds are to come into their own, rather than being exploited to express sentiments or ideas of order" (69).

That this view of music would have social implications was fully recognized by Cage himself. Indeed, Cage's social and philosophical views form a prominent part of the literature about him. In the Kostelanetz interviews from 1987, Cage explicitly addresses his own essential anarchism at several points (Kostelanetz 1987: 266). Connecting his view of sound to his anarchism, the composer expresses his need for "a music in which not only are sounds just sounds but in which people are just people, not subject, that is, to laws established by any one of them, even if he is 'the composer' or 'the conductor.'. . . Freedom of movement is basic to both this art and this society" (257).

Cage's notion of social instrumentality, however, does not connect this very American notion of freedom—perhaps reminiscent of the frontier myth—to any kind of struggle that might be required in order to obtain it. The composer denies the utility of protest, maintaining that "my notion of how to proceed in a society to bring change is not to protest the thing that is evil, but rather to let it die its own death. . . . Protests about these things, contrary to what has been said, will give it the kind of life that a fire is given when you fan it, and that it would be best to ignore it, put your attention elsewhere, take actions of another kind of positive nature" (Kostelanetz 1987: 265–66).

Composers such as Cage and Feldman located their work as an integral part of a sociomusical art world that explicitly bonded with the intellectual and musical traditions of Europe. The members of this art world, while critiquing aspects of contemporary European culture, were explicitly concerned with continuing to develop this "Western" tradition on the American continent. The composer's "History of Experimental Music in the United States" (Cage 1961: 67–75) identifies as relevant to his concerns both European and American composers and artists, including the European

Dada movement, composers such as Debussy and Varèse, and later European experimentalists such as Pierre Boulez, Karlheinz Stockhausen, Luigi Nono, and Luciano Berio. Among the American composers that Cage mentions as being part of America's "rich history" of music are Leo Ornstein, Dane Rudhyar, Lou Harrison, Harry Partch, and Virgil Thomson.

Though these and other composers do earn criticism, the only indigenous music that receives sharp denunciation from Cage is the African American music that he frequently refers to as "hot jazz." Criticizing the expression of Henry Cowell's interest in this and other American indigenous traditions, Cage appropriates the then-current conventional wisdom about the opposition between "jazz" music and "serious" music: "Jazz per se derives from serious music. And when serious music derives from it, the situation becomes rather silly" (Cage 1961: 72).

We may regard as more rhetorical device than historical fact Cage's brief account of the origins of jazz. In any event, despite such declarations as "the world is one world now" (Cage 1961: 75) or "when I think of a good future it certainly has music in it but it doesn't have one kind . . . it has all kinds" (Kostelanetz 1987: 257), it is clear that Cage has drawn very specific boundaries, not only as to which musics are relevant to his own musicality but as to which musics suit his own taste. The Cageian tendency is to confront this contradiction through the use of terms that essentially exnominate or disguise his likes and dislikes as such: "some music . . . which would not be useful to me at all might be very useful to someone else" (Kostelanetz 1987: 257).

Exnomination

Despite Cage's disavowal of jazz, however, the historical timeline shows that Cage's radical emphasis upon spontaneity and uniqueness—not generally found in either American or European music before Cage—arrives some eight to ten years after the innovations of bebop. And it is certain that bebop, a native American music with a strong base in New York City, was well known to what has come to be known as the "New York School" of artists and musicians of which Cage and Feldman were part. In the case of visual artists from that social circle, such as Jackson Pollock and Franz Kline, the connection with jazz has been remarked upon in a number of essays (see Mandeles 1981: 139).

The composer Anthony Braxton's pithy statement concerning the disavowal of Afrological forms by the art world that nurtured Cage's work advances the essential issue directly: "Both aleatory and indeterminism are words which have been coined . . . to bypass the word improvisation and as such the influence of non-white sensibility" (Braxton 1985: 366). Why improvisation and non-white sensibility would be perceived by anyone as objects to be avoided can usefully be theorized with respect to racialized power relations.

Commentators such as the media critic John Fiske, the cultural theorist George Lipsitz, and the legal scholar Cheryl I. Harris have identified "whiteness" as an important cultural construct in American society. For Harris and Lipsitz, whiteness is a historically emergent phenomenon; for Lipsitz, whiteness appears in large measure "because of realities created by slavery and segregation, immigration restriction and Indian policy, by conquest and colonialism" (Lipsitz 1995: 370).

Both Lipsitz and Harris have recourse to economic terms in describing the role of whiteness. Harris traces the evolution of the construction of whiteness as a form of legally constituted property, while Lipsitz refers to a "possessive investment in whiteness." Quoting legal theorist Kimberlé Crenshaw, Harris (1993: 1759) utilizes the language of investment in referring to the "actual stake in racism" that the previously Balkanized European ethnics developed, through the legal and social privileges that attend their classification as "white."

For Fiske, whiteness is "not an essential racial category that contains a set of fixed meanings, but a strategic deployment of power. . . . The space of whiteness contains a limited but varied set of normalizing positions from which that which is not white can be made into the abnormal; by such means whiteness constitutes itself as a universal set of norms by which to make sense of the world" (Fiske 1994: 42). Fiske identifies "exnomination" as a primary characteristic of whiteness as power: "Exnomination is the means by which whiteness avoids being named and thus keeps itself out of the field of interrogation and therefore off the agenda for change. . . . One practice of exnomination is the avoidance of self-recognition and self-definition. Defining, for whites, is a process that is always directed outward upon multiple 'others' but never inward upon the definer" (42).

It is my contention that, circumstantially at least, bebop's combination of spontaneity, structural radicalism, and uniqueness, antedating by several years the reappearance of improvisation in Eurological music, posed a challenge to that music which needed to be answered in some way. All too often, the space of whiteness provided a convenient platform for a racialized denial of the trenchancy of this challenge, while providing an arena for the articulation of an implicit sensibility which I have termed "Eurological."

In a transnational, transcultural musical environment where exchanges of musical information are increasingly commonplace, ethnicized or racialized grounds for classification of musical discourse, though not explicitly named, nevertheless become disclosed. Despite Baraka's contention that bebop was the African-American musical form that obliged the larger society to confront Afrological aesthetics in creative black music itself as "art" (Jones 1963: 190), the fact that both Bird and Cage expressed an experimental bent in describing their respective creative processes has not, so far, induced the authors of music history texts concerned with "American music since 1945" to classify the output of these two composers according to their relationship with the experimental. Instead, texts appropriating the term "experimental music" construct this classification as denoting a particular group of postwar music makers who come almost exclusively from either European or European-American heritage. Michael Nyman's important book *Experimental Music* (1974) is representative. This text, like most others, presents this group of composers as the intellectual heirs to what is vernacularly known as the "classical" or "Western" tradition, even when this tradition is subjected to critique through its inheritors' music.

Coded qualifiers to the word "music"—such as "experimental," "new," "art," "concert," "serious," "avant-garde," and "contemporary"—are used in these texts to delineate a racialized location of this tradition within the space of whiteness; either erasure or (brief) inclusion of Afrological music can then be framed as responsible chronicling and "objective" taxonomy. The passing reference to the Art Ensemble of Chicago in the Schwartz and Godfrey text on *Music Since 1945*, for example, was necessary "because their music was as much 'serious' or avant-garde music as jazz" (Schwartz and Godfrey 1993: 202). The quote demonstrates the role assumed by whiteness in defining the Art Ensemble as not quite so "other" as some of the others.

Similarly, David Cope's text rigorously avoids extended, serious treatment of major figures in postwar Afrological improvisation, while devoting considerable attention to something called "contemporary" improvisation. The reader is encouraged to assume that this kind of "contemporary" improvisation, despite the fact that a number of its proponents "are or were actively involved in jazz" (Cope 1993: 127), must have developed sui generis—perhaps in a sort of immaculate conception.

According to Cope, the likeliest origin of this sort of improvisation lay, not in any kind of musical miscegenation with jazz, but in "classical" performers' "inability to realize correctly the complexities of recent music; the composer, perhaps out of frustration, perhaps because the result was the same or better, chose to allow a certain freedom in performance" (127).

My own view is that in analyzing improvisative musical activity or behavior in structural terms, questions relating to how, when, and why are critical. It should be axiomatic that, both in our musical and in our human everyday-life improvisations, we interact with our environment, navigating through time, place, and situation, both creating and discovering form. On the face of it, this interactive, form-giving process appears to take root and flower freely, in many kinds of music, both with and without preexisting rules and regulations. Perhaps the most trenchant conception of what improvisation can be is to be found in this testament by Charlie Parker: "Music is your own experience, your thoughts, your wisdom. If you don't live it, it won't come out of your horn" (quoted in Levin and Wilson 1994: 24). The clear implication is that what you do live does come out of your horn.

References

Braxton, Anthony. *Tri-Axium Writings, Volume I*. Dartmouth, NH: Synthesis/Frog Peak, 1985.

Cage, John. *Silence: Lectures and Writings*. Middletown, CT: Wesleyan University Press, 1961.

Cope, David. *New Directions in Music*. Madison WI: Brown and Benchmark, 1993.

Fiske, John. *Media Matters: Everyday Culture and Political Change*. Minneapolis: University of Minnesota Press, 1994.

Gridley, Mark. *Jazz Styles: History and Analysis*. Englewood Cliffs, NJ: Prentice-Hall, 1994.

Harris, Cheryl I. "Whiteness as Property." *Harvard Law Review* 106:8, 1993, pp. 1707–91.

Jones, LeRoi. *Blues People*. New York: William Morrow, 1963.

Kofsky, Frank. *Black Nationalism and the Revolution in Music*. New York: Pathfinder, 1970.

Kostelanetz, Richard. *Conversing with Cage*. New York: Limelight, 1987.

Levin, Michael, and John S. Wilson. "No bop roots in jazz: Parker." *Down Beat* 61:2, 1994, pp. 24–25. (Originally published September 9, 1949).

Lipsitz, George. "The Possessive Investment in Whiteness: Racialized Social Democracy and the "White" Problem in American Studies." *American Quarterly* 47:3, 1995, pp. 369–427.

Mandeles, Chad. "Jackson Pollock and Jazz: Structural Parallels." *Arts Magazine* 57, 1981, pp. 139–41.

Nyman, Michael. *Experimental Music: Cage and Beyond*. Cambridge: Cambridge University Press, 1974.

Schwartz, Elliott, and Daniel Godfrey. *Music since 1945: Issues, Materials, and Literature*. New York: Schirmer, 1993.

Walton, Ortiz. *Music: Black, White, and Blue*. New York: William Morrow, 1972.

PART 10

The Second Century

65. Explaining the Art of a Trio

MUSICIANS HAVE OFTEN COMPLAINED OF BEING MISUNDERSTOOD by critics, but seldom with such sustained and detailed counterarguments as pianist Brad Mehldau (b. 1970) presents in this essay, first published as liner notes to one of his series of recordings called *Art of the Trio*. In this case, it's a standard piano trio, with Larry Grenadier on bass and Jorge Rossy on drums.

Mehldau begins with the pitfalls of style criticism, denouncing the tendency always to compare something to something else instead of accounting for how the first thing actually works and means. And he ends with—well, there still exists the assumption among some classical musicians that improvisation is what you do when your plans fail, that it is necessarily a kind of making do with less-than-optimal circumstances. Mehldau finishes his essay with a flourish, celebrating improvisation as potentially superior to written composition.

The constant comparison of this trio with the Bill Evans trio by critics has been a thorn in my side. I remember listening to his music only a little, when I was 13 or 14 years old, for several months. I'm not saying I "grew out of him." Nor am I denying Bill Evans's stature in jazz. But along with those of Lennie Tristano and Paul Bley, both of whom I never listened to, the nonstop claims of their influence on me are not about musical content. Notions of an introverted intellectualism and cloying overemotionalism give the piano trio its otherness in this false appraisal. What's really going on, I fear, is good old-fashioned racial troping—the piano trio as sensitive-white-guys club. If all this sounds defensive, it is. When you're trying to create something personal, it's frustrating to be categorized away with no explanation. The problem with a big portion of writing on jazz is that it lags behind the music. More like rock journalism, it draws on biographical hearsay about the artist, but

---

Source: Brad Mehldau, liner notes for Brad Mehldau, *Art of the Trio 4: Back at the Vanguard* (Warner Bros. Records 9 47463-2), 1999. Reprinted by permission of Brad Mehldau.

with an added pretense: it uses these speculations to make general, sweeping musical judgments. That's a form of sophistry with the worst aspects of classical and pop writing. It has all the mystification that comes along with pop's personality cult, with an air of self-righteous assurance that parodies classical criticism. Then throw in a fetishism for the past, fueled, ironically, by half-baked ideas about a recent renaissance. Let me clarify: how a player crooks his head into the piano or battles with substance abuse is not comparative criticism; what he does with melody, harmony, rhythm, and form is.

The way that Larry and I are abstracting harmony has nothing to do with Bill Evans, who to my knowledge generally stayed within the prescribed chords. Larry has found his own way to not walk a bass line per se but, within our texture, still play the bass role. He constantly supplies shifting pedal points that serve pragmatically as the root for whatever harmony I'm suggesting. He's totally unlike Evans's Scott Lafaro, who soloistically vied with the piano, often not supplying a root. Larry gives a bottom end to the harmony that allows me any possibility. You'll hear his constant inventiveness on a simple form like "Nice Pass." Listen only to Larry "behind" me here: his playing is melodically compelling in and of itself, yet acts as an anchor to my solo at the same time.

Often what I'm doing in my solo is basing its melodic content on the initial melody of the song. You won't find the model for this approach in Bill Evans. A predecessor is Monk, but there's no real harmonic resemblance. On top of Larry's shifting pedal points, my tonal center is shifting as well with its own logic. This is why we favor simple forms like those of "London Blues" or "Nice Pass." A blues or "rhythm changes" is just a frame. The music on our first live record, and now this one, is involved in exploiting that frame. The frame or form makes it possible to abstract harmonic and rhythmic ideas; without a form the possibility of abstraction is canceled out. A kind of formal improvisation is taking place, not *through* the tune, but *within* it. There's motion, but not in the time-sense of passing notes or rhythms; rather, there's a movement toward or away from the frame. The frame makes it art for me. To say that 32-bar or blues forms are outmoded is missing the point; it's like taking issue with the decimal system because it's based on tens. Playing "free" of a form has never been compelling to me because it feels like there's nowhere to go. The very limitations of a form imply the possibility of a destination; without them there's no project. That's just my personal aesthetic, and I offer it to illustrate what we're doing on this record. When criticism makes no attempt to account for specifically musical achievements—melodic, harmonic, rhythmic, formal—it sells everyone short, giving the false impression that nothing new is happening.

The odd meter on "All the Things You Are," the metric modulation on "Nice Pass," and the feel on "Sehnsucht" or "Exit Music" are not revolutionary but, to my knowledge, are not part of the Bill Evans Trio's rhythmic texture, which has a lot to do with Jorge. Whether on his ride cymbal, or on different parts of the kit, he plays rhythmic *phrases*, shapes that are constantly beginning and ending, instead of one continuous pattern. This approach is vital to me. It never delineates what I'm playing, and allows my phrases a different kind of freedom. They can start anywhere and end anywhere, and often suggest a different meter or tempo. Often, Jorge is the other side or negative imprint of whatever phrase I'm playing. None of this has been willed or planned ahead. My personal definition of jazz must include improvisation, which is what this recording captures. Improvisation takes place not only in performance but in the way a band develops. There is a group decision perpetually taking place, a collective intelligence that wants everyone to express themselves. That's the idea. Jazz's unique shot at greatness lies in its *active* creation, which is, as it were, off the cuff. So much of Western art has self-consciously strived to appear artless; jazz has the unique distinction of artlessly becoming artful.

I have a built-in wariness toward the term "renaissance" when applied to jazz music being played and recorded in recent years. A resurgence of interest took place, perhaps. But should we really paste a normative historical term to a music that evades the burden of history? The act of improvisation is a perpetual birthing, making a rebirth unnecessary. "America's classical music" doesn't work either. I identify an American ethos in the inception of jazz, if not in its present state (which hardly matters), but it has everything to do with *not* being classical. Classical wasn't called classical when it was being created. Someone came along after a point in time and lumped it all under one term, implying as well that an ending had taken place. This in turn implied that anything after that wasn't valid. "Classical" is a term ripe for deconstruction: it defines itself by a symbiotic Other that belatedly doesn't rise to its stature. Its shaky legitimacy depends on a dreary nostalgia for a time when distinctions between the high arts and everything else were more clear (if they ever were). People with this kind of backward longing are blind to their own irony. They feel that they missed an event that's no longer possible and, with their heads in these gray clouds, miss the present event. This lover of classics will always miss his art object in frustration because art can't achieve high or classical sainthood until at least a couple generations of posterity-testing. A dubious claim to jazz's legitimacy is its own watery-eyed parody of this species: the drunk at the bar who talks through the set, whining about how jazz will never be like it was in the days when Coltrane played here, oblivious to the music taking place in front of him.

The American artistic ethos I would identify in jazz was, as a precondition, always quite removed from all that historical gloom, and still is. It involved a perpetual newness, and freedom from a history, that, with all its old-age authority, tells you that you'll never be as great as it was, that you're already defeated. America's anti-legacy is pop. A seemingly innocent term, "pop" implies a disposable aspect, an inability to reveal any timeless truths. The highbrow tells us that pop's nonprofundity comes from a lack of autonomy in the criteria for its creation—integrity is sacrificed to make a buck. If we look under that assertion just a bit, there's a darker suggestion: that classical music, as high art, has a *moral* authority over its subject. Many of us buy into this trope in spite of ourselves, and it can initially alienate the listener from the work. Music of what we call classical was conceived in a subversive spirit. It wasn't as much concerned with autonomy from less noble interests of money and fame as it was freedom from the idea of any moral *function* in art at all. It's an irony of history, with its shifting perspectives, that classical music so often denotes a dominating, rule-making presence. Is that the fate of jazz?

Classical music, pragmatically speaking, was often the pop music of its own day. Pop, since it earned its own term, has often proved to be capable of staying power, not so disposable. Classical and pop as terms tell us nothing definitive about the aesthetic success or failure of the music they refer to. It's nobody's fault. Words have a peculiar penchant for deflating the sentiment out of any cognition, especially that of music. Language's precondition is its own hierarchic relation to whatever it's attempting to name. It wins a phony victory in the very act of its failure, serving us a metaphor that's limited at best, arriving too late. Music is often understood as a way of speaking in the abstract, having the best of both worlds as it were. Understanding music as a kind of utopian language is, alas, another trope of language, contingent on its very rules. "Classical" and "pop" refer more to the supposed life expectancy, and less to the content, of the actual music. They are often failed prophecies: what was initially called classic reveals itself as a pop anachronism; what was conceived as pop cheats its origins and wins the bid for immortality.

I suspect that the attraction of jazz is that it ideally seeks to inhabit the best part of both classical and pop, and, brazenly, moves beyond their limitations. Jazz inherits the grand narrative gestures of the classical legacy in its commitment to giving the listeners an experience that will enrich their lives permanently through the rigor of its craft, the organic integrity of its shape and form. Yet it out-pops pop in its quick-willed active creation, which takes place in the improvisation. Jazz musicians want to make the earth move now. They don't want to interpret how someone else did it and be told they're wrong. Again, there's something initially American in that project: after a thorough ransacking, a gleeful egg-tossing at the entire rule-list of Occidental music, in favor of a hit-or-miss attempt at a kind of quick-fix transcendence, to be felt here and now, for the first (and maybe last) time. This is what I love about jazz more than anything—the spirit in which it's created.

A Renaissance means we already have to go to the museum to witness jazz's "Antiquity," which is what so much concert programming feels like these days. The listener is treated like a tourist, while curator-musicians guide them through specific corridors of jazz history. To me, that smells of bad faith. Perhaps it's an American self-conscious attempt to ascribe a European legitimacy to jazz, the legitimacy of something already dead and enshrined under glass. If we're in a Renaissance, when exactly were the Dark Ages? The unspoken implication, of course, is the 1970s, a time when jazz succumbed to "lower" influences like rock 'n' roll and infected itself with electric instruments. What jazz in fact was doing was what it had always done: taking leads from pop music of its day, and reanimating the stylistic garment into something transfigured by the force of its composition and improvisation. This Dark Ages subtext perpetuates another misreading of jazz's short-lived history in the making—that acoustic music simply stopped until its supposed renaissance. One could easily have had the impression that jazz was a music played exclusively by the very young and very old. Thankfully, it seems like we're emerging from this condition, less indicative of musical quality than of the general fetishistic feeding frenzy of the media on Youth, the commodity. As a jazz musician of my generation, I have no pretense that the music presented here is part of some "return" to the real shit because it's piano trio, because it's acoustic music. The Renaissance misconception is limiting to jazz because it suggests that it already played itself out. It gives rise to a tired question like, "Can anything *still* be done with piano trio?" False hope leads to its flipside, a backlash of cynicism, and I wouldn't ever attempt to answer to either sentiment. An endgame attitude toward jazz gives us a premature, peanut-sized parody of the entire Western tradition in art. There's the familiar defeatist implication that the music degenerates over time, with a kind of Faustian inevitability, until it can be redeemed, which presumably is taking place now. Jazz never lost itself, so a redemption isn't necessary. The prelapsarian myth of art as a fallen thing from some earlier grace-state is a vestige of high art criticism that jazz need not willfully inherit. The Fall myth is usually less about art than it is a stapled-on projection, a misplaced anxiety about the mortality of the culture in which that art is created, which is in itself another evasion, fear of one's own mortality.

The same American attitude made two radically different genres possible that are certainly no longer exclusively American: really bad pop and really great jazz. It's a flipping-the-bird at the whole notion of mortality. Maybe that's partially the no-fear attitude of a young culture. Hegel prophesied a death of art; in his old-school terms, Coltrane and the Spice Girls start *after* that end in open-ended regions that have come to be called postmodern. They don't aspire to a lineage that will play itself out.

Lineage as an *idea* played *itself* out and willed its own critical death. We're now in a swamp of relativism artwise, which is fine with me, because the critical focus can be placed on the aesthetic. Pop engages in a kind of harmless nihilism when it offers up a reconstituted nothingness that dies as quickly as a mosquito (if it was ever alive). Jazz, in its most inspired moments, makes a kind of exalted fuck you to mortality in the flux of its improvisations. Jazz improvisation isn't born out of any previous text, which differentiates it from the interpretive art of classical performance. Music texts are the Prospero's Books of classical music. They insure a certain immortality. Part of the brazen quality of a music that puts improvisation at its center is that it simply did not *care* enough to write a text, and that not caring became its strength. I locate my personal aesthetic for jazz in that strength: it basks in the human capability to grasp at the transcendental with immediacy, free of the usual trial and error of art.

Often one says of a work by Beethoven, "Not one note could be changed." It's a retrospective feeling, a comment on the music's rich formal power. It's critically useless, because no one's *going* to change it. Nevertheless, when I listen to Miles on "Kind of Blue," I say, "Not one note could be changed." To figure out *why* a person feels that way is a good project for jazz criticism, but we first need to unpack a stigma from improvisation—that it won't yield something as formally profound as a written work. That's born out of simple ignorance, one that leads to a question often asked after the gig: "So like, were you guys just more or less 'jamming out?'" A listener doesn't need to know what chords or what structure we're blowing over any more they have to understand sonata-allegro form when they listen to a symphony, to dig the music. But it does help to know that there is a form there. There are lead-sheets, purposely limited texts that tell how and where to jump off. But jazz knew something from its beginning: Don't depend on a text! I am quite sure that the precondition of the Coltrane Quartet of the 1960s is that they absolutely could *not* have written out as inspiring a performance, note for note, ahead of time. This is an important distinction for an understanding of jazz. Improvisatory creation is not a medium that half-heartedly tries, but won't rise up to, a written composition; on the contrary, it gives jazz its grandeur, which is a potential to *eclipse* written music in its performance. One might point out that classical music originally had its great improvisers. We know this from biographical accounts, for instance, of cutting contests between Beethoven and Hummel. But what's kept Beethoven's music in circulation is his compositions, not his improvisation. Jazz's canon is its recorded legacy, so much of which is improvised. To close I offer a scenario: if all the written music in the world suddenly burned up in a flash, who could still do a gig the same night, with complete strangers, and no rehearsals?

66. Three Polemics on the State of Jazz

POET, NOVELIST, CULTURAL AND MUSICAL CRITIC STANLEY CROUCH (b. 1945) has been an outspoken and influential figure in the jazz criticism of the new millennium. His sensibility is conservative, and it's no surprise that he served as a Senior Creative Consultant for Ken Burns's film series *Jazz*.[1] His work as one of the best-known African-American commentators on jazz has often been taken to be too provocative, particularly in the case of the third of the essays reprinted here, which resulted in his departure from his position as a columnist for *JazzTimes*. He is obviously not afraid to confront the biggest and most consequential issues that can be raised about jazz, and to argue about them with the passion they might deserve.

The Jazz Tradition Is Not Innovation

I came of age in the 1960s and was accustomed then to a higher level of artistic discussion about jazz than we presently expect. When thinkers such as Gunther Schuller, Don Heckman, Martin Williams, George Russell, Richard B. Hadlock, Nat Hentoff, Charles Mingus, Dan Morgenstern, Bill Mathieu, Bill Russo, and others wrote about the traditions of jazz or about individual players or movements, or put their two cents into the whirlwind of controversy that dominated the air after Ornette Coleman opened at the Five Spot in November of 1959, they did so with more than a casual understanding of the music. Whether or not they were musicians, and whether or not one agreed with everything that those guys concluded, they came to the art with a great sense of what made it valuable and unique in the first place. They knew that jazz was not European concert music in disguise, that it was not African music, and that it was not merely improvised music. Those writers knew that jazz was not anything other than what it was, regardless of how many ways it had been played between the time Louis Armstrong left New Orleans to join King Oliver in Chicago in 1922 and Ornette Coleman packed up his plastic alto saxophone and headed out of Los Angeles for Manhattan.

This does not seem to be very true to me today. Now, critics maintain a perpetual pursuit of novelty, of something that might make the writers become famous for "discovering." There is little measured thinking about what is going on and little respect for those who are not bent on "innovation." We even have to endure imbecilic

---

Source: Stanley Crouch, *Considering Genius: Writings on Jazz* (New York: Basic Books, 2006), pp. 209–212, 232–34. Originally published in *JazzTimes*, January 2002, October 2002, and April 2003.

1. For more on this Ken Burns project, see the article by George Lipsitz in this volume.

statements like "the tradition of jazz is innovation." This means absolutely nothing since the vast majority of musicians at any time in history and in any idiom are not innovators themselves—even if they are among the first to embrace fresh vocabularies.

During the 1940s, the innovators were Charlie Parker, Dizzy Gillespie, Fats Navarro, Miles Davis, Lee Konitz, Warne Marsh, Bud Powell, Thelonious Monk, Lennie Tristano, Oscar Pettiford, Ray Brown, Kenny Clarke, Max Roach, Roy Haynes, and Art Blakey. Should everyone else of their generation have stopped playing, or should they have made the most that they could of what attracted them to the things they heard in those musicians? The answer is rather obvious, isn't it?

Innovators are no more—and no less—than individuals whose individuality demands dramatic reinterpretations of the present language, so much so that they add fresh choices to the community and to their idiom. They do not necessarily "advance" the music.

Adding is plenty. Is John Coltrane more advanced than Sonny Rollins or Charlie Parker or Lester Young or Coleman Hawkins? Hardly. He added some choices that they didn't, which is true of each of them as well. But a musician could ignore all of those players and put together a combination of Eddie "Lockjaw" Davis, Charlie Rouse, Paul Gonsalves, and Dewey Redman for something that would be highly individual as well, though it might not result in an entire school of thinking—that is proven by those four players themselves. Who is more of an individual than Davis or Rouse or Gonsalves or Redman?

Beyond the question of innovation, there is the absurd issue of what the music should be called and what gives it identity. Perhaps the most naïve are those who use Duke Ellington's discomfort with categories to justify their preferred idea that jazz should elude definition. They seem to think that Ellington himself had no idea what jazz was or that he was absolutely serious about his "beyond category" pronouncements.

Sure, he was serious, but not in the way that they think he was.

Ellington's music, whether secular or sacred, almost always addressed the irrefutable jazz fundamentals that have maintained themselves from generation to generation: 4/4 swing, blues, the meditative ballad, and the Spanish tinge. So it should be obvious that when he was attacking the reductive impact of categories, he was actually addressing the problem that anyone had in the arena of artistic respect when described as a jazz musician. After all, Ellington was born in 1899 and grew up when jazz was considered—in far too many circles—whorehouse music and was associated with the nightlife criminal types who came to power during the twenties, earning their slimy livings through the sale of illegal booze, prostitution, and gambling. Ellington, therefore, was dealing with academic, aesthetic, social, and racial prejudice. All the while, he was writing and playing jazz and leading a band of jazz musicians—jazz, and jazz alone.

The Negro Aesthetic of Jazz

Jazz has always been a hybrid. A mix of African, European, Caribbean, and Afro-Hispanic elements. But the distinctive results of that mix, which distinguished jazz as one of the new arts of the twentieth century, are now under assault by those who would love to make jazz no more than an "improvised music" free of definition. They would like to remove those elements that are essential to jazz and that came from the Negro. Troublesome person, that Negro.

Through the creation of blues and swing, the Negro discovered two invaluable things. With the blues, a fresh melodic idea could be framed within a short form of three chords that added a new feeling to Western music and inspired endless variations. In swing it was a unique way of phrasing that provided an equally singular pulsation. These two innovations were neither African nor European nor Asian nor Australian nor Latin nor South American; they were Negro-American.

Through the grand seer, Louis Armstrong, swinging and playing the blues moved to the high ground. After Armstrong straightened everyone out and indisputably pointed the way, there was a hierarchy in jazz, and that hierarchy was inarguably Negroid, so much so that many assumed Negro genius came from the skin and the blood, not from the mind. That is why one white musician brought a recording of the white New Orleans Rhythm Kings to Bix Beiderbecke and excitedly told him that they sounded "like real niggers." Ah, so. The issue was one of aesthetic skill, not color, not blood.

The white musician understood exactly what every black concert musician realized upon truly meeting the criteria of instrumental or vocal performance. At some point, perhaps even at the start, Leontyne Price learned that being black and from Laurel, Mississippi, did not shut her off from the art of Schubert, Wagner, or Puccini, no matter how far their European social worlds were from hers, in terms of history and geography. Nor did Price's becoming a master change those works she sang into German-Negro or Italian-Negro vocal art. They remained German and Italian and European, but were obviously available to anyone who could meet the measure of the music.

Hierarchy has always given Americans trouble. We believe that records are made to be broken, or to be broken free of, which is why, along with that pesky skin color, the Negroid elements central to jazz were rebelled against as soon as possible. Martin Williams, the late, great jazz critic and himself a white Southerner, told me once that there used to be a group of white jazz musicians who would say, when there were only white guys around, "Louis Armstrong and those people had a nice little primitive thing going, but we really didn't have what we now call jazz until Jack Teagarden, Bix, Trumbauer, and their gang gave it some sophistication. Bix is the one who introduced introspection to jazz. Without him you would have no Lester Young and no Miles Davis."

In such instances, Beiderbecke ceases to be a great musician and becomes a pawn in the ongoing attempt to deny the blues its primary identity as a Negro-developed, introspective music, which is about coming to understand oneself and the world through contemplation. To recognize that would be to recognize the possibility of the Negro having a mind and one that could conceive an aesthetic overview that distinguished the music as a whole. Troublesome person, that Negro—especially one with an aesthetic.

The most recent version of the movement to neutralize the Negro aesthetic was made clear to me by a European twenty-five years ago. He told me that someday we would all embrace the idea of a great jazz drummer like Ed Blackwell improvising with Asian Indians, North Africans, South Americans, Europeans, and so on, each playing in the language of his culture on instruments from his homeland. "This, to me, is the jazz of the future," he said.

It sounded like the United Nations in an instrumental session to me, not the jazz that is more than improvisation alone, not the jazz that always engages 4/4 swing, blues, the romantic to meditative ballad, and Afro-Hispanic rhythm as core aesthetic elements. If these people from all over the world want to truly play with jazz masters such as Blackwell and be considered jazz musicians, they have to learn how to play the blues, how to swing, how to play through chord progressions—just as Leontyne Price had to meet the essential refinements of the music to set free the talents that made her famous.

Jazz is an art, not a subjective phenomenon. Negroes in America, through extraordinary imagination and new instrumental techniques, provided a worldwide forum for the expression of the woes and the wonders of human life. Look like what you look like, come from wherever you come from, be either sex and any religion, but understand that blues and that swing are there for you too—if you want to play jazz.

Putting the White Man in Charge

Because Negroes invented jazz, and because the very best players have so often been Negroes, the art has always been a junction for color trouble in the world of evaluation and promotion. By the end of the 1920s, Duke Ellington was trying to get his buddies to call their art "Negro music," possibly because Paul Whiteman had been dubbed "King of Jazz." Variations on this phenomenon have risen and fallen throughout the history of the art.

Since the 1960s, however, certain Negroes who cannot play will claim to be of aesthetic significance on the basis of sociology and some irrelevant ancestral connection to Africa—which provided only part of the mix that became jazz. That had an ironic impact because we are now back to the Paul Whiteman phenomenon, as if all of those white people who had to put up with black nonsense now have their chance to express their rage. This time white musicians who can play are too frequently elevated far beyond their abilities in order to allow white writers to make themselves feel more comfortable about being in the role of evaluating an art from which they feel substantially alienated. Now, having long been devoted to creating an establishment based on "rebellion," or what Rimbaud called the "love of sacrilege," they have achieved a moment long desired: Now certain kinds of white men can focus their rebellion on the Negro. Oh, happy day.

In his essential *Blues Up and Down* (St. Martin's), Tom Piazza pulled the covers off of these men when he wrote, "Many jazz reviewers—especially among the generation that grew up in the 1960s and '70s—suffer from intense inferiority feelings in front of the musicians they write about. This results in a vacillation between an exaggerated hero-worship of musicians and an exaggerated sense of betrayal when the musicians don't meet their needs." Piazza surely knew what he was talking about, especially since he was a white man who had been among these jazz writers when nobody dark was around, which allowed him to understand them and their various insecurities and their various resentments close up.

In Francis Davis's *Like Young: Jazz, Pop, Youth and Middle Age* (2002; Da Capo: New York), one can get a good deal of insight into Piazza's thesis. It is a classic of its kind. Davis unintentionally makes it clear that he is intimidated by Negroes and also quite jealous of them. The intimidation arrives because of the troubles and the fun he imagines Negroes having when he is not around. The resentment flares if these Negroes have any power to define themselves and what they are doing or if they have reputations independent of Davis's permission or if they cannot be conventionally condescended to from the abolitionist's perspective that so many jazz writers have in common. Their job, they believe, is to speak up for the exotic Negro or use that Negro as a weapon against their own middle-class backgrounds or make that Negro into a symbol of their desire to do something bold, wild, and outside of convention. Even being in the presence of such stuff will do, since Davis points out that rap now allows the young white person to come in contact with the Negro most removed from the white world, which used to be the role of jazz. Is that so? Since the rap Negro is nothing more, at his most "street," than a theatrical version of Zip Coon, a character from the minstrel shows, how is he removed from the white world? Every

Negro inferior to a middlebrow white man like Davis fits comfortably in the white world, where black refinement is never expected or is dismissed as pompous.

Disturbed by the way things have gone over the last couple of decades, Davis's answer to his Negro problem is to create an alternative order of significance. He sees, as do so many of these men, jazz that is based on swing and blues as the enemy and, therefore, lifts up someone like, say, Dave Douglas as an antidote to too much authority from the dark side of the tracks. Douglas, a graduate of Exeter and a dropout from the New Jersey upper middle class, is the perfect white man to lead the music "forward." Unlike these misled uptown Negroes who spend too much time messing around with stuff like the blues and swinging, Downtown Dave brings truly new stuff into jazz, like Balkan folk material that surely predates the twentieth century in which blues and jazz were born.

There is nothing wrong with Douglas, who can play what he can play and who should continue to do whatever he wants to do, but there is something pernicious about Davis and all of those other white guys who want so badly to put white men in charge—American and European—and put Negroes in the background. Douglas, whom I have heard since he worked as a sideman years ago with Vincent Herring, is far from being a bad musician, but he also knows that he should keep as much distance as possible between himself and trumpet players like Wallace Roney, Terence Blanchard, and Nicholas Payton, to name but three, any one of whom on any kind of material—chordal, nonchordal, modal, free, whatever—would turn him into a puddle on the bandstand. Unlike the great white players of the past, such as Jack Teagarden, Bobby Hackett, Benny Goodman, Stan Getz, Lee Konitz—or, now, Joe Lovano—Douglas will never be seen standing up next to black masters of the idiom. The white critical establishment couldn't help him then.

But the deepest part of this is that it, finally, is not so much about color as it is about the destruction of the Negro aesthetic, which is why Negroes like Don Byron and Mark Turner are embraced. They accept an imposed aesthetic of "pushing the envelope" in ways that have nothing to do with blues and swing. Above all, they help these writers to bring things disguised as bulls into the middle-class china shops in which these critics themselves were born.

67. Exploding the Narrative

JAZZ MUSICIANS OFTEN SPEAK OF THE IMPORTANCE of "telling a story" or "saying something" in their improvisations, as opposed to merely playing notes that simply fit the context (for example, see the statement by Sidney Bechet that begins this volume). Here, Vijay Iyer (b. 1971) questions this metaphor and tries to go beyond it to find other kinds of meaning that improvisation can create. Iyer is best known as a jazz pianist and composer, but he also earned a Ph.D. with a dissertation on music cognition, and he has continued to contribute writings to that field. In particular, Iyer is interested in embodiment, in the ways that the physicality of musical performance creates significance through means that are just beginning to be understood.

Tell a story. This oft-repeated directive for an improvised solo has become a cliché of jazz musicology. Its validity is unarguable, having been restated in various forms by countless artists from Charlie Parker to Cecil Taylor. But we seem to lack the analytical tools to describe in detail how, under what circumstances, or indeed whether this wordless spinning of yarns even *could* happen, let alone what the content might be. In the constellations of jazz lore, the storytelling imperative seems to hang there, fixed in the firmament, along with "If you have to ask, you'll never know" and other hip tautologies.

In a renowned piece of jazz musicology, Gunther Schuller asserted that the musical "coherence" of a jazz solo—present, he claimed, only in the work of figures such as Louis Armstrong, Coleman Hawkins, and Charlie Parker—could be proven using the standard "reduction" tools of Western music analysis.[1] Brian Harker echoes this sentiment, stating that the coherence of an Armstrong improvisation amounts to a kind of "story."[2] For Harker the hallmarks of this story seem to include demonstrable relationships among musical phrases (a trait that seems more reminiscent of verse than narrative) and the gradual build to a climax. But perhaps we can view purely musical coherence as just one facet of a larger, richer, and more complex narrative structure.

Source: Vijay Iyer, "Exploding the Narrative in Jazz Improvisation," in Robert G. O'Meally, Brent Hayes Edwards, and Farah Jasmine Griffin, eds., *Uptown Conversation: The New Jazz Studies* (New York: Columbia University Press, 2004), pp. 393–403. Reprinted by permission of Copyright Clearance Center, Rightslink.

1. Gunther Schuller, "Sonny Rollins and the Challenge of Thematic Improvisation," in *Musings: The Musical Worlds of Gunther Schuller* (New York: Oxford University Press, 1986), pp. 86–97, reprinted from *Jazz Review* (November 1958). (Also reprinted in this volume)

2. Brian Harker, "'Telling a Story': Louis Armstrong and Coherence in Early Jazz," *Current Musicology* 63 (1999), pp. 46–83.

George Lewis furnishes a provocative description of African American improvised music as the encoded exchange of personal narratives.[3] Some guiding questions then become: What is the nature of these exchanged narratives, and how are they rendered musically? In the 1990s a wave of important scholarship on African American music addressed some of the ways in which meaning is generated in the course of jazz improvisation.[4] Much of this work focuses on the crucial role of interactivity and group interplay in the dialogical construction of multiplicities of meaning. Here one draws on a notion of communication as process, as a collective activity that harmonizes individuals rather than a telegraphic model of communication as mere transmission of literal, verbal meanings. For example, the musical notion of antiphony, or call and response, can function as a kind of communication, and nothing need be "said" at the literal level to make it so. What definitely *is* happening is that the interactive format, process, and feeling of conversational engagement are enacted by the musicians. In a context like jazz the presence of this kind of dialogical process is constant throughout a performance, as *sustained antiphony*.

But musical dialogue forms only part of the whole story. In the outtakes to John Coltrane's "Giant Steps," there emerges a revealing, poignant moment of candor among the musicians.[5] While rehearsing the precipitously difficult piece in the studio, John Coltrane can be heard saying to his struggling colleagues, "I don't think I'm gonna improve this, you know . . . I ain't goin be sayin nothin, (I goin do) tryin just, makin the *changes*, I ain't goin be, tellin no *story*. . . Like . . . tellin them *black* stories." Amidst the confounded mumbles of assent from his bandmates, one colleague rejoins, "Shoot. Really, you make the changes, *that*'ll tell 'em a story." Surprised by this idea, Coltrane responds, "You think the changes're the story!" Overlapping him, a second bandmate riffs, "(Right) . . . that'll change *all* the stories (up)." His voice crackling with laughter, Coltrane admits, "I don't want to tell no lies (on 'em)." After a group laugh, the second colleague trails off in a sort of denouement, "(The) changes *themselves* is *some* kind of story (man I'm tellin you)."[6]

These few seconds of banter could yield a symposium's worth of exegesis; the antiphonal, multilayered, Signifyin(g) exchange suggests striking notions of how musical stories can be told. "Making the changes"—i.e., negotiating the harmonic maze that forms the piece's improvisational structure—forms just one facet of the real-time construction of an improvised statement in this idiom. A list of other conventional ingredients might include conveying a steady rhythmic momentum ("swinging"), displaying a strong and personal timbre, constructing original melodic phrases, and amassing these phrases into a compelling "whole." From his concern that he isn't "tellin' no story," it is easy to suppose that Coltrane was thinking along

---

3. George E. Lewis, "Improvised Music since 1950: Afrological and Eurological Forms," *Black Music Research Journal* 16:1 (Spring 1996), pp. 91–119. (See also the abridged version of that essay in this volume.)

4. See, e.g., Samuel Floyd, *The Power of Black Music* (New York: Oxford University Press, 1995); Robert Walser, "'Out of Notes': Signification, Interpretation, and the Problem of Miles Davis," in K. Gabbard, ed., *Jazz Among the Discourses* (Durham, NC: Duke University Press, 1995), pp. 165–88 (also reprinted in this volume); Ingrid Monson, *Saying Something: Jazz Improvisation and Interaction* (Chicago: University of Chicago Press, 1996); George Lewis, "Singing Omar's Song: A (Re)construction of Great Black Music," *Lenox Avenue* 4 (1998), pp. 69–92.

5. John Coltrane, *The Heavyweight Champion*, compact disc compilation (Los Angeles: Atlantic Records, 1995), disc 7, track 1, originally recorded in 1959.

6. Transcribed by Steve Coleman and Vijay Iyer, 2000.

these lines, trying to create a "coherent," Schulleresque narrative arc over the scope of a given saxophone solo. However, his hint at larger concerns of cultural connection ("tellin' them black stories") suggests that his intentions transcend the étudelike nature of this clever harmonic progression, and even rise above this compositional idea of coherence. With these four words he seems to reach for musical statements in which no less than his whole community could hear its inexhaustible narrative multiplicity reflected. Indeed, his dogged pursuit of such an ideal is documented over the course of dozens of takes.

Moreover, his is a quest for veracity: "I don't want to tell no lies on 'em." One might wonder what notes, chords, and rhythms have to do with evaluations of truth, and one might be tempted to interpret the laughter that this comment elicits as an affirmation of the absurdity of this idea. But in fact this construction is common usage among jazz musicians, and the group outburst just might be a laugh of assent. Just weeks ago I heard a fellow musician criticize a bandmate for "telling lies" onstage; according to my colleague, his bandmate was playing what he thought their bandleader wanted to hear instead of following the general directive to make his own statement. For Coltrane, telling musical lies might have meant playing in an overly self-conscious, premeditated, or constructed fashion that rang false to his ears. This comment suggests that Coltrane strives to create an authentic representation of his community through telling his story as truthfully as he can. This trope of truthfulness has broad implications for the politics of authenticity and its role in the narrativity of black music; there is a clear connection between "telling your story" and "keeping it real."

My main interest in Coltrane's extemporaneous exchange with his quartet lies in his sideman's observation, "Really, you make the changes, *that*'ll tell 'em a story." Perhaps Coltrane's bandmate means to locate the kind of narrativity his leader seeks not only at the level of a philosophical imperative placed "on" the music but also precisely "in" the moment-to-moment act of making the changes. The sheer fact of Coltrane's maintenance of his musical balance in the face of such arduous challenges tells a compelling, even richly symbolic story. For what one hears is necessarily the result of much effort, time, and process—in short, of *labor* (meant with all of this word's attendant resonances).

This notion really does "change all the stories up": it implies a shift in emphasis from top-down notions of overarching coherence to bottom-up views of narrativity *emerging* from the minute laborious acts that make up musical activity. And given its focus on these acts and the rigors that they presuppose, the comment could also be read as a celebration of the athletics of black musical performance (or perhaps the performativity of black musical athletics). An improviser is engaged in a kind of highly disciplined physical activity, of which we only hear the sonic result. If we embrace this fact, we are led to consider the storytelling implications of this physical labor that we hear as music; surely the rigors of this embodied process tell "*some* kind of story."

In this vein, I would like to discuss what I call *traces of embodiment* in African-American music, and suggest what we might learn from them: how musical bodies tell us stories. I propose that the story that an improviser tells does not unfold merely in the overall form of a "coherent" solo, nor simply in antiphonal structures, but also in the microscopic musical details, as well as in the inherent structure of the performance itself. The story dwells not just in one solo at a time, but also in a single note, and equally in an entire lifetime of improvisations. In short, the story is revealed not as a simple linear narrative, but as a fractured, exploded one. It is what we take to be the shifting, multiple, continually reconstructed subjectivities of the improvisers, encoded in a diverse variety of sonic symbols, occurring at different levels and subject to different stylistic controls. Taking a similarly exploded form, this paper may seem fragmented. Indeed it must be, because it is only through this process of examining the puzzling shards of these exploded narratives that we may reveal a mosaic with a discernible underlying pattern.

Hearing the Body

In my previous work I have developed the claim that music perception and cognition are embodied, situated activities.[7] This means that they depend crucially on the physical constraints and enablings of our bodies and also on the ecological and sociocultural environment in which our music listening and producing capacities come into being. I argue that rhythm perception and production involve a complex, whole-body experience and that much of the musical structure found in rhythm-based music incorporates an awareness of the embodied, situated role of the participant. I show that certain kinds of rhythmic expression in African-derived music are directly related to the multiple roles of the body in making music and to certain cultural aesthetics that privilege this role.

Recent neurological studies have affirmed the cognitive role of body motion in music perception and production. According to these researchers, a perceived rhythmic pulse is literally an imagined movement; it seems to involve the same neural facilities as motor activity, most notably motor sequence planning.[8] Hence the act of listening to music involves the same mental processes that generate bodily motion. One might suppose that musical elements might be more efficacious in eliciting sympathetic behavior if they represent aspects of human motion somehow. Such sounds might include the dynamic swells associated with breathing, the steady pulse associated with walking, and the rapid rhythmic figurations associated with speech. Note that each of these three examples occurs at a different timescale. In fact, it is interesting to observe the rhythmic correspondences among these groups of behaviors:[9]

Bodily Activities	Musical Correlates	Timescale
Breathing, moderate arm gesture, body sway	Phrase, meter, harmonic rhythm, dynamics, vocal utterances	1–10 seconds
Heartbeat, walking, and running, sexual intercourse, head bob, toe tap	Pulse, "walking" basslines, dance rhythms	0.3–1 second (approximately 60–180 beats per minute)
Speech, lingual motion, syllables, rapid hand gesture, finger motion	Fast rhythmic activity, "bebop" melodies, etc.	0.1–0.3 second (3–10 notes per second)

7. Vijay Iyer, "Microstructures of Feel, Macrostructures of Sound: Embodied Cognition in West African and African-American Musics," Ph.D. thesis, University of California, Berkeley, 1998; "Embodied Mind, Situated Cognition, and Expressive Microtiming in African-American Music," *Music Perception* 19:3 (2002), pp. 387–414.

8. B. Carroll-Phelan and P. J. Hampson, "Multiple Components of the Perception of Musical Sequences: A Cognitive Neuroscience Analysis and Some Implications for Auditory Imagery," *Music Perception* 13 (1996), pp. 517–61; Neil Todd, C. Lee, and D. O'Boyle, "A Sensory-Motor Theory of Rhythm, Time Perception, and Beat Induction," *Journal of New Music Research* 28 (1999), pp. 5–29.

9. Paul Fraisse, "Rhythm and Tempo," in D. Deutsch, ed., *The Psychology of Music* (New York: Academic, 1982), pp. 149–80; Neil Todd, "The Auditory 'Primal Sketch': A Multiscale Model of Rhythmic Grouping," *Journal of New Music Research* 23 (1994), pp. 25–70.

It is plausible that musical activity on these three timescales might exploit these correspondences.

A variety of truisms support this view. For example, most wind-instrument phrase lengths are naturally constrained by lung capacity. Indeed, any instrument that produces sustained tones can be used to evoke the human voice. The throbbing of urban dance music often makes sonic references to foot stomping and to sexually suggestive slapping of skin. Blues guitarists, jazz pianists, and *quinto* players in Afro-Cuban *rumba* are said to "speak" with their hands and fingers. All such instances involve the embodiment of the musical performer and the listening audience.

A recent review by Shove and Repp highlights the often overlooked fact that musical motion is, first and foremost, audible human motion.[10] To amplify this view, Shove and Repp make use of the "ecological level" of perception as suggested by J. J. Gibson.[11] At this level "the listener does not merely hear the *sound* of a galloping horse or bowing violinist; rather the listener hears a *horse galloping* and a *violinist bowing*." In this ecological framework the source of perceived musical movement is the human performer, as is abundantly clear to the listener attending a music performance. We connect the perception of musical motion at the ecological level to human motion. This suggests that musical perception involves an understanding of bodily motion—that is, a mutual embodiment. For musical performers the difference between rhythmic motion and human motion collapses; the rhythmic motions of the performer and of the musical object are essentially one and the same.[12] Dance is then a natural response to the movement that music represents.

Kinesthetics

The term *kinesthetics* refers to the sensation of bodily position, presence, or movement resulting from tactile sensation and from vestibular input. We rely on such awareness whenever we engage in any physical activity; it helps us hold objects in our hands, walk upright, lean against walls, and guide food into our mouths. In these cases there is a strong interdependence between the kinesthetic and visual senses. Similarly, in the playing of musical instruments we must treat sonic and kinesthetic dimensions as interacting; we must bear in mind the spatiomotor mode of musical performance.[13] For musicians, musical competence involves the bodily coordination of limbs, digits, and, in the case of wind instruments, breathing.

John Blacking raised the issue of kinesthetics in musical performance by comparing two types of kalimba ("thumb piano") music among the Venda community of South Africa.[14] One very physical type, practiced by amateur boys, featured complex melodies that appeared to be secondary artifacts of patterned thumb movements; the regularity of the movements generated the jagged melodic result. The other type, a more popular style practiced by professional musicians, had simpler melodies with small intervals and flowing contours, directed more by an abstract melodic logic than by a spatiomotor one.

---

10. Paul Shove and Bruno Repp, "Musical Motion and Performance: Theoretical and Empirical Perspectives," in J. Rink, ed., *The Practice of Performance* (Cambridge: Cambridge University Press, 1995), pp. 55–83.

11. James J. Gibson, *The Ecological Approach to Visual Perception* (Boston: Houghton Mifflin, 1979).

12. Shove and Repp, "Musical Motion and Performance," pp. 59–60.

13. See John Baily, "Music Structure and Human Movement," in P. Howell, I. Cross, and R. West, eds., *Musical Structure and Cognition* (London: Academic, 1985), pp. 237–58.

14. John Blacking, *How Musical Is Man?* (Seattle: University of Washington Press, 1973).

From my experience with jazz improvisation on the piano, I have found that the kinesthetic or spatiomotor approach and the melodic approach form dual extremes of a continuum. We augment our aural imagination by exploring the possibilities suggested by the relationship between our bodies and our instruments, and we judge the result of such experimentation by appealing to our musical ear and aesthetics. Among pianists who have exploited this relationship in jazz, Thelonious Monk has been the most influential. His compositions and improvisations provide an exemplary nexus of kinesthetics and formalism. Often his pieces contained explicitly pianistic peculiarities, including the repeated use of pendular fourths, fifths, sixths, and sevenths (as in "Misterioso" and "Let's Call This"), whole-tone runs and patterns ("Four in One"), major- and minor-second dyads ("Monk's Point," "Light Blue"), and rapid figurations and ornamental filigrees ("Trinkle, Tinkle").[15] All of these idiosyncrasies fit, so to speak, in the palm of the pianist's hand, while often wreaking havoc for horn players (or, even worse, vocalists). Such physical patterns are simpler and apparently more primal for finger coordination than any nonconsecutive pattern. Monk was able to place these simple patterns in unconventional rhythmic and melodic relationships to yield new compositional and improvisational possibilities. The embodied-cognition viewpoint suggests that a musician's internal representations of music are intimately tied to his or her connection with the instrument, which forms part of the music-making environment. The musician's relationship with the instrument can leave its trace on the music itself—that is, it can be communicated musically, as Monk demonstrates so vividly.

Speech

As is commonly observed, jazz improvisation bears metaphorical attributes of speech and conversation. Ingrid Monson's book *Saying Something* provides an elaborate discussion of this metaphor. One often hears instances of the metaphor in African-American musical pedagogy, where "'to say' or 'to talk' often substitutes for 'to play.'"[16] Such usage underscores what musical performance does have in common with speech as an activity or behavior, as well as what music has in common with language as a symbolic system. Among the traits that link musical performance to speech, we see that:

- Like speech, musical performance is a *process*, a salient mental and physical activity that takes place in time.
- Like speech, musical performance is interactive, characterized by dialogue, call-and-response, and collective synchronization.
- Like speech, music has *semiotic* dimensions, which enable sonic symbols to refer actively to other parts of the same piece, to other music, or to contextual and extramusical phenomena—as with the rhythmic correspondences between finger motion and speech itself.

Note that these aspects of speech and performed music are not restricted to the domain of semantics; that is, they are not solely concerned with the "intrinsic" meanings of words or notes. Rather, these specific aspects depend upon the act of performance.

---

15. Recordings of all of these compositions can be found in the compact disc compilation *Thelonious Monk: The Complete Riverside Recordings* (Berkeley, CA: Riverside Records, 1986), originally recorded 1955–1961.

16. Monson, *Saying Something*, p. 84.

Performativity

Similarly one might imagine that visual and other contextual factors in a musical performance co-articulate musical meaning along with the sonic trace. We may call these elements *performatives*. In an essay entitled "The Grain of the Voice," Roland Barthes pointed out that the performance of composed music also carries this "extra" dimension.[17] In addition to the meaningful intramusical dynamics, supplemental meaning is generated by the presence of a music-making body, and the sonic traces it leaves behind. Hence the "grain" of the voice, by announcing the vocalist's physical presence, signifies a rupturing of the disembodied, self-contained world of the classical work. The personhood of the performer insinuates its way into (for Barthes, European classical) music performance through its roughness, its resistance, its departure from the ideal disembodied musical object. The physicality and resistance of the voice point to its producer, the performer, and to the act of it being produced. The grain of a musical performance reminds the listener of the physical sensation of using the voice, or other parts of the body: "The 'grain' is the body in the voice as it sings, the hand as it writes, the limb as it performs."[18] These physical encodings in musical performance have intensely expressive powers. The meaning of a vocal utterance is constituted not simply by its semantic content or its melodic logic, but also by its *sonorous* content.

Sound

Tellingly, among many jazz musicians, a most valued characterization is that a certain musician has his or her own, instantly recognizable *sound*, where "sound" means not only timbre, but also articulation, phrasing, rhythm, melodic vocabulary, and even analytical methods. Generally it came to mean a sort of "personality" or "character" that distinguishes different improvisers. Though it is a compliment if someone tells you that you "sound like Coleman Hawkins," it is even higher praise to be described as "having your own sound." Trombonist and improviser George Lewis writes,

> "[S]ound," sensibility, personality and intelligence cannot be separated from an improvisor's [sic] phenomenal (as distinct from formal) definition of music. Notions of personhood are transmitted via sounds, and sounds become signs for deeper levels of meaning beyond pitches and intervals.[19]

This view supports the widespread interpretation of improvisation as personal narrative, as that which gives voice to the meaningful experiences of the individual.[20] Cecil Taylor wrote of John Coltrane:

> In short, his tone is beautiful because it is functional. In other words, it is always involved in saying something. You can't separate the means that a man uses to say something from what he ultimately says. Technique is not separated from its content in a great artist.[21]

---

17. Roland Barthes, "The Grain of the Voice," in S. Heath, ed. and trans., *Image, Music, Text* (New York: Hill and Wang, 1977), pp. 179–89.

18. Ibid., p. 188.

19. Lewis, "Improvised Music since 1950," p. 117.

20. Ibid.

21. Cecil Taylor, "John Coltrane." *Jazz Review*, January 1959, p. 34.

Often, then, an improviser's original playing style is bound up with his or her (possibly idiosyncratic or self-styled) technique. In many cases the autodidactic approach plays a large role for improvisers, for whom the creation of music is embodied in one's relationship to one's instrument. Hence the inseparability of "sound," or embodied creative approach, from a "phenomenal definition of music"—a personal sense of what music is and what it is for.

The notion of personal sound functions as an analytical paradigm, a kind of down-home biographical criticism. An individual's tone, rhythmic feel, and overall musical approach are seen as an indicator of who he or she "is" as a person. Musicians' interactive strategies in music might be seen as an indicator of their interpersonal behavior; their rhythmic placement ahead of or behind the beat may reflect how "fiery" or "cool" their temperaments run; their melodic inventiveness and harmonic sophistication might parallel their offstage urbanity and wit. Admittedly, such stereotypical characterizations beg to be broken down; rarely does a musician's offstage personality fit such conventional wisdom. Indeed, one could also view "musical personality" as a kind of *mask* that the performer wears onstage, Signifyin(g) on his or her offstage identity as well as on performance itself. But in either case, the notion of personal sound, relating musical characteristics to personality traits, reveals much about how music, life, and personal narrative can be conceptualized together. In this sense, Sound provides a kind of Afrological animation of the "grain" in European performance.

Many have tried to establish "motivic development" in Coltrane's individual improvisations as that which creates structure and hence meaning.[22] But it seems to me that such structure is merely a consequence of a greater formation—Coltrane's "sound," his holistic approach to music, which yields these elements. I do not wish to imply that Coltrane had no mind for "structuring" an individual solo; but these sorts of analyses stem from the critical tools of the *listener* rather than the improviser. As a musician, I personally believe that the improviser is concerned more with making individual improvisations relate *to each other*, and to his or her conception of personal sound, than he or she might be with obeying some standard of coherence on the scale of the single improvisation.

Temporality of Musical Performance

Yet another fundamental consequence of physical embodiment and environmental situatedness is the fact that *things take time*. In intersubjective activities, such as speech, musical performance, or rehearsal, one remains aware of a sense of mutual embodiment, a presupposition of "shared time" between the listener and the performer. This sense is a crucial aspect of the temporality of performance. The experience of listening to live music is qualitatively different from that of reading a book. The former requires a "co-performance" on the part of the audience, one that must occur within a shared temporal domain.[23]

The experience of listening to music that we know to be improvised differs significantly from listening knowingly to composed music. A main source of drama in improvised music is the visceral fact of the shared sense of time: the sense that the

---

22. Roger Dean, *New Structures in Jazz and Improvised Music since 1960* (Philadelphia: Open University Press, 1992); Ekkehard Jost, *Free Jazz* (New York: Da Capo, 1981), pp. 92–94.

23. See A. Schutz, "Making Music Together," in *Collected Papers II: Studies in Social Theory* (The Hague: Martinus Nijhoff, 1964), pp. 159–78.

improviser is working, creating, generating musical material at the same time in which we are coperforming as listeners. As listeners, we seem to experience any music as an awareness of the physicality of the "grain," and a kind of *empathy* for the performer, an understanding of effort required to create music. In improvised music empathy extends beyond the concept of the physical body to an awareness of the performers' coincident physical and mental exertion, of their "in-the-moment" *process* of creative activity and interactivity. Listening to Coltrane on "Giant Steps," one cannot help but agree with his colleague, who suggested that the breathtaking *reality* of Coltrane improvising and creating his way through this maze tells quite an awesome story indeed, one that at the very least elicits our empathy.

Exploding the Narrative

In these and many other ways, the embodied view of music facilitates a nonlinear approach to musical narrative. Musical meaning is not conveyed only through motivic development, melodic contour, and other traditional musicological parameters; it is also *embodied* in improvisatory techniques. Musicians tell their stories, but not in the traditional linear narrative sense; an *exploded narrative* is conveyed through a holistic musical personality or *attitude*. That attitude is conveyed both musically, through the skillful, individualistic, improvisatory manipulation of expressive parameters in combination, as well as *extramusically*, in the sense that these sonic symbols "point" to a certain physical, social, and cultural comportment, a certain way of being embodied. Kinesthetics, performativity, personal sound, temporality—all these traces of embodiment generate, reflect, and refract stories into innumerable splinters and shards. Each one of these fragments is "saying something." The details of what the music is saying, and of how it does so, are as infinitely variable as are the individuals who enact and embody it.

In concluding, it is worth reminding ourselves that representations of African American culture have been plagued by racist mythologies surrounding the idea of the body. Historically, African American cultural practice has been seen by mainstream Western culture as the realm of the physical, the sensual, and the intuitive, in diametric opposition to the intellectual, the formal, and the logical. As Susan McClary and Robert Walser have argued, I must stress that "to discuss the bodily aspects of cultural texts or performances is not to *reduce* them" but rather to elevate the crucial role of embodiment in all aspects of cultural and perceptual activity.[24] An enlightened treatment of embodiment gets beyond that old mind-body binary, particularly in its racialist manifestations; and it also happens to affirm the African American aesthetics that gave birth to this powerfully embodied music.

---

24. Susan McClary and Robert Walser, "Theorizing the Body in African-American Music," *Black Music Research Journal* 14:1 (Spring 1994), p. 80.

68. The Jazz Left

CULTURAL POLITICS ARE OFTEN COMPLEX, BUT MUSICIANS' ATTITUDES about such qualities as innovation, individualism, tradition, and cooperation can certainly be understood to have political implications. Here, sociologist and cultural critic Herman S. Gray (b. 1950) draws upon published interviews with clarinetist Don Byron (b. 1958) and saxophonist Greg Osby (b. 1960) to propose the two of them as a political alternative—the jazz left—to the jazz conservatism of Wynton Marsalis, Stanley Crouch, and allied figures.

The cohort of contemporary avant-vangardists and experimenters expresses what I call road-and-street sensibility because of these musicians' willingness to transgress the boundaries of racial, musical, and aesthetic categories. Typical of this transgressive approach is clarinetist Don Byron, who works in a variety of settings and draws from myriad social, political, and cultural influences, including European classical, Jewish, folk, vernacular, and Cuban popular and traditional music. Explaining his use of the term the *jazz left*, which I have borrowed liberally, Byron says, "*I made the case that jazz's left half is being marginalized*. It is being marginalized by people who present jazz in institutions, on the radio, in print and everybody knows that."[1] Going right to the heart of the cultural politics that concern me here, Byron's elaboration is instructive: "*I thought jazz left of Lincoln Center needed an institutional home* because it didn't have one. . . . I think Carnegie Hall and Lincoln Center have really elevated jazz's status, and the music and musicians I know could use that sort of help. The way I see it, jazz is a two-headed monster, with a Democratic and Republican side, and without the Democratic side the beast dies."[2]

In their relationship to the music, the quest for institutional stability and longevity, and the cultural practices and sensibilities that define their music, players associated with what Byron calls the "Democratic side" of jazz approach the music like previous generations of experimenters and avant-gardists. In terms of technical competence, imagination, and openness to all kinds of musical influences and sources, Byron is one of the most gifted and prolific members of his generation. He is equally at home with the music of Duke Ellington as with klezmer great Mickey Katz, rock,

---

Source: Herman S. Gray, *Cultural Moves: African Americans and the Politics of Representation* (Berkeley: University of California Press, 2005), pp. 62–66.

1. Quoted in Peter Watrous, "Brooklyn Academy Finds Room for Outsiders of Jazz," *New York Times*, 12 October 1995; my emphasis.

2. Ibid.; my emphasis.

calypso, or classical chamber music.[3] Not surprisingly, Byron's sense of privilege to draw from such a wide range of music is an expression of his musical formation and commitment to stretching boundaries, as this *Wall Street Journal* profile explains:

> The upbringing that gave Byron his sense of entitlement combined rigorous classical training with the media sensibility of a child of the 60s. "The real basis of my aesthetic was the TV show *Shindig*. I identified with the backup band. Those cats could play behind anyone—Jackie Wilson, Chuck Berry, the Righteous Brothers, the Lettermen. My parents took me to the New York Philharmonic, but I was more interested in Lawrence Welk. His band featured a clarinet and they were on TV."[4]

Byron is passionate about his openness to popular and commercial influences and his refusal of a one-dimensional conception of the tradition. He rejects the press and music industry categories used to define him, his musical approach, and his choice of subjects. Here is Byron on the press's fascination with his interest in (and mastery of) klezmer music: "I'm not doing Jewish music instead of doing classical music instead of doing black music. I play what I like and I don't feel the need to live one genre of music like the young bebop cats who only listen to bebop and put down pop music."[5]

Technology has also given Byron access to a kind of global street traffic and musical marketplace, from which he and his contemporaries draw on pop and vernacular resources to extend their rich musical imaginations. Byron's ecumenical approach to the full range of musical options from James Brown to Mickey Katz is what makes Byron and his contemporaries so interesting and compelling musically, perhaps even threatening to the jazz traditionalist and canon defenders.[6] Byron and [Wynton] Marsalis might even be seen by some as working the same musical and cultural territory (thematically and in terms of their mastery of different musical idioms and styles). But Byron is clearly motivated by a sense of moving the music and the tradition beyond different musical and cultural borders, while Marsalis has devoted much of his public energy and credibility to establishing and then bolstering a narrow view of the jazz tradition. In this rather lengthy response, Byron comments on his conception of the tradition:

> I don't even think that preservation is really even relevant . . . in the sense that what the idiom is about isn't reproducing, isn't at least all about reproducing a past sound. Like Beethoven isn't a reproduction of Mozart, or Brahms isn't a reproduction of Bach, and they all consider themselves part of the same tradition, there is this sense that things have to move on and I consider both jazz and classical music not folk idioms. I think the jazz idiom has to decide whether it wants to be a folk

---

3. Wynton Marsalis has been duly celebrated for a similar musical dexterity and mastery, having won Grammys in both the jazz and the classical categories as well as a Pulitzer Prize for composition.

4. Jeremy Wolff, "A 'Cat' from the Bronx Makes His Mark on Klezmer," *Wall Street Journal*, September 19, 1991, p. A12.

5. Ibid.; Byron also includes running commentaries about the critics, the press, and racial discourse in his recorded work.

6. Politics are never far from Byron's music, expressed most directly in the titles of his compositions and recording sessions. In his music Byron has dealt with topics ranging from the Tuskegee Experiments and affirmative action to the marginalization of Jodi Al-Fyad, father of Princess Diana's boyfriend.

> idiom or whether it wants to treat itself as if it's art music, when what it's really doing is creating a folk music atmosphere. And you can't really have both. You're either art music and you're about what's gonna happen next or you're not. People who are the most conservative are dominating the talk, the press, the whole debate—a conservative tone. What little money is being spit out by the NEA, some of the conservative cats are dominating sort of who gets what and what kind of music gets funded.[7]

In taking this critical position Byron is by no means unique. His position is typical of other contemporary players on the jazz left.

Greg Osby, saxophonist and cofounder, with Steve Coleman, of the Brooklyn-based collective M-BASE, is, like Byron, passionate and outspoken, ecumenical, and eclectic in his use of popular and commercial influences in his work. Like Coleman, Osby counts among his cultural influences bebop, Motown, kung-fu movies, and funk. The M-BASE collective was "a group of black musicians, mostly in their late 20s or 30s (at the time of the collective's formation). All but a few of them migrated to New York City after growing up in other rich cradles of black music—St. Louis, Chicago, Mississippi, Detroit."[8]

In the early days of the collaborations that led to the M-BASE collective, two issues seemed to especially animate Osby and Coleman. One was the search for a distinctive individual voice on their instruments. The other was the need for autonomy and control over the creative process, especially control over the social conditions and cultural meanings of their creative labor. In a 1993 *Down Beat* interview, Osby explains the significance of a distinctive sound and its importance in the jazz vocabulary.

> I got the call to play with Lester Bowie's big band when I first came to town (in 1983). Lester is one of the cats that inspired me to pursue an individual voice in the music. I was playing with Jon Faddis at the time and the whole direction of that was what (Hamiet) Bluiette calls "model T-music." Playing with Lester's group—and close inspection of his history—showed me that his approach was more appealing than continuing to regurgitate everybody else's ideas. . . . People that we hold in so much esteem were inventors in their own time. Charlie Parker didn't make his mark by continuing to sound like Lester Young. Without your own sound you can't even hang out.[9]

In musical range and eclecticism, organizational flexibility and ingenuity, entrepreneurial imagination and drive, it is little surprise that funk guru George Clinton's performance units, including Parliament-Funkadelic, and the AACM were models for Osby, Coleman, and M-BASE. It is also striking that both Osby and Coleman, like Byron, have strong thoughts and clear ideas about the tradition, its exemplars, and the jazz left's relationship to them.[10]

---

7. Don Byron, quoted in interview with Josh Kun, unpublished ms., n.d.

8. Errol T. Louis, "Jazz Makes a New Sound with Soul, Pop, and Computers; Brooklyn Musical Collective: Macro-Basic Array of Structured Extemporizations," *Smithsonian*, October 1989, p. 176; George Lewis, "Experimental Music in Black and White: The AACM in New York, 1970–1985," *Current Musicology* 71–73 (Spring 2001-02): pp. 100–158.

9. Quoted in Kevin Whitehead, "Jazz Rebels: Lester Bowie and Greg Osby," *Down Beat*, August 1993, p. 17.

10. See Eric Porter, *What Is This Thing Called Jazz? African American Musicians as Artists, Critics, and Activists* (Berkeley: University of California Press, 2002).

The following exchange between Osby, Lester Bowie, and *Down Beat* interviewer Kevin Whitehead captures the passion that animates their collective commitment and vision about the tradition. Note too the intergenerational admiration between Osby and Bowie.

BOWIE: "Playing 'Bye Bye Blackbird' or sounding like Duke Ellington, that's got nothing to do with where we're coming from. That's the foundation. We got to do the rest of the house. With jazz, it's not so much what you play as how you play. It's not something you put into the repertoire. It's a living breathing young baby, music."

WHITEHEAD: [mock exasperation] "Jazz is America's classical music. We have to put it into the concert hall to get respect."

BOWIE: "I agree with you. Love to see jazz at Lincoln Center—it should have been there years ago. Every city should have a jazz orchestra with budgets equal to the Philharmonic's. But *don't negate the other things that are happening*, don't stunt the growth of the music. We're not gonna sacrifice the music to get to the concert hall."

OSBY: "These people [folks associated with Jazz at Lincoln Center] have to expand their tolerance of other branches of the tree. These are all facets coming from the same root source. I consider what I'm doing, what Lester's been doing, to be truer to jazz's historical motive than playing works reminiscent of other times, another climate."

BOWIE: "It's not a simple music anymore. So it does belong in the *street*, on the farm, it needs equal access everywhere, the same as country western, rap, anything. Because jazz is all these . . . *jazz is hip-hop, dixie-land anything people playing it want it to be*. 'Man don't listen to that Argentinean shit, it might influence you.' C'mon baby! Influence me![11]

---

11. Whitehead, "Jazz Rebels," p. 20; my emphasis.

69. "Resistance Is Futile!"

WHEN ONE THINKS OF "SMOOTH JAZZ," one of the most successful radio formats in the United States, one naturally thinks of saxophonist Kenny G, who has attracted a quantity of invective to match his extraordinary popularity.[1] And one might recall the famous denunciation by jazz guitarist Pat Metheny, who said of Kenny G's overdubbing himself onto Louis Armstrong's recording of "What a Wonderful World" that G had defiled "the greatest jazz musician that has ever lived by spewing his lame-ass, jive, pseudo bluesy, out-of-tune, noodling, wimped out, fucked up playing."[2]

But the smooth jazz world has nonetheless prospered, even though many fans of other styles of jazz would deny its denizens the now-prestigious label "jazz," and although even the musicians who are categorized as smooth might deny it. At the very least, the craft and the origins of smooth jazz in earlier styles demand careful consideration as to where it might seem to belong in the shifting typology of music (see also Robert Palmer's piece on "jazz pop" in this volume).

Sarah Rodman writes arts criticism for the *Boston Globe*, where this discussion of smooth jazz, drawing heavily on interviews with notable players of the style, first appeared in 2006.

Love it or hate it, smooth jazz is here to stay. And even musicians who reject the label are benefiting.

Call him pop. Call him jazz. Call him, if you must, a smooth operator. But whatever you do, don't call the music that trumpeter Chris Botti makes smooth jazz. "We're not smooth jazz," Botti says, curtly.

Try telling that to the radio programmers who routinely put his cool compositions and covers into rotation, and the listeners who have scooped up more than a million copies of his discs. Botti tries to be understanding. "To about 98 percent of the general public, if you put an instrument on the top and they can sort of figure out 'Well, you're playing in a little tiny club and it sounds like a math test' or 'You're

---

Source: Sarah Rodman, "Resistance Is Futile!" *Boston Globe*, July 16, 2006, p. N1.

1. For examples, see Robert Walser, "Analyzing Popular Music: Ten Apothegms and Four Instances," in Allen F. Moore, ed., *Analyzing Popular Music* (Cambridge: Cambridge University Press, 2003), pp. 33–37.

2. Pat Metheny, "Pat Metheny on Kenny G," http//jazzoasis.com/methenyonkennyg.htm, accessed April 17, 2010. Originally posted on patmetheny.com on June 5, 2000.

playing bigger venues and it's pleasing,' then the second one is always going to be smooth jazz," he says. "It doesn't matter what's going on underneath."

Indeed, a glance at smooth jazz radio playlists reveals a much wider collection of artists than you might guess. Of course, instrumentalists such as Botti, saxophonist Dave Koz, and keyboardist Brian Culbertson are staples. But so are plenty of vocalists and singer-songwriters: Norah Jones, Corinne Bailey Rae, India.Arie, Michael McDonald, Anita Baker, Alicia Keys, Luther Vandross, and Botti's former employer Sting. And the fact is, some of those artists—especially those who'd never be mistaken for jazz musicians—have no problem being adopted by the smooth jazz community, so long as it gets people listening to their music. Radio play is radio play, after all.

And yet, regardless of the music's popularity, or how many big-selling acts now fall under the genre's umbrella, many artists and fans, especially those who fancy themselves jazz purists, bristle at the very mention of smooth jazz. Others are simply resigned. George Benson, the virtuoso guitarist with unimpeachable straight-ahead jazz bona fides has, over the years, achieved a certain equanimity about the label. "It's here," the 63-year-old says with a laugh, "and you can't do nothing about it."

A Genre Is Born

Music fitting the description of smooth jazz existed long before the term ever did. Serious jazz musicians such as Benson, Bob James, David Sanborn, Herb Alpert, and Chuck Mangione played what would now be labeled smooth jazz as far back as the 1970s. And, yes, fans ate it up.

"The music just got more and more popular and so a whole radio format formed around it and they had to call it something because people like labels," Culbertson says. "You couldn't call it a [traditional] jazz station because it's not. They couldn't call it pop because there's not a lot of vocals. So it was like, 'Hmmm, the music's kind of smooth sounding and there's jazz influence—hey, let's put those two words together.'"

That's exactly what happened, according to Frank Cody, a former radio consultant who deserves the credit—or the blame, depending on your viewpoint—for the term "smooth jazz." "It was actually a listener," Cody concedes. In the early '90s, as a member of consulting firm Broadcast Architecture, Cody conducted focus groups. One Chicago woman strung together the infamous words when grappling for a description of a song snippet. "At that moment," Cody says, "light bulbs went off over everybody's heads." A format was born.

Around the same time, *Billboard* instituted its "Contemporary Jazz" chart to separate the popular smooth-jazz artists and harder-edged fusion groups from straight-ahead, or traditional, jazz artists. The reason? Smooth jazz sales were beginning to dwarf the traditional stuff. "The concern was that it would be easy for a [smooth jazz artist such as] Chuck Mangione or a Spyro Gyra to outsell [traditional artist] Dexter Gordon," says *Billboard's* director of charts and senior analyst Geoff Mayfield.

But what is smooth jazz? Ask ten different people, you'll get ten different answers. "It's almost like the Supreme Court justice's definition of pornography: I know it when I hear it," says Mayfield with a laugh.

The fundamental difference between smooth jazz and traditional jazz lies in the chief instrumentalist's approach to improvisation. Typically, at least on record, smooth jazz musicians just don't improvise. They often prefer to serve as a surrogate voice, "singing" the melody line over a simple pop or R&B groove. Play Kenny G's "Songbird" followed by John Coltrane's jazz classic "My Favorite Things" back to back and you'll get the picture. When it comes to vocalists, it's the difference between the mellow phrasing and textures of a Sade or a Norah Jones versus the energetic scatting of, say, Ella Fitzgerald. As the artists found on smooth jazz playlists make clear, the "smooth" is usually more important than the "jazz." "There's a quality to the vocals, a soulfulness to the vocals and an equal soulfulness to the instrumentals," Koz says. "Whether it's a vocal song or an instrumental song, it's melody driven and generally has some sort of rhythmic pulse on the bottom."

However it's described, almost all of the artists now loosely included in the category would tell you that they didn't set out to make smooth jazz. They created music from the heart, and the format abducted them. Which is exactly what smooth jazz programmers have been doing since the format's inception: gradually adopting artists and songs that dash the conventional image of smooth jazz as that blissed-out instrumental tootling you hear during massages or root canals. So while Kenny G's lyrical yet much maligned "Songbird" may be one of the most well known smooth jazz songs ever recorded, appropriated smooth jazz hits now include pop and R&B songs with vocals such as Benson's "On Broadway," Sade's "Smooth Operator," and Steely Dan's "Hey Nineteen."

Convincing listeners that if they like these songs then, by default, they like smooth jazz is an uphill battle, however. And musicians usually take one of three approaches: resist, tolerate, or embrace. "I could say to someone my last two CDs are all done basically live with an orchestra and it's way more coming from Miles Davis and Chet Baker than smooth jazz," says Botti, a resister. "But all people know is that it's smooth, so it translates into 'makes them feel relaxed.'" Because of that, listeners don't associate it with the more complex forms of bebop or fusion. "Most people think Sade is a badass jazz musician, and I love Sade. But is she a jazz musician? Heck no. So what do you do?"

Koz, meanwhile, embraces the genre. Known as the "ambassador of smooth jazz," he started a cottage industry to promote it. In addition to recording a half-dozen successful albums, Koz headlines popular summer and holiday tours with simpatico artists, cofounded the Rendezvous Entertainment record label with Cody—home to smooth jazz stars such as Wayman Tisdale and Kirk Whalum—and hosts a morning radio show and weekly syndicated program devoted to the music. "Maybe about 10 years ago I stopped letting that bother me," Koz says of dismissals of the genre as "elevator music." "For a lot of jazz critics, anything that is outside of that traditional box is not good or not worthy of attention. I recognize where that lives, but the most important critic to me is the listener."

Embracing the Term

These days, it seems that the less jazzy an artist is, the more likely he is to accept his inclusion in the smooth jazz pantheon. Pop singer Michael McDonald says he was thrilled when smooth jazz stations started playing cuts from his two recent collections of Motown covers. "It's a wonderful thing," says the former Doobie Brother, who has toured with Koz and Culbertson. "I mean, anytime that somebody's playing your music for an audience that's out there it can only be—I mean, thank God for smooth jazz [radio] for artists like myself."

British newcomer Corinne Bailey Rae is also grateful that her new single "Put Your Records On"—acoustic soul in the vein of Erykah Badu or India.Arie—has already made a splash stateside on the smooth jazz charts. In her home country, she gets spun on the rock and soul outposts of the BBC. "Wherever you go, people seem to hear things differently according to what culture or place it is," says the 27-year-old chanteuse. "I'm just happy to get played."

Of course, getting played can mean the difference between selling records or not. Smooth jazz artists typically outsell traditional artists, usually because they get more airplay on more stations. Traditional jazz outlets have shrunk over the years while smooth jazz outlets have expanded. "I will say we definitely sell a lot more than straight-ahead jazz, that is true," says Culbertson with just a touch of gloating. "We're selling 100,000 or more, they're not even coming close. They're lucky if they're selling 15,000."

And the fans don't just buy albums, they come out to hear the music live. "Straight-ahead jazz is a harder sell," says Fred Taylor, entertainment director of Sculler's Jazz Club in Cambridge. "All of the artists that we presented [in the early years of smooth jazz] I keep rebooking, and they are all big sellers," he says of acts such as Fourplay, Richard Eliot, and Koz. Taylor, known as a hard-core jazz purist himself, says that he tries to instruct the jazz police to be less elitist about the format since it helps subsidize the traditional acts that he brings in.

Benson, who's at work on an album with fellow Newport headliner and smooth jazz star Al Jarreau, certainly is. In fact, he admits that he tinkered with his style over the years to make himself more commercially viable. "There was a time when in the jazz world I didn't have a solid identity for the jazz masses," he says. "I couldn't fill up the clubs. So I had to do something that would. . . . And when I started getting hit records, they were records that were oriented on the pop thing and the R&B thing and I used my jazz experience to enhance those, to give them some pizazz."

But even when the music has pizazz, as much of it does—especially live when the instrumentalists engage in more inventive improvisation—the smooth jazz label itself is still a turn-off to some. "If we could change the name from smooth jazz to something that had a little bit more of a hip quality to it that would get the critics off our back, I think all the artists that have been around for a while would say let's do it!" Koz says with a laugh. "The problem is that radio stations have spent millions upon millions of dollars over 18 to 20 years branding themselves as smooth jazz stations, so you can't walk away from that."

Shirley Maldonado, who programs the jazz channels on Sirius satellite radio, concedes that by calling their straight-ahead station "Pure Jazz," Sirius is buying into the snobbishness directed at the easier-going style. "It's just more sophisticated taste," she says of traditional jazz. The Sirius smooth jazz station, called "Jazz Café," is more like "Jazz 101." "What we do with smooth jazz is for the novice," Maldonado says, "for the person who says 'I don't like jazz,' so we introduce them to a very palatable, easy-to-digest version of it."

Fans of smooth jazz, however, take exception to that "Jazz for Dummies" description. "It could be true in the same way that I can't appreciate Picasso in the same manner as someone who was an art history major," says smooth jazz fan Tracy Anderson, of West Yarmouth. "But that doesn't mean that I don't like to go look at his paintings." While trumpeter/keyboardist Jeff Cross of Charlestown enjoys listening to the straight-ahead artists such as Miles Davis and John Coltrane, he says the smooth stuff feeds a different part of his brain. "It makes me feel good," he says.

So what's wrong with that? Nothing, say the musicians who welcome one and all to the smooth jazz party. Even Botti grudgingly admits that "ultimately smooth jazz is a radio format that began with a lot of narrowness and in the last few years has opened substantially to other kinds of music that embrace jazz." "Even Slash has a smooth jazz hit called 'Obsession Confession'—so there," Koz says of the Guns N' Roses guitarist's surprise 1996 hit. "We are an equal opportunity employer in the smooth jazz community. If you're Slash and wearing that big top hat and you've got a good song, we'll take you."

70. The Nordic Tone in Jazz

JAZZ BECAME INTERNATIONAL IN SCOPE almost as quickly as it became national, but until recently the history of jazz has tended to focus overwhelmingly upon developments within the United States. British journalist Stuart Nicholson (b. 1948) here presents a study of the Scandinavian jazz scene—the musicians, the context, and the somewhat elusive "Nordic tone" that some people think differentiates the music of the Scandinavian countries. Nicholson is the author of biographies of Ella Fitzgerald, Billie Holiday, and Duke Ellington, as well as books on jazz-rock and other aspects of the more recent history of jazz.

Forces of globalization (sending the jazz aesthetic around the world) and glocalization (the need to adapt the music to local cultural conditions) have been at work to create new and exciting musical styles. Go to Africa or Brazil and you will hear music that takes American jazz as its starting point, but is shaped, both consciously and unconsciously, by elements from local culture. However, the effect of transculturation and the resulting jazz styles that have emerged around the globe continues to be a missing strand in the narrative of jazz history.

In fact, one key area in the growth of jazz outside America has been Europe, whose democracies, entertainment infrastructures, and social conditions provided similar circumstances to those that allowed jazz to flourish in the United States. As a jazz tradition was developing in America, a parallel tradition was being developed in Europe, shaped by its own aesthetic responses to the music. While this tradition hungrily absorbed the American vocabulary of jazz, spurred by the arrival in London in 1919 of the Original Dixieland Jazz Band (just eighteen months after they cut the first jazz recording), gradually some musicians sought to modify jazz from a European perspective. Yet today, "European jazz" is a vast catchall that includes "global" American styles—styles that have been disseminated around the world through recordings and personal appearances, and imitated and absorbed wholly or as a composite of several styles, by local musicians—that exist alongside a variety of hybridized "glocal" approaches to the music. Perhaps the most influential of all the European glocal styles is the so-called "Nordic tone," an important, if largely misunderstood voice within jazz. In fact, it is Scandinavian musicians who now seem to be at the forefront of the global jazz explosion. How, then, has the process of transculturation of jazz in Scandinavia occurred in practice to produce this quite distinct glocal dialect?

Source: Stuart Nicholson, *Is Jazz Dead? (Or Has It Moved to a New Address)* (New York: Routledge, 2005), pp. 195–222.

The Nordic tone, with its "encoding of multiple significances," has its roots in the existentially open, angst-ridden aspects of Scandinavian culture of the past century. A common theme in Nordic art was the struggle to assert individuality, revealed in the writings and paintings of Edvard Munch, for example, and equally apparent in the writing of Danish philosopher Søren Kierkegaard. In many ways this individuality found voice in what Swedish composer and conductor Wilhelm Stenhammar in 1910 called a "Nordic chastity and formal simplicity which I find so bracing in these sensually voluptuous times," a phrase that neatly encapsulates the essence and relevance of the Nordic tone in jazz today.

For European artists and thinkers down the years, the Scandinavian north, historically the "pagan north," is a place that mystically beckons, its rural tranquility, majestic scenery and uninhabited interior stretching up to the Arctic Circle appealing to something primal within. Throughout the nineteenth century, the notion of nature as a key to the renewal of inner life began to take hold, as much through the landscape and rigorous climate as through the art, literature, and music it helped inspire. For example, the Danish composer Per Nørgård considered the music of Jean Sibelius was associated with "the elementary, inmost and quite timeless forces of existence, with nature in its widest sense." The North brings an awareness of the closeness of man to nature, a place where the Danish artist Asger Jorn felt one might defeat the thousand and one distractions of everyday existence and feel life stirring once more in the depths of both oneself and the world. "Nordic art is dangerous," he said. "It compresses all its power *inside* ourselves."

The Nordic tone, equally drawing its power from within, is something that might be best described through analogy to Ingmar Bergman's approach to the cinema. Before Bergman, film was mostly about what could be seen and depicted in the "external" world, such as situation comedy, war, costume dramas, westerns, crime, and the chase. Very little important cinema made visible the internal drama of the self. Bergman found a way of exploring the human psyche, the "battlefield of the soul," initially through the encouragement of Victor Sjöström, when he was director of Svensk Filmindustri, who taught him about the "power of the naked face and to be simple, direct, and tell a story."

In the same way that Bergmann avoided the external world and the obviousness of the grand movie themes, and instead explored the intensely felt, internalized emotions, the Nordic tone avoids the "external," the patterns, the favorite licks, the quotations, and extroverted technical display of much of contemporary jazz, and instead zooms in close to deeply felt melody, exposing tone, space, and intensity. As saxophonist Jonas Knutsson points out, "Here we have a strong *chanson* tradition, strong melodies and strong folk songs for fiddles. Strong melodies with strong rhythmic and harmonic structure; here we know something about melodies—it would be stupid not to use it in jazz." Equally, bassist Arlid Andersen adds, "The sound is very important, the space in the music is very important, the transparency is important, the dynamic is important, not how clever you can play your instrument, how fast you can play or how impressive you could be, but how expressive you are."

With the benefit of hindsight, it is not hard to see why Scandinavia has become a major force in the global jazz explosion. Not only does it have a long history of performing the music, but also public money is used to provide a high level of free jazz education, a subsidized touring infrastructure, grants and bursaries for artists, and venue subsidy that create an environment where the music has flourished and grown. "The deepest musical education in Europe takes place in Sweden beginning at high school level," observed saxophonist and educator Dave Liebman. "There are many conservatories and programs in jazz as well as the other arts. For the working situation there is even a government-sponsored agency which sends groups out to countryside towns for performances as well as an association of nearly 100 jazz clubs country-wide. The typical Swedish jazz musician is the best overall equipped craftsman around."

In 1974, governmental support for jazz was instituted in the form of annual grants to music groups and eventually also to concert arrangers. The Swedish Jazz Federation, originally an organization of record collectors, reemerged as a network of over a hundred jazz societies throughout the country that arranged concerts on a regular basis, with some holding annual festivals partially underwritten by public funds. The 1970s also saw the evolution of municipal music schools that offered every child, starting from third grade, the chance to learn a musical instrument free of charge. These schools have stimulated and broadened musical life in Sweden, offering free lessons for a wide variety of musical instruments and genres, including big band music, rock, classical, folk, and jazz.

Parallel with this development, the Swedish Concert Institute regularly arranged concerts at the nation's schools, thus introducing jazz and other musical genres to young people. By the late 1970s, jazz had also become a recognized subject at the Royal College of Music in Stockholm and other higher education institutions. The club scene also began to enjoy governmental support. In 1977, after many years of arranging concerts at different venues, the Stockholm-based Federation of Swedish Jazz Musicians received municipal and governmental support to operate the club Fasching in the center of Stockholm. Since then, this former discothèque has been a center for jazz activity in the city, presenting both Swedish and international attractions. At about the same time, the club Nefertiti was established in Gothenburg.

Early in the 1970s the Swedish Concert Institute started to present jazz on its subsidized record label, Caprice. In the early 1980s the government began to support independent record companies that focused on jazz and other noncommercial types of music. By the decade's end, about fifty Swedish jazz albums were being released each year, a figure that has since doubled as a result of increased government subsidy.

But Sweden is not alone among the Scandinavian countries to build a subsidized infrastructure to support the arts, including jazz. Since the 1960s, Norway's Rikskonserterne created and established a national music program that today yields approximately 8,000 concerts per annum, mainly funded by government, of which jazz is a beneficiary. Music festivals—including jazz—have been established in several regions of the country under various auspices, together with support systems (touring, commissions, venue subsidies), which in turn play a part in the cultural job market in Norway. Finland and Denmark both enjoy government support for jazz, extending from education through to the bandstand. The result of such long-term strategies has been the emergence of several major Scandinavian musicians in recent times, with Norwegian and Swedish scenes described by the Edinburgh Jazz and Blues Festival in 2004 as "One of the most exciting jazz scenes in the world today."

The emergence of Scandinavian jazz, and the evolution of a specific glocalized jazz dialect, did not happen overnight. Since the end of the nineteenth century, African American music had been welcomed in Scandinavia; indeed, in either June or July 1899 Sweden can boast of making a recording of a Cakewalk. As the Original Dixieland Jazz Band arrived in England in 1919, their records were released in Scandinavia, prompting the Swedish singer Ernst Rolf to record with a "Swedish jazz band." But it was England that had a significant influence on early Swedish jazz, points out jazz historian Lars Westin:

> For many years, Swedish enthusiasts picked up on short-wave or middle-wave radios the dance music broadcasts from Savoy and other venues in London. From 1921 on, there were British bands playing in Sweden, most notably at the Grand Hotel in Stockholm, some with members that were influenced by ODJB and other visitors to London. The British influence was even more significant by way of records. Later on Jack Hylton's orchestra visited Stockholm in 1930, and by the end of the 1930s Nat Gonella had made several visits.

The roll call of American bands passing through Sweden from the 1920s through the 1950s was remarkable. Early visitors included Sam Wooding and his band in 1927 and 1929 (Wooding's group included Sidney Bechet on his first tour, although nobody seems to have noticed). In October 1933, Louis Armstrong visited and was followed by Coleman Hawkins in 1934. In 1939, Duke Ellington famously celebrated his fortieth birthday in Sweden, an event that prompted his instrumental tribute "Serenade to Sweden" on his return to America.

In 1950 American visitors increased with Nat King Cole, Duke Ellington, Benny Goodman, Coleman Hawkins, and most famously Charlie Parker, who toured the country between November 19 and 28. Later he would record his tribute to Sweden in his original composition entitled "Swedish Schnapps." Absorbing these influences firsthand, several Swedish musicians began forming their own jazz bands. Gradually, plausible imitation gave way to genuine creative talent. Already in 1947, two young Swedish musicians had moved to America to try their luck: trumpeter Rolf Ericson, who later became a member of Duke Ellington's Orchestra, and Ake "Stan" Hasselgard, a brilliant clarinetist, who quickly became a member of Benny Goodman's Septet. There were other brilliant young players emerging, too, including clarinetist Putte Wickman, saxophonist Arne Domnérus, and pianist Bengt Hallberg.

In 1951, 24-year-old saxophonist Stan Getz toured Sweden, employing the 18-year-old Hallberg, who had to get a release from his upper-secondary school to play the tour. On March 23, they recorded a version of an old Swedish folk song called "Ack Värmeland Du Sköna," which would become a jazz standard in the 1950s when, on May 9, 1952, Miles Davis recorded the song as "Dear Old Stockholm." In the eyes of many Swedish musicians, Getz's 1951 recording sanctioned the introduction of Swedish folkloric elements into jazz.

In the mid-1950s, Lars Gullin, who had emerged from Seymour Österwall's band, was the first European to win a jazz poll in the United States, topping *Downbeat* magazine's "New Star" category in 1954. Gullin's childhood and teenage years were spent on the island of Gotland in the Baltic Sea, where he developed a firsthand knowledge of rural and urban Swedish music traditions, providing the inspiration for a tonal vocabulary that evoked the Swedish folk tradition that he applied within the musical conventions of bebop. Inspired by Stan Getz's version of "Ack Värmeland Du Sköna,"—he was one of the Swedish musicians accompanying Getz at the 1951 session—he developed his own "Swedish" voice by incorporating elements of his own musical culture into jazz. By this time, Gullin was recognized by many as one of the finest baritone saxophonists in jazz.

In 1960, pianist and composer Nils Lindberg recorded an album called *Sax Appeal* that contained shimmering allusions to folk culture. "Surprisingly I did not realize I was influenced by the folk music," Lindberg told me in 2002. "When [*Sax Appeal*] came out in 1960 I thought my arrangements—it was for four saxes and rhythm section with among others Lars Gullin on baritone—I thought I was writing American jazz! West Coast—I didn't know I was influenced by folk music."

In contrast, trumpeter Bengt-Arne Wallin consciously drew on Swedish folkloric elements. In 1962, he became a pioneer in combining Nordic music and jazz with *Old Folklore in Swedish Modern*. "When we got to the 1960s I was dead tired of playing American standards," Wallin told me. "Mingus numbers, blues—I was so tired you cannot believe, that's why I started looking for other music, and I found it in my lap. The dialect we're playing comes from that mix-up between old Swedish folk music, old accordion music, which is completely different, and jazz."

At the time Wallin was a member of Arne Domnérus's band, whose pianist Jan Johansson was also mixing Swedish folk forms and jazz. In February 1961 Johansson recorded an album under his own name, *8 Bitar Johansson.* (It was later released in America as *Sweden Non-Stop*, and was awarded four and one-half stars by *Downbeat.*) The record was a mix of his own compositions and jazz standards, but it also included an unconventional piece for a jazz record of the time, a Swedish folk melody called "De salde sina hemman." It garnered a favorable critical response, particularly in Scandinavia, something that encouraged him to record more Swedish folk songs during the course of 1962 to 1963 with bassist Georg Riedel, which were collected together on the 1964 LP *Jazz pa Svenska.* "The record stands out as probably the most well-known and most sold record ever in the realms of Swedish jazz," wrote Erik Kjelberg.

The carefully nuanced sound of Johansson's piano, the gradation of his touch, the exquisite detail of every note revealed by the meticulous recording quality on *Jazz pa Svenska* captured a unique sound in jazz. "Nordic tonality is in fact a sort of blues, Nordic blues, Scandinavian blues if you will," explained drummer Egil Johansen. "For us jazz musicians it's but a short leap to experience that melancholy as a companion to joy." Sweden's best-selling jazz album to this day, two of its tracks, "Visa fran Utanmyra" and "Emigrantvisa," had wide exposure on Scandinavian radio, especially in Sweden where they are still played, and were seen as a symbol of the Nordic tradition in the midst of an increasingly pluralistic culture.

A defining moment in the evolution of contemporary Scandinavian jazz came in late 1964, when composer and theorist George Russell moved to Sweden. In 1966, Russell's Scandinavian big band recorded *The Essence of George Russell*, whose personnel included several important emerging young musicians including the Danish trumpeter Palle Mikkelborg and Norwegians Jan Garbarek on tenor saxophone and Jon Christensen on drums. By 1967, Garbarek had emerged as a key soloist with Russell, featuring on *Electronic Sonata for Souls Loved by Nature*, and was central to Russell's sextet version of the piece from 1969. Later, Russell described Garbarek as "the most original voice in European jazz since Django Reinhardt." Prior to the 1967 big band session, they performed at Stockholm's Gyllene Cirkeln (Golden Circle) for a concert that was reported at the time as one of the finest ever at the club. There, the seventeen-piece band was joined by a special guest, trumpeter Don Cherry, who had also taken up residence in Sweden. When Russell returned to America in 1969 to join the faculty of the New England Conservatory, Cherry's influence continued the impetus Russell had given to Scandinavian jazz. "He brought the avant garde tradition, but also the inspiration from Indian Raga, African music, Turkish folk music with oriental scales, meters in 5/8, 7/8, 9/8, etc.," recalled saxophonist Lennart Aberg.

In the 1970s, the Nordic tone was given considerable exposure with the formation of pianist Keith Jarrett's Belonging quartet on the ECM label, which took its title from the 1974 album of the same name, with Jan Garbarek on tenor saxophone, Palle Danielsson on bass, and Jon Christensen on drums. Garbarek's association with the Munich-based ECM label brought the Nordic tone to a worldwide audience. "I think about the cultural difference," says Manfred Eicher, who founded ECM and has produced the majority of the label's output:

> Even though [Garbarek] was influenced by a lot of American musicians and one could see the influence of Coltrane, Archie Shepp, and Albert Ayler on [his] early recordings—he very often says this in interviews—there was a kind of European "speech" and an idea that this could be something else. The sounds and ideas, what kind of harmonies to choose, that had to do with the surroundings. I just think people who live at that time in Scandinavia, somehow the musicians understood solitude and probably they lived in solitude. They understood transparency and clarity and somehow formulated a certain kind of approach towards music that was entirely different to an American musician living in New York. But that had to do with the sociological context.

Garbarek's music represented an ordered calm in the often frantic world of jazz, projecting the stark imagery of nature in the frozen north. He notes, "I can't say what extent growing up on Norway would influence you, but I imagine deep down it must have some influence. There are very dramatic changes of the seasons and the landscape is also dramatic." Rigorous and highly disciplined, he created an evocative tranquility strongly rooted in Nordic folk forms that gave prominence to his saxophone *tone* as the main expressive force. On the album *Dis*, he created a context where his haunting saxophone appeared to commune with nature, an effect heightened by his use of a wind harp. His working groups in the early 1980s included Bill Frisell on guitar, Eberhard Weber on bass, and Michael Pasqua on drums. Later work included his group with pianist Rainer Brüninghaus, solo recordings against electronic backdrops, and *Officium*, a collaboration with The Hilliard Ensemble.

The Nordic tone can be heard in the playing of musicians from all the Scandinavian countries. Drummer Edward Vesala emerged as one of the key musicians in the burgeoning Finnish free jazz scene of the late 1960s and early 1970s. He came to international attention in 1973 as a member of Jan Garbarek's trio on *Triptykon*, which stands as the saxophonist's most abstract statement on record. Subsequently, Vesala toured extensively as a coleader of the Tomasz Stanko-Edward Vesala Quartet, which ended in 1978 after recording five albums. In addition to his involvement in free jazz, Vesala also played blues, rock, tango, classical, and film music. In 1974 he recorded *Nan Madol*, which presented a mixture of brooding Scandinavian melancholia, freely improvised episodes, and sinister folk dance imagery. It established him as one of a handful of European jazz composers to make sense of his cultural heritage alongside the dominant African American ideology of jazz expressionism.

As Vesala observed the American jazz renaissance during the 1980s, he became disturbed at what he saw as glib revivalism, whose surface slickness, he believed, masked the music's loss of faith. His opposition to this perceived emotional sterility was voiced most forthrightly on his next album, *Ode to the Death of Jazz*, recorded in 1989, a denouncement of the status quo that he felt had come to prevail in jazz. "This music is first of all about feeling and the transmission of *feeling*," he wrote in the liner notes. "This empty echoing of old styles—I think it's tragic. If that is what the jazz tradition has become then what about the tradition of creativity, innovation, individuality, and personality?"

Although an integral part of Scandinavia, Denmark has a jazz scene that is perhaps less in tune with the tundra wastelands, pine forests, and dramatic scenery of its Nordic sister states, more in tune with the urban intensity of American jazz. "Denmark does not have a strong folk music tradition like its Scandinavian neighbors Sweden, Norway, and Finland," says Cim Meyer, editor of Denmark's leading jazz magazine *Jazz Special*:

> Denmark's geographical position on top of Germany has made us more continentally oriented than the rest of Scandinavia and also more cosmopolitan. Historically

> the German occupation during World War II had a huge effect, a period that's called "The Golden Swing Era of Danish Jazz," when Danish jazz music was isolated and the public interest became a way of showing resistance. Danish jazz today is often more influenced by [the] U.S. than our neighbors; that is, less ethereal and more hard swinging. Projects across borders are also happening more and more, so you could say the present Danish jazz music scene is an amalgamation of the "Nordic Tone" with the more energetic, powerful American style—something distinct in its own right that cannot be pigeonholed.

In the postwar years, the influence of American jazz on the flourishing Danish jazz scene was reinforced by several important American jazz musicians taking up residence in and around Copenhagen, including Dexter Gordon, Ben Webster, Ella Fitzgerald, Stan Getz, and others. Their inspiration helped produce several world-class Danish jazz musicians, including Niels-Henning Ørsted Pedersen, Alex Riel, and Jesper Thilo, fluent in American styles; indeed Pedersen, who as a young man had played with Bud Powell, was for several years Oscar Peterson's bassist.

In the early millennium years, Scandinavia had acquired a reputation as a jazz "hot spot" across Europe, with genuine curiosity and interest in its unique jazz scene. In addition to Jan Garbarek and others who had established themselves on the European circuit, an exciting generation of young Scandinavian musicians was emerging who were beginning to make a reputation for themselves across Europe, each in their own way reflecting a distinct Nordic tonality in their music. Musicians such as Nils Petter Molvaer and Bugge Wesseltoft enjoyed best-selling albums mixing jazz and rhythms from club culture and considerable success on the European jazz circuit.

The Finnish pianist Alexi Tuomarila emerged in the early millennium years as a musician of enormous ability and imagination. Tuomarila studied classical piano at the Espoo Music Institute in Finland, but came to jazz through his father's record collection. Pianist Brad Mehldau celebrated Tuomarila's achievement in the liner notes to his debut album *O2* (2003):

> What struck me first was his sound on the instrument. He gets a clear tone out of the piano that makes you focus on what he's playing. His playing "cuts through" the other instruments, demanding your attention, and never gets ambiguous or unclear. Even when he's playing only single note melodies, they have an authority to them that draws you in as a listener. That authority also comes from Alexi's strong, innate rhythmic sense. He's not just playing lines when he is soloing, but is really concerned with phrasing. You can hear sentences with a beginning and an end, punctuated by rhythmic accents that pull on the drummer's groove. Those sentences form paragraphs, and Alexi has a strong compositional sense to his soloing as well, allowing ideas to develop organically, taking his time, building a solo with patience. That kind of maturity in a musician is really more the exception than the rule and it's always a real pleasure when you hear a player who's addressing several things at once—melodic phrasing, compositional storytelling, a strong rhythmic dynamic and a concern for the sound of the instrument.

This is, in many ways, a wonderful description of the so-called Nordic tone. Tuomarila's playing, a rich, expansive vocabulary that is never flaunted but is put to compositional ends within the framework of his improvisations, has a very Scandinavian feel to it: a lyrical intensity that eschews prolixity, and a folk song-like flavor, such as on the track "Noáidi," mixed with a touch of the profound melodicism of Sibelius, as on "Sacrament."

In 2004, it was announced that the Esbjörn Svenssön Trio, or E.S.T. as they like to be known, were the winners of the European Jazz Award, voted by twenty-one industry professionals across Europe. The prize, which has a substantial bursary, is awarded to celebrate "outstanding musical achievement in the field of jazz." It was a fitting climax to an incredible few years that had seen the group—Svenssön on piano with Dan Berglund on bass and Magnus Öström on drums—pick up just about every jazz award in Europe (including a BBC Jazz Award in 2003) and become one of the top attractions on the European jazz circuit. Their rise has been so strong that it even caused consternation among the top American agents, anxious that their prime market was coming under pressure from the homegrown product. After almost fifteen years of constant touring, E.S.T. had become, in European jazz terms at least, regarded as something of a supergroup.

The knowledge Esbjörn had gained in working in the pop field—basically how to tell the world you exist and how to present the music—proved invaluable in establishing the group. Where possible, they toured with a sound engineer and a lighting designer because of the emphasis they placed on presentation. The trio points out that while they love jazz, they also grew up in one of the most creative periods in pop music. "I listen to rock music all my life, I grew up with pop music and hard rock in the 1970s, Black Sabbath and Rush and I still listen to them a lot," says bassist Berglund. "I used to say my biggest hero is Ritchie Blackmore [of Deep Purple], I love to hear him!"

It is this openness to contemporary music of all kinds that allows them to sound the way they do. By keeping their lines of musical input open, taking in new ideas and passing them through the "creative filter" of their own musical experiences, they have kept their music fresh and moving forward. By taking inspiration from popular culture and groups like Radiohead and Wilco, they are thinking outside the loop of the tradition-based jazz orthodoxy.

Just as in language, however, Scandinavians are going to Scandinavianize, whether consciously or not. "A lot of people talk about [the Nordic tone]," says Svenssön. "When I am in Germany, they talk a lot about it, in France, in Italy. Here we don't talk about it at all. If there is a Nordic tone, we are the Nordic tone! So we don't think about [it], but I think when I compare in general Nordic music to European music, there is some kind of difference, I don't really know what it is, maybe it has something to do with the folk music, or the less of light, but there is definitely something, there *is* something!"

The influence of the Nordic tone is being felt in the rest of Europe, and even on the U.S. jazz scene. It can be heard in the work of the Scots saxophonist Tommy Smith and the English saxophonist Andy Sheppard. In 2001, tenor saxophone virtuoso Michael Brecker told me he was greatly attracted to the "mountain jazz" style of Jan Garbarek, whose unhurried, intense lyricism and exploitation of the saxophone tone influenced his playing on *Ballad Book* (released in 2001). In 2001, pianist Herbie Hancock told the British magazine *Jazzwise* how, during the recording of his album *Future2Future*, he was listening to the work of Norwegian trumpeter Nils Petter Molvaer during the recording sessions: "Chuck Mitchell, who had been the president of Polygram's jazz division, sent over a bunch of discs for me to listen to by Nils Petter Molvaer and some other musicians . . . and suddenly it clicked, and I said to myself, 'Oh, I see!'"

Such examples of a glocal jazz style feeding back into global American jazz styles is similar to the way in which glocalized versions of pop music have fed back into international or global rock, such as on Paul Simon's *Graceland*. Regardless of what jazz used to be, it is now subject to the disciplines of the global cultural economy, and, as is every art form, interacting with other cultural forms, a process that is age old. No culture goes untouched by the world, and as cultures become increasingly subject to the disciplines and pressures of the global marketplace, change becomes more and more inevitable. Yet historically the purest cultural values are often products of complex strands of interaction; in jazz, cultural interaction (transculturation) has been a recurring theme in the evolution of the music outside the United States, revealing continuing dialogue with other musical forms to broaden the scope of jazz expressionism.

Today, the different glocal styles around the world hold the key to the future of jazz as they interact with the global American styles. As musicians adapt aspects of these glocal styles that they feel might work for them, various concepts and approaches are tried and either rejected or adapted in the constant quest to produce new contexts that broaden the expressive potential of the music. Where once the dynamic for this change and evolution in jazz came from within America, it is now shifting to its glocal communities around the world. As just one example, the Nordic tone's "chastity and formal simplicity" offers a different approach to playing and hearing jazz, its rural lucidity and folkloric allusions providing a contrast to the intensity of urban, big city life.

71. Now Who Listens to Jazz?

"CAN JAZZ BE SAVED?" ASKED ONE COMMENTATOR, alarmed at the implications of this 2008 government survey.[1] A follow-up to a similar survey done in 1992 (excerpted elsewhere in this volume), it shows that even as jazz has attained its greatest-ever degree of cultural prestige, its audience is aging and shrinking. In this respect, jazz has become ever more like the other "benchmark" arts activities included in the survey: classical music, opera, musicals, non-musical plays, ballet, and art museums. They are all niche markets, albeit highly respected ones. But is jazz's present (and foreseeable) lack of mass appeal a cause for despair? Or is it inevitable that cultures must change, as they always have, works and genres making way for new works and

---

Source: National Endowment for the Arts, *2008 Survey of Public Participation in the Arts: Research Report #49* (Washington, DC: NEA Office of Research and Analysis, November 2009), p. 80.

1. Terry Teachout, "Can Jazz Be Saved?," *The Wall Street Journal*, August 9, 2009.

genres that more directly speak to their historical moment, however universal their themes might seem? Fans of any cultural form have reason to bemoan its decline, but perhaps only a misanthrope can conclude that such change is simply and only bad.

Jazz

About 8 percent of adults attended a jazz performance in 2008, compared with 11 percent in 2002. The total number of attenders declined to 17.6 million adults, and the total number attending jazz performances declined to 51 million in 2008.

About 14 percent of U.S. adults watched or listened to jazz via media in 2008, which corresponds to 32 million people. The percentage of adults who reported liking jazz declined from 2002 to 2008 (from 28 percent to 24 percent, a statistically significant drop).

Demographic Profile of Attenders

The live audience for jazz performances was balanced between men (48 percent) and women (52 percent). Men make up a larger proportion of the jazz audience than any of the other benchmark activities. A similar distribution [exists] for those who listened to jazz via media.

More than half of jazz performance attenders in 2008 had a college or graduate degree. The highest income groups ($75,000 and over) represented about 48 percent of adults attending jazz performances.

Patterns of Attendance

African Americans were as likely as non-Hispanic whites to attend a jazz performance, and were more likely to watch or listen to jazz via media in 2008.

Adults ages 45 through 64 were the most likely to attend a jazz performance or concert. Jazz performance attendance among adults 44 and younger declined between 2002 and 2008, especially for the 35 to 44 age group.

Compared with people who have only a high school degree, people with college or graduate degrees were nearly eight times as likely to attend a jazz performance.

As with other benchmark activities, people with household incomes of at least $150,000 watched or listened to jazz more often than any other income group.

Residents of the Pacific region were among the most likely to attend a jazz performance in 2008.

Relationship with Other Art Forms

People who go to classical music, opera, or ballet often go to jazz performances. In 2008, about one-third of adults who said they attended an opera, ballet, or classical music performance in the past twelve months also went to a jazz performance.

Writers are also jazz attenders. One in five adults who said they had written poems, novels, or plays in the last twelve months also attended a jazz performance.

72. The Hidden Histories of Ken Burns's *Jazz*

KEN BURNS'S (b. 1953) TEN-PART DOCUMENTARY FILM *JAZZ*, first broadcast on PBS in January 2001, was a major event in the evolving public history of the art form. However, many criticisms appeared in its wake, most focusing on coverage—of both neglected individuals and the timescale of the series itself: the first nine episodes covered jazz history through the 1950s, with the next forty years crammed into the final installment.

George Lipsitz (b. 1947), a Professor of Black Studies at the University of California, Santa Barbara, grants great credit to Burns for his outreach on behalf of the people who have made and cared about jazz, yet pursues three points of critique, having to do with crucial assumptions about modernism, nationalism, and individualism.

Lipsitz is the author of several books on popular music, social movements, urban culture, and inequality, including *The Possessive Investment in Whiteness, Midnight at the Barrelhouse: The Johnny Otis Story,* and *Footsteps in the Dark: The Hidden Histories of Popular Music,* from which this excerpt is drawn. In the book, he uses the metaphor of the "long fetch" of ocean waves, the unfathomable distance between their origins and their arrivals, to evoke the hidden histories that historians try to illuminate.

New members of Harlan Leonard's "territory" jazz band in the 1940s began to hear about Darby Hicks as soon as they were hired. None of them recognized his name, but the musicians they played with in their new band seemed to know him well. "Oh yes, I heard about you," a band veteran would say upon being introduced to a new recruit, "Darby Hicks told me that you can't play a lick." If a musician failed to hit the right note or adjust to a difficult key change, someone would always say, "Darby Hicks would have nailed that."

Even worse, Darby Hicks seemed to know them. Senior members of the band would pull newcomers aside and confide to them "Darby Hicks was talking about you last night, man. He was saying some terrible things about you. He even talked about your sister, and about your mother, and even about your grandmother!" At this point the initiate often reached the breaking point, exploding in anger and vowing to settle things with Darby Hicks directly by challenging him to a fight.

Source: George Lipsitz, "Jazz: The Hidden History of Nationalist Multiculturalism," in *Footsteps in the Dark: The Hidden Histories of Popular Music* (Minneapolis: University of Minnesota Press, 2009), pp. 79–106. Reprinted by permission of George Lipsitz.

Yet this Darby Hicks did not exist. The musicians made up a name they could use to tease newcomers, to initiate them into the band with an "in joke." Eventually the new band members would become insiders themselves and play the same trick on those who joined the aggregation after them. The "Darby Hicks" story worked because musicians are competitive, proud, and sensitive to peer pressure, because reputations have professional and personal consequences. The story served a disciplinary function for the band as well, placing newcomers on notice that they were being watched, evaluated, and judged. Whatever the new band members thought of their own talent when they entered the band, they soon learned that they had not measured up to the standards of Darby Hicks. Whatever music they were about to play could never be as good as the music that Darby Hicks had already played.[1]

Historical narratives can have a lot of Darby Hicks in them. Instead of identifying the long waves of history accurately, chronological stories about the past built around golden age narratives of heroic origins function to make the present—even its unjust power relations—seem predestined. These long waves construct a past that makes the present seem inevitable, portraying it as the only possible outcome of previous events. History in these accounts is something that happens to people, not something created by them. It concerns itself mainly with sanctifying what has already happened, not with changing what might yet happen. This kind of past looms large and makes most people feel small, as if Darby Hicks has already done everything worth doing.

Much can be learned from these linear developmental narratives, but it is important to remember that they represent a way of thinking that is itself a historical creation—thinking about the past in this fashion is a creation of people in the modern era, an approach designed to serve particular purposes. It treats the past as little more than a simpler, more innocent, and less complex version of the present, valuable largely as the point of origin for contemporary institutions and practices. In this kind of history, national destiny, human progress, or the growing complexity of science and society give a kind of inevitability to the present, as if everything that has happened had to have happened, as if everything that did not happen could not have happened. In school textbooks, television and film productions, novels, and the official narratives of nation states, we often find the Darby Hicks version of history. It minimizes our ability to act and understand by maximizing what has already been done, said, written, and recorded by others.

Ken Burns's ten-part film, *Jazz,* has a lot of Darby Hicks in it. First broadcast on public television stations throughout the country in January 2001, it presented the public with a distinct way of understanding the national history and national culture of the United States. The film secured extraordinary critical acclaim and extensive commercial exposure, but its ultimate achievement came from its success in creating an accessible, enjoyable, and convincing story about national identity, progress, and heroic artistic achievement. Not just a film *about* history, this production *made* history by condensing the complex and conflicted history of jazz music into an allegory of national identity.

The series asserted a crucial connection between the artistry of individual musicians and the national character, between the achievements, practices, and institutions

1. There have been at least two people named Darby Hicks in show business, a Cajun singer and a dancer from Chicago, but *this* Darby Hicks comes from the folklore of the streets—a character who sleeps with other men's wives and girlfriends, something like the "Jody" character in the folklore of U.S. military personnel in the mid-twentieth century. See Jeff Hanusch, "The Legend of Jody Ryder," *Living Blues* n.163 (May/June) 2002, pp. 21–22.

of jazz music and the history of the nation state and the American people. It made its claims by organizing the history of jazz and the history of the United States around a focus on American space, modernist time, and individual heroism. This approach entailed glaring omissions and grievous distortions of the historical record. It transformed a history of exploitation, appropriation, conflict, and struggle into a fairy tale about cooperation, consent, and consensus.

Yet the film succeeded because its story conformed so clearly to the ruling ideas of its time, to the need by elites to recruit the populace to their political projects of triumphant nationalism and managerial multiculturalism. The message of *Jazz* echoed the insistence in elite circles at the start of the new millennium about the exceptional (and even divine) character of the U.S. nation state and its mission in the world, about the obsolescence of the anti-racist and egalitarian struggles of the mid-twentieth century, and about a new model of civic life that hides from the persistence of racial inequality by celebrating the incorporation of exemplary individuals from diverse backgrounds into the ranks of those who rule. It was a film for its time and about its time, yet it secured credibility by purporting to be a disinterested and true account of the past.

By emphasizing the U.S. nation as unique, exceptional, and extraordinary, *Jazz* obscures the history of the nation's role in the world and the presence of the whole world within the nation. By acknowledging the importance of racial difference in the nation, yet minimizing the significance of racial inequality, *Jazz* offers inspiring images of black-white unity that mark both groups as insiders, without honestly facing the differences between them, much less inquiring about what this axis of insider/outsider means for members of other aggrieved racial groups inside the nation and for people around the world relegated to roles as eternal outsiders in the U.S. national story.

Ken Burns's representation of the magnitude of black achievement in the United States is accurate and inspiring, yet his emphasis on the *inclusion* of African Americans within the history of cultural nationalism covers over their systematic *exclusion* from equal access to power and property in both the past and the present. As James Kyung-Jin Lee argues perceptively, this kind of managerial multiculturalism favors a modest redistribution of recognition and representation in U.S. society, while abandoning the struggle for the redistribution of resources and rights.[2]

As a means of staking a claim by blacks for inclusion into the celebratory nationalism of a nation that has routinely excluded them, the narrative strategy of *Jazz* makes sense. It urges white nationalists to acknowledge the importance of black people to the U.S. national project, while allowing blacks to see themselves as key contributors to something in which all Americans presumably take pride. Moreover, for all its flaws, *Jazz* does pay homage to artists who very much deserve to be honored, while recounting a history that very much needs to be told. Yet by telling the story as a narrative about modern time and American space, the film necessarily—and regrettably—occludes other temporal and spatial dimensions of jazz that also need to be illuminated. It paralyzes the present by locating all worthy achievement in the past. In an increasingly cosmopolitan world, it mourns nostalgically for a previous provincial nationalism. It minimizes the collective accomplishments of communities in order to magnify the reputations of heroic individual virtuosos.

---

2. James Kyung-Jin Lee, *Urban Triage: Race and the Fictions of Multiculturalism* (Minneapolis: University of Minnesota Press, 2004), p. ix.

The opening and establishing visual sequence in *Jazz* presents the skyscrapers of New York City illuminated at night during the 1920s. In the distance, viewers hear the sounds of automobile horns morphing into the sounds of the brass horns of a jazz ensemble. This opening serves to prefigure a connection between black music and modernity as a central focus of the series. A second connection becomes evident immediately as Wynton Marsalis's voice provides a sound bridge to a close-up of his face. Marsalis declares, "Jazz objectifies America," explaining that jazz music is something that can tell us who "we" are. The trumpet virtuoso identifies collective improvisation as jazz's core concept and key achievement. He notes that Bach improvised while playing his own compositions on the keyboard, but Marsalis relegates that accomplishment to a secondary level because Bach did not improvise with other musicians as jazz artists must do. Thus, in rapid order, in its first three scenes, *Jazz* (the film and television series) links "jazz" (the music) to three key signifiers—modernity, America, and heroic artistic genius.

The opening scenes of *Jazz* skillfully compress much of what follows during more than twenty hours of film stretched over ten episodes. Burns and his fellow filmmakers reduce the infinitely diverse and plural practices that make up the world of jazz into one time—modernity, into one place—"America," and into one subjectivity—the heroic artist who turns adversity and alienation into aesthetic triumph. As the opening shots of the New York skyline suggest, the film depicts jazz as the quintessential creation of modernity, as an art form shaped by the technological and social complexities of the twentieth-century city. A linear developmental narrative traces the journey of jazz across time and space, from its origins in the rural areas of the southern United States and the hinterlands of Europe before 1920, to the racially mixed and ethnically diverse cities of the twentieth century.

The same developmental narrative governs the growth of jazz's key styles. The film follows the presumably foundational ensemble style pioneered by "Dixieland" innovators in New Orleans during the 1910s and 1920s to the sophisticated section-playing, written arrangements, and compelling rhythms of "swing" bands in Kansas City, Chicago, and New York during the 1930s, to ultimate fulfillment in the sophisticated styles of bebop players in New York and Los Angeles in the 1940s and 1950s. The film presents jazz as an art form that emerged out of urbanization and industrialization, that fused folk forms with modern improvisation, and that responded to the upheavals of modernity with artistry oriented around originality and innovation. In this narrative, jazz has a beginning, a middle, and an end.

In addition to its designated proper time in this film, jazz also occupies a discrete physical space: the juridical and geographic boundaries of the United States of America. Jazz music's significance in this film comes from its identity as the most important art form to originate in the United States, from its value as a metaphorical representation of the tensions between diversity and unity that so often characterize "American" society. When Wynton Marsalis begins the film by proclaiming that "jazz objectifies America" and that it can tell us who "we" are, the audience is being interpellated as national subjects, as "Americans." As *Jazz* proceeds, however, we see that Marsalis's comments mean even more. In this film, jazz has metonymic rather than merely metaphorical significance. It not only reflects the nation, it somehow constitutes it. The story of jazz is exactly the story of America, according to this film. The ability of black and white jazz musicians to blend European and African musical traditions into a new synthesis despite the rigidly racist and segregated nature of the nation's social institutions is what makes the creation of jazz music a quintessentially American achievement.

The privileged time of modernity and the privileged space of America come together in *Jazz* to draw attention to one privileged social subject: the heroic creative artist. Louis Armstrong serves as the anchor of this project, the prototypical genius who played better (louder, higher, longer) than anyone else, whose creative innovations enabled him to influence and surpass everyone. Armstrong deserves this degree of praise, of course, but his innovations extend far beyond his remarkable physical abilities. They encompass his success in changing the language of jazz, in compelling others to respond to his playing in their own artistry. The film's narrative voices make the word "genius" the key category again and again, linking Louis Armstrong, Duke Ellington, and Charlie Parker to the canonical geniuses of European art music, to J. S. Bach, Wolfgang Amadeus Mozart, and Ludwig van Beethoven. The esteem this demonstrates for Armstrong, Ellington, and Parker is not wrong; in fact, it is fully justified and long overdue in popular discourse. This narrative strategy, however, expresses an approach to the history of jazz this is at odds with the social processes inherent in the music. Armstrong, Ellington, and Parker played in, and with, groups. Their virtuosity depended on dialogic relationships with other musicians, on their responses, additions, and augmentations to the music being played around them, and to the music that preceded them. Isolating their artistry from these contexts obscures more about their achievements than it reveals.

In Ken Burns's formulation, each instrument has its own history, and its own exemplary performer. Louis Armstrong perfects the possibilities of the trumpet, while Lester Young and Charlie Parker define the apex of artistry on the tenor and alto saxophones. Multi-instrumentalism can only be a footnote to this story. Yet the actual history of jazz tells a more interesting story. In the lives of individual musicians, moving from one instrument to another often led to innovations that would not have occurred had they stuck to a single instrument. Lionel Hampton and Lester Young explored scales extensively when they took up melodic instruments (vibraphone and saxophone) precisely because they started out as drummers who had not been required to think very much about harmony and melody. Under the tutelage of his father, Young had already learned to play clarinet, piano, flute, and piccolo. The unique sounds that he coaxed out of the tenor owed much to his previous playing on the C Melody and alto saxophones.[3] Young's friend Mutt Carey brought his experiences as a drummer to bear on his playing on cornet and trumpet.[4] Hamiet Bluiett felt he developed special skills as a baritone saxophone player precisely because most bands wanted an alto or tenor saxophonist instead. "I had to learn to play in all registers," he remembers, recounting his experiences playing parts written for the alto or the tenor on his baritone.[5]

The film's emphasis on individual instruments and instrumentalists relegates the complex textures of black experience and white supremacy in the United States to little more than dramatic background for the emergence of individuals who, the film tells us, cheerfully turn adversity into aesthetic perfection. Wynton Marsalis describes the overcoming of obstacles in the lives of Armstrong and the other geniuses of jazz as part of a universal process that takes place in all societies. For Marsalis,

---

3. Douglas Henry Daniels, *Lester Leaps In: The Life and Times of Lester "Pres" Young* (Boston: Beacon Books, 2002), pp. 69, 72, 101, 128.

4. Rich Koster, *Louisiana Music* (Boston: Da Capo Press, 2002), p. 17.

5. Richard Woodward, "Four Saxmen: One Great Voice," *New York Times Magazine* April 12, 1987, p. 47. David Ruben, "World Sax Quartet Swings to Its Own Beat, *San Francisco Chronicle* datebook, April 9, 1989, p. 47.

racism's relationship to jazz is incidental, only the historically specific obstacle to genius that these artists faced. "It happened to be racism," Marsalis observes, "but it is always something."

The narrative strategies deployed by the producers of *Jazz* are understandable, logical, and part of a long tradition. They reflect efforts by Houston Baker and Paul Gilroy to claim a central place for African Americans in the history of modernism. They echo the insistence of Albert Murray on "the inescapably mulatto" character of "American" culture, and on the inalienable contributions by blacks to the national narrative. They advance the arguments made by Billy Taylor, Grover Sales, Reginald Buckner, and many others for the canonization of jazz as "America's classical music." Yet, like any historical narrative, the evidence and arguments advanced in *Jazz* are partial, perspectival, and interested. In telling its own truths about time, place, and subjectivity, the film directs our attention away from the many other temporalities, spaces, and subject positions that are central to the story of jazz. It falls into the pitfalls identified by Vijay Iyer, himself a virtuoso jazz player and composer who warns, "Beware of the prevailing view of 'jazz' as some kind of history lesson that you have to sit through because it's good for you. . . . Understand that this is a living art form whose most esteemed practitioners are continually evolving and engaging with the world around them."[6]

It is not incorrect to view jazz as an exemplary modernist creation of the twentieth-century city, but doing so suppresses other temporalities and spaces equally responsible for the art. The migrant to the city who fashions a new art out of alienation is a recurrent story in the history of modernism, but to tell the story that way privileges the communities that the migrants come *to* in the city over the communities of shared historical experience that they depart *from* in order to become urban. Yet the two are not so easily separated. Musicians seeking work opportunities moved back and forth between different modern cities and between urban locations and the countryside. Music that originated in New Orleans, for example, did not just travel up the Mississippi to Chicago and then go eastward to New York. It developed significantly on the west coast, circulated nationwide through theater circuits, returned to New Orleans, and then branched out again.[7]

It is not at all implausible to do what Burns's film does: to view jazz as a quintessential expression of U.S. national identity, as a magnificent art form that emerged from contacts between European and African musical traditions on the North American continent. Yet the added prestige that jazz seems to acquire from its association with celebratory nationalism comes at the expense of appreciating jazz's capacity to create identities far more fluid and flexible than the citizen-subject of the nation state. Even the music itself becomes represented poorly through this strategy.

Duke Ellington may be a quintessential "American" to Wynton Marsalis and Ken Burns, but when the expatriate South African pianist Abdullah Ibrahim started playing with Ellington's band in Switzerland, he did not think of his boss as a citizen of any particular nation, but instead as "the wise old man in the village—the extended village."[8] Ellington expressed delight at finally arriving in Africa to play at

6. "Amazon.com Talks to Vijay Iyer," Author Interview. December 14, 2000. amazon.com/exec/obidos/show-interview/I-v-yerijay/002-2601507-4157631

7. George Lipsitz, "Music, Migration, and Myth: The California Connection," *Reading California: Art, Image, and Identity, 1900–2000* (Berkeley: University of California Press and the Los Angeles County Museum of Art, 2000), pp. 155–60.

8. Karen Bennett, "An Audience with Dollar Brand," *Musician* (March) 1990, p. 41.

the Dakar Festival in 1966 because he felt that he had been playing "African music" for thirty-five years.[9] Charlie Parker and Dizzy Gillespie invoked Africa as well as America when they performed with dancer Asadata Dafora and an assortment of Cuban and African drummers at New York benefits for the African Academy of Arts and Research in the 1940s. Mary Lou Williams and Dafora staged a two-day Carnegie Hall show in 1945 structured around the links between African and Western forms of music and dance.[10] Dafora proved to be a natural ally in these efforts because of his own complicated history. Born in Sierra Leone, his great-grandfather had been a slave in Nova Scotia, but later returned to Africa to live out his life in freedom. Dafora received classical training in opera in Germany and Italy, served in the British Army in World War I, and turned to "traditional" African dance in the late 1920s while pursuing a career in opera in New York City.

The story of jazz as the binary creation of black and white Americans does little to help us understand how light-skinned Puerto Ricans like Louis "King" Garcia and Miguel Angel Duchesne wound up playing for white bandleaders Benny Goodman, Tommy Dorsey, and Paul Whiteman, while dark-skinned Puerto Ricans played with bands led by Fletcher Henderson and Noble Sissle. It leaves little room for the stories of Latino, Asian American, and mixed-race musicians.

The celebratory equation between jazz and "America" cannot lead us to a productive understanding of how Rafael Hernandez came to play in James Reese Europe's African-American 15th Regimental Band in France during World War I, but with the Trio Borinquen (made up of two Puerto Ricans and a Dominican) in Cuba, Mexico, New York, and San Juan in the succeeding decades. It does not help us understand why Europe went to the Caribbean to recruit clarinetists for his New York-based Hell Fighters Orchestra.[11]

Was it something about "America" that led John Coltrane to name his son after Indian sitar genius Ravi Shankar?[12] Are we still dealing with "American" culture when Sidney Bechet moves to France, Albert Nicholas to Egypt, Buck Clayton to China, Randy Weston to Morocco, Art Blakey to Kenya, Budd Johnson to Haiti, Hampton Hawes to Japan, and Teddy Weatherford to India? Did Django Reinhardt cease being Romany or Belgian by playing jazz? Did Toshiko Akiyoshi cease being Japanese? Does music made in America (the continent) by Machito, Tito Puente, Mongo Santamaria, or Carlos "Patato" Valdes count as jazz in America (the country)? Was Mario Bauza making Latin American music when he served as musical director for Chick Webb? How central was the geography of the United States to jazz when the great Argentinean swing guitarist Oscar Aleman moved to the center of the musical world in Paris to conduct Josephine Baker's back-up band, the Baker Boys? [13]

The national chauvinism that pervades Ken Burns's film occludes the internationalism that has informed the art of so many jazz musicians. Randy Weston toured

---

9. Penny Von Eschen, *Satchmo Blows Up the World: Jazz Ambassadors Play the Cold War* (Cambridge: Harvard University Press, 2004), p. 154.

10. Eric Porter, *What Is This Thing Called Jazz? African American Musicians as Artists, Critics, and Activists* (Berkeley: University of California Press, 2002), p. 78.

11. John F. Szwed, *Crossovers: Essays on Race, Music and American Culture* (Philadelphia: University of Pennsylvania Press, 2005), p. 193.

12. James C. Hall, *Mercy, Mercy Me: African-American Culture and the American Sixties* (New York: Oxford University Press, 2001), p. 130.

13. Szwed, *Crossovers,* p. 194. Douglas Henry Daniels, "Vodun and Jazz: 'Jelly Roll' Morton and Lester 'Pres' Young: Substance and Shadow," *Journal of Haitian Studies* 9:1 (Spring 2003), p. 112.

Africa for the State Department in 1967, but thought of his mission in international terms. Raised in a Garveyite household committed to pan-African ideals where he learned to think of himself as an African born in America, Weston traced his ancestry on his father's side to Jamaica, Panama, and Costa Rica. He remains best known in Africa for his 1960 tribute to independence movements on that continent, *Uhuru Africa*.[14]

The celebratory America of *Jazz* does not prepare us adequately for the Charles Mingus compositions *They Trespass the Land of the Sacred Sioux, Remember Rockefeller at Attica,* and *Once There Was a Holding Corporation Called Old America.* The integrationist nationalism of *Jazz* cannot account for Dizzy Gillespie's suite *Burning Spear,* composed in honor of Kenyan independence fighter Jomo Kenyatta, a piece that blends South American, African, and African American elements. Gillespie called it "an international piece" because he considered Kenyatta an international figure.[15] *Jazz* does not help us understand why Dizzy Gillespie refused to attend a briefing arranged for him by the State Department while playing a government-sponsored tour overseas. Officials from the diplomatic corps offered to help Gillespie explain race relations in the United States. The trumpeter noted acerbically, "I've got three hundred years of briefing. I know what they've done to us and I'm not going to make any excuses."[16]

It is not totally incorrect to view jazz as Ken Burns does, as a crucible of heroic artistry forged by the contradictions of life in the United States and its connections to the rest of the world. Jazz musicians have discursively transcoded the hard facts of slavery, migration, industrialization and urbanization in U.S. history into aesthetically rich and complex creations. Their harmonious balance between individual solos and collective improvisation provides a metaphorical solution to one of the recurrent dilemmas of social life in the United States—how to encourage individuality without selfishness and how to encourage collective consciousness without totalitarianism. The formal complexities of jazz composition, the risks and rewards of collective improvisation, and the artistic virtuosity demonstrated by its most accomplished performers make jazz a logical and suitable site for the exploration of art as transcendence and existential fulfillment.

Yet this emphasis on the heroic individual depends upon hierarchies that are not universally—or perhaps even widely—accepted among jazz artists and audiences. The history of Western culture is replete with linear developmental narratives that attach art forms to celebratory nationalisms and to canons of great works and artists. Yet it does not necessarily follow that placing jazz within that pantheon elevates, or even helps explain, its artistry. The emphasis on immediacy, on involvement, and on engagement in jazz playing encourages a sensibility entirely at odds with the romanticization of the alienated artist that has been so central to the Western tradition since the beginning of the nineteenth century. The jazz tradition prizes connection rather than canonization; it finds value in the social relations that playing and listening create rather than in the notes and chords and rhythms all by themselves.

The story of jazz artists as heroic individualists also overlooks the unequal and exploitative gender relations that structured entry into the world of playing jazz for a living. Women musicians Melba Liston, Clora Bryant, and Mary Lou Williams can only be minor supporting players in Ken Burns's drama of heroic male artistry. Bessie Smith and Billie Holiday are revered as interpreters and icons, but not acknowledged

---

14. Von Eschen, *Satchmo Blows Up the World*, p. 170.

15. Von Eschen, *Satchmo Blows Up the World*, p. 236.

16. Von Eschen, *Satchmo Blows Up the World*, pp. 34, 154.

for their expressly musical contributions. Abbey Lincoln, Sarah Vaughan, and Betty Carter evidently do not qualify for admission into the pantheon. While *Jazz* acknowledges the roles played by supportive wives and partners in the success of individual male musicians, the broader structures of power that segregated women into "girl" bands, that relegated women players to local rather than national exposure, that defined the music of Nina Simone and Dinah Washington as somehow outside the world of jazz are never systematically addressed in the film. *Jazz* gives us no analysis of the practices and processes that obscure the important contributions made to music by women, to pick just one example, by keyboard artists Beryl Booker, Patty Bowen, Hazel Scott, and Valerie Capers.[17]

Even the much celebrated mingling between members of different races celebrated in *Jazz* took place with much more difficulty than the series acknowledges. In Oklahoma City, inter-racial dances did not take place until the Young Communist League deliberately crossed the color line in 1932 by promoting an inter-racial dance featuring the Blue Devils in that city's Forest Park.[18] In 1940, Los Angeles Police Department officials shut down a performance by the Benny Goodman Orchestra at the Shrine Auditorium because they feared the inter-racial dancing likely to take place among the band's white, Filipino, black, and Mexican fans.[19] Black musicians in Los Angeles routinely faced having to accept police "escorts" back to black neighborhoods by officers unwilling to let them remain in the white neighborhoods where the best paying musical venues tended to be located.[20]

The grand narrative of modernity, nationalism, and alienated artistry presented by *Jazz* is understandable and plausible, but incomplete. Its perspectival partiality is not random, however, but rather a way of looking at the world that serves a pernicious set of interests. The film purports to honor modernist innovation, struggle, and artistic indifference to popular success, yet its own form is calculatedly conservative and commercial. This history of jazz interpellates viewers as consumers rather than as creators. The important history of jazz has already happened, it tells us. The genre's consummate artists are already known, and their artistry has already been incorporated into the glory of the nation state. There is nothing left for viewers to do, but to honor—and more important to purchase—relics and souvenirs of an art greater than themselves. The film is a spectator's story aimed at generating a canon to be consumed. Viewers are not encouraged to make jazz music themselves, to support contemporary jazz artists, or even to advocate jazz education. They are, on the other hand, urged to buy the ten-part home video version of *Jazz* that is produced and distributed by Time Warner AOL, the nearly twenty albums of recorded music on Columbia/Sony promoting the show's artists and "greatest hits," and the book published by Knopf as a companion to the broadcast of the television program which was underwritten by General Motors.

---

17. Horace Silver, *Let's Get to the Nitty Gritty: The Autobiography of Horace Silver* (Berkeley: University of California Press, 2006), p. 53.

18. Daniels, *Lester Leaps In*, p. 130.

19. Ralph Eastman, "'Pitchin' Up a Boogie': African-American Musicians, Nightlife, and Music Venues in Los Angeles, 1930–1945," in Jacqueline Cogdell DjeDje and Eddie S. Meadows, eds., *California Soul: Music of African Americans in the West* (Berkeley and Los Angeles: University of California Press, 1998), p. 80.

20. Barney Hoskyns, *Waiting for the Sun: Strange Days, Weird Scenes, and the Sound of Los Angeles* (New York: St. Martin's Press, 1996), p. 8.

Thus a film honoring modernist innovation promotes nostalgic satisfaction. A film celebrating the centrality of African Americans to the national experience voices no demands for either rights or recognition on behalf of contemporary African American people. A film venerating the struggles of alienated artists to rise above the formulaic patterns of commercial culture comes into existence and enjoys wide exposure only because it fits so well within the commercial reach and scope of a fully integrated marketing campaign linking "educational" public television to media conglomerates.

The "reconciliation" of otherwise antagonistic social groups through a unified celebration of "America" that holds center stage in *Jazz* is ultimately a false reconciliation. The "Americans" united through shared vicarious appreciation of *Jazz* live in very different kinds of neighborhoods, experience very different relationships with the police and the courts, breathe different air, drink different water, and die from environmental hazards at very different rates. In fact, the very reconciliation promised by *Jazz* actually depends on these inequalities—without them, there would be no meaningful gaps to transcend.

Our entire understanding of music and society may hinge on what kinds of histories we valorize. Christopher Small rightly urges us to learn from the great African traditions that inform jazz music, to "learn to love the creative act more than the created object" and to not let our respect for the relics of the past inhibit our capacity to create culture relevant to our own experiences.[21] The history of jazz as creative act rather than created object can be represented in an infinitely diverse and plural number of equally true narratives.

The heroic narrative of *Jazz*, however, is designed as a genealogy of elitist blackness. It was consciously designed to counter a perceived excess of democratic thinking among black intellectuals. Marsalis contends that black professionals "are so gullible and worried about being accused of not identifying with the man in the street that they refuse to discern with the interest in quality that makes for a true elite."[22] This black elite, like the white elite it hopes to join, derives its legitimacy precisely from its distance from the majority of the population. It offers roles as cultural brokers to elite and accomplished African Americans, but only if they will collaborate in the organized abandonment of black communities. As James Kyung-Jin Lee argues, "Brokers are not simply middlemen, mediating and controlling access to societal power; brokers benefit from and, through their social being, affirm the asymmetrical relationships between the owners of capital and capital's owned, and manage that which is seen by the powerful and that which is left behind, all in the maintenance of this social order."[23]

Wynton Marsalis expresses his disdain of democracy openly. "The biggest problem with democracy, and with our education," he opines, "is that every opinion becomes law and fact, just because it exists. . . . Yet we mustn't forget that beneath all those opinions there is an underlying truth and reality."[24] Yet one might also say instead that "all those opinions" evidence multiple, conflicting, and contradictory realities and truths. Efforts to identify and honor a classical black tradition in a country historically ruled by elite whites follow an understandable and ideologically

---

21. Christopher Small, *Music of the Common Tongue: Survival and Celebration in African American Music* (Hanover, NH: Wesleyan/University Press of New England, 1998), p. 72.

22. Quoted in Porter, *What Is This Thing Called Jazz?*, p. 310.

23. Lee, *Urban Triage*, p. 101.

24. Quoted in Porter, *What Is This Thing Called Jazz?*, p. 307.

overdetermined logic. Yet there is more to be learned from the history and enduring creativity of black music than this. The true genius of black music has not been confined to the production of individual "geniuses," but rather has been manifest in the plurality of new social relationships that the music has helped bring into being. The created objects and creative artists celebrated in *Jazz* do not tell us enough about the broader African American imagination and activism that gave their art its determinate shape.

With its compression of modernist time, American space, and artistic struggle, the opening sequence of Ken Burns's *Jazz* captures a part of the truth about the history of jazz. But I suggest we turn to another compression of time, space, and struggle for an even truer and more useful understanding. It occurs in a story that trumpeter and arranger Clora Bryant tells in an oral history interview about jazz on Central Avenue. In my judgment, it encapsulates more of the experience of jazz in this country than all ten episodes of *Jazz*.

Bryant relates how hard it was for musicians to get paid by Curtis Mosby, owner of Central Avenue's Club Alabam. Mosby was an African American entrepreneur whose role as a cultural broker gave him power over the lives of aspiring black musicians. He promised them good wages, but was slow to keep his promises. Mosby's "deductions" for his purported expenses providing food and drink to the artists sometimes took back all they had earned. Occasionally he would pay the right amount to keep in good standing with the musicians' union, but then demand kickback from artists before he would let them play again. One night, blind singer Al Hibbler came to the club to demand money that Mosby owed him. As Bryant tells it, the blind singer shouted out, "You'd better give me my money or I'll shoot you" as he drew a pistol from his pocket. The blind man shouting and waving a pistol drew everyone's attention. Then, evidently remembering that his vision was impaired, Hibbler shouted to Mosby, "Say something so I'll know where you are."[25]

One joke about one artist and one club owner on one night in one city might not seem like an adequate substitute for the monumental reach and scope of *Jazz*. But Al Hibbler's anguish and anger helps us see a side of the music business and the American dream that Ken Burns and his corporate sponsors will never show us. It may be true that jazz objectifies America, but it does so at least as powerfully through the promises that it breaks as through the ones that it keeps. Even Darby Hicks understood that.

25. Clora Bryant et al., *Central Avenue Sounds: Jazz in Los Angeles* (Berkeley: University of California Press, 1998), p. 356.

Editing Notes

Obvious typographical and spelling errors have been corrected without comment, and some minor changes in punctuation have been made to facilitate readability. In most cases, cuts have not been marked with ellipses, so that readers might not, as Weiss and Taruskin put it, find "a profusion of little dots a hindrance to their concentration."[1] In one instance (Howard Becker's "The Professional Dance Musician and His Audience") I restored, with the author's encouragement, profanity that had been coyly bowdlerized in the original publication; Charles Mingus's idiosyncratic spelling of "schitt," on the other hand, was retained, since Sue Mingus told me it was typical of him and not evidence of a previous editor's intervention.

Musicians' names were misspelled seemingly more often than not in many of the sources; these have been corrected according to the authority of *The New Grove Dictionary of Jazz.* In interviews, musicians' last names have been used to attribute speaking voices throughout ("Marsalis" replacing "Wynton," "Armstrong" replacing "Louis" in the original sources). A small number of minor slips have been righted, as when John Hammond (or the transcriber of his talk) rendered the Theater Owners' Booking Association as the "Theater Bookers' Offices Association." Besides the several footnotes I added to help the reader make sense of Burnet Hershey's arch account of his whirlwind tour, I changed "Tinpan" to "Tin Pan" Alley. I adjusted the grammar of Max Roach's opening sentence so as to preserve his characteristic dignity. The titles of operas and other musical compositions to which Jelly Roll Morton refers have been corrected, which seems particularly just since the spelling errors were not his but those of the person who transcribed and edited his interview tapes. Some bibliographic citations were changed to footnotes.

I made one other editorial change that was not marked earlier. R. W. S. Mendl, in his 1927 book on the appeal of jazz, uses the words "negroes," "blacks," and "niggers" interchangeably to refer to African Americans. He does so without apparent malice or knowledge of the very different meanings those words have actually carried. Three times in the excerpt included here, I have replaced the last of those three terms with the first (following the singular or plural usage of the original text). Paradoxically, I believe I have done so in the interest of "keeping time": Mendl's thoughtless use of that cruel word might otherwise block us from appreciating the openness and intelligence with which he examines and defends the music of African Americans.

1. Piero Weiss and Richard Taruskin, eds., *Music in the Western World: A History in Documents* (New York: Schirmer, 1984), p. xiv.

Index